LEARN YOU SOME ERLANG
FOR GREAT GOOD!

Learn You Some Erlang for Great Good!

A Beginner's Guide

Fred Hébert

no starch
press

San Francisco

Printed in USA

First printing

17 16 15 14 13   1 2 3 4 5 6 7 8 9

ISBN-10: 1-59327-435-1
ISBN-13: 978-1-59327-435-1

Publisher: William Pollock
Production Editor: Alison Law
Cover Design: Sonia Brown
Developmental Editor: Keith Fancher
Technical Reviewer: Geoff Cant
Copyeditor: Marilyn Smith
Compositor: Susan Glinert Stevens
Proofreader: Greg Teague

For information on book distributors or translations, please contact No Starch Press, Inc. directly:

No Starch Press, Inc.
38 Ringold Street, San Francisco, CA 94103
phone: 415.863.9900; fax: 415.863.9950; info@nostarch.com; www.nostarch.com

Library of Congress Cataloging-in-Publication Data
A catalog record of this book is available from the Library of Congress.

BRIEF CONTENTS

CONTENTS IN DETAIL

3
SYNTAX IN FUNCTIONS   43

4
TYPES (OR LACK THEREOF)   55

5
HELLO RECURSION!   61

6
HIGHER-ORDER FUNCTIONS   77

7
ERRORS AND EXCEPTIONS

8
FUNCTIONALLY SOLVING PROBLEMS

9
A SHORT VISIT TO COMMON DATA STRUCTURES

10
THE HITCHHIKER'S GUIDE TO CONCURRENCY

ABOUT THE AUTHOR

Fred Hébert is a self-taught programmer with experience in frontend web development, web services, and general backend programming in various languages. His online tutorial, *Learn You Some Erlang for Great Good!*, is widely regarded as the best way to learn Erlang. While at Erlang Solutions Ltd., he wrote training materials and taught Erlang all around the Western world. He currently works with Erlang on a real-time bidding platform (AdGear) and was named Erlang User of the Year 2012.

FOREWORD

Learning to program is fun, or at least it should be
fun. If it's not fun, you won't enjoy doing it. During
my career as a programmer, I have taught myself several different programming languages, and it hasn't
always been fun. Whether or not learning a language
is fun depends to a large extent on how the language is
introduced.

When you start working with a new programming language, on the
surface it seems that all you are doing is learning a new language. But at
a deeper level, you are doing something much more profound—you are
learning a new way of thinking. It's this new way of thinking that is exciting,
not the minor details of the punctuation or how the language looks compared to your favorite programming language.

Functional programming is one of those areas of programming that
has acquired a reputation for being "hard" (concurrent programming even
more so), and so writing a book about Erlang that covers the ideas of functional programming *plus* concurrent programming is a daunting prospect.

Make no mistake about it: Introducing functional programming is not so easy, and introducing concurrent programming has its difficulties. Doing both with humor and ease requires a very particular kind of talent.

Fred Hebert has shown that he has this talent. He explains complex ideas in a way that makes them seem simple.

One of the biggest barriers to learning Erlang is not so much that the ideas involved are intrinsically difficult but that they are very different from the ideas in most of the other languages that you will have encountered. To learn Erlang, you have to temporarily unlearn what you have learned in other programming languages. Variables in Erlang do not vary. You're not supposed to program defensively. Processes are really, really cheap, and you can have thousands of them or even millions, if you feel like it. Oh, and then there is the strange syntax. Erlang doesn't look like Java; there are no methods or classes and no objects. And wait a moment . . . even the equals sign doesn't mean "equals"—it means "match this pattern."

Fred is completely undaunted by these issues; he treats the subject matter with a delicate dry humor and teaches complex subjects in such a way that we forget the complexity.

This is now the fourth major text on Erlang and is a great addition to the Erlang library. But it's not only about Erlang. Many of the ideas in Fred's book are equally applicable to Haskell or OCaml or F#.

I hope that many of you will enjoy reading Fred's book as much as I did and that you find learning Erlang to be an agreeable and thought-provoking process. If you type in the programs in this book and run them as you go along, you'll learn even more. Writing programs is much more difficult than reading them, and the first step is just letting your fingers get used to typing in the programs and getting rid of the small syntax errors that inevitably occur. As you get deeper into the book, you'll be writing programs that are pretty tricky to write in most other languages—but hopefully you won't realize this. Soon you'll be writing distributed programs. This is when the fun starts. . .

Thanks, Fred, for a great book.

Joe Armstrong
Stockholm, Sweden
November 6, 2012

PREFACE

This book initially started as a website, which is still available at *http://learnyousomeerlang.com/* (thanks to No Starch Press's open-mindedness regarding all things related to publishing and technical material).

Since the first chapters were made public in 2009, *Learn You Some Erlang* has grown from a three-chapter micro-tutorial with a request for proofreading on the *erlang-questions* mailing list into one of the official documentation's suggestions for learning Erlang, a book, and a major accomplishment in my life. I'm baffled and thankful for all it has brought me, from friends to jobs to the title of Erlang User of the Year 2012.

To the Foreigner

When you're looking at Erlang programmers from afar, as an outsider, they may seem like a weird little community of people who believe in principles that nearly nobody else needs or wants to follow. Their principles look impractical, limited in how they can be applied. To make matters worse, Erlang citizens may appear similar to members of a religious sect, entirely sure that they know the one true way to the heart of software. This is the same kind of "one true way" previously preached by fanatics of languages like those of the Lisp family, Haskellers, proud members of the formal proof school of thought, Smalltalk programmers, stack aficionados from the world of Forth, and so on. Same old, same old; they all offer great promises of success, and deliver in various ways, but the programs we programmers write are still buggy, too expensive, or unmaintainable.

With Erlang, it's likely the promise of concurrency or parallelism that brings you here. Maybe it's the distributed computing aspect of the language, or possibly its unusual approach to fault tolerance. Of course, approaching Erlang with skepticism is a good thing. It won't solve all your problems—that's your job, after all. Erlang is merely a nifty toolbox to help you do so.

To the Erlang Regular

You already know Erlang, possibly very well. In that case, I hope this book becomes an interesting read or a possible reference, or that a few of its chapters help you learn more about bits of the language and its environment that you weren't too familiar with before.

It's also possible that you know Erlang better than I do in every respect. In that case, I hope this book makes an adequate paperweight or space-filler in your library.

To the Person Who Has Read This Online

Thanks for your support, and I hope you enjoy what professional editing has brought to the original text, along with a boost into R15B+ versions of Erlang.

ACKNOWLEDGMENTS

Thanks to Miran Lipovača for coming up with the *Learn You a Language* idea first, and for letting me borrow the concept for this book and its related website.

Thanks to Jenn (my girlfriend) for the original website design, the long yeoman's work required to redraw most of the images of this book so they would be suitable for print, her support, and her patience in letting me spend so many hours working on this project.

Thanks to all the people who gave their time away to help review the online copy of this book, find errors, and offer support (in no particular order): Michael Richter, OJ Reeves, Dave Pawson, Robert Virding, Richard O'Keefe, Ulf Wiger, Lukas Larsson, Dale Harvey, Richard Carlsson, Nick Fitzgerald, Brendon Hogger, Geoff Cant, Andrew Thompson, Bartosz Fabianowski, Richard Jones, Tuncer Ayaz, William King, Mahesh Paolini-Subramanya, and Malcolm Matalka. There were also many other people who provided minor reviews and spotted typos and other errors.

A second thanks to Geoff Cant, who was the official tech reviewer for this version of the book.

Thanks to the team at No Starch Press (Keith, Alison, Leigh, Riley, Jessica, Tyler, and Bill) for their professional work.

Finally, thanks to the countless readers of the online copy of this book: those who bought this version, and those who read it without buying it.

INTRODUCTION

This is the beginning of *Learn You Some Erlang for Great Good!* Reading this book should be one of your first steps in learning Erlang, so let's talk about it a bit.

I got the idea to write this book after reading Miran Lipovača's *Learn You a Haskell for Great Good!* (LYAH) tutorial. I thought he did a great job making the language attractive and the learning experience friendly. As I already knew him, I asked him how he felt about me writing an Erlang version of his book. He liked the idea, being somewhat interested in Erlang.

So I began writing this book.

Of course, there were other sources to my motivation. When I began, I found the entry to the language to be hard (the Web had sparse documentation, and books are expensive), and I thought the community would benefit from a LYAH-like guide. Also, I had seen people attributing Erlang too little—or sometimes too much— merit based on sweeping generalizations.

This book is a way to learn Erlang for people who have a basic knowledge of programming in imperative languages (such as C/C++, Java, Python, Ruby, and so on) but may or may not be familiar with functional programming languages (such as Haskell, Scala, Clojure, and OCaml, as well as Erlang). I also wanted to write this book in an honest manner, selling Erlang for what it is, acknowledging its weaknesses and strengths.

So What's Erlang?

Erlang is a functional programming language. If you have ever worked with imperative languages, statements such as i++ may be normal to you, but in functional programming, they are not allowed. In fact, changing the value of any variable is strictly forbidden! This may sound weird at first, but if you remember your math classes, that's how you learned it:

```
y = 2
x = y + 3
x = 2 + 3
x = 5
```

If I added the following, you would have been very confused.

```
x = 5 + 1
x = x
∴ 5 = 6
```

Functional programming recognizes this. If I say x is 5, then I can't logically claim it is also 6! This would be dishonest. This is also why a function should return the same result every time it's called with the same parameter:

```
x = add_two_to(3) = 5
∴ x = 5
```

The concept of functions always returning the same result for the same parameter is called *referential transparency*. It's what lets us replace add_two_to(3) with 5, as the result of 3+2 will always be 5. That means we can glue dozens of functions together in order to resolve more complex problems while being sure nothing will break. Logical and clean, isn't it? There's a problem though:

```
x = today() = 2013/10/22
    -- wait a day --
x = today() = 2013/10/23
x = x
∴ 2013/10/22 = 2013/10/23
```

Oh no! My beautiful equations! They suddenly all turned wrong! How come my function returns a different result every day?

Obviously, there are some cases where it's useful to break referential transparency. Erlang has this very pragmatic approach with functional programming: Obey its purest principles (referential transparency, avoiding mutable data, and so on), but break away from them when real-world problems pop up.

Although Erlang is a functional programming language, there's also a large emphasis on concurrency and high reliability. To be able to have dozens of tasks being performed at the same time, Erlang uses the actor model, and each actor is a separate process in the virtual machine. In a nutshell, if you were an actor in Erlang's world, you would be a lonely person, sitting in a dark room with no window, waiting by your mailbox to get a message. Once you got a message, you would react to it in a specific way: You pay the bills, you respond to birthday cards with a "thank you" letter, and you ignore the letters you can't understand.

Erlang's actor model can be imagined as a world where everyone is sitting alone in a room and can perform a few distinct tasks. Everyone communicates strictly by writing letters, and that's it. While it sounds like a boring life (and a new age for the postal service), it means you can ask many people to perform very specific tasks for you, and none of them will ever do something wrong or make mistakes that will have repercussions on the work of others. They may not even know of the existence of people other than you (and that's great).

In practice, Erlang forces you to write actors (processes) that will share no information with other bits of code unless they pass messages to each other. Every communication is explicit, traceable, and safe.

Erlang is not just a language but also a development environment as a whole. The code is compiled to bytecode and runs inside a virtual machine. So Erlang, much like Java and kids with ADD, can run anywhere. Here are just some of the components of the standard distribution:

- Development tools (compiler, debugger, profiler, and test frameworks, optional type analyzer)
- The Open Telecom Platform (OTP) framework
- A web server
- Advanced tracing tools
- The Mnesia database (a key/value storage system able to replicate itself on many servers, which supports nested transactions and lets you store any kind of Erlang data)

The virtual machine and libraries also allow you to update the code of a running system without interrupting any program, distribute your code with ease on many computers, and manage errors and faults in a simple but powerful manner.

We'll cover how to use most of these tools and achieve safety in this book.

Speaking of safety, you should be aware of a related general policy in Erlang: Let it crash—not like a plane with dozens of passengers dying, but more like a tightrope walker with a safety net below. While you should avoid making mistakes, you won't need to check for every type or error condition in most cases.

Erlang's ability to recover from errors, organize code with actors, and scale with distribution and concurrency all sound awesome, which brings us to the next section . . .

Don't Drink Too Much Kool-Aid

This book has many little boxed sections named like this one (you'll recognize them when you see them). Erlang is currently gaining a lot of popularity due to zealous talks, which may lead people to believe it's more than what it really is. The following are some reminders to help you keep your feet on the ground if you're one of these overenthusiastic learners.

First is the talk of Erlang's massive scaling abilities due to its lightweight processes. It is true that Erlang processes are very light; you can have hundreds of thousands of them existing at the same time. But this doesn't mean you *should* use Erlang that way just because you *can*. For example, creating a shooter game where everything including bullets is its own actor is madness. The only thing you'll shoot with a game like that is your own foot. There is still a small cost in sending a message from actor to actor, and if you divide tasks too much, you will make things slower!

I'll cover this in more depth when we're far enough into the tutorial to actually worry about it, but just keep in mind that randomly throwing parallelism at a problem is not enough to make it go fast. (Don't be sad; occasionally, using hundreds of processes is both possible and useful!)

Erlang is also said to be able to scale in a directly proportional manner to how many cores your computer has, but this is usually not true. It is possible, but in most cases, problems do not behave in a way that lets you just run everything at the same time.

Something else to keep in mind is that while Erlang does some things very well, it's technically still possible to get the same results from other languages. The opposite is also true. You should evaluate each problem that you need to solve and choose the best tool for that problem and its solution. Erlang is no silver bullet and will be particularly bad at things like image and signal processing, operating system device drivers, and other functions. It will shine at things like large software for server use

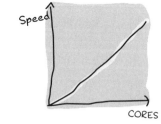

(for example, queue middleware, web servers, real-time bidding and distributed database implementations), doing some lifting coupled with other languages, higher-level protocol implementation, and so on. Areas in the middle will depend on you.

You should not necessarily limit yourself to server software with Erlang. People have done unexpected and surprising things with it. One example is IANO, a robot created by the Unict team (the Eurobot team of the University of Catania), which uses Erlang for its artificial intelligence. IANO won the silver medal at the 2009 Eurobot competition. Another example is Wings 3D, an open source, cross-platform 3D modeler (but not a renderer) written in Erlang.

What You Need to Dive In

All you need to get started is a text editor and the Erlang environment. You can get the source code and the Windows binaries from the official Erlang website.

For Windows systems, just download and run the binary files. Don't forget to add your Erlang directory to your PATH system variable to be able to access it from the command line.

On Debian-based Linux distributions, you should be able to install the package with this command:

```
$ sudo apt-get install erlang
```

On Fedora (if you have yum installed), you can install Erlang by typing this:

```
# yum install erlang
```

However, these repositories often hold outdated versions of the Erlang packages. Using an outdated version could give you some different results from those shown for the examples in this book, as well as a hit in performance with certain applications. I therefore encourage you to compile from source. Consult the *README* file within the package and Google to get all the installation details you'll need.

On FreeBSD, many options are available. If you're using portmaster, you can use this command:

```
$ portmaster lang/erlang
```

For standard ports, enter the following:

```
$ cd /usr/ports/lang/erlang; make install clean
```

Finally, if you want to use packages, enter this:

```
$ run pkg_add -rv erlang
```

If you're on a Mac OS X system, you can install Erlang with Homebrew:

```
$ brew install erlang
```

Or, if you prefer, use MacPorts:

```
$ port install erlang
```

NOTE *At the time of this writing, I'm using Erlang version R15B+, so for the best results, you should use that version or a newer one. However, most of the content in this book is also valid for versions as old as R13B.*

Along with downloading and installing Erlang, you should also download the complete set of files available for this book. They contain tested copies of any program and module written within these pages, and they might prove useful for fixing your own programs. They also can provide a base for later chapters if you feel like skipping around. The files are all packaged in a zip file, available at *http://learnyousomeerlang.com/static/erlang/learn-you-some-erlang.zip*. Otherwise, the examples in *Learn You Some Erlang* depend on no other external dependency.

Where to Get Help

If you're using Linux, you can access the man pages for good technical documentation. For example, Erlang has a `lists` module (as you'll see in Chapter 1). To get the documentation on lists, just type in this command:

```
$ erl -man lists
```

On Windows, the installation should include HTML documentation. You can download it at any time from the official Erlang site, or consult one of the alternative sites.

Good coding practices can be found at *http://www.erlang.se/doc/programming_rules.shtml* when you feel you need to get your code clean. The code in this book will attempt to follow these guidelines, too.

Now, there are times when just getting the technical details isn't enough. When that happens, I tend to turn to two main sources: the official Erlang mailing list (you should follow it just to learn a bunch) and the *#erlang* channel on *irc.freenode.net*.

1

STARTING OUT

In Erlang, you can test most of your code in an emulator. It will run your scripts when they are compiled and deployed, but it will also let you edit stuff live.

In this chapter, you'll learn how to use the Erlang shell and be introduced to some basic Erlang data types.

Using the Erlang Shell

To start the Erlang shell in a Linux or Mac OS X system, open a terminal, and then type **erl**. If you've set up everything correctly, you should see something like this:

```
$ erl
Erlang R15B (erts-5.9) [source] [64-bit] [smp:4:4] [async-threads:0] [hipe]
[kernel-poll:false]

Eshell V5.9  (abort with ^G)
```

Congratulations, you're running the Erlang shell!

If you're a Windows user, you can run the shell by executing *erl.exe* at the command prompt, but it's recommended that you use *werl.exe* instead, which can be found in your Start menu (choose **All Programs ▸ Erlang**). Werl is a Windows-only implementation of the Erlang shell that has its own window with scroll bars and supports line-editing shortcuts (which are not available with the standard *cmd.exe* shell in Windows). However, the *erl.exe* shell is still required if you want to redirect standard input or output, or use pipes.

Now we can enter code into the shell and run it in the emulator. But first, let's see how we can get around in it.

Entering Shell Commands

The Erlang shell has a built-in line editor based on a subset of Emacs, a popular text editor that has been in use since the 1970s. If you know Emacs, you should be fine. And even if you don't know Emacs, you'll do fine anyway.

To begin, type some text in the Erlang shell, and then press CTRL-A (^A). Your cursor should move to the beginning of the line. Similarly, pressing CTRL-E (^E) moves the cursor to the end of the line. You can also use the left and right arrow keys to move the cursor forward and backward, and cycle through previously written lines of code by using the up and down arrow keys.

Let's try something else. Type
li, and then press TAB. The shell
will expand the term for you to
lists:. Press TAB again, and the
shell will suggest all the functions
available in the lists module. You
may find the notation weird, but
don't worry, you'll become familiar
with it soon enough. (We'll learn
more about modules in Chapter 2.)

Exiting the Shell

At this point, you've seen most of the basic Erlang shell functionality, except for one very important thing: You don't know how to exit! Luckily, there's a fast way to find out: type **help().** into the shell and press ENTER. You'll see information about a bunch of commands, including functions to inspect processes, manage how the shell works, and so on. We'll use many of these in this book, but the only one of interest right now is the following expression:

```
q() -- quit - shorthand for init:stop()
```

So, this is one way to exit (two ways, in fact). But this won't help if the shell freezes!

If you were paying attention when you started the shell, you probably saw a comment about "aborting with ^G." So let's press CTRL-G, and then type **h** to get help.

```
User switch command
--> h
c [nn]             - connect to job
i [nn]             - interrupt job
k [nn]             - kill job
j                  - list all jobs
s [shell]          - start local shell
r [node [shell]]   - start remote shell
q                  - quit erlang
? | h              - this message
-->
```

If you are wearing a monocle, now would be the time to drop it. The Erlang shell isn't just a simple shell as with other languages. Instead, it is a bundle of shell instances, each running different *jobs*. Moreover, you can manage them like processes in an operating system. If you type k *N*, where *N* is a job number, you will terminate that shell and all the code it was running at the time. If you want to stop the code that is running without killing the shell, then i *N* is the command you need. You can also create new shell instances by typing in s, list them with j, and connect to them with c *N*.

At some point, you might see an asterisk (*) next to some shell jobs:

```
--> j
  1* {shell,start,[init]}
```

The * means that this is the last shell instance you were using. If you use the command c, i, or k without any number following it, that command will operate on this last shell instance.

If your shell ever freezes, a quick sequence to help is to press CTRL-G, type **i**, press ENTER, type **c**, and press ENTER (^G **i** ENTER **c** ENTER). This will get you to the shell manager, interrupt the current shell job, and then connect back to it:

```
Eshell V5.9  (abort with ^G)
1> "OH NO THIS SHELL IS UNRESPONSIVE!!! *hits ctrl+G*"
User switch command
 --> i
 --> c
** exception exit: killed
1> "YESS!"
```

There's one important thing to know before you start typing "real" stuff into the shell: *A sequence of expressions must be terminated with a period followed by whitespace* (a line break, a space, and so on); otherwise, it won't be executed. You can separate expressions with commas, but only the result of the last one will be shown (although the others are still executed). This is certainly unusual syntax for most people, and it comes from the days Erlang was implemented directly in Prolog, a logic programming language.

Now let's get things started (for real) by learning about the basic Erlang data types and how to write your first bits of programs in the shell.

Some Erlang Basics

Although you've just seen a rather advanced mechanism to handle different jobs and shell sessions, Erlang is considered to be a relatively small and simple language (in the way that C is simpler than C++). The language has only a few basic built-in data types (and few syntactic elements around them). First, we'll take a look at numbers.

Numbers

Open the Erlang shell as described earlier, and let's type some things:

```
1> 2 + 15.
17
2> 49 * 100.
4900
3> 1892 - 1472.
420
4> 5 / 2.
2.5
```

As you can see, Erlang doesn't care if you enter floating-point numbers or integers. Both types are supported when dealing with arithmetic.

Note that if you want to perform integer-to-integer division, rather than floating-point division, you should use div. To get the remainder (modulo) of an integer division, use rem (remainder).

```
5> 5 div 2.
2
6> 5 rem 2.
1
```

You can use several operators in a single expression, and mathematical operations obey the normal precedence rules:

```
7> (50 * 100) - 4999.
1
8> -(50 * 100 - 4999).
-1
9> -50 * (100 - 4999).
244950
```

If you want to express integers in other bases than base 10, just enter the number in the form *Base#Value* (as long as *Base* is in the range of 2 through 36), like this:

```
10> 2#101010.
42
11> 8#0677.
447
12> 16#AE.
174
```

Here, we're converting binary, octal, and hexadecimal values to base 10. Awesome! Erlang has the power of the calculator you have on the corner of your desk, but with a weird syntax on top of it. Absolutely exciting!

Invariable Variables

Doing arithmetic is all right, but you won't get far without being able to store the results somewhere. For that, you use variables. If you read the Introduction to this book, you know that variables can't be variable in functional programming.

In Erlang, variables begin with an uppercase letter by definition. The basic behavior of variables can be demonstrated with these six expressions:

```
1> One.
* 1: variable 'One' is unbound
2> One = 1.
1
3> Un = Uno = One = 1.
1
4> Two = One + One.
2
5> Two = 2.
2
6> Two = Two + 1.
** exception error: no match of right hand side value 3
```

The first thing these commands tell us is that you can assign a value to a variable exactly once. Then you can "pretend" to assign a value to a variable if it's the same value the variable already has. If the value is different, Erlang will complain. It's a correct observation, but the explanation is a bit more complex and depends on the = operator. The = operator (not the variables) has the role of comparing values and complaining if they're different. If they're the same, Erlang returns the value:

```
7> 47 = 45 + 2.
47
8> 47 = 45 + 3.
** exception error: no match of right hand side value 48
```

When you use the = operator with variables on both sides of it, with the variable on the left side being unbound (without any value associated with it), Erlang will automatically bind the value on the right to the variable on the left. Both variables will then have the same value. The comparison will consequently succeed, and the variable on the left side will keep the value in memory.

Here's another example:

```
9> two = 2.
** exception error: no match of right hand side value 2
```

The command fails because the word two begins with a lowercase letter.

NOTE   *Technically, variables can also start with an underscore (_), but by convention, their use is restricted to values you do not care about.*

This behavior of the = operator is the basis of something called *pattern matching*, which many functional programming languages have, although Erlang's way of doing things is usually regarded as more flexible and complete than the alternatives. You'll learn more about Erlang pattern matching when we visit other data types in this chapter, and also see how it works with functions in the following chapters.

Note that if you're testing in the shell and save the wrong value to a variable, it is possible to "erase" that variable by using the function f(Variable).. If you wish to clear all variable names, use f().. These functions are designed to help you when you're testing, and they only work in the shell. When you're writing real programs, you won't be able to destroy values this way. This restriction makes sense if you think about Erlang being usable in industrial scenarios. It's wholly possible that a shell will be active for years without interruption, and you can bet that a given variable will be used more than once in that time period.

Atoms

There is a reason why variables names can't begin with a lowercase character: *atoms*. Atoms are literals, which means that they're just constants whose only value is their own name. In other words, what you see is what you get—don't expect more. The atom cat means "cat," and that's it. You can't play with it. You can't change it. You can't smash it to pieces. It's cat. Deal with it.

While using single words starting with a lowercase letter is one way to write an atom, there are also other ways:

```
1> atom.
atom
2> atoms_rule.
atoms_rule
```

```
3> atoms_rule@erlang.
atoms_rule@erlang
4> 'Atoms can be cheated!'.
'Atoms can be cheated!'
5> atom = 'atom'.
atom
```

An atom should be enclosed in single quotes (') if it does not begin with a lowercase letter or if it contains any characters other than alphanumeric characters, an underscore (_), or an at sign (@). Line 5 also shows that an atom with single quotes is exactly the same as a similar atom without them.

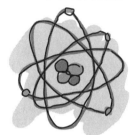

I compared atoms to constants that have their name as their values. You may have worked with code that used constants before. For example, let's say you have values for eye colors: 1 for blue, 2 for brown, 3 for green, and 4 for other. You need to match the name of the constant to some underlying value. Atoms let you forget about the underlying values. Your eye colors can simply be blue, brown, green, or other. These colors can be used anywhere in any piece of code. The underlying values will never clash, and it is impossible for such a constant to be undefined! (We'll see how to create constants with values associated with them in Chapter 2.)

Therefore, an atom is mainly useful to express or qualify data coupled with it, usually in a tuple (described in "Tuples" on page 16). Atoms are sometimes (but not often) useful when used alone. This is why we won't spend more time toying with them here. You'll see them coupled with other types of data in later examples.

DON'T DRINK TOO MUCH KOOL-AID

Atoms are really nice and a great way to send messages or represent constants. However, there are pitfalls to using atoms for too many things. An atom is referred to in an *atom table*, which consumes memory (4 bytes per atom in a 32-bit system and 8 bytes per atom in a 64-bit system). The atom table is not garbage collected, so atoms will accumulate until the system tips over, either from memory usage or because 1,048,577 atoms were declared.

This means atoms should not be generated dynamically. If your system needs to be reliable, and user input lets someone crash it at will by telling it to create atoms, you're in serious trouble.

Atoms should be seen as tools for the developer because, honestly, that's what they are. To reiterate: You should feel perfectly safe using atoms in your everyday code as long as you type them in yourself. It's only dynamic generation of atoms that is risky.

NOTE
Some atoms are reserved words and cannot be used except for what the language designers wanted them to be: function names, operators, expressions, and so on. These reserved words are as follows: after, and, andalso, band, begin, bnot, bor, bsl, bsr, bxor, case, catch, cond, div, end, fun, if, let, not, of, or, orelse, query, receive, rem, try, when, and xor.

Boolean Algebra and Comparison Operators

George
Boole

We would be in pretty deep trouble if we couldn't tell the difference between what's small and big, or what's true and false. Like any other language, Erlang has ways to let you use Boolean operations and to compare items.

Boolean algebra is dirt simple:

```
1> true and false.
false
2> false or true.
true
3> true xor false.
true
4> not false.
true
5> not (true and true).
false
```

NOTE
The Boolean operators and and or will always evaluate arguments on both sides of the operator. If you want a short-circuit operator (which will evaluate the right-side argument only if necessary), use andalso or orelse.

Testing for equality or inequality is also dirt simple, but involves slightly different symbols from those you see in many other languages:

```
6> 5 =:= 5.
true
7> 1 =:= 0.
false
8> 1 =/= 0.
true
9> 5 =:= 5.0.
false
10> 5 == 5.0.
true
11> 5 /= 5.0.
false
```

There's a good chance that your usual language uses == and != to test for and against equality, but Erlang uses =:= and =/=. The three last expressions (lines 9 through 11) also introduce a pitfall: Erlang doesn't care about the difference between floats and integers in arithmetic, but does distinguish between the two when comparing them. No worry though, because the == and /= operators are there to help you in these cases. Thus, it is important to consider whether or not you want exact equality. As a general rule of thumb, you should always start by using =:= and =/=, and switch to == and /= only when you know you do not need exact equality. This could help you avoid some unfortunate comparisons when the types of numbers you expect are not what you get.

Other operators for comparisons are < (less than), > (greater than), >= (greater than or equal to), and =< (less than or equal to). That last one is backward (in my opinion) and is the source of many syntax errors in my code. Keep an eye on that =<.

```
12> 1 < 2.
true
13> 1 < 1.
false
14> 1 >= 1.
true
15> 1 =< 1.
true
```

What happens when you enter something like 5 + llama or 5 =:= true? There's no better way to know than trying it and subsequently getting scared by error messages!

```
12> 5 + llama.
** exception error: bad argument in an arithmetic expression
    in operator  +/2
        called as 5 + llama
```

Erlang doesn't really like you misusing some of its fundamental types. The emulator returns an error message here, indicating it doesn't like one of the two arguments used around the + operator.

Erlang doesn't always get mad at you for using the wrong types though:

```
13> 5 =:= true.
false
```

Why does it refuse different types in some operations but not others? While Erlang doesn't let you *add* two operands of different types, it will let you *compare* them. This is because the creators of Erlang thought pragmatism beats theory and decided it would be great to be able to simply write things like general sorting algorithms that could order any terms. It's there to make your life simpler and can do so the vast majority of the time.

There is one last thing to keep in mind when doing Boolean algebra and comparisons:

```
14> 0 == false.
false
15> 1 < false.
true
```

Chances are you're pulling out your hair if you come from procedural languages or most object-oriented languages. Line 14 should evaluate to true and line 15 to false! After all, false means 0 and true is anything else! Except in Erlang. Because I lied to you. Yes, I did that. Shame on me.

Erlang has no such things as Boolean true and false. The terms true and false are atoms, but they are integrated well enough into the language that you shouldn't have a problem with them, as long as you don't expect false and true to mean anything but false and true.

NOTE *The correct ordering of each element in a comparison is the following:* number < atom < reference < fun < port < pid < tuple < list < bit string. *Some of these types won't be familiar to you, but you will get to know them through this book. Just remember that this is why you can compare anything with anything. To quote Joe Armstrong, one of the creators of Erlang, "The actual order is not important—but that a total ordering is well defined is important."*

Tuples

A *tuple* is a way to group together a set number of terms. In Erlang, a tuple is written in the form {Element1, Element2, ..., ElementN}. For example, you would give me the coordinates (x,y) if you wanted to tell me the position of a point in a Cartesian graph. We can represent this point as a tuple of two terms:

```
1> X = 10, Y = 4.
4
2> Point = {X,Y}.
{10,4}
```

In this case, a point will always be two terms. Instead of carrying the variables X and Y everywhere, you need to carry only one. However, what can you do if you receive a point and only want the x-coordinate? It's not hard to extract that information. Remember that when you assign values, Erlang will never complain if they are the same. Let's exploit that. (You may need to clear the variables we just set with f() before typing in the following example.)

```
3> Point = {4,5}.
{4,5}
4> {X,Y} = Point.
{4,5}
5> X.
4
6> {X,_} = Point.
{4,5}
```

From now on, we can use X to get the first value of the tuple. How did that happen? First, X and Y had no value and were thus considered unbound variables. When you set them in the tuple {X,Y} on the left side of the = operator, the = operator compares both values: {X,Y} versus {4,5}. Erlang is smart enough to unpack the values from the tuple and distribute them to the unbound variables on the left side. Then the comparison is only {4,5} = {4,5}, which obviously succeeds. That's one of the many forms of pattern matching.

Note that line 6 uses the don't care variable (_). This is exactly how it's meant to be used: to drop the value that would usually be placed there, since we won't use that value. The _ variable is always seen as unbound and acts as a wildcard for pattern matching. Pattern matching to unpack tuples will work only if the number of elements (the tuple's length) is the same.

MR.BRACKETS

```
7> {_,_} = {4,5}.
{4,5}
8> {_,_} = {4,5,6}.
** exception error: no match of right hand side value {4,5,6}
```

Tuples can also be useful when working with single values. For example, suppose that we want to store the following temperature:

```
9> Temperature = 23.213.
23.213
```

Looks like a good day to go to the beach! But wait—is this temperature in Kelvin, Celsius, or Fahrenheit? We can use a tuple to store the temperature's units along with its value:

```
10> PreciseTemperature = {celsius, 23.213}.
{celsius,23.213}
11> {kelvin, T} = PreciseTemperature.
** exception error: no match of right hand side value {celsius,23.213}
```

This raises an exception, but that's exactly what we want. This is, again, pattern matching at work. The = operator compares {kelvin, T} and {celsius, 23.213}, and even if the variable T is unbound, Erlang can see that the celsius atom is different from the kelvin atom. An exception is raised, which stops the execution of code. So, the part of the program that expects a temperature in Kelvin won't be able to process temperatures sent in Celsius. This makes it easier for the programmer to know what kind of data is being sent, and it also works as a debugging aid.

A tuple that contains an atom with one element following it is called a *tagged tuple*. Any element of a tuple can be of any type, even another tuple:

```
12> {point, {X,Y}}.
{point,{4,5}}
```

But what if we want to carry around more than one point? For that, we have *lists*.

Lists

Lists are the bread and butter of many functional languages. They're used to solve all kinds of problems and are undoubtedly the most-used data structure in Erlang. Lists can contain anything—numbers, atoms, tuples, other lists—your wildest dreams in a single structure.

The basic notation of a list is [*Element1*, *Element2*, ..., *ElementN*], and you can mix more than one type of data in it:

```
1> [1, 2, 3, {numbers,[4,5,6]}, 5.34, atom].
[1,2,3,{numbers,[4,5,6]},5.34,atom]
```

Simple enough, right? Let's try another one:

```
2> [97, 98, 99].
"abc"
```

Uh-oh! This is one of the most disliked things in Erlang: strings. Strings are lists, and the notation is exactly the same. Why do people dislike it? Because of this:

```
3> [97,98,99,4,5,6].
[97,98,99,4,5,6]
4> [233].
"é"
```

Erlang will print lists of numbers as numbers only when at least one of them could not also represent a letter. There is no such thing as a real string in Erlang! This will no doubt come to haunt you in the future, and you'll hate the language for it. Don't despair, because there are other ways to write strings, as you'll see in "Binary Strings" on page 27.

To glue lists together, use the ++ operator. To remove elements from a list, use --.

```
5> [1,2,3] ++ [4,5].
[1,2,3,4,5]
6> [1,2,3,4,5] -- [1,2,3].
[4,5]
7> [2,4,2] -- [2,4].
[2]
8> [2,4,2] -- [2,4,2].
[]
```

Both ++ and -- are right-associative. This means the elements of many -- or ++ operations will be done from right to left, as in the following examples:

```
9> [1,2,3] -- [1,2] -- [3].
[3]
10> [1,2,3] -- [1,2] -- [2].
[2,3]
```

In the first example, proceeding from right to left, we first remove [3] from [1,2], leaving us with [1,2]. Then we remove [1,2] from [1,2,3], leaving us with only [3]. For the last one, we first remove [2] from [1,2], giving [1]. Then we take [1] out of [1,2,3], producing the final result [2,3].

Let's keep going. The first element of a list is named the *head*, and the rest of the list is named the *tail*. We will use two built-in functions (BIFs) to get them:

```
11> hd([1,2,3,4]).
1
12> tl([1,2,3,4]).
[2,3,4]
```

NOTE *BIFs are usually functions that could not be implemented in pure Erlang, and as such are defined in C, or whichever language Erlang happens to be implemented in (it was Prolog in the 1980s). There are still some BIFs that could be done in Erlang but were implemented in C in order to provide more speed to common operations. One example of this is the length(List) function, which will return the (you've guessed it) length of the list passed in as the argument.*

Accessing or adding the head is fast and efficient. Virtually all applications where you need to deal with lists will operate on the head first. As it's used so frequently, Erlang provides an easier way to separate the head from the tail of a list, with the help of pattern matching: *[Head|Tail]*. For example, here's how you would add a new head to a list:

```
13> List = [2,3,4].
[2,3,4]
14> NewList = [1|List].
[1,2,3,4]
```

When processing lists, it's also helpful to have a quick way to store the tail, so you can operate on the tail later. If you remember the way tuples work and how we used pattern matching to unpack the values of a point ({X,Y}), you'll understand how we can get the first element (the head) sliced off a list in a similar manner:

```
15> [Head|Tail] = NewList.
[1,2,3,4]
16> Head.
1
17> Tail.
[2,3,4]
18> [NewHead|NewTail] = Tail.
[2,3,4]
19> NewHead.
2
```

The | we used is called the *cons* operator (constructor). In fact, any list can be built with only cons operators and values:

```
20> [1 | []].
[1]
21> [2 | [1 | []]].
[2,1]
22> [3 | [2 | [1 | []]]].
[3,2,1]
```

In other words, any list can be built with the following formula: *[Term1 | [Term2 | [... | [TermN]]]]*. Thus, you can define lists recursively as a head preceding a tail, which is itself a head followed by more heads. In this sense, you could imagine a list being a bit like an earthworm; you can slice it in half, and you'll then have two worms.

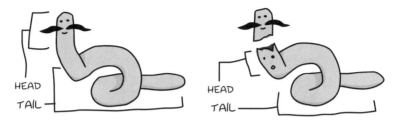

The ways Erlang lists can be built are sometimes confusing to people who are not used to similar constructors. To help you get familiar with the concept, read all of these examples (hint: they're all equivalent):

```
[a, b, c, d]
[a, b, c, d | []]
[a, b | [c, d]]
[a, b | [c | [d]]]
[a | [b | [c | [d]]]]
[a | [b | [c | [d | []]]]]
```

With this understood, you should be able to deal with list comprehensions, which are discussed in the next section.

Using the form [1 | 2] gives what is called an improper *list. Improper lists will work when you pattern match in the [Head|Tail] manner, but will fail when used with standard functions of Erlang (even* length()*). This is because Erlang expects* proper *lists. Proper lists end with an empty list as their last cell. When declaring an item like [2], the list is automatically formed in a proper manner. As such, [1|[2]] would work. Improper lists, although syntactically valid, are of very limited use outside of user-defined data structures.*

List Comprehensions

List comprehensions are ways to build or modify lists. They also make programs short and easy to understand compared to other ways of manipulating lists. They may be hard to grasp at first, but they're worth the effort. Don't hesitate to try the examples in this section until you understand them!

List comprehensions are based on the mathematical idea of *set notation*, so if you've ever taken a math class that dealt with set theory, list comprehensions may look familiar to you. Set notation describes how to build a set by specifying properties its members must satisfy. For instance, here's a basic example: $\{x \in \mathbb{R} : x = x^2\}$. This describes the set of all real numbers that are equal to their own square. (The result of that set would be {0,1}.) A simpler example of set notation is $\{x : x > 0\}$. This describes the set of all numbers greater than zero.

Like set notation, list comprehensions are about building sets from other sets. For example, given the set $\{2n : n \in L\}$, where L is the list

[1,2,3,4], we could read this as "for all n values in [1,2,3,4], give me n*2." The set built from this would be [2,4,6,8]. The Erlang implementation of this same set is as follows:

```
1> [2*N || N <- [1,2,3,4]].
[2,4,6,8]
```

Compare the mathematical notation to the Erlang one, and you'll see that not a lot changes: brackets ({}) become square brackets ([]), the colon (:) becomes two pipes (||), and the operator ∈ becomes the arrow (<-). In other words, we change symbols but keep the same logic. In the example, each value of [1,2,3,4] is sequentially pattern matched to N. The arrow acts exactly like the = operator, with the exception that it doesn't throw exceptions.

You can also add constraints to a list comprehension by using operations that return Boolean values. So if you want all the even numbers from one to ten, you could write something like this:

```
2> [X || X <- [1,2,3,4,5,6,7,8,9,10], X rem 2 =:= 0].
[2,4,6,8,10]
```

Here, X rem 2 =:= 0 checks if a number is even.

The recipe for list comprehensions in Erlang is as follows:

```
NewList = [Expression || Pattern <- List, Condition1, Condition2, ... ConditionN]
```

The *Pattern <- List* part is called a *generator expression*.

List comprehensions are useful when you want to apply a function to each element of a list, forcing it to respect constraints. For example, say you own a restaurant. A customer enters, sees your menu, and asks if he could have the prices of all the items costing between $3 and $10, with taxes (say 7 percent) counted in afterward.

```
3> RestaurantMenu = [{steak, 5.99}, {beer, 3.99}, {poutine, 3.50}, {kitten, 20.99}, {water, 0.00}].
[{steak,5.99},
 {beer,3.99},
 {poutine,3.5},
 {kitten,20.99},
 {water,0.0}]
4> [{Item, Price*1.07} || {Item,Price} <- RestaurantMenu, Price >= 3, Price =< 10].
[{steak,6.409300000000001},{beer,4.2693},{poutine,3.745}]
```

The decimals are not rounded in a readable manner, but you get the point.

Another nice thing about list comprehensions is that you can have more than one generator expression, as in this example:

```
5> [X+Y || X <- [1,2], Y <- [3,4]].
[4,5,5,6]
```

This runs the operations 1+3, 1+4, 2+3, 2+4. So if you want to make the list comprehension recipe more generic, you get this:

```
NewList = [Expression || GeneratorExp1, GeneratorExp2, ..., GeneratorExpN,
Condition1, Condition2, ... ConditionM]
```

Note that the generator expressions coupled with pattern matching can also act as a filter:

```
6> Weather = [{toronto, rain}, {montreal, storms}, {london, fog},
6>            {paris, sun}, {boston, fog}, {vancouver, snow}].
[{toronto,rain},
 {montreal,storms},
 {london,fog},
 {paris,sun},
 {boston,fog},
 {vancouver,snow}]
7> FoggyPlaces = [X || {X, fog} <- Weather].
[london,boston]
```

If an element of the list Weather doesn't match the {X, fog} pattern, it's simply ignored in the list comprehension, whereas the = operator would have raised an exception.

We'll look at using one more basic data type in this chapter. It is a surprising feature that makes interpreting binary data easy as pie.

Working with Binary Data

Unlike most other languages, Erlang provides useful abstractions when dealing with binary values with pattern matching, instead of requiring the old-fashioned bit twiddling with special operators. It makes dealing with raw binary data fun and easy (no, really), which was necessary for the telecom applications it was created  to help with. Bit manipulation has a unique syntax and idioms that may look kind of weird at first, but if you know how bits and bytes work generally, this should make sense to you. (You may want to skip the rest of this chapter if you're not familiar with binary operations.)

Bit Syntax

Erlang bit syntax encloses binary data between « and » and splits it in readable segments; each segment is separated by a comma. A segment is a sequence of bits of a binary (not necessarily on a byte boundary, although this is the default behavior).

Suppose you want to store an orange pixel of true color (24 bits). If you've ever checked colors in Photoshop or in a CSS style sheet for the Web, you know the hexadecimal notation has the format #*RRGGBB*. A tint of orange is #F09A29 in that notation, which could be expanded in Erlang to the following:

```
1> Color = 16#F09A29.
15768105
2> Pixel = <<Color:24>>.
<<240,154,41>>
```

This basically says, "Put the binary values of #F09A29 on 24 bits of space (red on 8 bits, green on 8 bits, and blue also on 8 bits) in the variable Pixel." That value can then be written to a file or a socket later. This may not look like much, but once written to a file, this value will turn into a bunch of unreadable characters that, in the proper context, can be decoded as a picture.

This syntax is especially nice because you can use clean, readable text to write things that need to look messy to the naked eye in order to work. Without good abstractions, your code would also need to be messy. Even better: When you read the file back in, Erlang will interpret the binary value into the nice <<240,151,41>> format again! You can jump back and forth between representations, using only the one that's the most useful to you when you need it.

What's more interesting is the ability to pattern match with binaries to unpack content:

```
3> Pixels = <<213,45,132,64,76,32,76,0,0,234,32,15>>.
<<213,45,132,64,76,32,76,0,0,234,32,15>>
4> <<Pix1,Pix2,Pix3,Pix4>> = Pixels.
** exception error: no match of right hand side value <<213,45,132,64,76,32,76,0,0,234,32,15>>
5> <<Pix1:24, Pix2:24, Pix3:24, Pix4:24>> = Pixels.
<<213,45,132,64,76,32,76,0,0,234,32,15>>
```

On line 3, we declare what would be precisely 4 pixels of RGB colors in binary. On line 4, we tried to unpack four values from the binary content. It throws an exception, because we have more than 4 segments—in fact, we have 12. So we tell Erlang that each variable on the left side will hold 24 bits of data using Pix1:24, Pix2:24, and so on. We can then take the first pixel and unpack it further into single color values:

```
6> <<R:8, G:8, B:8>> = <<Pix1:24>>.
<<213,45,132>>
7> R.
213
```

"Yeah, that's dandy. But what if I only want the first color from the start? Will I need to unpack all these values all the time?" Don't worry—Erlang introduces more syntactic sugar and pattern matching to help you out:

```
8> <<R:8, Rest/binary>> = Pixels.
<<213,45,132,64,76,32,76,0,0,234,32,15>>
9> R.
213
```

In this example, Rest/binary is a specific notation that lets you say that whatever is left in the binary, whatever length it is, is put into the Rest variable. So <<*Pattern*, Rest/binary>> is to binary pattern matching what [*Head*|*Tail*] is to list pattern matching.

Nice, huh? This works because Erlang allows more than one way to describe a binary segment. The following are all valid:

```
Value
Value:Size
Value/TypeSpecifierList
Value:Size/TypeSpecifierList
```

Here, *Size* is always in bits when no *TypeSpecifierList* is defined. *TypeSpecifierList* represents one or more of the following, separated by a hyphen (-):

Type

The possible values are integer, float, binary, bytes, bitstring, bits, utf8, utf16, and utf32. When no type is specified, Erlang assumes an integer type.

This represents the kind of binary data used. Note that bytes is shorthand for binary, and bits is shorthand for bitstring.

Signedness

The possible values are signed and unsigned. The default is unsigned. This only matters for matching when the type is integer.

Endianness

The possible values are big, little, and native. By default, endianness is set to big, as it is the standard used in network protocol encodings.

Endianness only matters when the type is integer, utf16, utf32, or float. This has to do with how the system reads binary data. For example, the BMP image header format holds the size of its file as an integer stored in 4 bytes. For a file that has a size of 72 bytes, a little-endian system would represent this as <<72,0,0,0>>, and a big-endian system would represent it as <<0,0,0,72>>. The former will be read as 72, while the latter will be read as 1207959552, so make sure you use the correct endianness.

There is also the option to use native, which will choose at runtime if the CPU uses little-endianness or big-endianness natively.

Unit

This is written as unit:Integer.

The unit is the size of each segment. The allowed range is 1 to 256. It is set by default to 1 bit for integer, float, and bitstring types, and to 8 bits for binary. The utf8, utf16, and utf32 types do not require a unit to be defined. The multiplication of size by unit is equal to the number of bits the segment will take, and must be evenly divisible by 8. The unit size is usually used to ensure byte alignment.

The default size of a data type can be changed by combining different parts of a binary. As an example, <<25:4/unit:8>> will encode the number 25 as a 4-byte integer, or <<0,0,0,25>> in its graphical representation. <<25:2/unit:16>> will give the same result, and so will <<25:1/unit:32>>. Erlang will generally accept <<25:*Size*/unit:*Unit*>> and multiply *Size* by *Unit* to figure out how much space it should take to represent the value. Again, the result of this should be divisible by 8.

Some examples may help you digest these definitions:

```
10> <<X1/unsigned>> = <<-44>>.
<<"Ô">>
11> X1.
212
12> <<X2/signed>> = <<-44>>.
<<"Ô">>
13> X2.
-44
14> <<X2/integer-signed-little>> = <<-44>>.
<<"Ô">>
15> X2.
-44
16> <<N:8/unit:1>> = <<72>>.
<<"H">>
17> N.
72
18> <<N/integer>> = <<72>>.
<<"H">>
19> <<Y:4/little-unit:8>> = <<72,0,0,0>>.
<<72,0,0,0>>
20> Y.
72
```

You can see that there is more than one way to read, store, and interpret binary data. This is a bit confusing, but still much simpler than using the usual tools given by most languages.

Bitwise Binary Operations

The standard binary operations (shifting bits to left and right, and binary and, or, xor, and not) also exist in Erlang. Just use the operators bsl (bit shift left), bsr (bit shift right), band, bor, bxor, and bnot.

```
2#00100 = 2#00010 bsl 1.
2#00001 = 2#00010 bsr 1.
2#10101 = 2#10001 bor 2#00101.
```

With this notation and bit syntax in general, parsing and pattern matching binary data are a piece of cake. For example, you could parse TCP segments with code like this:

```
<<SourcePort:16, DestinationPort:16,AckNumber:32,
DataOffset:4, _Reserved:4, Flags:8, WindowSize:16,
CheckSum: 16, UrgentPointer:16,
Payload/binary>> = SomeBinary.
```

If SomeBinary does contain a TCP segment from some networking code, it can be extracted with a similar pattern. All values are in bits (except for the Payload, which is of arbitrary length), and well defined by a standard. Whichever part of the segment your program needs can then be referred to by its corresponding variable.

The same logic can then be applied to anything binary: video encoding, images, other protocol implementations, and so on.

DON'T DRINK TOO MUCH KOOL-AID

Erlang can be slow compared to languages like C or C++. Unless you are a patient person (or a prodigy), it would likely be a bad idea to do stuff like converting videos or images with it, even though the binary syntax makes it extremely interesting. Erlang is traditionally just not that great at heavy number-crunching.

Take note, however, that Erlang is usually mighty fast for applications that do not require number-crunching, such as reacting to events, message-passing (with the help of atoms being extremely light), and so on. It can deal with events in matters of milliseconds, and as such, is a great candidate for soft real-time applications.

Binary Strings

There's a whole other aspect to binary notation: *binary strings*. Binary strings are bolted on top of the language in the same way strings are with lists, but they're much more efficient in terms of space. This is because normal lists are similar to linked lists (one "node" per letter, and then a reference to the next part of the list), while binary strings are more like C arrays (a tightly packed block of memory).

Binary strings use the syntax <<"this is a binary string!">>. The downside of binary strings compared to lists is a loss in simplicity when it comes to pattern matching and manipulation. Consequently, people tend to use binary strings when storing text that won't be manipulated too much or when space efficiency is a real issue.

Even though binary strings are pretty light, you should avoid using them to tag values. It might be tempting to use string literals to say, for example, {<<"temperature">>,50}, but you should always use atoms in that case. Using atoms results in almost no overhead when comparing different values, and such comparisons are done in constant time regardless of length, while binaries are compared in linear time. Conversely, do not use atoms to replace strings because they are lighter. Strings can be manipulated (splitting, regular expressions, and so on), while atoms can only be compared and nothing else.

Binary Comprehensions

Binary comprehensions are to bit syntax what list comprehensions are to lists: a way to make code short and concise when dealing with binaries. They can generally be used in the same manner as list comprehensions:

```
1> << <<X>> || <<X>> <= <<1,2,3,4,5>>, X rem 2 == 0>>.
<<2,4>>
```

The only change in syntax from regular list comprehensions is the <-, which becomes <= for binary generators, and using binaries (<<>>) instead of lists ([]).

Earlier in this chapter, you saw an example of using pattern matching to grab RGB values from a binary value that represented many pixels. That technique worked well in that example, but on larger structures, it could become harder to read and maintain. The same exercise can be done with a one-line binary comprehension, which is much cleaner:

```
2> Pixels = <<213,45,132,64,76,32,76,0,0,234,32,15>>.
<<213,45,132,64,76,32,76,0,0,234,32,15>>
3> RGB = [ {R,G,B} || <<R:8,G:8,B:8>> <= Pixels ].
[{213,45,132},{64,76,32},{76,0,0},{234,32,15}]
```

Changing <- to <= lets you use a binary as a generator. The complete binary comprehension basically changed binary data to integers inside tuples. Another binary comprehension syntax exists to let you do the exact opposite:

```
4> << <<R:8, G:8, B:8>> || {R,G,B} <- RGB >>.
<<213,45,132,64,76,32,76,0,0,234,32,15>>
```

Be careful, as the elements of the resulting binary require a clearly defined binary type if the generator returned binaries:

```
5> << <<Bin>> || Bin <- [<<3,7,5,4,7>>] >>.
** exception error: bad argument
6> << <<Bin/binary>> || Bin <- [<<3,7,5,4,7>>] >>.
<<3,7,5,4,7>>
```

By default, Erlang assumes that values you try to put into or extract from a binary are integers (unsigned, on 8 bits). When writing <<Bin>>, we're in fact declaring that we want a binary containing an integer that is stored in the variable Bin. The problem is that Bin holds another binary, and that just doesn't make sense to Erlang. We said we would give an integer, and we gave a binary. By specifying that the type is binary (as on line 6), Erlang is able to deal with the pattern because what we say Bin is and what Bin contains now make sense.

It's also possible to have a binary comprehension with a binary generator:

```
7> << <<(X+1)/integer>> || <<X>> <= <<3,7,5,4,7>> >>.
<<4,8,6,5,8>>
```

Note that specifying the type as integer is superfluous in this case, as Erlang assumes integers by default.

In this book, I won't go into much more detail on binaries and binary comprehensions. If you're interested in understanding more about bit syntax as a whole, you can read the white paper that defines their specification, at *http://user.it.uu.se/~pergu/papers/erlang05.pdf.*

2

MODULES

Working with the interactive shell is a vital part of using dynamic programming languages. It's useful to test all kinds of code and programs. In Chapter 1, we used the interactive shell to play with most of Erlang's basic data types without ever opening a text editor or saving a file. While you could stop reading here, go play ball outside, and call it a day, that would make you a terrible Erlang programmer. Code needs to be saved somewhere to be used! As you'll learn in this chapter, that's what modules are for.

What Are Modules?

A *module* is a bunch of functions grouped together in a single file, under a single name. All functions in Erlang must be defined in modules. You have already used modules, perhaps without realizing it. The

BIFs mentioned in Chapter 1, such as hd and tl, actually belong to the erlang module. All of the arithmetic, logic, and Boolean operators also are in the erlang module.

BIFs from the erlang module differ from other functions, as they are automatically imported when you use Erlang. Every other function defined in a module needs to be called with the form *Module:Function(Arguments)*, as in this example:

```
1> erlang:element(2, {a,b,c}).
b
2> element(2, {a,b,c}).
b
3> lists:seq(1,4).
[1,2,3,4]
4> seq(1,4).
** exception error: undefined shell command seq/2
```

Here, the seq function from the lists module was not automatically imported, while element was. The error "undefined shell command" comes from the shell looking for a shell command like f() and not being able to find it. Some functions from the erlang module are not imported automatically, but they are not used very frequently.

Logically, you should put functions that deal with similar things inside a single module. Common operations on lists are kept in the lists module, while functions to do input and output (such as writing to the terminal or in a file) are grouped in the io module or the file module. One of the only modules you will encounter that doesn't respect that pattern is the erlang module, which has functions that do math, perform conversions, deal with multiprocessing, fiddle with the VM's settings, and so on. They have nothing in common except being BIFs. You should avoid creating modules like erlang, and instead focus on clean and logical separations.

Creating Modules

When writing a module, you can declare two kinds of things: *functions* and *attributes*. Attributes are metadata describing the module itself, such as its name, the functions that should be visible to the outside world, the author of the code, and so on. This kind of metadata is useful because it gives hints to the compiler on how it should do its job, and also because it lets people retrieve information from compiled code without needing to consult the source.

A large variety of module attributes is currently used in Erlang code across the world. In fact, you can even declare your own attributes for whatever you please. However, some predefined attributes will appear more frequently than others in your code.

All module attributes follow the form *-Name(Attribute)..* Only one of them is necessary for your module to be compilable:

```
-module(Name).
```

This is always the first attribute (and statement) of a file, and for good reason: It's the name of the current module, where `Name` is an atom. This is the name you'll use to call functions from other modules. The calls are made with the form `M:F(A)`, where `M` is the module name, `F` the function, and `A` the arguments.

Note that the name of the module as defined in the `-module` attribute and the filename must match. For example, if the module name is `unimaginative_name`, then the file should be named *unimaginative_name.erl* (*.erl* is the standard Erlang source extension). If the names don't match, your module won't compile.

It's time to code already! Our first module will be very simple and useless. Open your text editor, type the following line, and then save the file as *useless.erl.*

```
-module(useless).
```

This line of text is actually a valid module. Really! Of course, it's useless without functions. Let's first decide which functions will be exported from our useless module. To do this, we will use another attribute:

```
-export([Function1/Arity, Function2/Arity, ..., FunctionN/Arity]).
```

This is used to define which functions of a module can be called by the outside world. It takes a list of functions with their respective arity. The *arity* of a function is an integer representing how many arguments can be passed to the function. This is critical information, because different functions defined within a module can share the same name if, and only if, they have a different arity. The functions `add(X,Y)` and `add(X,Y,Z)` would thus be considered different, and written in the form `add/2` and `add/3`, respectively.

NOTE   *Exported functions represent a module's interface. It is important to define an interface that reveals only the bare minimum of what is necessary to use the module's functions. This lets you fiddle with the internal details of your implementations without breaking code that might depend on your module.*

Our useless module will first export a useful function named `add`, which will take two arguments. Add the following `-export` attribute after the module declaration:

```
-export([add/2]).
```

And now we can write the function:

```
add(A,B) ->
    A + B.
```

The syntax of a function follows the form *Name(Args) -> Body.*, where *Name* must be an atom, and *Body* can be one or more Erlang expressions separated by commas. The function is ended with a period. Note that Erlang doesn't use the return keyword as many imperative languages do. A return is useless! Instead, the last logical expression of a function to be executed will have its value returned to the caller automatically, without you needing to mention it.

Next, add the following function to the file. (Yes, every tutorial needs a "Hello, world" example!) Don't forget to add it to the -export attribute as well (the -export attribute should then look like -export([add/2, hello/0]).).

```
%% Shows greetings.
%% io:format/1 is the standard function used to output text.
hello() ->
    io:format("Hello, world!~n").
```

The first thing to notice in this listing is the comments. In Erlang, comments are single-line only and begin with a % sign. (In this case, we've used %%, but this is purely a question of style.) The hello/0 function also demonstrates how to call functions from foreign modules inside your own module. In this case, io:format/1 is the standard function to output text, as written in the comments.

NOTE   *The convention in the Erlang community is to use three percent signs (%%%) for comments that are general to a module (what the module is used for, licenses, and so on) and divisions of different sections of a module (public code, private code, helper functions, and so on). Two percent signs (%%) are used for all other comments that are alone on their own line and at the same level of indentation as the surrounding code. A single % is used for comments at the end of a line where there is code.*

Let's add one last function to the module, using both functions add/2 and hello/0:

```
greet_and_add_two(X) ->
    hello(),
    add(X,2).
```

Again, don't forget to add greet_and_add_two/1 to the exported function list. The calls to hello/0 and add/2 don't need to have the module name prepended to them, because they were declared in the module itself.

If you wanted to be able to call io:format/1 in the same manner as add/2, or any other function defined within the current module, you could have added the following module attribute at the beginning of the file: -import(io, [format/1]).. Then you could have called format("Hello, World!~n"). directly. More generally, the -import attribute follows this recipe:

```
-import(Module, [Function1/Arity, ..., FunctionN/Arity]).
```

Importing a function is a handy shortcut, although most programmers strongly discourage the use of the -import attribute, as it can reduce the readability of code. For example, in the case of io:format/2, there's another function in a different library with the same name: io_lib:format/2. Determining which one is used requires going to the top of the file to see from which module it was imported, if it was imported in the first place. Consequently, including the module name is considered good practice and will help the many Erlang users who love to use grep to find their way across projects. Usually, the only functions you'll see imported come from the lists module; its functions are used with a higher frequency than those from most other modules.

Your useless module should now look like the following:

```
-module(useless).
-export([add/2, hello/0, greet_and_add_two/1]).

add(A,B) ->
    A + B.

%% Shows greetings.
%% io:format/1 is the standard function used to output text.
hello() ->
    io:format("Hello, world!~n").

greet_and_add_two(X) ->
    hello(),
    add(X,2).
```

We are now finished with the useless module. Save your *useless.erl* file, and then we can try to compile it.

Compiling Code

Erlang code is compiled to bytecode so it can be used by the VM. You can call the compiler from many places. The most common way is to call it from the command line, like so:

```
$ erlc flags file.erl
```

When in the shell or in a module, you can compile it like this:

```
compile:file(Filename)
```

Another way, often used when developing code, is to compile from the shell:

```
c()
```

It's time to compile our useless module and try it out. But first we need to tell the Erlang shell where to find our module. Open the Erlang shell and type the following, filling in the full path where your file is saved.

```
1> cd("/path/to/where/you/saved/the-module/").
"Path Name to the directory you are in"
ok
```

By default, the shell will only look for files in the same directory it was started in and the standard library. The cd/1 function is defined exclusively for the Erlang shell, telling it to change the directory to a new one, so it's less annoying to browse for files.

Next, enter the following:

```
2> c(useless).
{ok,useless}
```

If you get a different message—one that looks something like useless.erl:*Line*: *Some Error Message*—make sure the file is named correctly; that you are in the right directory; and that you've made no mistakes in your module, such as using unmatched parentheses, forgetting about full stops (.), and so on.

After you've successfully compiled your code, you'll notice that a *useless.beam* file has been added next to *useless.erl* in your working directory. This is the compiled module.

The .beam filename extension stands for Bogdan/Björn's Erlang Abstract Machine, which is the VM itself. Other VMs for Erlang exist, but most are not used anymore. For example, Joe's Abstract Machine (JAM), inspired by Prolog's WAM and old BEAM, attempted to compile Erlang to C, and then to native code. Benchmarks demonstrated little benefit in this practice, and the concept was given up. More recently, there has been an effort to port Erlang to the JVM, giving the Erjang *language. While the results are impressive, few developers have switched over to the Java platform for their Erlang development.*

Now let's try our first functions!

```
3> useless:add(7,2).
9
4> useless:hello().
Hello, world!
ok
5> useless:greet_and_add_two(-3).
Hello, world!
-1
6> useless:not_a_real_function().
** exception error: undefined function useless:not_a_real_function/0
```

The functions work as expected: add/2 adds numbers, hello/0 outputs Hello, world!, and greet_and_add_two/1 does both. Of course, you might be asking why hello/0 returns the atom ok after outputting text. This is because Erlang functions and expressions must *always* return something, even if they would not need to in other languages. As such, io:format/1 returns ok to denote a normal condition: the absence of errors.

Line 6 shows an error being thrown because the function we tried to call doesn't exist in our module. If you forget to export a function, this is the kind of error message you will see when you try to call it.

Compiler Options

Erlang includes many compilation flags that can give you more control over how a module is compiled. You can get a list of all of them in the Erlang documentation. The following are the most common flags:

-debug_info
    Erlang tools such as debuggers, code-coverage utilities, and static-analysis utilities will use the debug information of a module to do their work. In general, it is recommended to always turn on this option. You are more likely to need this option than the little bits of extra space you would save by not having it in your compiled code.

-{outdir,*Dir*}

> By default, the Erlang compiler will create the *.beam* files in the current directory. This will let you choose where to put the compiled file.

-export_all

> This flag causes the compiler to ignore the -export module attribute and instead export all functions defined. This is mainly useful when testing and developing new code, but should not be used in production.

-{d,*Macro*} or {d,*Macro,Value*}

> This flag defines a macro to be used in the module, where `Macro` is an atom. This is most frequently used when unit testing, as it ensures that a module will have its testing functions created and exported only when they are explicitly wanted. By default, `Value` is `true` if it's not defined as the third element of the tuple.

To compile our useless module with some flags, we could do one of the following:

```
7> compile:file(useless, [debug_info, export_all]).
{ok,useless}
8> c(useless, [debug_info, export_all]).
{ok,useless}
```

You can also be sneaky and define compile flags from within a module, with a module attribute. To get the same results as from lines 7 and 8, you could add the following to the module:

```
-compile([debug_info, export_all]).
```

NOTE   *Another option is to compile your Erlang module to native code. Native code compiling is* not *available for every platform and operating system, but on those that support this feature, it can make your programs go faster (about 20 percent faster, based on anecdotal evidence). To compile to native code, you need to use the* `hipe` *module and call it the following way:* `hipe:c`(Module,OptionsList). *You could also use* `c`(Module,[native]). *when in the shell to achieve similar results. Note that the .beam file generated will no longer be portable across platforms. In general, compiling with* `hipe` *is seen as a last resort to get performance out of CPU-intensive operations.*

Defining Macros

Erlang *macros* are similar to C's #define statements, and are mainly used to define short functions and constants. They are simple expressions represented by text that will be replaced before the code is compiled for the VM. Such macros are mainly useful to avoid having "magic values" floating around your modules. For example, if you were to see code that compares some variable to a hard-coded number 3600, you'd have no idea if it represented 1 hour (3600 seconds), 60 hours (3600 minutes), some monetary amount, etc. However, if you encounter a value such as ?HOUR, which is an Erlang macro, then you instantly have an idea of what you are dealing with. Even better, if you eventually switch your representation from seconds (3600) to, say, milliseconds (3,600,000), you need only change the macro definition in order to update all the instances of the macro in your code.

You can define such a macro as a module attribute in the following way:

```
-define(MACRO, some_value).
```

You can then use the macro as ?MACRO inside any function defined in the module, and it will be replaced by *some_value* before the code is compiled. For the hour example above, we would define the macro as follows:

```
-define(HOUR, 3600). % in seconds
```

Defining a "function" macro is similar. Here's a simple macro used to subtract one number from another:

```
-define(sub(X,Y), X-Y).
```

To use this macro, simply call it in the same way that you would call any other macro. For example, if you called ?sub(23,47), this would be replaced with 23-47 by the compiler.

There are also a few predefined macros, such as the following:

- ?MODULE, which is replaced by the current module name as an atom
- ?FILE, which is replaced by the filename as a string
- ?LINE, which returns the line number of wherever the macro is placed

You can also check whether particular macros are defined in your code and conditionally define other macros based on that result. To do this, use the attributes -ifdef(MACRO)., -else., and -endif. as in this example:

```
-ifdef(DEBUGMODE).
-define(DEBUG(S), io:format("dbg: "++S)).
-else.
-define(DEBUG(S), ok).
-endif.
```

When used in code, the macro will look like ?DEBUG("entering some function"), and will only output information if the module is compiled with a DEBUGMODE macro present. Otherwise, the atom ok is declared and does nothing at all.

As another example, you could also define tests to exist only if some test macro is first defined:

```
-ifdef(TEST).
my_test_function() ->
    run_some_tests().
-endif.
```

Then, using the compile flags mentioned previously, we can choose whether to define DEBUGMODE or TEST as c(*Module*, [{d,'TEST'},{d,'DEBUGMODE'}])..

More About Modules

Before we move on to writing more powerful functions and fewer useless snippets of code, we'll look at a few other miscellaneous bits of information about modules that might be useful to you in the future.

Metadata

As mentioned earlier in the chapter, module attributes are metadata describing properties of the module itself. Where can we find this metadata when we don't have an access to the source? Well, the compiler plays nice with us—when compiling a module, it will pick up most module attributes and store them (along with other information) in a module_info/0 function.

You can see the metadata of the useless module like this:

```
9> useless:module_info().
[{exports,[{add,2},
           {hello,0},
           {greet_and_add_two,1},
           {module_info,0},
           {module_info,1}]},
 {imports,[]},
 {attributes,[{vsn,[174839656007867314473085021121413256129]}]},
 {compile,[{options,[]},
 {version,"4.8"},
 {time,{2013,2,13,2,56,32}},
 {source,"/home/ferd/learn-you-some-erlang/useless.erl"}]}]
10> useless:module_info(attributes).
[{vsn,[174839656007867314473085021121413256129]}]
```

This snippet also shows an additional function, module_info/1, which will let you grab one specific piece of information. You can see exported functions, imported functions (none in this case), attributes (this is where your custom metadata would go), and compile options and information. Had you decided to add -author("An Erlang Champ"). to your module, it would have ended up in the same section as vsn.

NOTE *vsn is an automatically generated unique value that differentiates each version of your code, excluding comments. It is used in code hot-loading (upgrading an application while it runs, without stopping it) and by some tools related to release handling. You can also specify a vsn value yourself by adding -vsn(VersionNumber) to your module.*

There are limited uses for module attributes when it comes to production code, but they can be nice when doing little tricks to help yourself out. For example, I'm using them in my testing script for this book to annotate functions for which unit tests could be better. The script looks up module attributes, finds the annotated functions, and shows a warning about them. If you're interested in looking at this script, you can find it at *http://learnyousomeerlang.com/static/erlang/tester.erl*.

Circular Dependencies

Another point to keep in mind about module design is to avoid circular dependencies. A module A should not call a module B that also calls module A. Such dependencies usually end up making code maintenance difficult.

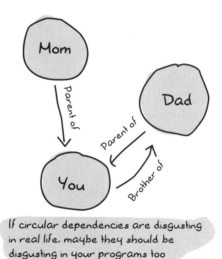

If circular dependencies are disgusting in real life, maybe they should be disgusting in your programs too

In fact, code that depends on too many modules—even if they're not in a circular dependency—can make maintenance harder. The last thing you want is to wake up in the middle of the night only to find a maniac software engineer trying to gouge your eyes out because of terrible code you have written.

Well, that's enough of the pedantic moralizing. In Chapter 3, we'll continue our exploration of Erlang, focusing on functions.

3

SYNTAX IN FUNCTIONS

Now that we have the ability to store and compile our code, we can begin to write more advanced functions. The functions that we have written so far are extremely simple and a bit underwhelming. Now let's get to more interesting stuff. In this chapter, we'll work with functions that behave differently depending on the arguments passed to them and expressions that let us make decisions based on different conditions.

Pattern Matching

The first function we'll write will greet someone differently according to gender. To achieve this in most procedural languages, you would need to write something similar to the following pseudocode:

```
function greet(Gender,Name)
    if Gender == male then
        print("Hello, Mr. %s!", Name)
    else if Gender == female then
        print("Hello, Mrs. %s!", Name)
    else
```

```
        print("Hello, %s!", Name)
    end
```

Erlang can save you a whole lot of boilerplate code with pattern matching, which we used in Chapter 1. That chapter showed how we can compare and assign variables in structures like lists and tuples (remember patterns like {point,{X,Y}}).

Erlang lets us use similar patterns when defining functions. An Erlang version of the greet function looks like this:

```
greet(male, Name) ->
    io:format("Hello, Mr. ~s!", [Name]);
greet(female, Name) ->
    io:format("Hello, Mrs. ~s!", [Name]);
greet(_, Name) ->
    io:format("Hello, ~s!", [Name]).
```

When we were in the shell and a given pattern could not be matched, Erlang would throw a fit and yell at us with an error message. When a pattern fails in a function (such as greet(male, Name)), Erlang just looks for the next part of the function with a different pattern (here, it would be greet(female, Name)) and runs that one if it matches.

The main difference between the two versions of greet is that in Erlang, we use pattern matching to define which parts of a function should be used and bind the values we need at the same time. There is no need to first bind the values and then compare them. So instead of this form:

```
function(Args)
    if X then
        Expression
    else if Y then
        Expression
    else
        Expression
```

we write this:

```
function(X) ->
    Expression;
function(Y) ->
    Expression;
function(_) ->
    Expression.
```

This allows us to get similar results, but in a much more declarative style.

Each of these function declarations is called a *function clause*. Function clauses must be separated by semicolons (;) and together form a *function declaration*. A function declaration counts as one larger statement, which is why the final function clause ends with a period. It's a strange use of tokens to determine workflow, but you'll get used to it. At least you'd better hope so, because there's no way out of it!

FORMATTING WITH IO:FORMAT

`io:format`'s formatting is done with the help of tokens being replaced in a string. The tilde (~) character is used to denote a token. Some tokens are built in, such as ~n, which will be changed to a line break. Most other tokens denote a way to format data. For example, the function call `io:format("~s!~n",["Hello"])`. includes the token ~s, which accepts strings and binary strings as arguments. The final output message would be `"Hello!\n"`. Another widely used token is ~p, which will print an Erlang term in the same way terms are output for you by the Erlang shell (adding indentation and everything).

　　We'll pick more uses of `io:format` as we go, but in the meantime, you can try the following calls to see what they do:

```
io:format("~s~n",[<<"Hello">>])
io:format("~p~n",[<<"Hello">>])
io:format("~~~n")
io:format("~f~n", [4.0])
io:format("~30f~n", [4.0])
```

　　This is just a small sample of `io:format`'s possibilities. You can read the online documentation to find out more.

Fancier Patterns

Pattern matching in functions can be quite complex and powerful. As you may remember from Chapter 1, we can pattern match on lists to get their heads and tails. Let's do that!

　　Start a new module called `functions`:

```
-module(functions).
-compile(export_all). % Replace with -export() later, for sanity's sake!
```

　　In this module, we'll write a bunch of functions to explore many of the available pattern-matching avenues. The first function we'll write is head/1, which will act exactly like erlang:hd/1: It will take a list as an argument and return its first element. We'll do this with the help of the cons operator (|) and the "don't care" variable (_):

```
head([H|_]) -> H.
```

If you type functions:head([1,2,3,4]). in the shell (once the module is compiled), you can expect the value 1 to be returned. Consequently, to get the second element of a list, you would create this function:

```
second([_,X|_]) -> X.
```

Erlang will be smart enough to look inside the list and fetch what it needs in order for the pattern match to succeed. Try it in the shell:

```
1> c(functions).
{ok, functions}
2> functions:head([1,2,3,4]).
1
3> functions:second([1,2,3,4]).
2
```

Retrieving values with pattern matching could be done for lists as long as you want, although it would be impractical to do it up to thousands of values. The smarter way to accomplish this is to use recursive functions, which are covered in Chapter 5. For now, let's concentrate on more pattern matching.

Variables in a Bind

The concept of free and bound variables discussed in Chapter 1 still holds true for functions. Let's review bound and unbound variables, using a wedding scenario.

Here, the bridegroom is sad because in Erlang, variables can never change value—no freedom! On the other hand, unbound

variables don't have any values attached to them (like our little bum on the right). Binding a variable is simply attaching a value to an unbound variable. In the case of Erlang, when you want to assign a value to a variable that is already bound, an error occurs *unless the new value is the same as the old one.* Let's imagine our guy on the left has married one of two twins. If the second twin comes around, he won't differentiate them and will act normally. If a different woman comes around, he'll complain. (You can review "Invariable Variables" on page 11 if this concept is not clear to you.)

Using pattern matching and functions, we can compare and know if two parameters passed to a function are the same. For this, we'll create a function named same/2 that takes two arguments and tells if they're identical:

```
same(X,X) ->
    true;
same(_,_) ->
    false.
```

And it's that simple.

When you call same(a,a), the first X is seen as unbound; it automatically takes the value a. Then when Erlang goes to the second argument, it sees X is already bound. Erlang then compares the value to the a passed as the second argument and checks if it matches. The pattern matching succeeds, and the function returns true. If the two values aren't the same, pattern matching will fail and go to the second function clause, which doesn't care about its arguments (when you're the last to choose, you can't be picky!) and will instead return false. Note that this function can effectively take any kind of argument whatsoever. It works for any type of data, not just lists or single variables.

Now let's look at a more advanced example. The following function prints a date, but only if it is formatted correctly.

```
valid_time({Date = {Y,M,D}, Time = {H,Min,S}}) ->
    io:format("The Date tuple (~p) says today is: ~p/~p/~p,~n",[Date,Y,M,D]),
    io:format("The time tuple (~p) indicates: ~p:~p:~p.~n", [Time,H,Min,S]);
valid_time(_) ->
    io:format("Stop feeding me wrong data!~n").
```

Note that it is possible to use the = operator in the function head, allowing us to match both the content inside a tuple ({Y,M,D}) and the tuple as a whole (Date). We can test the function like this:

```
4> c(functions).
{ok, functions}
5> functions:valid_time({{2013,12,12},{09,04,43}}).
The Date tuple ({2013,9,6}) says today is: 2013/9/6,
The time tuple ({9,4,43}) indicates: 9:4:43.
ok
6> functions:valid_time({{2013,09,06},{09,04}}).
Stop feeding me wrong data!
ok
```

There is a problem though. This function could take anything for values, even text or atoms, as long as the tuples are in the form {{A,B,C},{D,E,F}}. This is one of the limits of pattern matching. It can either specify really precise values, such as a known number or atom, or abstract values, such as the head or tail of a list, a tuple of N elements, or anything (_ and unbound variables). To solve this problem, we use guards.

Guards, Guards!

Guards are additional clauses that can go in a function's head to make pattern matching more expressive. As mentioned earlier, pattern matching is somewhat limited, as it cannot express things like a range of values or certain types of data.

One concept that cannot be represented with pattern matching is counting: Is this 12-year-old basketball player too short to play with the pros? Is this distance too long to walk on your hands? Are you too old or too young to drive a car? You couldn't answer these questions with simple pattern matching. You could represent the driving question in a very impractical way like this:

```
old_enough(0) -> false;
old_enough(1) -> false;
old_enough(2) -> false;
...
old_enough(14) -> false;
old_enough(15) -> false;
old_enough(_) -> true.
```

You can do that if you want, but you'll be alone to work on your code forever. If you want to eventually make friends, start a new guards module, and then type in the following solution to the driving question:

```
old_enough(X) when X >= 16 -> true;
old_enough(_) -> false.
```

And you're finished! As you can see, this is much shorter and cleaner than the previous version.

A basic rule for guard expressions is that they must return true to succeed. The guard will fail if it returns false or if it raises an exception.

Suppose we now forbid people who are over 104 years old from driving. Our valid ages for drivers are from 16 years old up to 104 years old. We need to take care of that, but how? Let's just add a second guard clause:

```
right_age(X) when X >= 16, X =< 104 ->
    true;
right_age(_) ->
    false.
```

In guard expressions, the comma (,) acts in a similar manner to the operator andalso, and the semicolon (;) acts a bit like orelse (described in Chapter 1). Because right_age/1 uses the comma, both guard expressions need to succeed for the whole guard to pass. In fact, if you have any number of guards separated by commas, they all need to succeed for the entire guard to pass.

We could also represent the function in the opposite way:

```
wrong_age(X) when X < 16; X > 104 ->
    true;
wrong_age(_) ->
    false.
```

And we get correct results from this approach, too. Test it if you want (you should always test stuff!).

NOTE *I've compared , and ; in guards to the operators* andalso *and* orelse. *They're not exactly the same, though. The former pair will catch exceptions as they happen, while the latter will not. What this means is that if there is an error thrown in the first part of the guard* X >= N; N >= 0, *the second part can still be evaluated, and the guard might succeed. If an error was thrown in the first part of* X >= N orelse N >= 0, *the second part will also be skipped, and the whole guard will fail. However (there is always a "however"), only* andalso *and* orelse *can be nested inside guards. This means* (A orelse B) andalso C *is a valid guard, while* (A; B), C *is not. Given their different use, the best strategy is often to mix them as necessary.*

In addition to using comparisons and Boolean evaluation in your guards, you can use math operations (for example, A*B/C >= 0) and functions about data types, such as is_integer/1, is_atom/1, and so on. (We'll talk more about these kinds of functions in Chapter 4.)

One negative point about guards is that they will not accept user-defined functions because of side effects. Erlang is not a purely functional programming language (like Haskell) because it relies on side effects a lot. You can do I/O, send messages between actors, or raise exceptions as you want and when you want. There is no trivial way to determine if a function you would use in a guard would print text or catch important errors every time it is tested over many function clauses. So instead, Erlang just doesn't trust you (and it may be right not to!).

That being said, you should now know enough to understand the basic syntax of guards and to understand them when you encounter them.

What the If?!

An if clause acts like a guard and shares the guard syntax, but outside a function clause's head. In fact, if clauses are called *guard patterns*.

Erlang's ifs are different from the ifs you'll ever encounter in most other languages. Compared to those other if clauses, Erlang's versions are weird creatures that might have been more accepted it they had a different name. When entering Erlang country, you should leave all you know about ifs at the door.

To see how similar the if expression is to guards, enter the following examples in a module named what_the_if.erl:

```
-module(what_the_if).
-export([heh_fine/0]).

heh_fine() ->
    if 1 =:= 1 ->
        works
    end,
    if 1 =:= 2; 1 =:= 1 ->
        works
    end,
 ❶ if 1 =:= 2, 1 =:= 1 ->
        fails
    end.
```

Save the module and let's try it:

```
1> c(what_the_if).
./what_the_if.erl:12: Warning: no clause will ever match
./what_the_if.erl:12: Warning: the guard for this clause evaluates to 'false'
{ok,what_the_if}
2> what_the_if:heh_fine().
** exception error: no true branch found when evaluating an if expression
in function  what_the_if:heh_fine/0
```

Uh-oh! The compiler is warning us that no clause from the if at ❶ will ever match because its only guard evaluates to false. Remember that in Erlang, everything must return something, and if expressions are no exception to the rule. As such, when Erlang can't find a way to have a guard succeed, it will crash; it cannot *not* return something (this explains why the VM threw a "no true branch found" error when it got mad). We need to add a catchall branch that will always succeed no matter what. In most languages, this would be called an else. In Erlang, we use true, like this:

```
oh_god(N) ->
    if N =:= 2 -> might_succeed;
    true -> always_does  %% This is Erlang's if's 'else!'
end.
```

And now we can test this new function (the old one will keep spitting warnings; ignore them or take them as a reminder of what not to do):

```
3> c(what_the_if).
./what_the_if.erl:12: Warning: no clause will ever match
./what_the_if.erl:12: Warning: the guard for this clause evaluates to 'false'
{ok,what_the_if}
4> what_the_if:oh_god(2).
might_succeed
5> what_the_if:oh_god(3).
always_does
```

Here's another function that shows how to use many guards in an `if` expression:

```
%% Note that this one would be better as a pattern match in function heads!
%% I'm doing it this way for the sake of the example.
help_me(Animal) ->
    Talk = if Animal == cat  -> "meow";
              Animal == beef -> "mooo";
              Animal == dog  -> "bark";
              Animal == tree -> "bark";
              true -> "fgdadfgna"
           end,
    {Animal, "says " ++ Talk ++ "!"}.
```

This function also demonstrates how any expression must return something. Talk has the result of the `if` expression bound to it, and is then concatenated in a string, inside a tuple. When reading the code, it's easy to see how the lack of a true branch would mess things up, considering Erlang has no such thing as a null value (such as Lisp's nil, C's NULL, and Python's None).

Let's try it:

```
6> c(what_the_if).
./what_the_if.erl:12: Warning: no clause will ever match
./what_the_if.erl:12: Warning: the guard for this clause evaluates to 'false'
{ok,what_the_if}
7> what_the_if:help_me(dog).
{dog,"says bark!"}
8> what_the_if:help_me("it hurts!").
{"it hurts!","says fgdadfgna!"}
```

You might be one of the many Erlang programmers wondering why `true` has taken over `else` as an atom to control flow—after all, `else` is much more familiar. Richard O'Keefe gave the following answer on the Erlang mailing lists, which I'll quote directly because I couldn't have put it better:

> It may be more FAMILIAR, but that doesn't mean 'else' is a good thing. I know that writing '; true ->' is a very easy way to get 'else' in Erlang, but we have a couple of decades of psychology-of-programming results to show that it's a bad idea. I have started to replace   by

```
if X > Y -> a()           if X > Y  -> a()
 ; true  -> b()            ; X =< Y -> b()
end                       end


if X > Y -> a()           if X > Y -> a()
 ; X < Y -> b()            ; X < Y -> b()
 ; true  -> c()            ; X ==Y -> c()
end                       end
```

> which I find mildly annoying when _writing_ the code but enormously helpful when _reading_ it.[1]

In other words, `else` or `true` branches should be avoided altogether. The `if` expressions are usually easier to read when you cover all logical ends, rather than relying on a catchall clause.

NOTE   *All this horror expressed by the function names in* what_the_if.erl *is in regard to the* if *language construct when seen from the perspective of any other language's* if. *In Erlang, it turns out to be a perfectly logical construct with a confusing name.*

As mentioned earlier, only a limited set of functions can be used in guard expressions (we'll look at more of them in Chapter 4). This is where the real conditional powers of Erlang must be conjured. I present to you . . . the case expression!

In case ... of

If the `if` expression is like a guard, a `case ... of` expression is like the whole function head. You can have the complex pattern matching available for each argument of a function, and you can have guards, too.

For this example, we'll write the `insert` function for sets (a collection of unique values) that we will represent as an unordered list. This may be the

---

1. *http://erlang.org/pipermail/erlang-questions/2009-January/041229.html*

worst implementation possible in terms of efficiency, but what we want here is the syntax. Enter the following code in a file named cases.erl:

```
insert(X,[]) ->
    [X];
insert(X,Set) ->
    case lists:member(X,Set) of
        true  -> Set;
        false -> [X|Set]
    end.
```

If we send in an empty set (list) and a term X to be added, this code returns a list containing only X. Otherwise, the function lists:member/2 checks whether an element is part of a list, and returns true if it is or false if it is not. If we already have the element X in the set, we do not need to modify the list. Otherwise, we add X as the list's first element.

In this case, the pattern matching is really simple. However, it can get more complex, as in this example (still in the cases module):

```
beach(Temperature) ->
    case Temperature of
        {celsius, N} when N >= 20, N =< 45 ->
            'favorable';
        {kelvin, N} when N >= 293, N =< 318 ->
            'scientifically favorable';
        {fahrenheit, N} when N >= 68, N =< 113 ->
            'favorable in the US';
        _ ->
            'avoid beach'
    end.
```

Here, the answer to "Is it the right time to go to the beach?" is given in three different temperature systems: Celsius, Kelvin, and Fahrenheit. Pattern matching and guards are combined in order to return an answer satisfying all uses.

As pointed out earlier, case ... of expressions are pretty much the same thing as a bunch of function heads with guards. In fact, we could have written our code the following way:

```
beachf({celsius, N}) when N >= 20, N =< 45 ->
    'favorable';
...
beachf(_) ->
    'avoid beach'.
```

This raises the question of whether we should use if, case ... of, or functions for conditional expressions.

Which Should We Use?

Which of these three expressions—if, case … of, or functions—to use is rather hard to answer. The differences between function calls and case … of are minimal. In fact, they are represented the same way at a lower level, and they both effectively have the same performance cost. One obvious difference arises when more than one argument needs to be evaluated. For example, function(A,B) -> ... can have guards and values to match against A and B, but a case expression would need to be formulated a bit, like this:

```
case {A,B} of
    Pattern Guards -> ...
end.
```

This form might seem a bit surprising. In similar situations, using a function call might be more appropriate. On the other hand, the insert/2 function we wrote earlier is arguably cleaner the way it is, rather than having an immediate function call to track down a simple true or false clause.

And why would you ever use if, given that case expressions and functions are flexible enough to even encompass if through guards? The rationale behind if is quite simple: It was added to the language as a short way to have guards without needing to write the whole pattern-matching part when it wasn't needed.

Of course, all of this is mostly a matter of personal preference. There is no good, solid answer. In fact, this topic is still debated by the Erlang community from time to time. No one is going to try to beat you up because of the method you've chosen, as long as it is easy to understand. As Ward Cunningham, inventor of the wiki, once put it, "Clean code is when you look at a routine and it's pretty much what you expected."

4

TYPES (OR LACK THEREOF)

Modern functional languages are often known for their fancy type systems, which are powerful systems that let programmers obtain more safety and speed while doing less. Static type systems vary a lot—from C- and Java-like systems where annotations are provided to the compiler, to rather complex systems that depend on advanced mathematical concepts to guarantee the crash-free nature of a program. Other type systems are rather crude—not static at all, but dynamic. They give no guarantees about the safety of a piece of software, and just check everything while it runs.

This chapter introduces Erlang's type system, the reasons behind its use, and how that affects you, as a brand-new Erlang programmer.

Dynamite-Strong Typing

As you might have noticed when trying the examples in Chapter 1, and then creating modules and functions in Chapters 2 and 3, we never needed to specify the type of a variable or the type of a function. When pattern matching, the code we wrote didn't need to know what it would be matched against. The tuple {X,Y} could be matched with {atom, 123}, as well as {"A string", <<"binary stuff!">>}, {2.0, ["strings","and",atoms]}, or really anything at all.

When it didn't work, an error was thrown in your face, but only once you ran the code. This is because Erlang is *dynamically typed*. Every error is caught at runtime, and the compiler won't always yell at you when compiling modules where things may result in failure, as in the 5 + llama example in Chapter 1.

One classic friction point between proponents of static and dynamic typing has to do with the safety of the software being written. Some programmers claim that good static type systems will catch most errors before you can even execute the code. As such, statically typed languages are typi-

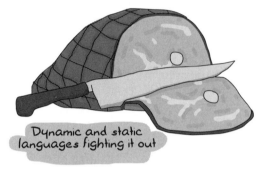

Dynamic and static languages fighting it out

cally seen as safer than their dynamic counterparts. While this might be true in comparison with many dynamic languages, Erlang begs to differ, and it has a track record to prove it.

The best example of Erlang's robustness is the often-reported nine nines (99.9999999 percent) of availability offered on the Ericsson AXD 301 ATM switches, which consist of more than a million lines of Erlang code. Please note that this is not an indication that none of the components in an Erlang-based system failed, but that a general switch system was available 99.9999999 percent of the time, planned outages included. This is partially because Erlang is built on the notion that a failure in one of the components should not affect the whole system. It accounts for errors coming from the programmer, hardware failures, and some network failures. The language includes features that allow distributing a program to different nodes. It can handle unexpected errors and never stop running.

To put it simply, while most languages and type systems aim to allow error-free programs, Erlang assumes that errors will happen and includes features that make those errors easier to handle smoothly and without unnecessary downtime. So Erlang's dynamic type system is not a barrier to the reliability and safety of programs. This sounds like a lot of prophetic talking, but you'll see the gritty details in later chapters.

NOTE *Dynamic typing was historically chosen for simple reasons. The programmers who first implemented Erlang mostly came from dynamically typed languages, and as such, making Erlang dynamic was a natural choice for them. Indirectly, this also proved to be the simplest way to allow hot-reloading (updating code without stopping it first). Doing static type checking on systems where any of its components might be replaced at any time proves to be quite difficult compared to doing it dynamically.*

Erlang is also *strongly typed*. A weakly typed language would do implicit type conversions between terms. For example, if Erlang were weakly typed, we could do the operation 6 = 5 + "1". But because of Erlang's strong typing, trying this operation raises an exception for bad arguments:

```
1> 6 + "1".
** exception error: bad argument in an arithmetic expression
in operator  +/2
called as 6 + "1"
```

Of course, there are times when you may want to convert one kind of data to another type. For example, you might want to change regular strings into binary strings to store them, or convert an integer to a floating-point number. The Erlang standard library provides a number of functions to do these conversions.

Type Conversions

Erlang, like many languages, changes the type of a term by casting it into another one. This is done with the help of BIFs, as many of the conversions could not be implemented in Erlang itself. Each of these functions takes the form *TypeA_to_TypeB*, and they are implemented in the erlang module. Here are a few of them:

```
1> erlang:list_to_integer("54").
54
2> erlang:integer_to_list(54).
"54"
3> erlang:list_to_integer("54.32").
** exception error: bad argument
in function  list_to_integer/1
called as list_to_integer("54.32")
4> erlang:list_to_float("54.32").
54.32
5> erlang:atom_to_list(true).
"true"
6> erlang:list_to_binary("hi there").
<<"hi there">>
7> erlang:binary_to_list(<<"hi there">>).
"hi there"
```

We're hitting on a language wart here: Because the scheme *Type_to_Type* is used, every time a new type is added to the language, a whole lot of conversion BIFs need to be added by the OTP team!

Here's the whole list already there:

atom_to_binary/2	integer_to_list/1	list_to_integer/2
atom_to_list/1	integer_to_list/2	list_to_pid/1
binary_to_atom/2	iolist_to_atom/1	list_to_tuple/1
binary_to_existing_atom/2	iolist_to_binary/1	pid_to_list/1
binary_to_list/1	list_to_atom/1	port_to_list/1
binary_to_term/1	list_to_binary/1	ref_to_list/1
binary_to_term/2	list_to_bitstring/1	term_to_binary/1
bitstring_to_list/1	list_to_existing_atom/1	term_to_binary/2
float_to_list/1	list_to_float/1	tuple_to_list/1
fun_to_list/1		

That's a lot of conversion functions. You'll see most, if not all, of these types in this book, although we probably won't need all of these functions in our code.

NOTE *The BIF binary_to_term/2 lets you unserialize data the same way binary_to_term/1 does. The big difference is that the second argument is an option list. If you pass in [safe], the binary won't be decoded if it contains unknown atoms or anonymous functions, which could exhaust the memory of a node or represent a security risk. Use binary_to_term/2 rather than binary_to_term/1 if you are decoding data that could be unsafe.*

To Guard a Data Type

Erlang basic data types are easy to spot: Tuples have curly brackets, lists have square brackets, strings are enclosed in double quotation marks, and so on. So, we've been able to enforce a certain data type with pattern matching. For example, a function head/1 taking a list could accept only lists because otherwise the matching ([H|_]) would fail.

However, we ran into a problem when pattern matching with numeric values because we couldn't specify ranges. So, in Chapter 3, we used guards in functions that needed to test for certain ranges, such as temperatures, ages, and so on. We're hitting another roadblock now. How could we write a guard that ensures that patterns match against data of a single specific type, like numbers, atoms, or binaries?

There are functions dedicated to the task of guard-ing data types. They take a single argument and return

MY NAME IS
Tuple

true if the type is correct; otherwise, they return false. They are part of the few functions allowed in guard expressions and are named the *type-test BIFs*. The following are the Erlang type-test BIFs:

is_atom/1	is_function/1	is_port/1
is_binary/1	is_function/2	is_record/2
is_bitstring/1	is_integer/1	is_record/3
is_boolean/1	is_list/1	is_reference/1
is_builtin/3	is_number/1	is_tuple/1
is_float/1	is_pid/1	

These functions can be used like any other guard expression, wherever guard expressions are allowed.

You might be wondering why there is no function that just gives the type of the term being evaluated (something akin to type_of(X) -> Type). The answer is simple: Erlang is about programming for the right cases. You program only for what you know will happen and what you expect, and everything else should cause an error as soon as possible. As such, having a single function type_of(X) would encourage people to write conditional branches to code, a bit like this:

```
my_function(Exp) ->
    case type_of(Exp) of
        binary -> Expression1;
        list -> Expression2
    end.
```

This code is equivalent to the following:

```
my_function(Exp) when is_binary(Exp) -> Expression1;
my_function(Exp) when is_list(Exp) -> Expression2.
```

The declarative nature of the language favors the latter form, where we do branching through function heads by specifying what we expect, rather than handling one of many types that a function like type_of(X) might return.

NOTE *Type-test BIFs constitute more than half of the functions allowed in guard expressions. The rest are also BIFs, but do not represent type tests. These include abs(Number), bit_size(Binary), byte_size(Binary), element(N, Tuple), float(Term), hd(List), length(List), node(), node(Pid|Ref|Port), round(Number), self(), tl(List), trunc(Number), and tuple_size(Tuple). The functions node/1 and self/0 are related to distributed Erlang and processes/actors.*

It may seem like Erlang data structures are relatively limited, but lists and tuples are usually enough to build other complex structures. For example, the basic node of a binary tree could be represented as {node, Value, Left, Right}, where Left and Right are either similar nodes or empty tuples. I could also represent myself as follows:

```
{person, {name, <<"Fred T-H">>},
{qualities, ["handsome", "smart", "honest", "objective"]},
{faults, ["liar"]},
{skills, ["programming", "bass guitar", "underwater breakdancing"]}}.
```

This shows that by nesting tuples and lists, and filling them with data, we can obtain complex data structures and build functions to operate on them.

For Type Junkies

If you're a programmer who somehow can't live without a static type system, I invite you to jump to Chapter 30, which covers Dialyzer.

In that chapter, I will briefly describe tools used to do static type analysis in Erlang, allowing you to define custom types and get more safety that way. The types are entirely optional, and although useful, they are not necessary to make good Erlang programs.

5

HELLO RECURSION!

Some readers accustomed to imperative and object-oriented programming languages might be wondering why we haven't covered loops already. The answer to this is a question: What is a loop? The truth is that functional programming languages usually do not offer looping constructs like for and while. Instead, functional programmers rely on a silly concept called *recursion*, which is the topic of this chapter.

How Recursion Works

Recall how invariable variables were explained in Chapter 1 (if you can't, reread "Invariable Variables" on page 11). Recursion can also be explained with the help of mathematical concepts and functions.

A basic mathematical function such as the factorial of a value is a good example of a function that can be expressed recursively. The factorial of a number n is the product of the sequence $1 \times 2 \times 3 \times \ldots \times n$, or alternatively $n \times n - 1 \times n - 2 \times \ldots \times 1$. In mathematical notation, the factorial of a number is represented as the number followed by an exclamation point (!). To give some examples, the factorial of 3 is $3! = 3 \times 2 \times 1 = 6$, and the factorial of 4 is $4! = 4 \times 3 \times 2 \times 1 = 24$. Such a function can be expressed the following way in mathematical notation:

$$n! = \begin{cases} 1 & \text{if } n = 0 \\ n((n-1)!) & \text{if } n > 0 \end{cases}$$

This tells us that if the value of n is 0, we return the result 1. For any value above 0, we return n multiplied by the factorial of $n - 1$, which unfolds until it reaches 1:

$$4! = 4 \times 3!$$
$$4! = 4 \times 3 \times 2!$$
$$4! = 4 \times 3 \times 2 \times 1!$$
$$4! = 4 \times 3 \times 2 \times 1 \times 1$$

How can such a function be translated from mathematical notation to Erlang? The conversion is simple enough. Take a look at the parts of the notation: $n!$, 1, and $n((n-1)!)$, and then the if expressions. What we have here is a function name (n!), guards (the ifs), and a function body (1 and n((n-1)!)). We'll rename n! to fac(N) to restrict our syntax a bit, and we get the following:

```
-module(recursive).
-export([fac/1]).

fac(N) when N == 0 -> 1;
fac(N) when N > 0  -> N*fac(N-1).
```

And this factorial function is now complete! It's pretty similar to the mathematical definition, really. With the help of pattern matching, we can shorten the definition a bit:

```
fac(0) -> 1;
fac(N) when N > 0 -> N*fac(N-1).
```

We looped by using a function that calls itself! And you know what? "A function that calls itself" is one way to define recursion.

However, having a function that calls itself is not enough. If the function just calls itself forever, it will, unsurprisingly, continue forever. What we need is a stopping condition (called a *base case*), which is a function clause where we return a value rather than calling the function again. In our case, the stopping condition is when n is equal to 0. At that point, we no longer tell our function to call itself, and it stops its execution right there by returning 1.

Length of a List

Let's try a slightly more practical example. We'll implement a function to count how many elements a list contains. So we know from the beginning that we will need the following:

- A base case
- A function that calls itself
- A list to test our function

With most recursive functions, I find it easier to write the base case first. What's the simplest input we'll need to find the length of? Surely an empty list, with a length of 0, is the simplest case. So let's make a mental note that [] = 0 when dealing with lengths. Then the next simplest list has a length of 1: [_] = 1. This sounds like enough to get going with our definition. We can write this down:

```
len([]) -> 0;
len([_]) -> 1.
```

Awesome! We can calculate the length of lists, given the length is either 0 or 1. Very useful indeed! Of course, it's useless, because it's not yet recursive, which brings us to the hardest part: extending our function so it calls itself for lists longer than 1 or 0.

I mentioned in Chapter 1 that lists are defined recursively as [1 | [2| ... [n | []]]]. This means we can use the [H|T] pattern to match against lists of one or more elements, as a list of length 1 will be defined as [X|[]], and a list of length 2 will be defined as [X|[Y|[]]]. Note that the second element is a list itself. This means that we need to count only the first one, and the function can call itself on the second element. Given each value in a list counts as a length of 1, the function can be rewritten the following way:

```
len([]) -> 0;
len([_|T]) -> 1 + len(T).
```

And now you have your own recursive function to calculate the length of a list. To see how len/1 behaves when it runs, let's try it on a given list, say [1,2,3,4]:

```
len([1,2,3,4]) = len([1 | [2,3,4]])
               = 1 + len([2 | [3,4]])
               = 1 + 1 + len([3 | [4]])
               = 1 + 1 + 1 + len([4 | []])
               = 1 + 1 + 1 + 1 + len([])
               = 1 + 1 + 1 + 1 + 0
               = 1 + 1 + 1 + 1
               = 1 + 1 + 2
               = 1 + 3
               = 4
```

And we get the correct answer. Congratulations on your first useful recursive function in Erlang!

Length of a Tail Recursion

You might have noticed that for a list of four terms, we expanded our function call to a single chain of five additions. While this does the job fine for short lists, it can become problematic if your list has a few million values in it. You don't want to keep millions of numbers in memory for such a simple calculation. It's wasteful, and there's a better way. Enter *tail recursion*.

Tail recursion is a way to transform the preceding linear process (it grows as much as there are elements) to an iterative one (there is not really any growth). To make a function call tail recursive, it needs to be "alone," which requires a bit of explanation.

What made our previous calls grow is how the answer to the first part depends on evaluating the second part. The answer to 1 + len(Rest) needs the answer to len(Rest) to be found. The function len(Rest) itself then needs the result of another function call to be found. The additions are stacked until the last one is found, and only then is the final result calculated. Tail recursion aims to eliminate this stacking of operations by reducing them as they happen.

To achieve this, we will need to hold an extra temporary variable as a parameter in our function. I'll illustrate the concept with the help of the factorial function, but this time defining it to be tail recursive. The aforementioned temporary variable is sometimes called an *accumulator*, and it acts as a place to store the results of our computations as they happen in order to limit the growth of our calls:

```erlang
tail_fac(N) -> tail_fac(N,1).

tail_fac(0,Acc) -> Acc;
tail_fac(N,Acc) when N > 0 -> tail_fac(N-1,N*Acc).
```

Here, we define both tail_fac/1 and tail_fac/2. This is necessary because Erlang doesn't allow default arguments in functions (different arity means different function), so we do that manually. In this specific case, tail_fac/1 acts like an abstraction over the tail recursive tail_fac/2 function. The details about the hidden accumulator of tail_fac/2 don't interest anyone, so we would export only tail_fac/1 from our module. When running this function, we can expand it to the following:

```erlang
tail_fac(4)     = tail_fac(4,1)
tail_fac(4,1)   = tail_fac(4-1, 4*1)
tail_fac(3,4)   = tail_fac(3-1, 3*4)
tail_fac(2,12)  = tail_fac(2-1, 2*12)
tail_fac(1,24)  = tail_fac(1-1, 1*24)
tail_fac(0,24)  = 24
```

Do you see the difference? Now we never need to hold more than two terms in memory, so the space usage is constant. It will take as much space to calculate the factorial of 4 as it will to calculate the factorial of 1,000,000 (that is, if we forget that 4! is a smaller number than 1,000,000! in its complete representation).

With an example of tail recursive factorials under your belt, you might be able to see how this pattern could be applied to our len/1 function. We need to make our recursive call alone. If you like visual examples, just imagine you're going to put the +1 part inside the function call by adding a parameter. So this:

```erlang
len([]) -> 0;
len([_|T]) -> 1 + len(T).
```

becomes the following:

```erlang
tail_len(L) -> tail_len(L,0).

tail_len([], Acc) -> Acc;
tail_len([_|T], Acc) -> tail_len(T,Acc+1).
```

And now our length function is tail recursive.

More Recursive Functions

We'll write a few more recursive functions, just to get in the habit. After all, since recursion is the only looping construct that exists in Erlang (except list comprehensions), it's one of the most important concepts to understand. It's also useful in every other functional programming language you'll try, so take notes!

A Duplicate Function

The first function we'll write is duplicate/2. This function takes an integer as its first parameter and any other term as its second parameter. It then creates a list of as many copies of the term as specified by the integer.

Again, thinking of the base case first might help us get going. For duplicate/2, asking to repeat something zero times is the most basic thing that can be done. All we need to do is return an empty list, no matter what the term is. Every other case needs to try to get to the base case by calling the function itself. We will also forbid negative values for the integer, because you can't duplicate something −*n* times. Here are these cases:

```
duplicate(0,_) ->
    [];
duplicate(N,Term) when N > 0 ->
    [Term|duplicate(N-1,Term)].
```

Once the basic recursive function is found, it becomes easier to transform it into a tail recursive one by moving the list construction into a temporary variable:

```
tail_duplicate(N,Term) ->
    tail_duplicate(N,Term,[]).

tail_duplicate(0,_,List) ->
    List;
tail_duplicate(N,Term,List) when N > 0 ->
    tail_duplicate(N-1, Term, [Term|List]).
```

Success!

A Reverse Function

There's also an interesting property that we can discover when we compare recursive and tail recursive functions by writing a reverse/1 function, which will reverse a list of terms. For such a function, the base case is an empty list, for which we have nothing to reverse. We can just return an empty list when that happens. Every other possibility should try to converge to the base case by calling itself, as with `duplicate/2`. Our function is going to iterate through the list by pattern matching [H|T], and then putting H after the rest of the list:

```
reverse([]) -> [];
reverse([H|T]) -> reverse(T)++[H].
```

On long lists, this will be a true nightmare. Not only will we stack up all our append operations, but we will need to traverse the whole list for every single append operation until the last one! For visual readers, the many checks can be represented as follows:

```
reverse([1,2,3,4]) = [4]++[3]++[2]++[1]
                       ↑    ↵
                   = [4,3]++[2]++[1]
                      ↑ ↑      ↵
                   = [4,3,2]++[1]
                      ↑ ↑ ↑     ↵
                   = [4,3,2,1]
```

This is where tail recursion comes to the rescue. Because we will use an accumulator and will add a new head to it every time, our list will be reversed automatically.

Let's first see the implementation:

```
tail_reverse(L) -> tail_reverse(L,[]).

tail_reverse([],Acc) -> Acc;
tail_reverse([H|T],Acc) -> tail_reverse(T, [H|Acc]).
```

If we represent this one in a similar manner as the normal version, we get the following:

```
tail_reverse([1,2,3,4]) = tail_reverse([2,3,4], [1])
                        = tail_reverse([3,4], [2,1])
                        = tail_reverse([4], [3,2,1])
                        = tail_reverse([], [4,3,2,1])
                        = [4,3,2,1]
```

This shows that the number of elements visited to reverse our list is now linear. Not only do we avoid growing the stack, we also do our operations much more efficiently!

A Sublist Function

Another function we'll implement is sublist/2, which takes a list L and an integer N, and returns the N first elements of the list. As an example, sublist([1,2,3,4,5,6],3) returns [1,2,3].

Again, the base case is trying to obtain zero elements from a list. But we need to be careful, because sublist/2 is a bit different. We have a second base case when the list passed is empty! If we do not check for empty lists, an error will be thrown when calling recursive:sublist([1],2), when we want [1] instead. Once this is defined, the recursive part of the function only needs to cycle through the list, keeping elements as it goes, until it hits one of the base cases, as follows:

```
sublist(_,0) -> [];
sublist([],_) -> [];
sublist([H|T],N) when N > 0 -> [H|sublist(T,N-1)].
```

This can then be transformed to a tail recursive form in the same manner as before:

```
tail_sublist(L, N) -> tail_sublist(L, N, []).

tail_sublist(_, 0, SubList) -> SubList;
tail_sublist([], _, SubList) -> SubList;
tail_sublist([H|T], N, SubList) when N > 0 ->
    tail_sublist(T, N-1, [H|SubList]).
```

There's a flaw in this function—a *fatal* flaw! We use a list as an accumulator in exactly the same manner as we did to reverse our list. If you compiled this function as is, sublist([1,2,3,4,5,6],3) would not return [1,2,3] but instead would give you [3,2,1]. The only thing we can do is take the final result and reverse it ourselves. Just change the `tail_sublist/2` call and leave all our recursive logic intact:

```
tail_sublist(L, N) -> reverse(tail_sublist(L, N, [])).
```

The final result will be ordered correctly. It might seem like reversing our list after a tail recursive call is a waste of time, and that's partially right (we still save memory doing this). On shorter lists, you might find your code is running faster with normal recursive calls than with tail recursive calls for this reason, but as your data sets grow, reversing the list will be comparatively lighter.

NOTE   *Instead of writing your own* reverse/1 *function, you should use* lists:reverse/1. *It has been used so much for tail recursive calls that the maintainers and developers of Erlang decided to turn it into a BIF. Your lists can now benefit from extremely fast reversal (thanks to functions written in C), which will make the reversal disadvantage a lot less obvious. The rest of the code in this chapter will make use of our own reversal function, but after that, you should never use it again.*

A Zip Function

To push things a bit further, we'll write a zipping function. A zipping function takes two lists of the same length as parameters and joins them as a list of tuples, which all hold two terms. Our own `zip/2` function will behave this way:

```
1> recursive:zip([a,b,c],[1,2,3]).
[{a,1},{b,2},{c,3}]
```

Given that we want both our parameters to have the same length, the base case will be zipping two empty lists:

```
zip([],[]) -> [];
zip([X|Xs],[Y|Ys]) -> [{X,Y}|zip(Xs,Ys)].
```

However, if we wanted a more lenient zipping function, we could decide to have it finish whenever one of the two lists is done. In this scenario, we have two base cases:

```
lenient_zip([],_) -> [];
lenient_zip(_,[]) -> [];
lenient_zip([X|Xs],[Y|Ys]) -> [{X,Y}|lenient_zip(Xs,Ys)].
```

Notice that no matter what our base cases are, the recursive part of the function remains the same.

I suggest that you try to make your own tail recursive versions of zip/2 and lenient_zip/2, just to make sure you fully understand how to make tail recursive functions. They will be one of the central concepts of larger applications, where the main loops will be made that way.

If you want to check your answers, take a look at my implementation of *recursive.erl* (*http://learnyousomeerlang.com/static/erlang/recursive.erl*), particularly the tail_zip/2 and tail_lenient_zip/3 functions.

Quick, Sort!

Just to ensure that recursion and tail recursion make sense to you, we'll push forward with a more complex example: quicksort. Yes, this is the canonical "Hey look, I can write short functional code" example.

A naive implementation of quicksort works by taking the first element of a list, the *pivot*, and then putting all the elements smaller than or equal to the pivot in a new list and all those larger than the pivot in another list. We then take each of these lists and do the same thing on them until each list gets smaller and smaller. This goes on until we have nothing but an empty list to sort, which will be our base case. This implementation is said to be naive because smarter versions of quicksort will try to pick optimal pivots to be faster. We don't really care about that for our example.

We will need two functions for this one: a function to partition the list into smaller and larger parts, and another function to apply the partition

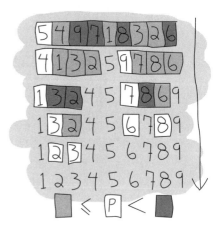

function on each of the new lists and to glue them together. First, we'll write the glue function (you can do this in recursive.erl):

```erlang
quicksort([]) -> [];
quicksort([Pivot|Rest]) ->
    {Smaller, Larger} = partition(Pivot,Rest,[],[]),
    quicksort(Smaller) ++ [Pivot] ++ quicksort(Larger).
```

This shows the base case, a list already partitioned in larger and smaller parts by another function, and the use of a pivot with both lists quicksorted appended before and after it. So this should take care of assembling lists.

Next, we write the partitioning function:

```erlang
partition(_,[], Smaller, Larger) -> {Smaller, Larger};
partition(Pivot, [H|T], Smaller, Larger) ->
    if H =< Pivot -> partition(Pivot, T, [H|Smaller], Larger);
       H >  Pivot -> partition(Pivot, T, Smaller, [H|Larger])
    end.
```

And you can now run our quicksort function.

If you've looked for Erlang examples on the Internet, you might have seen another implementation of quicksort—one that is simpler and easier to read, but makes use of list comprehensions. The easy-to-replace parts are the ones that create new lists, the partition/4 function:

```erlang
lc_quicksort([]) -> [];
lc_quicksort([Pivot|Rest]) ->
    lc_quicksort([Smaller || Smaller <- Rest, Smaller =< Pivot])
    ++ [Pivot] ++
    lc_quicksort([Larger || Larger <- Rest, Larger > Pivot]).
```

DON'T DRINK TOO MUCH KOOL-AID

All this conciseness is good for educational purposes, but not for performance. Many functional programming tutorials never mention this! First of all, both implementations of quicksort shown here need to process values that are equal to the pivot more than once. We could have decided to instead return three lists—elements smaller, larger, and equal to the pivot—to make this more efficient.

Another problem relates to how we need to traverse all the partitioned lists more than once when attaching them to the pivot. It is possible to reduce the overhead a little by doing the concatenation while partitioning the lists in three parts. If you're curious about this, look at the last function (bestest_qsort/1) of recursive.erl for an example.

A nice point about all of these quicksort versions is that they will work on lists of any data type you have, even tuples of lists and whatnot. Try them, and you'll see that they work.

This version is much easier to read, but in exchange, it must traverse the list to partition it in two parts. This is a battle of clarity vs. performance, although the real loser here is you, because a lists:sort/1 function already exists. Use that one instead.

More Than Lists

At this point, you might think that recursion in Erlang mainly concerns lists. While lists are a good example of a data structure that can be defined recursively, there's certainly more to recursion than working with lists. For the sake of diversity, we'll look at how to build binary trees and then read data from them.

First, it's important to define what a tree is. In our case, a tree has nodes all the way down. Nodes are tuples that contain a key, a value associated with the key, and then two other nodes. Of these two nodes, we need one that has a smaller key and one that has a larger key than the node holding them. So here's recursion! A tree is a node containing nodes, each of which contains nodes, which, in turn, also contain nodes. This can't keep going forever (we don't have infinite data to store), so we'll say that our nodes can also contain empty nodes.

To represent nodes, tuples are an appropriate data structure. For our implementation, we can then define these tuples as {node, {Key, Value, Smaller, Larger}} (a tagged tuple!), where Smaller and Larger can be another similar node or an empty node ({node, nil}). We don't need a concept more complex than that.

Let's start building a module for our very basic tree implementation. The first function, empty/0, returns an empty node. The empty node is the starting point of a new tree, also called the *root*.

```
-module(tree).
-export([empty/0, insert/3, lookup/2]).

empty() -> {node, 'nil'}.
```

By using that function and then encapsulating all representations of nodes the same way, we hide the implementation of the tree so people don't need to know how it's built. All that information can be contained by the module alone. If you ever decide to change the representation of a node, you can then do it without breaking external code.

To add content to a tree, you must first understand how to recursively navigate through it. Let's proceed in the same way as we did for every other recursion example: by first trying to find the base case.

Given that an empty tree is an empty node, our base case is thus logically an empty node. So whenever we hit an empty node, that's where we can add our new key/value. The rest of the time, our code must go through the tree to try to find an empty node in which to put content.

To find an empty node starting from the root, we must use the fact that the presence of Smaller and Larger nodes lets us navigate by comparing the new key we have to insert to the current node's key. If the new key is smaller than the current node's key, we try to find the empty node inside Smaller; if it's larger, we look inside Larger. There is one last case, though: What if the new key is equal to the current node's key? We have two options there: let the program fail or replace the value with the new one. We'll take the latter option. Put into a function, all this logic works the following way:

```
insert(Key, Val, {node, 'nil'}) ->
    {node, {Key, Val, {node, 'nil'}, {node, 'nil'}}};
insert(NewKey, NewVal, {node, {Key, Val, Smaller, Larger}}) when NewKey < Key ->
    {node, {Key, Val, insert(NewKey, NewVal, Smaller), Larger}};
insert(NewKey, NewVal, {node, {Key, Val, Smaller, Larger}}) when NewKey > Key ->
    {node, {Key, Val, Smaller, insert(NewKey, NewVal, Larger)}};
insert(Key, Val, {node, {Key, _, Smaller, Larger}}) ->
    {node, {Key, Val, Smaller, Larger}}.
```

Note here that the function returns a completely new tree. This is typical of functional languages that have only single assignment. While this can be seen as inefficient, updating a tree or adding an element usually requires changing only the nodes that were modified up to the change. The other nodes can be shared between both versions of the tree, strongly reducing the memory overhead. In the following image, the node containing "E" is added, which requires updating all of its parents. However, the entire left side of the tree (starting with "B") doesn't change and can be kept the same across versions. This concept is more regularly known to functional programmers as using *persistent data structures*.

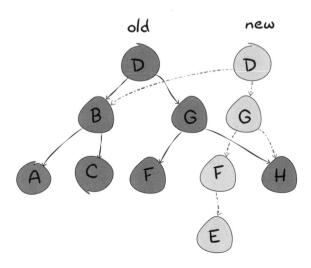

The last thing we need to do with our example tree implementation is to create a `lookup/2` function that will let us find a value from a tree by giving its key. The logic needed is extremely similar to the logic used to add new content to the tree: We step through the nodes, checking if the lookup key is equal to, smaller than, or larger than the current node's key. We have two base cases: one when the node is empty (the key isn't in the tree) and one when the key is found. Because we don't want our program to crash each time we look for a key that doesn't exist, we'll return the atom `undefined`. Otherwise, we'll return {ok, Value}. If we only returned Value, and the node contained the atom `undefined`, we would have no way to know if the tree did return the correct value or failed to find it. By wrapping successful cases in such a tuple, we make it easy to understand which is which. Here's the implemented function:

```
lookup(_, {node, 'nil'}) ->
    undefined;
lookup(Key, {node, {Key, Val, _, _}}) ->
    {ok, Val};
lookup(Key, {node, {NodeKey, _, Smaller, _}}) when Key < NodeKey ->
    lookup(Key, Smaller);
lookup(Key, {node, {_, _, _, Larger}}) ->
    lookup(Key, Larger).
```

And we're finished. Let's test it by making a little email address book. Compile the file and start the shell:

```
1> T1 = tree:insert("Jim Woodland", "jim.woodland@gmail.com", tree:empty()).
{node,{"Jim Woodland","jim.woodland@gmail.com",
       {node,nil},
       {node,nil}}}
2> T2 = tree:insert("Mark Anderson", "i.am.a@hotmail.com", T1).
{node,{"Jim Woodland","jim.woodland@gmail.com",
       {node,nil},
       {node,{"Mark Anderson","i.am.a@hotmail.com",
              {node,nil},
              {node,nil}}}}}
3> Addresses = tree:insert("Anita Bath", "abath@someuni.edu",
3>      tree:insert("Kevin Robert", "myfairy@yahoo.com",
3>          tree:insert("Wilson Longbrow", "longwil@gmail.com", T2))).
{node,{"Jim Woodland","jim.woodland@gmail.com",
       {node,{"Anita Bath","abath@someuni.edu",
              {node,nil},
              {node,nil}}},
       {node,{"Mark Anderson","i.am.a@hotmail.com",
              {node,{"Kevin Robert","myfairy@yahoo.com",
                     {node,nil},
                     {node,nil}}},
              {node,{"Wilson Longbrow","longwil@gmail.com",
                     {node,nil},
                     {node,nil}}}}}}}
```

And now you can look up email addresses with it:

```
4> tree:lookup("Anita Bath", Addresses).
{ok, "abath@someuni.edu"}
5> tree:lookup("Jacques Requin", Addresses).
undefined
```

That concludes our functional address book example built from a recursive data structure other than a list! *Anita Bath* now . . .

NOTE   *Our tree implementation is very naive. We do not support common operations such as deleting nodes or rebalancing the tree to make the following lookups faster. If you're interested in implementing and/or exploring these, studying the implementation of Erlang's* gb_trees *module (*YourErlangInstallPath/lib/stdlib/src/gb_trees.erl*) is a good idea. This is also the module you should use when dealing with trees in your code, rather than reinventing the wheel.*

Thinking Recursively

If you've understood everything in this chapter, thinking recursively is probably becoming more intuitive. A different aspect of recursive definitions when compared to their imperative counterparts (usually in while or for loops) is that instead of taking a step-by-step approach ("do this, then that, then this, then you're finished"), our approach is more declarative ("if you get this input, do that; otherwise, do this"). This property is made more obvious with the help of pattern matching in function heads.

If you still haven't grasped how recursion works, maybe reading this sentence will help you.

Joking aside, recursion coupled with pattern matching is sometimes an optimal solution to the problem of writing concise algorithms that are easy to understand. By subdividing each part of a problem into separate functions until they can no longer be simplified, the algorithm becomes nothing but assembling a bunch of correct answers coming from short routines (that's a bit similar to what we did with quicksort). This kind of mental abstraction is also possible with your everyday loops, but I believe the practice is easier with recursion. Your mileage may vary.

**AND NOW LADIES AND GENTLEMEN, A DISCUSSION:
THE AUTHOR VS. HIMSELF**

Self: Okay, I think I understand recursion. I get the declarative aspect of it. I get it has mathematical roots, like with invariable variables. I get that you find it easier in some cases. What else?

Author: It respects a regular pattern. Find the base cases and write them down. Then all the other cases should try to converge to these base cases to get your answer. It makes writing functions pretty easy.

Self: Yeah, I got that. You repeated it a bunch of times already. My loops can do the same thing.

Author: Yes, they can. I can't deny that.

Self: And another thing: Why bother writing all these non-tail recursive versions if they're not as good as tail recursive ones?

Author: Oh, it's simply to make things easier to grasp. Moving from regular recursion, which is prettier and easier to understand, to tail recursion, which is theoretically more efficient, sounded like a good way to show all of the options.

Self: Right, so they're useless except for educational purposes. I get it.

Author: Not exactly. In practice, you'll see little difference in the performance between tail recursive and normal recursive calls. The areas to take care of are in functions that are supposed to loop infinitely, like main loops. There are also types of functions that will always generate very large stacks, be slow, and possibly crash early if you don't make them tail recursive. The best example of this is the Fibonacci function, which grows exponentially if it's not iterative or tail recursive. You should profile your code, see what slows it down, and fix it.

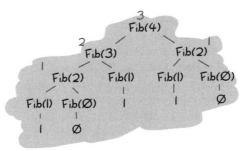

Self: But loops are always iterative and make this a nonissue.

Author: Yes, but . . . but . . . my beautiful Erlang . . .

Self: Well isn't that great? All that learning because there is no while or for in Erlang. Thank you very much. I'm going back to programming my toaster in C!

Author: Not so fast there! Functional programming languages have other assets! If we've found a few basic common points between many recursive functions (accumulators, reversing at the end, and so on), a bunch of smart people found many more common points and patterns. In fact, they found enough of them that most frequent operations have been abstracted away in libraries. You'll rarely need to write recursive functions yourself. If you stay around, you'll see how such abstractions can be built. But for this, we will need more power. Let me tell you about higher-order functions . . .

6

HIGHER-ORDER FUNCTIONS

An important part of all functional programming languages is the ability to take a function you defined and then pass it as a parameter to another function. This binds that function parameter to a variable, which can be used like any other variable within the function. A function that can accept other functions transported around this way is called a *higher-order function*. As you'll learn in this chapter, higher-order functions are a powerful means of abstraction and one of the best tools to master in Erlang.

Let's Get Functional

The concept behind carrying functions around and passing them to higher-order functions is rooted in mathematics, mainly lambda calculus. Basically, in pure lambda calculus, everything is a function—even numbers, operators, and lists. Because everything is represented as a function, functions must accept other

functions as parameters, and must be able to operate on them with even more functions! (If you want a good, quick introduction to lambda calculus, read the Wikipedia entry for it.)

This concept might be a bit hard to grasp, so let's start with an example (this is nowhere close to real lambda calculus, but it illustrates the point).

```erlang
-module(hhfuns).
-compile(export_all).

one() -> 1.
two() -> 2.

add(X,Y) -> X() + Y().
```

Now open the Erlang shell, compile the module, and get going:

```erlang
1> c(hhfuns).
{ok, hhfuns}
2> hhfuns:add(one,two).
** exception error: bad function one
in function  hhfuns:add/2
3> hhfuns:add(1,2).
** exception error: bad function 1
in function  hhfuns:add/2
4> hhfuns:add(fun hhfuns:one/0, fun hhfuns:two/0).
3
```

Confusing? Not so much, once you know how it works (isn't that always the case?). In line 2, the atoms one and two are passed to add/2, which then uses both atoms as function names (X() + Y()). If function names are written without a parameter list, then those names are interpreted as atoms, and atoms cannot be functions, so the call fails. This is why the expression on line 3 also fails: The values 1 and 2 cannot be called as functions, and functions are what we need!

To handle this issue, a new notation must be added to the language in order to pass functions from outside a module. This is the purpose of fun Module:Function/Arity:, which tells the VM to use that specific function and then bind it to a variable.

So what are the gains of using functions in that manner? Well, a little example might help answer that question. We'll add a few functions to hhfuns that work recursively over a list to add or subtract one from each integer of a list.

```erlang
increment([]) -> [];
increment([H|T]) -> [H+1|increment(T)].

decrement([]) -> [];
decrement([H|T]) -> [H-1|decrement(T)].
```

Do you see how similar these functions are? They basically do the same thing: cycle through a list, apply a function on each element (+ or -), and then call themselves again. Almost nothing changes in that code; only the applied function and the recursive call are different. The core of a recursive call on a list like that is always the same. We'll abstract all the similar parts in a single function (map/2) that will take another function as an argument.

```
map(_, []) -> [];
map(F, [H|T]) -> [F(H)|map(F,T)].

incr(X) -> X + 1.
decr(X) -> X - 1.
```

Now let's test this in the shell.

```
1> c(hhfuns).
{ok, hhfuns}
2> L = [1,2,3,4,5].
[1,2,3,4,5]
3> hhfuns:increment(L).
[2,3,4,5,6]
4> hhfuns:decrement(L).
[0,1,2,3,4]
5> hhfuns:map(fun hhfuns:incr/1, L).
[2,3,4,5,6]
6> hhfuns:map(fun hhfuns:decr/1, L).
[0,1,2,3,4]
```

Here, the results are the same, but we have just created a very smart abstraction! Every time we want to apply a function to each element of a list, we only need to call map/2 with our function as a parameter. However, it is a bit annoying to need to put every function we want to pass as a parameter to map/2 in a module, name it, export it, compile it, and so on. In fact, it's plainly unpractical. What we need are functions that can be declared on the fly—the type of functions discussed next.

Anonymous Functions

Anonymous functions, or *funs*, address the problem of using functions as parameters by letting you declare a special kind of function inline, without naming that function. Anonymous functions can do pretty much everything normal functions can do, except call themselves recursively (how could they do that if they are anonymous?).

Anonymous functions have the following syntax:

```
fun(Args1) ->
    Expression1, Exp2, ..., ExpN;
  (Args2) ->
    Expression1, Exp2, ..., ExpN;
```

```
  (Args3) ->
    Expression1, Exp2, ..., ExpN
end
```

Here's an example of using an anonymous function:

```
7> Fn = fun() -> a end.
#Fun<erl_eval.20.67289768>
8> Fn().
a
9> hhfuns:map(fun(X) -> X + 1 end, L).
[2,3,4,5,6]
10> hhfuns:map(fun(X) -> X - 1 end, L).
[0,1,2,3,4]
```

And now you're seeing one of the things that make people like functional programming so much: the ability to make abstractions on a very low level of code. Basic concepts such as looping can thus be ignored, letting you focus on what is done, rather than how to do it.

More Anonymous Function Power

Anonymous functions are pretty dandy for such abstractions, but they have more hidden powers. Let's look at another example:

```
11> PrepareAlarm = fun(Room) ->
11>      io:format("Alarm set in ~s.~n",[Room]),
11>      fun() -> io:format("Alarm tripped in ~s! Call Batman!~n",[Room]) end
11> end.
#Fun<erl_eval.20.67289768>
12> AlarmReady = PrepareAlarm("bathroom").
Alarm set in bathroom.
#Fun<erl_eval.6.13229925>
13> AlarmReady().
Alarm tripped in bathroom! Call Batman!
ok
```

Hold the phone, Batman! What's going on here? Well, first of all, we declare an anonymous function assigned to PrepareAlarm. This function has not run yet. It is executed only when PrepareAlarm("bathroom") is called. At that point, the call to io:format/2 is evaluated, and the "Alarm set" text is output. The second expression (another anonymous function) is returned to the caller and then assigned to AlarmReady. Note that in this function, the Room variable's value is taken from the "parent" function (PrepareAlarm). This is related to a concept called *closures*. But before we can talk about closures, we need to address the idea of scope.

Function Scope and Closures

A function's *scope* can be imagined as the place where all the variables and their values are stored. In the function base(A) -> B = A + 1., for example, A and B are both defined to be part of base/1's scope. This means that anywhere inside base/1, you can refer to A and B and expect a value to be bound to them. And when I say "anywhere," I ain't kidding, kid. This includes anonymous functions, too.

```
base(A) ->
    B = A + 1,
    F = fun() -> A * B end,
    F().
```

In this example, B and A are still bound to base/1's scope, so the function F can still access them. This is because F inherits base/1's scope. As with most kinds of real-life inheritance, the parents can't get what the children have.

```
base(A) ->
    B = A + 1,
    F = fun() -> C = A * B end,
    F(),
    C.
```

In this version of the function, B is still equal to A + 1, and F will still execute fine. However, the variable C is only in the scope of the anonymous function in F. When base/1 tries to access C's value on the last line, it finds only an unbound variable. In fact, if you tried to compile this function, the compiler would throw a fit. Inheritance goes only one way.

It is important to note that the inherited scope follows the anonymous function wherever it is, even when it is passed to another function. Here's an example:

```
a() ->
    Secret = "pony",
    fun() -> Secret end.

b(F) ->
    "a/0's password is "++F().
```

Now we can compile it.

```
14> c(hhfuns).
{ok, hhfuns}
15> hhfuns:b(hhfuns:a()).
"a/0's password is pony"
```

Who told a/0's password? Well, a/0 did. While the anonymous function has a/0's scope when it's declared in there, the function can still carry it when executed in b/1, as explained earlier. This is very useful because it lets us carry around parameters and content out of their original context, where the whole context itself is no longer needed (exactly as we did with Batman in the previous section).

You're most likely to use anonymous functions to carry state around when you have defined functions that take many arguments, but one of these arguments remains the same all the time, as in the following example.

```
16> math:pow(5,2).
25.0
17> Base = 2.
2
18> PowerOfTwo = fun(X) -> math:pow(Base,X) end.
#Fun<erl_eval.6.13229925>
17> hhfuns:map(PowerOfTwo, [1,2,3,4]).
[2.0,4.0,8.0,16.0]
```

By wrapping the call to math:pow/2 inside an anonymous function with the Base variable bound in that function's scope, we made it possible to have each of the calls to PowerOfTwo in hhfuns:map/2 use the integers from the list as the exponents of our base.

A little trap you might fall into when writing anonymous functions is when you try to redefine the scope, like this:

```
base() ->
    A = 1,
    (fun() -> A = 2 end)().
```

This will declare an anonymous function and then run it. As the anonymous function inherits base/0's scope, trying to use the = operator compares 2 with the variable A (bound to 1). This is guaranteed to fail. However, we can redefine the variable if we do that in the nested function's head:

```
base() ->
    A = 1,
    (fun(A) -> A = 2 end)(2).
```

And this works. If you try to compile it, you'll get a warning about shadowing: "Warning: variable 'A' shadowed in 'fun'." *Shadowing* is the term used to describe the act of defining a new variable that has the same name as one that was in the parent scope. This warning is there to prevent some mistakes (usually rightly so), so you might want to consider renaming your variables in these circumstances.

Now that we've covered scope, we can turn to closures. Closure is just the idea of having a function that references some environment along with it (the value's part of the scope). In other words, a closure is what happens when anonymous functions meet the concept of scope and carrying variables around.

We'll set the anonymous function theory aside for now and explore more common abstractions to avoid needing to write more recursive functions, as I promised at the end of Chapter 5.

Maps, Filters, Folds, and More

At the beginning of this chapter, we took a brief look at how to abstract away two similar functions to get a map/2 function:

```
map(_, []) -> [];
map(F, [H|T]) -> [F(H)|map(F,T)].
```

Such a function can be used for any list where we want to act on each element. However, there are many other similar abstractions to build from commonly occurring recursive functions.

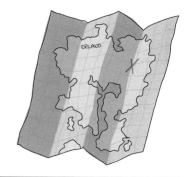

Filters

First, we'll look at filters. Consider the following functions:

```
%% Only keep even numbers.
even(L) -> lists:reverse(even(L,[])).

even([], Acc) -> Acc;
even([H|T], Acc) when H rem 2 == 0 ->
    even(T, [H|Acc]);
even([_|T], Acc) ->
    even(T, Acc).

%% Only keep men older than 60.
old_men(L) -> lists:reverse(old_men(L,[])).

old_men([], Acc) -> Acc;
old_men([Person = {male, Age}|People], Acc) when Age > 60 ->
    old_men(People, [Person|Acc]);
old_men([_|People], Acc) ->
    old_men(People, Acc).
```

The first of these functions takes a list of numbers and returns only those that are even. The second one goes through a list of people of the form {Gender, Age} and keeps only those that are males over 60.

The similarities are a bit harder to find here than in the previous examples, but we have some common points. Both functions operate on lists and have the same objective of keeping elements that succeed some test (also called a *predicate*) and then dropping the others. From this generalization, we can extract all the useful information we need and abstract them away, like this:

```
filter(Pred, L) -> lists:reverse(filter(Pred, L,[])).

filter(_, [], Acc) -> Acc;
filter(Pred, [H|T], Acc) ->
    case Pred(H) of
        true  -> filter(Pred, T, [H|Acc]);
        false -> filter(Pred, T, Acc)
    end.
```

To use the filtering function, we now only need to pass in a predicate outside of the function. Compile the hhfuns module and try it.

```
1> c(hhfuns).
{ok, hhfuns}
2> Numbers = lists:seq(1,10).
[1,2,3,4,5,6,7,8,9,10]
3> hhfuns:filter(fun(X) -> X rem 2 == 0 end, Numbers).
[2,4,6,8,10]
4> People = [{male,45},{female,67},{male,66},{female,12},{unkown,174},{male,74}].
[{male,45},{female,67},{male,66},{female,12},{unkown,174},{male,74}]
5> hhfuns:filter(fun({Gender,Age}) -> Gender == male andalso Age > 60 end, People).
[{male,66},{male,74}]
```

These two examples show that with the use of the filter/2 function, the programmer needs to worry only about producing the predicate and the list. The act of cycling through the list to throw out unwanted items is no longer a consideration. This is one important thing about abstracting functional code: Try to get rid of what's always the same, and let the programmer supply the parts that change.

Fold Everything

In Chapter 5, we looked at another kind of recursive list manipulation, where we applied some operation to each element of a list successively to reduce the elements to a single value. This is called a *fold* and can be used to reduce the size of the following functions:

```
%% Find the maximum of a list.
max([H|T]) -> max2(T, H).

max2([], Max) -> Max;
max2([H|T], Max) when H > Max -> max2(T, H);
max2([_|T], Max) -> max2(T, Max).
```

```
%% Find the minimum of a list.
min([H|T]) -> min2(T,H).

min2([], Min) -> Min;
min2([H|T], Min) when H < Min -> min2(T,H);
min2([_|T], Min) -> min2(T, Min).

%% Find the sum of all the elements of a list.
sum(L) -> sum(L,0).

sum([], Sum) -> Sum;
sum([H|T], Sum) -> sum(T, H+Sum).
```

To find how the `fold` function should be used, we need to determine all the common points of the actions made by these functions, as well as what is different. As mentioned earlier, we always have a reduction from a list to a single value. Consequently, our fold function should consider iterating only while keeping a single item—no list building is needed. We need to ignore the guards, because they exist in only some of these functions, not all of them. The guards will need to be included in the function that we pass to fold. In this regard, our `fold` function will probably look a lot like `sum`.

A subtle element of all three functions is that every function needs to have an initial value to start counting with. In the case of `sum/2`, we use 0, as we're doing addition, and given X = X + 0, the value is neutral, so we can't mess up the calculation by starting there. If we were doing multiplication, we would use 1 given X = X * 1.

The functions `min/1` and `max/1` can't have a default starting value. If the list were only negative numbers and we started at 0, the answer would be wrong. So we need to use the first element of the list as a starting point. Sadly, we can't always decide the starting value this way, so we'll leave that decision to the programmer.

By taking all these elements, we can build the following abstraction:

```
fold(_, Start, []) -> Start;
fold(F, Start, [H|T]) -> fold(F, F(H,Start), T).
```

Let's try it.

```
6> c(hhfuns).
{ok, hhfuns}
7> [H|T] = [1,7,3,5,9,0,2,3].
[1,7,3,5,9,0,2,3]
8> hhfuns:fold(fun(A,B) when A > B -> A; (_,B) -> B end, H, T).
9
9> hhfuns:fold(fun(A,B) when A < B -> A; (_,B) -> B end, H, T).
0
```

```
10> hhfuns:fold(fun(A,B) -> A + B end, 0, lists:seq(1,6)).
21
```

Pretty much any function you can think of that reduces lists to one element can be expressed as a fold.

Strangely enough, you can represent an accumulator as a single element (or a single variable), and an accumulator can be a list. Therefore, we can use a fold to build a list. This means folding is universal in the sense that you can implement pretty much any other recursive function on lists with a fold, even maps and filters, like so:

```
reverse(L) ->
    fold(fun(X,Acc) -> [X|Acc] end, [], L).

map2(F,L) ->
    reverse(fold(fun(X,Acc) -> [F(X)|Acc] end, [], L)).

filter2(Pred, L) ->
    F = fun(X,Acc) ->
            case Pred(X) of
                true  -> [X|Acc];
                false -> Acc
            end
        end,
    reverse(fold(F, [], L)).
```

These all work in the same way as those written by hand before. How's that for powerful abstractions?

More Abstractions

Map, filters, and folds are only a few of many abstractions over lists provided by the Erlang standard library (see lists:map/2, lists:filter/2, lists:foldl/3, and lists:foldr/3). Other functions include all/2 and any/2, which both take a predicate and test if all the elements return true or if at least one of them returns true, respectively.

Also available is dropwhile/2, which will ignore elements of a list until it finds one that fits a certain predicate. Its opposite, takewhile/2, will keep all elements until there is one that doesn't return true to the predicate. A complementary function to these is partition/2, which will take a list and return two lists: one that has the terms that satisfy a given predicate and one for the others.

Other frequently used list functions include flatten/1, flatlength/1, flatmap/2, merge/1, nth/2, nthtail/2, and split/2. You can look up all of these functions in the documentation if you want to learn more about them.

You'll also find other functions such as zipping functions (as shown in Chapter 5), unzipping functions, combinations of maps and folds, and so on. I encourage you to read the documentation on lists to see what can be done. You'll find yourself rarely needing to write recursive functions as long as you use what's already been abstracted away by smart people.

7

ERRORS AND EXCEPTIONS

There's no right place for a chapter such as this one. So far, you've seen plenty of errors but not much about the mechanisms for handling them. That's a bit because Erlang has two main paradigms: *functional* and *concurrent*. The functional subset is the one I've been explaining since the beginning of the book: referential transparency, recursion, higher-order functions, and so on. The concurrent subset is the one that makes Erlang famous: actors, thousands and thousands of concurrent processes, supervision trees, and more.

Although Erlang includes a few ways to handle errors in functional code, most of the time you'll be told to just let it crash. The error-handling mechanisms are in the concurrent part of the language. But because it's essential to understand the functional part before moving on to the concurrent part, this chapter covers only the functional subset of the language. If we are to manage errors, we must first understand them.

A Compilation of Errors

There are many kinds of errors: compile-time errors, logical errors, and runtime errors. First, let's look at compile-time errors.

Compile-Time Errors

Compile-time errors are often syntactic mistakes. Check your function names, the tokens in the language (such as brackets, parentheses, periods, and commas), the arity of your functions, and so on.

Here's a list of some of the common compile-time error messages and potential resolutions in case you encounter them:

`module.beam: Module name 'madule' does not match file name 'module'`
> The module name you've entered in the -module attribute doesn't match the filename.

`./module.erl:2: Warning: function some_function/0 is unused`
> You have not exported a function, or the place where it's used has the wrong name or arity. It's also possible you've written a function that is no longer needed. Check your code!

`./module.erl:2: function some_function/1 undefined`
> The function does not exist. You've written the wrong name or arity either in the -export attribute or when declaring the function. This error is also output when the given function could not be compiled, usually because of a syntax error like forgetting to end a function with a period.

`./module.erl:5: syntax error before: 'SomeCharacterOrWord'`
> This happens for a variety of reasons. Common causes are unclosed parentheses, tuples, or wrong expression termination (like closing the last branch of a case with a comma). Other reasons include the use of a reserved atom in your code and Unicode characters not being converted correctly between different encodings (I've seen it happen!).

`./module.erl:5: syntax error before:`
> This message is certainly not as descriptive as the previous one. It usually comes up when your line termination is not correct. This is a specific case of the previous error, so just keep an eye out.

./module.erl:5: Warning: this expression will fail with a 'badarith' exception
Erlang is all about dynamic typing, but remember that the types are strong. In this case, the compiler is smart enough to find that one of your arithmetic expressions will fail (say, llama + 5). It won't find type errors much more complex than that, though.

./module.erl:5: Warning: variable 'Var' is unused
You declared a variable and never used it. This might be a bug with your code, so double-check what you have written. Otherwise, you might want to switch the variable name to _, or just prefix it with an underscore if you feel the name helps make the code readable.

./module.erl:5: Warning: a term is constructed, but never used
In one of your functions, you're doing something such as building a list, or declaring a tuple or an anonymous function without ever binding it to a variable or returning it. This warning tells you that you're doing something useless or have made some mistake.

./module.erl:5: head mismatch
It's possible your function has more than one head, and each of them has a different arity. Don't forget that different arity means different functions, and you can't interleave function declarations that way. Similarly, this error is raised when you insert a function definition between the head clauses of another function.

./module.erl:5: Warning: this clause cannot match because a previous clause at line 4 always matches
A function defined in the module has a specific clause defined after a catchall one. As such, the compiler can warn you that you'll never even need to go to the other branch.

./module.erl:9: variable 'A' unsafe in 'case' (line 5)
You're using a variable declared within one of the branches of a case ... of outside of it. This is considered unsafe. If you want to use such variables, you're better off doing MyVar = case ... of.

This covers most of the errors you'll get at compile-time at this point. There aren't too many, and most of the time, the hardest part is finding which error caused a huge cascade of errors listed against other functions. It is better to resolve compiler errors in the order they were reported to avoid being misled by errors that may not actually be errors at all.

No, YOUR Logic Is Wrong!

Logical errors are the hardest kind of errors to find and debug. They're most likely errors coming from the programmer: branches of conditional statements such as ifs and cases that don't consider all the cases, using a multiplication that should have been a division, and so on. They do not make your programs crash, but can lead to unseen bad data or your program working in an unintended manner.

You're most likely on your own when it comes to dealing with logical errors, but Erlang has many facilities to help you, such as test frameworks, the TypEr and Dialyzer tools, and a debugger and tracing module. Testing your code is likely your best defense. Sadly, there are enough of these kinds of errors in every programmer's career to write a few dozen books about them. Here, we'll focus on those that make your programs crash, because it happens right there and won't bubble up to 50 levels to search through. Note that this is pretty much the origin of the "let it crash" ideal I've mentioned previously.

Runtime Errors

Runtime errors are pretty destructive in the sense that they crash your code. While Erlang has ways to deal with them, recognizing these errors is always helpful. We'll look at some common runtime errors and examples of code that generate them.

Function Clause Errors

The most likely reasons you'll run into a function clause error is when you fail all guard clauses of a function or fail all pattern matches, as in this example:

```
1> lists:sort([3,2,1]).
[1,2,3]
2> lists:sort(fffffff).
** exception error: no function clause matching lists:sort(fffffff) (lists.erl, line 414)
```

Case Clause Errors

Case clause errors occur when you've forgotten a specific case, sent in the wrong kind of data, or need a catchall clause. Here's an example:

```
3> case "Unexpected Value" of
3>     expected_value -> ok;
3>     other_expected_value -> 'also ok'
3> end.
** exception error: no case clause matching "Unexpected Value"
```

If Clause Errors

If clause errors are similar to case clause errors. They arise when Erlang cannot find a branch that evaluates to true.

```
4> if 2 > 4 -> ok;
4>    0 > 1 -> ok
4> end.
** exception error: no true branch found when evaluating an if expression
```

Making sure you consider all cases or adding the catchall true clause might be what you need.

Bad Match Errors

Bad match errors happen whenever pattern matching fails. This most likely means you're trying to do impossible pattern matches (such as the following), trying to bind a variable for the second time, or just using anything that isn't equal on both sides of the = operator (which is pretty much what makes rebinding a variable fail!).

```
5> [X,Y] = {4,5}.
** exception error: no match of right hand side value {4,5}
```

Note that this error sometimes happens because the programmer believes that a variable of the form _MyVar is the same as _. Variables with an underscore are normal variables, except the compiler won't complain if they're not used. It is not possible to bind them more than once.

Bad Argument Errors

Bad argument errors are similar to function clause errors, as they are about calling functions with incorrect arguments.

```
6> erlang:binary_to_list("heh, already a list").
** exception error: bad argument
    in function  binary_to_list/1
        called as binary_to_list("heh, already a list")
```

The main difference here is that this error is usually triggered by the programmer after validating the arguments from within the function, outside of the guard clauses. It is also the error of choice thrown by BIFs or any other function written in C. I'll show you how to raise such errors in "Raising Exceptions" on page 93.

Undefined Function Errors

An undefined function error happens when you call a function that doesn't exist.

```
7> lists:random([1,2,3]).
** exception error: undefined function lists:random/1
```

Make sure the function is exported from the module with the correct arity (if you're calling it from outside the module), and double-check that you typed the name of the function and the name of the module correctly.

You might also get this error message when the module is not in Erlang's search path. By default, Erlang's search path is set to be in the current directory. You can add paths to the list by using code:add_patha("/*some/path*/") or code:add_pathz("*some/path*"). If this still doesn't work, make sure you compiled the module to begin with!

Bad Arithmetic Errors

Bad arithmetic errors occur when you try to do arithmetic that doesn't exist, like divisions by zero or between atoms and numbers.

```
8> 5 + llama.
** exception error: bad argument in an arithmetic expression
     in operator  +/2
         called as 5 + llama
```

Bad Function Errors

The most frequent reason for bad function errors is when you use variables as functions, but the variable's value is not a function. The following example uses the hhfuns function from Chapter 6, with two atoms as functions. This doesn't work, and a bad function error is thrown.

```
9> hhfuns:add(one,two).
** exception error: bad function one
     in function  hhfuns:add/2 (hhfuns.erl, line 7)
```

Bad Arity Errors

The bad arity error is a specific case of a bad function error. It happens when you use higher-order functions, but you pass them more or fewer arguments than they can handle.

```
10> F = fun(_) -> ok end.
#Fun<erl_eval.6.13229925>
11> F(a,b).
** exception error: interpreted function with arity 1 called with two arguments
```

System Limit Errors

A system limit error may be raised for many reasons, including the following:

- Too many processes
- Atoms that are too long
- Too many arguments in a function
- Too many atoms
- Too many nodes connected

To get a full list and details of these errors, read the Erlang Efficiency Guide on system limits, at *http://www.erlang.org/doc/efficiency_guide/advanced .html#2265856*. Note that some of these errors are serious enough to crash the whole VM.

Raising Exceptions

In trying to monitor code's execution and protect against logical errors, it's often a good idea to provoke runtime crashes so problems will be spotted early.

There are three kinds of exceptions in Erlang: *errors*, *exits*, and *throws*. They all have different uses (kind of), as explained in the following sections.

Error Exceptions

Calling erlang:error(Reason) will end the execution in the current process and include a stack trace of the last functions called with their arguments when you catch the exception. These are the kind of exceptions that provoke runtime errors.

Errors are the means for a function to stop its execution when you can't expect the calling code to handle what just happened. If you get an if clause error, what can you do? Change the code and recompile—that's what you can do (other than just displaying a pretty error message).

When Not to Use Errors

An example of when *not* to use errors could be our tree module from Chapter 5. That module might not always be able to find a specific key in a tree when doing a lookup. In this case, it makes sense to expect the users to deal with unknown results. They could use a default value, check to insert a new one, delete the tree, or use some other approach. This is when it's appropriate to return a tuple of the form {ok, Value} or an atom like undefined, rather than raising errors.

Custom Errors

Errors aren't limited to the ones provided by Erlang. You can define your own kinds of errors, as in this example:

```
1> erlang:error(badarith).
** exception error: bad argument in an arithmetic expression
2> erlang:error(custom_error).
** exception error: custom_error
```

Here, custom_error is not recognized by the Erlang shell, and it has no custom translation, such as "bad argument in …," but it's usable in the same way and can be handled by the programmer in an identical manner (as discussed in "Dealing with Exceptions" on page 96).

Exit Exceptions

Two kinds of exits exist in Erlang:

- *Internal exits* are triggered by calling the function exit/1 and making the current process stop its execution.
- *External exits* are called with exit/2 and have to do with multiple processes in the concurrent aspect of Erlang.

Here, we'll focus on internal exits. We will visit the external kind in Chapter 12.

Internal exits are similar to errors. In fact, historically speaking, they were the same, and only exit/1 existed. Errors and exits have roughly the same use cases. So how do you choose which one to use? Well, the choice is not obvious. To decide when to use one or the other, you need to understand the most generic principles behind Erlang processes.

Processes can send each other messages. A process can also *listen* for messages, or wait for them.

You can also choose which messages to listen to. You can discard some messages, ignore others, give up listening after a certain time, and so on.

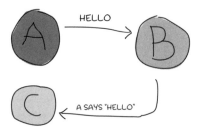

These basic concepts let the implementers of Erlang use a special kind of message (an *exit signal*) to communicate exceptions between processes. They act a bit like a process's last breath; they're sent right before a process dies, and the code it contains stops executing. Other processes that were listening for that specific kind of message can then know about the event and do whatever they please with it. This includes logging, restarting the process that died, and so on.

With this concept explained, the difference in using erlang:error/1 and exit/1 is easier to understand. While both can be used in an extremely similar manner, the real difference is intent. Is what you have simply an error, or is it a condition worthy of killing the current process? This point is made stronger by the fact erlang:error/1 returns a stack trace and exit/1 doesn't. If you had a pretty large stack trace or a lot of arguments to the current function, copying the exit message to every listening process would mean copying the data. In some cases, this could become impractical.

Throw Exceptions

A throw is a class of exceptions used for cases that the programmer can be expected to handle. Unlike exits and errors, throws don't really carry any "crash that process!" intent behind them but rather control flow.

To throw an exception, the syntax is as follows:

```
1> throw(permission_denied).
** exception throw: permission_denied
```

You can replace permission_denied with anything you want (including 'everything is fine', but that is not helpful, and you will lose friends).

NOTE *If you use throws while expecting the programmer to handle them, it's usually a good idea to document the throws within a module using them.*

Throws can also be used for nonlocal returns when in deep recursion. An example of this is the ssl module, which uses throw/1 as a way to push {error, Reason} tuples back to a top-level function. That function then simply returns that tuple to the user. This lets the implementer write code only for the successful cases and have one function deal with the exceptions on top of it all.

Another example of using throws can be found in the array module, where there is a lookup function that can return a user-supplied default value if it can't find the element needed. When the element can't be found, the value default is thrown as an exception, and the top-level function handles that and replaces it with the user-supplied default value. This keeps the programmer of the module from needing to pass the default value as a parameter of every function of the lookup algorithm, again, focusing only on the successful cases.

As a rule of thumb, try to limit the use of your throws for nonlocal returns to a single module in order make it easier to debug your code. This approach will also let you change the innards of your module without requiring changes in its interface.

Dealing with Exceptions

As I've mentioned, throws, errors, and exits can be handled. The way to do this is by using a try ... catch expression.

A try ... catch is a way to evaluate an expression while letting you handle the successful case as well as the errors encountered. Here's the general syntax for such an expression:

```
try Expression of
    SuccessfulPattern1 [Guards] ->
        Expression1;
    SuccessfulPattern2 [Guards] ->
        Expression2
catch
    TypeOfError:ExceptionPattern1 ->
        Expression3;
    TypeOfError:ExceptionPattern2 ->
        Expression4
end.
```

NOTE   *In the syntax shown here, the brackets around [Guards] only denote that the guards are optional. There is no need to put them in a list.*

The *Expression* between try and of is said to be *protected*. This means that any kind of exception happening within that call will be caught.

The patterns and expressions between the try ... of and catch behave in exactly the same manner as a case ... of. They are not protected, and allow pattern matching, variable bindings, and guards.

In the catch part, you can replace *TypeOfError* with error, throw, or exit, for each respective exception type. If no type is provided, throw is assumed. So let's put this in practice.

Handling Different Types of Exceptions

We'll start by creating a module named exceptions (we're going for simplicity here).

```
-module(exceptions).
-compile(export_all).
```

```
throws(F) ->
    try F() of
        _ -> ok
    catch
        Throw -> {throw, caught, Throw}
    end.
```

We can compile it and try it with different kinds of exceptions.

```
1> c(exceptions).
{ok,exceptions}
2> exceptions:throws(fun() -> throw(thrown) end).
{throw,caught,thrown}
3> exceptions:throws(fun() -> erlang:error(pang) end).
** exception error: pang
     in function  exceptions:throws/1 (exceptions.erl, line 5)
```

As you can see, this try ... catch is receiving only throws. This is because when no type is specified, a throw is assumed. We can add functions with catch clauses of each type.

```
errors(F) ->
    try F() of
        _ -> ok
    catch
        error:Error -> {error, caught, Error}
    end.

exits(F) ->
    try F() of
        _ -> ok
    catch
        exit:Exit -> {exit, caught, Exit}
    end.
```

Let's try this version.

```
4> c(exceptions).
{ok,exceptions}
5> exceptions:errors(fun() -> erlang:error("Die!") end).
{error,caught,"Die!"}
6> exceptions:exits(fun() -> exit(goodbye) end).
{exit,caught,goodbye}
```

The next example on the menu shows how to combine all types of exceptions in a single try ... catch. We'll first declare a function to generate all the exceptions we need.

```
sword(1) -> throw(slice);
sword(2) -> erlang:error(cut_arm);
sword(3) -> exit(cut_leg);
```

```
sword(4) -> throw(punch);
sword(5) -> exit(cross_bridge).

black_knight(Attack) when is_function(Attack, 0) ->
    try Attack() of
        _ -> "None shall pass."
    catch
        throw:slice -> "It is but a scratch.";
        error:cut_arm -> "I've had worse.";
        exit:cut_leg -> "Come on you pansy!";
        _:_ -> "Just a flesh wound."
    end.
```

Here, is_function/2 is a BIF that makes sure the variable Attack is a function of arity 0. Then we add this line for good measure:

```
talk() -> "blah blah".
```

And now for something completely different.

```
7> c(exceptions).
{ok,exceptions}
8> exceptions:talk().
"blah blah"
9> exceptions:black_knight(fun exceptions:talk/0).
"None shall pass."
10> exceptions:black_knight(fun() -> exceptions:sword(1) end).
"It is but a scratch."
11> exceptions:black_knight(fun() -> exceptions:sword(2) end).
"I've had worse."
12> exceptions:black_knight(fun() -> exceptions:sword(3) end).
"Come on you pansy!"
13> exceptions:black_knight(fun() -> exceptions:sword(4) end).
"Just a flesh wound."
14> exceptions:black_knight(fun() -> exceptions:sword(5) end).
"Just a flesh wound."
```

The expression on line 9 demonstrates normal behavior for the black knight, when normal function execution happens. Each line that follows that one demonstrates pattern matching on exceptions according to their class (throw, error, or exit) and the reason associated with them (slice, cut_arm, or cut_leg).

Lines 13 and 14 show a catchall clause for exceptions. You need to use the _:_ pattern to make sure to catch any exception from any type. In practice, you should be careful when using catchall patterns. Try to protect your code from what you can handle but not more. Erlang has other facilities in place to take care of the rest.

After the Catch

You can also add a clause after a try ... catch that will always be executed, as follows:

```
try Expression of
    Pattern -> Expr1
catch
    Type:Exception -> Expr2
after
    Expr3
end
```

This is equivalent to the finally block in many other languages. Whether or not there are errors, the expressions inside the after part are guaranteed to run.

However, you cannot get any return value out of the after construct. Therefore, after is mostly used to run code with side effects. The canonical use of this approach is when you want to make sure a file you were reading gets closed, whether or not exceptions were raised.

Trying Multiple Expressions

We've covered how to handle the three classes of exceptions in Erlang with catch blocks. However, I've hidden information from you: It's actually possible to have more than one expression between the try and the of!

```
whoa() ->
    try
        talk(),
        _Knight = "None shall pass!",
        _Doubles = [N*2 || N <- lists:seq(1,100)],
        throw(up),
        _WillReturnThis = tequila
    of
        tequila -> "Hey, this worked!"
    catch
        Exception:Reason -> {caught, Exception, Reason}
    end.
```

By calling exceptions:whoa(), we'll get the obvious {caught, throw, up} because of throw(up). So yeah, it's possible to have more than one expression between try and of.

What exceptions:whoa/0 highlighted that you might not have noticed is that when we use many expressions in this manner, we might not always care what the return value is. So, the of part becomes a bit useless. Well, good news—you can just give it up:

```
im_impressed() ->
    try
        talk(),
```

```
        _Knight = "None shall pass!",
        _Doubles = [N*2 || N <- lists:seq(1,100)],
        throw(up),
        _WillReturnThis = tequila
    catch
        Exception:Reason -> {caught, Exception, Reason}
    end.
```

And now it's a bit leaner!

PROTECTING THE RIGHT THING

The protected part of an exception can't be tail recursive. The VM must always keep a reference there in case there's an exception popping up. Because the try ... catch construct without the of part has nothing but a protected part, calling a recursive function from there might be dangerous for programs that are supposed to run for a long time (which is Erlang's niche). After enough iterations, you'll run out of memory, or your program will get slower. When you put your recursive calls between the of and catch, they are not in a protected part, and you will benefit from last call optimization (discussed in Chapter 5). However, this effect is canceled if you use after in your try expression, as it needs to run *after* anything else, and thus needs to keep track of where it is in the list of function calls.

Some people use try ... of ... catch rather than try ... catch by default to avoid unexpected behaviors of that kind, except for obviously nonrecursive code with a result they don't care about. You're most likely able to make your own decision on what to do!

Wait, There's More!

As if the preceding constructs weren't already enough to put Erlang on par with most languages, it has yet another error-handling construct. This construct is defined as the keyword catch and basically captures all types of exceptions on top of the good results. It's a bit of a weird one because it displays a different representation of exceptions. Here's an example:

```
1> catch throw(whoa).
whoa
2> catch exit(die).
{'EXIT',die}
3> catch 1/0.
{{'EXIT',{badarith,[{erlang,'/',[1,0],[]},
                {erl_eval,do_apply,6,[{file,"erl_eval.erl"},{line,576}]},
                {erl_eval,expr,5,[{file,"erl_eval.erl"},{line,360}]},
                {shell,exprs,7,[{file,"shell.erl"},{line,668}]},
                {shell,eval_exprs,7,[{file,"shell.erl"},{line,623}]},
                {shell,eval_loop,3,[{file,"shell.erl"},{line,608}]}]}}}
4> catch 2+2.
4
```

As you can see, the throws remain the same, but exits and errors are both represented as {'EXIT', Reason}. That's consequent to errors being bolted to the language after exits (the Erlang implementers kept a similar representation for backward compatibility).

Let's try another example.

```
5> catch doesnt:exist(a,4).
{'EXIT',{undef,[{doesnt,exist,[a,4],[]},
               {erl_eval,do_apply,6,[{file,"erl_eval.erl"},{line,576}]},
               {erl_eval,expr,5,[{file,"erl_eval.erl"},{line,360}]},
               {shell,exprs,7,[{file,"shell.erl"},{line,668}]},
               {shell,eval_exprs,7,[{file,"shell.erl"},{line,623}]},
               {shell,eval_loop,3,[{file,"shell.erl"},{line,608}]}]}}
```

The type of error is undef, which means the function you called is not defined.

The list immediately after the type of error is a stack trace. Here's how to read the stack trace:

- The tuple on top of the stack trace represents the last function to be called ({Module, Function, Arguments}). That's your undefined function.
- The tuples after that are the functions called before the error. This time, they're of the form {Module, Function, Arity, Details}.
- The Details field is a list of tuples containing the filename and the line within the file. In this case, the files are erl_eval.erl and shell.erl because they're in charge of interpreting the code you input in the Erlang shell.

That's all there is to it, really.

NOTE   *Before the R15B release, Erlang didn't have the Details part of stack traces. For two decades, Erlang programmers found the origin of errors by using short functions and a strong sense of deduction.*

You can also manually get a stack trace by calling erlang:get_stacktrace/0 in the process that crashed.

You'll often see catch written in the following manner (we're still in *exceptions.erl*):

```
catcher(X,Y) ->
    case catch X/Y of
        {'EXIT', {badarith,_}} -> "uh oh";
        N -> N
    end.
```

And as expected, here's what happens when you run this:

```
6> c(exceptions).
{ok,exceptions}
7> exceptions:catcher(3,3).
1.0
8> exceptions:catcher(6,3).
2.0
9> exceptions:catcher(6,0).
"uh oh"
```

This sounds like a compact and easy way to catch exceptions, but there are a few problems with catch. This example shows one of them:

```
10> X = catch 4+2.
* 1: syntax error before: 'catch'
10> X = (catch 4+2).
6
```

We would expect the first case to behave exactly like the second one. Yet, it looks like Erlang can't cope with the way we declared things. That's because of the operator precedence defined by the language. The catch conflicts with =, and the only way to keep them from clashing is to wrap catch in parentheses. That's not exactly intuitive, given that most expressions do not need to be wrapped in parentheses this way.

Another problem with catch is that you can't see the difference between what looks like the underlying representation of an exception and a real exception, as in this example:

```
11> catch erlang:boat().
{'EXIT',{undef,[{erlang,boat,[],[]},
            {erl_eval,do_apply,6,[{file,"erl_eval.erl"},{line,576}]},
            {erl_eval,expr,5,[{file,"erl_eval.erl"},{line,360}]},
            {shell,exprs,7,[{file,"shell.erl"},{line,668}]},
            {shell,eval_exprs,7,[{file,"shell.erl"},{line,623}]},
            {shell,eval_loop,3,[{file,"shell.erl"},{line,608}]}]}}
12> catch exit({undef,[{erlang,boat,[],[]},
12>          {erl_eval,do_apply,6,[{file,"erl_eval.erl"},{line,576}]},
12>          {erl_eval,expr,5,[{file,"erl_eval.erl"},{line,360}]},
12>          {shell,exprs,7,[{file,"shell.erl"},{line,668}]},
12>          {shell,eval_exprs,7,[{file,"shell.erl"},{line,623}]},
12>          {shell,eval_loop,3,[{file,"shell.erl"},{line,608}]}]}).
{'EXIT',{undef,[{erlang,boat,[],[]},
            {erl_eval,do_apply,6,[{file,"erl_eval.erl"},{line,576}]},
            {erl_eval,expr,5,[{file,"erl_eval.erl"},{line,360}]},
            {shell,exprs,7,[{file,"shell.erl"},{line,668}]},
            {shell,eval_exprs,7,[{file,"shell.erl"},{line,623}]},
            {shell,eval_loop,3,[{file,"shell.erl"},{line,608}]}]}}
```

Also, you can't know the difference between an error and an actual exit, as both results are identical. You could also have used throw/1 to generate the preceding exception. In fact, a throw/1 in a catch might also be problematic in another scenario:

```
one_or_two(1) -> return;
one_or_two(2) -> throw(return).
```

And now the killer problem:

```
13> c(exceptions).
{ok,exceptions}
14> catch exceptions:one_or_two(1).
return
15> catch exceptions:one_or_two(2).
return
```

Because we're behind a catch, we can never know if the function threw an exception or it returned an actual value! This might not happen a whole lot in practice, but it's still a wart big enough to have warranted the addition of the try ... catch construct in the Erlang/OTP R10B release.

Try a try in a Tree

To put exceptions in practice, we'll do a little exercise requiring us to dig out our tree module from Chapter 5. We're going to add a function that lets us do a lookup in the tree to find out if a value is already present. Because the tree is ordered by its keys, and in this case we do not care about the keys, we'll need to traverse the whole thing until we find the value.

The traversal of the tree will be roughly similar to what we did in tree:lookup/2, except this time, we will always search down both the left branch and then the right branch. To write the function, you'll just need to remember that a tree node is either {node, {Key, Value, NodeLeft, NodeRight}} or {node, 'nil'} when empty. With this in mind, we can write a basic implementation without exceptions:

```
%% looks for a given value 'Val' in the tree
has_value(_, {node, 'nil'}) ->
    false;
has_value(Val, {node, {_, Val, _, _}}) ->
    true;
has_value(Val, {node, {_, _, Left, Right}}) ->
    case has_value(Val, Left) of
        true -> true;
        false -> has_value(Val, Right)
    end.
```

The problem with this implementation is that every node of the tree we branch at must test for the result of the previous branch.

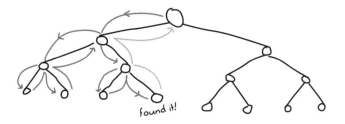

This is a bit annoying. With the help of throws, we can make something that will require fewer comparisons.

```
has_value(Val, Tree) ->
    try has_value1(Val, Tree) of
        false -> false
    catch
        true -> true
    end.

has_value1(_, {node, 'nil'}) ->
    false;
has_value1(Val, {node, {_, Val, _, _}}) ->
    throw(true);
has_value1(Val, {node, {_, _, Left, Right}}) ->
    has_value1(Val, Left),
    has_value1(Val, Right).
```

The execution of this code is similar to the previous version, except that we never need to check for the return value—we don't care about it at all. In this version, only a throw means the value was found. When this happens, the tree evaluation stops, and it falls back to the catch on top. Otherwise, the execution keeps going until the last false is returned, and that's what the user sees.

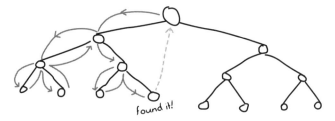

Of course, this implementation is longer than the previous one. However, it is possible to gain in speed and clarity by using nonlocal returns with a throw, depending on the operations you're doing. The current example is a simple comparison, and there's not much to see, but the practice still makes sense with more complex data structures and operations.

That being said, we're probably ready to solve real problems in sequential Erlang.

8

FUNCTIONALLY SOLVING PROBLEMS

So we're ready to do something practical with all that Erlang juice we drank. In this chapter, we'll apply some of the techniques covered in previous chapters to solve some interesting problems.

The problems in this chapter were taken from Miran Lipovača's *Learn You a Haskell for Great Good!* (No Starch Press, 2011; available from *http://learnyouahaskell.com*). I decided to use the same problems so curious readers can compare solutions in Erlang and Haskell as they wish. If you do so, you might find the final results to be pretty similar for two languages with such different syntaxes. This is because once you understand functional concepts, you'll find that they're relatively easy to carry over to other functional languages.

Reverse Polish Notation Calculator

Most people have learned to write arithmetic expressions with the operators in between the numbers ((2 + 2) / 5). This is how most calculators let you insert mathematical expressions, and it's probably the notation you were taught in school. This notation has the downside of needing you to know about operator precedence. For example, multiplication and division are more important (have a higher precedence) than addition and subtraction.

In another notation, called *prefix notation* or *Polish notation*, the operator comes before the operands. Under this notation, (2 + 2) / 5 becomes (/ (+ 2 2) 5). If we decide to say + and / always take two arguments, then (/ (+ 2 2) 5) can simply be written as / + 2 2 5.

However, we will instead focus on *Reverse Polish notation (RPN)*, which is the opposite of prefix notation: the operator follows the operands. In RPN, our example is written as 2 2 + 5 /. The expression 9 * 5 + 7 becomes 9 5 * 7 +, and 10 * 2 * (3 + 4) / 2 is translated to 10 2 * 3 4 + * 2 /. This notation was used a whole lot in early models of calculators, as it takes little memory to use. In fact, some people still carry around RPN calculators. We'll write one of these.

How RPN Calculators Work

First, let's consider how to read RPN expressions. One way is to find the operators one by one, and then regroup them with their operands by arity:

```
10 4 3 + 2 * -
10 (4 3 +) 2 * -
10 ((4 3 +) 2 *) -
(10 ((4 3 +) 2 *) -)
(10 (7 2 *) -)
(10 14 -)
-4
```

However, in the context of a computer or a calculator, a simpler way to read RPN expressions is to make a *stack* of all the operands as we see them. For example, in the mathematical expression 10 4 3 + 2 * -, the first operand we see is 10. We add that to the stack. Then there is 4, so we also push that on top of the stack. In third place, we have 3—let's push that one on the stack, too. Our stack should now look like this:

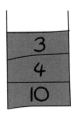

The next character to parse is +. That one is a function of arity 2. In order to use it, we will need to feed it two operands, which will be taken from the stack:

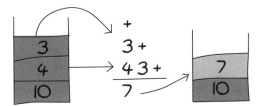

So we take that 7 and push it back on top of the stack (yuck, we don't want to keep these filthy numbers floating around!). The stack is now [7,10], and what's left of the expression is 2 * -. We can take the 2 and push it on top of the stack. We then see *, which needs two operands to work. Again, we take them from the stack:

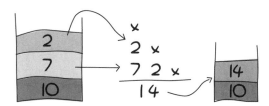

And we push 14 back on top of our stack. All that remains is -, which also needs two operands. Oh glorious luck! There are two operands left in our stack. Use them!

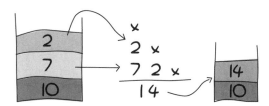

And so we have our result. This stack-based approach is relatively foolproof, and the low amount of parsing needed before starting to calculate results explains why it was a good idea for old calculators to use this approach.

Creating an RPN Calculator

Making our own RPN calculator in Erlang is not too hard once we've done the complex stuff. It turns out the tough part is figuring out what steps need to be done in order to get our end result, and we just did that. So let's get started by opening a file named *calc.erl*.

The first part to worry about is how we're going to represent a mathematical expression. To make things simple, we'll probably input them as a string: "10 4 3 + 2 * -". This string has whitespace, which isn't part of our problem-solving process, but is necessary in order to use a simple tokenizer. What would be usable then is a list of terms of the form ["10","4","3","+","2","*","-"] after going through the tokenizer. It turns out the function string:tokens/2 does just that:

```
1> string:tokens("10 4 3 + 2 * -", " ").
["10","4","3","+","2","*","-"]
```

This will be a good representation for our expression.

The next part to define is the stack. How are we going to do that? You might have noticed that Erlang's lists act a lot like stacks. Using the cons operator (|) in [Head|Tail] effectively produces the same behavior as pushing Head on top of a stack (Tail, in this case). Using a list for a stack will be good enough.

To read the expression, we just need to do the same thing as we did when solving the problem by hand. Read each value from the expression, and if it's a number, put it on the stack. If it's a function, pop all the values it needs from the stack, and then push the result back in. To generalize, we need to go over the whole expression as a loop only once and accumulate the results. Sounds like the perfect job for a fold!

What we need to plan for is the function that lists:foldl/3 will apply on every operator and operand of the expression. This function, because it will be run in a fold, will need to take two arguments: the first one will be the element of the expression to work with, and the second one will be the stack.

We can start writing our code in the *calc.erl* file. First, we'll write the function responsible for all the looping and also the removal of spaces in the expression:

```
-module(calc).
-export([rpn/1]).

rpn(L) when is_list(L) ->
    [Res] = lists:foldl(fun rpn/2, [], string:tokens(L, " ")),
    Res.
```

Next, we'll implement rpn/2. Note that because each operator and operand from the expression ends up being put on top of the stack, the solved expression's result will be on that stack. We need to get that last value out of there before returning it to the user. This is why we pattern match over [Res] and return only Res.

Now to the harder part. Our rpn/2 function will need to handle the stack for all values passed to it. The head of the function will probably look like rpn(Op,Stack), and its return value will look like [NewVal|Stack]. When we get regular numbers, the operation will be as follows:

```
rpn(X, Stack) -> [read(X)|Stack].
```

Here, read/1 is a function that converts a string to an integer or a floating-point value. Sadly, there is no built-in function to do this in Erlang (it just has functions that convert to only one or the other). So we'll add the function ourselves, like this:

```
read(N) ->
    case string:to_float(N) of
        {error,no_float} -> list_to_integer(N);
        {F,_} -> F
    end.
```

Here, string:to_float/1 does the conversion from a string such as "13.37" to its numeric equivalent. However, if there is no way to read a floating-point value, it returns {error,no_float}. When that happens, we need to call list_to_integer/1 instead.

Now let's get back to rpn/2. The numbers we encounter are all added to the stack. However, because our pattern matches on anything (see Chapter 5 for a discussion of pattern matching), operators will also get pushed on the stack. To avoid this, we'll put them all in preceding clauses. The first one we'll try this with is the addition:

```
rpn("+", [N1,N2|S]) -> [N2+N1|S];
rpn(X, Stack) -> [read(X)|Stack].
```

You can see that whenever we encounter the "+" string, we take two numbers from the top of the stack (N1,N2) and add them before pushing the result back onto that stack. This is exactly the same logic we applied when solving the problem by hand. Trying the program, we can see that it works:

```
1> c(calc).
{ok,calc}
2> calc:rpn("3 5 +").
8
3> calc:rpn("7 3 + 5 +").
15
```

The rest is trivial, as we just need to add all the other operators:

```
rpn("+", [N1,N2|S]) -> [N2+N1|S];
rpn("-", [N1,N2|S]) -> [N2-N1|S];
rpn("*", [N1,N2|S]) -> [N2*N1|S];
rpn("/", [N1,N2|S]) -> [N2/N1|S];
rpn("^", [N1,N2|S]) -> [math:pow(N2,N1)|S];
rpn("ln", [N|S])    -> [math:log(N)|S];
rpn("log10", [N|S]) -> [math:log10(N)|S];
rpn(X, Stack) -> [read(X)|Stack].
```

Note that functions that take only one argument such as logarithms need to pop only one element from the stack. It is left as an exercise for the reader to add functions such as sum and prod, which return the sum of all the elements read so far and the products of all the elements, respectively. To help you out, they are already implemented in my version of *calc.erl*.

Testing the Code

To make sure this all works, we'll write some very simple unit tests. Erlang's = operator can act as an *assertion* function. Assertions should crash whenever they encounter unexpected values, which is exactly what we need. Of course, there are more advanced testing frameworks for Erlang, including EUnit and Common Test. We'll check them out in Chapters 25 and 28 but for now, the basic = will do the job.

```erlang
rpn_test() ->
    5 = rpn("2 3 +"),
    87 = rpn("90 3 -"),
    -4 = rpn("10 4 3 + 2 * -"),
    -2.0 = rpn("10 4 3 + 2 * - 2 /"),
    ok = try
        rpn("90 34 12 33 55 66 + * - +")
    catch
        error:{badmatch,[_|_]} -> ok
    end,
    4037 = rpn("90 34 12 33 55 66 + * - + -"),
    8.0 = rpn("2 3 ^"),
    true = math:sqrt(2) == rpn("2 0.5 ^"),
    true = math:log(2.7) == rpn("2.7 ln"),
    true = math:log10(2.7) == rpn("2.7 log10"),
    50 = rpn("10 10 10 20 sum"),
    10.0 = rpn("10 10 10 20 sum 5 /"),
    1000.0 = rpn("10 10 20 0.5 prod"),
    ok.
```

The test function tries all operations. If no exception is raised, the tests are considered successful. The first four tests check that the basic arithmetic functions work correctly. In the fifth test, the try ... catch expects a badmatch error to be thrown because the expression can't work:

```
90 34 12 33 55 66 + * - +
90 (34 (12 (33 (55 66 +) *) -) +)
```

At the end of rpn/1, the values -3947 and 90 are left on the stack because there is no operator to work on the 90 that hangs there. There are two possible ways to handle this problem: ignore it and take only the value on top of the stack (which would be the last result calculated), or crash because the arithmetic is wrong. Given that Erlang's policy is to let it crash, that's the path chosen here. The part that actually crashes is the [Res] in rpn/1. That one makes sure only one element—the result—is left in the stack.

The few tests that are of the form true = *FunctionCall1* == *FunctionCall2* are there because you can't have a function call on the left-hand side of =. It still works as an assertion because we compare the comparison's result to true.

I've also added the test cases for the sum and prod operations, so you can test them after implementing these functions. If all tests are successful, you should see the following:

```
1> c(calc).
{ok,calc}
2> calc:rpn_test().
ok
3> calc:rpn("1 2 ^ 2 2 ^ 3 2 ^ 4 2 ^ sum 2 -").
28.0
```

Here, 28.0 is indeed equal to sum(1^2 + 2^2 + 3^2 + 4^2) - 2. Try as many calculations as you wish.

NOTE *One way to improve our calculator is to make sure it raises* badarith *errors when it crashes because of unknown operators or values left on the stack, rather than raising* badmatch *errors. It would certainly make debugging easier for the user of the* calc *module.*

Heathrow to London

Our next problem is also taken from *Learn You a Haskell.* You're on a plane due to land at Heathrow Airport in the next few hours. You need to get to London as fast as possible. Your rich uncle is dying, and you want to be the first one there to claim dibs on his estate.

There are two roads going from Heathrow to London, and a bunch of smaller streets linking them together. Because of speed limits and traffic, some parts of the roads and smaller streets take longer to travel than others. Before you land, you decide to maximize your chances by finding the optimal path to your uncle's house. Here's the map you've found on your laptop:

Having become a huge fan of Erlang after reading online books, you decide to solve the problem using that language. To make it easier to work with the map, you enter the following data in a file named *road.txt*:

```
50
10
30
5
90
20
40
2
25
10
8
0
```

The path is laid out in the pattern A1, B1, X1, A2, B2, X2, ..., A*n*, B*n*, X*n*, where *X* is one of the roads joining the A side to the B side of the map. We insert a 0 as the last X segment, because no matter what we do, we're at our destination already. Data can probably be organized in tuples of three elements of the form {A,B,X}.

The next thing you realize is that it's worthless to try to solve this problem in Erlang when you don't even know how to solve it by hand. In order to do this, we'll use what recursion taught us.

Solving the Problem Recursively

When writing a recursive function, the first thing to do is to find the base case. For the problem at hand, this would be if we had only one tuple to analyze; that is, if we only had to choose between A, B (and crossing X, which in this case is useless because we're at our destination):

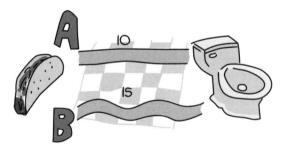

Then the only choice is picking whether path A or path B is the shortest. By understanding how recursion works, we know that we should try to converge toward the base case. This means that on each step we'll take, we'll want to reduce the problem to choosing between A and B for the next step.

Let's extend our map and start over:

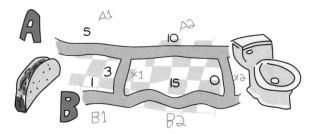

Ah! It gets interesting! How can we reduce the triple {5,1,3} to a strict choice between A and B? Let's see how many options are possible for A. To get to the intersection of A1 and A2 (we'll call this point A1), we can either take road A1 directly (5) or come from B1 (1) and then cross over X1 (3). In this case, the first option (5) is longer than the second one (4). For option A, the shortest path is [B, X]. So what are the options for B? We can either proceed from A1 (5) and then cross over X1 (3) or strictly take the path B1 (1).

So we now have a length 4 with the path [B, X] toward the first intersection A and a length 1 with the path [B] toward the intersection of B1 and B2. Now we must decide how to go to the second point A (the intersection of A2 and the endpoint or X2) and the second point B (intersection of B2 and X2). To make a decision, I suggest we do the same as before (and you don't have much choice but to obey, given that I'm the guy writing this book). Here we go!

We can get to the next point A by either taking the path A2 from [B, X], which gives us a length of 14 (14 = 4 + 10), or by taking B2 then X2 from [B], which gives us a length of 16 (16 = 1 + 15 + 0). In this case, the path [B, X, A] is better than [B, B, X].

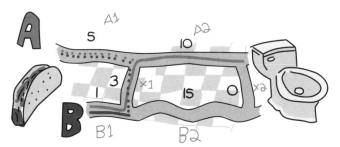

We can also get to the next point B by either taking the path A2 from [B, X], and then crossing over X2 for a length of 14 (14 = 4 + 10 + 0), or by taking the road B2 from [B] for a length of 16 (16 = 1 + 15). Here, the best path is to pick the first option: [B, X, A, X].

When this whole process is complete, we're left with two paths: A or B, both of length 14. Either of them is the right one. The last selection will always have two paths of the same length, given the last X segment has a length of 0. By solving our problem recursively, we've made sure to always get the shortest path at the end. Not too bad, eh?

Subtly enough, we've given ourselves the basic logical parts we need to build a recursive function. We could implement it, but I promised we would have very few recursive functions to write ourselves. Instead, we'll use a fold.

NOTE   *While I have shown folds being used and constructed with lists, folds represent a broader concept of iterating over a data structure with an accumulator. As such, folds can be implemented over trees, dictionaries, arrays, database tables, and so on. It is sometimes useful when experimenting to use abstractions like maps and folds because they make it easier to later change the data structure you use to work with your own logic.*

Writing the Code

So where were we? Ah, yes! We have the file we're going to feed as input ready. To do file manipulations, the file module is our best tool. It contains a lot of functions common to many programming languages in order to deal with files themselves (setting permissions, moving files around, renaming files, deleting files, and so on).

The file module also contains the usual functions to read and/or write from files, such as file:open/2 and file:close/1 to do as their names say (open and close files!), file:read/2 to get the content of a file (either as string or a binary), file:read_line/1 to read a single line, and file:position/3 to move the pointer of an open file to a given position.

The module also contains a bunch of shortcut functions, such as file:read_file/1 (opens and reads the contents as a binary), file:consult/1 (opens and parses a file as Erlang terms), file:pread/2 (changes the position and then reads content), and file:pwrite/2 (changes the position and writes content).

With all these choices available, it's going to be easy to find a function to read our *road.txt* file. Because we know our road is relatively small, we'll call file:read_file("road.txt").:

```
1> {ok, Binary} = file:read_file("road.txt").
{ok,<<"50\r\n10\r\n30\r\n5\r\n90\r\n20\r\n40\r\n2\r\n25\r\n10\r\n8\r\n0\r\n">>}
2> S = string:tokens(binary_to_list(Binary), "\r\n\t ").
["50","10","30","5","90","20","40","2","25","10","8","0"]
```

Note that in this case, we added a space (" ") and a tab ("\t") to the valid tokens, so the file could also have been written in the form "50 10 30 5 90 20 40 2 25 10 8 0".

Given that list, we'll need to transform the strings into integers.

```
3> [list_to_integer(X) || X <- S].
[50,10,30,5,90,20,40,2,25,10,8,0]
```

Let's start a new module called *road.erl* and write down this logic:

```erlang
-module(road).
-compile(export_all).

main() ->
    File = "road.txt",
    {ok, Bin} = file:read_file(File),
    parse_map(Bin).

parse_map(Bin) when is_binary(Bin) ->
    parse_map(binary_to_list(Bin));
parse_map(Str) when is_list(Str) ->
    [list_to_integer(X) || X <- string:tokens(Str,"\r\n\t ")].
```

The function `main/0` is responsible for reading the content of the file and passing it on to `parse_map/1`. Because we use the function `file:read_file/1` to get the contents of *road.txt*, the result we obtain is a binary. For this reason, we've made the function `parse_map/1` match on both lists and binaries. In the case of a binary, we just call the function again with the string being converted to a list (our function to split the string works only on lists).

The next step in parsing the map would be to regroup the data into the {A,B,X} form described earlier. Sadly, there's no simple generic way to pull elements from a list three at a time, so we'll need to pattern match our way in a recursive function in order to accomplish this:

```erlang
group_vals([], Acc) ->
    lists:reverse(Acc);
group_vals([A,B,X|Rest], Acc) ->
    group_vals(Rest, [{A,B,X} | Acc]).
```

That function works in a standard tail-recursive manner; there's nothing too complex going on here. We'll just need to call it by modifying `parse_map/1` a bit:

```erlang
parse_map(Bin) when is_binary(Bin) ->
    parse_map(binary_to_list(Bin));
parse_map(Str) when is_list(Str) ->
    Values = [list_to_integer(X) || X <- string:tokens(Str,"\r\n\t ")],
    group_vals(Values, []).
```

Let's try to compile it all and see if we now have a road that makes sense.

```erlang
1> c(road).
{ok,road}
2> road:main().
[{50,10,30},{5,90,20},{40,2,25},{10,8,0}]
```

Ah yes, that looks right. We get the blocks we need to write our function that will then fit in a fold. For this to work, finding a good accumulator is necessary.

To decide what to use as an accumulator, the method I find the easiest to employ is to imagine myself in the middle of the algorithm while it runs. For this specific problem, we'll imagine that we're currently trying to find the shortest path of the second triple ({5,90,20}). To decide on which path is the best, we need to have the result from the previous triple. Luckily, we know how to get that, because we don't need an accumulator, and we have all that logic already worked out. So for A, we have the following:

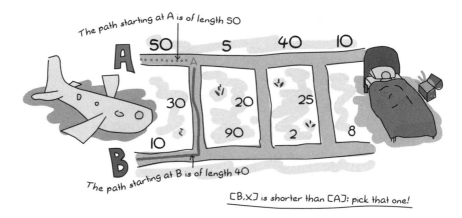

The path starting at A is of length 50

The path starting at B is of length 40

[B,X] is shorter than [A]: pick that one!

And we take the shorter of these two paths.
For B, the choice is similar:

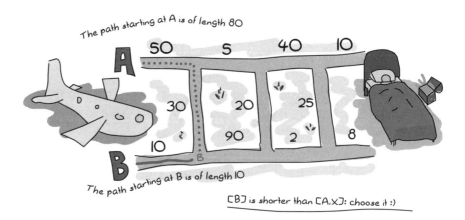

The path starting at A is of length 80

The path starting at B is of length 10

[B] is shorter than [A,X]: choose it :)

So now we know that the current best path coming from A is [B, X]. We also know it has a length of 40. For B, the path is simply [B], and the length is 10. We can use this information to find the next best paths for A and B by reapplying the same logic, but counting the previous ones in the expression.

The other data we need is the path traveled so we can show it to the user. Given that we need two paths (one for A and one for B) and two accumulated lengths, our accumulator can take the form {{*DistanceA*, *PathA*}, {*DistanceB*, *PathB*}}. That way, each iteration of the fold has access to all the state, and we build it up to show it to the user in the end.

This gives us all the parameters our function will need: the {A,B,X} tuples and an accumulator of the form {{*DistanceA*,*PathA*}, {*DistanceB*,*PathB*}}.

We can put this into code in order to get our accumulator as follows:

```
shortest_step({A,B,X}, {{DistA,PathA}, {DistB,PathB}}) ->
    OptA1 = {DistA + A, [{a,A}|PathA]},
    OptA2 = {DistB + B + X, [{x,X}, {b,B}|PathB]},
    OptB1 = {DistB + B, [{b,B}|PathB]},
    OptB2 = {DistA + A + X, [{x,X}, {a,A}|PathA]},
    {erlang:min(OptA1, OptA2), erlang:min(OptB1, OptB2)}.
```

Here, OptA1 gets the first option for A (going through A), and OptA2 gets the second one (going through B then X). The variables OptB1 and OptB2 get the similar treatment for point B. Finally, we return the accumulator with the paths obtained.

For the paths saved in this code, I decided to use the form [{x,X}] rather than [x] for the simple reason that it might be nice for the user to know the length of each segment. We're also accumulating the paths backward ({x,X} comes before {b,B}). This is because we're in a fold, which is tail recursive. The whole list is reversed given how we accumulate it, so we must put the last one traversed before the others.

Finally, we use erlang:min/2 to find the shortest path. It might sound weird to use such a comparison function on tuples, but remember that every Erlang term can be compared to any other! Because the length is the first element of the tuple, we can sort them that way.

What's left to do is to stick that function into a fold:

```
optimal_path(Map) ->
    {A,B} = lists:foldl(fun shortest_step/2, {{0,[]}, {0,[]}}, Map),
    {_Dist,Path} = if hd(element(2,A)) =/= {x,0} -> A;
                      hd(element(2,B)) =/= {x,0} -> B
                   end,
    lists:reverse(Path).
```

At the end of the fold, both paths should end up having the same distance, except one is going through the final {x,0} segment. The if looks at the last visited element of both paths and returns the one that doesn't go through {x,0}. Picking the path with the fewest steps (compare with length/1) would also work. Once the shortest path has been selected, it is reversed (it was built in a tail-recursive manner; you *must* reverse it). You can then display it to the world, or keep it secret and get your rich uncle's estate. To do that, we need to modify the main function to call optimal_path/1. Then it can be compiled.

```
main() ->
    File = "road.txt",
    {ok, Bin} = file:read_file(File),
    optimal_path(parse_map(Bin)).
```

And we can try it as follows:

```
1> c(road).
{ok,road}
2> road:main().
[{b,10},{x,30},{a,5},{x,20},{b,2},{b,8}]
```

Oh, look! We have the right answer. Great job!
Or, to put it in a visual way:

Running the Program Without the Erlang Shell

You know what would be really useful? Being able to run our program from
outside the Erlang shell. To do this, we'll need to change our main function
again:

```
main([FileName]) ->
    {ok, Bin} = file:read_file(FileName),
    Map = parse_map(Bin),
    io:format("~p~n",[optimal_path(Map)]),
    erlang:halt().
```

The main function now has an arity of 1, needed to receive parameters
from the command line. We've also added the function erlang:halt/0, which
will shut down the Erlang VM after being called. We've wrapped the call to
optimal_path/1 into io:format/2 because that's the only way to have the text
visible outside the Erlang shell.

With all of this, your *road.erl* file should now look like this (minus
comments):

```
-module(road).
-compile(export_all).

main([FileName]) ->
    {ok, Bin} = file:read_file(FileName),
```

```
    Map = parse_map(Bin),
    io:format("~p~n",[optimal_path(Map)]),
    erlang:halt(0).

%% Transform a string into a readable map of triples.
parse_map(Bin) when is_binary(Bin) ->
    parse_map(binary_to_list(Bin));
parse_map(Str) when is_list(Str) ->
    Values = [list_to_integer(X) || X <- string:tokens(Str,"\r\n\t ")],
    group_vals(Values, []).

group_vals([], Acc) ->
    lists:reverse(Acc);
group_vals([A,B,X|Rest], Acc) ->
    group_vals(Rest, [{A,B,X} | Acc]).

%% Picks the best of all paths, woo!
optimal_path(Map) ->
    {A,B} = lists:foldl(fun shortest_step/2, {{0,[]}, {0,[]}}, Map),
    {_Dist,Path} = if hd(element(2,A)) =/= {x,0} -> A;
                      hd(element(2,B)) =/= {x,0} -> B
                   end,
    lists:reverse(Path).

%% actual problem solving
%% Change triples of the form {A,B,X}
%% where A,B,X are distances and a,b,x are possible paths
%% to the form {DistanceSum, PathList}.
shortest_step({A,B,X}, {{DistA,PathA}, {DistB,PathB}}) ->
    OptA1 = {DistA + A, [{a,A}|PathA]},
    OptA2 = {DistB + B + X, [{x,X}, {b,B}|PathB]},
    OptB1 = {DistB + B, [{b,B}|PathB]},
    OptB2 = {DistA + A + X, [{x,X}, {a,A}|PathA]},
    {erlang:min(OptA1, OptA2), erlang:min(OptB1, OptB2)}.
```

And we can run the code like this:

```
$ erlc road.erl
$ erl -noshell -run road main road.txt
[{b,10},{x,30},{a,5},{x,20},{b,2},{b,8}]
```

And yep, we get the right answer! That's pretty much all you need to do to get things to work, though you could also make yourself a bash/batch script to wrap the line into a single executable, or you could check out the escript command (which provides scripting support) to get similar results.

As you've seen with these two exercises, solving problems is much easier when you break them into small parts that you can solve individually before piecing everything together. It's also important not to dive right in before you fully understand the problem, since this will usually end up creating more work in the long run. Finally, a few tests are always appreciated. They allow you to make sure everything works initially and will return the same results down the road, even if you change the particulars of the implementation.

USING ESCRIPT

The Erlang `escript` command provides a simple way to run Erlang programs without starting the `erl` application directly. Basically, the command takes a module and allows you to interpret it without needing to compile it first.

The structure of the module remains similar to what you had before, but you need to change its head. Instead of having a `-module(Name)` attribute, the following is required:

```
#!/usr/bin/env escript
%% -*- erlang -*-
%%! -pa 'ebin/' [Other erl Arguments]
main([StringArguments]) ->
    ...
```

The function `main/1` will automatically be called when you start the script, either as *./script-name*.erl or `escript` *script-name*.erl (the latter makes it easier to run on Windows). The module will run as a normal script.

If you want the benefits of `escript` without needing to interpret the code (which is slower) and would prefer compiling the code, just add the `-mode(compile).` module attribute somewhere in the file.

To find out more about `escript`, read the documentation that comes with Erlang, which is also available online at *http://erlang.org/doc/man/escript.html*.

9

A SHORT VISIT TO COMMON DATA STRUCTURES

Chances are that you now understand the functional subset of Erlang pretty well and could read many programs without a problem. However, I bet it's still a bit hard to think about how to build a real, useful program, even though Chapter 8 was about solving problems in a functional manner. Well, that's how I felt at this point in my Erlang studies—if you're doing better, congratulations!

So far, we've covered a bunch of topics, including most of the basic data types, the shell, how to write modules and functions (with recursion), different ways to compile, how to control the flow of the program, how to handle exceptions, and how to abstract away some common operations. We've also gone over how to store data with tuples, lists, and an incomplete implementation of a binary search tree. What we haven't talked about yet is the other data structures provided to the programmer in the Erlang standard library. This chapter fills that void, with information about records, key/value stores, sets, directed graphs, and queues.

Records

Records are, first of all, a hack. They are more or less an afterthought to the language and can have their share of inconveniences. However, they're still pretty useful when you have a small data structure and you want to access the attributes by name directly. Used this way, Erlang records are a lot like structs in C.

Defining Records

Records are declared as module attributes in the following manner:

```
-module(records).
-compile(export_all).

-record(robot, {name,
                type=industrial,
                hobbies,
                details=[]}).
```

Here, we have a record representing robots with four fields: name, type, hobbies, and details. There are also default values for type and details, which are industrial and [], respectively.

Here's how to create an instance of a record in the module records:

```
first_robot() ->
    #robot{name="Mechatron",
           type=handmade,
           details=["Moved by a small man inside"]}.
```

Let's try running the code:

```
1> c(records).
{ok,records}
2> records:first_robot().
{robot,"Mechatron",handmade,undefined,
       ["Moved by a small man inside"]}
```

Whoops! Here comes the hack! Erlang records are just syntactic sugar on top of tuples. Fortunately, there's a way to keep the illusion going. The Erlang shell has the command rr(*Module*), which lets you load record definitions from *Module*. Try it with our records module.

```
3> rr(records).
[robot]
4> records:first_robot().
#robot{name = "Mechatron",type = handmade,
       hobbies = undefined,
       details = ["Moved by a small man inside"]}
```

NOTE *The* rr() *function can take more than a module name. It can also take a wildcard (like* rr("*")) *and a list as a second argument to specify which records to load.*

Ah, there! This makes it much easier to work with records. You'll notice that in first_robot/0, we did not define the hobbies field, and it has no default value in its declaration. By default, Erlang sets the value to undefined for you.

To see the behavior of the defaults we set in the robot definition, let's compile the following function:

```
car_factory(CorpName) ->
    #robot{name=CorpName, hobbies="building cars"}.
```

Now run it.

```
5> c(records).
{ok,records}
6> records:car_factory("Jokeswagen").
#robot{name = "Jokeswagen",type = industrial,
    hobbies = "building cars",details = []}
```

Now we have an industrial robot that likes to spend time building cars.

OTHER RECORD FUNCTIONS FOR THE ERLANG SHELL

Along with rr(), Erlang provides a few other functions to deal with records in the shell:

- Use rd(*Name*, *Definition*) to define a record in a manner similar to the -record(*Name*, *Definition*) function used in our module.

- Use rf() to "unload" all records.

- Use rf(*Name*) or rf([*Names*]) to get rid of specific definitions.

- Use rl() to print all record definitions currently defined in the shell in a way that makes it easy to copy and paste them into the module. Use rl(*Name*) or rl([*Names*]) to print only specific records.

Reading Values from Records

Simply writing records isn't very useful. We need a way to extract values from them. There are basically two ways to do this: with a special dot syntax or through pattern matching. Assuming you have the record definition for robots loaded, we'll take a look at the dot syntax first.

```
5> Crusher = #robot{name="Crusher", hobbies=["Crushing people","petting cats"]}.
#robot{name = "Crusher",type = industrial,
    hobbies = ["Crushing people","petting cats"],
    details = []}
```

```
6> Crusher#robot.hobbies.
["Crushing people","petting cats"]
```

Ugh—not a pretty syntax. This is due to the nature of records as tuples. Because they're just a kind of compiler trick, you need to include keywords to define which record goes with which variable; hence, the #robot part of Crusher#robot.hobbies. It's sad, but there's no way out of it. Worse than that, nested records can get pretty ugly:

```
7> NestedBot = #robot{details=#robot{name="erNest"}}.
#robot{name = undefined,type = industrial,
       hobbies = undefined,
       details = #robot{name = "erNest",type = industrial,
                        hobbies = undefined,details = []}}
8> (NestedBot#robot.details)#robot.name.
"erNest"
```

And no, the parentheses are not mandatory. You could also type NestedBot#robot.details#robot.name. For backward compatibility (with Erlang versions before R14A) and to suit my personal preferences, I tend to use the version with parentheses, because I think that they make the code more readable.

The following example further demonstrates the dependence of records on tuples.

```
9> #robot.type.
3
```

This outputs which element of the underlying tuple type is.

One redeeming feature of records is that you can use them in function heads to pattern match and also in guards. To see how this works, declare a new record at the top of the file, and then add the functions under the declaration.

```
-record(user, {id, name, group, age}).

%% Use pattern matching to filter.
admin_panel(#user{name=Name, group=admin}) ->
    Name ++ " is allowed!";
admin_panel(#user{name=Name}) ->
    Name ++ " is not allowed".

%% Can extend user without problem.
adult_section(U = #user{}) when U#user.age >= 18 ->
    %% Show stuff that can't be written in such a text.
    allowed;
adult_section(_) ->
    %% Redirect to Sesame Street site.
    forbidden.
```

The syntax to bind a variable to any field of a record is demonstrated in the admin_panel/1 function (it's possible to bind variables to more than one field).

Regarding the adult_section/1 function, note that you need to do *SomeVar* = #*some_record*{} in order to bind the whole record to a variable.

Then we do the compiling as usual.

```
10> c(records).
{ok,records}
11> rr(records).
[robot,user]
12> records:admin_panel(#user{id=1, name="ferd", group=admin, age=96}).
"ferd is allowed!"
13> records:admin_panel(#user{id=2, name="you", group=users, age=66}).
"you is not allowed"
14> records:adult_section(#user{id=21, name="Bill", group=users, age=72}).
allowed
15> records:adult_section(#user{id=22, name="Noah", group=users, age=13}).
forbidden
```

This shows that it's not necessary to match on all parts of the tuple, or even know how many there are when writing the function. We can match on only the age or the group, if that's what's needed, and forget about all the rest of the structure. If we were to use a normal tuple, the function definition might need to look a bit like function({record, _, _, ICareAboutThis, _, _}) -> .... Then, whenever someone decided to add an element to the tuple, someone else (probably angry about it) would need to update all the functions where that tuple is used.

Updating Records

The following function illustrates how to update a record (they wouldn't be very useful otherwise).

```
repairman(Rob) ->
    Details = Rob#robot.details,
    NewRob = Rob#robot{details=["Repaired by repairman"|Details]},
    {repaired, NewRob}.
```

Now compile it.

```
16> c(records).
{ok,records}
17> records:repairman(#robot{name="Ulbert", hobbies=["trying to have feelings"]}).
{repaired,#robot{name = "Ulbert",type = industrial,
                 hobbies = ["trying to have feelings"],
                 details = ["Repaired by repairman"]}}
```

As you can see, the robot has been repaired. The syntax to update records is a bit special here. It looks like we're updating the record in place (Rob#robot{*Field=NewValue*}), but it's all compiler trickery to call the underlying erlang:setelement/3 function.

Sharing Records

Because records can be useful and code duplication is annoying, Erlang programmers frequently share records across modules with the help of header files. Erlang *header files* are similar to their C counterparts. A header file is nothing but a snippet of code that gets added to the module as if it were written there in the first place.

Create a file named *records.hrl* with the following content:

```
%% This is a .hrl (header) file.
-record(included, {some_field,
                   some_default = "yeah!",
                   unimaginative_name}).
```

To include it in records.erl, just add the following line to the module:

```
-include("records.hrl").
```

And then add the following function to try it:

```
included() -> #included{some_field="Some value"}.
```

Now compile it as usual.

```
18> c(records).
{ok,records}
19> rr(records).
[included,robot,user]
20> records:included().
#included{some_field = "Some value",some_default = "yeah!",
          unimaginative_name = undefined}
```

Hooray! That's about it for records. As you've seen, their syntax is not pretty, and they're not much more than a hack, but they're relatively important for the maintainability of your code.

WARNING *You will often see open source software using the method shown here of having a project-wide* .hrl *file for records that are shared across all modules. While I felt obligated to document this use, I strongly recommend that you keep all record definitions local, within one module. If you want some other module to look at a record's innards, write functions to access its fields and keep its details as private as possible. This helps prevent name clashes, avoids problems when upgrading code, and just generally improves the readability and maintainability of your code.*

Key/Value Stores

Back in Chapter 5, we built a tree and then used it as a key/value store for an address book. That address book sucked. We couldn't delete or convert it to anything useful. It was a good demonstration of recursion, but not much more.

Now is the time to introduce you to a bunch of useful data structures and modules to store data under a certain key. I won't define what every function does, show entire examples, or go through all the modules, because you can easily find that information in Erlang's documentation. Consider me as "someone responsible for raising awareness about key/value stores in Erlang" (sounds like a good title—I just need one of those ribbons).

Stores for Small Amounts of Data

For storing small amounts of data, basically two types of data structures can be used: a *property list (proplist)* or an ordered *dictionary (orddict)*.

Proplists

A proplist is any list of tuples of the form [{*Key*,*Value*}]. Proplists are a weird kind of structure because that's the only rule that applies to them. In fact, the rules are so relaxed that the list can also contain Boolean values, integers, and whatever else you want. Here, we're interested in the idea of a tuple with a key and a value in a list.

To work with proplists, use the proplists module. It contains functions such as proplists:delete/2, proplists:get_value/2, proplists:get_all_values/2, proplists:lookup/2, and proplists:lookup_all/2. You can get their definitions from Erlang's documentation.

You'll notice there is no function to add or update an element of the list. This shows how loosely defined proplists are as a data structure. In fact, a proplist is more often appropriate when you need a list of properties. For example, we could describe a dog as the proplist [{name, buddy}, {race, husky}, friendly], where the value friendly is equivalent to {friendly, true}.

If you want to add an element to a proplist, you must use the cons operator to insert your element manually (*NewList* = [*NewElement*|*OldList*]). This works well even for updates, because the proplists module will look through the list in order and stop as soon as it finds a matching element. You can also use functions such as lists:keyreplace/4 to update a proplist if you need to do it a lot, as this approach avoids making the proplist longer as time goes on. Using two modules for one small data structure is not the cleanest technique, but because proplists are so loosely defined, they're often used to deal with configuration lists.

Orddicts

If you want a more complete key/value store for small amounts of data, the orddict module is what you need. Orddicts are proplists with a taste for formality. Each key can be there only once. The whole list is sorted so, on average, lookups are faster. The items need to respect a strict {Key, Value} structure. You're not expected to edit orddicts as lists, as with proplists, but to use the functional interface for all the operations you need.

Common functions for CRUD (Create, Read, Update, and Delete) usage include orddict:store/3, orddict:find/2 (when you do not know whether the key is in the dictionaries), orddict:fetch/2 (when you know it is there or that it must be there), and orddict:erase/2. You can create an orddict by using orddict:new/0 or orddict:from_list/1. Again, you can look up these functions in the Erlang documentation.

WARNING *To create and manipulate the orddict, you might be tempted to manually modify the key/value list, but you should* always *use the functions provided by the* orddict *module to avoid ordering errors.*

Orddicts are generally a good compromise between complexity and efficiency for up to about 75 elements (see my benchmark, *keyval_benchmark.erl*, available with the rest of the code for this book). After that amount, you should switch to different key/value stores, such as the ones discussed next.

Larger Dictionaries: Dicts and GB Trees

Erlang provides two key/value structures to deal with larger amounts of data: *dictionaries (dicts)* and *general balanced (GB) trees*. Dicts have the same interface as orddicts: dict:store/3, dict:find/2, and dict:fetch/2, dict:erase/2. They also have every other function from orddict, such as dict:map/2  and dict:fold/2 (pretty useful to work on the whole data structure!). Dicts are thus very good choices for scaling up orddicts whenever it is needed.

GB trees, handled through the gb_trees module, have many more functions that give you more direct control over how the structure is to be used. There are basically two modes for gb_trees: the mode where you know your structure inside and out (I call this the *smart mode*), and the mode where you can't assume much about it (I call this the *naive mode*). In naive mode, the functions are gb_trees:enter/2, gb_trees:lookup/2, and gb_trees:delete_any/2. The related smart functions are gb_trees:insert/3, gb_trees:get/2, gb_trees:update/3, and gb_trees:delete/2. There is also gb_trees:map/2, which is a tree-based equivalent to lists:map/2 (always a nice thing to have when you need it).

The disadvantage of naive functions over smart ones is that because GB trees are balanced trees, whenever you insert a new element (or delete a bunch of elements), the tree may need to balance itself. This can take time and memory (even in useless checks that end up changing nothing but seek to make sure the tree is still balanced). The smart functions all assume that the key is present in the tree. This lets you skip all the safety checks and results in faster operations.

DON'T DRINK TOO MUCH KOOL-AID

What about code that requires data structures with only numeric keys? For that, most languages usually have arrays. Erlang has arrays, too. They allow you to access elements with numeric indices and to fold over the whole structure while possibly ignoring undefined slots. However, very few people use them.

Erlang arrays, unlike their imperative counterparts, do not have such things as constant-time insertion or lookup. Instead, they are said to be *persistent*, as they allow no destructive updates. For this reason, they're usually slower than those in languages that support destructive assignment. People who know and use that type of array usually do so with a given set of algorithms and a precise style in mind. Erlang's arrays hardly allow that. They tend to sit in a dark corner, alone.

Erlang programmers who need to do matrix manipulations and other jobs that require arrays tend to use concepts called *ports* to let other languages do the heavy lifting, or *C nodes*, *linked-in drivers*, and *native implemented functions (NIFs)*. See the Erlang documentation for more details.

When should you use the gb_trees module rather than dict functions? Well, it's not a clear decision. As the benchmark module I wrote (*keyval_benchmark.erl*) shows, GB trees and dicts have somewhat similar performances in many respects. However, the benchmark demonstrates that dicts have the best read speeds, and the GB trees tend to be a little quicker on other operations.

Also note that while dicts have a fold function, GB trees don't. Instead, they have an iterator function, which returns a bit of the tree on which you can call gb_trees:next(Iterator) to get the following values in order. This means that you need to write your own recursive functions on top of using gb_trees, rather than using a generic fold. On the other hand, gb_trees lets you have quick access to the smallest and largest elements of the structure with gb_trees:smallest/1 and gb_trees:largest/1. This is because a GB tree preserves the order of all elements inside of it, from the smallest to the largest. A dict, on the other hand, will not provide this ordering. As such, if you need to be able to traverse your key/value store in order, GB trees might be a good option.

So, your application's needs are what should govern which key/value store you choose. You'll need to consider factors such as how much data you have to store and what you need to do with it. Measure, profile, and benchmark to make sure.

Some special key/value stores exist to deal with resources of different sizes. Such stores are ETS tables, Dets tables, and the Mnesia database. Their use is strongly related to the concepts of multiple processes and distribution, so we'll get to them in Chapter 25. I'm mentioning them now just to pique your curiosity and as a reference for those who are interested.

A Set of Sets

If you've ever studied set theory in a mathematics class, you have an idea about what sets can do. If you haven't, you might want to skip this section.

Sets are groups of unique elements that you can compare and operate on—find which elements are in two groups, in none of them, in only one or the other, and so on. There are advanced operations that let you define relations and operate on these relations, and much more. I'm not going to dive into the theory here but just give you an idea of what is available.

Erlang has four main modules to deal with sets. This seems a bit weird at first, but it's because the implementers agreed that there was no "best" way to build a set. The four modules are as follows:

ordsets

ordsets module sets are implemented as sorted lists. They're mainly useful for small sets, and are the slowest kind of set, but they have the simplest and most readable representation of all sets. Some of the many standard functions for them are ordsets:new/0, ordsets:is_element/2, ordsets:add_element/2, ordsets:del_element/2, ordsets:union/1, and ordsets:intersection/1.

sets

sets (the module) is implemented on top of a structure similar to the one used by dicts. The sets module implements the same interface as ordsets, but its sets scale much better. Like dicts, they're especially good for read-intensive manipulations, such as checking whether some element is part of the set.

gb_sets

gb_sets module sets are constructed above a GB tree structure similar to the one used in the gb_trees module. gb_sets is to sets what gb_trees is to dict: an implementation that is faster when considering operations other than reading, leaving you with more control. While gb_sets implements the same interface as sets and ordsets, it adds more functions. As with gb_trees, we have smart versus naive functions, iterators, and quick access to the smallest and largest values.

sofs

Sets of sets, created with the sofs module, are implemented with sorted lists, stuck inside a tuple with some metadata. This is the module to use if you want to have full control over relationships between sets and families, enforce set types, and so on. These sets are what you want if you need the mathematics concept of sets, rather than just groups of unique elements.

It's a bit confusing to have so many options available. Björn Gustavsson, from the Erlang/OTP team and programmer of Wings 3D, suggests using gb_sets in most circumstances, using ordset when you need a clear representation that you want to process with your own code, and using sets when you need the =:= operator (see *http://erlang.org/pipermail/erlang-questions/2010-March/050333.html*).

In any case, as with key/value stores, the best solution is usually to benchmark and see which approach best suits your application.

> ### DON'T DRINK TOO MUCH KOOL-AID
>
> While such a variety of sets can be seen as something great, some implementation details can be downright frustrating. As an example, gb_sets, ordsets, and sofs all use the == operator to compare values; if you have the numbers 2 and 2.0, they'll be seen as the same number.
>
> However, the sets module uses the =:= operator, which means you can't necessarily switch over every implementation as you wish. There are cases where you need one precise behavior, and at that point, you might lose the benefit of having multiple implementations.

Directed Graphs

One other data structure intimately related to mathematics is the directed graph. Directed graphs in Erlang are implemented as two modules: digraph and digraph_utils. The digraph module basically allows the construction and modification of a directed graph—manipulating edges and vertices, finding paths and cycles, and so on. The digraph_utils module allows you to navigate a graph (postorder and preorder); test for cycles, arborescences, and trees; find neighbors; and so on.

Because directed graphs are closely related to set theory, the sofs module contains a few functions that let you convert families to directed graphs and directed graphs to families.

Because of the way the directed graphs modules are built, they aren't really appropriate without a good basic knowledge of either graphs or set theory. If you know your stuff and you are interested in learning more about these modules, you'll have no problem figuring them out by their standard documentation.

Queues

The queue module implements a double-ended first in, first out (FIFO) queue. Queues are implemented a bit as illustrated here: two lists (in this context, stacks) that allow you to both append and prepend elements rapidly.

Because a single list doesn't allow efficiently adding *and* removing elements from both ends at once (it's only fast to add and remove the head), the idea behind the queue module is that if you have two lists, then you can use one to add elements and one to remove elements. One of the lists then behaves as one end of the queue, where you push values, and the other list acts as the other end, where you pop them. When the latter is empty, you take the former and reverse it, and it becomes the new list to pop from. This allows an efficient queue implementation on the average of all operations over the life of the queue.

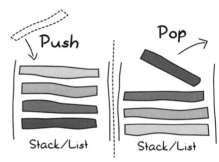

The queue module has different functions that are separated into three interfaces (or APIs) of varying complexity:

Original API

The original API contains the functions at the base of the queue concept. These include new/0, for creating empty queues; in/2, for inserting new elements; and out/1, for removing elements. It also has functions to convert to lists, reverse the queue, check if a particular value is part of the queue, and so on.

Extended API

The extended API mainly adds some introspection power and flexibility. It lets you do things such as look at the front of the queue without removing the first element (get/1 or peek/1), remove elements without caring about them (drop/1), and so on. These functions are not essential to the concept of queues, but they're still useful in general.

Okasaki API

The Okasaki API is a bit weird. It's derived from Chris Okasaki's *Purely Functional Data Structures* (Cambridge University Press, 1999). The API provides operations similar to those available in the other APIs, but some of the function names are written backward, and the whole thing is relatively peculiar. Unless you have a specific reason for using this API, I wouldn't bother with it.

You'll generally want to use queues when you need to ensure that the first item ordered is indeed the first one processed. So far, the examples I've shown mainly used lists as accumulators that would then be reversed. In cases where you can't just do all the reversing at once, and elements are frequently added, the queue module is what you want. (Well, you should test and measure first. Always test and measure first!)

End of the Short Visit

That's about it for our trip through the most common data structures of Erlang. Thank you for having kept your arms inside the vehicle the whole time. There are a few more data structures available to solve different problems. Here, I've covered those that you're likely to encounter or need the most, given the strengths of general use cases of Erlang. I encourage you to explore the standard library and the extended one, too, to find more information.

You might be glad to learn that this completes our trip into sequential (functional) Erlang. I know a lot of people get into Erlang to see all the concurrency and processes and whatnot. This is understandable, given these are the areas where Erlang really shines. It offers supervision trees, fancy error management, distribution, and more. I know that I've been very impatient to write about these subjects, so I guess some readers are very impatient to read about them.

However, it makes more sense to be comfortable with functional Erlang before moving on to concurrent Erlang. Now we can focus on all the new concepts. Here we go!

10

THE HITCHHIKER'S GUIDE TO CONCURRENCY

Far out in the uncharted backwaters of the unfashionable beginning of the 21st century lies a small subset of human knowledge. Within this subset of human knowledge is an utterly insignificant little discipline whose Von Neumann–descended architecture is so amazingly primitive that it is still thought that RPN calculators are a pretty neat idea.

This discipline has—or rather had—a problem, which was this: Most of the people studying it were unhappy for pretty much of the time when trying to write parallel software. Many solutions were suggested for this problem, but most of these were largely concerned with the handling of little pieces of logic called *locks* and *mutexes* and whatnot, which is odd because on the whole, it wasn't the small pieces of logic that needed parallelism.

And so the problem remained. Lots of people were mean, and most of them were miserable, even those with RPN calculators.

Many were increasingly of the opinion that they'd all made a big mistake in trying to add parallelism to their programming languages, and that no program should have ever left its initial thread.

NOTE *Parodying* The Hitchhiker's Guide to the Galaxy *is fun. Read the book if you haven't already. It's good!*

Don't Panic

Hi. Today (or whatever day you are reading this—even tomorrow), I'm going to tell you about concurrent Erlang. Chances are you've read about or dealt with concurrency before. You might also be curious about the emergence of multicore programming. Anyway, the probabilities are high that you're reading this book because of all the talk about concurrency going on these days.

A warning though: This chapter is mostly theory. If you have a headache, a distaste for programming language history, or a desire just to program, you might be better off skipping to the end of the chapter, or moving on to the next one (where more practical content is shown).

In the Introduction to this book, I explained that Erlang's concurrency is based on message passing and the actor model, using the example of people communicating with nothing but letters. We'll get to more details about concurrency later in this chapter, but first, it is important to define the difference between *concurrency* and *parallelism*.

In many places, both words refer to the same concept, but in the context of Erlang, *concurrency* refers to having many actors running independently but not necessarily all at the same time, while *parallelism* is having actors running at exactly the same time. This is how I'll use these terms in this text, but don't be surprised if other sources or people use the same terms to mean different things. There doesn't seem to be any consensus on these definitions in the computer science world.

Erlang had concurrency from the beginning, even when everything was done on a single core processor in the 1980s. Each Erlang process would have its own slice of time to run, much like desktop applications did before multicore systems. Parallelism was still possible back then; all you needed to do was to have a second computer running the code and communicating with the first one. Even then, only two actors could be run in parallel in this setup. Nowadays, multicore systems allow for parallelism on a single computer (some industrial chips have many dozens of cores), and Erlang takes full advantage of this possibility.

The distinction between concurrency and parallelism is important to make, because many programmers hold the belief that Erlang was ready for multicore computers years before it actually was. Erlang was adapted to true *symmetric multiprocessing (SMP)* in the mid-2000s, and only got most of the implementation right with the R13B release of the language in 2009. Before that, SMP often needed to be disabled to avoid performance losses. Then to get parallelism on a multicore computer without SMP, you would need to start many instances of the VM.

An interesting fact is that because Erlang concurrency is all about isolated processes, it took no conceptual change at the language level to bring true parallelism to the language. All the changes were transparently done in the VM, away from the eyes of the programmers.

Concurrency Concepts

Back in the day, Erlang's development as a language was extremely quick, with frequent feedback from engineers working on telephone switches in Erlang itself. These interactions proved process-based concurrency and asynchronous message passing to be a good way to model the problems the engineers faced. Moreover, the telephony world already had a certain culture going toward concurrency before Erlang came to be. This was inherited from PLEX, a language created earlier at Ericsson, and AXE, a switch developed with it. Erlang followed this tendency and attempted to improve on previous tools available.

Erlang had a few requirements to satisfy before being considered good. The main ones were being able to scale up and support many thousands of users across many switches, and to achieve high reliability—to the point of never stopping the code.

Scalability

Some properties were seen as necessary to achieve scalability. Because users would be represented as processes that reacted only upon the occurrence of certain events (such as receiving a call or hanging up), an ideal system would support processes doing small computations, switching between them very quickly as events came through. To make the system efficient, it made sense for processes to be started and destroyed very quickly. Having them be lightweight was mandatory to achieve this efficiency. It was also mandatory because you didn't want to have things like process pools (a fixed amount of processes you split the work among). Instead, it would be much easier to design programs that could use as many processes as they needed.

NOTE *Another important aspect of scalability is to be able to bypass your hardware's limitations. There are two ways to do this: make the hardware better or add more hardware. The first option is useful up to a certain point, after which it becomes extremely expensive. The second option is usually cheaper and requires you to add more computers to do the job. This is where distribution can be useful to have as a part of your language.*

Because telephony applications needed a lot of reliability, it was decided that the cleanest approach was to forbid processes from sharing memory. Shared memory could leave things in an inconsistent state after some crashes (especially on data shared across different nodes) and had some complications. Instead, processes should communicate by sending messages where all the data is copied. This might end up being slower but safer.

Fault Tolerance

The first writers of Erlang always kept in mind that failure is common. You can try to prevent bugs all you want, but most of the time, some will still creep in. And even if by some miracle your code doesn't have any bugs, nothing can stop the eventual hardware failure. Therefore, the idea is to find good ways to handle errors and problems, rather than trying to prevent them all.

It turns out that taking the design approach of multiple processes with message passing was a good idea, because error handling could be grafted onto it relatively easily. Take lightweight processes (made for quick restarts and shutdowns) as an example. Some studies proved that the main sources of downtime in large-scale software systems are intermittent or transient bugs (see *http://dslab.epfl.ch/pubs/crashonly/*). Also, there's a principle that says that errors that corrupt data should cause the faulty part of the system to die as fast as possible in order to avoid propagating errors and bad data to the rest of the system.

Another concept here is that a system can terminate in many different ways, two of which are clean shutdowns and crashes (terminating with an unexpected error).

Here, the worst case is obviously the crash. A safe solution would be to make sure all crashes are the same as clean shutdowns. This can be done through practices such as *shared-nothing* (all memory is separated for subparts of the system) and single assignment (which can further isolate a process's memory), avoiding locks (if certain data was locked during a crash, it would keep other processes from accessing the data or leave it in an inconsistent state), and other safeguards, which were all part of Erlang's design.

The ideal solution in Erlang is thus to kill processes as fast as possible to avoid data corruption and transient bugs. Lightweight processes are a key element in this. Further error-handling mechanisms are also part of the language to allow processes to monitor other processes (which are described in Chapter 12), in order to know when processes die and to decide what to do about it.

Assuming that restarting processes quickly is enough to deal with crashes, the next problem is handling hardware failures. How do you make sure your program keeps running when someone kicks the computer it's running on? Although a fancy defense mechanism consisting of laser detection and strategically placed cacti could do the job for a while, it would not last forever. The solution is simply to have your program running on more than one computer at once—something that's necessary for scaling anyway. This is another advantage of independent processes with no communication channel outside message passing. You can have them working the same way whether they're local or on a different computer, making fault tolerance through distribution nearly transparent to the programmer.

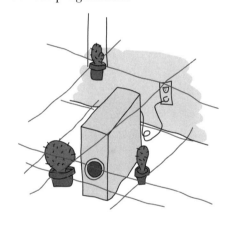

Being distributed has direct consequences on how processes can communicate with each other. One of the biggest hurdles of distribution is that you can't assume that because a node (a remote computer) was there when you made a function call, it will still be there for the whole transmission of the call, or that it will even execute the call correctly. Someone tripping over a cable or unplugging the machine would leave your application hanging. Or maybe it would make it crash. Who knows?

Well, it turns out the choice of asynchronous message passing was a good design pick there, too. Under the processes-with-asynchronous-messages model, messages are sent from one process to a second one and stored in a *mailbox* inside the receiving process until they are taken out to be read. It's important to mention that messages are sent without even checking if the receiving process exists, because it would not be useful to do so. As implied in the previous paragraph, it's impossible to know if a process will crash between the time a message is sent and received. And if the message is received, it's impossible to know whether the message will be acted upon or if the receiving process will die before that. Asynchronous messages allow safe remote function calls because there is no assumption about what will happen; the programmer is the one to know. If you need to have a confirmation of delivery, you must send a second message as a reply to the original process. This message will have the same safe semantics, and so will any program or library you build on this principle.

Concurrency Implementation

So now you know why it was decided that lightweight processes with asynchronous message passing were the approach to take for Erlang. But how could Erlang's implementers make this work?

First of all, the operating system can't be trusted to handle the processes. Operating systems have many different ways to handle processes, and their performance varies a lot. Most, if not all, of them are too slow or heavy for what is needed by standard Erlang applications. By handling processes in the VM, the Erlang implementers kept control of optimization and reliability. Nowadays, Erlang's processes take about 300 words of memory each and can be created in a matter of microseconds—not something currently doable on major operating systems.

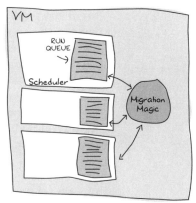

To handle all these potential processes your programs could create, the VM starts one thread per core that acts as a *scheduler*. Each of these schedulers has a *run queue*, or a list of Erlang processes on which to spend a slice of time. When one of the schedulers has too many tasks in its run queue, some tasks are migrated to another queue. This means that each Erlang VM takes care of doing all the load balancing, and the programmer doesn't need to worry about it. The VM also does some other optimizations, such as limiting the rate at which messages can be sent to overloaded processes in order to regulate and distribute the load.

All the hard stuff is in there, managed for you. That is what makes it easy to go parallel with Erlang. Going parallel means your program should go twice as fast if you add a second core, four times faster if there are four cores, and so on, right? It depends. Such a phenomenon is named *linear scaling* in relation to speed gain versus the number of cores or processors (see the graph in the next section). In real life, there is no such thing as a free lunch (well, maybe at funerals, but someone, somewhere, still has to pay).

Not Entirely Unlike Linear Scaling

The difficulty of obtaining linear scaling is not due to the language itself, but rather to the nature of the problems to solve. Problems that scale very well are often said to be *embarrassingly parallel*. If you look up "embarrassingly parallel problems" on the Internet, you're likely to find examples such as ray-tracing (a method to create 3D images), brute-forcing searches in cryptography, and weather prediction.

From time to time, messages pop up in IRC channels, forums, and mailing lists asking if Erlang could be used to solve that kind of problem, or if it could be used to program on a graphical processing unit (GPU).

The answer is almost always no. The reason is relatively simple: All these problems usually involve numerical algorithms with a lot of data crunching. Erlang is not very good at this.

Erlang's embarrassingly parallel problems are present at a higher level. Usually, they have to do with concepts such as chat servers, phone switches, web servers, message queues, web crawlers, or any other application where the work done can be represented as independent logical entities (actors, anyone?). This kind of problem can be solved efficiently with close-to-linear scaling.

Many problems will never show such scaling properties. In fact, you need only one centralized sequence of operations to lose it all. *Your parallel program goes only as fast as its slowest sequential part.* An example of that phenomenon is observable any time you go to a mall. Hundreds of people can be shopping at once, rarely interfering with each other. Then once it's time to pay, queues form as soon as there are fewer cashiers than there are customers ready to leave. It would be possible to add cashiers until one exists for each customer, but then you would need a door for each customer, because the shoppers couldn't get inside or outside the mall all at once.

To put this another way, even though customers could pick each of their items in parallel and take as much time to shop whether they're alone or one of a thousand in the store, they would still need to wait to pay. Therefore, their shopping experience could never be shorter than the time it takes them to wait in the queue and pay.

A generalization of this principle is called *Amdahl's law*. It indicates how much of a speedup you can expect your system to have when you add parallelism to it, and in what proportion:

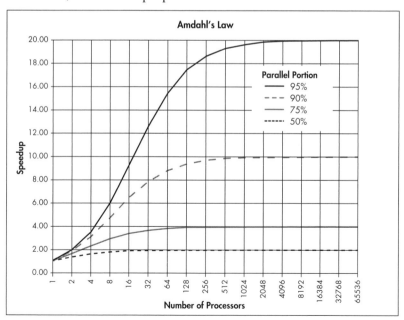

(Adapted from an image created by Daniel; used under a Creative Commons license. Original can be found at http://en.wikipedia.org/wiki/File:AmdahlsLaw.svg.)

According to Amdahl's law, code that is 50 percent parallel can never get faster than twice what it was before, and code that is 95 percent parallel can theoretically be expected to be about 20 times faster if you add enough processors. What's interesting to see on this graph is how getting rid of the last few sequential parts of a program allows a relatively huge theoretical speedup compared to removing as much sequential code in a program that is not very parallel to begin with.

DON'T DRINK TOO MUCH KOOL-AID

Parallelism is *not* the answer to every problem. In some cases, going parallel will even slow down your application. This can happen when your program is 100 percent sequential but still uses multiple processes.

One of the best examples of this is the *ring benchmark*. A ring benchmark is a test where many thousands of processes will pass a piece of data to one after the other in a circular manner. Think of it as a game of telephone. In this benchmark, only one process at a time does something useful, but the Erlang VM still spends time distributing the load across cores and giving every process its share of time.

This plays against many common hardware optimizations and makes the VM spend time doing useless stuff.

This load distribution often makes purely sequential applications run much slower on many cores than on a single one. If this kind of algorithm is central to your system, disabling SMP (`$ erl -smp disable`) might be a good idea. However, in other cases, sequential algorithms that aren't central to the execution of the whole program will usually be drowned by other events. In these cases, disabling SMP shouldn't have a big impact.

So Long and Thanks for All the Fish!

Of course, this chapter would not be complete if it didn't show the three primitives required for concurrency in Erlang: spawning new processes, sending messages, and receiving messages. In practice, more mechanisms are required for making really reliable applications; but for now, these three will suffice.

Spawning Processes

I've skirted around the issue a lot but have yet to explain what a process really is. It's actually nothing but a function. A process runs a function, and once it's finished, it disappears. Technically, a process also has some hidden state (such as a mailbox for messages), but functions are our focus for now.

To start a new process, Erlang provides the function spawn/1, which takes a single function and runs it:

```
1> F = fun() -> 2 + 2 end.
#Fun<erl_eval.20.67289768>
2> spawn(F).
<0.44.0>
```

The result of spawn/1 (<0.44.0>) is called a *process identifier*, often just written as *pid* (the form I'll use), *Pid*, or *PID* by the Erlang community. The pid is an arbitrary value representing any process that exists (or might have existed) at some point in the VM's life. It is used as an address to communicate with the process.

You'll notice that we can't see the result of function F. We get only its pid. That's because processes do not return anything.

How can we see the result of F then? Well, there are two ways. The easiest one is to just output whatever we get:

```
3> spawn(fun() -> io:format("~p~n",[2 + 2]) end).
4
<0.46.0>
```

This isn't practical for a real program, but it is useful for seeing how Erlang dispatches processes. Fortunately, using io:format/2 is enough to let us experiment. We'll quickly start 10 processes and pause each of them for a while with the help of the function timer:sleep/1, which takes an integer value *N* and waits for *N* milliseconds before resuming. After the delay, the value present in the process is output:

```
4> G = fun(X) -> timer:sleep(10), io:format("~p~n", [X]) end.
#Fun<erl_eval.6.13229925>
5> [spawn(fun() -> G(X) end) || X <- lists:seq(1,10)].
[<0.273.0>,<0.274.0>,<0.275.0>,<0.276.0>,<0.277.0>,
 <0.278.0>,<0.279.0>,<0.280.0>,<0.281.0>,<0.282.0>]
2
1
4
3
5
8
7
6
10
9
```

The order doesn't make sense. Welcome to parallelism! Because the processes are running at the same time, the ordering of events isn't guaranteed anymore. That's because the Erlang VM uses many tricks to decide which process to run, making sure each gets a good share of time. Many Erlang services are implemented as processes, including the shell you're typing in. Your processes must be balanced with those the system itself needs, and this might be the cause of the weird ordering.

SYMMETRIC MULTIPROCESSING AND YOU

The results are similar whether or not SMP is enabled. To prove this, you can just test it by starting the Erlang VM with $ erl -smp disable.

To see if your Erlang VM runs with or without SMP support, start a new VM without any options and look for the first line output. If you can spot the text [smp:2:2], it means you're running with SMP enabled, and that you have two run queues running on two cores. If you don't see it, that means you're running with SMP disabled.

The [smp:2:2] means that two cores are available, with two schedulers (each having a run queue). In earlier versions of Erlang, you could have multiple schedulers, but with only one shared run queue for all of them. Since R13B, there is one run queue per scheduler, which allows for better parallelism.

To prove the shell itself is implemented as a regular process, let's use the BIF self/0, which returns the pid of the current process:

```
6> self().
<0.41.0>
7> exit(self()).
** exception exit: <0.41.0>
8> self().
<0.285.0>
```

And the pid changes because the process has been restarted.

The next concern is how to send messages around, because no one wants to be stuck with outputting the resulting values of processes all the time, and then entering them by hand in other processes (at least, I know I don't).

Sending Messages

The next primitive required to do message passing is the operator !, also known as the *bang* symbol. On the left-hand side, it takes a pid; on the right-hand side, it takes any Erlang term. The term is then sent to the process represented by the pid, which can access it. Here's an example:

```
9> self() ! hello.
hello
```

The message has been put in the process's mailbox, but it hasn't been read yet. The second `hello` shown here is the return value of the send function. This means it is possible to send the same message to many processes by doing this:

```
10> self() ! self() ! double.
double
```

This is equivalent to self() ! (self() ! double).

Something to note about a process's mailbox is that the messages are kept in the order they are received. Every time a message is read, it is taken out of the mailbox. Again, this is a bit similar to the analogy of people writing letters.

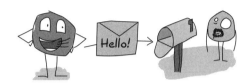

To see the contents of the current mailbox, you can use the `flush()` command while in the shell:

```
11> flush().
Shell got hello
Shell got double
Shell got double
ok
```

The `flush/0` function is just a shortcut that outputs received messages. This means we still can't bind the result of a process to a variable, but at least we know how to send it from a process to another one and check if it has been received.

Receiving Messages

Sending messages that no one will read is as useful as writing emo poetry (in other words, not very useful). This is why we need the receive expression. Rather than playing too long in the shell, we'll write a short program about dolphins to demonstrate how receiving messages works. Here's our new program:

```
-module(dolphins).
-compile(export_all).

dolphin1() ->
    receive
        do_a_flip ->
            io:format("How about no?~n");
        fish ->
            io:format("So long and thanks for all the fish!~n");
        _ ->
            io:format("Heh, we're smarter than you humans.~n")
    end.
```

As you can see, receive is syntactically similar to case ... of. In fact, the patterns work exactly the same way, except they bind variables coming from messages rather than the expression between case and of. The receive expressions can also have guards. Here's their general syntax:

```
receive
    Pattern1 when Guard1 -> Expr1;
    Pattern2 when Guard2 -> Expr2;
    Pattern3 -> Expr3
end
```

Knowing this, we can now compile the module, run it, and start communicating with dolphins:

```
11> c(dolphins).
{ok,dolphins}
12> Dolphin = spawn(dolphins, dolphin1, []).
<0.40.0>
13> Dolphin ! "oh, hello dolphin!".
Heh, we're smarter than you humans.
"oh, hello dolphin!"
14> Dolphin ! fish
fish
```

Here, we introduce a new way of spawning with spawn/3. Rather than taking a single function, spawn/3 takes the module, function, and its arguments as its own arguments. Once the function is running, the following events take place:

1. The function hits the receive expression. Given that the process's mailbox is empty, our dolphin waits until it gets a message.

2. The message "oh, hello dolphin!" is received. The function tries to pattern match against do_a_flip. This fails, and so the pattern fish is tried, and this also fails. Finally, the message meets the catchall clause (_) and matches.

3. The process outputs the message "Heh, we're smarter than you humans."

Note that if the first message we sent works, the second provokes no reaction whatsoever from the process <0.40.0>. This is due to the fact that once our function output Heh, we're smarter than you humans., it terminated, and so did the process. We'll need to restart the dolphin:

```
8> f(Dolphin).
ok
9> Dolphin = spawn(dolphins, dolphin1, []).
<0.53.0>
10> Dolphin ! fish.
So long and thanks for all the fish!
fish
```

And this time, the fish message works.

Wouldn't it be useful to be able to receive a reply from the dolphin rather than needing to use io:format/2? Of course it would! (Why am I even asking?)

I mentioned earlier in this chapter that the only way to know if a process has received a message is to send a reply. Our dolphin process will need to know who to reply to. This works in the same way as it does with the postal service. If we want someone to answer our letter, we need to add our address. In Erlang terms, this is done by packaging a process's pid in a tuple, given that messages are otherwise anonymous. The end result is a message that looks a bit like {*Pid, Message*}. Let's create a new dolphin function that will accept such messages:

```
dolphin2() ->
    receive
        {From, do_a_flip} ->
            From ! "How about no?";
        {From, fish} ->
            From ! "So long and thanks for all the fish!";
        _ ->
            io:format("Heh, we're smarter than you humans.~n")
    end.
```

As you can see, rather than accepting do_a_flip and fish for messages, we now require a variable From. That's where the pid will go.

```
11> c(dolphins).
{ok,dolphins}
12> Dolphin2 = spawn(dolphins, dolphin2, []).
<0.65.0>
13> Dolphin2 ! {self(), do_a_flip}.
{<0.32.0>,do_a_flip}
14> flush().
Shell got "How about no?"
ok
```

It seems to work pretty well. We can receive replies to messages we sent (we need to add an address to each message, a bit like an e-mail's Reply To field), but we still need to start a new process for each call. Recursion is the way to solve this problem. We just need the function to call itself so it never ends and always expects more messages. Here's a dolphin3/0 function that puts this in practice:

```
dolphin3() ->
    receive
        {From, do_a_flip} ->
            From ! "How about no?",
            dolphin3();
```

```
            {From, fish} ->
                From ! "So long and thanks for all the fish!";
            _ ->
                io:format("Heh, we're smarter than you humans.~n"),
                dolphin3()
    end.
```

Here, the catchall clause and the do_a_flip clause both loop with the help of dolphin3/0. Note that the function will not blow the stack because it is tail recursive. As long as only these messages are sent, the dolphin process will loop indefinitely. However, if we send the fish message, the process will stop:

```
15> Dolphin3 = spawn(dolphins, dolphin3, []).
<0.75.0>
16> Dolphin3 ! Dolphin3 ! {self(), do_a_flip}.
{<0.32.0>,do_a_flip}
17> flush().
Shell got "How about no?"
Shell got "How about no?"
ok
18> Dolphin3 ! {self(), unknown_message}.
Heh, we're smarter than you humans.
{<0.32.0>,unknown_message}
19> Dolphin3 ! Dolphin3 ! {self(), fish}.
{<0.32.0>,fish}
20> flush().
Shell got "So long and thanks for all the fish!"
ok
```

And that's it for *dolphins.erl*. As you see, it does respect our expected behavior of replying once for every message and continuing execution afterwards, except for the fish call. The dolphin got fed up with our crazy human antics and left us for good.

There you have it. This is the core of all of Erlang's concurrency. We've covered processes and basic message passing. There are more concepts to understand in order to make truly useful and reliable programs. We'll look at some of these in the following chapters.

11

MORE ON MULTIPROCESSING

The examples shown in Chapter 10 were suitable for demonstrative purposes, but they won't take you very far in your own projects. It's not that the examples were bad; it's just that there's no huge advantage to processes and actors if they're just functions with messages. To reap the benefits, we need to be able to hold state in a process.

In this chapter, we will apply the concurrency concepts and primitives to practical examples that are able to hold state.

State Your State

Let's first create a function in a new *kitchen.erl* module that will let a process act like a refrigerator. The process will allow two operations: storing food in the fridge and taking food from the fridge. It should only be possible to take food that has been stored beforehand, and only as many times as it was stored. The following function can act as the base for our process:

```erlang
-module(kitchen).
-compile(export_all).

fridge1() ->
    receive
        {From, {store, _Food}} ->
            From ! {self(), ok},
            fridge1();
        {From, {take, _Food}} ->
            %% uh....
            From ! {self(), not_found},
            fridge1();
        terminate ->
            ok
    end.
```

Something's wrong here. When we ask to store the food, the process should reply with ok, but there is nothing actually storing the food; fridge1() is called, and then the function starts from scratch, without state. Also, when we call the process to take food from the fridge, there is no state to take it from, and so the only reply is not_found. In order to store and take food items, we'll need to add state to the function.

With the help of recursion, the state of a process can be held entirely in the parameters of the function. In the case of our fridge process, one possibility would be to store all the food as a list, and then look in that list when someone needs to eat something:

```erlang
fridge2(FoodList) ->
    receive
        {From, {store, Food}} ->
            From ! {self(), ok},
            fridge2([Food|FoodList]);
        {From, {take, Food}} ->
            case lists:member(Food, FoodList) of
                true ->
                    From ! {self(), {ok, Food}},
                    fridge2(lists:delete(Food, FoodList));
```

```
                    false ->
                        From ! {self(), not_found},
                        fridge2(FoodList)
                end;
            terminate ->
                ok
    end.
```

Notice that fridge2/1 takes one argument, FoodList. You can see that when
we send a message that matches {From, {store, Food}}, the function will add
Food to FoodList before recursing. Once that recursive call is made, it will then
be possible to retrieve the same item. In fact, we've implemented that here.

The function uses lists:member/2 to check whether Food is part of FoodList.
Depending on the result, the item is sent back to the calling process (and
removed from FoodList) or not_found is sent:

```
1> c(kitchen).
{ok,kitchen}
2> Pid = spawn(kitchen, fridge2, [[baking_soda]]).
<0.51.0>
3> Pid ! {self(), {store, milk}}.
{<0.33.0>,{store,milk}}
4> flush().
Shell got {<0.51.0>,ok}
ok
```

Storing items in the fridge seems to work. Now let's try to store something else and then take it from the fridge:

```
5> Pid ! {self(), {store, bacon}}.
{<0.33.0>,{store,bacon}}
6> Pid ! {self(), {take, bacon}}.
{<0.33.0>,{take,bacon}}
7> Pid ! {self(), {take, turkey}}.
{<0.33.0>,{take,turkey}}
8> flush().
Shell got {<0.51.0>,ok}
Shell got {<0.51.0>,{ok,bacon}}
Shell got {<0.51.0>,not_found}
ok
```

As expected, we can take bacon from the fridge because we have put it
in there first (along with the milk and baking soda), but the fridge process has no turkey to find when we request some. This is why we get the
last {<0.51.0>,not_found} message. More interestingly, because of the way
mailboxes work, it is guaranteed that even if a thousand people suddenly
reached for the last piece of turkey in the fridge at the same time, only one
of them could get it.

We Love Messages, But We Keep Them Secret

Something annoying with the previous example is that the programmer who's going to use the fridge must know about the protocol that has been invented for that process. That's a useless burden. A good way to solve this is to abstract messages away with the help of functions dealing with receiving and sending them:

```erlang
store(Pid, Food) ->
    Pid ! {self(), {store, Food}},
    receive
        {Pid, Msg} -> Msg
    end.

take(Pid, Food) ->
    Pid ! {self(), {take, Food}},
    receive
        {Pid, Msg} -> Msg
    end.
```

Now the interaction with the process is much cleaner:

```erlang
9> c(kitchen).
{ok,kitchen}
10> f().
ok
11> Pid = spawn(kitchen, fridge2, [[baking_soda]]).
<0.73.0>
12> kitchen:store(Pid, water).
ok
13> kitchen:take(Pid, water).
{ok,water}
14> kitchen:take(Pid, juice).
not_found
```

We don't need to care about how the messages work anymore. If you want to send self() or a precise atom like take or store, you just need a pid and to know which functions to call. This hides all of the dirty work and makes it easier to build on the fridge process.

Now let's hide that whole part about needing to spawn a process. We dealt with hiding messages, but then we still expect the user to handle the creation of the process. Let's add the following start/1 function:

```erlang
start(FoodList) ->
    spawn(?MODULE, fridge2, [FoodList]).
```

Here, ?MODULE is a macro that returns the current module's name. At first glance, it might not seem like there are any advantages to writing such a function, but there are. The essential advantage is consistency with the calls to take/2 and store/2—everything about the fridge process is now handled by the kitchen module. If we wanted to add logging when the fridge process is started or start a second process (say a freezer), that would be really easy to do inside our start/1 function. However, if the spawning is left for the user to do through spawn/3, then every place that starts a fridge now needs to add the new calls. That's prone to errors, and errors suck.

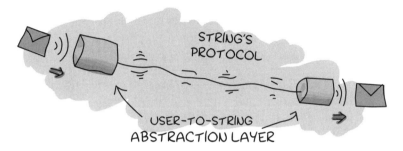

Let's see this function put to use:

```
15> f().
ok
16> c(kitchen).
{ok,kitchen}
17> Pid = kitchen:start([rhubarb, dog, hotdog]).
<0.84.0>
18> kitchen:take(Pid, dog).
{ok,dog}
19> kitchen:take(Pid, dog).
not_found
```

Yay! The dog has gotten out of the fridge, and our abstraction is complete!

Time Out

Let's try a test with the help of the command pid(A,B,C), which lets us change the three integers A, B and C into a pid. Here, we'll deliberately feed kitchen:take/2 a fake pid:

```
20> kitchen:take(pid(0,250,0), dog).
```

Whoops. The shell is frozen. This happened because of how take/2 was implemented. To understand what goes on, let's first revisit what happens in the normal case:

1. A message to store food is sent from you (the shell) to the fridge process.
2. Your process switches to receive mode and waits for a new message.
3. The fridge stores the item and sends ok to your process.
4. Your process receives it and moves on with its life.

And here's what happens when the shell freezes:

1. A message to store food is sent from you (the shell) to an unknown process.
2. Your process switches to receive mode and waits for a new message.
3. The unknown process either doesn't exist or doesn't expect such a message and does nothing with it.
4. Your shell process is stuck in receive mode.

That's annoying, especially because there is no error handling possible here. Nothing illegal happened; the program is just waiting—forever, which is a *deadlock*. In general, anything dealing with asynchronous operations (how message passing is done in Erlang) needs a way to give up after a certain period of time if it gets no sign of receiving data. A web browser does this when a page or image takes too long to load, and you do it when someone takes too long to answer the phone or is late for a meeting. Erlang certainly has an appropriate mechanism for handling timeouts, and it's part of the receive construct:

```
receive
    Match -> Expression1
after Delay ->
    Expression2
end.
```

The part between receive and after is exactly the same as what you've seen so far. The after part will be triggered if the Delay (in milliseconds) has passed without receiving a message that matches the Match pattern. When this happens, Expression2 is executed.

We'll write two new interface functions, store2/2 and take2/2, which will act exactly like store/2 and take/2, except that they will stop waiting after three seconds:

```
store2(Pid, Food) ->
    Pid ! {self(), {store, Food}},
    receive
        {Pid, Msg} -> Msg
    after 3000 ->
        timeout
    end.

take2(Pid, Food) ->
    Pid ! {self(), {take, Food}},
    receive
        {Pid, Msg} -> Msg
    after 3000 ->
        timeout
    end.
```

When it takes too long, we return timeout. This doesn't tell us how to deal with the fact that something took too long, and the message might come back later to haunt us in unexpected ways, but at least we won't be deadlocked if the other process is dead. Something called a *monitor* will help us make this type of code more robust, as you'll see in Chapter 12; but for now, you can just unfreeze the shell by pressing CTRL-G and try the new interface functions:

```
User switch command
--> i
--> s
--> c
Eshell V5.7.5  (abort with ^G)
1> c(kitchen).
{ok,kitchen}
2> kitchen:take2(pid(0,250,0), dog).
timeout
```

And now it works.

NOTE   *I said that after takes only milliseconds as a value, but it is actually possible to use the atom infinity. While this is not useful in many cases (you might as well just remove the after clause altogether), it is sometimes used when the programmer can submit the wait time to a function where receiving a result is expected. That way, if the programmer really wants to wait forever, he can.*

Timers have uses other than just giving up after too long. One such use is in the implementation of the timer:sleep/1 function, which we used in Chapter 10. Here's how it is implemented (let's put it in a new *multiproc.erl* module):

```
sleep(T) ->
    receive
    after T -> ok
    end.
```

In this specific case, no message will ever be matched in the receive part of the construct because there is no pattern. Instead, the after part of the construct will be called once the delay T has passed.

Another special case is when the timeout is at 0:

```
flush() ->
    receive
        _ -> flush()
    after 0 ->
        ok
    end.
```

When that happens, the Erlang VM will try to find a message that fits one of the available patterns. In the preceding case, anything matches. As long as there are messages, the flush/0 function will recursively call itself until the mailbox is empty. After that, the after 0 -> ok part of the code is executed, and the function returns.

Selective Receives

Erlang's "flushing" concept makes it possible to implement a selective receive, which can give a priority to the messages you receive by nesting calls:

```erlang
important() ->
    receive
        {Priority, Message} when Priority > 10 ->
            [Message | important()]
    after 0 ->
        normal()
    end.

normal() ->
    receive
        {_, Message} ->
            [Message | normal()]
    after 0 ->
        []
    end.
```

This function will build a list of all messages, placing those with a priority above 10 first:

```erlang
1> c(multiproc).
{ok,multiproc}
2> self() ! {15, high}, self() ! {7, low}, self() ! {1, low}, self() ! {17, high}.
{17,high}
3> multiproc:important().
[high,high,low,low]
```

Because we used the after 0 bit, every message will be obtained until no messages remain, but the process will try to grab all those with a priority above 10 before even considering the other messages, which are accumulated in the normal/0 call. This practice is called a *selective receive*. If it looks interesting, be aware that it is sometimes unsafe due to the way it's handled by Erlang.

The Pitfalls of Selective Receives

When messages are sent to a process, they're stored in the mailbox until the process reads them and they match a pattern there, even if the process that originally sent them has died since then. The messages are stored in the order they were received. This means every time you enter a receive to match a message, the mailbox is scanned, beginning with the first (and oldest) message received.

That oldest message is then tried against every pattern of the receive until one of them matches. When it does, the message is removed from the mailbox, and the code for the process executes normally until the next receive. When this next receive is executed, the VM will look for the oldest message currently in the mailbox (the one after the one you removed), and so on.

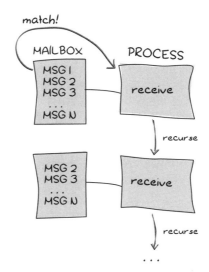

When there is no way to match a given message, it is put in a *save queue*, and the next message is tried. If the second message matches, the first message is put back on top of the mailbox to be retried later.

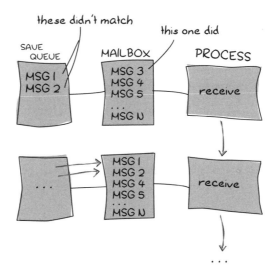

This lets you care only about the messages that are useful. Ignoring some messages to handle them later in the manner described is the essence of selective receives. While they're useful, the problem with selective receives is that if your process has a lot of messages you never care about, reading useful messages will actually take longer and longer (and the processes will grow in size, too).

In the last illustration of matching messages, imagine we want the 367th message, but the first 366 messages are junk ignored by our code. To get the 367th message, the process needs to try to match those 366 junk messages. Once it has done that, and the messages have all been put in the queue, the 367th message is taken out, and the first 366 are put back on top of the mailbox. The next useful message could be burrowed much deeper and take even longer to be found.

This kind of receive is a frequent cause of performance problems in Erlang. If your application is running slowly and you know there are a lot of messages going around, this could be the cause. If such selective receives are effectively causing a massive slowdown in your code, the first thing to do is to ask yourself why you are getting messages you do not want. Are the messages sent to the right processes? Are the patterns correct? Are the messages formatted incorrectly? Are you using one process where there should be many? Answering one or many of these questions could solve your problem.

CONVERSATIONAL OPTIMIZATIONS

Since R14A, a new optimization has been added to Erlang's compiler. It simplifies selective receives in very specific cases of back-and-forth communications between processes. An example of such a function is optimized/1 in *multiproc.erl*.

To make this optimization work, a reference must be created (either by using make_ref() or by starting a monitor, as described in Chapter 12) in a function and then sent in a message. In the same function, a selective receive is then made. If no message can match unless it contains the same reference, the compiler automatically makes sure the VM will skip messages received before the creation of that reference.

Note that you shouldn't try to coerce your code to fit such optimizations. The Erlang developers only look for patterns that are frequently used and then make them faster. If you write idiomatic code, optimizations should come to you, not the other way around.

More Mailbox Pitfalls

Because of the risks of having useless messages polluting a process's mailbox, Erlang programmers sometimes take a defensive measure against such events. A standard defense might look like this:

```
receive
    Pattern1 -> Expression1;
    Pattern2 -> Expression2;
    Pattern3 -> Expression3;
    ...
    PatternN -> ExpressionN;
    Unexpected ->
        io:format("unexpected message ~p~n", [Unexpected])
end.
```

This makes sure that any message will match at least one clause. The *Unexpected* variable will match anything, take the unexpected message out of the mailbox, and show a warning. Depending on your application, you might want to store the message in some kind of logging facility where you will be able to find information about it later on. If the messages are going to the wrong process, it would be a shame to lose them for good and have a hard time finding out why that other process doesn't receive what it should, given that's pretty much guaranteed to be a bug.

In cases where you do need to work with a priority in your messages and can't use such a catchall clause, a smarter way to handle them is to implement a *min-heap* (see *https://secure.wikimedia.org/wikipedia/en/wiki/Min-heap*) or use the gb_trees module (discussed in Chapter 9) and dump every received message in it (make sure to put the priority number first in the key so it gets used for sorting the messages). Then you can just search for the smallest or largest element in the data structure according to your needs.

In most cases, this technique should let you receive messages with a priority more efficiently than selective receives. However, it could slow you down if most messages you receive have the highest priority possible. As usual, the trick is to profile and measure before optimizing.

Now that we've covered how to hold state in processes, the next step is to do efficient error handling with multiple processes, which is the topic of Chapter 12.

12

ERRORS AND PROCESSES

In most languages, exceptions are managed from within the execution flow of the program, the way we've done it with try ... catch in previous examples. The problem with this very common approach is that your regular code needs to handle outstanding errors on every level, or you just delegate the burden of making things safe to the layer above it until you end up having the eternal top-level try ... catch, which catches everything but doesn't know anything about it. It's more complex than that in the real world, but that's generally what it looks like. Erlang supports this model too, as you've already seen.

However, Erlang also supports a different level of exception handling that allows you to move the handling of exceptions outside the normal flow of execution of the program, into a different, concurrent process. This usually leads to very clean code, where only the "happy case" is considered. In this chapter, we discuss the basic tools that make this possible: links, monitors, and named processes. We'll also cover some general practices that make the use of these tools more efficient.

Links

A *link* is a specific kind of relationship that can be created between two processes. When that relationship is set up and one of the processes dies from an unexpected throw, error, or exit (see Chapter 7), the other linked process also dies, binding their separate life cycles into a single, related one.

This is a useful concept from the perspective of failing as soon as possible to stop errors. If the process that has an error crashes, but those that depend on it continue to run, then all these depending processes must deal with a dependency disappearing. Letting them die and then restarting the whole group is usually an acceptable alternative. Links let us do exactly this.

To set a link between two processes, Erlang has the primitive function link/1, which takes a pid as an argument. When called, the function will create a link between the current process and the one identified by the pid. To get rid of a link, use unlink/1.

When one of the linked processes crashes, a special kind of message is sent, with information relative to what happened. No such message is sent if the process dies of natural causes (read: is done running its functions).

Let's look at how this new function works, as part of the *linkmon.erl* file.

```
myproc() ->
    timer:sleep(5000),
    exit(reason).
```

If you try the following calls (and wait 5 seconds between each spawn command), you should see the shell crashing for reason only when a link has been set between the two processes:

```
1> c(linkmon).
{ok,linkmon}
2> spawn(fun linkmon:myproc/0).
<0.52.0>
3> link(spawn(fun linkmon:myproc/0)).
true
** exception error: reason
```

Here's a picture of how it works:

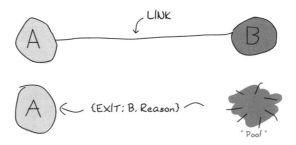

However, this {'EXIT', B, Reason} message cannot be caught with a try ... catch as usual. Other mechanisms need to be used to do this, as discussed in "It's a Trap" on page 164.

If you wanted to kill another process from the shell, you could use the function exit/2, which makes use of these mechanisms to kill processes. It is called this way: exit(Pid, Reason). Try it if you wish.

Links are used to establish larger groups of processes that should all die together. Here's an example:

```
chain(0) ->
    receive
        _ -> ok
    after 2000 ->
        exit("chain dies here")
    end;
chain(N) ->
    Pid = spawn(fun() -> chain(N-1) end),
    link(Pid),
    receive
        _ -> ok
    end.
```

This function will take an integer N, start N processes that are linked together. To pass the N-1 argument to the next "chain" process (which calls spawn/1), the example wraps the call inside an anonymous function so it doesn't need arguments anymore. Calling spawn(?MODULE, chain, [N-1]) would have done a similar job.

Here, we'll have many processes linked together, dying as each of their successors exits.

```
4> c(linkmon).
{ok,linkmon}
5> link(spawn(linkmon, chain, [3])).
true
** exception error: "chain dies here"
```

And as you can see, the shell does receive the death signal from some other process. Here's a drawn representation of the spawned processes and links going down:

```
[shell] == [3] == [2] == [1] == [0]
[shell] == [3] == [2] == [1] == *dead*
[shell] == [3] == [2] == *dead*
[shell] == [3] == *dead*
[shell] == *dead*
*dead, error message shown*
[shell] <-- restarted
```

After the process running `linkmon:chain(0)` dies, the error is propagated down the chain of links until the shell process itself dies because of it. The crash could have happened in any of the linked processes. Because links are bidirectional, you need only one of them to die for the others to follow suit.

NOTE   *Links cannot be stacked. If you call `link/1` fifteen times for the same two processes, only one link will still exist between those processes, and a single call to `unlink/1` will be enough to tear it down.*

Note that `link(spawn(Function))` or `link(spawn(M,F,A))` happen in more than one step. In some cases, it is possible for a process to die before the link has been set up and then provoke unexpected behavior. For this reason, the function `spawn_link/1-3` has been added to the language. It takes the same arguments as `spawn/1-3`, creates a process, and links it as if `link/1` had been there, except it's all done as an atomic operation (the operations are combined as a single one, which can either fail or succeed, but nothing else). This is generally considered safer, and you save a set of parentheses, too.

It's a Trap!

Error propagation across processes is done through a process similar to message passing, but with a special type of message called *signals*. Exit signals are "secret" messages that automatically act on processes, killing them.

I have mentioned many times that in order to be reliable, an application needs to be able to both kill and restart a process quickly. Right now, links can serve to do the killing part. What's missing is the restarting. To restart a process, we first need a way to know that it died. This can be done by adding a layer on top of links (the delicious frosting on the cake) with a concept called *system processes*.

System processes are basically normal processes, except they can convert exit signals to regular messages. This is done by calling `process_flag(trap_exit, true)` in a running process. Nothing speaks as much as an example. Let's just redo the chain example with a system process at the beginning.

```
1> process_flag(trap_exit, true).
true
2> spawn_link(fun() -> linkmon:chain(3) end).
<0.49.0>
3> receive X -> X end.
{'EXIT',<0.49.0>,"chain dies here"}
```

Ah! Now things get interesting. To get back to our drawings, what happens is now more like this:

```
[shell] == [3] == [2] == [1] == [0]
[shell] == [3] == [2] == [1] == *dead*
[shell] == [3] == [2] == *dead*
[shell] == [3] == *dead*
[shell] <-- {'EXIT,Pid,"chain dies here"} -- *dead*
[shell] <-- still alive!
```

And this is the mechanism that allows for a quick restart of processes. By writing programs using system processes, it's easy to create a process whose only role is to check if something dies and then restart it whenever it fails. We'll cover more of this in Chapter 13, when we really apply these techniques.

Old Exceptions, New Concepts

Let's return to the exception functions introduced in Chapter 7 and see how they behave around processes that trap exits. First, we'll set the bases to experiment without a system process. We'll look at the results of uncaught throws, errors, and exits in neighboring processes.

Exceptions and Traps

There's a load of reasons why processes ususaly die. Let's look at a few of them and what the reasons look like when exits are trapped.

Exception source: `spawn_link(fun() -> ok end)`

> **Untrapped result:** Nothing
>
> **Trapped result:** `{'EXIT', <0.61.0>, normal}`
>
> The process exited normally, without a problem. Note that this looks a bit like the result of `catch exit(normal)`, except a pid is added to the tuple to identify which process failed.

Exception source: `spawn_link(fun() -> exit(reason) end)`

> **Untrapped result:** `** exception exit: reason`
>
> **Trapped result:** `{'EXIT', <0.55.0>, reason}`
>
> The process has terminated for a custom reason. If there is no trapped exit, the process crashes. While trapping exits, you get a message.

Exception source: `spawn_link(fun() -> exit(normal) end)`

> **Untrapped result:** Nothing
>
> **Trapped result:** `{'EXIT', <0.58.0>, normal}`
>
> This successfully emulates a process terminating normally. In some cases, you might want to kill a process as part of the normal flow of a program, without anything exceptional going on. This is the way to do it.

Exception source: spawn_link(fun() -> 1/0 end)

Untrapped result:
Error in process <0.44.0> with exit value: {badarith, [{erlang, '/', [1,0]}]}

Trapped result: {'EXIT', <0.52.0>, {badarith, [{erlang, '/', [1,0]}]}}

The error ({badarith, Reason}) is never caught by a try ... catch block and bubbles up into an 'EXIT'. At this point, it behaves exactly the same as exit(reason) does, but with a stack trace giving more details about what happened.

Exception source: spawn_link(fun() -> erlang:error(reason) end)

Untrapped result:
Error in process <0.47.0> with exit value: {reason, [{erlang, apply, 2}]}

Trapped result: {'EXIT', <0.74.0>, {reason, [{erlang, apply, 2}]}}

This is pretty much the same as with 1/0. That's normal—erlang:error/1 is meant to allow you to do just that.

Exception source: spawn_link(fun() -> throw(rocks) end)

Untrapped result:
Error in process <0.51.0> with exit value: {{nocatch, rocks}, [{erlang, apply, 2}]}

Trapped result: {'EXIT', <0.79.0>, {{nocatch, rocks}, [{erlang, apply, 2}]}}

Because the throw is never caught by a try ... catch, it bubbles up into an error, which in turn bubbles up into an EXIT. Without trapping exits, the process fails. While trapping exits, it deals with the error just fine.

And that's about it for usual exceptions. Things are normal, and everything goes fine. Exceptional stuff happens, and processes die and different signals are sent around.

exit/2 Changes Everything

Then there's exit/2. This one is the Erlang process equivalent of a gun. It allows a process to kill another one from a distance, safely. The following are some of the possible calls.

Exception source: exit(self(), normal)

Untrapped result: ** exception exit: normal

Trapped result: {'EXIT', <0.31.0>, normal}

When not trapping exits, exit(self(), normal) acts the same as exit(normal). Otherwise, you receive a message with the same format you would have received by listening to links from foreign processes dying.

Exception source: `exit(spawn_link(fun() -> timer:sleep(50000) end), normal)`

Untrapped result: Nothing

Trapped Result: Nothing

This basically is a call to exit(Pid, normal). This command doesn't do anything useful, because a process cannot be remotely killed with the reason normal as an argument.

Exception source: `exit(spawn_link(fun() -> timer:sleep(50000) end), reason)`

Untrapped result: `** exception exit: reason`

Trapped result: `{'EXIT', <0.52.0>, reason}`

This is the foreign process terminating for reason itself. It looks the same as if the foreign process called exit(reason) on itself.

Exception source: `exit(spawn_link(fun() -> timer:sleep(50000) end), kill)`

Untrapped result: `** exception exit: killed`

Trapped result: `{'EXIT', <0.58.0>, killed}`

Surprisingly, the message gets changed from the dying process to the spawner. The spawner now receives killed instead of kill. That's because kill is a special exit signal, as explained in the next section.

Exception source: `exit(self(), kill)`

Untrapped result: `** exception exit: killed`

Trapped result: `** exception exit: killed`

Oops, look at that. It seems like this one is actually impossible to trap. The following exception doesn't make it easier.

Exception source: `spawn_link(fun() -> exit(kill) end)`

Untrapped result: `** exception exit: killed`

Trapped result: `{'EXIT', <0.67.0>, kill}`

Now that's getting confusing. When another process kills itself with exit(kill), and we don't trap exits, our own process dies with the reason killed. However, when we trap exits, things don't happen that way.

Killing Me (Not So) Softly

While you can trap most exit reasons, there are situations where you might want to brutally murder a process. Maybe one of your processes is trapping exits but is also stuck in an infinite loop, never reading any message. The kill reason acts as a special signal that

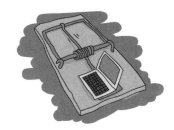

can't be trapped. This ensures any process you terminate with it will really be dead. Usually, `kill` is a bit of a last resort to apply when everything else has failed.

As the kill reason can never be trapped, it needs to be changed to `killed` when other processes receive the message. If it weren't changed, every other process linked to it would in turn die for the same `kill` reason, and would in turn kill its neighbors, and so on. A death cascade would ensue.

This also explains why `exit(kill)` looks like `killed` when received from another linked process (the signal is modified so it doesn't cascade), but still looks like `kill` when trapped locally.

If you find this all confusing, don't worry. Many programmers feel the same way. Exit signals are a bit of a strange beast. Luckily, there aren't other special cases than the ones described here. Once you understand these, you can understand most of Erlang's concurrent error management without a problem.

Monitors

Maybe murdering processes isn't what you want. Maybe you don't feel like taking the world down with you once you're gone. Maybe you're more of a stalker. In that case, *monitors* might be what you want, given that they don't kill processes. Monitors are a special type of link, with two differences:

- They are unidirectional.
- You can have many of them between two processes (they *stack* and they have an *identity*).

Monitors are useful when a process wants to know what's going on with a second process, but neither of them is really vital to each other. They're also useful for stacking references that are individually identifiable. This might seem useless at first, but it's great for writing libraries that need to know what's going on with other processes. Why aren't links appropriate for this? Because links do not stack, a library setting up a link and then removing it afterward might be playing with important links unrelated to it. Monitors (and stacking) allow library programmers to separate their use of monitoring from other, unrelated ones. Since each monitor has a unique identity, it is possible to choose which one to listen to or to manipulate.

Links are more of an organizational construct than monitors are. When you design the architecture of your application, you determine which process will do which jobs, and what will depend on what. Some processes will supervise others, some couldn't live without a twin process, and so on. This structure is usually something fixed and known in advance. Links are useful in this case, but should not necessarily be used outside it.

But what happens if you have two or three different libraries that you call and they all need to know whether a process is alive? If you were to use links for this, you would quickly hit a problem whenever you needed to unlink a process. Links aren't stackable, so the moment you unlink one, you unlink them all and mess up all the assumptions made by the other libraries. So you need stackable links, and monitors are your solution, since they can be removed individually. Plus, being unidirectional is handy in libraries because other processes shouldn't need to be aware of those libraries.

So what does a monitor look like? To see, let's set one up. The function is erlang:monitor/2, where the first argument is always the atom process and the second one is the pid.

```
1> erlang:monitor(process, spawn(fun() -> timer:sleep(500) end)).
#Ref<0.0.0.77>
2> flush().
Shell got {'DOWN',#Ref<0.0.0.77>,process,<0.63.0>,normal}
ok
```

Every time a process you monitor goes down, you will receive such a message, in the form {'DOWN', MonitorReference, process, Pid, Reason}. The reference is there to allow you to demonitor the process. Remember that monitors are stackable, so it's possible to take more than one down. References allow you to track each of them in a unique manner. Also note that as with links, there is an atomic function to spawn a process while monitoring it: spawn_monitor/1-3.

```
3> {Pid, Ref} = spawn_monitor(fun() -> receive _ -> exit(boom) end end).
{<0.73.0>,#Ref<0.0.0.100>}
4> erlang:demonitor(Ref).
true
5> Pid ! die.
die
6> flush().
ok
```

In this case, we demonitored the other process before it crashed, so we had no trace of it dying. The function demonitor/2 also exists and gives a little more information. The second parameter can be a list of options. Only two exist: info and flush.

```
7> f().
ok
8> {Pid, Ref} = spawn_monitor(fun() -> receive _ -> exit(boom) end end).
{<0.35.0>,#Ref<0.0.0.35>}
9> Pid ! die.
die
10> erlang:demonitor(Ref, [flush, info]).
false
11> flush().
ok
```

The info option tells you if a monitor existed when you tried to remove it. This is why line 10 returned false. Using flush as an option removes the DOWN message from the mailbox if it existed, resulting in flush() finding nothing in the current process's mailbox.

Naming Processes

With links and monitors covered, there is another problem still left to be solved: What do we do when we detect that a process we rely on has died? Let's use the following functions of the *linkmon.erl* module:

```erlang
start_critic() ->
    spawn(?MODULE, critic, []).

judge(Pid, Band, Album) ->
    Pid ! {self(), {Band, Album}},
    receive
        {Pid, Criticism} -> Criticism
    after 2000 ->
        timeout
    end.

critic() ->
    receive
        {From, {"Rage Against the Turing Machine", "Unit Testify"}} ->
            From ! {self(), "They are great!"};
        {From, {"System of a Downtime", "Memoize"}} ->
            From ! {self(), "They're not Johnny Crash but they're good."};
        {From, {"Johnny Crash", "The Token Ring of Fire"}} ->
            From ! {self(), "Simply incredible."};
        {From, {_Band, _Album}} ->
            From ! {self(), "They are terrible!"}
    end,
    critic().
```

Now we'll just pretend we're going around stores, shopping for music. There are a few albums that sound interesting, but we're never quite sure. We decide to call our friend, the critic.

```erlang
1> c(linkmon).
{ok,linkmon}
2> Critic = linkmon:start_critic().
<0.47.0>
3> linkmon:judge(Critic, "Genesis", "The Lambda Lies Down on Broadway").
"They are terrible!"
```

Because of a solar storm (I'm trying to find something realistic here), the connection is dropped.

```
4> exit(Critic, solar_storm).
true
5> linkmon:judge(Critic, "Genesis", "A trick of the Tail Recursion").
timeout
```

This is annoying. We can no longer get criticism for the albums. To keep the critic alive, we'll write a basic "supervisor" process whose only role is to restart the critic when it goes down.

```
start_critic2() ->
    spawn(?MODULE, restarter, []).

restarter() ->
    process_flag(trap_exit, true),
    Pid = spawn_link(?MODULE, critic, []),
    receive
        {'EXIT', Pid, normal} -> % not a crash
            ok;
        {'EXIT', Pid, shutdown} -> % manual termination, not a crash
            ok;
        {'EXIT', Pid, _} ->
            restarter()
    end.
```

Here, the restarter will be its own process. It will in turn start the critic's process, and if it ever dies of an abnormal cause, restarter/0 will loop and create a new critic. Note that we added a clause for {'EXIT', Pid, shutdown} as a way to manually kill the critic if we ever need to.

The problem with our approach is that there is no way to find the pid of the critic, and thus we can't call him to get his opinion. One of the solutions Erlang provides is to give names to processes. The act of giving a name to a process allows you to replace the unpredictable pid with an atom. This atom can then be used exactly as a pid when sending messages.

To give a process a name, use the function erlang:register(Name,Pid). If the process dies, it will automatically lose its name. Alternatively, you can use unregister/1 to do it manually. You can get a list of all registered processes with registered/0, or a more detailed one with the shell command regs(). We can rewrite the restarter/0 function as follows:

```
restarter() ->
    process_flag(trap_exit, true),
    Pid = spawn_link(?MODULE, critic, []),
    register(critic, Pid),
    receive
        {'EXIT', Pid, normal} -> % not a crash
            ok;
        {'EXIT', Pid, shutdown} -> % manual termination, not a crash
            ok;
```

```
    {'EXIT', Pid, _} ->
        restarter()
end.
```

As you can see, register/2 will always give our critic the name critic, no matter what the pid is. Then we need to remove the need to pass in a pid from the abstraction functions. Let's try this:

```
judge2(Band, Album) ->
    critic ! {self(), {Band, Album}},
    Pid = whereis(critic),
    receive
        {Pid, Criticism} -> Criticism
    after 2000 ->
        timeout
    end.
```

Here, the line Pid = whereis(critic) is used to find the critic's pid in order to pattern match against it in the receive expression. We want to match with this pid because it makes sure we will match on the right message. (There could be 500 of them in the mailbox as we speak!) This can be the source of a problem though. This code assumes that the critic's pid will remain the same between the first two lines of the function. However, it is completely plausible the following will happen:

```
1. critic ! Message
                        2. critic receives
                        3. critic replies
                        4. critic dies
5. whereis fails
                        6. critic is restarted
7. code crashes
```

This is also a possibility:

```
1. critic ! Message
                        2. critic receives
                        3. critic replies
                        4. critic dies
                        5. critic is restarted
6. whereis picks up
   wrong pid
7. message never matches
```

Things could go wrong in a different process and make another process have problems if we don't do things correctly. In this case, the value of the critic atom can be seen from multiple processes. This is known as *shared state*. The problem here is that the value of critic can be accessed and modified by different processes at virtually the same time, resulting in inconsistent information and software errors. The common term for such things is a *race condition.*

Race conditions are particularly dangerous because they depend on the timing of events. In pretty much every concurrent and parallel language out there, this timing depends on unpredictable factors, such as how busy the processor is, where the processes go, and what data is being processed by your program.

DON'T DRINK TOO MUCH KOOL-AID

You might have heard that Erlang is usually free of race conditions or deadlocks and makes parallel code safe. This is true in many circumstances, but only because message passing through a mailbox forces some ordering of events and because the language seriously restricts how much shared state you can have. Generally, you should never assume your code is entirely free of race conditions.

Named processes are only one example of the multiple ways in which parallel code can go wrong.

Other examples include when accessing files on the computer (to modify them) and when updating the same database records from many different processes.

Luckily for us, it's relatively easy to fix the sample code if we don't assume the named process remains the same. Instead, we'll use references (created with make_ref()) as unique values to identify messages and make sure we receive the correct messages from the right process. We'll need to rewrite the critic/0 function into critic2/0 and judge/3 into judge2/2.

```erlang
judge2(Band, Album) ->
    Ref = make_ref(),
    critic ! {self(), Ref, {Band, Album}},
    receive
        {Ref, Criticism} -> Criticism
    after 2000 ->
        timeout
    end.

critic2() ->
    receive
        {From, Ref, {"Rage Against the Turing Machine", "Unit Testify"}} ->
            From ! {Ref, "They are great!"};
        {From, Ref, {"System of a Downtime", "Memoize"}} ->
            From ! {Ref, "They're not Johnny Crash but they're good."};
        {From, Ref, {"Johnny Crash", "The Token Ring of Fire"}} ->
            From ! {Ref, "Simply incredible."};
        {From, Ref, {_Band, _Album}} ->
            From ! {Ref, "They are terrible!"}
    end,
    critic2().
```

And then change restarter/0 to fit by making it spawn critic2/0 rather than critic/0.

Now the other functions should keep working fine, and the users won't see a difference. Well, they will because we renamed functions and changed the number of parameters, but they won't know what implementation details were changed and why it was important. All they will see is that their code got simpler and they no longer need to send a pid around function calls. Here's an example:

```
6> c(linkmon).
{ok,linkmon}
7> linkmon:start_critic2().
<0.55.0>
8> linkmon:judge2("The Doors", "Light my Firewall").
"They are terrible!"
9> exit(whereis(critic), kill).
true
10> linkmon:judge2("Rage Against the Turing Machine", "Unit Testify").
"They are great!"
```

And now, even though we killed the critic, a new one instantly came back to solve our problems. That's the usefulness of named processes. Had we tried to call linkmon:judge/2 without a registered process, a bad argument error would have been thrown by the ! operator inside the function, making sure that processes that depend on named ones can't run without them.

In Chapter 13, we'll put concurrent programming with Erlang into practice by writing a real application.

NAME WHAT'S WORTH NAMING

Remember that atoms can be used in a limited (though high) number. You should never create dynamic atoms. This means naming processes should be reserved for important services unique to an instance of the VM and processes that should be there for the whole time your application runs.

If you need named processes but they are transient or none of them can be unique to the VM, it may mean they need to be represented as a group instead. Linking and restarting them together if they crash might be the sane option, rather than trying to use dynamic names.

13

DESIGNING A CONCURRENT APPLICATION

All is fine and dandy. You understand the concepts. But then again, all we've had since the beginning of the book were toy examples: calculators, trees, Heathrow to London, and so on. It's time for something more fun and educational. In this chapter, we'll write a small application in concurrent Erlang. The application will be small and line-based, but still useful and moderately extensible.

I'm a somewhat disorganized person. I'm lost with homework, things to do around the apartment, this book, work, meetings, appointments, and so on. I end up having a dozen lists everywhere, listing tasks I still forget to do. I hope that you also sometimes need reminders of what to do (but you don't have a mind that wanders as much as mine does), because we're going to write one of those event reminder applications that prompt you to do stuff and remind you about appointments.

Understanding the Problem

The first step is to know what the hell we're doing. "A reminder app," you say. "Of course," I say. But there's more. How do we plan on interacting with the software? What do we want it to do for us? How do we represent the program with processes? How do we know what messages to send?

As the quote goes, "Walking on water and developing software from a specification are easy if both are frozen" (Edward V. Berard). So let's set up a spec and stick to it.

Our little piece of software will allow us to do the following:

- Add an event. Events contain a deadline (the time to warn), an event name, and a description.
- Show a warning when the time for our event has come.
- Cancel an event by name.
- Interact with the software via the command line, although it could be extended to allow other means (such as a GUI, web page access, instant messaging software, or e-mail).

This application will not have persistent disk storage. It's not needed to demonstrate the architectural concepts we'll cover in this chapter. But I will show you where it could be inserted if you wanted to add it for a real application, and also point to a few helpful functions. Given we have no persistent storage, we must be able to update the code while it is running.

Here's the structure of the program we'll build, where the client, event server, x, y, and z are all processes:

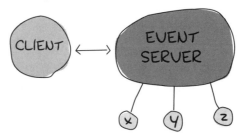

The event server has these tasks:

- Accept subscriptions from clients
- Forward notifications from event processes to each of the subscribers
- Accept messages to add events (and start the x, y, and z processes needed)
- Accept messages to cancel an event and subsequently kill the event processes

The event server can be terminated by a client, and it can have its code reloaded via the shell.

The client has these tasks:

- Subscribe to the event server and receive notifications as messages
- Ask the server to add an event with all its details
- Ask the server to cancel an event
- Monitor the server (to know if it goes down)
- Shut down the event server if needed

It should be easy to design a bunch of clients all subscribing to the event server. Each of these could potentially be a gateway to the different interaction points (GUI, web page, instant messaging software, email, and so on).

The x, y, and z processes represent a notification waiting to fire (they're basically just timers linked to the event server). They have the following tasks:

- Send a message to the event server when the time is up
- Receive a cancellation message and die

Note that all clients (instant messaging, mail, and others that are not implemented in this example) are notified about all events, and a cancellation is not something to warn the clients about. Here, the software is written for you and me, and it's assumed only one user will run it.

Here's a more complex graph with all the possible messages:

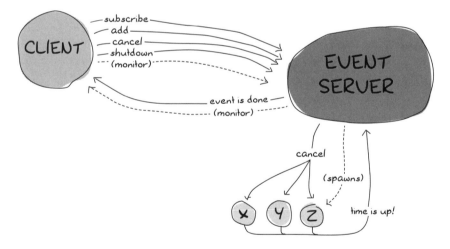

This represents every process we'll have. By drawing all the arrows there and saying they're messages, we've written a high-level protocol, or at least its skeleton.

In a real-world application, using one process per event to be reminded of would likely be overkill and hard to scale. However, since you are going to be the sole user of the application, this is good enough. A different approach could be using functions such as `timer:send_after/2-3` to avoid spawning too many processes.

Defining the Protocol

Now that we know what each component needs to do and what it should communicate, it's a good idea to make a list of all messages that will be sent and specify what they will look like. Let's start with the communication between the client and the event server:

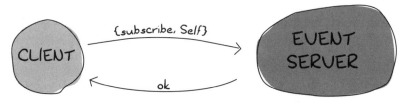

Note: – the client monitors the server
– the server monitors the client

Here, we're using two monitors because there is no obvious dependency between the client and the server. Of course, the client doesn't work without the server, but the server can live without a client. A link could have done the job right here, but because we want our system to be extensible with many clients, we can't assume other clients will all want to crash when the server dies. Nor can we assume the client can really be turned into a system process and trap exits in case the server dies.

Now to the next message set:

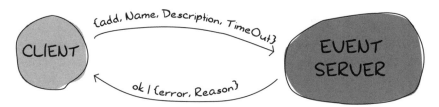

This adds an event to the event server. A confirmation is sent back under the form of the ok atom, unless something goes wrong (maybe the TimeOut is in the wrong format). The inverse operation, removing events, can be done as follows:

The event server can then later send a notification when the event is due:

Then we need only the two following special cases for when we want to shut the server down or when it crashes:

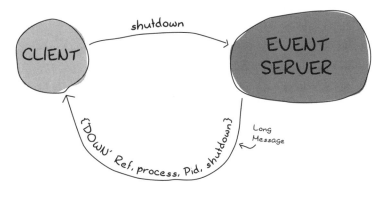

No direct confirmation is sent when the server dies because the monitor will already warn us of that. That's pretty much all that will happen between the client and the event server.

Now we need to deal with the messages between the event server and the event processes themselves. Something to note here before we start is that it would be very useful to have the event server linked to the events. This is because we want all events to die if the server does; they make no sense without it.

When the event server starts the events, it gives each of them a special identifier (the event's name). Once one of these event's time has come, it needs to send a message saying so:

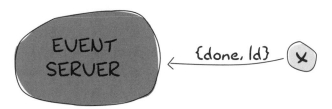

On the other hand, the event needs to watch for cancel calls from the event server:

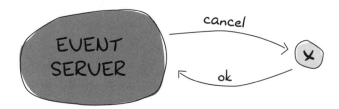

One last message will be needed for our protocol—the one that lets us upgrade the server:

No reply is necessary. When we actually program this feature, you'll see this makes sense.

Having both the protocol defined and the general idea of how our process hierarchy will look in place, we can actually start working on the project.

Lay Them Foundations

To begin, we should lay down a standard Erlang directory structure, which looks like this:

```
ebin/
include/
priv/
src/
```

These directories store files as follows:

- The *ebin/* directory is where files will go once they are compiled.
- The *include/* directory is used to store *.hrl* files that are to be included by other applications (the private *.hrl* files are usually kept inside the *src/* directory).
- The *priv/* directory is used for executables that might need to interact with Erlang, such as specific drivers and whatnot. We won't actually use that directory for this project.
- The *src/* directory is where all *.erl* files stay.

In standard Erlang projects, this directory structure can vary a little. A *conf/* directory can be added for specific configuration files, *doc/* for documentation, and *lib/* or *deps/* for third-party libraries required for your application to run. Erlang products

on the market often use different directory names, but the four in our structure usually stay the same, given that they're part of the standard OTP practices.

An Event Module

We'll start with the event module because it's the one with the fewest dependencies. We should be able to run it without needing to implement the event server or client functions.

Navigate to the *src/* directory and start an *event.erl* module, which will implement the x, y, and z events for the application.

Before we begin writing any code, I have to mention that the protocol is incomplete. It helps represent what data will be sent from process to process, but not the intricacies: how the addressing works, whether we use references or names, and so on. Most messages will be wrapped in the form {Pid, Ref, Message}, where Pid is the sender and Ref is a unique message identifier to help determine which reply came from which sender. If we were to send many messages before looking for replies, we would not know which reply went with which message without a reference.

Events and Loops

The core of the processes that will run *event.erl*'s code will be the function loop/1, which, if you remember the protocol, will look a bit like the following skeleton:

```
loop(State) ->
    receive
        {Server, Ref, cancel} ->
            ...
    after Delay ->
            ...
    end.
```

This shows the timeout we need to support to announce an event has come to term and the way a server can call for the cancellation of an event. You'll notice a State variable in the loop. The State variable will need to contain data such as the timeout value (in seconds) and the name of the event (in order to send the message {done, Id}). It will also need to know the event server's pid in order to send it notifications.

This is all stuff that's fit to be held in the loop's state. So let's declare a state record at the top of the file:

```
-module(event).
-compile(export_all).
-record(state, {server,
                name="",
                to_go=0}).
```

Note that -compile(export_all). is used to avoid needing to modify lists of exported functions all the time. Once the development of the module is done, replacing it with a real sequence of -export([...]). is recommended.

With this state defined, it should be possible to refine the loop a bit more:

```
loop(S = #state{server=Server}) ->
    receive
        {Server, Ref, cancel} ->
            Server ! {Ref, ok}
    after S#state.to_go*1000 ->
        Server ! {done, S#state.name}
    end.
```

Here, the multiplication by a thousand is to change the to_go value from seconds to milliseconds. You could alternatively call timer:seconds/1, which converts seconds to milliseconds, to get the same result.

DON'T DRINK TOO MUCH KOOL-AID

Language wart ahead! We need to bind the variable Server in the function head because it's used in pattern matching in the receive section. Remember that records are hacks! The expression S#state.server is secretly expanded to element(2, S), which isn't a valid pattern to match.

This still works fine for S#state.to_go after the after part, because that one can be an expression left to be evaluated later.

Now let's test the loop:

```
6> c(event).
{ok,event}
7> rr(event, state).
[state]
8> spawn(event, loop, [#state{server=self(), name="test", to_go=5}]).
<0.60.0>
9> flush().
ok
```

```
10> flush().
Shell got {done,"test"}
ok
11> Pid = spawn(event, loop, [#state{server=self(), name="test", to_go=500}]).
<0.64.0>
12> ReplyRef = make_ref().
#Ref<0.0.0.210>
13> Pid ! {self(), ReplyRef, cancel}.
{<0.50.0>,#Ref<0.0.0.210>,cancel}
14> flush().
Shell got {#Ref<0.0.0.210>,ok}
ok
```

First, we import the record from the event module with rr(Mod). Then we spawn the event loop with the shell as the server (self()). This event should fire after 5 seconds. The ninth expression was run after 3 seconds, and the tenth one after 6 seconds. You can see we did receive the {done, "test"} message on the second try.

Right after that, we try the cancel feature (with an ample 500 seconds to type it). We created the reference, sent the message, and got a reply with the same reference, so we know the ok we received was coming from this process and not any other on the system.

The cancel message is wrapped with a reference, but the done message is not, simply because we don't expect it to come from anywhere specific (anyplace will do; we won't match on the receive), nor should we want to reply to it.

Let's try another test. What about an event happening next year?

```
15> spawn(event, loop, [#state{server=self(), name="test", to_go=365*24*60*60}]).
<0.69.0>
16>
=ERROR REPORT==== DD-MM-YYYY::HH:mm:SS ===
Error in process <0.69.0> with exit value: {timeout_value,[{event,loop,1}]}
```

Ouch. It seems like we hit an implementation limit. It turns out Erlang's timeout value is limited to about 50 days in milliseconds. It might not be significant, but I'm showing this error for three reasons:

- It bit me in the ass when writing the module and testing it, halfway through the chapter.

- Erlang is certainly not perfect for every task. What we're seeing here is the consequences of using timers in ways not intended by the implementers.

- It's not really a problem. We can work around it.

The fix we'll apply for this problem is to write a function that splits the timeout value into many parts if turns out to be too long. This will require some support from the loop/1 function, too. So the way to split the time is to divide it in equal parts of 49 days (because the limit is about 50), and then put the remainder with all these equal parts. The sum of the list of seconds should now be the original time:

```
%% Because Erlang is limited to about 49 days (49*24*60*60*1000) in
%% milliseconds, the following function is used.
normalize(N) ->
    Limit = 49*24*60*60,
    [N rem Limit | lists:duplicate(N div Limit, Limit)].
```

The function lists:duplicate/2 will take a given expression as a second argument and reproduce it as many times as the value of the first argument ([a,a,a] = lists:duplicate(3, a)). If we were to send normalize/1 the value 98*24*60*60+4, it would return [4,4233600,4233600].

The loop/1 function should now look like this to accommodate the new format:

```
%% Loop uses a list for times in order to go around the ~49 days limit
%% on timeouts.
loop(S = #state{server=Server, to_go=[T|Next]}) ->
    receive
        {Server, Ref, cancel} ->
            Server ! {Ref, ok}
    after T*1000 ->
        if Next =:= [] ->
            Server ! {done, S#state.name};
           Next =/= [] ->
            loop(S#state{to_go=Next})
        end
    end.
```

This takes the first element of the to_go list and waits for its whole duration. When this is done, the next element of the timeout list is verified. If it's empty, the timeout is over and the server is notified. Otherwise, the loop keeps going with the rest of the list until it's finished.

You can test the revised loop. It should work as normal, but now support years and years of timeout.

Adding An Interface

It would be very annoying to need to manually call something like event:normalize(N) every time an event process is started, especially since our work-around shouldn't be of concern to programmers using our code. The standard way to do this is to instead have an init function handle all initialization of data required for the loop function to work well. While we're at it, we'll add the standard start and start_link functions.

```
start(EventName, Delay) ->
    spawn(?MODULE, init, [self(), EventName, Delay]).
```

```
start_link(EventName, Delay) ->
    spawn_link(?MODULE, init, [self(), EventName, Delay]).

%%% event's innards
init(Server, EventName, Delay) ->
    loop(#state{server=Server,
                name=EventName,
                to_go=normalize(Delay)}).
```

The interface is now much cleaner. Before testing, though, it would be nice to have the only message we can send, cancel, also have its own interface function.

```
cancel(Pid) ->
    %% Monitor in case the process is already dead.
    Ref = erlang:monitor(process, Pid),
    Pid ! {self(), Ref, cancel},
    receive
        {Ref, ok} ->
            erlang:demonitor(Ref, [flush]),
            ok;
        {'DOWN', Ref, process, Pid, _Reason} ->
            ok
    end.
```

Oh, a new trick! Here, we're using a monitor to see if the process is there. If the process is already dead, we avoid useless waiting time and return ok as specified in the protocol. If the process replies with the reference, then we know it will soon die, so we remove the reference to avoid receiving them when we no longer care about them. Note that we also supply the flush option, which will purge the DOWN message if it was sent before we had the time to demonitor.

Let's test these functions:

```
17> c(event).
{ok,event}
18> f().
ok
19> event:start("Event", 0).
<0.103.0>
20> flush().
Shell got {done,"Event"}
ok
21> Pid = event:start("Event", 500).
<0.106.0>
22> event:cancel(Pid).
ok
```

And it works!

The last thing annoying with the event module is that we need to input the time left in seconds. It would be much better if we could use a standard format such as Erlang's datetime ({{*Year, Month, Day*}, {*Hour, Minute, Second*}}). Just add the following function, which will calculate the difference between the current time on your computer and the delay you inserted.

```
time_to_go(TimeOut={{_,_,_}, {_,_,_}}) ->
    Now = calendar:local_time(),
    ToGo = calendar:datetime_to_gregorian_seconds(TimeOut) -
           calendar:datetime_to_gregorian_seconds(Now),
    Secs = if ToGo > 0  -> ToGo;
              ToGo =< 0 -> 0
    end,
    normalize(Secs).
```

Oh yeah, the calendar module has pretty funky function names. This calculates the number of seconds between now and when the event is supposed to fire. If the event is in the past, we instead return 0 so it will notify the server as soon as it can. Now fix the init function to call this function instead of normalize/1. You can also rename Delay variables to say DateTime if you want the names to be more descriptive.

```
init(Server, EventName, DateTime) ->
    loop(#state{server=Server,
                name=EventName,
                to_go=time_to_go(DateTime)}).
```

Now that the event module is finished, we can take a break. Start a new event, go drink a pint (half liter) of milk/beer, and come back just in time to see the event message coming in.

The Event Server

Let's deal with the event server. According to the protocol, its skeleton should look a bit like this:

```
-module(evserv).
-compile(export_all).

loop(State) ->
    receive
        {Pid, MsgRef, {subscribe, Client}} ->
            ...
        {Pid, MsgRef, {add, Name, Description, TimeOut}} ->
            ...
        {Pid, MsgRef, {cancel, Name}} ->
            ...
        {done, Name} ->
            ...
        shutdown ->
            ...
```

```
        {'DOWN', Ref, process, _Pid, _Reason} ->
            ...
        code_change ->
            ...
        Unknown ->
            io:format("Unknown message: ~p~n",[Unknown]),
            loop(State)
    end.
```

You'll notice calls that require replies are wrapped with the same
{Pid, Ref, Message} format as earlier.

The server will need to keep two things in its state: a list of subscribing
clients and a list of all the event processes it spawned.

The protocol says that when an event is done, the event server should
receive {done, Name}, but send {done, Name, Description}. The idea here is to
have as little traffic as necessary and have the event processes care only about
what is strictly required. So here is the list of clients and list of events:

```
-record(state, {events,    %% list of #event{} records
                clients}). %% list of Pids

-record(event, {name="",
                description="",
                pid,
                timeout={{1970,1,1},{0,0,0}}}).
```

And the loop now has the record definition in its head:

```
loop(S = #state{}) ->
    receive
        ...
    end.
```

It would be nice if both events and clients were orddicts. We're unlikely
to have many hundreds of them at once. As you'll recall from Chapter 9,
orddicts fit that need very well. We'll write an init function to handle this.

```
init() ->
    %% Loading events from a static file could be done here.
    %% You would need to pass an argument to init telling where the
    %% resource to find the events is. Then load it from here.
    %% Another option is to just pass the events straight to the server
    %% through this function.
    loop(#state{events=orddict:new(),
                clients=orddict:new()}).
```

With the skeleton and initialization complete, we'll implement each
message one by one.

Handling Messages

The first message is the one about subscriptions. We want to keep a list of all subscribers because when an event is done, we need to notify them. Also, our protocol mentions that we should monitor them. It makes sense because we don't want to hold onto crashed clients and send useless messages for no reason. The code should look like this:

```
{Pid, MsgRef, {subscribe, Client}} ->
    Ref = erlang:monitor(process, Client),
    NewClients = orddict:store(Ref, Client, S#state.clients),
    Pid ! {MsgRef, ok},
    loop(S#state{clients=NewClients});
```

This section of loop/1 starts a monitor and stores the client information in the orddict under the key Ref. The reason for this is simple: The only other time we'll need to fetch the client ID will be if we receive a monitor's EXIT message, which will contain the reference (which will let us get rid of the orddict's entry).

The next message we care about is the one where we add events. Now, it is possible to return an error status. The only validation we'll do is to check the timestamps we accept. While it's easy to subscribe to the {{*Year,Month,Day*}, {*Hour,Minute,seconds*}} layout, we need to make sure we don't do things like accept events on February 29 when we're not in a leap year, or on any other date that doesn't exist. Moreover, we don't want to accept impossible date values such as "5 hours, minus 1 minute and 75 seconds." A single function can take care of validating all of that.

The first building block we'll use is the function calendar:valid_date/1. As its name says, this function checks if the date is valid. Sadly, the weirdness of the calendar module doesn't stop at funky names; there is actually no function to confirm that {H,M,S} has valid values. We'll need to implement that one, too, following the funky naming scheme.

```
valid_datetime({Date,Time}) ->
    try
        calendar:valid_date(Date) andalso valid_time(Time)
    catch
        error:function_clause -> %% not in {{D,M,Y},{H,Min,S}} format
            false
    end;
valid_datetime(_) ->
    false.

valid_time({H,M,S}) -> valid_time(H,M,S).
valid_time(H,M,S) when H >= 0, H < 24,
                       M >= 0, M < 60,
                       S >= 0, S < 60 -> true;
valid_time(_,_,_) -> false.
```

The valid_datetime/1 function can now be used in the part where we try to add the message.

```
{Pid, MsgRef, {add, Name, Description, TimeOut}} ->
    case valid_datetime(TimeOut) of
        true ->
            EventPid = event:start_link(Name, TimeOut),
            NewEvents = orddict:store(Name,
                                      #event{name=Name,
                                             description=Description,
                                             pid=EventPid,
                                             timeout=TimeOut},
                                      S#state.events),
            Pid ! {MsgRef, ok},
            loop(S#state{events=NewEvents});
        false ->
            Pid ! {MsgRef, {error, bad_timeout}},
            loop(S)
    end;
```

If the time is valid, we spawn a new event process, and then store its data in the event server's state before sending a confirmation to the caller. If the timeout is wrong, we notify the client, rather than having the error pass silently or crashing the server. Additional checks could be added for name clashes or other restrictions. (Just remember to update the protocol documentation!)

The next message defined in our protocol is the one where we cancel an event. Canceling an event never fails on the client side, so the code is simpler there. Just check whether the event is in the process's state record. If it is, use the event:cancel/1 function we defined to kill it and send ok. If it's not found, tell the user everything went okay anyway—the event is not running, and that's what the user wanted.

```
{Pid, MsgRef, {cancel, Name}} ->
    Events = case orddict:find(Name, S#state.events) of
                 {ok, E} ->
                     event:cancel(E#event.pid),
                     orddict:erase(Name, S#state.events);
                 error ->
                     S#state.events
             end,
    Pid ! {MsgRef, ok},
    loop(S#state{events=Events});
```

So now all voluntary interaction coming from the client to the event server is covered. Let's deal with the stuff that's going between the server and the events themselves. There are two messages to handle: canceling the events (which is done) and the events timing out. That message is simply {done, Name}:

```
{done, Name} ->
    case orddict:find(Name, S#state.events) of
        {ok, E} ->
            send_to_clients({done, E#event.name, E#event.description},
            S#state.clients),
            NewEvents = orddict:erase(Name, S#state.events),
            loop(S#state{events=NewEvents});
        error ->
            %% This may happen if we cancel an event and
            %% it fires at the same time.
            loop(S)
    end;
```

The function send_to_clients/2 does as its name says and is defined as follows:

```
send_to_clients(Msg, ClientDict) ->
    orddict:map(fun(_Ref, Pid) -> Pid ! Msg end, ClientDict).
```

That should be it for most of the loop code. What's left is the handling of different status messages: clients going down, shutdown, code upgrades, and so on. Here they come:

```
shutdown ->
    exit(shutdown);
{'DOWN', Ref, process, _Pid, _Reason} ->
    loop(S#state{clients=orddict:erase(Ref, S#state.clients)});
code_change ->
    ?MODULE:loop(S);
Unknown ->
    io:format("Unknown message: ~p~n",[Unknown]),
    loop(S)
```

The first case (shutdown) is pretty explicit. You get the kill message; let the process die. If you wanted to save state to disk, that could be a possible place to do it. If you wanted safer save/exit semantics, this could be implemented on every add, cancel, or done message. Loading events from disk could then be done in the init function, spawning them as they come.

The 'DOWN' message's actions are also simple enough. It means a client died, so we remove it from the client list in the state.

Unknown messages will just be shown with io:format/2 for debugging purposes, although a real production application would likely use a dedicated logging module. Otherwise, all that useful information would be wasted in output that no one ever looks for in production.

Next comes the code change message. This one is interesting enough to have its own section.

Hot Code Loving

In order to do hot code loading, Erlang has the *code server*. The code server is basically a VM process in charge of an ETS table (an in-memory database table, native to the VM, discussed later in Chapter 25). The code server can hold two versions of a single module in memory, and both versions can run at once. A new version of a module is loaded automatically when compiling it with c(Module), loading with l(Module), or loading it with one of the many functions of the code module, which you can read about in the Erlang documentation.

An important concept to understand is that Erlang has both local and external calls. Local calls are those function calls you can make with functions that might not be exported. They have the format Name(Args). An external call can be done only with exported functions and has the form Module:Function(Args). The precise name for an external call is *fully qualified call*.

When there are two versions of a module loaded in the VM, all local calls are done through the currently running version in a process. However, fully qualified calls are *always* done on the newest version of the code available in the code server. Then, if local calls are made from within the fully qualified one, they are in the new version of the code.

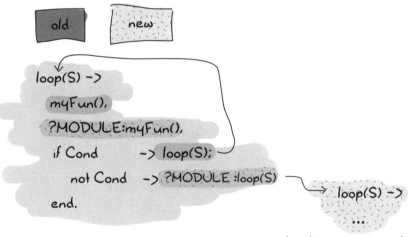

`new` becomes the default

Given that every process/actor in Erlang needs to do a recursive call in order to change state, it is possible to load entirely new versions of an actor by having an external recursive call.

NOTE   *If you load a third version of a module while a process still runs with the first one, that process will be killed by the VM, which assumes it was an orphan process without a supervisor or a way to upgrade itself. If no one runs the oldest version, it is simply dropped and the newest ones are kept instead.*

There are ways to bind your code to a system module that will send messages whenever a new version of a module is loaded. By doing this, you can trigger a module reload only when receiving such a message, and always do it with a code upgrade function, say MyModule:Upgrade(CurrentState), which will then be able to transform the state data structure according to the new version's specification. This "subscription" handling is done automatically by the OTP framework, which we'll start studying in Chapter 14. For the reminder application, we won't use the code server and will instead use a custom code_change message from the shell, doing very basic reloading. That's pretty much all you need to know to do hot code loading. Nevertheless, here's a more generic example:

```
-module(hotload).
-export([server/1, upgrade/1]).

server(State) ->
    receive
        update ->
            NewState = ?MODULE:upgrade(State),
            ?MODULE:server(NewState);  %% Loop in the new version of the module.
        SomeMessage ->
            %% Do something here.
            server(State)  %% Stay in the same version no matter what.
    end.

upgrade(OldState) ->
%% Transform and return the state here.
```

As you can see, our ?MODULE:loop(S) fits this pattern.

I Said, Hide Your Messages

Hide messages! If you expect people to build on your code and processes, you must hide the messages in interface functions. Here's what we used for the evserv module:

```
start() ->
    register(?MODULE, Pid=spawn(?MODULE, init, [])),
    Pid.

start_link() ->
    register(?MODULE, Pid=spawn_link(?MODULE, init, [])),
    Pid.

terminate() ->
    ?MODULE ! shutdown.
```

We registered the server module because, for now, we should have only one running at a time. If you were to expand the reminder application to support many users, it would be a decent idea to instead register the names with the global module, and it would be even better to use the gproc library. For the sake of this example app, what we have here will be enough.

NOTE *The gproc library is a process dictionary for Erlang, which provides a number of useful features beyond what the built-in dictionary has, such as he use of any term as an alias, multiple names for a process, waiting for registration of other processes, atomic name giveaway, and counters. It's available from* http://github.com/uwiger/gproc.

The first message we wrote is the next we should abstract away: how to subscribe. The little protocol or specification we wrote earlier called for a monitor, so this one is added there. At any point, if the reference returned by the subscribe message is in a `DOWN` message, the client will know the server has gone down.

```
subscribe(Pid) ->
    Ref = erlang:monitor(process, whereis(?MODULE)),
    ?MODULE ! {self(), Ref, {subscribe, Pid}},
    receive
        {Ref, ok} ->
            {ok, Ref};
        {'DOWN', Ref, process, _Pid, Reason} ->
            {error, Reason}
    after 5000 ->
        {error, timeout}
    end.
```

The next message to abstract away is the event adding:

```
add_event(Name, Description, TimeOut) ->
    Ref = make_ref(),
    ?MODULE ! {self(), Ref, {add, Name, Description, TimeOut}},
    receive
        {Ref, Msg} -> Msg
    after 5000 ->
        {error, timeout}
    end.
```

Note that we forward the {error, bad_timeout} message that could be received to the client. We could have also decided to crash the client by raising erlang:error(bad_timeout). Whether crashing the client or forwarding the error message is the thing to do is still debated in the community. Here's the alternative crashing function:

```
add_event2(Name, Description, TimeOut) ->
    Ref = make_ref(),
    ?MODULE ! {self(), Ref, {add, Name, Description, TimeOut}},
    receive
        {Ref, {error, Reason}} -> erlang:error(Reason);
        {Ref, Msg} -> Msg
    after 5000 ->
```

```
    {error, timeout}
end.
```

Then there's event cancellation, which just takes a name:

```
cancel(Name) ->
    Ref = make_ref(),
    ?MODULE ! {self(), Ref, {cancel, Name}},
    receive
        {Ref, ok} -> ok
    after 5000 ->
        {error, timeout}
    end.
```

Last of all is a small nicety provided for the client—a function used to accumulate all messages during a given period of time. If messages are found, they're all taken, and the function returns as soon as possible.

```
listen(Delay) ->
    receive
        M = {done, _Name, _Description} ->
            [M | listen(0)]
    after Delay*1000 ->
        []
    end.
```

This is mostly useful when working with applications where the client polls for updates, whereas applications that are always listening can use a push-based mechanism, and thus would not need such a function.

A Test Drive

You should now be able to compile the application and give it a test run. To make things a bit simpler, we'll write a specific Erlang makefile to build the project. Open a file named *Emakefile* and put it in the project's base directory. The file contains Erlang terms and gives the Erlang compiler the recipe to cook wonderful and crispy *.beam* files.

```
{'src/*', [debug_info,
        {i, "src"},
        {i, "include"},
        {outdir, "ebin"}]}.
```

This tells the compiler to add debug_info to the files (this is rarely an option you want to give up), to look for header files in the *src/* and *include/* directories to help compile modules in *src/*, and to output them in *ebin/*.

Go to your command line and run erl -make from the project's base directory, and the files should all be compiled and put inside the *ebin/* directory for you. Start the Erlang shell by enterng erl -pa ebin/. The

-pa *directory* option tells the Erlang VM to add that path to the places it can look for modules.

Another option is to start the shell as usual and call make:all([load]). This will look for a file named *Emakefile* in the current directory, recompile it (if it changed), and load the new files.

You should now be able to track thousands of events. Try it out.

```
1> evserv:start().
<0.34.0>
2> evserv:subscribe(self()).
{ok,#Ref<0.0.0.31>}
3> evserv:add_event("Hey there", "test", FutureDateTime).
ok
4> evserv:listen(5).
[]
5> evserv:cancel("Hey there").
ok
6> evserv:add_event("Hey there2", "test", NextMinuteDateTime).
ok
7> evserv:listen(2000).
[{done,"Hey there2","test"}]
```

This works nicely. Writing any client should now be simple enough, given the few basic interface functions we have created.

Adding Supervision

In order to make our example a more stable application, we should write a "restarter," as we did in Chapter 12. Open a file named *sup.erl* where our supervisor will be:

```
-module(sup).
-export([start/2, start_link/2, init/1, loop/1]).

start(Mod,Args) ->
    spawn(?MODULE, init, [{Mod, Args}]).

start_link(Mod,Args) ->
    spawn_link(?MODULE, init, [{Mod, Args}]).

init({Mod,Args}) ->
    process_flag(trap_exit, true),
    loop({Mod,start_link,Args}).

loop({M,F,A}) ->
    Pid = apply(M,F,A),
    receive
```

```
        {'EXIT', _From, shutdown} ->
            exit(shutdown); % will kill the child too
        {'EXIT', Pid, Reason} ->
            io:format("Process ~p exited for reason ~p~n",[Pid,Reason]),
            loop({M,F,A})
    end.
```

This is somewhat similar to the restarter from Chapter 12, although this one is a tad more generic. It can take any module, as long as it has a start_link function. It will restart the process it watches indefinitely, unless the supervisor itself is terminated with a shutdown exit signal. Here it is in use:

```
1> c(evserv), c(sup).
{ok,sup}
2> SupPid = sup:start(evserv, []).
<0.43.0>
3> whereis(evserv).
<0.44.0>
4> exit(whereis(evserv), die).
true
Process <0.44.0> exited for reason die
5> exit(whereis(evserv), die).
Process <0.48.0> exited for reason die
true
6> exit(SupPid, shutdown).
true
7> whereis(evserv).
undefined
```

As you can see, killing the supervisor will also kill its child.

NOTE   *We'll explore much more advanced and flexible supervisors in Chapter 18. Those are the ones people are thinking of when they mention supervision trees. The supervisor demonstrated here is only the most basic form that exists and is not exactly fit for production environments compared to the real thing.*

Namespaces (or Lack Thereof)

Because Erlang has a flat module structure (there is no hierarchy), some applications may have naming conflicts among
their modules. One example of this is the
frequently used user module that almost
every project attempts to define at least
once. This clashes with the user module
shipped with Erlang. You can test for any
clashes with the function code:clash/0.

Because of the potential for conflicts, the common pattern is to prefix every module name with the name of your project. In this case, our reminder application's modules should be renamed to `reminder_evserv`, `reminder_sup`, and `reminder_event`.

Some programmers then decide to add a module, named after the application itself, which wraps common calls that programmers could make when using their own application. Examples of calls could be functions such as starting the application with a supervisor, subscribing to the server, and adding and canceling events. It's important to be aware of other namespaces, too, such as registered names that must not clash, database tables, and so on.

That's pretty much it for a very basic concurrent Erlang application. This one showed we could have a bunch of concurrent processes without thinking too hard about it: supervisors, clients, servers, processes used as timers (and we could have thousands of them), and so on. There's no need to synchronize them, no locks, and no real main loop. Message passing has made it simple to compartmentalize our application into a few modules with separated concerns and tasks.

The basic calls inside *evserv.erl* could now be used to construct clients that could interact with the event server from somewhere outside the Erlang VM and make the program truly useful.

Before doing that, though, I suggest you read up on the OTP framework. The next few chapters will cover some of its building blocks, which allow for much more robust and elegant applications. A huge part of Erlang's power comes from using the OTP framework. It's a carefully crafted and well-engineered tool that any self-respecting Erlang programmer must know.

14

AN INTRODUCTION TO OTP

In this chapter, we'll get started with Erlang's OTP framework. OTP stands for Open Telecom Platform, though these days it's more about software that has the properties of telecom applications than telecom itself. If half of Erlang's greatness comes from its concurrency and distribution, and the other half comes from its error handling capabilities, then the OTP framework provides the third half.

During the previous chapters we've seen a few examples of common practices of how to write concurrent applications with the language's built-in facilities: links, monitors, servers, timeouts, trapping exits, and so on. There were a few "gotchas" involved in concurrent programming: Things must be done in a certain order, race conditions need to be avoided, and a process could die at any time. We also covered hot code loading, naming processes, adding supervisors, and other techniques.

Doing all of this manually is time consuming and error prone. There are corner cases to be forgotten about and pits to fall in to. The OTP framework takes care of this by grouping these essential practices into a set of libraries that have been carefully engineered and battle hardened over the years. Every Erlang programmer should use them.

The OTP framework is also a set of modules and standards designed to help you build applications. Given that most Erlang programmers end up using OTP, most Erlang applications you'll encounter in the wild will tend to follow these standards.

The Common Process, Abstracted

One of the things we've done many times in the previous process examples is divide everything in accordance to very specific tasks. In most processes, we had a function in charge of spawning the new process, a function in charge of giving the process its initial values, a main loop, and so on. These parts, as it turns out, are usually present in all concurrent programs you'll write, no matter what the process might be used for.

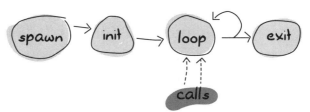

The engineers and computer scientists behind the OTP framework spotted these patterns and included them in a bunch of common libraries.

The OTP libraries are built with code that is equivalent to most of the abstractions we used (like using references to tag messages), with the advantages of being used for years in the field and built with far more caution than we used in our implementations. They contain functions to safely spawn and initialize processes, send messages to them in a fault-tolerant manner, and perform many other tasks. But you should rarely need to use these libraries yourself. The abstractions they contain are so basic and universal that a lot more interesting things, called *behaviors*, were built on top of them.

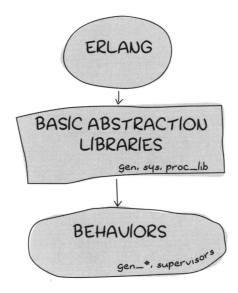

In this and the following chapters, we'll look at a few of the common uses of processes, and how they can be abstracted and then made generic. Then for each of these, we'll explore the corresponding implementation with the OTP framework's behaviors.

The Basic Server

The common pattern we'll explore in this chapter is one we've already used. For the event server we wrote in Chapter 13, we used a *client/server* model. The event server receives calls from the client, acts on them, and then replies to the client if the protocol says to do so.

Introducing the Kitty Server

For this chapter, we'll use a very simple server, allowing us to focus on its essential properties. Here's the kitty_server:

```erlang
%%%% Naive version
-module(kitty_server).
-export([start_link/0, order_cat/4, return_cat/2, close_shop/1]).

-record(cat, {name, color=green, description}).

%%% Client API
start_link() -> spawn_link(fun init/0).

%% Synchronous call
order_cat(Pid, Name, Color, Description) ->
    Ref = erlang:monitor(process, Pid),
    Pid ! {self(), Ref, {order, Name, Color, Description}},
    receive
```

```erlang
        {Ref, Cat} ->
            erlang:demonitor(Ref, [flush]),
            Cat;
        {'DOWN', Ref, process, Pid, Reason} ->
            erlang:error(Reason)
    after 5000 ->
        erlang:error(timeout)
    end.

%% This call is asynchronous.
return_cat(Pid, Cat = #cat{}) ->
    Pid ! {return, Cat},
    ok.

%% Synchronous call
close_shop(Pid) ->
    Ref = erlang:monitor(process, Pid),
    Pid ! {self(), Ref, terminate},
    receive
        {Ref, ok} ->
            erlang:demonitor(Ref, [flush]),
            ok;
        {'DOWN', Ref, process, Pid, Reason} ->
            erlang:error(Reason)
    after 5000 ->
        erlang:error(timeout)
    end.

%%% Server functions
init() -> loop([]).

loop(Cats) ->
    receive
        {Pid, Ref, {order, Name, Color, Description}} ->
            if Cats =:= [] ->
                Pid ! {Ref, make_cat(Name, Color, Description)},
                loop(Cats);
               Cats =/= [] -> % got to empty the stock
                Pid ! {Ref, hd(Cats)},
                loop(tl(Cats))
            end;
        {return, Cat = #cat{}} ->
            loop([Cat|Cats]);
        {Pid, Ref, terminate} ->
            Pid ! {Ref, ok},
            terminate(Cats);
        Unknown ->
            %% Do some logging here too.
            io:format("Unknown message: ~p~n", [Unknown]),
            loop(Cats)
    end.
```

```
%%% Private functions
make_cat(Name, Col, Desc) ->
    #cat{name=Name, color=Col, description=Desc}.

terminate(Cats) ->
    [io:format("~p was set free.~n",[C#cat.name]) || C <- Cats],
    ok.
```

So this is a kitty server/store. The behavior is extremely simple: You describe a cat, and you get that cat. If someone returns a cat, it's added to a list, and then automatically sent as the next order instead of what the client actually asked for (we're in this kitty store for the money, not smiles).

```
1> c(kitty_server).
{ok,kitty_server}
2> rr(kitty_server).
[cat]
3> Pid = kitty_server:start_link().
<0.57.0>
4> Cat1 = kitty_server:order_cat(Pid, carl, brown, "loves to burn bridges").
#cat{name = carl,color = brown,
description = "loves to burn bridges"}
5> kitty_server:return_cat(Pid, Cat1).
ok
6> kitty_server:order_cat(Pid, jimmy, orange, "cuddly").
#cat{name = carl,color = brown,
description = "loves to burn bridges"}
7> kitty_server:order_cat(Pid, jimmy, orange, "cuddly").
#cat{name = jimmy,color = orange,description = "cuddly"}
8> kitty_server:return_cat(Pid, Cat1).
ok
9> kitty_server:close_shop(Pid).
carl was set free.
ok
10> kitty_server:close_shop(Pid).
** exception error: no such process or port
in function  kitty_server:close_shop/1
```

Looking back at the source code for the module, we can see patterns we've previously applied. The sections where we set monitors up and down, apply timers, receive data, use a main loop, handle the init function, and so on should be familiar. It should be possible to abstract away these things we end up repeating all the time. Let's start with the client API.

Generalizing Calls

The first thing to notice in the source code is that both synchronous calls are extremely similar. These are the calls that would likely go in abstraction libraries, as mentioned earlier. For now, we'll just abstract these away as a single function in a new module that will hold all the generic parts of the kitty server.

```
-module(my_server).
-compile(export_all).

call(Pid, Msg) ->
    Ref = erlang:monitor(process, Pid),
    Pid ! {self(), Ref, Msg},
    receive
        {Ref, Reply} ->
            erlang:demonitor(Ref, [flush]),
            Reply;
        {'DOWN', Ref, process, Pid, Reason} ->
            erlang:error(Reason)
    after 5000 ->
        erlang:error(timeout)
    end.
```

This takes a message and a pid, sticks them into the function, and then forwards the message for you in a safe manner.

From now on, we can just substitute the message sending we do with a call to this function. So if we were to rewrite a new kitty server to be paired with the abstracted my_server, it could begin like this:

```
-module(kitty_server2).
-export([start_link/0, order_cat/4, return_cat/2, close_shop/1]).

-record(cat, {name, color=green, description}).

%%% Client API
start_link() -> spawn_link(fun init/0).

%% Synchronous call
order_cat(Pid, Name, Color, Description) ->
    my_server:call(Pid, {order, Name, Color, Description}).

%% This call is asynchronous.
return_cat(Pid, Cat = #cat{}) ->
    Pid ! {return, Cat},
    ok.

%% Synchronous call
close_shop(Pid) ->
    my_server:call(Pid, terminate).
```

Generalizing the Server Loop

The next big generic chunk of code we have is not as obvious as the call/2 function. Note that every process we've written so far has a loop where all the messages are pattern matched. This part is a bit touchy, but here we

need to separate the pattern matching from the loop itself. One quick way
to do it would be to add this:

```
loop(Module, State) ->
    receive
        Message -> Module:handle(Message, State)
    end.
```

And then the specific module would look like this:

```
handle(Message1, State) -> NewState1;
handle(Message2, State) -> NewState2;
...
handle(MessageN, State) -> NewStateN.
```

This is better, but there are ways to make it even cleaner.

If you paid attention when reading or entering the kitty_server module
(and I hope you did!), you will have noticed we have a specific way to call
synchronously and another way to call asynchronously. It would be pretty
helpful if our generic server implementation could provide a clear way to
know which kind of call is which.

To accomplish this, we will need to match different kinds of messages
in my_server:loop/2. This means we'll need to change the call/2 function a
bit so synchronous calls are made obvious. We'll do this by adding the atom
sync to the message on the function's second line, as follows:

```
call(Pid, Msg) ->
    Ref = erlang:monitor(process, Pid),
    Pid ! {sync, self(), Ref, Msg},
    receive
        {Ref, Reply} ->
            erlang:demonitor(Ref, [flush]),
            Reply;
        {'DOWN', Ref, process, Pid, Reason} ->
            erlang:error(Reason)
    after 5000 ->
        erlang:error(timeout)
    end.
```

We can now provide a new function for asynchronous calls. The function cast/2 will handle this.

```
cast(Pid, Msg) ->
    Pid ! {async, Msg},
    ok.
```

Now the loop looks like this:

```erlang
loop(Module, State) ->
    receive
        {async, Msg} ->
            loop(Module, Module:handle_cast(Msg, State));
        {sync, Pid, Ref, Msg} ->
            loop(Module, Module:handle_call(Msg, Pid, Ref, State))
    end.
```

And then you could also add specific slots to handle messages that don't fit the sync/async concept (maybe they were sent by accident) or to have your debug functions and other stuff like hot code reloading in there.

One disappointing thing about our loop is that the abstraction is leaking. The programmers who will use my_server will still need to know about references when sending synchronous messages and replying to them. That makes the abstraction useless. To use it, you still need to understand all the boring details. Here's a quick fix:

```erlang
loop(Module, State) ->
    receive
        {async, Msg} ->
            loop(Module, Module:handle_cast(Msg, State));
        {sync, Pid, Ref, Msg} ->
            loop(Module, Module:handle_call(Msg, {Pid, Ref}, State))
    end.
```

With both the variables Pid and Ref placed in a tuple, they can be passed as a single argument to the other function as a variable with a name like From. Then the user doesn't need to know anything about the variable's innards. Instead, we'll provide a function to send replies that should understand what From contains:

```erlang
reply({Pid, Ref}, Reply) ->
    Pid ! {Ref, Reply}.
```

Starter Functions

What is left to do is specify the starter functions (start, start_link, and init) that pass around the module names and whatnot. Once they're added, the module should look like this:

```erlang
-module(my_server).
-export([start/2, start_link/2, call/2, cast/2, reply/2]).

%%% Public API
start(Module, InitialState) ->
    spawn(fun() -> init(Module, InitialState) end).
```

```erlang
start_link(Module, InitialState) ->
    spawn_link(fun() -> init(Module, InitialState) end).

call(Pid, Msg) ->
    Ref = erlang:monitor(process, Pid),
    Pid ! {sync, self(), Ref, Msg},
    receive
        {Ref, Reply} ->
            erlang:demonitor(Ref, [flush]),
            Reply;
        {'DOWN', Ref, process, Pid, Reason} ->
            erlang:error(Reason)
    after 5000 ->
        erlang:error(timeout)
    end.

cast(Pid, Msg) ->
    Pid ! {async, Msg},
    ok.

reply({Pid, Ref}, Reply) ->
    Pid ! {Ref, Reply}.

%%% Private stuff
init(Module, InitialState) ->
    loop(Module, Module:init(InitialState)).

loop(Module, State) ->
    receive
        {async, Msg} ->
            loop(Module, Module:handle_cast(Msg, State));
        {sync, Pid, Ref, Msg} ->
            loop(Module, Module:handle_call(Msg, {Pid, Ref}, State))
    end.
```

Generalizing Kitty Server

Next, we need to re-implement the kitty server, now kitty_server2, as a call-back module that will respect the interface we defined for my_server. We'll keep the same interface as the previous implementation, except all the calls are now redirected to go through my_server.

```erlang
-module(kitty_server2).

-export([start_link/0, order_cat/4, return_cat/2, close_shop/1]).
-export([init/1, handle_call/3, handle_cast/2]).

-record(cat, {name, color=green, description}).

%%% Client API
start_link() -> my_server:start_link(?MODULE, []).
```

```
%% Synchronous call
order_cat(Pid, Name, Color, Description) ->
    my_server:call(Pid, {order, Name, Color, Description}).

%% This call is asynchronous.
return_cat(Pid, Cat = #cat{}) ->
    my_server:cast(Pid, {return, Cat}).

%% Synchronous call
close_shop(Pid) ->
    my_server:call(Pid, terminate).
```

Note that we added a second -export() at the top of the module. These are the functions my_server will need to call to make everything work:

```
%%% Server functions
init([]) -> []. %% no treatment of info here!

handle_call({order, Name, Color, Description}, From, Cats) ->
    if Cats =:= [] ->
        my_server:reply(From, make_cat(Name, Color, Description)),
        Cats;
       Cats =/= [] ->
        my_server:reply(From, hd(Cats)),
        tl(Cats)
    end;

handle_call(terminate, From, Cats) ->
    my_server:reply(From, ok),
    terminate(Cats).

handle_cast({return, Cat = #cat{}}, Cats) ->
    [Cat|Cats].
```

And then we need to reinsert the private functions:

```
%%% Private functions
make_cat(Name, Col, Desc) ->
    #cat{name=Name, color=Col, description=Desc}.

terminate(Cats) ->
    [io:format("~p was set free.~n",[C#cat.name]) || C <- Cats],
    exit(normal).
```

Just make sure to replace the ok we had before with exit(normal) in terminate/1; otherwise, the server will keep running.

You should be able to compile and test the code, and run it in exactly the same manner as the previous version. The code is quite similar, but let's see what has changed.

Specific vs. Generic

Our kitty server example demonstrates the core of OTP (conceptually speaking). This is what OTP really is all about: taking all the generic components, extracting them in libraries, making sure they work well, and then reusing that code when possible. Then all that's left to do is focus on the specific stuff—things that will always change from application to application.

Obviously, you don't benefit much by doing things that way with only the kitty server. It looks a bit like abstraction for abstraction's sake. If the application you needed to ship to a customer were nothing but the kitty server, then the first version might be fine. However, for larger applications, it might be worth the effort to separate generic parts of your code from the specific sections.

Imagine that we have some Erlang software running on a server. Our software has a few kitty servers running, a veterinary process (you send your broken kitties, and it returns them fixed), a kitty beauty salon, a server for pet food, and so on. Most of these can be implemented with a client/server pattern. As time passes, your complex system becomes full of different servers running around.

Adding servers adds complexity in terms of code, and also in terms of testing, maintenance, and understanding. Each implementation might be different, programmed in different styles by various people, and so on. However, if all these servers share the same common `my_server` abstraction, you substantially reduce that complexity. You understand the basic concept of the module instantly ("Oh, it's a server!"), and there's a single generic implementation of it to test and document. The rest of the effort can be put into each specific implementation of the server.

This means you reduce a lot of time tracking and solving bugs (just do it in one place for all servers). It also means that you reduce the number of bugs you introduce. If you were to rewrite the `my_server:call/3` or the process's main loop all the time, not only would it be more time-consuming, but chances of forgetting one step or another would skyrocket, and so would bugs. Fewer bugs mean fewer calls during the night to go fix something, which is definitely good for all of us (I bet you don't appreciate going to the office on days off to fix bugs either).

Another interesting outcome of separating the generic from the specific is that we instantly made it much easier to test our individual modules. If you wanted to unit test the old kitty server implementation, you would need to spawn one process per test, give it the right state, send your messages, and hope for the reply you expected. On the other hand, our second kitty server requires us to run the function calls over only the `handle_call/3`

and handle_cast/2 functions, and see what they output as a new state. There is no need to set up servers. Just pass the state in as a function parameter. Note that this also means the generic aspect of the server is much easier to test, given you can just implement very simple functions that do nothing other than let you focus on the behavior you want to observe.

A less obvious advantage of using common abstractions in this way is that if everyone uses the exact same backend for their processes, when someone optimizes that single backend to make it a little faster, every process using it out there will run a little faster, too. For this principle to work in practice, it's usually necessary to have a whole lot of people using the same abstractions and putting effort in them. Luckily for the Erlang community, that's what happens with the OTP framework.

In our kitty server modules, there are a bunch of things we haven't yet addressed: named processes, configuring the timeouts, adding debug information, what to do with unexpected messages, how to tie in hot code loading, handling specific errors, abstracting away the need to write most replies, handling most ways to shut down a server, making sure the server plays nice with supervisors, and more. Going over all of this is superfluous for this text, but it would be necessary in real products that need to be shipped. Again, you might see why doing all of this by yourself is a bit of a risky task. Luckily for you (and the people who will support your applications), the Erlang/OTP team managed to handle all of that with the gen_server behavior. gen_server is a bit like my_server on steroids, except it has years and years of testing and production use behind it.

Callback to the Future

Similar to the interface we started designing in this chapter, the OTP gen_server asks us to provide functions to deal with initialization and termination of processes, the handling of synchronous and asynchronous requests done through message passing, and a few other tasks.

The init Function

The first callback is an init/1 function. It is similar to the one we used with my_server in that it is used to initialize the server's state and do all of these one-time tasks that the server will depend on. The function can return {ok, State}, {ok, State, TimeOut}, {ok, State, hibernate}, {stop, Reason}, or ignore.

The normal {ok, State} return value doesn't really need explaining other than that State will be passed directly to the main loop of the process as the state to keep later on. The TimeOut variable is meant to be added to the tuple whenever you need a deadline before which you expect the server to receive a message. If no message is received before the deadline, a special one (the atom `timeout`) is sent to the server, which should be handled with `handle_info/2` (described later in this chapter). This option is seldom used in production code, because you can't always know which messages you will receive, and any of them will be enough to reset the timer. It is usually better to use a function such as `erlang:start_timer/3` and handle things manually for better control.

On the other hand, if you do expect the process to take a long time before getting a reply and are worried about memory, you can add the hibernate atom to the tuple. Hibernation basically reduces the size of the process's state until it gets a message, at the cost of some processing power. If you are in doubt about using hibernation, you probably don't need it.

Returning {stop, Reason} should be done when something went wrong during the initialization.

A CLOSER LOOK AT HIBERNATION

There's a more technical definition of process hibernation, if you're interested. When the BIF `erlang:hibernate(M,F,A)` is called, the call stack for the currently running process is discarded (the function never returns). The garbage collection then kicks in, and what's left is one continuous heap that is shrunken to the size of the data in the process. This basically compacts all the data so the process takes less space.

Once the process receives a message, the function `M:F` with `A` as arguments is called, and the execution resumes.

NOTE *While `init/1` is running, execution is blocked in the process that spawned the server. This is because it is waiting for a "ready" message sent automatically by the `gen_server` module to make sure everything went fine.*

The handle_call Function

The function `handle_call/3` is used to work with synchronous messages. It takes three arguments: `Request`, `From`, and `State`. It's pretty similar to how we programmed our own `handle_call/3` in `my_server`. The biggest difference is how you reply to messages. In our own abstraction of a server, it was necessary to use `my_server:reply/2` to talk back to the process. In the case of `gen_server`, eight different return values are possible, taking the form of tuples:

```
{reply,Reply,NewState}
{reply,Reply,NewState,TimeOut}
{reply,Reply,NewState,hibernate}
{noreply,NewState}
{noreply,NewState,TimeOut}
{noreply,NewState,hibernate}
{stop,Reason,Reply,NewState}
{stop,Reason,NewState}
```

For all of these values, `TimeOut` and `hibernate` work the same way as for `init/1`. Whatever is in `Reply` will be sent back to whoever called the server in the first place.

Notice that there are three possible `noreply` options. When you use `noreply`, the generic part of the server will assume you're taking care of sending the reply back yourself. This can be done with `gen_server:reply/2`, which can be used in the same way as `my_server:reply/2`.

Most of the time, you'll need only the `reply` tuples. However, there are a few valid reasons to use `noreply`, such as when you want another process to send the reply for you, or when you want to send an acknowledgment ("Hey! I received the message!") but still process it afterward (without replying this time). If this is what you choose to do, it is absolutely necessary to use `gen_server:reply/2`; otherwise, the call will time out and cause a crash.

The handle_cast Function

The `handle_cast/2` callback works a lot like the one in `my_server`. It takes the parameters `Message` and `State` and is used to handle asynchronous calls. You do whatever you want in there, in a manner quite similar to what's doable with `handle_call/3`. On the other hand, only tuples without replies are valid return values:

```
{noreply,NewState}
{noreply,NewState,TimeOut}
{noreply,NewState,hibernate}
{stop,Reason,NewState}
```

The handle_info Function

Earlier, I mentioned that our own server didn't really deal with messages that do not fit our interface. Well, `handle_info/2` is the solution. It's very similar to `handle_cast/2`, and in fact, returns the same tuples. The difference is that this callback is there only for messages that were sent directly with the ! operator and special ones like `init/1`'s timeout, monitors' notifications, and `EXIT` signals.

The terminate Function

The callback `terminate/2` is called whenever one of the three `handle_something` functions returns a tuple of the form {stop, Reason, NewState} or {stop, Reason, Reply, NewState}. It takes two parameters, `Reason` and `State`, corresponding to the same values from the stop tuples.

The `terminate/2` function will also be called when its parent (the process that spawned it) dies, if and only if the gen_server is trapping exits.

If any reason other than normal, shutdown, *or* {shutdown, Term} *is used when* terminate/2 *is called, the OTP framework will see this as a failure and start logging the process's state, reason for failures, last messages received, and so on. This makes debugging easier, which might save your life quite a few times.*

This function is pretty much the direct opposite of init/1, so whatever was done in there should have its opposite in terminate/2. It's your server's janitor—the function in charge of locking the door after making sure everyone is gone. Of course, the function is helped by the VM itself, which should usually delete all ETS tables (see Chapter 25), close all sockets (see Chapter 23), and handle other tasks for you. Note that the return value of this function doesn't really matter, because the code stops executing after it has been called.

The code_change Function

The function code_change/3 lets you upgrade code. It takes the form code_change(PreviousVersion, State, Extra). Here, the variable PreviousVersion is either the version term itself (see Chapter 2 if you forgot what this is) in the case of an upgrade or {down, Version} in the case of a downgrade (just reloading older code). The State variable holds all of the current server state so you can convert it.

Imagine for a moment that we used an orddict to store all of our data. However, as time passes, the orddict becomes too slow, and we decide to replace it with a regular dict. In order to avoid the process crashing on the next function call, the conversion from one data structure to the other can be done in there, safely. All we need to do is return the new state with {ok, NewState}. We'll make use of this feature in Chapter 22, when we see relups as well as the Extra variable. We won't worry about these things for now.

So now we have all the callbacks defined. Don't worry if you're a little lost. The OTP framework is a bit circular sometimes; to understand part A of the framework, you need to understand part B, but then part B requires that you understand part A. The best way to get over that confusion is to actually implement a gen_server.

.BEAM Me Up, Scotty!

Now we'll build kitty_gen_server. It will be similar to kitty_server2, with only minimal API changes. First start a new module with the following lines in it:

```
-module(kitty_gen_server).
-behavior(gen_server).
```

Both behavior and behaviour are accepted by the Erlang compiler.

And try to compile it. You should get something like this:

```
1> c(kitty_gen_server).
./kitty_gen_server.erl:2: Warning: undefined callback function code_change/3
(behavior 'gen_server')
./kitty_gen_server.erl:2: Warning: undefined callback function handle_call/3
(behavior 'gen_server')
./kitty_gen_server.erl:2: Warning: undefined callback function handle_cast/2
(behavior 'gen_server')
./kitty_gen_server.erl:2: Warning: undefined callback function handle_info/2
(behavior 'gen_server')
./kitty_gen_server.erl:2: Warning: undefined callback function init/1
(behavior 'gen_server')
./kitty_gen_server.erl:2: Warning: undefined callback function terminate/2
(behavior 'gen_server')
{ok,kitty_gen_server}
```

The compilation worked, but there are warnings about missing callbacks. This is because of the gen_server behavior. A *behavior* is basically a way for a module to specify functions it expects another module to have. The behavior is the contract sealing the deal between the well-behaved generic part of the code and the specific, error-prone part of the code (yours).

DEFINING BEHAVIORS

Defining your own behaviors is really simple. You just need to export a function called behavior_info/1, implemented as follows:

```
-module(my_behavior).
-export([behavior_info/1]).

%% init/1, some_fun/0 and other/3 are now expected callbacks.
behavior_info(callbacks) -> [{init,1}, {some_fun, 0}, {other, 3}];
behavior_info(_) -> undefined.
```

And that's about it for behaviors. You can just use -behavior(my_behavior). in a module, implementing behaviors to get compiler warnings if you forgot a function.

The first function we had for our kitty server was start_link/0. This one can be changed to the following:

```
start_link() -> gen_server:start_link(?MODULE, [], []).
```

The first parameter is the callback module, the second one is a term to pass to init/1, and the third one is about debugging options for running servers. You could add a fourth parameter in the first position: {local, *Name*}, which is the name to register the server with. Note that while the previous version of the function simply returned a pid, this one instead returns {ok, Pid}.

The next functions are now as follows:

```
%% Synchronous call
order_cat(Pid, Name, Color, Description) ->
    gen_server:call(Pid, {order, Name, Color, Description}).

%% This call is asynchronous.
return_cat(Pid, Cat = #cat{}) ->
    gen_server:cast(Pid, {return, Cat}).

%% Synchronous call
close_shop(Pid) ->
    gen_server:call(Pid, terminate).
```

All of these calls are equivalent to those we had in my_server. Note that a third parameter can be passed to gen_server:call to give a timeout, in milliseconds. If you don't give a timeout to the function (or the atom infinity), the default is set to 5 seconds. If no reply is received before the time is up, the call crashes. This is an entirely arbitrary value, and many Erlang regulars will tell you that it should be changed to default to infinity. In my own experience, I often wanted replies to come in faster than 5 seconds, and having this timer force crashes has generally helped me diagnose more important problems.

Now we'll be able to add the gen_server callbacks. Table 14-1 shows the relationship we have between calls and callbacks.

Table 14-1: Relationship Between Calls and Callbacks

gen_server	YourModule
start/3-4	init/1
start_link/3-4	init/1
call/2-3	handle_call/3
cast/2	handle_cast/2

And then we have the other callbacks, which are more about special cases: handle_info/2, terminate/2, and code_change/3.

Let's begin by changing those we already have to fit the model: init/1, handle_call/3, and handle_cast/2.

```
%%% Server functions
init([]) -> {ok, []}. %% no treatment of info here!

handle_call({order, Name, Color, Description}, _From, Cats) ->
    if Cats =:= [] ->
        {reply, make_cat(Name, Color, Description), Cats};
    Cats =/= [] ->
        {reply, hd(Cats), tl(Cats)}
    end;
```

```
handle_call(terminate, _From, Cats) ->
    {stop, normal, ok, Cats}.

handle_cast({return, Cat = #cat{}}, Cats) ->
    {noreply, [Cat|Cats]}.
```

Again, very little has changed here. In fact, the code is now shorter, thanks to smarter abstractions.

Now we get to the new callbacks. The first one is handle_info/2. Given this is a toy module and we have no logging system predefined, just outputting the unexpected messages will be enough.

```
handle_info(Msg, Cats) ->
    io:format("Unexpected message: ~p~n",[Msg]),
    {noreply, Cats}.
```

As a general rule of thumb, always log unexpected messages in handle_cast/2 and handle_info/2. You might also want to log them in handle_call/3, but generally speaking, not replying to calls (coupled with the default 5 seconds timeout) is enough to achieve the same result.

The next one is the terminate/2 callback. It will be very similar to the terminate/1 private function we used earlier.

```
terminate(normal, Cats) ->
    [io:format("~p was set free.~n",[C#cat.name]) || C <- Cats],
    ok.
```

And here's the last callback, code_change/3:

```
code_change(_OldVsn, State, _Extra) ->
    %% No change planned. The function is there for the behavior,
    %% but will not be used.
    {ok, State}.
```

Just remember to keep in the make_cat/3 private function:

```
%%% Private functions
make_cat(Name, Col, Desc) ->
    #cat{name=Name, color=Col, description=Desc}.
```

And we can now try the brand-new code:

```
1> c(kitty_gen_server).
{ok,kitty_gen_server}
2> rr(kitty_gen_server).
[cat]
3> {ok, Pid} = kitty_gen_server:start_link().
{ok,<0.253.0>}
```

```
4> Pid ! <<"Test handle_info">>.
Unexpected message: <<"Test handle_info">>
<<"Test handle_info">>
5> Cat = kitty_gen_server:order_cat(Pid, "Cat Stevens",
5>      white, "not actually a cat").
#cat{name = "Cat Stevens",color = white,
     description = "not actually a cat"}
6> kitty_gen_server:return_cat(Pid, Cat).
ok
7> kitty_gen_server:order_cat(Pid, "Kitten Mittens",
7>     black, "look at them little paws!").
#cat{name = "Cat Stevens",color = white,
     description = "not actually a cat"}
```

Because we returned the Cat cat to the server, it's given back to us before we can order anything new. If we try again, we should get what we want:

```
8> kitty_gen_server:order_cat(Pid, "Kitten Mittens",
8>     black, "look at them little paws!").
#cat{name = "Kitten Mittens",color = black,
     description = "look at them little paws!"}
9> kitty_gen_server:return_cat(Pid, Cat).
ok
10> kitty_gen_server:close_shop(Pid).
"Cat Stevens" was set free.
ok
```

Hot damn, it works!

So what can we say about this generic adventure? Probably the same generic stuff as before: Separating the generic from the specific is a great idea on every point. Maintenance is simpler. Complexity is reduced. The code is safer, easier to test, and less prone to bugs. And if there are bugs, they are easier to fix.

Generic servers are only one of the many available abstractions, but they're certainly one of the most used ones. We'll explore more of these abstractions and behaviors in the next chapters.

15

RAGE AGAINST THE FINITE-STATE MACHINES

Finite-state machines are a central part of numerous implementations of important protocols in the industrial world. They allow programmers to represent complex procedures and sequences of events in a way that can be understood with ease.

Although the most mathematically inclined readers might know finite-state machines under stricter mathematical definitions, the finite-state machines used in Erlang are more inspired by them than a direct implementation. A typical Erlang finite-state machine can be implemented as a process running a given set of functions (their states) and receiving messages (events) that force a state transition.

They were used so frequently in the telecom world that the OTP engineers ended up writing a behavior for them: gen_fsm.

This chapter introduces the concept of finite-state machines as used in the Erlang world and its OTP counterpart. We'll experiment with them by designing a fully asynchronous, message-based protocol for a client-to-client trading system that could be added to a video game.

What Is a Finite-State Machine?

A finite-state machine (FSM) is not really a machine, but it does have a finite number of states. I've always found FSMs easier to understand with graphs and diagrams. For example, the following is a simplistic diagram for a (very dumb) dog as a state machine:

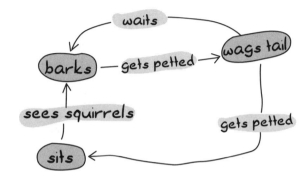

Here, the dog has three states: sitting, barking, or wagging his tail. Different events or inputs may force the dog to change his state. If a dog is calmly sitting and sees a squirrel, he will start barking and won't stop until you pet him again. However, if the dog is sitting and you pet him, we have no idea what might happen. In the Erlang world, the dog could crash (and eventually be restarted by his supervisor). In the real world, restarting your dog would be pretty unusual (and a little freaky), though that would mean the dog could come back after being run over by a car, so it's not all bad.

Here's a cat's state diagram for comparison:

This cat has a single state, and no event can ever change it. Implementing the cat state machine in Erlang is a fun and simple task:

```erlang
-module(cat_fsm).
-export([start/0, event/2]).

start() ->
    spawn(fun() -> dont_give_crap() end).

event(Pid, Event) ->
    Ref = make_ref(), % won't care for monitors here
    Pid ! {self(), Ref, Event},
    receive
        {Ref, Msg} -> {ok, Msg}
```

```
    after 5000 ->
        {error, timeout}
    end.

dont_give_crap() ->
    receive
        {Pid, Ref, _Msg} -> Pid ! {Ref, meh};
        _ -> ok
    end,
    io:format("Switching to 'dont_give_crap' state~n"),
    dont_give_crap().
```

We can try the module to see that the cat really never gives a crap:

```
1> c(cat_fsm).
{ok,cat_fsm}
2> Cat = cat_fsm:start().
<0.67.0>
3> cat_fsm:event(Cat, pet).
Switching to 'dont_give_crap' state
{ok,meh}
4> cat_fsm:event(Cat, love).
Switching to 'dont_give_crap' state
{ok,meh}
5> cat_fsm:event(Cat, cherish).
Switching to 'dont_give_crap' state
{ok,meh}
```

The same can be done for the dog FSM, except more states are available:

```
-module(dog_fsm).
-export([start/0, squirrel/1, pet/1]).

start() -> spawn(fun() -> bark() end).

squirrel(Pid) -> Pid ! squirrel.

pet(Pid) -> Pid ! pet.

bark() ->
    io:format("Dog says: BARK! BARK!~n"),
    receive
        pet ->
            wag_tail();
        _ ->
            io:format("Dog is confused~n"),
            bark()
    after 2000 ->
        bark()
    end.

wag_tail() ->
    io:format("Dog wags its tail~n"),
```

```
    receive
        pet ->
            sit();
        _ ->
            io:format("Dog is confused~n"),
            wag_tail()
    after 30000 ->
        bark()
    end.

sit() ->
    io:format("Dog is sitting. Gooooood boy!~n"),
    receive
        squirrel ->
            bark();
        _ ->
            io:format("Dog is confused~n"),
            sit()
    end.
```

It should be relatively simple to match each of the states and transitions to those shown in the dog's state diagram. Here's the FSM in use:

```
6> c(dog_fsm).
{ok,dog_fsm}
7> Pid = dog_fsm:start().
Dog says: BARK! BARK!
<0.46.0>
Dog says: BARK! BARK!
Dog says: BARK! BARK!
Dog says: BARK! BARK!
8> dog_fsm:pet(Pid).
pet
Dog wags its tail
9> dog_fsm:pet(Pid).
Dog is sitting. Gooooood boy!
pet
10> dog_fsm:pet(Pid).
Dog is confused
pet
Dog is sitting. Gooooood boy!
11> dog_fsm:squirrel(Pid).
Dog says: BARK! BARK!
squirrel
Dog says: BARK! BARK!
12> dog_fsm:pet(Pid).
Dog wags its tail
pet
❶ 13> %% wait 30 seconds
Dog says: BARK! BARK!
Dog says: BARK! BARK!
Dog says: BARK! BARK!
```

```
13> dog_fsm:pet(Pid).
Dog wags its tail
pet
14> dog_fsm:pet(Pid).
Dog is sitting. Gooooood boy!
pet
```

You can follow along with the schema if you want (I usually do, since it helps me to make sure that nothing is wrong). Note that at ❶, the command entered is strictly a comment intended for the reader, although the Erlang shell deals with it fine.

That's really the core of FSMs implemented as Erlang processes. There are things that could have been done differently. We could have passed state in the arguments of the state functions in a way similar to what we do with a server's main loop. We could also have added init and terminate functions, handled code updates, and so on.

A difference between the dog and cat FSMs is that the cat's events are *synchronous* and the dog's events are *asynchronous*. In a real FSM, both could be used in a mixed manner, but I went for the simplest representation out of pure, untapped laziness.

There is also another event form the examples do not show: global events that can happen in any state. One example of such an event could be when the dog gets a sniff of food. Once the "smell food" event is triggered, no matter which state the dog is in, he will go looking for the source of food.

We won't spend too much time implementing all of this in our "written-on-a-napkin" FSM. Instead, we'll move directly to the gen_fsm behavior.

Generic Finite-State Machines

The gen_fsm behavior is somewhat similar to gen_server in that it is a specialized version of that behavior. The biggest difference is that rather than handling *calls* and *casts*, we're handling *synchronous* and *asynchronous* events. Similar to our dog and cat examples, each state is represented by a function. Here, we'll go through the callbacks our modules need to implement in order to work.

The init Function

The init function for FSMs is the same init/1 as used for generic servers, except the return values accepted are {ok, StateName, Data}, {ok, StateName, Data, Timeout}, {ok, StateName, Data, hibernate}, and {stop, Reason}. The stop tuple works in the same manner as for gen_server, and both hibernate and Timeout keep the same semantics.

What's new here is the StateName variable. StateName is an atom and represents the next callback function to be called. For our dog, this would be the bark state.

The StateName Function

The functions StateName/2 and StateName/3 are placeholder names, and you decide what they will be. Let's suppose the init/1 function returns the tuple {ok, sitting, dog}. This means the FSM will be in the sitting state. This is not the same kind of state as we have seen with gen_server, but more like the sit, bark, and wag_tail states of our dog FSM. These states dictate a context in which you handle a given event.

As an example, consider someone calling you on your phone. If you're in the state "sleeping on a Saturday morning," your reaction might be to yell at the phone. If your state is "waiting for a job interview," chances are you'll pick up the phone and answer politely. On the other hand, if you're in the state "dead," then I am surprised you can even read this text at all.

In our FSM, the init/1 function said we should be in the sitting state. Whenever the gen_fsm process receives an event, either the function sitting/2 or sitting/3 will be called. The sitting/2 function is called for asynchronous events, and sitting/3 is called for synchronous events.

The arguments for sitting/2 (or generally StateName/2) are Event, the actual message sent as an event, and StateData, the data that was carried over the calls. The sitting/2 function can then return the tuples {next_state, NextStateName, NewStateData}, {next_state, NextStateName, NewStateData, Timeout}, {next_state, NextStateName, hibernate}, and {stop, Reason, NewStateData}.

The arguments for sitting/3 are similar, except there is a From variable in between Event and StateData. The From variable is used in exactly the same way as it is for gen_server, including gen_fsm:reply/2. The StateName/3 functions can return the following tuples:

```
{reply, Reply, NextStateName, NewStateData}
{reply, Reply, NextStateName, NewStateData, Timeout}
{reply, Reply, NextStateName, NewStateData, hibernate}

{next_state, NextStateName, NewStateData}
{next_state, NextStateName, NewStateData, Timeout}
{next_state, NextStateName, NewStateData, hibernate}

{stop, Reason, Reply, NewStateData}
{stop, Reason, NewStateData}
```

Note that there's no limit on how many of these functions you can have, as long as they are exported. The atoms returned as NextStateName in the tuples will determine whether or not the function will be called.

The handle_event Function

Earlier, I mentioned global events, which trigger a specific reaction no matter what state we're in (the dog smelling food will drop whatever he is doing and look for food). For these events that should be treated the same way in every state, the handle_event/3 callback is what you want. The function takes arguments similar to StateName/2, with the exception that it accepts a StateName variable in between them (handle_event(Event, StateName, Data)), telling you what the state was when the event was received. It returns the same values as StateName/2.

The handle_sync_event Function

The handle_sync_event/4 callback is to StateName/3 what handle_event/2 is to StateName/2. It handles synchronous global events, takes the same parameters, and returns the same kind of tuples as StateName/3.

Now might be a good time to explain how we know whether an event is global or if it's meant to be sent to a specific state. To determine this, we can look at the function used to send an event to the FSM. Asynchronous events aimed at any StateName/2 function are sent with gen_fsm:send_event/2, and synchronous events to be picked up by StateName/3 are sent with gen_fsm:sync_send_event/2-3 (the optional third argument is the timeout).

The two equivalent functions for global events are gen_fsm:send_all_state_event/2 and gen_fsm:sync_send_all_state_event/2-3 (quite a long name).

The code_change and terminate Functions

The code_change function works exactly the same as it does for gen_server, except that it takes an extra state parameter when called, such as code_change(OldVersion, StateName, Data, Extra), and returns a tuple of the form {ok, NextStateName, NewStateData}.

Similarly, terminate acts a bit like what we have for generic servers. terminate(Reason, StateName, Data) should do the opposite of init/1.

A Trading System Specification

It's time to put all of this information about FSMs into practice. Many Erlang tutorials about FSMs use examples containing telephone switches and the like. It's my guess that most programmers will rarely need to deal with telephone switches for state machines. Here, we'll look at an example that is more fitting for many developers. We'll design and implement an item trading system for a fictional video game.

The design I have picked is somewhat challenging. Rather than using a central broker through which players route items and confirmations (which, frankly, would be easier), we're going to implement a server where both players speak to each other directly (which has the advantage of being easily distributable).

Show Me Your Moves

To begin, we should define the actions that can be taken by our players when trading. The first is asking for a trade to be set up. The other user should also be able to accept that trade. We won't give the players the right to deny a trade, though, because we want to keep things simple. It would be easy to add that feature later.

Once the trade is set up, our users should be able to negotiate with each other. This means they should be able to make offers and also to retract those offers. When both players are satisfied with the offer, they can declare themselves as ready to finalize the trade. The data should then be saved somewhere on both sides. At any point in time, the players should be able to cancel the whole trade. Some pleb could be offering only items deemed unworthy to the other party (who might be very busy), and so it should be possible to backhand that player with a well-deserved cancellation.

In short, the following actions should be possible:

- Ask for a trade.
- Accept a trade.
- Offer items.
- Retract an offer.
- Declare self as ready.
- Brutally cancel the trade.

When each of these actions is taken, the other player's FSM should be made aware of it. This makes sense, because when you're playing the game and Jim tells his FSM to send an item to you, your FSM must be made aware of it. This means both players can talk to their own FSM, which will talk to the other's FSM. This gives us something a bit like this:

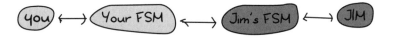

The first thing to notice when we have two identical processes communicating with each other is that we need to avoid synchronous calls as much as possible. If Jim's FSM sends a message to your FSM and then waits for its reply, while at the same time, your FSM sends a message over to Jim's FSM and waits for its own specific reply, both end up waiting for the other without ever replying. This effectively freezes both FSMs. We have a *deadlock*.

One solution is to wait for a timeout and then move on, but then there will be leftover messages in both processes' mailboxes, and the protocol will be messed up. This certainly is a can of worms, and so we want to avoid it.

The simplest way to handle this is to go fully asynchronous. Note that Jim might still make a synchronous call to his own FSM; there's no risk here because the FSM won't need to call Jim, and so no deadlock can occur between them.

When two of these FSMs communicate together, the whole exchange might look a bit like this:

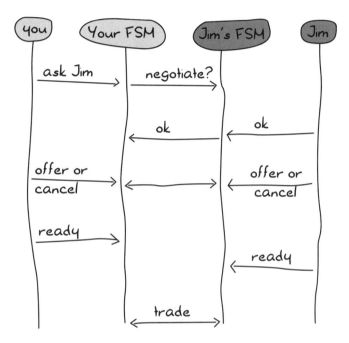

Both FSMs are in an idle state. When you ask Jim to trade, Jim needs to accept before things move on. Then both you and Jim can offer items or withdraw them. When both players declare themselves ready, the trade can take place. This is a simplified version of all that can happen. We'll consider all possible cases as we implement the trading system.

Defining the State Diagrams and Transitions

Here comes the tough part: defining the state diagrams and how state transitions happen. Usually, a good bit of thinking goes into this, because you need to consider all the small things that could go wrong (and some things might go wrong even after you've reviewed the definitions many times). Here's the one I decided to implement:

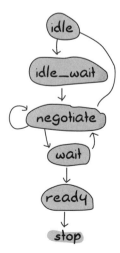

At first, both FSMs start in the idle state. At this point, one thing we can do is ask some other player to negotiate with us:

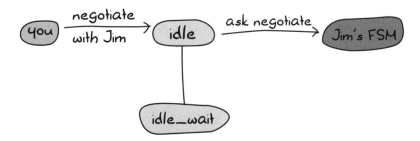

We go into idle_wait mode in order to wait for an eventual reply after our FSM forwarded the request. Once the other FSM sends the reply, ours can switch to negotiate:

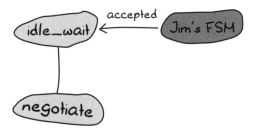

The other player should also be in the negotiate state after this. Obviously, if we can invite the other player, the other player can invite us. If all goes well, the diagram should end up looking like this:

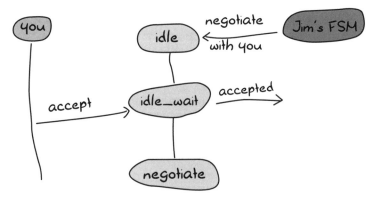

So this is pretty much the opposite of the two previous state diagrams bundled into one. Note that we expect the player to accept the offer in this case.

What happens if, by pure chance, we ask the other player to trade with us at the same time he asks us to trade?

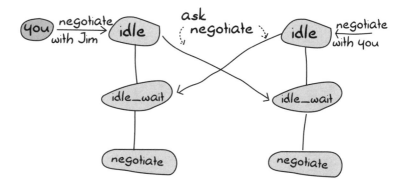

In this case, both clients ask their own FSM to negotiate with the other one. As soon as the ask negotiate messages are sent, both FSMs switch to `idle_wait` state. Then they will be able to process the negotiation question. Reviewing the previous state diagrams, we see that this combination of events is the only time we'll receive ask negotiate messages while in the `idle_wait` state. Consequently, we know that getting these messages in `idle_wait` means that we hit the race condition and can assume both users want to talk to each other. We can move both of them to the `negotiate` state.

So now we're negotiating. Good for us! According to the actions listed earlier, we must support users offering items and then retracting the offer:

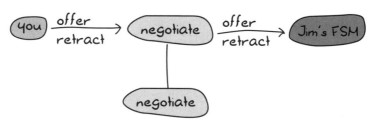

All this does is forward our client's message to the other FSM. Both FSMs will need to hold a list of items offered by either player, so they can update that list when receiving such messages. We stay in the `negotiate` state after this; maybe the other player wants to offer items:

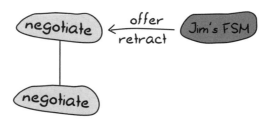

Here, our FSM basically acts in a similar manner by remaining in the `negotiate` state. This is normal.

Once we get tired of offering things and think we're generous enough, we need to say we're ready to officialize the trade. Because we must synchronize both players, we'll need to use an intermediary state, as we did for idle and idle_wait:

Here, as soon as our player is ready, our FSM asks Jim's FSM if he is ready. Pending its reply, our own FSM falls into its wait state. The reply we'll get will depend on Jim's FSM state. If it's in wait state, it will tell us that it's ready. Otherwise, it will tell us that it's not ready yet. That's precisely what our FSM automatically replies to Jim if he asks us if we are ready when in negotiate state:

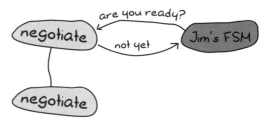

Our FSM will remain in negotiate mode until our player says he is ready. Let's assume he did and we're now in the wait state. However, Jim's not there yet. This means that when we declared ourselves as ready, we'll have asked Jim if he was also ready and his FSM will have replied "not yet":

He is not ready, but we are. We can't do much but keep waiting. While waiting for Jim (who is still negotiating, by the way), it is possible that he will try to send us more items or maybe cancel his previous offers:

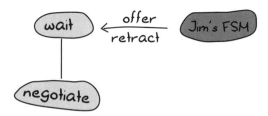

Of course, we want to avoid Jim removing all of his items and then clicking "I'm ready," screwing us over in the process. As soon as he changes the items offered, we go back into the negotiate state so we can either modify our own offer or examine the current one and decide we're ready. Rinse and repeat.

At some point, Jim will be ready to finalize the trade, too. When this happens, his FSM will ask ours if we are ready:

Then our FSM replies that we indeed are ready. We stay in the wait state and refuse to move to the ready state though. Why is this? Because there's a potential race condition! Imagine that the following sequence of events takes place, without doing this necessary step:

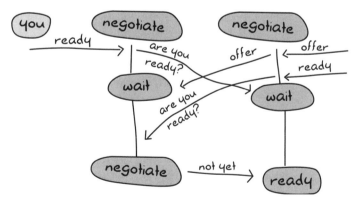

Because of the way messages are received, we could possibly process the item offer only *after* we declared ourselves ready and also *after* Jim declared himself as ready. This means that as soon as we read the offer message, we switch back to the negotiate state. During that time, Jim will have told us he is ready. If he were to change states right there and move on to ready (as in the preceding illustration), he would be caught waiting indefinitely, while we wouldn't know what the hell to do. This could also happen the other way around!

One way to solve this is by adding a layer of indirection (thanks to David Wheeler). This is why we stay in wait mode and send "ready!" (as shown in our previous state diagram).

NOTE *David Wheeler, a computer scientist* (http://en.wikipedia.org/wiki/David_Wheeler_(computer_scientist)), *is often quoted as saying, "All problems in computer science can be solved by another level of indirection . . . except for the problem of too many layers of indirection."*

Here's how we deal with that "ready!" message, assuming we were already in the ready state because we told our FSM we were ready beforehand:

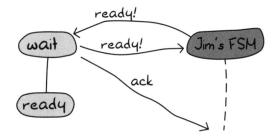

When we receive "ready!" from the other FSM, we send "ready!" back again. This is to make sure that we won't have the double race condition mentioned earlier. This will create a superfluous "ready!" message in one of the two FSMs, but we'll just have to ignore it in this case. We then send an "ack" message (and Jim's FSM will do the same) before moving to the ready state. The "ack" message exists due to some implementation details about synchronizing clients, which we'll look at later in the chapter. Whew—we finally managed to synchronize both players.

So now there's the ready state. This one is a bit special. Both players are ready and have basically given the FSMs all the control they need. This lets us implement a bastardized version of a *two-phase commit* to make sure things go right when making the trade official:

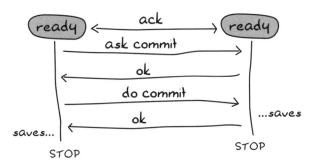

Our version (as described above) will be rather simplistic. Writing a truly correct two-phase commit would require a lot more code than what is necessary for us to understand FSMs. (For more information about two-phase commits, see *http://en.wikipedia.org/wiki/Two_phase_commit*.)

Finally, we need to allow the trade to be canceled at any time. This means that somehow—no matter what state we're in—we'll need to listen to the "cancel" message from either side and quit the transaction. It should also be common courtesy to let the other side know we're going before leaving.

At this point, we've covered a whole lot of information. Don't worry if it takes a while to fully grasp the concepts. A bunch of people looked over my protocol to see if it was right, and even then, we all missed a few race conditions, which I caught a few days later when reviewing the code. It's normal to need to read the code more than once, especially if you are not used to asynchronous protocols. If this is the case, I fully encourage you to try to design your own protocol. Then ask yourself these questions:

- What happens if two people do the same actions very fast?
- What if they chain two other events quickly?
- What do I do with messages I don't handle when changing states?

You'll see that the complexity grows quickly. You might find a solution similar to mine, or possibly a better one (let me know if this is the case!). No matter the outcome, it's a very interesting problem to work on, and our FSMs are still relatively simple.

Once you've digested all of this (or before, if you're a rebel reader), you can move on to the next section, where we implement the gaming system. For now, you can take a nice coffee break if you feel like doing so.

Game Trading Between Two Players

Now we'll implement our trading system protocol with OTP's gen_fsm. The first step is to create the interface.

The Public Interface

There will be three callers for our module: the player, the gen_fsm behavior, and the other player's FSM. We will need to export only the player function and gen_fsm functions, though. This is because the other FSM will also run within the trade_fsm module and can access them from the inside.

```
-module(trade_fsm).
-behavior(gen_fsm).

%% public API
-export([start/1, start_link/1, trade/2, accept_trade/1,
         make_offer/2, retract_offer/2, ready/1, cancel/1]).
%% gen_fsm callbacks
-export([init/1, handle_event/3, handle_sync_event/4, handle_info/3,
         terminate/3, code_change/4,
         % custom state names
         idle/2, idle/3, idle_wait/2, idle_wait/3, negotiate/2,
         negotiate/3, wait/2, ready/2, ready/3]).
```

So that's our API. You can see we'll have some functions that will be both synchronous and asynchronous (idle/2 and idle/3, for example). This is mostly because we want our client to call us synchronously in some cases, but the other FSM can do it asynchronously. Having the client synchronous simplifies our logic a whole lot by limiting the number of contradicting messages that can be sent one after the other. We'll get to that part when we add the gen_fsm callbacks later. Let's first implement the actual public API according to the preceding protocol definition.

```
%%% PUBLIC API
start(Name) ->
    gen_fsm:start(?MODULE, [Name], []).

start_link(Name) ->
    gen_fsm:start_link(?MODULE, [Name], []).

%% Ask for a begin session. Returns when/if the other accepts.
trade(OwnPid, OtherPid) ->
    gen_fsm:sync_send_event(OwnPid, {negotiate, OtherPid}, 30000).

%% Accept someone's trade offer.
accept_trade(OwnPid) ->
    gen_fsm:sync_send_event(OwnPid, accept_negotiate).

%% Send an item on the table to be traded.
make_offer(OwnPid, Item) ->
    gen_fsm:send_event(OwnPid, {make_offer, Item}).

%% Cancel trade offer.
retract_offer(OwnPid, Item) ->
    gen_fsm:send_event(OwnPid, {retract_offer, Item}).

%% Mention that you're ready for a trade. When the other
%% player also declares they're ready, the trade is done.
ready(OwnPid) ->
    gen_fsm:sync_send_event(OwnPid, ready, infinity).
```

```
%% Cancel the transaction.
cancel(OwnPid) ->
    gen_fsm:sync_send_all_state_event(OwnPid, cancel).
```

This is rather standard, and we've already covered these gen_fsm functions (except start/3-4 and start_link/3-4, which I believe you can figure out) in this chapter.

FSM-to-FSM Functions

Next, we'll implement the FSM-to-FSM functions. The first ones have to do with trade setups, when we want to invite the other user to join us in a trade.

```
%% Ask the other FSM's Pid for a trade session.
ask_negotiate(OtherPid, OwnPid) ->
    gen_fsm:send_event(OtherPid, {ask_negotiate, OwnPid}).

%% Forward the client message accepting the transaction.
accept_negotiate(OtherPid, OwnPid) ->
    gen_fsm:send_event(OtherPid, {accept_negotiate, OwnPid}).
```

The first function asks the other pid if it wants to trade, and the second one is used to reply (asynchronously, of course).

We can then write the functions to offer and cancel offers. According to our protocol, this is how these functions should look:

```
%% Forward a client's offer.
do_offer(OtherPid, Item) ->
    gen_fsm:send_event(OtherPid, {do_offer, Item}).

%% Forward a client's offer cancellation.
undo_offer(OtherPid, Item) ->
    gen_fsm:send_event(OtherPid, {undo_offer, Item}).
```

The next calls relate to being ready for trade or not. Again, given our protocol, we have three messages in total. The first is are_you_ready, which can have the two messages not_yet or 'ready!' as replies.

```
%% Ask the other side if he's ready to trade.
are_you_ready(OtherPid) ->
    gen_fsm:send_event(OtherPid, are_you_ready).

%% Reply that the side is not ready to trade,
%% i.e. is not in 'wait' state.
not_yet(OtherPid) ->
    gen_fsm:send_event(OtherPid, not_yet).

%% Tells the other fsm that the user is currently waiting
%% for the ready state. State should transition to 'ready'.
am_ready(OtherPid) ->
    gen_fsm:send_event(OtherPid, 'ready!').
```

The other functions are those that are to be used by both FSMs when doing the commit in the ready state. Their precise usage will be described in more detail later in the chapter, but their names and the sequence/state diagram shown earlier should give you an idea of their purpose, and you can still transcribe them to your own version of trade_fsm.

```
%% Acknowledge that the fsm is in a ready state.
ack_trans(OtherPid) ->
    gen_fsm:send_event(OtherPid, ack).

%% Ask if ready to commit.
ask_commit(OtherPid) ->
    gen_fsm:sync_send_event(OtherPid, ask_commit).

%% Begin the synchronous commit.
do_commit(OtherPid) ->
    gen_fsm:sync_send_event(OtherPid, do_commit).
```

Oh, and there's also the courtesy function allowing us to warn the other FSM we canceled the trade:

```
notify_cancel(OtherPid) ->
    gen_fsm:send_all_state_event(OtherPid, cancel).
```

The gen_fsm Callbacks

We can now move to the really interesting part: the gen_fsm callbacks. The first callback is init/1. In our case, we'll want each FSM to hold a name for the user it represents (that way, our output will be nicer) in the data it keeps passing on to itself as the last argument of each callback. What else do we want to hold in memory? In our case, we want the other player's (Jim's) FSM pid, the items we offer, and the items the other player's FSM offers. We'll also add the reference of a monitor (so we know to abort if the other dies) and a from field, used to do delayed replies.

```
-record(state, {name="",
                other,
                ownitems=[],
                otheritems=[],
                monitor,
                from}).
```

In the case of init/1, we'll only care about our name for now. Note that we'll begin in the idle state.

```
init(Name) ->
    {ok, idle, #state{name=Name}}.
```

The next callbacks to consider are the states themselves. So far, we have covered the state transitions and calls that can be made, but we'll need a way to make sure everything goes all right. We'll write a few utility functions first.

```erlang
%% Send players a notice. This could be messages to their clients
%% but for our purposes, outputting to the shell is enough.
notice(#state{name=N}, Str, Args) ->
    io:format("~s: "++Str++"~n", [N|Args]).

%% Allows to log unexpected messages.
unexpected(Msg, State) ->
    io:format("~p received unknown event ~p while in state ~p~n",
              [self(), Msg, State]).
```

And we can start with the idle state. For the sake of convention, we'll cover the asynchronous version first. This part of the idle state callbacks shouldn't need to care about anything but the *other player* asking for a trade. This is because our own player, if you look at the API functions, will use a synchronous call and will therefore need a different callback, with three arguments.

```erlang
idle({ask_negotiate, OtherPid}, S=#state{}) ->
    Ref = monitor(process, OtherPid),
    notice(S, "~p asked for a trade negotiation", [OtherPid]),
    {next_state, idle_wait, S#state{other=OtherPid, monitor=Ref}};
idle(Event, Data) ->
    unexpected(Event, idle),
    {next_state, idle, Data}.
```

A monitor is set up to allow us to handle the other dying, and its reference is stored in the FSM's data along with the other's pid, before moving to the idle_wait state. Note that we will report all unexpected events and ignore them by staying in the state we were already in. We can have a few out-of-band messages here and there that could be the result of race conditions. It's usually safe to ignore them, but we can't easily get rid of them. It's just better not to crash the whole FSM on receipt of these unknown but somewhat expected messages.

When our own client asks the FSM to contact another player for a trade, it will send a synchronous event. The idle/3 callback will be needed.

```erlang
idle({negotiate, OtherPid}, From, S=#state{}) ->
    ask_negotiate(OtherPid, self()),
    notice(S, "asking user ~p for a trade", [OtherPid]),
    Ref = monitor(process, OtherPid),
    {next_state, idle_wait, S#state{other=OtherPid, monitor=Ref, from=From}};
idle(Event, _From, Data) ->
    unexpected(Event, idle),
    {next_state, idle, Data}.
```

We proceed in a way similar to the asynchronous version, except we need to actually ask the other side whether it wants to negotiate with us. You'll notice that we do not reply to the client yet. This is because we have nothing interesting to say, and we want the client locked and waiting for the trade to be accepted before doing anything. The reply will be sent only if the other side accepts once we're in idle_wait.

When we're there, we need to deal with the other player agreeing to negotiate following our invitation or asking to negotiate at the same time we did (a race condition, as described in the protocol).

```erlang
idle_wait({ask_negotiate, OtherPid}, S=#state{other=OtherPid}) ->
    gen_fsm:reply(S#state.from, ok),
    notice(S, "starting negotiation", []),
    {next_state, negotiate, S};
%% The other side has accepted our offer. Move to negotiate state.
idle_wait({accept_negotiate, OtherPid}, S=#state{other=OtherPid}) ->
    gen_fsm:reply(S#state.from, ok),
    notice(S, "starting negotiation", []),
    {next_state, negotiate, S};
idle_wait(Event, Data) ->
    unexpected(Event, idle_wait),
    {next_state, idle_wait, Data}.
```

This gives us two transitions to the negotiate state, but remember that we must use gen_fsm:reply/2 to reply to our client to say it's okay to start offering items. There's also the case of our FSM's client accepting the trade suggested by the other party.

```erlang
idle_wait(accept_negotiate, _From, S=#state{other=OtherPid}) ->
    accept_negotiate(OtherPid, self()),
    notice(S, "accepting negotiation", []),
    {reply, ok, negotiate, S};
idle_wait(Event, _From, Data) ->
    unexpected(Event, idle_wait),
    {next_state, idle_wait, Data}.
```

Again, this one moves on to the negotiate state. Here, we must handle asynchronous queries to add and remove items coming both from the client and the other FSM. However, we have not yet decided how to store items. Let's say we're somewhat lazy and assume users won't trade that many items, so simple lists will do it for now. However, we might need to change that later, so it would be a good idea to wrap item operations in their own functions. Add the following functions at the bottom of the file with notice/3 and unexpected/2:

```erlang
%% Adds an item to an item list.
add(Item, Items) ->
    [Item | Items].
```

```
%% Removes an item from an item list.
remove(Item, Items) ->
    Items -- [Item].
```

These functions are simple, but they have the role of isolating the actions (adding and removing items) from their implementation (using lists). We could easily move to proplists, dicts, or any other data structure without disrupting the rest of the code.

Using both of these functions, we can implement offering and removing items:

```
negotiate({make_offer, Item}, S=#state{ownitems=OwnItems}) ->
    do_offer(S#state.other, Item),
    notice(S, "offering ~p", [Item]),
    {next_state, negotiate, S#state{ownitems=add(Item, OwnItems)}};
%% Own side retracting an item offer.
negotiate({retract_offer, Item}, S=#state{ownitems=OwnItems}) ->
    undo_offer(S#state.other, Item),
    notice(S, "cancelling offer on ~p", [Item]),
    {next_state, negotiate, S#state{ownitems=remove(Item, OwnItems)}};
%% Other side offering an item.
negotiate({do_offer, Item}, S=#state{otheritems=OtherItems}) ->
    notice(S, "other player offering ~p", [Item]),
    {next_state, negotiate, S#state{otheritems=add(Item, OtherItems)}};
%% Other side retracting an item offer.
negotiate({undo_offer, Item}, S=#state{otheritems=OtherItems}) ->
    notice(S, "Other player cancelling offer on ~p", [Item]),
    {next_state, negotiate, S#state{otheritems=remove(Item, OtherItems)}};
```

This is an ugly aspect of using asynchronous messages on both sides. One set of messages has the form "make" and "retract," while the other has "do" and "undo." This is entirely arbitrary and only used to differentiate between player-to-FSM communications and FSM-to-FSM communications. Note that in those messages coming from our own player, we need to tell the other side about the changes we're making.

Another responsibility is to handle the are_you_ready message in the protocol. This is the last asynchronous event to handle in the negotiate state.

```
negotiate(are_you_ready, S=#state{other=OtherPid}) ->
    io:format("Other user ready to trade.~n"),
    notice(S,
           "Other user ready to transfer goods:~n"
           "You get ~p, The other side gets ~p",
           [S#state.otheritems, S#state.ownitems]),
    not_yet(OtherPid),
    {next_state, negotiate, S};
negotiate(Event, Data) ->
    unexpected(Event, negotiate),
    {next_state, negotiate, Data}.
```

As described in the protocol, whenever we're not in the `wait` state and receive this message, we must reply with `not_yet`. We're also outputting trade details to the user so a decision can be made.

When such a decision is made and the user is ready, the `ready` event will be sent. This one should be synchronous because we don't want the user to keep modifying his offer by adding items while claiming he is ready.

```
negotiate(ready, From, S = #state{other=OtherPid}) ->
    are_you_ready(OtherPid),
    notice(S, "asking if ready, waiting", []),
    {next_state, wait, S#state{from=From}};
negotiate(Event, _From, S) ->
    unexpected(Event, negotiate),
    {next_state, negotiate, S}.
```

At this point, a transition to the `wait` state should be made. Note that just waiting for the other player is not interesting. We save the `From` variable so we can use it with `gen_fsm:reply/2` when we have something to tell the client.

The `wait` state is a funny beast. New items might be offered and retracted because the other player might not be ready. So it makes sense to automatically roll back to the `negotiate` state. It would suck to have great items offered to us, only for the other player to remove them and declare himself ready, stealing our loot. Going back to negotiation is a good decision.

```
wait({do_offer, Item}, S=#state{otheritems=OtherItems}) ->
    gen_fsm:reply(S#state.from, offer_changed),
    notice(S, "other side offering ~p", [Item]),
    {next_state, negotiate, S#state{otheritems=add(Item, OtherItems)}};
wait({undo_offer, Item}, S=#state{otheritems=OtherItems}) ->
    gen_fsm:reply(S#state.from, offer_changed),
    notice(S, "Other side cancelling offer of ~p", [Item]),
    {next_state, negotiate, S#state{otheritems=remove(Item, OtherItems)}};
```

Now that's something meaningful, and we reply to the player with the coordinates we stored in `S#state.from`.

The next messages we need to worry about are those related to synchronizing both FSMs so they can move to the `ready` state and confirm the trade. For this set, we should really focus on the protocol defined earlier.

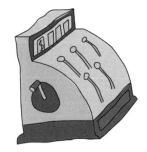

The three messages we could have are `are_you_ready` (because the other player just declared himself ready), `not_yet` (because we asked the other player if he was ready and he was not), and 'ready!' (because we asked the other player if he was ready and he was).

We'll start with `are_you_ready`. Remember that in the protocol we said that a race condition could be hidden there. The only thing we can do is send the 'ready!' message with `am_ready/1` and deal with the rest later.

```
wait(are_you_ready, S=#state{}) ->
    am_ready(S#state.other),
    notice(S, "asked if ready, and I am. Waiting for same reply", []),
    {next_state, wait, S};
```

We'll be stuck waiting again, so it's not worth replying to our client yet. Similarly, we won't reply to the client when the other side sends a not_yet reply to our invitation.

```
wait(not_yet, S = #state{}) ->
    notice(S, "Other not ready yet", []),
    {next_state, wait, S};
```

On the other hand, if the other player is ready, we send an extra 'ready!' message to the other FSM, reply to our own player, and then move to the ready state.

```
wait('ready!', S=#state{}) ->
    am_ready(S#state.other),
    ack_trans(S#state.other),
    gen_fsm:reply(S#state.from, ok),
    notice(S, "other side is ready. Moving to ready state", []),
    {next_state, ready, S};
%% Don't care about these!
wait(Event, Data) ->
    unexpected(Event, wait),
    {next_state, wait, Data}.
```

You might have noticed that we've used ack_trans/1. In fact, both FSMs should use it. Why is this? To understand, we need to start looking at what goes on in the ready state.

When in the ready state, both players' actions become useless (except canceling). We won't care about new item offers. This gives us some liberty. Basically, both FSMs can talk to each other freely without worrying about the rest of the world. This lets us implement our bastardization of a two-phase commit. To begin this commit without either player acting, we'll need an event to trigger an action from the FSMs. The ack event from ack_trans/1 is used for that. As soon as we're in the ready state, the message is treated and acted upon, and the transaction can begin.

Two-phase commits require synchronous communications, though. This means we can't have both FSMs starting the transaction at once, because they will end up deadlocked. The secret is to find a way to decide that one FSM should initiate the commit, while the other will sit and wait for orders from the first one.

It turns out that the engineers and computer scientists who designed Erlang were pretty smart (well, we knew that already). The pids of any processes can be compared to each other and sorted. This can be done no matter when the process was spawned, whether it's still alive or not, or if it comes from another VM (we'll see more about this when we get into distributed Erlang in Chapter 26).

Knowing that two pids can be compared and one will be greater than the other, we can write a function priority/2 that will take two pids and tell a process whether it has been elected.

```
priority(OwnPid, OtherPid) when OwnPid > OtherPid -> true;
priority(OwnPid, OtherPid) when OwnPid < OtherPid -> false.
```

And by calling this function, we can have one process starting the commit and the other following orders.

Here's what this gives us when included in the ready state, after receiving the ack message:

```
ready(ack, S=#state{}) ->
    case priority(self(), S#state.other) of
        true ->
            try
                notice(S, "asking for commit", []),
                ready_commit = ask_commit(S#state.other),
                notice(S, "ordering commit", []),
                ok = do_commit(S#state.other),
                notice(S, "committing...", []),
                commit(S),
                {stop, normal, S}
            catch Class:Reason ->
                %% Abort! Either ready_commit or do_commit failed.
                notice(S, "commit failed", []),
                {stop, {Class, Reason}, S}
            end;
        false ->
            {next_state, ready, S}
    end;
ready(Event, Data) ->
    unexpected(Event, ready),
    {next_state, ready, Data}.
```

This big try ... catch expression is the leading FSM deciding how the commit works. Both ask_commit/1 and do_commit/1 are synchronous. This lets the leading FSM call them freely. You can see that the other FSM just waits. It will then receive the orders from the leading process. The first message should be ask_commit. This is just to make sure both FSMs are still there—nothing bad happened, and they're both dedicated to completing the task.

```erlang
ready(ask_commit, _From, S) ->
    notice(S, "replying to ask_commit", []),
    {reply, ready_commit, ready, S};
```

Once this is received, the leading process will ask to confirm the transaction with do_commit. That's when we must commit our data.

```erlang
ready(do_commit, _From, S) ->
    notice(S, "committing...", []),
    commit(S),
    {stop, normal, ok, S};
ready(Event, _From, Data) ->
    unexpected(Event, ready),
    {next_state, ready, Data}.
```

And once it's done, we leave. The leading FSM will receive ok as a reply and will know to commit on its own end afterward. This explains why we need the big try ... catch: If the replying FSM dies or its player cancels the transaction, the synchronous calls will crash after a timeout. The commit should be aborted in this case.

Just so you know, the commit function is defined as follows:

```erlang
commit(S = #state{}) ->
    io:format("Transaction completed for ~s. "
              "Items sent are:~n~p,~n received are:~n~p.~n"
              "This operation should have some atomic save "
              "in a database.~n",
              [S#state.name, S#state.ownitems, S#state.otheritems]).
```

Pretty underwhelming, eh? It's generally not possible to do a true safe commit with only two participants; a third party is usually required to judge if both players did everything right. A true commit function should contact that third party on behalf of both players, and then do the safe write to a database for them or roll back the whole exchange. We won't go into such details here, and the current commit/1 function will be enough for this example.

We're not finished yet. We have not yet covered two types of events: a player canceling the trade and the other player's FSM crashing. The former can be dealt with by using the callbacks handle_event/3 and handle_sync_event/4. Whenever the other user cancels, we'll receive an asynchronous notification.

```erlang
%% The other player has sent this cancel event.
%% Stop whatever we're doing and shut down!
handle_event(cancel, _StateName, S=#state{}) ->
    notice(S, "received cancel event", []),
    {stop, other_cancelled, S};
handle_event(Event, StateName, Data) ->
    unexpected(Event, StateName),
    {next_state, StateName, Data}.
```

And we must not forget to tell the other player before we quit, like this:

```
%% This cancel event comes from the client. We must warn the other
%% player that we have a quitter!
handle_sync_event(cancel, _From, _StateName, S = #state{}) ->
    notify_cancel(S#state.other),
    notice(S, "cancelling trade, sending cancel event", []),
    {stop, cancelled, ok, S};
%% Note: DO NOT reply to unexpected calls. Let the call-maker crash!
handle_sync_event(Event, _From, StateName, Data) ->
    unexpected(Event, StateName),
    {next_state, StateName, Data}.
```

The last event to take care of is when the other FSM goes down. Fortunately, we set a monitor back in the idle state. We can match on this and react accordingly:

```
handle_info({'DOWN', Ref, process, Pid, Reason}, _, S=#state{other=Pid, monitor=Ref}) ->
    notice(S, "Other side dead", []),
    {stop, {other_down, Reason}, S};
handle_info(Info, StateName, Data) ->
    unexpected(Info, StateName),
    {next_state, StateName, Data}.
```

Note that even if the cancel or 'DOWN' events happen while we're in the commit, everything should be safe, and the players will still have their own items. No exploit allowing people to steal others' items hides in there.

NOTE   *We used io:format/2 for most of our messages to let the FSMs communicate with their own clients. In a real-world application, you might want something more flexible. One approach is to let the client send in a pid, which will receive the notices sent to it. That process could be linked to a GUI or any other system to make the player aware of the events. The io:format/2 solution was chosen for its simplicity, allowing us to focus on the FSM and the asynchronous protocols.*

There are only two callbacks left to cover: code_change/4 and terminate/3. For now, we don't need to do anything with code_change/4. We just export it so the next version of the FSM can call it when it will be reloaded. Our terminate function is also really short because we didn't handle real resources in this example.

```
code_change(_OldVsn, StateName, Data, _Extra) ->
    {ok, StateName, Data}.

%% Transaction completed.
terminate(normal, ready, S=#state{}) ->
    notice(S, "FSM leaving.", []);
terminate(_Reason, _StateName, _StateData) ->
    ok.
```

Whew, we're finally finished.

We can now try our trading system. Well, trying it is a bit annoying because we need two processes to communicate with each other. To solve this, I've written the tests in the file *trade_calls.erl* (available from *http://learnyousomeerlang.com/static/erlang/trade_calls.erl*), which can run three different scenarios:

- `main_ab/0` will run a standard trade and output everything.
- `main_cd/0` will cancel the transaction halfway through.
- `main_ef/0` is very similar to `main_ab/0`, except it contains a different race condition.

If you try these, the first and third tests should succeed, while the second one should fail (with a load of error messages, but that's how it goes).

That Was Really Something

If you've found this chapter a bit harder than the others, I must admit that I've just gone crazy and decided to make something difficult out of the generic FSM behavior. If you feel confused, consider these questions:

Am I a Snake?

- Can you understand how different events are handled depending on the state your process is in?
- Do you understand how you can transition from one state to the other?
- Do you know when to use `send_event/2` and `sync_send_event/2-3` as opposed to `send_all_state_event/2` and `sync_send_all_state_event/3`?

If you answered yes to these questions, you understand what `gen_fsm` is about.

The rest of it—the asynchronous protocols, delaying replies and carrying the `From` variable, giving a priority to processes for synchronous calls, bastardized two-phase commits, and so on—*are not essential to understand.* They're mostly there to show what can be done and to highlight the difficulty of writing truly concurrent software, even in a language like Erlang. Erlang doesn't excuse you from planning or thinking, and Erlang won't solve your problems for you. It will only give you tools.

That being said, if you understood everything about these points, you can be proud of yourself (especially if you had never written concurrent software before). You are now starting to really think concurrently.

Fit for the Real World?

A real game would have a lot of stuff going on that could make trading even more complex. Items could be worn by the characters and damaged by enemies while they're being traded. Maybe items could be moved in and out of the inventory while being exchanged. Are the players on the same server? If not, how do you synchronize commits to different databases?

Our trade system is sane when detached from the reality of any game. Before trying to fit it in a game (if you dare), make sure everything goes right. Test it, test it, and test it again. You'll likely find that testing concurrent and parallel code is a complete pain. You'll lose hair, friends, and a piece of your sanity. Even after this, you'll need to keep in mind that your system is always as strong as its weakest link, and thus potentially very fragile nonetheless.

WARNING *While the model for this trade system seems sound, subtle concurrency bugs and race conditions can often rear their ugly heads a long time after they were written, and even if they have been running for years. While my code is generally bulletproof (yeah, right), you sometimes must face swords and knives. Beware the dormant bugs.*

Fortunately, we can put all of this madness behind us. We'll next see how OTP allows you to handle various events, such as alarms and logs, with the help of the gen_event behavior.

16

EVENT HANDLERS

Back in Chapter 13, when we built the reminder application, I mentioned that we could notify clients, whether by instant messaging, email, or some other method. In Chapter 15, our trading system used `io:format/2` to notify people of what was going on.

You can probably see the common link between these cases: They're all about letting people (or some process or application) know about an event that happened at some point in time. In one case, we output only the results; in the other, we took the pid of subscribers before sending them a message.

This chapter covers the OTP event handlers, one of the many strategies to handle notifications. After reviewing the handlers, we will put this knowledge in practice by implementing a notification system for sports events.

Handle This! *pumps shotgun*

The output approach we have used for notifications is minimalist and cannot be extended with ease. The one with subscribers is certainly valid. In fact, it's pretty useful when each of the subscribers has a long-running operation to do after receiving an event. In simpler cases, where you do not necessarily want a standby process waiting for events for each of the callbacks, a third approach can be taken.

This third approach simply takes a process that accepts functions and lets them run on any incoming event. This process is usually called an *event manager*, and it might end up looking a bit like this:

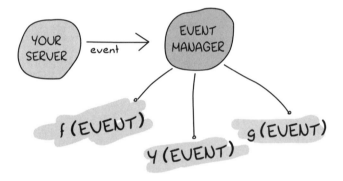

Taking this approach has a few advantages:

- If your server has many subscribers, it can keep going because it needs to forward events only once—to the manager.
- If there is a lot of data to be transferred, the data transfer happens only once, and all callbacks operate on that same instance of the data.
- You don't need to spawn processes for short-lived tasks.

And, of course, there are some downsides, too:

- If all functions need to run for a long time, they're going to block each other. This can be prevented by actually having the function forward the event to a process, basically using the event manager as an event forwarder (similar to what we did for the reminder app in Chapter 13).
- A function that loops indefinitely can prevent any new event from being handled until something crashes.

The way to resolve these issues is actually a bit underwhelming. Basically, you need to turn the event manager approach into the subscriber one. Luckily, the event manager approach is flexible enough to make this change relatively easy, and you'll see how in this chapter.

I usually start by writing a basic version of the OTP behavior in pure Erlang beforehand, but in this case, we'll just go straight to the point. Here comes gen_event.

Generic Event Handlers

The gen_event behavior differs quite a bit from the gen_server and gen_fsm behaviors in that you are never really starting a process. The part about "accepting a callback" is the reason for this.

The gen_event behavior basically runs the process that accepts and calls functions, and you only need to provide a module with these functions. This means that you have nothing to do with event manipulation except to place your callback functions in a format that pleases the event manager. All managing is done for free; you provide only what's specific to your application. This is not really surprising, given that OTP is all about separating the generic from the specific.

This separation, however, means that the standard spawn/initialize/loop/terminate pattern will be applied only to event handlers. Recall that event handlers are a bunch of functions running in the manager. This means the currently presented model:

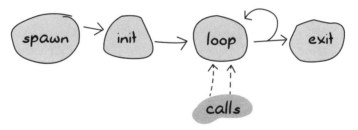

switches to something more like this for the programmer:

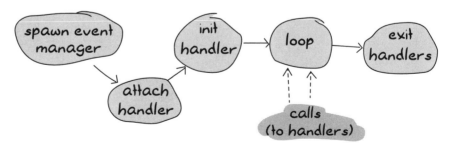

Each event handler can hold its own state, which is carried around by the manager. Each event handler can then take this form:

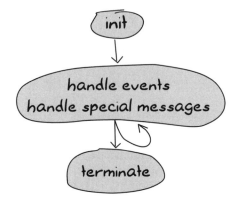

Now let's look at the event handlers' callbacks.

The init and terminate Functions

The init and terminate functions are similar to what we've seen in the previous behaviors with servers and FSMs. The init/1 function takes a list of arguments and returns {ok, State}. Whatever happens in init/1 should have its counterpart in terminate/2.

The handle_event Function

The handle_event(Event, State) function is more or less the core of gen_event's callback modules. Like gen_server's handle_cast/2, handle_event/2 works asynchronously. However, it differs in what it can return:

- {ok, NewState}
- {ok, NewState, hibernate}, which puts the event manager itself into hibernation until the next event
- remove_handler
- {swap_handler, Args1, NewState, NewHandler, Args2}

The tuple {ok, NewState} works in a way similar to what we've seen with gen_server:handle_cast/2. It simply updates its own state and doesn't reply to anyone. In the case of {ok, NewState, hibernate}, the whole event manager will be put in hibernation. Remember that event handlers run in the same process as their manager.

Then remove_handler drops the handler from the manager. This can be useful whenever your event handler knows it's finished and it has nothing else to do.

Finally, there's {swap_handler, Args1, NewState, NewHandler, Args2}. This one is not used too frequently. It removes the current event handler and replaces that handler with a new one. Returning such a tuple will result in the manager first calling CurrentHandler:terminate(Args1, NewState) and removing the current handler, and then adding a new one by calling NewHandler:init(Args2, ResultFromTerminate). This can be useful in the cases where you know some specific event happened and you're better off giving control to a new handler. Generally, this is one of those things that you'll simply know when you need it and apply it then.

All incoming events can come from gen_event:notify/2, which is asynchronous, like gen_server:cast/2. There is also gen_event:sync_notify/2, which is synchronous. This is a bit funny to say, because handle_event/2 remains asynchronous. The idea here is that the function call returns only after all the event handlers have seen and treated the new message. Until then, the event manager will keep blocking the calling process by not replying.

The handle_call Function

The handle_call function is similar to a gen_server's handle_call callback, except that it can return {ok, Reply, NewState}, {ok, Reply, NewState, hibernate}, {remove_handler, Reply}, or {swap_handler, Reply, Args1, NewState, Handler2, Args2}. The gen_event:call/3-4 function is used to make the call.

This raises a question: How does this work when we have something like 15 different event handlers? Do we expect 15 replies, or just 1 that contains them all? Well, in fact, we'll be forced to choose only one handler to reply to us. We'll get into the details of how this is done when we attach handlers to our event manager in "Game Events" on page 253, but if you're impatient, you can refer to the gen_event:add_handler/3 function's documentation to try to figure it out.

The handle_info Function

The handle_info/2 callback is pretty much the same as handle_event (it has the same return values and such), with the exception that it treats only out-of-band messages, such as exit signals and messages sent directly to the event manager with the ! operator. It has use cases similar to those of handle_info in gen_server and gen_fsm.

The code_change Function

The code_change function works in the same manner as it does for gen_server, except it's for each individual event handler. It takes the arguments OldVsn, State, and Extra, which are, in order, the version number, the current handler's state, and data we can ignore for now. All it needs to do is return {ok, NewState}.

It's Curling Time!

Now it's time to see what we can do with gen_event. For this example, we'll make a set of event handlers to track game updates of one of the most entertaining sports in the world: curling.

For those who have never seen or played curling (which is a shame!), the rules are relatively simple. Two teams try to send a curling stone (a thick stone disc weighing between 38 and 44 pounds (17 and 20 kilograms) with a handle attached to the top) sliding on the ice to the middle of the red circle:

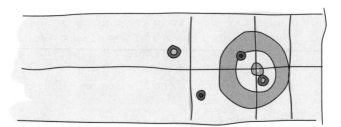

The teams do this with 16 stones, and the team with the stone closest to the center wins a point at the end of the round (called an *end*). If the team has the two closest stones, it earns two points; if it has the three closest stones, it's worth three points, and so on. There are 10 ends, and the team with the most points at the completion of the 10 ends wins the game.

There are more rules, making the game more fascinating, but this is a book on Erlang, not extremely fascinating winter sports. If you want to learn more about curling, I suggest you head over to the Wikipedia article on the topic.

For this entirely real-world-relevant scenario, we'll be working for the next winter Olympic Games. The city where everything happens has just finished building the arena where the matches will take place, and they're working on getting the scoreboard ready. It turns out that we need to program a system that will let some official enter game events—such as when a stone has been thrown, when a round ends, and when a game is over—and then route these events to the scoreboard, to a stats system, to news reporters' feeds, and so on.

Being as clever as we are, we know this is a chapter on gen_event and deduce we will likely use it to accomplish our task. We won't implement all the rules in this example, but feel free to do so after you've built the sample app—I promise not to be mad.

The Scoreboard

We'll start with the scoreboard. Because they're installing it right now, we'll make use of a fake module that would usually let us interact with it, but for this example, it will use only standard output to show what's going on. This is called a *mock*, and it's there to help us develop code about parts of the system that do not exist yet. This is where the following *curling_scoreboard_hw.erl* file comes in.

```erlang
-module(curling_scoreboard_hw).
-export([add_point/1, next_round/0, set_teams/2, reset_board/0]).

%% This is a 'dumb' module that's only there to replace what a real hardware
%% controller would likely do. The real hardware controller would likely hold
%% some state and make sure everything works right, but this one doesn't mind.

%% Shows the teams on the scoreboard.
set_teams(TeamA, TeamB) ->
    io:format("Scoreboard: Team ~s vs. Team ~s~n", [TeamA, TeamB]).

next_round() ->
    io:format("Scoreboard: round over~n").

add_point(Team) ->
    io:format("Scoreboard: increased score of team ~s by 1~n", [Team]).

reset_board() ->
    io:format("Scoreboard: All teams are undefined and all scores are 0~n").
```

So this is all the functionality the scoreboard has. Scoreboards usually have a timer and other awesome features, but it seems like the Olympics Committee didn't feel like having us implementing trivialities for a tutorial.

Game Events

This hardware interface lets us have a bit of design time to ourselves. We know that there are a few events to handle for now: adding teams, going to the next round, and setting the number of points. We will use only the reset_board functionality when starting a new game and won't need it as part of our protocol. The events we need might take the following form in our protocol:

- {set_teams, TeamA, TeamB}, where this is translated to a single call to curling_scoreboard_hw:set_teams(TeamA, TeamB)
- {add_points, Team, N}, where this is translated to *N* calls to curling_scoreboard_hw:add_point(Team)
- next_round, which gets translated to a single call to the function with the same name

We can start our implementation with this basic event handler skeleton:

```erlang
-module(gen_event_callback).
-behavior(gen_event).
```

```
-export([init/1, handle_event/2, handle_call/2, handle_info/2, code_change/3,
terminate/2]).

init([]) -> {ok, []}.

handle_event(_, State) -> {ok, State}.

handle_call(_, State) -> {ok, ok, State}.

handle_info(_, State) -> {ok, State}.

code_change(_OldVsn, State, _Extra) -> {ok, State}.

terminate(_Reason, _State) -> ok.
```

This is a skeleton that we can use for every gen_event callback module out there. For now, the scoreboard event handler itself won't need to do anything special except forward the calls to the hardware module. We expect the events to come from gen_event:notify/2, so the handling of the protocol should be done in handle_event/2. The file *curling_scoreboard.erl* contains the changes to the skeleton, as follows:

```
-module(curling_scoreboard).
-behavior(gen_event).

-export([init/1, handle_event/2, handle_call/2, handle_info/2, code_change/3,
terminate/2]).

init([]) ->
    {ok, []}.

handle_event({set_teams, TeamA, TeamB}, State) ->
    curling_scoreboard_hw:set_teams(TeamA, TeamB),
    {ok, State};
handle_event({add_points, Team, N}, State) ->
    [curling_scoreboard_hw:add_point(Team) || _ <- lists:seq(1,N)],
    {ok, State};
handle_event(next_round, State) ->
    curling_scoreboard_hw:next_round(),
    {ok, State};
handle_event(_, State) ->
    {ok, State}.

handle_call(_, State) ->
    {ok, ok, State}.

handle_info(_, State) ->
    {ok, State}.
```

You can see the updates done to the `handle_event/2` function. Now let's try it:

```
1> c(curling_scoreboard_hw).
{ok,curling_scoreboard_hw}
2> c(curling_scoreboard).
{ok,curling_scoreboard}
3> {ok, Pid} = gen_event:start_link().
{ok,<0.43.0>}
4> gen_event:add_handler(Pid, curling_scoreboard, []).
ok
5> gen_event:notify(Pid, {set_teams, "Pirates", "Scotsmen"}).
Scoreboard: Team Pirates vs. Team Scotsmen
ok
6> gen_event:notify(Pid, {add_points, "Pirates", 3}).
ok
Scoreboard: increased score of team Pirates by 1
Scoreboard: increased score of team Pirates by 1
Scoreboard: increased score of team Pirates by 1
7> gen_event:notify(Pid, next_round).
Scoreboard: round over
ok
8> gen_event:delete_handler(Pid, curling_scoreboard, turn_off).
ok
9> gen_event:notify(Pid, next_round).
ok
```

A few things are going on here. The first is that we're starting gen_event as a stand-alone process. We then attach our event handler to it dynamically with gen_event:add_handler/3. This can be done as many times as you want. However, as mentioned in the handle_call discussion earlier, this might cause problems when you want to work with a particular event handler.

If you want to call, add, or delete a specific handler when there's more than one instance of it, you'll need to find a way to uniquely identify it. My favorite way of doing this (which works great if you don't have anything more specific in mind) is to just use make_ref() as a unique value. To give this value to the handler, you add it by calling add_handler/3 as gen_event:add_handler(Pid, {Module, Ref}, Args). From this point on, you can use {Module, Ref} to talk to that specific handler, and the problem is solved.

Next, we send messages to the event handler, which successfully calls the hardware module. We then remove the handler. Here, turn_off is an argument to the terminate/2 function, which our implementation currently doesn't care about. The handler is gone, but we can still send events to the event manager. Hooray.

One awkward aspect of the preceding code snippet is that we're forced to call the gen_event module directly and show everyone what our protocol looks like. A better option would be to provide an *abstraction module* on top of it that just wraps up all the calls we need. This will look a lot nicer to everyone using our code and will, again, let us change the implementation if (when) we need to do so. It will also let us specify which handlers are necessary to include for a standard curling game.

```erlang
-module(curling).
-export([start_link/2, set_teams/3, add_points/3, next_round/1]).

start_link(TeamA, TeamB) ->
    {ok, Pid} = gen_event:start_link(),
    %% The scoreboard will always be there.
    gen_event:add_handler(Pid, curling_scoreboard, []),
    set_teams(Pid, TeamA, TeamB),
    {ok, Pid}.

set_teams(Pid, TeamA, TeamB) ->
    gen_event:notify(Pid, {set_teams, TeamA, TeamB}).

add_points(Pid, Team, N) ->
    gen_event:notify(Pid, {add_points, Team, N}).

next_round(Pid) ->
    gen_event:notify(Pid, next_round).
```

And now we can run it.

```erlang
1> c(curling).
{ok,curling}
2> {ok, Pid} = curling:start_link("Pirates", "Scotsmen").
Scoreboard: Team Pirates vs. Team Scotsmen
{ok,<0.78.0>}
3> curling:add_points(Pid, "Scotsmen", 2).
Scoreboard: increased score of team Scotsmen by 1
Scoreboard: increased score of team Scotsmen by 1
ok
4> curling:next_round(Pid).
Scoreboard: round over
ok
```

This doesn't look like much of an advantage, but it's really about making the code nicer to use (and it reduces the possibilities of writing the messages incorrectly).

This being done, the code should now be usable by officials. Olympics do require us to do a little bit more, say, satisfying the press.

Alert the Press!

We want international reporters to be able to get live data from the official in charge of updating our system. Because this is an example program, we won't go through the steps of setting up a socket and writing a protocol for the updates, but we'll set up the system to do it by putting an intermediary process in charge of it.

Basically, whenever a news organization feels like getting into the game feed, the organization will register its own handler that just forwards the data the organization needs. We'll effectively turn our gen_event server into a kind of message hub, just routing messages to whoever needs them.

First, we'll update the *curling.erl* module with the new interface. Because we want things to be easy to use, we'll add only two functions: join_feed/2 and leave_feed/2. Joining the feed should be doable just by inputting the correct pid for the event manager and the pid to forward all the events to. This should return a unique value that can then be used to unsubscribe from the feed with leave_feed/2.

```
%% Subscribes the pid ToPid to the event feed.
%% The specific event handler for the newsfeed is
%% returned in case someone wants to leave.
join_feed(Pid, ToPid) ->
    HandlerId = {curling_feed, make_ref()},
    gen_event:add_handler(Pid, HandlerId, [ToPid]),
    HandlerId.

leave_feed(Pid, HandlerId) ->
    gen_event:delete_handler(Pid, HandlerId, leave_feed).
```

Note that we're using the technique described earlier for multiple handlers ({curling_feed, make_ref()}). You can see that this function expects a gen_event callback module named curling_feed. If we used only the name of the module as a HandlerId, things would have still worked fine, except that we would have no control over which handler to delete when we're finished with one instance of it. The event manager would just pick one of the handlers in an undefined manner. Using a reference makes sure that some guy from the *Head-Smashed-In Buffalo Jump* (Alberta, Canada) press leaving the place won't disconnect a journalist from *The Economist* (no idea why that magazine would do a report on curling, but you never know). Anyway, here is the implementation for the curling_feed module:

```
-module(curling_feed).
-behavior(gen_event).
```

```
-export([init/1, handle_event/2, handle_call/2, handle_info/2, code_change/3,
terminate/2]).

init([Pid]) -> {ok, Pid}.

handle_event(Event, Pid) ->
    Pid ! {curling_feed, Event},
    {ok, Pid}.

handle_call(_, State) -> {ok, ok, State}.

handle_info(_, State) -> {ok, State}.

code_change(_OldVsn, State, _Extra) -> {ok, State}.

terminate(_Reason, _State) -> ok.
```

The only interesting thing here is still the handle_event/2 function, which blindly forwards all events to the subscribing pid.

Now let's use the new modules.

```
1> c(curling), c(curling_feed).
{ok,curling_feed}
2> {ok, Pid} = curling:start_link("Saskatchewan Roughriders",
2>                                 "Ottawa Roughriders").
Scoreboard: Team Saskatchewan Roughriders vs. Team Ottawa Roughriders
{ok,<0.165.0>}
3> HandlerId = curling:join_feed(Pid, self()).
{curling_feed,#Ref<0.0.0.909>}
4> curling:add_points(Pid, "Saskatchewan Roughriders", 2).
Scoreboard: increased score of team Saskatchewan Roughriders by 1
ok
Scoreboard: increased score of team Saskatchewan Roughriders by 1
5> flush().
Shell got {curling_feed,{add_points,"Saskatchewan Roughriders",2}}
ok
6> curling:leave_feed(Pid, HandlerId).
ok
7> curling:next_round(Pid).
Scoreboard: round over
ok
8> flush().
ok
```

Here, we added ourselves to the feed, got the updates, and then left and stopped receiving them. You can actually try to add many subscribers many times, and it will work fine.

This introduces a problem though. What if one of the curling feed subscribers crashes? Do we just keep the handler going on there? Ideally, we wouldn't need to do that, and in fact, we don't have to. All that needs to be done is to change the call from gen_event:add_handler/3 to gen_event:add_sup_handler/3. If we crash, the handler is gone. Then on the opposite end, if the gen_event manager crashes, the message {gen_event_EXIT, Handler, Reason} is sent back to us so we can handle it. Easy enough, right? Think again.

DON'T DRINK TOO MUCH KOOL-AID

At some time in your childhood, you probably went to your aunt or grandmother's place for a party or some other event. While there, you would have several adults watching over you in addition to your parents. If you misbehaved, you would get scolded by your mom, dad, aunt, grandmother, and so on, and then everyone would keep harassing you long after you clearly knew you had done something wrong. Well, gen_event:add_sup_handler/3 is a bit like that—seriously.

Whenever you use gen_event:add_sup_handler/3, a link is set up between your process and the event manager so both of them are supervised and the handler knows if its parent process fails. In the section on monitors in Chapter 12, I mentioned that monitors are great for writing libraries that need to know what's going on with other processes because, unlike links, monitors can be stacked. Well, gen_event predates the appearance of monitors in Erlang, and a strong commitment to backward-compatibility introduced this pretty bad wart. Basically, because you could have the same process acting as the parent of many event handlers, the library doesn't ever unlink the processes (except when it terminates for good) just in case. Monitors would actually solve the problem, but they aren't being used there.

This mean that everything goes okay when your own process crashes—the supervised handler is terminated (with the call to YourModule:terminate(({stop, Reason}, State)). Everything goes okay when your handler itself crashes (but not the event manager)—you will receive {gen_event_EXIT, HandlerId, Reason}. When the event manager is shut down though, either of the following will happen:

- You will receive the {gen_event_EXIT, HandlerId, Reason} message, and then crash because you're not trapping exits.

- You will receive the {gen_event_EXIT, HandlerId, Reason} message, and then a standard 'EXIT' message that is either superfluous or confusing.

That's quite a wart, but at least you know about it. You can try to switch your event handler to a supervised one if you feel like it. It will be safer, even if it risks being more annoying in some cases. Safety first.

We're not finished yet! What happens if some members of the media are not there on time? We need to be able to tell them from the feed what the current state of the game is. For this, we'll write an additional event handler named curling_accumulator. Again, before writing it entirely, we might want to add it to the curling module with the few calls we want, as follows:

```
-module(curling).
-export([start_link/2, set_teams/3, add_points/3, next_round/1]).
-export([join_feed/2, leave_feed/2]).
-export([game_info/1]).

start_link(TeamA, TeamB) ->
    {ok, Pid} = gen_event:start_link(),
    %% The scoreboard will always be there.
    gen_event:add_handler(Pid, curling_scoreboard, []),
    %% Start the stats accumulator.
    gen_event:add_handler(Pid, curling_accumulator, []),
    set_teams(Pid, TeamA, TeamB),
    {ok, Pid}.

...

%% Returns the current game state.
game_info(Pid) ->
    gen_event:call(Pid, curling_accumulator, game_data).
```

Notice that the game_info/1 function here uses only curling_accumulator as a handler ID. In the cases where you have many versions of the same handler, the hint about using make_ref() (or any other means) to ensure you write to the correct handler still holds. Also note that the curling_accumulator handler starts automatically along with the scoreboard.

Now let's put together the module itself. It should be able to hold state for the curling game. So far, we have teams, score, and rounds to track. This information can all be held in a state record and changed on each event received. Then we will only need to reply to the game_data call, as follows:

```
-module(curling_accumulator).
-behavior(gen_event).

-export([init/1, handle_event/2, handle_call/2, handle_info/2, code_change/3,
terminate/2]).

-record(state, {teams=orddict:new(), round=0}).

init([]) -> {ok, #state{}}.

handle_event({set_teams, TeamA, TeamB}, S=#state{teams=T}) ->
    Teams = orddict:store(TeamA, 0, orddict:store(TeamB, 0, T)),
    {ok, S#state{teams=Teams}};
handle_event({add_points, Team, N}, S=#state{teams=T}) ->
    Teams = orddict:update_counter(Team, N, T),
    {ok, S#state{teams=Teams}};
```

```erlang
handle_event(next_round, S=#state{}) ->
    {ok, S#state{round = S#state.round+1}};
handle_event(_Event, State=#state{}) ->
    {ok, State}.

handle_call(game_data, S=#state{teams=T, round=R}) ->
    {ok, {orddict:to_list(T), {round, R}}, S};
handle_call(_, State) ->
    {ok, ok, State}.

handle_info(_, State) -> {ok, State}.

code_change(_OldVsn, State, _Extra) -> {ok, State}.

terminate(_Reason, _State) -> ok.
```

So, we basically just update the state until someone asks for game
details, at which point, we'll be sending them back. We did this in a very
basic way. Perhaps a smarter way to organize the code would have been to
simply keep a list of all the events to ever happen in the game so we could
send them all back each time a new process subscribed to the feed. That's
not necessary for our purposes here, however, so let's focus on using our
new code. Give it a try:

```erlang
1> c(curling), c(curling_accumulator).
{ok,curling_accumulator}
2> {ok, Pid} = curling:start_link("Pigeons", "Eagles").
Scoreboard: Team Pigeons vs. Team Eagles
{ok,<0.242.0>}
3> curling:add_points(Pid, "Pigeons", 2).
Scoreboard: increased score of team Pigeons by 1
ok
Scoreboard: increased score of team Pigeons by 1
4> curling:next_round(Pid).
Scoreboard: round over
ok
5> curling:add_points(Pid, "Eagles", 3).
Scoreboard: increased score of team Eagles by 1
ok
Scoreboard: increased score of team Eagles by 1
Scoreboard: increased score of team Eagles by 1
6> curling:next_round(Pid).
Scoreboard: round over
ok
7> curling:game_info(Pid).
{[{"Eagles",3},{"Pigeons",2}],{round,2}}
```

Enthralling! Surely the Olympic Committee will love our code. We can
pat ourselves on the back, cash in a fat check, and go play video games all
night.

We haven't covered all that can be done with gen_event as a module. In
fact, we haven't discussed the most common use of event handlers: logging

and system alarms. I decided against showing them because pretty much any other source on Erlang out there uses gen_event strictly for those purposes. If you're interested in learning more about these uses, check out the error_logger module of the standard library first.

Even though we have not covered the most common uses of gen_event, we've explored all the concepts necessary to understand them, to build our own, and to integrate them into our applications. More important, we've finally covered the three main OTP behaviors used in active code development. We still have a few behaviors left to visit—those that act as a bunch of glue between all of our worker processes, such as the supervisor, which is what Chapter 17 is all about.

17

WHO SUPERVISES THE SUPERVISORS?

Supervisors are one of the most useful parts of OTP. We've encountered basic supervisors in Chapters 12 and 13, where they offered a way to keep our software going in case of errors by just restarting the faulty processes. This chapter introduces OTP's take on supervisors, which is much better than ours.

In our earlier examples, our supervisors would start a worker process, link to it, and trap exit signals with `process_flag(trap_exit,true)` to know when the process died and restart it. This is fine when we want restarts, but it's also pretty dumb. Imagine that you're using the remote control to turn on the TV. If it doesn't work the first time, you might try again once or twice, just in case you didn't press the right button or the signal went wrong. But our supervisor would keep trying to turn on that TV forever, even if it turned out that the remote had no batteries or didn't belong to that TV. That's a pretty dumb supervisor.

Something else that was dumb about our supervisors was that they could watch only one worker at a time. Although it's sometimes useful to have one supervisor for a single worker, in large applications, this would mean you could have only a chain of supervisors, not a tree. How would you supervise a task where you need two or three workers at once? With our implementation, it just couldn't be done.

The OTP supervisors, fortunately, provide the flexibility to handle such cases (and more). As you'll see in this chapter, they let you define how many times a worker should be restarted in a given period before giving up. They let you have more than one worker per supervisor, and even let you pick from a few patterns to determine how they should depend on each other in case of a failure.

Supervisor Concepts

Supervisors are one of the simplest behaviors to use and understand, but one of the hardest behaviors to write a good design with. There are various strategies related to supervisors and application design, but before getting to the hard stuff, we need to cover some basic concepts.

One of the terms I've used previously in this book without much of a definition is *worker*. Workers are defined a bit in opposition of supervisors. If supervisors are supposed to be processes that do nothing but make sure their children are restarted when they die, workers are processes that are in charge of doing actual work and that may die while doing so. They are usually not trusted to be safe.

Supervisors can supervise workers and other supervisors. Workers should never be used in any position except under a supervisor:

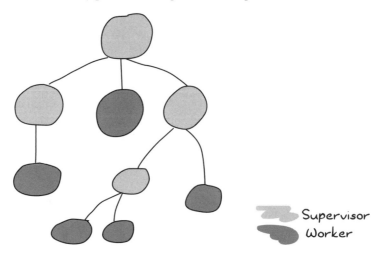

Supervisor
Worker

Why should every process be supervised? Well, the idea is simple: If you're spawning unsupervised processes, how can you be sure they are gone? If you can't measure something, it doesn't exist. If a process resides in the void away from all your supervision trees, how do you know whether it actually exists? How did it get there? Will it happen again?

If it does happen, you'll find yourself leaking memory very slowly—so slowly your VM might suddenly die because the VM no longer has memory, and so slowly you might not be able to easily track the problem until it happens again and again. Of course, you might say, "If I take care and know what I'm doing, things will be fine." Maybe they will be fine, but maybe they won't. In a production system, you don't want to be taking chances. And in the case of Erlang, it's why you have garbage collection to begin with. Keeping things supervised is pretty useful.

Supervision is also useful because it allows you to terminate applications in good order. You'll write Erlang software that is not meant to run forever, but you'll still want it to terminate cleanly. How do you know everything is ready to be shut down? With supervisors, it's easy. Whenever you want to terminate an application, you have the top supervisor of the VM shut down (this is done for you with functions like init:stop/1). Then that supervisor asks each of its children to terminate. If some of the children are supervisors, they do the same:

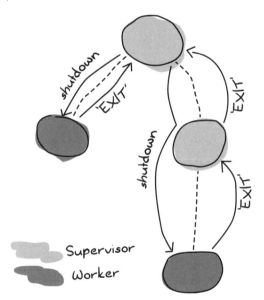

This gives you a well-ordered VM shutdown, which is very hard to achieve without having all of your processes being part of the tree. Of course, there are times when your process will be stuck for some reason and won't terminate correctly. When that happens, supervisors have a way to brutally kill the process.

So, we have workers, supervisors, supervision trees, ways to specify dependencies, ways to tell supervisors when to give up on trying or waiting for their children, and so on. This is not all that supervisors can do; but for now, we have enough information to start looking at how to use them.

Using Supervisors

This has been a very violent chapter so far: Parents spend their time binding their children to trees, forcing them to work before brutally killing them. But we wouldn't be real sadists without actually implementing it all.

When I said supervisors were simple to use, I wasn't kidding. There is a single callback function to provide: init/1. The catch is that its return is quite complex. Here's an example return from a supervisor:

```
{ok, {{one_for_all, 5, 60},
     [{fake_id,
       {fake_mod, start_link, [SomeArg]},
       permanent,
       5000,
       worker,
       [fake_mod]},
      {other_id,
       {event_manager_mod, start_link, []},
       transient,
       infinity,
       worker,
       dynamic}]}}.
```

Say what? A general definition might be a bit simpler to work with:

```
{ok, {{RestartStrategy, MaxRestart, MaxTime},[ChildSpec]}}.
```

Let's take a look at each of these pieces.

Restart Strategies

The RestartStrategy part of the definition can be one_for_one, one_for_all, rest_for_one, or simple_one_for_one.

one_for_one

one_for_one is an intuitive restart strategy. It basically means that if your supervisor supervises many workers and one of them fails, only that one should be restarted. You should use one_for_one whenever the processes being supervised are independent and not really related to each other, or when the process can restart and lose its state without impacting its siblings.

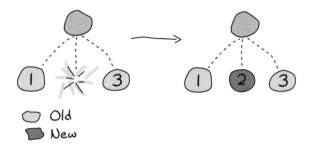

○ Old
● New

one_for_all

one_for_all has little to do with musketeers. It's to be used whenever all your processes under a single supervisor heavily depend on each other to be able to work normally. Let's say you have decided to add a supervisor on top of the trading system we implemented in Chapter 15. If a trader crashed, it wouldn't make sense to restart only that one of the two traders, because the traders' states would be out of sync. Restarting both of them at once would be a saner choice, and one_for_all is the strategy for that.

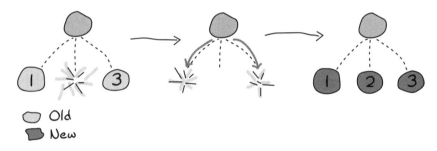

○ Old
● New

rest_for_one

rest_for_one is a more specific kind of strategy. Whenever you need to start processes that depend on each other in a chain (A starts B, which starts C, which starts D, and so on), you can use rest_for_one. It's also useful in the case of services where you have similar dependencies (X works alone, but Y depends on X and Z depends on both). Basically, with a rest_for_one restarting strategy, if a process dies, all the processes that were started after it (depend on it) are restarted, but not the other way around.

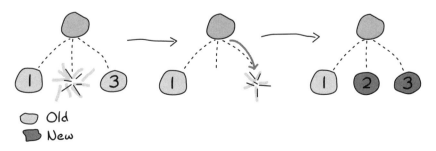

○ Old
● New

simple_one_for_one

Despite its name, the `simple_one_for_one` restart strategy isn't all that simple. This type of supervisor takes only one kind of child, and it's used when you want to dynamically add children to the supervisor, rather than having them started statically.

To say it a bit differently, a `simple_one_for_one` supervisor just sits around, and it knows it can produce one kind of child only. Whenever you want a new child, you ask for it and you get it. This could theoretically be done with the standard `one_for_one` supervisor, but there are practical advantages to using the simple version, as you'll see when we look at dynamic supervision later in the chapter.

NOTE *One of the big differences between `one_for_one` and `simple_one_for_one` is that `one_for_one` holds a list of all the children it has started (and had started, if you don't clear it after manipulating it manually), ordered by their starting order, while `simple_one_for_one` holds a single definition for all its children and works using a dictionary to hold its data. Basically, when a process crashes, the `simple_one_for_one` supervisor will be much faster if you have a large number of children.*

Restart Limits

The last part of the `RestartStrategy` tuple contains the variables `MaxRestart` and `MaxTime`. The idea is that if more than the `MaxRestart` limit happens within `MaxTime` (in seconds), the supervisor just gives up on your code, shuts it down, and then kills itself, never to return. And that is based on restarts for *all* children of the supervisor, not any one of them individually. Fortunately, that supervisor's supervisor might still have hope in its children and start them all over again.

Child Specifications

And now for the `ChildSpec` part of the return value. `ChildSpec` stands for *child specification*. Earlier we had the following two child specifications:

```
[{fake_id,
  {fake_mod, start_link, [SomeArg]},
  permanent,
  5000,
  worker,
  [fake_mod]},
 {other_id,
  {event_manager_mod, start_link, []},
  transient,
  infinity,
  worker,
  dynamic}]
```

The child specification can be described in a more abstract form, as follows:

```
{ChildId, StartFunc, Restart, Shutdown, Type, Modules}.
```

And now we can look at how each part works.

ChildId

ChildId is just a name used by the supervisor internally. You will rarely need to use it yourself, although it might happen to be useful for debugging purposes, and sometimes when you decide to actually get a list of all the children of a supervisor. Any term can be used for this identifier, but I suggest making it something readable, just in case you do need it for debugging.

StartFunc

StartFunc is a tuple that specifies how to start the supervisor. It's the standard {M,F,A} format we've used a few times already. Note that it is *very* important that the starting function here is OTP-compliant and links to its caller when executed. (Hint: Use gen_*:start_link() wrapped in your own module, all the time.)

Restart

Restart tells the supervisor how to react when that particular child dies. This can take one of three values:

- permanent
- temporary
- transient

A permanent process should always be restarted, no matter what. The supervisors we implemented in our previous applications used this strategy only. This is usually used by vital, long-living processes (or services) running on your node.

On the other hand, a temporary process is a process that should never be restarted. These processes are for short-lived workers that are expected to fail and have few bits of code that depend on them. You usually still want to supervise them to know where they are, and to be able to shut them down cleanly via the supervisor.

Transient processes are a bit of an in-between breed. They're meant to run until they terminate normally, and then they won't be restarted. However, if they die of abnormal causes (the exit reason is anything but normal, shutdown, or {shutdown, Reason}), they will be restarted. This restart option is often used for workers that need to succeed at their task, but it won't be used after they do so.

You can have children of all three kinds mixed under a single supervisor. This might affect the restart strategy. A one_for_all restart won't be triggered by a temporary process dying, but that temporary process might be restarted under the same supervisor if a permanent process dies first!

Shutdown

Earlier in the chapter, I mentioned being able to shut down entire applications with the help of supervisors. Here's how it's done: When the top-level supervisor is asked to terminate, it calls exit(ChildPid, shutdown) on each of the pids. If the child is a worker and trapping exits, it will call its own terminate function; otherwise, it's just going to die. When a supervisor gets the shutdown signal, it will forward that signal to its own children in the same way.

The Shutdown value of a child specification is thus used to give a deadline for the termination. On certain workers, you know you might need to do things like properly close files, notify a service that you're leaving, and so on. In these cases, you might want to use a certain cutoff time, either in milliseconds or set as infinity if you are really patient. If the time passes and nothing happens, the process is then brutally killed with exit(Pid, kill). If you don't care about the child and it can die without any consequences without any timeout needed, the atom brutal_kill is also an acceptable value. brutal_kill will make it so the child is killed with exit(Pid, kill), which is untrappable and instantaneous.

Choosing a good Shutdown value is sometimes complex or tricky. If you have a chain of supervisors with Shutdown values like $5 \to 2 \to 5 \to 5$, the two last ones will likely end up brutally killed, because the second one had a shorter cutoff time. The proper value is entirely application-dependent, and few general tips can be given on the subject.

NOTE *Before Erlang R14B03, simple_one_for_one children did not respect this rule with the Shutdown time. In the case of simple_one_for_one, the supervisor would just exit, and it would be left to each of the workers to terminate on its own after its supervisor was gone.*

Type

Type lets the supervisor know whether the child is a supervisor (it implements either the supervisor or supervisor_bridge behavior) or a worker (any other OTP process). This will be important when upgrading applications with more advanced OTP features, but you do not really need to care about it at the moment—just tell the truth and everything should be fine. You have to trust your supervisors!

Modules

Modules is a list of one element: the name of the callback module used by the child behavior. The exception is when you have callback modules whose identity you do not know beforehand (such as event handlers in an event manager). In this case, the value of Modules should be dynamic so that the whole OTP system knows who to contact when using more advanced features, such as releases.

Hooray, we now have covered the basic knowledge required to start supervised processes. You can take a break and digest it all, or move forward to see how supervisors work in practice.

Band Practice

Some practice is in order. And speaking of practice, the perfect example in this case is a band practice! (Well, not *that* perfect, but bear with me for a while.)

Let's say we're managing a band named *RSYNC, made up of a handful of musically inclined programmers: a drummer, a singer, a bass player, and a keytar player (in memory of all the forgotten 1980s glory). Despite a few retro hit cover songs, such as "Thread Safety Dance" and "Saturday Night Coder," the band has a hard time getting a venue. Annoyed with the whole situation, I storm into your office with yet another sugar rush-induced idea of simulating a band in Erlang. You're tired because you live in the same apartment as the drummer (who is the weakest link in this band to be honest, but they stick with him because they don't know any other drummers), so you accept.

Musicians

The first thing we can do is write the individual band members. For our use case, the musicians module will implement a gen_server. Each musician will take an instrument and a skill level as a parameter (so we can say the drummer sucks, while the others are all right). Once a musician has spawned, it will start playing. We'll also have an option to stop musicians, if needed. This gives us the following module and interface:

```
-module(musicians).
-behavior(gen_server).

-export([start_link/2, stop/1]).
-export([init/1, handle_call/3, handle_cast/2,
         handle_info/2, code_change/3, terminate/2]).
```

```
-record(state, {name="", role, skill=good}).
-define(DELAY, 750).

start_link(Role, Skill) ->
    gen_server:start_link({local, Role}, ?MODULE, [Role, Skill], []).

stop(Role) -> gen_server:call(Role, stop).
```

We've defined a ?DELAY macro that we'll use as the standard time span between each time a musician will show himself as playing. As the record definition shows, we'll also need to give each of the musicians a name, as follows:

```
init([Role, Skill]) ->
    %% To know when the parent shuts down.
    process_flag(trap_exit, true),
    %% Sets a seed for random number generation for the life of the process.
    %% Uses the current time to do it. Unique value guaranteed by now().
    random:seed(now()),
    TimeToPlay = random:uniform(3000),
    Name = pick_name(),
    StrRole = atom_to_list(Role),
    io:format("Musician ~s, playing the ~s entered the room~n",
              [Name, StrRole]),
    {ok, #state{name=Name, role=StrRole, skill=Skill}, TimeToPlay}.
```

Two things go on in the init/1 function. First, we start trapping exits. As you'll recall from the description of the terminate/2 function for generic servers in Chapter 14, we need to do this if we want terminate/2 to be called when the server's parent shuts down its children. The rest of the init/1 function sets a random seed (so that each process gets different random numbers) and then creates a random name for itself. The following are the functions to create the names:

```
%% Yes, the names are based off the magic school bus characters'
%% 10 names!
pick_name() ->
    %% The seed must be set for the random functions. Use within the
    %% process that started with init/1.
    lists:nth(random:uniform(10), firstnames())
    ++ " " ++
    lists:nth(random:uniform(10), lastnames()).

firstnames() ->
    ["Valerie", "Arnold", "Carlos", "Dorothy", "Keesha",
     "Phoebe", "Ralphie", "Tim", "Wanda", "Janet"].

lastnames() ->
    ["Frizzle", "Perlstein", "Ramon", "Ann", "Franklin",
     "Terese", "Tennelli", "Jamal", "Li", "Perlstein"].
```

Now we can move on to the implementation. This one is going to be pretty trivial for handle_call and handle_cast.

```erlang
handle_call(stop, _From, S=#state{}) ->
    {stop, normal, ok, S};
handle_call(_Message, _From, S) ->
    {noreply, S, ?DELAY}.

handle_cast(_Message, S) ->
    {noreply, S, ?DELAY}.
```

The only call we have is to stop the musician server, which we agree to do pretty quickly. If we receive an unexpected message, we do not reply to it, and the caller will crash. This is not our problem. We set the timeout in the {noreply, S, ?DELAY} tuples, for one simple reason that we'll see right now.

```erlang
handle_info(timeout, S = #state{name=N, skill=good}) ->
    io:format("~s produced sound!~n",[N]),
    {noreply, S, ?DELAY};
handle_info(timeout, S = #state{name=N, skill=bad}) ->
    case random:uniform(5) of
        1 ->
            io:format("~s played a false note. Uh oh~n",[N]),
            {stop, bad_note, S};
        _ ->
            io:format("~s produced sound!~n",[N]),
            {noreply, S, ?DELAY}
    end;
handle_info(_Message, S) ->
    {noreply, S, ?DELAY}.
```

Each time the server times out, our musicians are going to play a note. If they're good, everything will be completely fine. If they're bad, they will have one chance out of five to miss and play a bad note, which will make them crash. Again, we set the ?DELAY timeout at the end of each nonterminating call.

Then we add an empty code_change/3 callback, as required by the gen_server behavior.

```erlang
code_change(_OldVsn, State, _Extra) ->
    {ok, State}.
```

And we can set the terminate function, as follows:

```erlang
terminate(normal, S) ->
    io:format("~s left the room (~s)~n",[S#state.name, S#state.role]);
terminate(bad_note, S) ->
    io:format("~s sucks! kicked that member out of the band! (~s)~n",
    [S#state.name, S#state.role]);
terminate(shutdown, S) ->
    io:format("The manager is mad and fired the whole band! "
```

```
                   "~s just got back to playing in the subway~n",
                   [S#state.name]);
terminate(_Reason, S) ->
        io:format("~s has been kicked out (~s)~n", [S#state.name, S#state.role]).
```

We have many different messages here. If we terminate with a normal reason, it means we've called the stop/1 function, and so we display the musician left on his own free will. In the case of a bad_note message, the musician will crash, and we'll say that it's because the manager (the supervisor we'll soon add) kicked him out of the band.

Then we have the shutdown message, which will come from the supervisor. Whenever that happens, it means the supervisor decided to kill all of its children, or in our case, fire all of the musicians. We then add a generic error message for the rest.

Here's a simple use case of a musician:

```
1> c(musicians).
{ok,musicians}
2> musicians:start_link(bass, bad).
Musician Ralphie Franklin, playing the bass entered the room
{ok,<0.615.0>}
Ralphie Franklin produced sound!
Ralphie Franklin produced sound!
Ralphie Franklin played a false note. Uh oh
Ralphie Franklin sucks! kicked that member out of the band! (bass)
3>
=ERROR REPORT==== 6-June-2013::03:22:14 ===
** Generic server bass terminating
** Last message in was timeout
** When Server state == {state,"Ralphie Franklin","bass",bad}
** Reason for termination ==
** bad_note
** exception error: bad_note
```

So we have Ralphie playing and crashing after a bad note. If you try the same with a good musician, you'll need to call our musicians:stop(Instrument) function in order to stop all the playing.

Band Supervisor

We can now work with the band supervisor. We'll have three grades of supervisors: a lenient one, an angry one, and a total jerk. The lenient supervisor, while still a very pissy person, will fire a single member of the band at a time (one_for_one)—the one who fails—until he gets fed up, fires them all, and gives up on bands. The angry supervisor, on the other hand, will fire some of the musicians (rest_for_one) on each mistake and wait a shorter amount of time before firing them all and giving up. The jerk supervisor will fire the whole band each time someone makes a mistake, and give up if the band members fail even less often.

```
-module(band_supervisor).
-behavior(supervisor).

-export([start_link/1]).
-export([init/1]).

start_link(Type) ->
    supervisor:start_link({local,?MODULE}, ?MODULE, Type).

%% The band supervisor will allow its band members to make a few
%% mistakes before shutting down all operations, based on what
%% mood he's in. A lenient supervisor will tolerate more mistakes
%% than an angry supervisor, who'll tolerate more than a
%% complete jerk supervisor.
init(lenient) ->
    init({one_for_one, 3, 60});
init(angry) ->
    init({rest_for_one, 2, 60});
init(jerk) ->
    init({one_for_all, 1, 60});
```

The init definition doesn't finish here, but this lets us set the tone for each kind of supervisor we want. The lenient one will restart only one musician and will fail on the fourth failure in 60 seconds. The angry one will accept only two failures, and the jerk supervisor will have very strict standards!

Now let's finish the function and actually implement the band starting functions and whatnot.

```
init({RestartStrategy, MaxRestart, MaxTime}) ->
    {ok, {{RestartStrategy, MaxRestart, MaxTime},
         [{singer,
            {musicians, start_link, [singer, good]},
            permanent, 1000, worker, [musicians]},
          {bass,
            {musicians, start_link, [bass, good]},
            temporary, 1000, worker, [musicians]},
          {drum,
            {musicians, start_link, [drum, bad]},
            transient, 1000, worker, [musicians]},
          {keytar,
            {musicians, start_link, [keytar, good]},
            transient, 1000, worker, [musicians]}
         ]}}.
```

So we'll have three good musicians: the singer, bass player, and keytar player. The drummer is terrible (which makes you pretty mad). The musicians have different Restart values (permanent, transient, or temporary). The singer is permanent, so the band could never work without a singer, even if the current one left by choice. The bass player is temporary, because the band could still play fine without a bass player (frankly, who gives a crap about bass players?). Other musicians are transient, and so they can leave on their own, but they might still need to be replaced in case of errors.

That gives us a functional band_supervisor module, which we can now try.

```
3> c(band_supervisor).
{ok,band_supervisor}
4> band_supervisor:start_link(lenient).
Musician Carlos Terese, playing the singer entered the room
Musician Janet Terese, playing the bass entered the room
Musician Keesha Ramon, playing the drum entered the room
Musician Janet Ramon, playing the keytar entered the room
{ok,<0.623.0>}
Carlos Terese produced sound!
Janet Terese produced sound!
Keesha Ramon produced sound!
Janet Ramon produced sound!
Carlos Terese produced sound!
Keesha Ramon played a false note. Uh oh
Keesha Ramon sucks! kicked that member out of the band! (drum)
... <snip> ...
Musician Arnold Tennelli, playing the drum entered the room
Arnold Tennelli produced sound!
Carlos Terese produced sound!
Janet Terese produced sound!
Janet Ramon produced sound!
Arnold Tennelli played a false note. Uh oh
Arnold Tennelli sucks! kicked that member out of the band! (drum)
... <snip> ...
Musician Carlos Frizzle, playing the drum entered the room
... <snip for a few more firings> ...
Janet Jamal played a false note. Uh oh
Janet Jamal sucks! kicked that member out of the band! (drum)
The manager is mad and fired the whole band!
  Janet Ramon just got back to playing in the subway
The manager is mad and fired the whole band!
  Janet Terese just got back to playing in the subway
The manager is mad and fired the whole band!
  Carlos Terese just got back to playing in the subway
** exception error: shutdown
```

Magic! We can see that at first only the drummer is fired, and then after a while, everyone else gets kicked out, too. And off to the subway (tubes for the UK readers) they go!

You can try the code with other kinds of supervisors, and it will end the same. The only difference will be the restart strategy. Here's the angry supervisor at work:

```
5> band_supervisor:start_link(angry).
Musician Dorothy Frizzle, playing the singer entered the room
Musician Arnold Li, playing the bass entered the room
Musician Ralphie Perlstein, playing the drum entered the room
Musician Carlos Perlstein, playing the keytar entered the room
```

```
... <snip> ...
Ralphie Perlstein sucks! kicked that member out of the band! (drum)
... <snip> ...
The manager is mad and fired the whole band!
   Carlos Perlstein just got back to playing in the subway
```

With the angry supervisor, both the drummer and the keytar player get fired when the drummer makes a mistake. This is nothing compared to the jerk's behavior:

```
6> band_supervisor:start_link(jerk).
Musician Dorothy Franklin, playing the singer entered the room
Musician Wanda Tennelli, playing the bass entered the room
Musician Tim Perlstein, playing the drum entered the room
Musician Dorothy Frizzle, playing the keytar entered the room
... <snip> ...
Tim Perlstein played a false note. Uh oh
Tim Perlstein sucks! kicked that member out of the band! (drum)
The manager is mad and fired the whole band! Dorothy Franklin just got back to
playing in the subway
The manager is mad and fired the whole band! Wanda Tennelli just got back to
playing in the subway
The manager is mad and fired the whole band! Dorothy Frizzle just got back to
playing in the subway
```

And that's about it for static restart strategies.

Dynamic Supervision

So far, the kind of supervision we've covered has been static. We specified all the children we would have directly in the source code, and let everything run after that. This is how most of your supervisors might be set up in real-world applications, usually for the supervision of architectural components.

On the other hand, you may have supervisors who supervise undetermined workers. They're usually there on a per-demand basis. Think of a web server that spawns a process per connection it receives. In this case, you would want dynamic supervisors to look over all the different processes you'll have.

Using Standard Supervisors Dynamically

Every time a worker is added to a supervisor using the one_for_one, rest_for_one, or one_for_all strategy, the child specification is added to a list in the supervisor, along with a pid and some other information. The child specification can then be used to restart the child and perform other tasks. Because things work that way, the following interface exists:

start_child(SupervisorNameOrPid, ChildSpec)
   Adds a child specification to the list and starts the child with it.

terminate_child(SupervisorNameOrPid, ChildId)
> Terminates or brutal_kills the child. The child specification is left in the supervisor.

restart_child(SupervisorNameOrPid, ChildId)
> Uses the child specification to get things rolling.

delete_child(SupervisorNameOrPid, ChildId)
> Gets rid of the ChildSpec of the specified child.

check_childspecs([ChildSpec])
> Makes sure a child specification is valid. You can use this to try the specification before using start_child/2.

count_children(SupervisorNameOrPid)
> Counts all the children under the supervisor and gives you a little comparative list of who is active, how many specs there are, how many are supervisors, and how many are workers.

which_children(SupervisorNameOrPid)
> Gives you a list of all the children under the supervisor.

Let's see how this works with musicians, with the output removed (you need to be quick to outrace the failing drummer!).

```
1> band_supervisor:start_link(lenient).
{ok,0.709.0>}
2> supervisor:which_children(band_supervisor).
[{keytar,<0.713.0>,worker,[musicians]},
 {drum,<0.715.0>,worker,[musicians]},
 {bass,<0.711.0>,worker,[musicians]},
 {singer,<0.710.0>,worker,[musicians]}]
3> supervisor:terminate_child(band_supervisor, drum).
ok
4> supervisor:terminate_child(band_supervisor, singer).
ok
5> supervisor:restart_child(band_supervisor, singer).
{ok,<0.730.0>}
6> supervisor:count_children(band_supervisor).
[{specs,4},{active,3},{supervisors,0},{workers,4}]
7> supervisor:delete_child(band_supervisor, drum).
ok
8> supervisor:restart_child(band_supervisor, drum).
{error,not_found}
9> supervisor:count_children(band_supervisor).
[{specs,3},{active,3},{supervisors,0},{workers,3}]
```

And you can see how this could work well for anything dynamic that you need to manage (start, terminate, and so on) and when few children are involved. Because the internal representation is a list, this won't work well when you need quick access to many children.

In those cases, what you want is simple_one_for_one.

Using a simple_one_for_one Supervisor

With a supervisor that uses the simple_one_for_one strategy, all the children are held in a dictionary, which makes looking them up faster. There is also a single child specification for all children under the supervisor. This will save you memory and time—you will never need to delete a child yourself or store any child specifications.

For the most part, writing a simple_one_for_one supervisor is similar to writing any other type of supervisor, except for one thing: The argument list in the {M,F,A} tuple is not the whole thing, but will be appended to what you call it with when you do supervisor:start_child(Sup, Args). That's right—supervisor:start_child/2 changes meaning. So instead of doing supervisor:start_child(Sup, Spec), which would call erlang:apply(M,F,A), we now have supervisor:start_child(Sup, Args), which calls erlang:apply(M,F,Args++A).

We could use this strategy with our band_supervisor just by adding the following clause somewhere in it:

```erlang
init(jamband) ->
    {ok, {{simple_one_for_one, 3, 60},
        [{jam_musician,
            {musicians, start_link, []},
            temporary, 1000, worker, [musicians]}
        ]}};
```

We've made all the musicians temporary in this case, and the supervisor is quite lenient:

```erlang
1> supervisor:start_child(band_supervisor, [djembe, good]).
Musician Janet Tennelli, playing the djembe entered the room
{ok,<0.690.0>}
2> supervisor:start_child(band_supervisor, [djembe, good]).
{error,{already_started,<0.690.0>}}
```

Whoops! This happens because we register the djembe player as djembe as part of the start call to our gen_server. If we didn't name the child processes or used a different name for each, it wouldn't cause a problem. Here's one with the name drum instead:

```erlang
3> supervisor:start_child(band_supervisor, [drum, good]).
Musician Arnold Ramon, playing the drum entered the room
{ok,<0.696.0>}
3> supervisor:start_child(band_supervisor, [guitar, good]).
Musician Wanda Perlstein, playing the guitar entered the room
{ok,<0.698.0>}
```

```
4> supervisor:terminate_child(band_supervisor, djembe).
ok
```

That seems right.

DON'T DRINK TOO MUCH KOOL-AID

Before Erlang version R14B03, it wasn't possible to terminate children with the function `supervisor:terminate_child(SupRef, Pid)`. The function would instead return `{error,simple_one_for_one}` and fail to terminate children. Instead, the following would have been the best way to terminate a child with a `simple_one_for_one` supervisor:

```
5> musicians:stop(drum).
Arnold Ramon left the room (drum)
ok
```

Backward-compatible code should take this kind of behavior into account.

As a general (though sometimes wrong) recommendation, use standard supervisors dynamically only when you know with certainty that you will have few children to supervise and/or they won't need to be manipulated frequently or with any high speed requirement. For other kinds of dynamic supervision, use `simple_one_for_one` where possible.

That's about it for the supervision strategies and child specifications. Right now, you might be having doubts and thinking. "How the hell am I going to get a working application out of that?" If that's the case, you'll be happy to get to Chapter 18, which actually builds a simple application with a short supervision tree to demonstrate how it could be done in the real world.

18

BUILDING AN APPLICATION

We've now covered how to use generic servers, FSMs, event handlers, and supervisors. However, we haven't gotten to how to put them all together to build complete applications and tools.

An Erlang application is a group of related code and processes. An OTP application specifically uses OTP behaviors for its processes, and then wraps them in a very specific structure that tells the VM how to set everything up and then tear it down. In this chapter, we're going to build an application with OTP components, although it won't be a full OTP application because we won't do the "wrapping up" just yet. The details of complete OTP applications are a bit complex and warrant their own chapter (the next one). This chapter is about using OTP components to implement an application, in our case, a process pool. The idea behind such a process pool is to manage and limit resources running in a system in a generic manner.

A Pool of Processes

A pool allows us to limit how many processes run at once. A pool can also queue up jobs when the running workers' limit is hit. The jobs can then be run as soon as resources are freed up, or they can simply block by telling the user they can't do anything else.

We might want to use process pools for several purposes, such as the following:

- Limit a server to at most N concurrent connections.
- Limit how many files can be opened by an application.
- Give different priorities to different subsystems of a release by allowing more resources for some and fewer for others. For example, you might want to allow more processes for client requests than processes in charge of generating reports for management.
- Allow an application under occasional heavy loads coming in bursts to remain more stable during its entire life by queuing the tasks.

The process pool application we'll build in this chapter will need to implement a few functions to handle the following:

- Start and stop the application.
- Start and stop a particular process pool (all the pools sit within the process pool application).
- Run a task in the pool and tell you it can't be started if the pool is full.

- Run a task in the pool if there is room; otherwise, keep the calling process waiting while the task is in the queue. Free the caller once the task can be run.

- Run a task asynchronously in the pool, as soon as possible. If no place is available, queue it up and run it whenever.

These needs will help drive our program design. Also keep in mind that we can now use supervisors, and, of course, we want to. However, though supervisors give us new powers in terms of robustness, they also impose a certain limit on flexibility. We'll explore that trade-off next.

The Onion Layer Theory

To help ourselves design an application with supervisors, it helps to have an idea of what needs supervision and how it needs to be supervised. As you'll recall from Chapter 17, we have different supervision strategies with different settings, which will fit for different kinds of code with different kinds of errors. A rainbow of mistakes can be made!

One thing newcomers and even experienced Erlang programmers have trouble dealing with is how to cope with the loss of state. Supervisors kill processes; state is lost; woe is me. To help with this, we will identify different kinds of states:

OTP:

Onion Theory Platform

- A static state that can easily be fetched from a configuration file, another process, or the supervisor restarting the application.

- A dynamic state that is composed of data you can recompute. This includes state that you needed to transform from its initial form to get where it is right now.

- A dynamic state that you cannot recompute. This might include user input, live data, sequences of external events, and so on.

Static data is somewhat easy to deal with; most of the time, you can get it straight from the supervisor. The same is true for the dynamic but recomputable data. In this case, you might want to grab it and compute it within the init/1 function (or anywhere else in your code, really). The most problematic kind of state is the dynamic data you can't recompute and that you just hope not to lose. In some cases, you'll be pushing that data to a database, although that won't always be a good option.

The idea of an onion-layered system is to allow all of these different states to be protected correctly by isolating different kinds of code from each other. In other words, it's process segregation. The static state can be handled by supervisors, as it is generally known as soon as the system starts up. Each time a child dies, the supervisor restarts it and can inject it with some form of static state, which is always available. Because most supervisor definitions are rather static by nature, each layer of supervision you add acts as a shield protecting your application against their failure and the loss of their state.

The dynamic state that can be recomputed has a whole lot of available solutions. For example, you can build it from the static data sent by the supervisors, or you could go fetch it back from some other process, database, text file, the current environment, or whatever. It should be relatively easy to get the data back on each restart. The fact that you have supervisors that do a restarting job can be enough to help you keep that state alive.

The dynamic non-recomputable kind of state needs a more thoughtful solution. The real nature of an onion-layered approach takes shape here. The idea is that the most important data (or the data that is most annoying to lose) must be the most protected type. The place where you are actually not allowed to fail is called the *error kernel* of your application.

The error kernel is likely the place you'll want to use try ... catch expressions more than anywhere else, since handling exceptional cases is vital there. This is the area that you want to be error-free. Careful testing must be done around the error kernel, especially in cases where there is no way to go back. You don't want to lose a customer's order halfway through processing it, do you?

Some operations are going to be considered safer than others. Because of this, we want to keep vital data in the safest core possible and keep everything somewhat dangerous outside it. In specific terms, this means that all related operations should be part of the same supervision trees, and the unrelated ones should be kept in different trees. Within the same tree, operations that are more failure-prone can be placed deeper in the tree, and the processes that cannot afford to crash are closer to the root of the tree.

These principles result in systems where all related pieces of software are part of the same trees, with the riskiest operations low in the tree, decreasing the risk of the core processes dying until the system can't cope with the errors properly anymore. We'll see an example of this when designing our actual process pool's supervision tree.

A Pool's Tree

So how should we organize these process pools? There are two schools of thought here. One tells people to design bottom-up (write all individual components, and put them together as required), and another one tells us to write things top-down (design as if all the parts were there, and then build them). Both approaches are equally valid depending on the circumstances and your personal style. For the sake of making things understandable, we're going to do things top-down here.

So what should our tree look like? Well, our requirements include being able to start the pool application as a whole, having many pools, and having many workers that can be queued for each pool. This already suggests a few possible design constraints.

We will need one gen_server per pool. The server's job will be to maintain the counter of how many workers are in the pool. For convenience, the same server should also hold the queue of tasks. Who should be in charge of overlooking each of the workers, though? The server itself?

Doing it with the server is interesting. After all, the server needs to track the processes to count them, and supervising them itself is a nifty way to do this. Moreover, neither the server nor the processes can crash without losing the state of all the others (otherwise, the server can't track the tasks after it has restarted). It has a few disadvantages, too: The server has many responsibilities, can be seen as more fragile, and duplicates the functionality of existing, better-tested modules.

A good way to make sure all workers are properly accounted for would be to use a supervisor just for them:

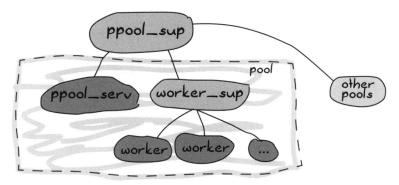

In this example, there is a single supervisor for all of the pools. Each pool is a set of a pool server and a supervisor for workers. The pool server knows of the existence of its worker supervisor and asks it to add items. Given that adding children is a very dynamic thing with unknown limits so far, we'll use a simple_one_for_one supervisor.

NOTE   *The name ppool was chosen because the Erlang standard library already has a pool module. Plus it's a terrible pool-related pun.*

The advantage of this approach is that because the worker_sup supervisor will need to track only OTP workers of a single type, each pool is guaranteed to be about a well-defined kind of worker, with simple management and restart strategies that are easy to define. This is one example of an error kernel being better defined. If we're using a pool of sockets for web connections and another pool of servers in charge of log files, we are making sure that incorrect code or messy permissions in the log file section of our application won't be drowning out the processes in charge of the sockets. If the log files' pool crashes too much, they will be shut down and their supervisor will stop. Oh wait—their supervisor stopping is a serious problem!

Because all pools are under the same supervisor, a given pool or server restarting too many times in a short time span can take all the other pools down. A solution might be to add one level of supervision. This will also make it much simpler to handle more than one pool at a time, so let's say the following will be our application architecture:

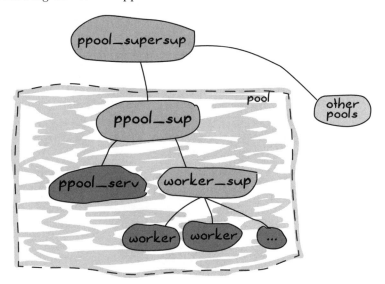

And that makes a bit more sense. From the onion-layer perspective, all pools are independent, the workers are independent from each other and the ppool_serv server is going to be isolated from all the workers. That's good enough for the architecture. Everything we need seems to be there. We can start working on the implementation—again, using a top-to-bottom approach.

Implementing the Supervisors

We can start with the top-level supervisor, ppool_supersup. All this one needs to do is start the supervisor of a pool when required. We'll give it a few functions: start_link/0, which starts the whole application; stop/0, which stops it; start_pool/3, which creates a specific pool; and stop_pool/1, which does the opposite. We also can't forget init/1, which is the only callback required by the supervisor behavior.

```
-module(ppool_supersup).
-behavior(supervisor).
-export([start_link/0, stop/0, start_pool/3, stop_pool/1]).
-export([init/1]).
```

```
start_link() ->
    supervisor:start_link({local, ppool}, ?MODULE, []).
```

Here, we gave the top-level process pool supervisor the name ppool (this explains the use of {local, Name}, an OTP convention about registering gen_* processes on a node; another one exists for distributed registration). This is because we know we will have only one ppool per Erlang node, and we can give it a name without worrying about clashes. Fortunately, the same name can then be used to stop the whole set of pools, like this:

```
%% Technically, a supervisor cannot be killed in an easy way.
%% Let's do it brutally!
stop() ->
    case whereis(ppool) of
        P when is_pid(P) ->
            exit(P, kill);
        _ -> ok
    end.
```

As the comments in the code explain, we cannot terminate a supervisor gracefully. The OTP framework provides a well-defined shutdown procedure for all supervisors, but we can't use it from where we are right now. We'll address how to do that in Chapter 19; but for now, brutally killing the supervisor is the best we can do.

What is the top-level supervisor exactly? Well, its only task is to hold pools in memory and supervise them. In this case, it will be a childless supervisor.

```
init([]) ->
    MaxRestart = 6,
    MaxTime = 3600,
    {ok, {{one_for_one, MaxRestart, MaxTime}, []}}.
```

We can now focus on starting each individual pool's supervisor and attaching them to ppool. Given our initial requirements, we can determine that we'll need two parameters: the number of workers the pool will accept and the {M,F,A} tuple that the worker supervisor will need to start each worker. We'll also add a name for good measure. We then pass this ChildSpec to the process pool's supervisor as we start it.

```
start_pool(Name, Limit, MFA) ->
    ChildSpec = {Name,
                 {ppool_sup, start_link, [Name, Limit, MFA]},
                 permanent, 10500, supervisor, [ppool_sup]},
    supervisor:start_child(ppool, ChildSpec).
```

You can see each pool supervisor is asked to be permanent and has the arguments needed (notice how we're changing programmer-submitted data into static data this way). The name of the pool is both passed to the supervisor and used as an identifier in the child specification. There's also a maximum shutdown time of 10500. There is no easy way to pick this value—just make sure it's large enough that all the children will have time to stop, if they need any. Play with the value according to your needs, and test and adapt to your application. If you're really not sure what value to use, you can try the infinity option.

To stop the pool, we need to ask the ppool super supervisor (the *supersup*!) to kill its matching child.

```
stop_pool(Name) ->
    supervisor:terminate_child(ppool, Name),
    supervisor:delete_child(ppool, Name).
```

This is possible because we gave the pool's name as the child specification identifier. Great! We can now focus on each pool's direct supervisor! Each ppool_sup will be in charge of the pool server and the worker supervisor:

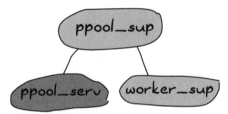

Can you see the funny thing here? The ppool_serv process should be able to contact the worker_sup process. If they're both started by the same supervisor at the same time, we won't have any way to let ppool_serv know about worker_sup, unless we were to do some trickery with supervisor:which_children/1 (which would be sensitive to timing and somewhat risky), or unless we give a name to both the ppool_serv process (so that users can call it) and the supervisor. However, we don't want to give names to the supervisors for several reasons:

- The users don't need to call them directly.
- We would need to dynamically generate atoms, and that makes me nervous.
- There is a better way.

The solution is to get the pool server to dynamically attach the worker supervisor to its ppool_sup. Don't worry if this sounds vague—you'll get it soon. For now, we only start the server.

```
-module(ppool_sup).
-export([start_link/3, init/1]).
-behavior(supervisor).

start_link(Name, Limit, MFA) ->
    supervisor:start_link(?MODULE, {Name, Limit, MFA}).
```

```
init({Name, Limit, MFA}) ->
    MaxRestart = 1,
    MaxTime = 3600,
    {ok, {{one_for_all, MaxRestart, MaxTime},
          [{serv,
            {ppool_serv, start_link, [Name, Limit, self(), MFA]},
            permanent,
            5000, % Shutdown time
            worker,
            [ppool_serv]}]}}.
```

And that's about it. Note that the `Name` is passed to the server, along with
`self()`, the supervisor's own pid. This will let the server call for the spawning
of the worker supervisor; the `MFA` variable will be used in that call to let the
`simple_one_for_one` supervisor know which kind of workers to run.

We'll get to how the server handles everything in the next section.
For now, we'll finish creating all of the application's supervisors by writing
`ppool_worker_sup`, which is in charge of all the workers.

```
-module(ppool_worker_sup).
-export([start_link/1, init/1]).
-behavior(supervisor).

start_link(MFA = {_,_,_}) ->
    supervisor:start_link(?MODULE, MFA).

init({M,F,A}) ->
    MaxRestart = 5,
    MaxTime = 3600,
    {ok, {{simple_one_for_one, MaxRestart, MaxTime},
          [{ppool_worker,
            {M,F,A},
            temporary, 5000, worker, [M]}]}}.
```

This is simple stuff. We
picked a `simple_one_for_one`
supervisor because workers
could be added in very high
numbers with a requirement
for speed, plus we want to
restrict their type. All the
workers are temporary, and
because we use an `{M,F,A}`
tuple to start the worker, we
can use any kind of OTP
behavior there.

The reason to make the workers temporary is twofold. First, we cannot know for sure whether they need to be restarted in case of failure, or what kind of restart strategy would be required for them. Second, the pool might be useful only if the worker's creator can have access to the worker's pid, depending on the use case. For this to work in any safe and simple manner, we can't just restart workers as we please without tracking their creator and sending it a notification. This would make things quite complex just to grab a pid. Of course, you are free to write your own ppool_worker_sup that doesn't return pids but restarts them. There's nothing inherently wrong in that design.

Working on the Workers

The pool server is the most complex part of the application, where all the clever business logic happens. Here's a reminder of the operations we must support:

- Running a task in the pool and indicating that it can't be started if the pool is full
- Running a task in the pool if there's room; otherwise, keeping the calling process waiting while the task is in the queue, until it can be run
- Running a task asynchronously in the pool, as soon as possible; if no place is available, queuing it up and running it whenever

The first operation will be done by a function named run/2, the second by sync_queue/2, and the last one by async_queue/2.

```
-module(ppool_serv).
-behavior(gen_server).
-export([start/4, start_link/4, run/2, sync_queue/2, async_queue/2, stop/1]).
-export([init/1, handle_call/3, handle_cast/2, handle_info/2,
         code_change/3, terminate/2]).

start(Name, Limit, Sup, MFA) when is_atom(Name), is_integer(Limit) ->
    gen_server:start({local, Name}, ?MODULE, {Limit, MFA, Sup}, []).

start_link(Name, Limit, Sup, MFA) when is_atom(Name), is_integer(Limit) ->
    gen_server:start_link({local, Name}, ?MODULE, {Limit, MFA, Sup}, []).

run(Name, Args) ->
    gen_server:call(Name, {run, Args}).

sync_queue(Name, Args) ->
    gen_server:call(Name, {sync, Args}, infinity).

async_queue(Name, Args) ->
    gen_server:cast(Name, {async, Args}).
```

```
stop(Name) ->
    gen_server:call(Name, stop).
```

For start/4 and start_link/4, Args will be the additional arguments passed to the A part of the {M,F,A} tuple sent to the supervisor. Note that for the synchronous queue, we've set the waiting time to infinity.

As mentioned earlier, we must start the supervisor from within the server. If you're adding the code as we go, you might want to include an empty gen_server template (or use the completed file available online) to follow along, because we'll do things on a per-feature basis, rather than from top to bottom.

The first thing we do is handle the creation of the supervisor. As discussed in "Dynamic Supervision" on page 277, we do not need a simple_one_for_one for cases where only a few children will be added, so supervisor:start_child/2 ought to do it. We'll first define the child specification of the worker supervisor.

```
%% The friendly supervisor is started dynamically!
-define(SPEC(MFA),
        {worker_sup,
         {ppool_worker_sup, start_link, [MFA]},
         permanent,
         10000,
         supervisor,
         [ppool_worker_sup]}).
```

We can then define the inner state of the server. We know we will need to track a few pieces of data: the number of processes that can be running, the pid of the supervisor, and a queue for all the jobs. To know when a worker's finished running and to fetch one from the queue to start it, we will need to track each worker from the server. The sane way to do this is with monitors, so we'll also add a refs field to our state record to keep all the monitor references in memory.

```
-record(state, {limit=0,
                sup,
                refs,
                queue=queue:new()}).
```

With this ready, we can start implementing the init function. The natural thing to try is this:

```
init({Limit, MFA, Sup}) ->
    {ok, Pid} = supervisor:start_child(Sup, ?SPEC(MFA)),
    {ok, #state{limit=Limit, refs=gb_sets:empty()}}.
```

However, this code is wrong. With gen_* behaviors, the process that spawns the behavior waits until the init/1 function returns before resuming its processing. This means that by calling supervisor:start_child/2 in there, we create the following deadlock:

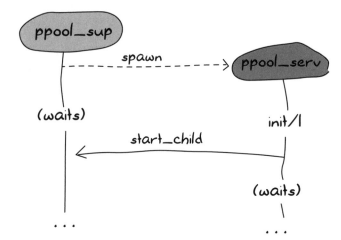

Both processes will keep waiting for each other until there is a crash. The cleanest way to get around this is to create a special message that the server will send to itself and later handle in handle_info/2 as soon as the init function has returned (and the pool supervisor has become free):

```
init({Limit, MFA, Sup}) ->
    %% We need to find the Pid of the worker supervisor from here,
    %% but alas, this would be calling the supervisor while it waits for us!
    self() ! {start_worker_supervisor, Sup, MFA},
    {ok, #state{limit=Limit, refs=gb_sets:empty()}}.
```

This one is cleaner. We can then head out to the handle_info/2 function and add the following clauses:

```
handle_info({start_worker_supervisor, Sup, MFA}, S = #state{}) ->
    {ok, Pid} = supervisor:start_child(Sup, ?SPEC(MFA)),
    {noreply, S#state{sup=Pid}};
handle_info(Msg, State) ->
    io:format("Unknown msg: ~p~n", [Msg]),
    {noreply, State}.
```

The first clause is the interesting one here. We find the message we sent ourselves (which will necessarily be the first one received), ask the pool supervisor to add the worker supervisor, track this pid, and *voilà*! Our tree is now fully initialized. You can try compiling everything to make sure no mistake has been made so far. Unfortunately, we still can't test the application because too much stuff is missing.

*Don't worry if you do not like the idea of building the whole application before run-
ning it. Things are being done this way to show a cleaner reasoning of the whole
thing. While I did have the general design in mind (the same one I illustrated earlier), I started writing this pool application in a little test-driven manner, with a few
tests here and there and a bunch of refactoring to get everything to a functional state.
Few Erlang programmers (much like programmers of most other languages) will be
able to produce production-ready code on their first try, and the author is not as clever
as the examples might make him seem.*

Now that we've solved this bit, we'll take care of the run/2 function. This
one is a synchronous call with the message of the form {run, Args} and works
as follows:

```
handle_call({run, Args}, _From, S = #state{limit=N, sup=Sup, refs=R}) when N > 0 ->
    {ok, Pid} = supervisor:start_child(Sup, Args),
    Ref = erlang:monitor(process, Pid),
    {reply, {ok,Pid}, S#state{limit=N-1, refs=gb_sets:add(Ref,R)}};
handle_call({run, _Args}, _From, S=#state{limit=N}) when N =< 0 ->
    {reply, noalloc, S};
```

We have a long function head, but we can see most of the management
taking place there. Whenever there are places left in the pool (the original limit N being decided by the programmer adding the pool in the first
place), we accept to start the worker. We then set up a monitor to know
when it's done, store all of this in our state, decrement the counter, and off
we go. In the case no space is available, we simply reply with noalloc.

The calls to sync_queue/2 will give a very similar implementation:

```
handle_call({sync, Args}, _From, S = #state{limit=N, sup=Sup, refs=R}) when N > 0 ->
    {ok, Pid} = supervisor:start_child(Sup, Args),
    Ref = erlang:monitor(process, Pid),
    {reply, {ok,Pid}, S#state{limit=N-1, refs=gb_sets:add(Ref,R)}};
handle_call({sync, Args}, From, S = #state{queue=Q}) ->
    {noreply, S#state{queue=queue:in({From, Args}, Q)}};
```

If there is space for more workers, then the first clause will do exactly
the same thing as we did for run/2. The difference comes in the case where
no workers can run. Rather than replying with noalloc as we did with run/2,
this one doesn't reply to the caller, keeps the From information, and queues
it for a later time when there is space for the worker to be run. We'll see
how we dequeue workers and handle them soon enough, but for now, we'll
finish the handle_call/3 callback with the following clauses:

```
handle_call(stop, _From, State) ->
    {stop, normal, ok, State};
handle_call(_Msg, _From, State) ->
    {noreply, State}.
```

These handle the unknown cases and the stop/1 call. We can now focus on getting async_queue/2 working. Because async_queue/2 basically does not care when the worker is run and expects absolutely no reply, we'll make it a cast rather than a call. You'll find the logic of it very similar to the two previous options.

```erlang
handle_cast({async, Args}, S=#state{limit=N, sup=Sup, refs=R}) when N > 0 ->
    {ok, Pid} = supervisor:start_child(Sup, Args),
    Ref = erlang:monitor(process, Pid),
    {noreply, S#state{limit=N-1, refs=gb_sets:add(Ref,R)}};
handle_cast({async, Args}, S=#state{limit=N, queue=Q}) when N =< 0 ->
    {noreply, S#state{queue=queue:in(Args,Q)}};
%% Not going to explain the one below!
handle_cast(_Msg, State) ->
    {noreply, State}.
```

Again, the only big difference apart from not replying is that when there is no place left for a worker, it is queued. This time though, we have no From information and just send the worker to the queue without it. The limit doesn't change in this case.

When do we know it's time to dequeue something? Well, we have monitors set all over the place, and we're storing their references in a gb_sets. Whenever a worker goes down, we're notified of it. Let's work from there.

```erlang
handle_info({'DOWN', Ref, process, _Pid, _}, S = #state{limit=L, sup=Sup, refs=Refs}) ->
    io:format("received down msg~n"),
    case gb_sets:is_element(Ref, Refs) of
        true ->
            handle_down_worker(Ref, S);
        false -> %% not our responsibility
            {noreply, S}
    end;
handle_info({start_worker_supervisor, Sup, MFA}, S = #state{}) ->
    ...
handle_info(Msg, State) ->
    ...
```

In this snippet, we make sure the 'DOWN' message we get comes from a worker. If it doesn't come from one (which would be surprising), we just ignore it. However, if the message really is what we want, we call a function named handle_down_worker/2:

```erlang
handle_down_worker(Ref, S = #state{limit=L, sup=Sup, refs=Refs}) ->
    case queue:out(S#state.queue) of
        {{value, {From, Args}}, Q} ->
            {ok, Pid} = supervisor:start_child(Sup, Args),
            NewRef = erlang:monitor(process, Pid),
            NewRefs = gb_sets:insert(NewRef, gb_sets:delete(Ref,Refs)),
            gen_server:reply(From, {ok, Pid}),
            {noreply, S#state{refs=NewRefs, queue=Q}};
```

```
    {{value, Args}, Q} ->
        {ok, Pid} = supervisor:start_child(Sup, Args),
        NewRef = erlang:monitor(process, Pid),
        NewRefs = gb_sets:insert(NewRef, gb_sets:delete(Ref,Refs)),
        {noreply, S#state{refs=NewRefs, queue=Q}};
    {empty, _} ->
        {noreply, S#state{limit=L+1, refs=gb_sets:delete(Ref,Refs)}}
end.
```

This is quite a complex function. Because our worker is dead, we can look in the queue for the next one to run. We do this by popping one element out of the queue and looking at the result. If there is at least one element in the queue, it will be of the form {{value, Item}, NewQueue}. If the queue is empty, it returns {empty, SameQueue}. Furthermore, we know that when we have the value {From, Args}, it means this came from sync_queue/2; otherwise, it came from async_queue/2.

Both cases where the queue has tasks in it will behave roughly the same: A new worker is attached to the worker supervisor, and the reference of the old worker's monitor is removed and replaced with the new worker's monitor reference. The only different aspect is that in the case of the synchronous call, we send a manual reply, and in the other case, we can remain silent. In the case the queue was empty, we need to do nothing but increment the worker limit by one.

The last thing to do is add the standard OTP callbacks:

```
code_change(_OldVsn, State, _Extra) ->
    {ok, State}.

terminate(_Reason, _State) ->
    ok.
```

That's it—our pool is ready to be used! It is a very unfriendly pool, though. All the functions we need to use are scattered throughout the code. Some are in ppool_supersup; some are in ppool_serv. Also, the module names are long for no reason. To make things nicer, add the following API module (just abstracting the calls away) to the application's directory:

```
%%% API module for the pool
-module(ppool).
-export([start_link/0, stop/0, start_pool/3,
         run/2, sync_queue/2, async_queue/2, stop_pool/1]).

start_link() ->
    ppool_supersup:start_link().

stop() ->
    ppool_supersup:stop().
```

```
start_pool(Name, Limit, {M,F,A}) ->
    ppool_supersup:start_pool(Name, Limit, {M,F,A}).

stop_pool(Name) ->
    ppool_supersup:stop_pool(Name).

run(Name, Args) ->
    ppool_serv:run(Name, Args).

async_queue(Name, Args) ->
    ppool_serv:async_queue(Name, Args).

sync_queue(Name, Args) ->
    ppool_serv:sync_queue(Name, Args).
```

And now we're finished with our pool for real!

POOL LIMITS

You'll have noticed that our process pool doesn't limit the number of items that can be stored in the queue. In some cases, a real server application will need to put a ceiling on how many things can be queued to avoid crashing when too much memory is used, although the problem can be circumvented if you use run/2 and sync_queue/2 only with a fixed number of callers (if all content producers are stuck waiting for free space in the pool, they stop producing so much content in the first place).

Adding a limit to the queue size is left as an exercise to the reader, but fear not because it is relatively simple to do. You will need to pass a new parameter to all functions up to the server, which will then check the limit before any queuing.

Additionally, to control the load of your system, you sometimes want to impose limits closer to their source by using synchronous calls. Synchronous calls allow you to block incoming queries when the system is getting swamped by producers faster than consumers. This approach generally helps keep it more responsive than a free-for-all load.

Writing a Worker

Look at me go—I'm lying all the time! The pool isn't really ready to be used. We don't have a worker at the moment. I forgot. This is a shame because we all know that in the chapter about writing a concurrent application (Chapter 13), we built a nice task reminder. It apparently isn't enough for me, so for this example, we'll write a *nagger*.

It will basically be a worker for each task, and the worker will keep nagging us by sending repeated messages until a given deadline.

The nagger will be able to take the following elements:

- A time delay for which to nag
- An address (pid) to say where the messages should be sent
- A nagging message to be sent in the process mailbox, including the nagger's own pid to be able to call
- A stop function to say the task is done and that the nagger can stop nagging

Here we go:

```
%% demo module, a nagger for tasks,
%% because the previous one wasn't good enough
-module(ppool_nagger).
-behavior(gen_server).
-export([start_link/4, stop/1]).
-export([init/1, handle_call/3, handle_cast/2,
         handle_info/2, code_change/3, terminate/2]).

start_link(Task, Delay, Max, SendTo) ->
    gen_server:start_link(?MODULE, {Task, Delay, Max, SendTo} , []).

stop(Pid) ->
    gen_server:call(Pid, stop).
```

Yes, we're going to be using yet another gen_server. You'll find out that people use them all the time—sometimes even when not appropriate! It's important to remember that our pool can accept any OTP-compliant process, not just a gen_server.

```
init({Task, Delay, Max, SendTo}) ->
    {ok, {Task, Delay, Max, SendTo}, Delay}.
```

This just takes the basic data and forwards it:

- Task is the thing to send as a message.
- Delay is the time spent in between each sending.
- Max is the number of times it's going to be sent.
- SendTo is a pid or a name where the message will go.

Note that Delay is passed as a third element of the tuple, which means the timeout will be sent to handle_info/2 after Delay milliseconds.
Given our API, most of the server is rather straightforward.

```
%%% OTP Callbacks
handle_call(stop, _From, State) ->
    {stop, normal, ok, State};
```

```
handle_call(_Msg, _From, State) ->
    {noreply, State}.

handle_cast(_Msg, State) ->
    {noreply, State}.

handle_info(timeout, {Task, Delay, Max, SendTo}) ->
    SendTo ! {self(), Task},
    if Max =:= infinity ->
        {noreply, {Task, Delay, Max, SendTo}, Delay};
       Max =< 1 ->
        {stop, normal, {Task, Delay, 0, SendTo}};
       Max > 1  ->
        {noreply, {Task, Delay, Max-1, SendTo}, Delay}
    end.
%% We cannot use handle_info below: if that ever happens,
%% we cancel the timeouts (Delay) and basically zombify
%% the entire process. It's better to crash in this case.
%% handle_info(_Msg, State) ->
%%     {noreply, State}.

code_change(_OldVsn, State, _Extra) ->
    {ok, State}.

terminate(_Reason, _State) -> ok.
```

The only somewhat complex part here lies in the handle_info/2 function. As seen back in Chapter 14's introduction to gen_server, every time a timeout is hit (in this case, after Delay milliseconds), the timeout message is sent to the process. Based on this, we check how many nags were sent to know if we should send more or just quit.

With this worker complete, we can actually try this process pool!

Run Pool Run

We can now play with the pool. Compile all the files and start the pool top-level supervisor itself:

```
$ erlc *.erl
$ erl
... <snip> ...
1> ppool:start_link().
{ok,<0.33.0>}
```

From this point, we can try a bunch of different features of the nagger as a pool:

```
2> ppool:start_pool(nagger, 2, {ppool_nagger, start_link, []}).
{ok,<0.35.0>}
```

```
3> ppool:run(nagger, ["finish the chapter!", 10000, 10, self()]).
{ok,<0.39.0>}
4> ppool:run(nagger, ["Watch a good movie", 10000, 10, self()]).
{ok,<0.41.0>}
5> flush().
Shell got {<0.39.0>,"finish the chapter!"}
Shell got {<0.39.0>,"finish the chapter!"}
ok
6> ppool:run(nagger, ["clean up a bit", 10000, 10, self()]).
noalloc
7> flush().
Shell got {<0.41.0>,"Watch a good movie"}
Shell got {<0.39.0>,"finish the chapter!"}
Shell got {<0.41.0>,"Watch a good movie"}
Shell got {<0.39.0>,"finish the chapter!"}
Shell got {<0.41.0>,"Watch a good movie"}
... <snip> ...
```

Everything seems to work rather well for the synchronous nonqueued runs. The pool is started, tasks are added, and messages are sent to the right destination. When we try to run more tasks than allowed, allocation is denied to us. No time for cleaning up, sorry! The others still run fine though.

NOTE   *The ppool is started with start_link/0. If at any time you make an error in the shell, you take down the whole pool and need to start over again. This issue will be addressed in Chapter 19.*

Now let's try the queuing facilities (asynchronous):

```
8> ppool:async_queue(nagger, ["Pay the bills", 30000, 1, self()]).
ok
9> ppool:async_queue(nagger, ["Take a shower", 30000, 1, self()]).
ok
10> ppool:async_queue(nagger, ["Plant a tree", 30000, 1, self()]).
ok
❶ ... <wait a bit> ...
received down msg
received down msg
11> flush().
Shell got {<0.70.0>,"Pay the bills"}
Shell got {<0.72.0>,"Take a shower"}
❷ ... <wait some more> ...
received down msg
12> flush().
Shell got {<0.74.0>,"Plant a tree"}
ok
```

Great! So the queuing works. The log here doesn't show everything in a very clear manner (although you should wait at ❶ and ❷ for best effect).

What happens is that the two first naggers run as soon as possible. Then the worker limit is hit, and we need to queue the third one (planting a tree). When the nags for paying the bills are finished, the tree nagger is scheduled and sends the message a bit later.

The synchronous one will behave differently:

```
13> ppool:sync_queue(nagger, ["Pet a dog", 20000, 1, self()]).
{ok,<0.108.0>}
14> ppool:sync_queue(nagger, ["Make some noise", 20000, 1, self()]).
{ok,<0.110.0>}
15> ppool:sync_queue(nagger, ["Chase a tornado", 20000, 1, self()]).
received down msg
{ok,<0.112.0>}
received down msg
16> flush().
Shell got {<0.108.0>,"Pet a dog"}
Shell got {<0.110.0>,"Make some noise"}
ok
received down msg
17> flush().
Shell got {<0.112.0>,"Chase a tornado"}
ok
```

Again, the log isn't as clear as if you tried it yourself (which is recommended). The basic sequence of events is that two workers are added to the pool. They aren't finished running, and when we try to add a third one, the shell gets locked up until ppool_serv (under the process name nagger) receives a worker's down message (received down msg). After this, our call to sync_queue/2 can return and give us the pid of our brand-new worker.

We can now get rid of the pool as a whole:

```
18> ppool:stop_pool(nagger).
ok
19> ppool:stop().
** exception exit: killed
```

All pools will be terminated if you decide to just call ppool:stop(), but you'll receive a bunch of error messages. This is because we brutally kill the ppool_supersup process, rather than taking it down correctly, which in turns crashes all child pools. In Chapter 19, I will cover how to terminate the pool cleanly.

Cleaning the Pool

In this chapter, we managed to write a process pool to do some resource allocation in
a somewhat simple manner. Everything can
be handled in parallel, can be limited, and
can be called from other processes. Pieces
of your application that crash can, with the
help of supervisors, be replaced transparently without breaking the entirety of it.
Once the pool application was ready, we
even rewrote a surprisingly large part of our
reminder app with very little code.

Failure isolation for a single computer has been taken into account, and
concurrency is handled. We now have enough architectural blocks to write
some pretty solid server-side software, even though we still haven't really
covered good ways to run them from the shell.

Chapter 19 will show how to package the ppool application into a
real OTP application, ready to be shipped and used by other products.
Although we haven't explored all the advanced features of OTP, you're now
on a level where you should be able to understand most intermediate to
somewhat advanced discussions on OTP and Erlang (the nondistributed
part, at least). That's pretty good!

19

BUILDING APPLICATIONS
THE OTP WAY

After seeing our whole application's supervision tree start at once with a simple function call, you might wonder why we would want to package it in any way. What could be simpler than a single function call?

The concepts behind supervision trees are a bit complex already, and I could see myself just starting all of these trees and subtrees manually with a script when the system is first set up. Then after that, I would be free to go outside and try to find clouds that look like animals for the rest of the afternoon.

This is entirely true, yes. This is an acceptable way to do things (especially the part about clouds, because these days, everything is about

cloud computing). However, like most abstractions made by programmers and engineers, OTP applications are the result of many ad hoc systems being generalized and made clean.

If you were to make an array of scripts and commands to start your supervision trees, and other developers you work with had their own, you would quickly run into massive issues. Then someone would ask something like, "Wouldn't it be nice if everyone used the same kind of system to start everything? And wouldn't it even be nicer if they all had the same kind of application structure?"

OTP applications attempt to solve this type of problem by providing the following:

- A directory structure
- A way to handle configurations
- A way to create environment variables and configurations
- Ways to start and stop applications while respecting dependencies
- A lot of safe control in detecting conflicts and handling live upgrades without shutting your applications down

So unless you don't want these aspects (nor the niceties they give, like consistent structures and tools), this chapter should be of some interest to you, as it introduces all the necessary concepts to get a good understanding of OTP applications.

My Other Car Is a Pool

Merely using OTP components isn't enough to guarantee we're creating an *OTP application*, much like putting pieces of humans together won't guarantee you get a human being instead of some kind of Frankenstein's monster. We're going to reuse the ppool application we wrote in Chapter 18 and turn it into a proper OTP application.

The first step in doing so is to copy all the ppool-related files into a neat directory structure:

```
ebin/
include/
priv/
src/
 - ppool.erl
 - ppool_sup.erl
 - ppool_supersup.erl
 - ppool_worker_sup.erl
 - ppool_serv.erl
 - ppool_nagger.erl
test/
 - ppool_tests.erl
```

Most directories will remain empty for now. As explained in Chapter 13, the *ebin/* directory will hold compiled files; the *include/* directory will contain public Erlang header (*.hrl*) files; *priv/* will hold executables, other programs, and various specific files needed for the application to work; and *src/* will hold the Erlang source files you will need (as well as private *.hrl* files).

You'll note that we added a *test/* directory, which holds the test file *ppool_tests.erl* that I wrote for Chapter 18, if you downloaded the related code. Tests are somewhat common, but you don't necessarily want them distributed as part of your application. You just need the tests when developing your code and justifying yourself to your manager ("Tests pass. I don't understand why the app killed people."). Other directories end up being added as required, depending on the case. One example is the *doc/* directory, created whenever you have EDoc documentation (which is a way to annotate Erlang code to generate documentation) to add to your application. For more information on EDoc, see *http://www.erlang.org/doc/apps/ edoc/chapter.html*.

The four basic directories to have are *ebin/*, *include/*, *priv/*, and *src/*. These are common to pretty much every OTP application, although only *ebin/* and *priv/* will be exported when real OTP systems are deployed.

The Application Resource File

Where do we go from here? Well, the first thing to do is add an application file. This file will tell the Erlang VM what the application is, where it begins, and where it ends. This file lives in the *ebin/* directory, along with all the compiled modules.

This file is usually named *yourapp.app* (in our case *ppool.app*) and contains a bunch of Erlang terms defining the application in a way that the VM can understand. (The VM is pretty bad at guessing stuff!)

NOTE *Some people prefer to keep the application file outside* ebin/ *and instead have a file named* myapp.app.src *as part of* src/. *Whatever build system they use then copies this file over to* ebin/ *or even generates an app file in order to keep everything clean.*

The basic structure of the application file is simply as follows:

```
{application, ApplicationName, Properties}.
```

`ApplicationName` is an atom, and `Properties` is a list of `{Key, Value}` tuples describing the application. They're used by OTP to figure out what your application does. They're all optional, but they can be useful to debug running systems and make sure different applications interact in an orderly manner. They're also necessary for some tools. We'll look at a subset of them for now, and introduce the others as we need them.

{description, "Some description of your application"}

This gives the system a short description of the application. The field defaults to an empty string. Although this field is optional, I suggest always defining a description, if only because it makes things easier to read.

{vsn, "1.2.3"}

This is the version of your application. This string can take any format you want. It's usually a good idea to stick to a scheme of the form *Major.Minor.Patch*, or something similar. When you start using tools to help with upgrades and downgrades, this string is used to identify your application's version.

{modules, ModuleList}

This contains a list of all the modules that your application introduces to the system. A module always belongs to at most one application and cannot be present in two applications' app files at once. This list lets the system and tools look at dependencies of your application, making sure everything is where it needs to be and that you have no conflicts with other applications already loaded in the system. If you're using a standard OTP structure and are using an Erlang build tool like rebar, this is handled for you.

NOTE *Rebar is an Erlang build tool used by the community in general. It understands the principles behind OTP applications and can act the way Emakefiles do. It can also fetch dependencies from git and mercurial repositories as needed.*

{registered, AtomList}

This contains a list of all the names registered by the application. It lets OTP know if there will be name clashes when you try to bundle a bunch of applications together, but is entirely based on trusting the developers to give good data. We all know this isn't always the case, so blind faith shouldn't be used in this case, and some testing is always recommended.

{env, [{Key, Val}]}

This is a list of key/values that can be used as a configuration for your application. They can be obtained at runtime by calling application:get_env(Key) or application:get_env(AppName, Key). The former will try to find the value in the application file of whatever application you are in at the moment of the call. The latter allows you to specify a particular application. These values can be overwritten as required (either at boot time or by using application:set_env(Application, Key, Value)). Because it's possible to overwrite these values, the env part of the application resource file is usually used for default values. This helps make the application usable with minimal user configuration.

All in all, this is a pretty useful place to store configuration data rather than having a bunch of configuration files to read in some arbitrary format, without really knowing where to store them and whatnot. People often tend to roll their own system to handle it anyway, since not everyone is a fan of using Erlang syntax in their configuration files.

{maxT, Milliseconds}

This is the maximum time that the application can run, after which it will be shut down. This is a rarely used item. `Milliseconds` defaults to `infinity`, so you often don't need to bother with this one at all.

{applications, AtomList}

This is a list of applications on which yours depends. The application system of Erlang will make sure they were loaded and/or started before allowing yours to do so. All applications depend at least on `kernel` and `stdlib`, but if your application were to depend on `ppool` being started, then you should add `ppool` to the list. It is important to add your dependencies, given OTP has mechanisms to know whether an application can be loaded or started based on this list. Not adding them is doing a disservice to yourself.

NOTE *Yes, the standard library and the VM's kernel are applications themselves, which means that Erlang is a language used to build OTP, but whose runtime environment depends on OTP to work. It's circular. This gives you some idea of why the language is officially named Erlang/OTP.*

{mod, {CallbackMod, Args}}

This defines a callback module for the application, using the application behavior (described shortly). This tells OTP that when starting your application, it should call `CallbackMod:start(normal, Args)`. It will also call `CallbackMod:stop(Args)` when stopping it. People will tend to name `CallbackMod` after their application.

And this covers most of what we need for now (and for most applications you'll ever write).

Converting the Pool

Now let's put this into practice! We'll turn the `ppool` set of processes from Chapter 18 into a basic OTP application. The first step for this is to redistribute everything under the correct directory structure:

```
ebin/
include/
```

```
priv/
src/
      - ppool.erl
      - ppool_serv.erl
      - ppool_sup.erl
      - ppool_supersup.erl
      - ppool_worker_sup.erl
test/
      - ppool_tests.erl
      - ppool_nagger.erl
```

You'll notice we moved the *ppool_nagger.erl* to the *test* directory. This is for a good reason: It is not much more than a demo case and will have nothing to do with our application, but is still necessary for the tests. We can actually try it later on once the app has been packaged to make sure everything still works, but for the moment, it's kind of useless.

We'll add an Emakefile (appropriately named Emakefile, placed in the app's base directory) to help us compile and run things later on.

```
{"src/*", [debug_info, {i,"include/"}, {outdir, "ebin/"}]}.
{"test/*", [debug_info, {i,"include/"}, {outdir, "ebin/"}]}.
```

This just tells the compiler to include debug_info for all files in *src/* and *test/*, go look in the *include/* directory (if it's ever needed), and then shove the files up its *ebin/* directory.

Speaking of which, let's add the app file in the *ebin/* directory.

```
{application, ppool,
 [{vsn, "1.0.0"},
  {modules, [ppool, ppool_serv, ppool_sup, ppool_supersup, ppool_worker_sup]},
  {registered, [ppool]},
  {mod, {ppool, []}}
]}.
```

This one contains only fields we find necessary; env, maxT, and applications are not used.

We now need to change how the callback module (ppool) works. How do we do that exactly?

First, let's see the application behavior.

NOTE *Even though all applications depend on the* kernel *and the* stdlib *applications, I haven't included them.* ppool *will still work because starting the Erlang VM starts these applications automatically. You might feel like adding them for the sake of explicitness, but there's no need for it right now.*

The Application Behavior

Remember that behaviors are always about splitting generic code away from specific code. They denote the idea that your specific code gives up its own execution flow and inserts itself as a bunch of callbacks to be used by the generic code. To put it simply, behaviors handle the boring parts while you connect the dots. In the case of applications, this generic part is quite complex and not nearly as simple as other behaviors.

Whenever the VM first starts up, a process called the *application controller* is started (with the name application_controller). It starts all other applications and sits on top of most of them. In fact, you could say the application controller acts a bit like a supervisor for all applications. We'll cover the available supervision strategies in the next section.

THE EXCEPTION THAT CONFIRMS THE RULE

The application controller technically doesn't sit over all the applications. One exception is the kernel application, which itself starts a process named user. The user process acts as a group leader to the application controller, and the kernel application thus needs some special treatment. We don't need to care about this, but I felt like it should be included for the sake of precision.

In Erlang, the I/O system depends on a concept called a *group leader*. The group leader represents standard input and output and is inherited by all processes. There is a hidden I/O protocol (*http://erlang.org/doc/apps/stdlib/io_protocol.html*) that the group leader and any process-calling I/O functions use to communicate. The group leader then takes the responsibility of forwarding these messages to whatever I/O channels there are, weaving some magic that doesn't concern us within the confines of this text.

When someone decides to start an application, the application controller (often referred to as *AC* in OTP parlance) starts an *application master*. The application master is two processes taking charge of each individual application. They set up the application and act like a middleman between your application's top supervisor and the application controller. OTP is a bureaucracy, and we have many layers of middle management! I won't get into the details of what happens in there, as most Erlang developers never actually need to care about this, and very little documentation exists (the code is the documentation). Just know that the application master acts a bit like the app's nanny (well, a pretty insane nanny). It looks over its children and grandchildren, and when things go awry, it goes berserk and terminates its whole family tree. Brutally killing children is a common topic among Erlangers.

An Erlang VM with a bunch of applications might look a bit like this:

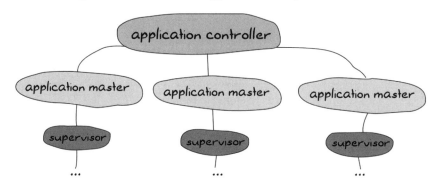

Up to now, we've been looking at the generic part of the behavior, but what about the specific stuff? After all, this is all we actually have to program. Well, the application callback module requires very few functions to be functional: start/2 and stop/1.

The start/2 function takes the form YourMod:start(Type, Args). For now, the Type will always be normal (the other possibilities accepted have to do with distributed applications, which we'll cover in Chapter 27). Args is what is coming from your app file (in the {mod, {YourMod, Args}} tuple). The function initializes everything for your app and needs to return only the pid of the application's top-level supervisor in one of the two following forms: {ok, Pid} or {ok, Pid, SomeState}. If you don't return SomeState, it simply defaults to [].

The stop/1 function takes the state returned by start/2 as an argument. It runs after the application is finished running and does only the necessary cleanup.

That's it—a huge generic part and a tiny specific one. Be thankful for that, because you wouldn't want to write the generic part yourself too often. (Just look at the source if you feel like it!) There are a few more functions that you can optionally use to have more control over the application, but we don't need them for now. This means we can move forward with our ppool application!

From Chaos to Application

We have the app file and a general idea of how applications work. Two simple callbacks are needed. Open *ppool.erl* and locate these lines:

```
-export([start_link/0, stop/0, start_pool/3,
         run/2, sync_queue/2, async_queue/2, stop_pool/1]).
```

```
start_link() ->
    ppool_supersup:start_link().

stop() ->
    ppool_supersup:stop().
```

Change this code to the following instead:

```
-behavior(application).
-export([start/2, stop/1, start_pool/3,
         run/2, sync_queue/2, async_queue/2, stop_pool/1]).

start(normal, _Args) ->
    ppool_supersup:start_link().

stop(_State) ->
    ok.
```

We can then make sure the tests are still valid. Open the old *ppool_tests.erl* file and replace the single call to ppool:start_link/0 with application:start(ppool), as follows:

```
find_unique_name() ->
    application:start(ppool),
    Name = list_to_atom(lists:flatten(io_lib:format("~p",[now()]))),
    ?assertEqual(undefined, whereis(Name)),
    Name.
```

You should also take the time to remove stop/0 from ppool_supersup (and remove the export), because the OTP application tools will take care of that for us.

We can finally recompile the code and run all the tests to make sure everything still works (we'll cover how that eunit thing works in Chapter 24).

```
$ erl -make
Recompile: src/ppool_worker_sup
Recompile: src/ppool_supersup
... <snip> ...
$ erl -pa ebin/
... <snip> ...
1> make:all([load]).
Recompile: src/ppool_worker_sup
Recompile: src/ppool_supersup
Recompile: src/ppool_sup
Recompile: src/ppool_serv
Recompile: src/ppool
Recompile: test/ppool_tests
Recompile: test/ppool_nagger
up_to_date
2> eunit:test(ppool_tests).
  All 14 tests passed.
ok
```

The tests take a while to run due to `timer:sleep(X)` being used to synchronize everything in a few places, but you should find that they work, as shown here. Good news: Our app is healthy!

We can now study the wonders of OTP applications by using our new awesome callbacks:

```
3> application:start(ppool).
ok
4> ppool:start_pool(nag, 2, {ppool_nagger, start_link, []}).
{ok,<0.142.0>}
5> ppool:run(nag, [make_ref(), 500, 10, self()]).
{ok,<0.146.0>}
6> ppool:run(nag, [make_ref(), 500, 10, self()]).
{ok,<0.148.0>}
7> ppool:run(nag, [make_ref(), 500, 10, self()]).
noalloc
9> flush().
Shell got {<0.146.0>,#Ref<0.0.0.625>}
Shell got {<0.148.0>,#Ref<0.0.0.632>}
... <snip> ...
received down msg
received down msg
```

The magic command here is `application:start(ppool)`. This tells the application controller to launch our ppool application. It starts the `ppool_supersup` supervisor, and from that point on, everything can be used as normal. We can see all the applications currently running by calling `application:which_applications()`:

```
10> application:which_applications().
[{ppool,[],"1.0.0"},
 {stdlib,"ERTS  CXC 138 10","1.17.4"},
 {kernel,"ERTS  CXC 138 10","2.14.4"}]
```

What a surprise—ppool is running (the [] means we have put no description in the *.app* file). As mentioned earlier, we can see that all applications depend on `kernel` and `stdlib`, which are both running. We can close the pool as follows:

```
11> application:stop(ppool).

=INFO REPORT==== DD-MM-YYYY::23:14:50 ===
    application: ppool
    exited: stopped
    type: temporary
ok
```

And it is finished. You should notice that we now get a clean shutdown with a little informative report rather than the messy ** exception exit: killed from Chapter 18.

You'll sometimes see people do something like MyApp:start(...) *instead of* application:start(MyApp). *While this works for testing purposes, it loses a lot of the advantages of actually having an application. It's no longer part of the VM's supervision tree, cannot access its environment variables, will not check dependencies before being started, and so on. Try to stick to* application:start/1 *if possible.*

But wait! What's that thing about our app being *temporary*? We write Erlang and OTP stuff because it's supposed to run forever, not just for a while! How dare the VM say this? The secret is that we can give different arguments to application:start/1. Depending on the arguments, the VM will react differently to termination of one of its applications. In some cases, the VM will be a loving beast ready to die for its children. In other cases, it's rather a cold, heartless, and pragmatic machine willing to tolerate many of its children dying for the survival of its species.

Application started with application:start(AppName, temporary)

If it ends normally, nothing special happens, and the application has stopped.

If it ends abnormally, the error is reported, and the application terminates without restarting.

Application started with application:start(AppName, transient)

If it ends normally, nothing special happens, and the application has stopped.

If it ends abnormally, the error is reported, all the other applications are stopped, and the VM shuts down.

Application started with application:start(AppName, permanent)

If it ends normally, all other applications are terminated, and the VM shuts down.

If it ends abnormally, the same thing happens: All applications are terminated, and the VM shuts down.

You can see something new in the supervision strategies when it comes to applications. No longer will the VM try to save you. At this point, something has gone very, very wrong to cause it to travel up the whole supervision tree of one of its vital applications—enough to crash it. When this does happen, the VM has lost all hope in your program. Given the definition of insanity is to keep doing the same thing while expecting different outcomes each time, the VM prefers to die sanely and just give up. Of course, the real reason has to do with something being broken that needs to be fixed, but you catch my drift. Note that all applications can be terminated by calling application:stop(AppName) without affecting others, as if a crash had occurred.

Library Applications

What happens when we want to wrap flat modules in an application but we have no process to start and thus no need for an application callback module?

After pulling our hair and crying in rage for a few minutes, the only other thing left to do is to remove the tuple {mod, {Module, Args}} from the application file. That's it. This is called a *library application*. The Erlang stdlib (standard library) application is an example of one of these.

If you have the source package of Erlang, you can go to *otp_src_<release>/lib/stdlib/src/stdlib.app.src* and see the following:

```
{application, stdlib,
 [{description, "ERTS  CXC 138 10"},
  {vsn, "%VSN%"},
  {modules, [array,
            ...
            gen_event,
            gen_fsm,
            gen_server,
            io,
            ...
            lists,
            ...
            zip]},
  {registered,[timer_server,rsh_starter,take_over_monitor,pool_master,
              dets]},
  {applications, [kernel]},
  {env, []}]}.
```

You can see it's a pretty standard application file, but without the callback module. Again, it's a library application.

How about we go deeper with applications and try building more complex ones?

20

THE COUNT OF APPLICATIONS

Our ppool app has become a valid OTP application, and we now understand what this means. But wouldn't it be nice to build an application that actually uses our process pool to do something useful? To push our knowledge of applications a bit further, we will write a second application. This one will depend on ppool but will be able to benefit from some more automation than our "nagger" from Chapter 19.

This application, which we will name erlcount, will have a somewhat simple objective: recursively look into some directory, find all Erlang files (ending in *.erl*), and then run a regular expression over the result to count all instances of a given string within the modules. The results are then accumulated to give the final result, which will be output to the screen.

From OTP Application to Real Application

The erlcount application will be relatively simple, relying heavily on our process pool to do the work. It will have a structure as follows:

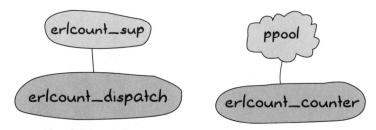

In this diagram, ppool represents the whole application but only means to show that erlcount_counter will be the worker for the process pool. It will open files, run the regular expression, and return the count. The process/module erlcount_sup will be our supervisor. erlcount_dispatch will be a single server in charge of browsing the directories, asking ppool to schedule workers, and compiling the results. We'll also add an erlcount_lib module, taking charge of hosting all the functions to read directories, compile data, and so on, leaving the other modules with the responsibility of coordinating these calls. Last will be an erlcount module, with the single purpose of being the application callback module.

The first step is to create the required directory structure. You can also add a few file stubs if you feel like doing so.

```
ebin/
 - erlcount.app
include/
priv/
src/
 - erlcount.erl
 - erlcount_counter.erl
 - erlcount_dispatch.erl
 - erlcount_lib.erl
 - erlcount_sup.erl
test/
Emakefile
```

This has nothing too different from the structure we used in Chapter 19, and you can even copy our old Emakefile.

We can probably start writing most parts of the application pretty quickly. The *.app* file, counter, library, and supervisor should be relatively simple. On the other hand, the dispatch module will need to accomplish some complex tasks if we want the application to be useful.

The Application File

Let's start with the app file, which looks like this:

```
{application, erlcount,
 [{vsn, "1.0.0"},
  {modules, [erlcount, erlcount_sup, erlcount_lib,
             erlcount_dispatch, erlcount_counter]},
  {applications, [ppool]},
  {registered, [erlcount]},
  {mod, {erlcount, []}},
  {env,
   [{directory, "."},
    {regex, ["if\\s.+->", "case\\s.+\\sof"]},
    {max_files, 10}]}
 ]}.
```

This app file is a bit more complex than the ppool one. We can still recognize some of the fields as being the same: this app will also be in version 1.0.0, and the modules are listed. The next part is something we didn't have for ppool: an application dependency. As explained earlier, the applications tuple gives a list of all the applications that should be started before erlcount. If you try to start it without that, you'll get an error message.

We then need to count the registered processes with {registered, [erlcount]}. Technically, none of our modules started as part of the erlcount app will need a name. Everything we do can be anonymous. However, because we know ppool registers the ppool_serv to the name we give it, and because we know we will use a process pool, we're going to call it erlcount and note it here. If all applications that use ppool do the same, we should be able to detect conflicts in the future. The mod tuple is similar to the one we used earlier. In it, we define the application behavior callback module.

The last new thing in here is the env tuple. This entire tuple gives us a key/value store for application-specific configuration variables. These variables will be accessible from all the processes running within the application, stored in memory for your convenience. They can basically be used as a substitute configuration file for your app.

In this case, we define three variables:

- directory tells the app where to look for *.erl* files. Assuming we run the app in an Erlang virtual machine started in the *learn-you-some-erlang* root (if you downloaded the package of files for this book), "." will refer to that directory.

- max_files tells us how many file descriptors should be opened at once. We don't want to open 10,000 files at once if we end up having that many, so this variable will match the maximum number of workers in ppool.

- regex, the most complex variable, will contain a list of all regular expressions we want to run over each of the files to count the results.

We won't get into the syntax of Perl Compatible Regular Expressions (PCRE) here (if you're interested, the re module's documentation contains full details), but we will look at what we're doing for our application. In this case, the first regular expression says, "Look for a string that contains if followed by any single whitespace character (\s, with a second backslash for escaping purposes) and finishes with ->. Moreover, there can be anything in between the if and the -> (.+)." The second regular expression says, "Look for a string that contains case followed by any single whitespace character (\s), and finishes with of preceded by a single whitespace character. Between the case and the of, there can be anything (.+)." To make things simple, we'll try to count how many times we use case ... of versus how many times we use if ... end in our libraries.

DON'T DRINK TOO MUCH KOOL-AID

Using regular expressions is not an optimal choice to analyze Erlang code. The problem is there are a lot of cases that will make your results inaccurate, including strings in the text and comments that match the patterns you're looking for but are technically not code.

To get more accurate results, you would need to look at the parsed and expanded version of your modules directly in Erlang. While more complex, this would make sure that you handle things like macros, exclude comments, and just generally do it the right way. You can look into erl_syntax or xref if this is something you wish to explore.

The Application Callback Module and Supervisor

With the app file out of the way, we can start writing the application callback module.

```
-module(erlcount).
-behavior(application).
-export([start/2, stop/1]).

start(normal, _Args) ->
    erlcount_sup:start_link().

stop(_State) ->
    ok.
```

It's not complex—basically it just starts the supervisor. And now let's set up the supervisor itself:

```
-module(erlcount_sup).
-behavior(supervisor).
-export([start_link/0, init/1]).

start_link() ->
    supervisor:start_link(?MODULE, []).

init([]) ->
    MaxRestart = 5,
    MaxTime = 100,
    {ok, {{one_for_one, MaxRestart, MaxTime},
          [{dispatch,
            {erlcount_dispatch, start_link, []},
            transient,
            60000,
            worker,
            [erlcount_dispatch]}]}}.
```

This is a standard supervisor, which will be in charge of only erlcount_dispatch, as it was shown in the previous little schema. The MaxRestart, MaxTime, and 60 seconds value for shutdown were chosen pretty randomly, but in real cases, you would want to study the needs you have. Because this is a demo application, it didn't seem that important. The author reserves the right to laziness.

The Dispatcher

The next process and module in the chain is the dispatcher. The dispatcher will have a few complex requirements to fulfill for it to be useful:

- When we search the directories to find files ending in *.erl*, we should go through the whole list of directories only once, even when we apply multiple regular expressions.

- We should be able to start scheduling files for result counting as soon as we find there is one that matches our criteria. We should not need to wait for a complete list to do so.

- We need to hold a counter per regular expression so we can compare the results in the end.

- It is possible that we will start getting results from the erlcount_counter workers before we're finished looking for *.erl* files.

- It is possible that many erlcount_counters will be running at once.

- It is likely we will keep getting results after we have finished looking up files in the directories (especially if we have many files or complex regular expressions).

The two big points we must consider right now are how we're going to go through a directory recursively while still being able to get results from there in order to schedule them, and then accept results back while that goes on, without getting confused.

Returning Results through CPS

At a first glance, the easiest way to gain the ability to return results while in the middle of recursion would be to use a process to do it. However, it's a bit annoying to change our previous structure just to be able to add another process to the supervision tree, and then to get the processes working together. There is, in fact, a simpler way to do things: Use a style of programming called *continuation-passing style (CPS)*.

The basic idea behind CPS is to take one function that's usually deeply recursive and break down every step. We return each step (which would usually be the accumulator), and then call a function that will allow us to keep going after that. In our case, our function will have two possible return values:

```
{continue, Name, NextFun}
done
```

Whenever we receive the first one, we can schedule FileName into ppool and then call NextFun to keep looking for more files. We can implement this function in erlcount_lib, like this:

```
-module(erlcount_lib).
-export([find_erl/1]).
-include_lib("kernel/include/file.hrl").

%% Finds all files ending in .erl.
find_erl(Directory) ->
    find_erl(Directory, queue:new()).
```

Ah, something new here! What a surprise; my heart is racing and my blood is pumping. The include file up there is something given to us by the file module. It contains a record (#file_info{}) with a bunch of fields explaining details about the file, including its type, size, permissions, and so on.

Our design includes a queue. Why is that? Well, it is entirely possible that a directory contains more than one file. So when we hit a directory and it contains something like 15 files, we want to handle the first one (and if it's a directory, open it, look inside, and so on), and then handle the 14 others later. In order to do this, we will just store their names in memory until we have the time to process them. We use a queue for that, but a stack or any other data structure would still be fine, given we don't really care about the order in which we read files. The point is that this queue acts a bit like a to-do list for files in our algorithm.

Let's start by reading the first file passed from the first call:

```
%%% Private
%% Dispatches based on file type.
find_erl(Name, Queue) ->
    {ok, F = #file_info{}} = file:read_file_info(Name),
    case F#file_info.type of
        directory -> handle_directory(Name, Queue);
        regular -> handle_regular_file(Name, Queue);
        _Other -> dequeue_and_run(Queue)
    end.
```

This function tells us a few things. One is that we want to deal with only regular files and directories. In each case, we will write a function to handle these specific occurrences (handle_directory/2 and handle_regular_file/2). For other files, we will dequeue anything we had prepared before with the help of dequeue_and_run/2. For now, we first start dealing with directories, as follows:

```
%% Opens directories and enqueues files in there.
handle_directory(Dir, Queue) ->
    case file:list_dir(Dir) of
        {ok, []} ->
            dequeue_and_run(Queue);
        {ok, Files} ->
            dequeue_and_run(enqueue_many(Dir, Files, Queue))
    end.
```

So if there are no files, we keep searching with dequeue_and_run/1. If there are many files, we enqueue them before searching further. The function dequeue_and_run will take the queue of filenames and get one element out of it. The filename it fetches from there will be used by calling find_erl(Name, Queue), and we just keep going as if we were just getting started.

```
%% Pops an item from the queue and runs it.
dequeue_and_run(Queue) ->
    case queue:out(Queue) of
        {empty, _} -> done;
        {{value, File}, NewQueue} -> find_erl(File, NewQueue)
    end.
```

Note that if the queue is empty ({empty, _}), the function considers itself done (a keyword chosen for our CPS function); otherwise, we keep going over again.

The other function we need to consider is enqueue_many/3. This one is designed to enqueue all the files found in a given directory. It works as follows:

```
%% Adds a bunch of items to the queue.
enqueue_many(Path, Files, Queue) ->
    F = fun(File, Q) -> queue:in(filename:join(Path,File), Q) end,
    lists:foldl(F, Queue, Files).
```

Basically, we use the function filename:join/2 to merge the directory's path to each filename (so that we get a complete path). We then add this new full path to a file to the queue. We use a fold to repeat the same procedure with all the files in a given directory. The new queue we get out of it is then used to run find_erl/2 again, but this time with all the new files we found added to the to-do list.

We digressed a bit. Where were we? Oh yes, we were handling directories, and now we're finished with them. We then need to check for regular files and whether they end in *.erl*.

```
%% Checks if the file finishes in .erl.
handle_regular_file(Name, Queue) ->
    case filename:extension(Name) of
        ".erl" ->
            {continue, Name, fun() -> dequeue_and_run(Queue) end};
        _NonErl ->
            dequeue_and_run(Queue)
    end.
```

You can see that if the name matches (according to filename:extension/1), we return our continuation. The continuation gives the Name to the caller, and then wraps the operation dequeue_and_run/1 with the queue of files left to visit into an anonymous function. That way, the user can call that anonymous function and keep going as if we were still in the recursive call, while still getting results in the meantime. In the case where the filename doesn't end in *.erl*, the user has no interest in us returning yet, and we keep going by dequeuing more files. That's it.

Hooray, the CPS thing is complete. We can now focus on the other issue.

Dispatching and Receiving

How are we going to design the dispatcher so that it can both dispatch and receive at once? My suggestion, which you will no doubt accept because I'm the one writing the text, is to use an FSM.

The FSM will have two states. The first one will be the "dispatching" state. It's the one used whenever we're waiting for our find_erl CPS function to hit the done entry. While we're in there, we will never think about being finished with the counting. That will happen in only the second and final state, "listening," but we will still receive notices from ppool all the time:

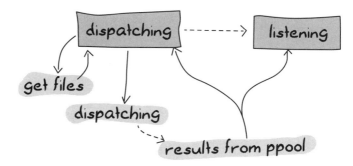

This will thus require us to have the following:

- A dispatching state with an asynchronous event for when we get new files to dispatch

- A dispatching state with an asynchronous event for when we are finished getting new files

- A listening state with an asynchronous event for when we are finished getting new files

- A global event to be sent by the ppool workers when they are finished running their regular expression

We'll slowly start building our gen_fsm:

```
-module(erlcount_dispatch).
-behavior(gen_fsm).
-export([start_link/0, complete/4]).
-export([init/1, dispatching/2, listening/2, handle_event/3,
         handle_sync_event/4, handle_info/3, terminate/3, code_change/4]).

-define(POOL, erlcount).
```

Our API will have two functions: one for the supervisor (start_link/0) and one for the ppool callers (complete/4, which we'll get to soon). The other functions are the standard gen_fsm callbacks, including our listening/2 and dispatching/2 asynchronous state handlers. We also defined a ?POOL macro, used to give our ppool server the name erlcount.

What should the gen_fsm's data look like, though? Because we're going asynchronous and we will always call ppool:run_async/2 instead of anything else, we will have no real way of knowing if we're ever done scheduling files. Basically, we could have a timeline like this:

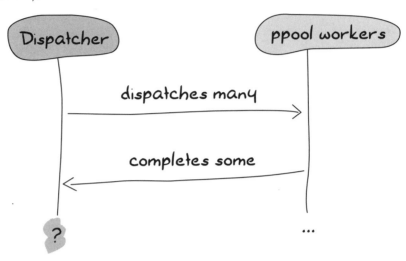

One way to solve the problem could be to use a timeout, but this is always annoying. Is the timeout too long or too short? Has something crashed? This much uncertainty is probably as much fun as a toothbrush made of lemon. Instead, we could use a concept where each worker is given some kind of identity, which we can track and associate with a reply, a bit like a secret password to enter the private club of "workers who succeeded." This concept will let us match one-on-one whatever message we get and let us know when we are absolutely finished. We now know what our state data might look like:

```
-record(data, {regex=[], refs=[]}).
```

The first list will be tuples of the form {RegularExpression, NumberOfOccurrences}, and the second will be a list of some kind of references to the messages. Anything will do, as long as it's unique. We can then add the two following API functions:

```
%%% PUBLIC API
start_link() ->
    gen_fsm:start_link(?MODULE, [], []).

complete(Pid, Regex, Ref, Count) ->
    gen_fsm:send_all_state_event(Pid, {complete, Regex, Ref, Count}).
```

And here is our secret complete/4 function. Unsurprisingly, the workers will need to send back only three pieces of data: what regular expression they were running, what their associated score was, and then the reference mentioned earlier. Awesome—now we can get into the real interesting stuff!

```
init([]) ->
    {ok, Re} = application:get_env(regex),
    {ok, Dir} = application:get_env(directory),
    {ok, MaxFiles} = application:get_env(max_files),
    ppool:start_pool(?POOL, MaxFiles, {erlcount_counter, start_link, []}),
    case lists:all(fun valid_regex/1, Re) of
        true ->
            self() ! {start, Dir},
            {ok, dispatching, #data{regex=[{R,0} || R <- Re]}};
        false ->
            {stop, invalid_regex}
    end.
```

The init function first loads all the information we need to run from the application file. Once that's done, we plan on starting the process pool with erlcount_counter as a callback module. The last step before actually starting to dispatch workers is to make sure all regular expressions are valid. The reason for this is simple: If we do not check it right now, then we will need to add an error-handling call somewhere else instead. This is likely going to be in the erlcount_counter worker. If it happens there, we now need to define what we do to handle workers crashing when regular expressions are invalid. It's just simpler to handle when starting the app and crash early. Here's the valid_regex/1 function:

```
valid_regex(Re) ->
    try re:run("", Re) of
        _ -> true
    catch
        error:badarg -> false
    end.
```

We try to run the regular expression on only an empty string. This will take no time and let the re module try to run things. So the regular expressions are valid, and we start the app by sending ourselves {start, Directory} and with a state defined by [{R,0} || R <- Re]. This will basically change a list of the form [a,b,c] to the form [{a,0},{b,0},{c,0}], the idea being to add a counter set to 0 to each of the regular expressions.

The first message we need to handle is {start, Dir} in handle_info/2. Remember that because Erlang's behaviors are pretty much all based on messages, we need to take the step of sending ourselves messages if we want to trigger a function call and do things our way. This is annoying but manageable.

```
handle_info({start, Dir}, State, Data) ->
    gen_fsm:send_event(self(), erlcount_lib:find_erl(Dir)),
    {next_state, State, Data}.
```

We send ourselves the result of erlcount_lib:find_erl(Dir). It will be received in the dispatching callback, given that's the value of State as it was set by the init function of the FSM. This snippet solves our problem, but also illustrates the general pattern we'll have during the whole FSM. Because our find_erl/1 function is written in CPS, we can just send ourselves an asynchronous event and deal with it in each of the correct callback states. It is likely that the first result of our continuation will be {continue, File, Fun}. We will also be in the "dispatching" state, because that's what we put as the initial state in the init function:

```
dispatching({continue, File, Continuation}, Data = #data{regex=Re, refs=Refs}) ->
    F = fun({Regex, _Count}, NewRefs) ->
        Ref = make_ref(),
        ppool:async_queue(?POOL, [self(), Ref, File, Regex]),
        [Ref|NewRefs]
    end,
    NewRefs = lists:foldl(F, Refs, Re),
    gen_fsm:send_event(self(), Continuation()),
    {next_state, dispatching, Data#data{refs = NewRefs}};
```

That's a bit ugly. For each of the regular expressions, we create a unique reference, schedule a ppool worker that knows this reference, and then store this reference (to know if a worker has finished). Doing this in a foldl makes it easier to accumulate all the new references. Once that dispatching is complete, we call the continuation again to get more results, and then wait for the next message with the new references as our state.

What's the next kind of message we can get? We have two choices here: Either none of the workers have given us our results back (even though they have not been implemented yet) or we get the done message because all files have been looked up. Let's go with the second type to finish implementing the dispatching/2 function:

```
dispatching(done, Data) ->
    %% This is a special case. We cannot assume that all messages have NOT
    %% been received by the time we hit 'done'. As such, we directly move to
    %% listening/2 without waiting for an external event.
    listening(done, Data).
```

The comment is pretty explicit about what is going on. When we schedule jobs, we can receive results while in dispatching/2 or while in listening/2. This can take the following form:

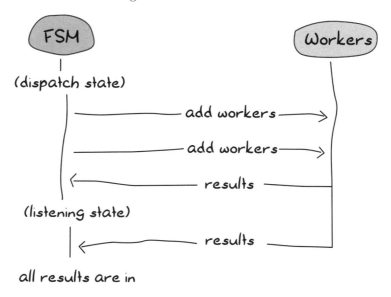

In this case, the listening state can just wait for results and declare everything is in. But remember that this is Erlang Land (Erland), and we work in parallel and asynchronously! This scenario is as probable:

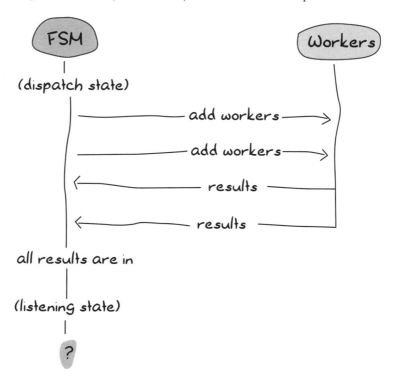

Ouch. Our application would then be hanging forever, waiting for messages. This is why we need to manually call listening/2. We will force it to do some kind of result detection to make sure everything has been received, just in case we already have all the results. Here's what this looks like:

```
listening(done, #data{regex=Re, refs=[]}) -> % all received!
    [io:format("Regex ~s has ~p results~n", [R,C]) || {R, C} <- Re],
    {stop, normal, done};
listening(done, Data) -> % entries still missing
    {next_state, listening, Data}.
```

If no refs are left, then everything was received and we can output the results. Otherwise, we can keep listening to messages. Take another look at complete/4 and our events diagram:

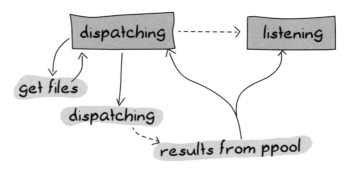

The result messages are global because they can be received in either dispatching or listening states. Here's the implementation:

```
handle_event({complete, Regex, Ref, Count}, State, Data = #data{regex=Re, refs=Refs}) ->
    {Regex, OldCount} = lists:keyfind(Regex, 1, Re),
    NewRe = lists:keyreplace(Regex, 1, Re, {Regex, OldCount+Count}),
    NewData = Data#data{regex=NewRe, refs=Refs--[Ref]},
    case State of
        dispatching ->
            {next_state, dispatching, NewData};
        listening ->
            listening(done, NewData)
    end.
```

The first thing this does is find the regular expression that just completed in the Re list, which also contains the count for all of them. We extract that value (OldCount) and update it with the new count (OldCount+Count) with the help of lists:keyreplace/4. We update our Data record with the new scores while removing the Ref of the worker, and then send ourselves to the next state.

In normal FSMs, we would just have done {next_state, State, NewData}, but here, because of the problem with knowing when we're finished, we must manually call listening/2 again. This may be a pain, but alas, it's a necessary step.

And that's it for the dispatcher. We just add in the rest of the filler behavior functions, as follows:

```erlang
handle_sync_event(Event, _From, State, Data) ->
    io:format("Unexpected event: ~p~n", [Event]),
    {next_state, State, Data}.

terminate(_Reason, _State, _Data) ->
    ok.

code_change(_OldVsn, State, Data, _Extra) ->
    {ok, State, Data}.
```

Next, we'll move on to the counter. You might want to take a little break before then. Hard-core readers can go bench-press their own weight a few times to relax themselves and then come back for more.

The Counter

The counter is simpler than the dispatcher. While we still need a behavior to do things (in this case, a gen_server), it will be quite minimalist. We need it to do only three things:

- Open a file
- Run a regular expression on it and count the instances
- Return the result

For the first task, we have plenty of functions in file to help us. For the third task, we defined erlcount_dispatch:complete/4 to handle it. For the second, we can use the re module with run/2-3, but it doesn't quite do what we need, as you can see here:

```erlang
1> re:run(<<"brutally kill your children (in Erlang)">>, "a").
{match,[{4,1}]}
2> re:run(<<"brutally kill your children (in Erlang)">>, "a",
2>        [global]).
{match,[[{4,1}],[{35,1}]]}
3> re:run(<<"brutally kill your children (in Erlang)">>, "a",
3>        [global, {capture, all, list}]).
{match,[["a"],["a"]]}
4> re:run(<<"brutally kill your children (in Erlang)">>, "child",
4>        [global, {capture, all, list}]).
{match,[["child"]]}
```

While the function does take the arguments we need (re:run(String, Pattern, Options)), it doesn't give us the correct count. Let's add the following function to erlcount_lib so we can start writing the counter:

```
regex_count(Re, Str) ->
    case re:run(Str, Re, [global]) of
        nomatch -> 0;
        {match, List} -> length(List)
    end.
```

This one basically just counts the results and returns that value. Don't forget to add it to the export attribute.

Now let's continue by defining the worker, as follows:

```
-module(erlcount_counter).
-behavior(gen_server).
-export([start_link/4]).
-export([init/1, handle_call/3, handle_cast/2, handle_info/2,
         terminate/2, code_change/3]).

-record(state, {dispatcher, ref, file, re}).

start_link(DispatcherPid, Ref, FileName, Regex) ->
    gen_server:start_link(?MODULE, [DispatcherPid, Ref, FileName, Regex], []).

init([DispatcherPid, Ref, FileName, Regex]) ->
    self() ! start,
    {ok, #state{dispatcher=DispatcherPid,
                ref = Ref,
                file = FileName,
                re = Regex}}.

handle_call(_Msg, _From, State) ->
    {noreply, State}.

handle_cast(_Msg, State) ->
    {noreply, State}.

handle_info(start, S = #state{re=Re, ref=Ref}) ->
    {ok, Bin} = file:read_file(S#state.file),
    Count = erlcount_lib:regex_count(Re, Bin),
    erlcount_dispatch:complete(S#state.dispatcher, Re, Ref, Count),
    {stop, normal, S}.

terminate(_Reason, _State) ->
    ok.

code_change(_OldVsn, State, _Extra) ->
    {ok, State}.
```

The two interesting sections here are the init/1 callback, where we order ourselves to start, and then a single handle_info/2 clause, where we open the file (file:read_file(Name)) and get back a binary, which we pass to our new regex_count/2 function, and then send it back with complete/4. We then stop the worker. The rest is just standard OTP callback stuff.

We can now compile and run the whole thing!

```
$ erl -make
Recompile: src/erlcount_sup
Recompile: src/erlcount_lib
Recompile: src/erlcount_dispatch
Recompile: src/erlcount_counter
Recompile: src/erlcount
Recompile: test/erlcount_tests
```

Hell, yes. Pop the champagne because we have no whine!

Run App Run

There are many ways to get our app running. Make sure you're in a directory where you somehow have these two directories next to each other:

```
erlcount-1.0
ppool-1.0
```

Now start Erlang the following way:

```
$ erl -env ERL_LIBS "."
```

ERL_LIBS is a special variable defined in your environment that lets you specify where Erlang can find OTP applications. The VM is then able to automatically look there to find the *ebin/* directories for you. The erl executable can also take an argument of the form -env NameOfVar Value to override this setting quickly, so that's what we used here. The ERL_LIBS variable is pretty useful, especially when installing libraries, so try to remember it!

With the VM we started, we can test that the modules are all there:

```
1> application:load(ppool).
ok
```

This function will try to load all the application modules in memory if they can be found. If you don't call it, the loading will be done automatically when starting the application, but this provides an easy way to test our paths. We can start the apps:

```
2> application:start(ppool), application:start(erlcount).
ok
```

```
Regex if\s.+-> has 20 results
Regex case\s.+\sof has 26 results
```

Your results may vary depending on what you have in your directories. Note that depending how many files you have, this can take a while.

What if we want different variables to be set for our applications, though? Do we need to change the application file all the time? No, we don't! Erlang also supports that. So let's say we wanted to see how many times the developers of Erlang are angry in their source files?

The erl executable supports a special set of arguments of the form -AppName Key1 Val1 Key2 Val2 ... KeyN ValN. In this case, we could then run the following regular expression over the Erlang source code from the R15B01 distribution with two regular expressions, as follows:

```
$ erl -env ERL_LIBS "." -erlcount directory '"/home/ferd/otp_src_R15B01/lib/"' regex '["shit","damn"]'
... <snip> ...
1> application:start(ppool), application:start(erlcount).
ok
Regex shit has 3 results
Regex damn has 1 results
2> q().
ok
```

Note that in this case, all expressions given as arguments are wrapped in single quotation marks ('). That's because I want them to be taken literally by my Unix shell. Different shells might have different rules.

We could also try our search with more general expressions, allowing values to start with capital letters and more file descriptors:

```
$ erl -env ERL_LIBS "." -erlcount directory '"/home/ferd/otp_src_R15B01/lib/"'
  regex '["[Ss]hit","[Dd]amn"]' max_files 50
... <snip> ...
1> application:start(ppool), application:start(erlcount).
ok
Regex [Ss]hit has 13 results
Regex [Dd]amn has 6 results
2> q().
ok
```

Oh, OTP programmers, what makes you so angry ("working with Erlang" not being an acceptable answer)?

This one might take even longer to run due to the more complex checks required over the hundreds of files there. This all works pretty well, but there are a few annoying things here. Why are we always manually starting both applications? Isn't there a better way?

Included Applications

Included applications are one way to get things working. The basic idea of an included application is that you define an application (in this case ppool) as an application that is part of another one (erlcount here). To do this, a bunch of changes need to be made to both applications.

The gist of this approach is that you modify your application file a bit, and then you need to add something called *start phases* to them, and respect a given protocol described at length in the Erlang documentation.

It is more and more recommended *not* to use included applications for a simple reason: They seriously limit code reuse. We've spent a lot of time working on ppool's architecture to make it so anyone can use it, get their own pool, and be free to do whatever they want with it. If we were to push it into an included application, then it can no longer be included in any other application on this VM. Also, if erlcount dies, then ppool will be taken down with it, ruining the work of any third-party application that wanted to use ppool.

For these reasons, included applications are usually excluded from many Erlang programmers' toolbox, although some still love them. As we will discuss in the following chapter, releases can basically help us do the same (and much more) in a more generic manner.

But before we get to that, we have a one more application topic left to discuss.

Complex Terminations

In some cases, we need more steps to be taken before terminating our application. The stop/1 function from the application callback module might not be enough, especially since it is called *after* the application has already terminated. What do we do if we need to clean up things before the application is actually gone?

The trick is simple: Just add a function prep_stop(State) to your application callback module. State will be the state returned by your start/2 function, and whatever prep_stop/1 returns will be passed to stop/1. The function prep_stop/1 thus technically inserts itself between start/2 and stop/1, and is executed while your application is still alive, but just before it shuts down. For your own code, you will know when you need to use this kind of callback. We don't require it for our application right now.

Now that we have basic applications working, we're going to start thinking about packaging our applications into releases.

21

RELEASE IS THE WORD

How far have we really gotten? All this work, all these concepts, and we haven't shipped a single Erlang executable yet! You might agree with me that getting an Erlang system up and running requires a lot of effort, especially compared to many languages where you call the compiler and off you go.

Of course this is entirely right. We can compile files, run applications, check for some dependencies, handle crashes, and so on, but it's not very useful without a functioning Erlang system you can easily deploy or ship with the code we wrote. What use is having a great pizza when it can only be delivered cold? (People who enjoy cold pizza might feel excluded here. I am sorry.)

The OTP team didn't leave us on our own when it comes to making sure real systems come to life. OTP releases are part of a system made to help package applications with the minimal resources and dependencies. In this chapter, we'll look at the two major ways to handle releases, Systools and Reltool.

Fixing the Leaky Pipes

For our first release, we will reuse our ppool and erlcount applications from the previous chapters. However, before we do so, we'll need to change a few things here and there.

If you're following along with the book and writing your own code, you might want to copy both of our apps into a new directory called *release/*, which I will assume you have done for the rest of the chapter.

Terminating the VM

The first thing that's really bothersome about erlcount is that once it's finished running, the VM stays up, doing nothing. We might want most applications to stay running forever, but that's not the case here. Keeping it running makes sense during development, because we might want to play with a few things in the shell and need to manually start applications, but this should no longer be necessary.

For this reason, we'll add a command that will shut down the Erlang VM in an orderly manner. The best place to do this is within erlcount_dispatch.erl's own terminate function, given it's called after we obtain the results. The perfect function to tear everything down is init:stop/0. This function is quite complex, but will take care of terminating our applications in order. It will get rid of file descriptors, sockets, and so on for us. The new stop function should now look like this:

```
terminate(_Reason, _State, _Data) ->
    init:stop().
```

And that's it for the code itself. However, we still have a bit more work to do.

Updating the Application Files

When we defined our app files in the preceding chapters, we did so while using the absolute minimal amount of information necessary to get them running. A few more fields are required for releases so that Erlang isn't completely mad at us.

First, the Erlang tools to build releases require us to be a little more precise in our application descriptions. You see, although tools for releases don't understand documentation, they still have this intuitive fear of code where the developers were too impolite to at least leave an idea of what the application does. For this reason, we'll need to add a description tuple to both our *ppool.app* and *erlcount.app* files.

For ppool, add the following:

```
{description, "Run and enqueue different concurrent tasks"}
```

For erlcount, add this:

```
{description, "Run regular expressions on Erlang source files"}
```

Now we'll be able to get a better idea of what's going on when we inspect our different systems.

The most attentive readers will also remember I've mentioned at some point that *all* applications depend on stdlib and kernel. However, our two app files do not mention these. Let's add both applications to each of our app files. Add the following tuple to the ppool app file:

```
{applications, [stdlib, kernel]}
```

Also add the two applications to the existing erlcount app file, giving us:

```
{applications, [stdlib, kernel, ppool]}.
```

DON'T DRINK TOO MUCH KOOL-AID

While adding the stdlib and kernel applications to the list in the app file might have virtually no impact when we start releases manually (and even when we generate them with systools, which we'll explore soon), it is absolutely vital to do so.

People who generate releases with Reltool (the other tool we'll cover in this chapter) will definitely need these applications in order for their release to run well, and even to be able to shut down the VM in a respectable manner. I'm not kidding—it's *really* necessary. I forgot to do it when writing this chapter, and lost a night of work trying to find what was wrong, only to discover that it was just me not doing things right in the first place.

It could be argued that, ideally, the release systems of Erlang could implicitly add these applications, given pretty much all of them (except very special cases) will depend on them. Alas, they don't.

Compiling the Applications

We have a termination in place and have updated the app files. The last step before we start working with releases is to *compile all your applications.*

Successively run your Emakefile files (with erl -make) in each directory containing one. Otherwise, Erlang's tools won't do it for you, and you'll end up with a release without code to run. Ouch.

Releases with systools

The systools application is the simplest one to use to build Erlang releases. It's the Easy-Bake Oven of Erlang releases. To get your delicious releases out of the systools oven, you first need a basic recipe and list of ingredients. Here's a list of the ingredients of a successful minimal Erlang release for our erlcount application (erlcount 1.0.0):

- An Erlang Run-Time System (ERTS) of your choice
- A standard library
- A kernel library
- The ppool application, which should not fail
- The erlcount application

Did I mention that I'm a terrible cook? I'm not sure I can even make pancakes, but at least I know how to build an OTP release. The ingredient list for an OTP release with systools looks like this file, named *erlcount-1.0.rel* and placed at the top level of the *release/* directory:

```
{release,
 {"erlcount", "1.0.0"},
 {erts, "5.9.1"},
 [{kernel, "2.15.1"},
  {stdlib, "1.18.1"},
  {ppool, "1.0.0", permanent},
  {erlcount, "1.0.0", transient}]}.
```

This has the same content as the textual list of ingredients for the recipe, although we can specify how we want the applications to be started (temporary, transient, or permanent). We can also specify versions so we can mix and match different libraries from different Erlang versions depending on our needs. To get all the version numbers in there, we can just make the following sequence of calls:

```
$ erl
Erlang R15B01 (erts-5.9.1) [source] [64-bit] [smp:4:4] [async-threads:0]
[hipe] [kernel-poll:false]

Eshell V5.9.1  (abort with ^G)
1> application:which_applications().
[{stdlib,"ERTS  CXC 138 10","1.18.1"},
 {kernel,"ERTS  CXC 138 10","2.15.1"}]
```

For this example, I was running R15B01. You can see the ERTS version in there right after the release number (the version is 5.9.1). Then by calling application:which_applications() on a running system, I can see the two versions I need from kernel (2.15.1) and stdlib (1.18.1). The numbers will vary from Erlang version to version. However, being explicit about the versions you need is helpful because it means that if you have many different

Erlang installations on a system, you can still use an older version of stdlib that won't badly influence whatever you're doing.

You'll also note that I chose to name the *release* as erlcount and make it version 1.0.0. This is unrelated to the ppool and erlcount applications, which are both also running version 1.0.0, as specified in their app file.

So now we have all our applications compiled, our list of ingredients, and the wonderful concept of a metaphorical Easy-Bake Oven. What we need is the actual recipe.

A recipe will tell you a few things: in what order to add ingredients, how to mix them, how to cook them, and so on. The part about the order used to add them is covered by our list of dependencies in each app file. The systools application will be clever enough to look at the app files and figure out what needs to run before what. But we do need to handle relaying the other instructions.

Creating a Boot File

Erlang's VM can start itself with a basic configuration taken from something called a *boot file*. In fact, when you start your own erl executable from the shell, it implicitly calls the ERTS with a default boot file. That boot file will give basic instructions such as "load the standard library," "load the kernel application," "run a given function," and so on. That boot file is a binary file created from a *boot script* (*http://www.erlang.org/doc/man/script.html*), which contains tuples that will represent these instructions. We'll write such a boot script now.

First we start with the following:

```
{script, {Name, Vsn},
 [
  {progress, loading},
  {preLoaded, [Mod1, Mod2, ...]},
  {path, [Dir1,"$ROOT/Dir",...]}.
  {primLoad, [Mod1, Mod2, ...]},
  ...
```

I'm just kidding. No one really takes the time to do that, and we won't either. The boot script is something easy to generate from the *.rel* file. Just start an Erlang VM from the *release/* directory and call the following line:

```
$ erl -env ERL_LIBS .
... <snip> ...
1> systools:make_script("erlcount-1.0", [local]).
ok
```

Now if you look in your directory, you will have a bunch of new files, including *erlcount-1.0.script* and *erlcount-1.0.boot*. Here, the `local` option means that we want the release to be able to run from anywhere, and not just the current installation. The systools application has many more options (see *http://www.erlang.org/doc/man/systools.html*), but because systools isn't as powerful as Reltool (which we'll discuss in the next section), we won't look into them with too much depth.

At this point, we have the boot script, but not enough to distribute our code yet.

Packaging the Release

Go back to your Erlang shell and run the following command:

```
2> systools:make_tar("erlcount-1.0", [{erts, "/usr/local/lib/erlang/"}]).
ok
```

Or, on Windows 7, run this:

```
2> systools:make_tar("erlcount-1.0",
2>                    [{erts, "C:/Program Files (x86)/erl5.9.1"}]).
ok
```

Here, systools will look for your release files and the ERTS (because of the erts option). If you omit the erts option, the release won't be self-executable and will depend on Erlang already being installed on a system.

Running this function call creates an archive file named *erlcount-1.0.tar.gz*. Unarchive the files inside the archive, and you should see a directory like this:

```
erts-5.9.1/
lib/
releases/
```

The *erts-5.9.1/* directory will contain the ERTS. The *lib/* directory holds all the applications we need, and the *releases/* directory has the boot files and other files related to releases.

Move into the directory where you extracted these files. From there, we can build a command-line call for erl. First, we specify where to find the erl executable and the boot file (without the *.boot* extension). In Linux, this gives us the following:

```
$ ./erts-5.9.1/bin/erl -boot releases/1.0.0/start
```

The command is the same on Windows 7, using Windows PowerShell.

You can optionally use absolute paths if you want the command to work from anywhere on your computer. Don't run it right now, though. It's going to be useless because there is no source file to analyze in the current directory. If you use absolute paths, you can go to the directory you want to analyze and call the file from there.

> **DON'T DRINK TOO MUCH KOOL-AID**
>
> There is no guarantee that a release will work on any system ever. If you're using pure Erlang code without native compiling with HiPE (a native compiler for Erlang code, which gives somewhat faster code, especially for CPU-bound applications), then that code will be portable. The issue is that the ERTS you ship with it might itself not work. You will need to either create many binary packages for many different platforms for large-scale distribution or just ship the BEAM files without the associated ERTS and ask people to run them with an Erlang system they have on their own computer.

The erlcount application's implementation would use the current directory as its default point to start searching. It is, however, possible to configure which directory to scan by overriding the application's env variables. Let's add -erlcount directory "'<path to the directory>'" to the command. Then because we want this to not look like Erlang, let's add the -noshell argument. This gives me something like this on my own computer:

```
$ ./erts-5.9.1/bin/erl -boot releases/1.0.0/start -erlcount directory
'"/home/ferd/code/otp_src_R14B03/"' -noshell
Regex if\s.+-> has 3846 results
Regex case\s.+\sof has 55894 results
```

I was running erlcount on old Erlang and OTP releases. You can try it on more recent ones. Using absolute file paths, I get something like this long command:

```
$ /home/ferd/code/learn-you-some-erlang/release/rel/erts-5.9.1/bin/erl -boot
/home/ferd/code/learn-you-some-erlang/release/rel/releases/1.0.0/start -noshell
```

Wherever I run it from, that's the directory that's going to be scanned. Wrap this up in a shell script or a batch file, and you should be good to go.

Releases with Reltool

There are a bunch of aspects of systools that are annoying. We have very little control over how things are done. Manually specifying the path to the boot file and whatnot is kind of painful. Moreover, the files are a bit large. The whole release takes more than 20MB on disk, and it would be a lot worse if we were to package more applications. It is possible to do better with Reltool, as we get a lot more power, although the trade-off is increased complexity.

Reltool works from a configuration file that looks like this:

```
{sys, [
    {lib_dirs, ["/home/ferd/code/learn-you-some-erlang/release/"]},
    {rel, "erlcount", "1.0.0",
     [kernel,
      stdlib,
      {ppool, permanent},
      {erlcount, transient}
      % {LibraryApp, load} is also an option for stuff that never starts.
     ]},
    {boot_rel, "erlcount"},
    {relocatable, true},
    {profile, standalone},
    {app, ppool, [{vsn, "1.0.0"},
                  {app_file, all},
                  {debug_info, keep}]},
    {app, erlcount, [{vsn, "1.0.0"},
                     {incl_cond, include},
                     {app_file, strip},
                     {debug_info, strip}]]
]}.
```

Behold the user-friendliness of Erlang! To be quite honest, there's no easy way to introduce Reltool. You need a bunch of these options at once or nothing will work. It might sound confusing, but there's logic behind it.

First of all, Reltool will take different levels of information. The first level will contain release-wide information. The second level will be application-specific, before allowing fine-grained control at a module-specific level.

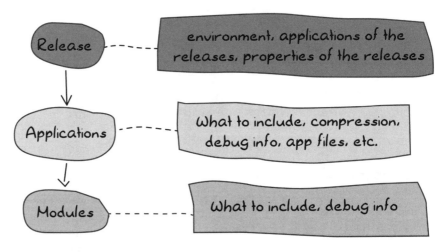

For each of these levels, different options will be available. Rather than taking the encyclopedic approach with all the options possible, we'll visit a few essential options and then a few possible configurations.

The first option is one that helps us get rid of the somewhat annoying need to be sitting in a given directory or to set the correct -env arguments to the VM. The option is lib_dirs, and it takes a list of directories where applications reside. So instead of adding -env ERL_LIBS *list:of:directories*, you put in {lib_dirs, [*ListOfDirectories*]} and get the same result.

Another vital option for the Reltool configuration files is rel. This tuple is very similar to the *.rel* file we wrote for systools. In the demo file, we have this:

```
{rel, "erlcount", "1.0.0",
 [kernel,
  stdlib,
  {ppool, permanent},
  {erlcount, transient}
 ]},
```

This is what we need to define which apps must be started correctly. After that tuple, we want to add a tuple of this form:

```
{boot_rel, "erlcount"}
```

This will tell Reltool that whenever someone runs the erl binary included in the release, we want the apps from the erlcount release to be started. With just these three options—lib_dirs, rel, and boot_rel—we can get a valid release.

To do so, we'll put these tuples into a format Reltool can parse:

```
{sys, [
    {lib_dirs, ["/home/ferd/code/learn-you-some-erlang/release/"]},
    {rel, "erlcount", "1.0.0",
     [kernel,
      stdlib,
      {ppool, permanent},
      {erlcount, transient}
     ]},
    {boot_rel, "erlcount"}
]}.
```

We just wrap them into a {sys, [Options]} tuple. I saved this in a file named *erlcount-1.0.config* in the *release/* directory. You can put it anywhere you want (except */dev/null*, even though it has exceptional write speeds!).

Then we'll need to open an Erlang shell:

```
1> {ok, Conf} = file:consult("erlcount-1.0.config").
{ok,[{sys,[{lib_dirs,["/home/ferd/code/learn-you-some-erlang/release/"]},
    {rel,"erlcount","1.0.0",
        [kernel,stdlib,{ppool,permanent},{erlcount,transient}]},
    {boot_rel,"erlcount"}]}]}
2> {ok, Spec} = reltool:get_target_spec(Conf).
{ok,[{create_dir,"releases",
... <snip> ...
3> reltool:eval_target_spec(Spec, code:root_dir(), "rel").
ok
```

The first step here is to read the configuration and bind it to the Conf variable. Then we send that into reltool:get_target_spec(Conf). The function will take a while to run and return way too much information for us to proceed. We don't care, so we just save the result in Spec.

The third command takes the specification and tells Reltool, "I want you to take my release specification, using whatever path where my Erlang installations are, and shove it into the *rel* directory." That's it. Look in the *rel* directory, and you should find a bunch of subdirectories there.

For now, we don't care and can just call this:

```
$ ./bin/erl -noshell
Regex if\s.+-> has 0 results
Regex case\s.+\sof has 0 results
```

Ah, this is a bit simpler to run. You can put these files pretty much anywhere, as long as they keep the same file tree, and run them from wherever you want.

Have you noticed something different? I hope you have. We didn't need to specify any version numbers. Reltool is a bit more clever than systools there. If you do not specify a version, it will automatically look for the newest one possible in the paths you have (either in the directory returned by code:root_dir() or what you put in the lib_dirs tuple).

But what if I'm not hip and cool and trendy and all about the latest apps, but rather a retro lover? I'm still wearing my disco pants, and I want to use older ERTS versions and older library versions (I've never stayed more alive than I was in 1977!).

Thankfully, Reltool can handle releases that need to work with older versions of Erlang. Respecting your elders is an important concept for Erlang tools.

If you have older versions of Erlang installed, you can add an {erts, [{vsn, Version}]} entry to the configuration file:

```
{sys, [
    {lib_dirs, ["/home/ferd/code/learn-you-some-erlang/release/"]},
    {erts, [{vsn, "5.8.3"}]},
    {rel, "erlcount", "1.0.0",
     [kernel,
      stdlib,
      {ppool, permanent},
      {erlcount, transient}
     ]},
    {boot_rel, "erlcount"}
]}.
```

Now you want to clear out the *rel/* directory to get rid of the newer release. Then you run the rather ugly sequence of calls again:

```
4> f(),
4> {ok, Conf} = file:consult("erlcount-1.0.config"),
4> {ok, Spec} = reltool:get_target_spec(Conf),
4> reltool:eval_target_spec(Spec, code:root_dir(), "rel").
ok
```

A quick reminder here: f() is used to unbind the variables in the shell.

Now if I go to the *rel* directory and call $ **./bin/erl**, I get the following output:

```
Erlang R14B02 (erts-5.8.3) [source] ...

Eshell V5.8.3  (abort with ^G)
1> Regex if\s.+-> has 0 results
Regex case\s.+\sof has 0 results
```

Awesome! This runs on version 5.8.3, even though I have newer ones available (Ah, ha, ha, ha, stayin' alive . . .). For the preceding snippet to work for you, you must have Erlang R14B02 installed beforehand.

NOTE *If you look at the* rel/ *directory, you'll see things are kind of similar to what they were with systools. One difference will be in the* lib/ *directory, which will now contain a bunch of directories and .ez files. The directories in* lib/ *will contain the* include/ *files required when you want to do development using the libraries from the release, and the* priv/ *directories when there are files that need to be kept there, such as C drivers or specific files required by running applications. The .ez files, on the other hand, are just zipped BEAM files. The Erlang VM will unpack them for you come runtime; this setup is just to make things lighter.*

But wait, what about the other modules?

Ah, now we move away from the release-wide settings and enter the realm of settings that have to do with applications. There are still a lot of release-wide options to see, but we're on such a roll that we can't be asked to stop right now. We'll revisit them in the next section.

For applications, we can specify versions by adding more tuples:

```
{app, AppName, [{vsn, Version}]}
```

Put in one per app that needs it.

Reltool Options

Now we have many more options for everything. We can specify if we want the release to include debug information or strip it away, whether to try to make more compact app files or keep the existing ones, which stuff to include or exclude, how strict to be when it comes to including applications and modules on which your own applications might depend, and so on. Moreover, these options can usually be defined both release-wide and application-wide, so you can specify defaults and then values to override.

Here, we'll take a quick look at the Reltool options. If you find these complex, just skip to the next section, where you'll find a few Reltool cookbook recipes to follow.

Release-Only Options

The following are Reltool release-only options.

{lib_dirs, [ListOfDirs]}
> This lets you specify which directories to search for libraries.

{excl_lib, otp_root}
> Added in R15B02, this option lets you specify OTP applications as part of your release, without including whatever comes from the standard Erlang/OTP path in the final release. This lets you create releases that are essentially libraries bootable from an existing virtual machine installed in a given system. When using this option, you must start the virtual machine as $ erl -boot_var RELTOOL_EXT_LIB path/to/release directory/lib -boot path/to/boot/file. This will allow the release to use the current Erlang/OTP install, but with your own libraries for your custom release.

{app, AppName, [AppOptions]}
> This lets you specify application-wide options, which are usually more specific than the release-wide options.

{boot_rel, ReleaseName}
> This lets you specify the default release to boot with the erl executable. This means you won't need to specify the boot file when calling erl.

{rel, Name, Vsn, [Apps]}
> This lets you specify the applications to be included in the release.

{relocatable, true | false}
> It is possible to run the release from everywhere or from a hard-coded path in your system. By default, this option is set to true, and I tend to leave it that way unless there is a good reason to do otherwise. You'll know when you need it.

{profile, development | embedded | standalone}
> This option serves as a way to specify default *_filters (described in the next list) based on your type of release. By default, development is used. That one will include more files from each app and ERTS blindly. The standalone profile will be more restrictive, and the embedded profile even more so, dropping more default ERTS applications and binaries.

Release-wide and Application-wide Options

The following are Reltool release-wide and application-wide options, Note that for all of these, setting the option on the level of an application will simply override the value you gave at a system level.

{incl_sys_filters, [RegularExpressions]} and {excl_sys_filters, [RegularExpressions]}

These check whether a file matches the include filters without matching the exclude filters before including it. You might drop or include specific files this way.

{incl_app_filters, [RegularExpressions]} and {excl_app_filters, [RegularExpressions]}

These are similar to incl_sys_filters and excl_sys_filters, but for application-specific files.

{incl_archive_filters, [RegularExpressions]} and {excl_archive_filters, [RegularExpressions]}

These specify which top-level directories must be included or excluded in *.ez* archive files (more on this in the next section). Files not included in the archive may still be included in the release, but just not compressed.

{incl_cond, include | exclude | derived}

This decides how to include applications not necessarily specified in the rel tuple. Picking include means that Reltool will include pretty much everything it can find. Picking derived means that Reltool will include only applications that it detects can be used by any of the applications in your rel tuple. This is the default value. Picking exclude means that you will include no apps at all by default. You usually set this on a release level when you want minimal includes, and then override it on an application-by-application basis for the stuff you feel like adding.

{mod_cond, all | app | ebin | derived | none}

This controls the module inclusion policy. Picking none means no modules will be kept (which isn't very useful). The derived option means that Reltool will try to figure out which modules are used by other modules that are already included and add them. Setting the option to app means that Reltool keeps all the modules mentioned in the app file and those that were derived. Setting it to ebin keeps those in the *ebin/* directory and the derived ones. Using the option all, which is the default, is a mix of using ebin and app.

{app_file, keep | strip | all}

This option handles how the app files are going to be managed for you when you include an application. Picking keep guarantees that the app file used in the release is the same one you wrote for your application. That's the default option. If you choose strip, Reltool will try to generate a new app file that removes the modules you don't want in there (those that were excluded by filters and other options). Choosing all keeps the original file, but also adds specifically included modules. The nice thing with all is that it can generate app files for you if none are available.

Module-Specific Options

The following are Reltool module-specific options.

{incl_cond, include | exclude | derived}
> This lets you override the mod_cond option defined at the release level and application level.

All-levels Options

The following options work on all levels. The lower the level, the more precedence it takes.

{debug_info, keep | strip}
> Assuming your files were compiled with debug_info on (which I suggest), this option lets you decide whether to keep that information or drop it. The debug_info is useful when you want to decompile files or debug them, but will take some space.

That's Dense

Oh yes, we've covered a lot of information about Reltool options. I didn't include all the possible options, but it's still a decent reference. If you want the whole thing, check out the official documentation at *http://www.erlang .org/doc/man/reltool.html*.

Reltool Recipes

Now we'll consider a few general tips and tricks on how to write your *.rel* files in order to obtain specific results, such as small-sized releases or releases that contain enough libraries to allow development work.

Development Versions

Getting a release packed with libraries useful for development of specific projects should be relatively easy, and often the defaults are good enough. Just stick to getting the basic items we've covered so far, and you should be in good shape.

```
{sys, [
    {lib_dirs, ["/home/ferd/code/learn-you-some-erlang/release/"]},
    {rel, "erlcount", "1.0.0", [kernel, stdlib, ppool, erlcount]},
    {boot_rel, "erlcount"}
]}.
```

Reltool will take care of importing enough libraries for the new release to be fine. In some cases, you might want to have everything from a regular

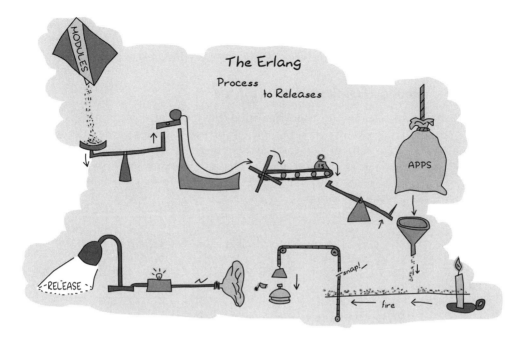

The Erlang Process to Releases

VM as created by the OTP team, plus some of your own libraries. You might be distributing an entire VM for a team, with some libraries included. In that case, what you want to do is something more like this:

```
{sys, [
    {lib_dirs, ["/home/ferd/code/learn-you-some-erlang/release/"]},
    {rel, "start_clean", "1.0.0", [kernel, stdlib]},
    {incl_cond, include},
    {debug_info, keep}
]}.
```

By setting incl_cond to include, all applications found in the current ERTS installation and the lib_dirs will be part of your release.

NOTE   *When no boot_rel is specified, you need to have a release named start_clean for Reltool to be happy. That one will be picked by default when you start the associated erl executable.*

If we want to exclude a specific application—let's say megaco because I never looked into it—we can instead get a file, like this:

```
{sys, [
    {lib_dirs, ["/home/ferd/code/learn-you-some-erlang/release/"]},
    {rel, "start_clean", "1.0.0", [kernel, stdlib]},
    {incl_cond, include},
    {debug_info, keep},
    {app, megaco, [{incl_cond, exclude}]}
]}.
```

Here, we can specify one or more applications (each having its own `app` tuple), and each of them overrides the `incl_cond` setting put at the release level. So, in this case, we will include everything except `megaco`.

Importing or Exporting Only Part of a Library

In our release, one annoying thing that happened was that apps like ppool and others also kept their test files in the release, even though they didn't need them. You can see them by going into *rel/lib/* and unzipping *ppool-1.0.0.ez* (you might need to change the extension first).

The easiest way to get rid of these files is to specify exclusion filters, such as the following:

```
{sys, [
    {lib_dirs, ["/home/ferd/code/learn-you-some-erlang/release/"]},
    {rel, "start_clean", "1.0.0", [kernel, stdlib, ppool, erlcount]},
    {excl_app_filters, ["_tests.beam$"]}
]}.
```

When you want to import only specific files of an application, things get a bit more complex. Here's an example of importing only `erlcount_lib` for its functionality, but nothing else from `erlcount`:

```
{sys, [
    {lib_dirs, ["/home/ferd/code/learn-you-some-erlang/release/"]},
    {rel, "start_clean", "1.0.0", [kernel, stdlib]},
    {incl_cond, derived}, % Exclude would also work, but not include.
    {app, erlcount, [{incl_app_filters, ["^ebin/erlcount_lib.beam$"]},
                    {incl_cond, include}]}
]}.
```

In this case, we switched from `{incl_cond, include}` to the more restrictive `incl_conds`. This is because if you go large and rake everything in, then the only way to include a single library is to exclude all the others with an `excl_app_filters`. However, when our selection is more restrictive (in this case, we're derived and wouldn't include `erlcount` because it's not part of the rel tuple), we can specifically tell the release to include the `erlcount` app with only files that match the regular expression having to do with `erlcount_lib`. This prompts the question as to how to make the smallest release possible, right?

Smaller Apps for Programmers with Big Hearts

Release size reduction is where Reltool becomes a good bit more complex, with a rather verbose configuration file:

```
{sys, [
    {lib_dirs, ["/home/ferd/code/learn-you-some-erlang/release/"]},
    {erts, [{mod_cond, derived},
            {app_file, strip}]},
```

```
        {rel, "erlcount", "1.0.0", [kernel, stdlib, ppool, erlcount]},
        {boot_rel, "erlcount"},
        {relocatable, true},
        {profile, embedded},
        {app_file, strip},
        {debug_info, strip},
        {incl_cond, exclude},
        {excl_app_filters, ["_tests.beam$"]},
        {app, stdlib, [{mod_cond, derived}, {incl_cond, include}]},
        {app, kernel, [{incl_cond, include}]},
        {app, ppool, [{vsn, "1.0.0"}, {incl_cond, include}]},
        {app, erlcount, [{vsn, "1.0.0"}, {incl_cond, include}]}
]}.
```

A lot more stuff is going on here. We can see that in the case of erts, we ask for Reltool to keep only what's necessary. Setting mod_cond to derived and app_file to strip will ask Reltool to check and keep only what's used for something else. That's why {app_file, strip} is also used on the release level.

The profile is set to embedded. If you looked at the .ez archives in the previous cases, they contained the source files, test directories, and so on. When switching over to embedded, only include files, binaries, and the *priv/* directories are kept. We're also removing debug_info from all files, even if they were compiled with it. This means we're going to lose some debugging ability, but it will reduce the size of files.

We're still stripping away test files, and setting things so that no application is included until explicitly told to be ({incl_cond, exclude}). Then we override this setting in each app we do want to include. If something is missing, Reltool will warn you, so you can try to move things around and play with settings until you get the results you want. It might involve having some application settings with {mod_cond, derived}, as we did with the stdlib, so that the minimal files of some applications are what is kept.

What's the difference in the end? Some of our more general releases would weigh in at more than 35MB. The one described here is reduced to less than 20MB. We're shaving off a good part of it, although it's still fairly large. That's because of ERTS, which itself takes around 18.5MB. If you want to, you can dig deeper and really micromanage how ERTS is built to get something smaller. You can alternatively pick and delete some binary files in the ERTS that you know won't be used by your application: executables for scripts, remote running of Erlang, binaries from test frameworks, and different running commands (such as Erlang with or without SMP).

The lightest release will be the one that assumes that other users have Erlang installed already. When you pick this option, you need to add the *rel/* directory's content as part of your ERL_LIBS environment variable and call the boot file yourself (a bit like with systools), but it will work. Programmers might want to wrap this up in scripts to get things going.

These days, Erlang programmers seem to really love the idea of having all these releases handled for them by a tool called rebar, which will act as a wrapper over Emakefile files and Reltool. There is no loss in understanding how Reltool works. The rebar tool uses configuration files that are nearly the same, and the gap between the two tools isn't that big.

Released from Releases

Well, that's it for the two major ways to handle releases. It's a complex topic, but a standard way to handle distributions. Applications might be enough for many readers, and there's nothing wrong with sticking to them for a good while. However, now and then, releases might be useful if you want your operations guy to like you a bit better, given you know (or at least have some idea about) how to deploy Erlang applications when necessary.

Of course, what could make your operations guy happier than no downtime? The next challenge will be to do software upgrades while a release is running.

22

LEVELING UP IN THE PROCESS QUEST

Code hot-loading is simple in Erlang. You recompile, make a fully qualified function call, and then enjoy. However, doing it the right (and safe) way is much more difficult.

A plethora of things can go wrong in practice.

In this chapter, we'll explore the problems that hot code loading can bring and some principles that prove helpful to solve them. Then we'll go through a practical demonstration of how to take an existing OTP release, upgrade it, and reload the new version of it while it runs with the help of OTP mechanisms, through *appups* and *relups* (application and release upgrades).

NOTE *This chapter does not include all of the code used in the examples. Before you start this chapter, you might want to get the required code from* http://learnyousomeerlang.com/static/erlang/processquest.zip. *If you've downloaded the whole code package from the* Learn You Some Erlang *website, you already have everything you need.*

The Hiccups of Appups and Relups

One very simple challenge makes code reloading problematic. To understand it, let's use our amazing Erlang-programming brain and imagine a `gen_server` process. This process has a `handle_cast/2` function that accepts one kind of argument. You update it to one that takes a different kind of argument, compile it, and push it in production. All is fine and dandy, but because you have an application that you don't want to shut down, you decide to load it on the production VM to make it run.

Then a bunch of error reports start pouring in.

It turns out that your different `handle_cast` functions are incompatible. So when they were called a second time, no clause matched. The customer is pissed off and so is your boss. Then the operations guy is also angry because he needs to get on location and roll back the code, extinguish fires, and so on. If you're lucky, you're that operations guy. You're staying late and ruining the janitor's night (he likes to hum along with his music and dance a little as he works, but he is ashamed to do that in your presence). You come home late, your spouse/friends/World of Warcraft raid party/children are mad at you. They yell, scream, slam the door, and you're left alone. You had promised that nothing could go wrong—no downtime. You're using Erlang after all, right? But it didn't happen like that. You're alone, curled up in a ball in the corner of the kitchen, eating frozen Hot Pockets.

Of course, things aren't always that bad, but the point stands. Doing live code upgrades on a production system can be very dangerous if you're changing the interface your modules give to the world, changing internal data structures, changing function names, modifying records (remember that they're tuples!), and so on. These all have the potential to cause a crash.

When we were first playing with code reloading in Chapter 13, we had a process with some kind of hidden message to handle doing a fully qualified call. If you recall, a process could have looked like this:

```
loop(N) ->
    receive
        some_standard_message -> N+1;
```

```
        other_message -> N-1;
        {get_count, Pid} ->
            Pid ! N,
            loop(N);
        update -> ?MODULE:loop(N);
    end.
```

However, this way of doing things wouldn't fix our problems if we were to change the arguments to loop/1. We would need to extend it a bit, like this:

```
loop(N) ->
    receive
        some_standard_message -> N+1;
        other_message -> N-1;
        {get_count, Pid} ->
            Pid ! N,
            loop(N);
        update -> ?MODULE:code_change(N);
    end.
```

And then code_change/1 could take care of calling a new version of the loop. But this kind of trick wouldn't work with generic loops. Consider this example:

```
loop(Mod, State) ->
    receive
        {call, From, Msg} ->
            {reply, Reply, NewState} = Mod:handle_call(Msg, State),
            From ! Reply,
            loop(Mod, NewState);
        update ->
            {ok, NewState} = Mod:code_change(State),
            loop(Mod, NewState)
    end.
```

Do you see the problem? If we want to update Mod and load a new version, there is no way to do it safely with that implementation. The call Mod:handle_call(Msg, State) is already fully qualified, and it's possible that a message of the form {call, From, Msg} could be received in between the time we reload the code and handle the update message. In that case, we would update the module in an uncontrolled manner. Then we would crash.

The secret to getting it right is buried within the entrails of OTP. We must freeze the sands of time! To do so, we require more secret messages: messages to put a process on hold, messages to change the code, and then messages to resume the actions we had before. Deep inside OTP behaviors is hidden a special protocol to take care of all that kind of management. This is handled through the sys module and the release_handler module, which is part of the System Architecture Support Libraries (SASL) application. They take care of everything.

The trick is that you can call sys:suspend(*PidOrName*) to suspend OTP processes (you can find all of the processes by using the supervision trees and looking at the children each supervisor has). Then you use sys:change_code(*PidOrName*, Mod, OldVsn, Extra) to force the process to update itself. Finally, you call sys:resume(*PidOrName*) to make things go again.

It wouldn't be very practical for us to call these functions manually by writing ad hoc scripts all the time. Instead, we can look at how relups are done.

The Ninth Circle of Erl

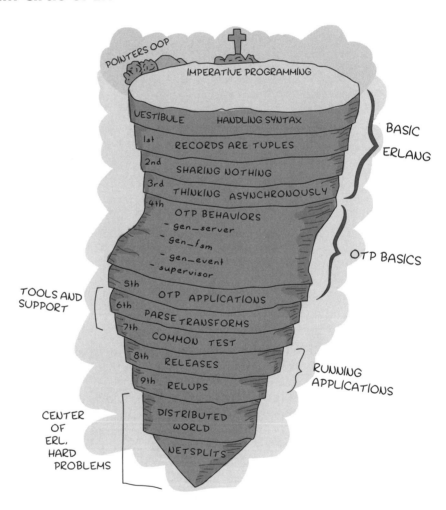

The act of taking a running release, making a second version of it, and updating it while it runs is perilous. What seems like a simple assembly of *appups* (files containing instructions on how to update individual applications) and *relups* (files containing instructions to update an entire release) quickly turns into a struggle through APIs and undocumented assumptions.

We're getting into one of the most complex parts of OTP, a part that is difficult to comprehend and get right, on top of being time-consuming. In fact, if you can avoid the whole procedure (which will be called *relup* from now on) and do simple rolling upgrades by restarting VMs and booting new applications, I recommend you do so. Relups should be one of these "do or die" tools—something you use when you have few other choices.

There are a bunch of steps to execute when dealing with release upgrades, each of which can be more complex than the preceding one:

1. Write OTP applications.
2. Turn a bunch of them into a release.
3. Create new versions of one or more of the OTP applications.
4. Create an appup file that explains what to change to make the transition between the old and the new application work.
5. Create a new release with the new applications.
6. Generate an appup file from these releases.
7. Install the new app in a running Erlang shell.

We've only covered how to do the first three steps so far. To demonstrate how to work with an application that is more adapted to long-running upgrades than the previous ones (eh, who cares about running regular expressions without restarting?), we'll introduce a superb video game.

Process Quest

Progress Quest (*http://progressquest.com/*) is a revolutionary role-playing game (RPG). I would call it the OTP of RPGs, in fact. If you've ever played an RPG before, you'll notice that many steps are similar: run around, kill enemies, gain experience, get money, level up, get skills, complete quests—rinse and repeat forever. Power players will have shortcuts such as macros or even bots to go around and do their bidding for them.

Progress Quest took all of these generic steps and turned them into one streamlined game where you can sit back and enjoy your character doing all the work:

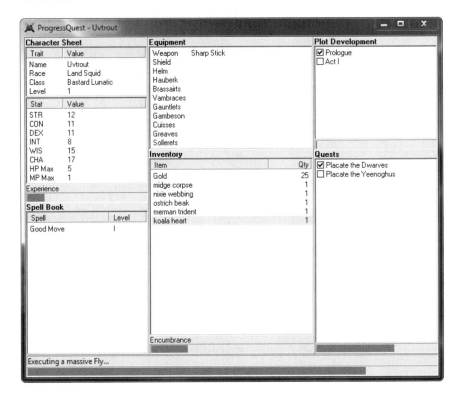

With the permission of the creator of this fantastic game, Eric Fredricksen, I've made a very minimal Erlang clone of it called Process Quest. Process Quest is similar in principle to Progress Quest, but rather than being a single-player application, it's a server able to hold many raw socket connections (usable through *telnet*) to let someone use a terminal and temporarily play the game.

The game is made up of the regis, processquest, and sockserv applications.

The regis-1.0.0 Application

The regis application is a process registry. It has an interface somewhat similar to the regular Erlang process registry, but it can accept any term at all and is meant to be dynamic. It might make things slower because all the calls will be serialized when they enter the server, but it will be better than using the regular process registry, which is not made for this kind of dynamic work. If this book could automatically update itself with external libraries (it's too much work), I would have used gproc instead.

The application has three modules: regis.erl, regis_server.erl, and regis_sup.erl. The first one is a wrapper around the other two (and an application callback module). regis_server is the main registration gen_server, and regis_sup is the application's supervisor.

The processquest-1.0.0 Application

The processquest application is the core of the release. It includes all the game logic—enemies, market, killing fields, and statistics. The player itself is a gen_fsm that sends messages to itself in order to keep going all the time. It contains the following modules:

pq_enemy.erl
> This module randomly picks an enemy to fight, of the form {<<"Name">>, [{drop, {<<"DropName">>, Value}}, {experience, ExpPoints}]}. This lets the player fight an enemy.

pq_market.erl
> This implements a market that allows players to find items of a given value and a given strength. All items returned are of the form {<<"Name">>, Modifier, Strength, Value}. There are functions to fetch weapons, armors, shields, and helmets.

pq_stats.erl
> This is a small attribute generator for your character.

pq_events.erl
> This is a wrapper around a gen_event event manager. This acts as a generic hub to which subscribers connect themselves with their own handlers to receive events from each player. It also takes care of waiting a given delay for the player's actions to avoid the game being instantaneous.

pq_player.erl
> This is the central module. It is a gen_fsm that goes through the state loop of killing, then going to the market, then killing again, and so on. It uses all of the preceding modules to function.

pq_sup.erl
> This is a supervisor that sits above a pair of pq_event and pq_player processes. They both need to be together in order to work; otherwise, the player process is useless and isolated or the event manager will never get any events.

pq_supersup.erl
> This is the top-level supervisor of the application. It sits over a bunch of pq_sup processes. This lets you spawn as many players as you like.

processquest.erl
> This is a wrapper and application callback module. It gives the basic interface to a player. You start one, and then subscribe to events.

The sockserv-1.0.0 Application

The sockserv application is a customized raw socket server, made to work only with the processquest app. It will spawn gen_servers, each in charge of a TCP socket that will push strings to some client. Again, you may use telnet to work with it. (Telnet was technically not made for raw socket connections and is its own protocol, but most modern clients accept it without any problems.) Here are sockserv's modules:

sockserv_trans.erl
> This translates messages received from the player's event manager into printable strings.

sockserv_pq_events.erl
> This is a simple event handler that takes whatever events come from a player and casts them to the socket gen_server.

sockserv_serv.erl
> This is a gen_server in charge of accepting a connection, communicating with a client, and forwarding information to it.

sockserv_sup.erl
> This supervises a bunch of socket servers.

sockserv.erl
> This is an application callback module for the app as a whole.

The Release

I've set everything up in a directory called *processquest* with the following structure:

```
apps/
 - processquest-1.0.0
   - ebin/
   - src/
   - ...
 - regis-1.0.0
   - ...
```

```
 - sockserv-1.0.0
   - ...
rel/
  (will hold releases)
processquest-1.0.0.config
```

Based on that, we can build a release.

> **MORE RELEASE CONFIGURATION**
>
> If you look into *processquest-1.0.0.config*, you will see that applications such as Crypto and SASL are included. Crypto is necessary to have good initialization of pseudo-random number generators, and SASL is mandatory to be able to do appups on a system. *If you forget to include SASL in your release, it will be impossible to upgrade the system.*
>
> A new filter has appeared in the configuration file: {excl_archive_filters, [".*"]}. This filter makes sure that no *.ez* file is generated; only regular files and directories are created. This is necessary because the tools we're going to use cannot look into *.ez* files to find the items they need.
>
> You will also see that there are no instructions asking to strip the debug_info. Without debug_info, doing an appup will fail for some reason. It's always useful to have debug_info anyway.

Following Chapter 21's instructions for releases, we start by calling erl -make for all applications. Once this is done, start an Erlang shell from the *processquest* directory and enter the following:

```
1> {ok, Conf} = file:consult("processquest-1.0.0.config"),
1> {ok, Spec} = reltool:get_target_spec(Conf),
1> reltool:eval_target_spec(Spec, code:root_dir(), "rel").
ok
```

We should have a functional release. Let's try it. Start any version of the VM by entering ./rel/bin/erl -sockserv port 8888 (or any other port number you want; the default is 8082). This will show a lot of logs about processes being started (that's one of the functions of SASL), and then a regular Erlang shell. Start a telnet session on your localhost using whatever client you want:

```
$ telnet localhost 8888
Trying 127.0.0.1...
Connected to localhost.
Escape character is '^]'.
What's your character's name?
hakvroot
```

```
Stats for your character:
  Charisma: 7
  Constitution: 12
  Dexterity: 9
  Intelligence: 8
  Strength: 5
  Wisdom: 16

Do you agree to these? y/n
```

That's a bit too much wisdom and charisma for me. So, I type **n** and hit ENTER:

```
n
Stats for your character:
  Charisma: 6
  Constitution: 12
  Dexterity: 12
  Intelligence: 4
  Strength: 6
  Wisdom: 10

Do you agree to these? y/n
```

Yes, that's ugly, dumb, and weak—exactly what I'm looking for in a hero based on me.

```
y
Executing a Wildcat...
Obtained Pelt.
Executing a Pig...
Obtained Bacon.
Executing a Wildcat...
Obtained Pelt.
Executing a Robot...
Obtained Chunks of Metal.
...
Executing a Ant...
Obtained Ant Egg.
Heading to the marketplace to sell loot...
Selling Ant Egg
Got 1 bucks.
Selling Chunks of Metal
Got 1 bucks.
...
Negotiating purchase of better equipment...
Bought a plastic knife
Heading to the killing fields...
Executing a Pig...
Obtained Bacon.
Executing a Ant...
```

That's enough for me. I type **quit** and then press ENTER to close the connection:

```
quit
Connection closed by foreign host.
```

If you want, you can leave it open, see yourself level up, gain stats, and so on. The game basically works, and you can try it with many clients. It should keep going without a problem.

Awesome, right? Well, we can do better.

Making Process Quest Better

There are a few issues with the current versions of the applications of Process Quest. First, we have very little variety in terms of enemies to beat. Second, we have text that looks a bit weird (what is it with "Executing a Ant..."?). A third issue is that the game is a bit too simple; let's add a mode for quests! Another one is that the value of items you sell at the market is directly bound to your level in Progress Quest,  while Process Quest doesn't do anything like that. Finally—and you can't see this unless you read the code and try to close the client on your own end—a client closing its connection will leave the player process alive on the server. Uh-oh, memory leaks!

We'll need to fix these problems!

NOTE *I started by making a new copy of both applications that need fixes. I then had* processquest-1.1.0 *and* sockserv-1.0.1 *on top of the others. (I use the version scheme of* MajorVersion.Enhancements.BugFixes.*) In the copies, I implemented all the changes I needed. I won't go through all of them here, because we're here to upgrade an app, not to walk through all the details and intricacies of this specific app. In case you do want to know all the little intricacies, I commented the code so you can find the information you need to understand it.*

Updating code_change Functions

In processquest-1.1.0, changes were made to *pq_enemy.erl*, *pq_events.erl*, and *pq_player.erl*. I also added a file named *pq_quest.erl*, which implements quests based on how many enemies were killed by a player. Of these files, only *pq_player.erl* had incompatible changes that required a time suspension. This record:

```
-record(state, {name, stats, exp=0, lvlexp=1000, lvl=1,
                equip=[], money=0, loot=[], bought=[], time=0}).
```

was changed to this one:

```
-record(state, {name, stats, exp=0, lvlexp=1000, lvl=1,
                equip=[], money=0, loot=[], bought=[],
                time=0, quest}).
```

where the quest field will hold a value given by pq_quest:fetch/0.

Because of that change, we'll need to modify the code_change/4 function in version 1.1.0. In fact, we'll need to modify it twice: once in the case of an upgrade (moving from 1.0.0 to 1.1.0) and another in the case of a downgrade (1.1.0 to 1.0.0). Fortunately, OTP will pass different arguments in each case. When we upgrade, we get a version number for the module. We don't exactly care for that one at this point, and we'll likely just ignore it. When we downgrade, we get {down, Version}. This lets us easily match on each operation:

```
code_change({down, _}, StateName, State, _Extra) ->
    ...;
code_change(_OldVsn, StateName, State, _Extra) ->
    ...
```

But hold on a second! We can't just blindly take the state as we usually do. We need to upgrade it. The problem is we can't do something like this:

```
code_change(_OldVsn, StateName, S = #state{}, _Extra) ->
    ...
```

We have two options. The first is to declare a new state record that will have a new form and a new name. We would end up having something like this:

```
-record(state, {...}).
-record(new_state, {...}).
```

And then we would need to change the record in each of the function clauses of the module. That's annoying and not worth the risk. It will be simpler to expand the record to its underlying tuple form (remember the discussion of records in Chapter 9), as follows:

```
code_change({down, _},
            StateName,
            #state{name=N, stats=S, exp=E, lvlexp=LE, lvl=L, equip=Eq,
                   money=M, loot=Lo, bought=B, time=T},
            _Extra) ->
    Old = {state, N, S, E, LE, L, Eq, M, Lo, B, T},
    {ok, StateName, Old};
code_change(_OldVsn,
            StateName,
            {state, Name, Stats, Exp, LvlExp, Lvl, Equip, Money, Loot,
             Bought, Time},
```

```
        _Extra) ->
State = #state{
    name=Name, stats=Stats, exp=Exp, lvlexp=LvlExp,
    lvl=Lvl, equip=Equip, money=Money, loot=Loot,
    bought=Bought, time=Time, quest=pq_quest:fetch()
},
{ok, StateName, State}.
```

And there's our code_change/4 function! All it does is convert between both tuple forms. For new versions, we also take care of adding a new quest—it would be boring to add quests but have all our existing players unable to use them.

You'll notice that we still ignore the _Extra variable. This one is passed from the appup file (described next), and you'll be the one to pick its value. For now, we don't care because we can upgrade and downgrade to and from only one release. In some more complex cases, you might want to pass release-specific information in there.

For the sockserv-1.0.1 application, only *sockserv_serv.erl* required changes. Fortunately, they didn't need a restart, and only added a new message to match on.

The two versions of the two applications have been fixed. That's not enough to go on our merry way, though. We need to find a way to let OTP know what kinds of changes require different kinds of actions.

Adding Appup Files

Appup files are lists of Erlang commands that need to be done to upgrade a given application. They contain lists of tuples and atoms telling what to do and in what case. The general format for them is as follows:

```
{NewVersion,
 [{VersionUpgradingFrom, [Instructions]}]
 [{VersionDownGradingTo, [Instructions]}]}.
```

They ask for lists of versions because it's possible to upgrade and downgrade to many different versions. In our case, for processquest-1.1.0, this would be the following:

```
{"1.1.0",
 [{"1.0.0", [Instructions]}],
 [{"1.0.0", [Instructions]}]}.
```

The instructions contain both high-level and low-level commands. We usually need to care about only high-level ones, though:

{add_module, Mod}
    The module Mod is loaded for the first time.

{load_module, Mod}
    The module Mod is already loaded in the VM and has been modified.

{delete_module, Mod}

> The module `Mod` is removed from the VM.

{update, Mod, {advanced, Extra}}

> This will suspend all processes running `Mod`, call the `code_change` function of your module with `Extra` as the last argument, and then resume all processes running `Mod`. `Extra` can be used to pass in arbitrary data to the `code_change` function, in case it's required for upgrades.

{update, Mod, supervisor}

> Calling this lets you redefine the `init` function of a supervisor to influence its restart strategy (`one_for_one`, `rest_for_one`, and so on) or change child specifications (this will not affect existing processes).

{apply, {M, F, A}}

> This will call `apply(M,F,A)`.

Module dependencies

> You can use `{load_module, Mod, [ModDependencies]}` or `{update, Mod, {advanced, Extra}, [ModDeps]}` to make sure that a command happens only after some other modules were handled beforehand. This is especially useful if `Mod` and its dependencies are *not* part of the same application. There is sadly no way to give similar dependencies to `delete_module` instructions.

Note that when generating relups, we won't need any special instructions to remove or add applications. The function that generates relup files (files to upgrade releases) will take care of detecting this for us.

Using these instructions, we can write the two following appup files for our applications. The file must be named *NameOfYourApp.appup* and be put in the app's *ebin/* directory.

Here's processquest-1.1.0's appup file:

```
{"1.1.0",
 [{"1.0.0", [{add_module, pq_quest},
             {load_module, pq_enemy},
             {load_module, pq_events},
             {update, pq_player, {advanced, []}, [pq_quest, pq_events]}]}],
 [{"1.0.0", [{update, pq_player, {advanced, []}},
             {delete_module, pq_quest},
             {load_module, pq_enemy},
             {load_module, pq_events}]}]}.
```

You can see that we need to add the new module, load the two ones that require no suspension, and then update `pq_player` in a safe manner. When we downgrade the code, we do the same thing, but in reverse. The funny thing is that in one case, `{load_module, Mod}` will load a new version, and in the other, it will load the old version. It all depends on the context between an upgrade and a downgrade.

Because socketserv-1.0.1 had only one module to change and it required no suspension, its appup file is brief, as follows:

```
{"1.0.1",
 [{"1.0.0", [{load_module, sockserv_serv}]}],
 [{"1.0.0", [{load_module, sockserv_serv}]}]}.
```

The next step is to build a new release using the new modules. Here's the file *processquest-1.1.0.config*:

```
{sys, [
    {lib_dirs, ["/home/ferd/code/learn-you-some-erlang/processquest/apps"]},
    {erts, [{mod_cond, derived},
            {app_file, strip}]},
    {rel, "processquest", "1.1.0",
     [kernel, stdlib, sasl, crypto, regis, processquest, sockserv]},
    {boot_rel, "processquest"},
    {relocatable, true},
    {profile, embedded},
    {app_file, strip},
    {incl_cond, exclude},
    {excl_app_filters, ["_tests.beam"]},
    {excl_archive_filters, [".*"]},
    {app, stdlib, [{mod_cond, derived}, {incl_cond, include}]},
    {app, kernel, [{incl_cond, include}]},
    {app, sasl, [{incl_cond, include}]},
    {app, crypto, [{incl_cond, include}]},
    {app, regis, [{vsn, "1.0.0"}, {incl_cond, include}]},
    {app, sockserv, [{vsn, "1.0.1"}, {incl_cond, include}]},
    {app, processquest, [{vsn, "1.1.0"}, {incl_cond, include}]}
]}.
```

It's just a copy/paste of the old one with a few versions changed. First, compile both new applications with erl -make (the new versions are in the zip file mentioned earlier). Then we can generate a new release. First, compile the two new applications, and then enter the following:

```
$ erl -env ERL_LIBS apps/
1> {ok, Conf} = file:consult("processquest-1.1.0.config"),
1> {ok, Spec} = reltool:get_target_spec(Conf),
1> reltool:eval_target_spec(Spec, code:root_dir(), "rel").
ok
```

But wait, there's more manual work required!

1. Copy *rel/releases/1.1.0/processquest.rel* as *rel/releases/1.1.0/processquest-1.1.0.rel*.

2. Copy *rel/releases/1.1.0/processquest.boot* as *rel/releases/1.1.0/processquest-1.1.0.boot*.

3. Copy *rel/releases/1.1.0/processquest.boot* as *rel/releases/1.1.0/start.boot*.

4. Copy *rel/releases/1.0.0/processquest.rel* as *rel/releases/1.0.0/processquest-1.0.0.rel*.

5. Copy *rel/releases/1.0.0/processquest.boot* as *rel/releases/1.0.0/ processquest-1.0.0.boot*.

6. Copy *rel/releases/1.0.0/processquest.boot* as *rel/releases/1.0.0/start.boot*.

DON'T DRINK TOO MUCH KOOL-AID

Why didn't we just use systools to build our release? Well, systools has its share of issues. First, it will generate appup files that sometimes have weird versions in them and won't work perfectly. It will also assume a directory structure that is barely documented, but somewhat close to what Reltool uses. The biggest issue, though, is that it will use your default Erlang installation as the root directory, which might create all kinds of permission issues and whatnot when the time comes to unpack stuff.

There's just no easy way to build the release with either tool, and it will require a lot of manual work. We thus make a chain of commands that uses both modules in a rather complex manner, because it ends up being a bit less work.

Now we can generate the relup file. To do this, start an Erlang shell and call the following:

```
erl -env ERL_LIBS apps/ -pa apps/processquest-1.0.0/ebin/ -pa apps/sockserv-1.0.0/ebin/
1> systools:make_relup("./rel/releases/1.1.0/processquest-1.1.0",
1>                       ["rel/releases/1.0.0/processquest-1.0.0"],
1>                       ["rel/releases/1.0.0/processquest-1.0.0"]).
ok
```

Because the ERL_LIBS environment variable will look for only the newest versions of applications, we also need to add the -pa *Path_to_older_applications* in there so that the systools relup generator will be able to find everything. Once this is done, move the relup file to *rel/releases/1.1.0/*. That directory will be looked into when updating the code in order to find the right stuff. One problem we'll have, though, is that the release handler module will depend on a bunch of files it assumes to be present, but won't necessarily be there.

Upgrading the Release

Sweet—we have a relup file. There's still stuff to do before being able to use it though. The next step is to generate a tar file for the whole new version of the release:

```
2> systools:make_tar("rel/releases/1.1.0/processquest-1.1.0").
ok
```

The file will be in *rel/releases/1.1.0/*. We now need to manually move it to *rel/releases*, and rename it to add the version number when doing so. More hard-coded junk! Here's our way out of this:

```
$ mv rel/releases/1.1.0/processquest-1.1.0.tar.gz rel/releases/
```

The next step is a step you want to do at *any time before you start the real production application*. This step needs to be done before you start the application, as it will allow you to roll back to the initial version after a relup. If you do not do this, you will be able to downgrade production applications only to releases newer than the first one, but not the first one!

Open a shell and run this:

```
1> release_handler:create_RELEASES(
1>    "rel",
1>    "rel/releases",
1>    "rel/releases/1.0.0/processquest-1.0.0.rel",
1>    [{kernel,"2.14.4", "rel/lib"}, {stdlib,"1.17.4","rel/lib"},
1>     {crypto,"2.0.3","rel/lib"},{regis,"1.0.0", "rel/lib"},
1>     {processquest,"1.0.0","rel/lib"},{sockserv,"1.0.0", "rel/lib"},
1>     {sasl,"2.1.9.4", "rel/lib"}]
1> ).
```

The general format of the function is as follows:

```
release_handler:create_RELEASES(RootDir, ReleasesDir, Relfile, [{AppName, Vsn, LibDir}])
```

This will create a file named *RELEASES* inside the *rel/releases* directory (or any other *ReleasesDir*), which will contain basic information on your releases when relup is looking for files and modules to reload.

We can now start running the old version of the code. If you start *rel/bin/erl*, it will start the 1.1.0 release by default. That's because we built the new release before starting the VM. For this demonstration, we'll need to start the release with this command:

```
$ ./rel/bin/erl -boot rel/releases/1.0.0/processquest
```

You should see everything starting up. Start a telnet client to connect to your socket server so you can see the live upgrade taking place.

Whenever you feel ready for an upgrade, go to the Erlang shell currently running Process Quest and call the following function:

```
1> release_handler:unpack_release("processquest-1.1.0").
{ok,"1.1.0"}
2> release_handler:which_releases().
[{"processquest","1.1.0",
  ["kernel-2.14.4","stdlib-1.17.4","crypto-2.0.3",
   "regis-1.0.0","processquest-1.1.0","sockserv-1.0.1",
   "sasl-2.1.9.4"],
  unpacked},
 {"processquest","1.0.0",
  ["kernel-2.14.4","stdlib-1.17.4","crypto-2.0.3",
   "regis-1.0.0","processquest-1.0.0","sockserv-1.0.0",
   "sasl-2.1.9.4"],
  permanent}]
```

The second prompt here tells you that the release is ready to be upgraded, but not installed or made permanent yet. To install it, enter the following:

```
3> release_handler:install_release("1.1.0").
{ok,"1.0.0",[]}
4> release_handler:which_releases().
[{"processquest","1.1.0",
  ["kernel-2.14.4","stdlib-1.17.4","crypto-2.0.3",
   "regis-1.0.0","processquest-1.1.0","sockserv-1.0.1",
   "sasl-2.1.9.4"],
  current},
 {"processquest","1.0.0",
  ["kernel-2.14.4","stdlib-1.17.4","crypto-2.0.3",
   "regis-1.0.0","processquest-1.0.0","sockserv-1.0.0",
   "sasl-2.1.9.4"],
  permanent}]
```

Now release 1.1.0 should be running, but it's still not there forever. Still, you could keep your application running that way. Call the following function to make things permanent:

```
5> release_handler:make_permanent("1.1.0").
ok.
```

Ah, damn—a bunch of our processes are dying now (error output removed from the preceding sample). But if you look at our telnet client, it did seem to upgrade fine. The issue is that all the gen_servers that were waiting for connections in sockserv could not listen to messages because accepting a TCP connection is a blocking operation. Thus, the servers couldn't upgrade when new versions of the code were loaded and were killed by the VM. Here's how we can confirm this:

```
6> supervisor:which_children(sockserv_sup).
[{undefined,<0.51.0>,worker,[sockserv_serv]}]
7> [sockserv_sup:start_socket() || _ <- lists:seq(1,20)].
[{ok,<0.99.0>},
 {ok,<0.100.0>},
 ... <snip> ...
 {ok,<0.117.0>},
 {ok,<0.118.0>}]
8> supervisor:which_children(sockserv_sup).
[{undefined,<0.112.0>,worker,[sockserv_serv]},
 {undefined,<0.113.0>,worker,[sockserv_serv]},
 ... <snip> ...
 {undefined,<0.109.0>,worker,[sockserv_serv]},
 {undefined,<0.110.0>,worker,[sockserv_serv]},
 {undefined,<0.111.0>,worker,[sockserv_serv]}]
```

The first command shows that all children that were waiting for connections have already died. The processes left will be those with an active session going on. This shows the importance of keeping code responsive. Had our processes been able to receive messages and act on them, things would have been fine.

In the two last commands, we just start more workers to fix the problem. While this works, it requires manual action from the person running the upgrade. In any case, this is far from optimal.

A better way to solve the problem would be to change the way our application works in order to have a monitor process watching how many children sockserv_sup has. When the number of children falls under a given threshold, the monitor starts more of them.

Another strategy would be to change the code so accepting connections is done by blocking on intervals of a few seconds at a time, and keep retrying after pauses where messages can be received. This would give the gen_servers the time to upgrade themselves as required, assuming you would wait the right delay between the installation of a release and making it permanent. Implementing either or both of these solutions is left as an exercise to the reader (because I am somewhat lazy).

These kinds of crashes are why you want to test your code *before* doing these updates on a live system. If you want to really test your planned relups, you should be ready to test both for upgrades and downgrades, and restarting the node in case of failure, just to make sure.

In any case, we've solved the problem for now. Let's check how the upgrade procedure went:

```
9> release_handler:which_releases().
[{"processquest","1.1.0",
  ["kernel-2.14.4","stdlib-1.17.4","crypto-2.0.3",
   "regis-1.0.0","processquest-1.1.0","sockserv-1.0.1",
   "sasl-2.1.9.4"],
  permanent},
 {"processquest","1.0.0",
  ["kernel-2.14.4","stdlib-1.17.4","crypto-2.0.3",
   "regis-1.0.0","processquest-1.0.0","sockserv-1.0.0",
   "sasl-2.1.9.4"],
  old}]
```

That's worth a fist pump. You can try downgrading an installation by doing release_handler:install(OldVersion).. This should work fine, although it could risk killing more processes that never updated themselves.

DON'T DRINK TOO MUCH KOOL-AID

If rolling back always fails when trying to roll back to the first version of the release using the techniques shown in this chapter, you probably forgot to create the *RELEASES* file. You can tell this is the case if you see an empty list in {YourRelease,Version,[],Status} when calling release_handler:which_releases(). This is a list of where to find modules to load and reload, and it is first built when booting the VM and reading the *RELEASES* file, or when unpacking a new release.

Relup Review

In summary, here's a list of all the actions that must be taken to have functional relups:

1. Write OTP applications for your first software iteration.

2. Compile them.

3. Build a release (1.0.0) using Reltool. It must have debug info and no *.ez* archive.

4. Make sure you create the *RELEASES* file at some point before starting your production application. You can do it with release_handler:create_RELEASES(RootDir, ReleasesDir, Relfile, [{AppName, Vsn, LibDir}]).

5. Run the release!

6. Find bugs in it.

7. Fix bugs in new versions of applications.

8. Write appup files for each of the applications.

9. Compile the new applications.

10. Build a new release (1.1.0 in our case). It must have debug info and no *.ez* archive.

11. Copy *rel/releases/NewVsn/RelName.rel* as *rel/releases/NewVsn/RelName-NewVsn.rel*.

12. Copy *rel/releases/NewVsn/RelName.boot* as *rel/releases/NewVsn/RelName-NewVsn.boot*.

13. Copy *rel/releases/NewVsn/RelName.boot* as *rel/releases/NewVsn/start.boot*.

14. Copy *rel/releases/OldVsn/RelName.rel* as *rel/releases/OldVsn/RelName-OldVsn.rel*.

15. Copy *rel/releases/OldVsn/RelName.boot* as *rel/releases/OldVsn/RelName-OldVsn.boot*.

16. Copy *rel/releases/OldVsn/RelName.boot* as *rel/releases/OldVsn/start.boot*.

17. Generate a relup file with systools:make_relup("rel/releases/Vsn/RelName-Vsn", ["rel/releases/OldVsn/RelName-OldVsn"], ["rel/releases/DownVsn/RelName-DownVsn"]).

18. Move the relup file to *rel/releases/Vsn*.

19. Generate a tar file of the new release with systools:make_tar("rel/releases/ Vsn/RelName-Vsn").

20. Move the tar file to *rel/releases/*.

21. Have some shell opened that still runs the first version of the release.

22. Call release_handler:unpack_release("NameOfRel-Vsn").

23. Call release_handler:install_release(Vsn).

24. Call release_handler:make_permanent(Vsn).

25. Make sure things went fine. If not, roll back by installing an older version.

You might want to write a few scripts to automate this.

Again, relups are a very messy part of OTP—a part that is hard to grasp. You will likely find yourself finding plenty of new errors, which are all more impossible to understand than the previous ones. Some assumptions are made about how you're going to run things, and choosing different tools when creating releases will change how things should be done. You might even be tempted to write your

own update code using the sys module's functions! Or maybe you'll want to use tools like rebar that automate some of the painful steps. In any case, this chapter and its examples have been written to the best knowledge of the author, a person who sometimes enjoys writing about himself in third person.

If it is possible to upgrade your application in ways that do not require relups, I recommend doing so. It is said that divisions of Ericsson that do use relups spend as much time testing them as they do testing their applications themselves. Relups are a tool to be used when working with products that can imperatively never be shut down. You will know when you will need them, mostly because you'll be ready to go through the hassle of using them (got to love that circular logic!). When the need arises, relups are entirely useful.

How about we move on to some of the friendlier features of Erlang now? Chapter 23 explores socket programming with Erlang.

23

BUCKETS OF SOCKETS

So far, we've had some fun dealing with Erlang itself, but we've barely communicated with the outside world. And even when we did, it was only by reading the occasional text file. Though relationships with yourself might be fun, it's time to get out of our lair and start talking to the rest of the world. One way to do this is by using sockets.

This chapter covers three components of using sockets: IO lists, UDP sockets, and TCP sockets.

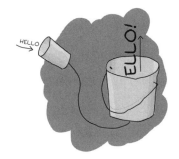

IO Lists

As you've learned, for text, we can use either strings (lists of integers) or binaries (binary data structures that hold data).

Sending things over the wire such as "Hello World" can be done as a string ("Hello World") or as a binary (<<"Hello World">>)—similar notation, similar results.

The difference lies in how you can assemble things.

A string is a bit like a linked list of integers. For each character, you need to store the character itself plus a link to the rest of the list. Moreover, if you want to add elements to a list—either in the middle or at the end—you must traverse the whole list up to the point you're modifying, and then add your elements. This isn't the case when you prepend, however:

```
A = [a]
B = [b|A] = [b,a]
C = [c|B] = [c,b,a]
```

In the case of prepending, whatever is held in A, B, or C never needs to be rewritten. The representation of C can be seen as [c,b,a], [c|B], or [c,|[b|[a]]] (among others). In the last case, you can see that the shape of A is the same at the end of the list as when it was declared, and it works similarly for B. Here's how it looks with appending:

```
A = [a]
B = A ++ [b] = [a] ++ [b] = [a|[b]]
C = B ++ [c] = [a|[b]] ++ [c] = [a|[b|[c]]]
```

Do you see all that rewriting? When we create B, we need to rewrite A. When we write C, we must rewrite B (including the [a|...] part it contains). If we were to add D in a similar manner, we would need to rewrite C. Over long strings, this becomes way too inefficient, and it creates a lot of garbage left to be cleaned up by the Erlang VM.

With binaries, things are not quite as bad:

```
A = <<"a">>
B = <<A/binary, "b">> = <<"ab">>
C = <<B/binary, "c">> = <<"abc">>
```

In this case, binaries know their own length, and data can be joined in constant time. That's good—much better than lists. They're also more compact. For these reasons, we'll try to stick to binaries when using text in the future.

There are a few downsides, however. Binaries were meant to handle things in certain ways, and there is still a cost to modifying binaries, splitting them, and so on. Moreover, sometimes we'll work with code that uses strings, binaries, and individual characters interchangeably. Constantly converting between types would be a hassle.

In these cases, *IO lists* are our savior. IO lists are a weird type of data structure. They are lists of bytes (integers from 0 to 255), binaries, or other IO lists. This means that functions that accept IO lists can accept items such as [$H, $e, [$l, «"lo"»], " "], [[["W","o"], «"rl"»]] | [«"d"»]]. When this happens, the Erlang VM will just flatten the list as it needs to in order to obtain the sequence of characters *Hello World*.

What are the functions that accept such IO lists? Most of the functions that have to do with outputting data will accept them, and any function from the io module, file module, TCP and UDP sockets will be able to handle them. Some library functions, such as several from the unicode module and all of the functions from the re (for regular expressions) module, will also handle them, as will many others.

Just to see, try the previous Hello World IO list in the shell with io:format("~s~n", [IoList]). It should work without a problem.

All in all, IO lists are a pretty clever way of building strings to avoid the problems of immutable data structures when it comes to dynamically building content to be output.

UDP and TCP: Bro-tocols

The first kind of socket that we can use in Erlang is based on the User Datagram Protocol (UDP). UDP is a protocol built on top of the IP layer that provides a few helpful abstractions, such as port numbers.

UDP is a *connectionless* protocol. The data that is received from the UDP port is broken into small untagged parts without a session (datagrams), and there is no guarantee that the fragments you received were sent in the same order as you got them. In fact, there is no guarantee that if someone sends a packet, you'll receive it at all. For these reasons, people tend to use UDP in the following situations:

- When the packets are small
- When packets can sometimes be lost with little consequences
- When there aren't too many complex exchanges taking place
- When low latency is absolutely necessary

This is in opposition to *connection-based* protocols like the Transmission Control Protocol (TCP), where the protocol takes care of handling lost packets, reordering them, maintaining isolated sessions between multiple senders and receivers, and so on. TCP allows reliable exchange of information, but can be slower and heavier to set up. UDP will be fast but less reliable. Choose carefully depending on what you need.

Using UDP in Erlang is relatively simple. We set up a socket over a given port, and that socket can both send and receive data:

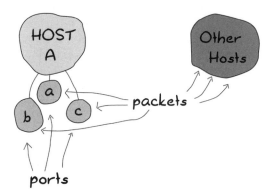

This is a bit like having a bunch of mailboxes for your house (each mailbox being a port) and receiving tiny slips of paper in each of them with small messages. They can have any content, from "I like how you look in these pants" to "The slip is coming from *inside* the house!" When some messages are too large for a slip of paper, many of them are dropped in the mailbox. It's your job to reassemble them in a way that makes sense, then drive up to some house, and drop slips as a reply. If the messages are purely informative ("Hey there, your door is unlocked") or very tiny ("What are you wearing? —Ron"), it should be fine, and you could use one mailbox for all of the queries. If they are complex, though, you might want to use one port per session, right? Ugh, no! Use TCP!

In the case of TCP, the protocol is said to be stateful, connection-based. Before being able to send messages, you must do a handshake. This means that someone is delivering messages to a mailbox (similar to what we have in the UDP analogy), and sending a message saying something like, "Hey dude, this is IP 94.25.12.37 calling. Wanna chat?" And you reply something like, "Sure. Tag your messages with number N, and then add an increasing number to them." From that point on, when you or IP 92.25.12.37 want to communicate with each other, it will be possible to order slips of paper, ask for missing ones, reply to them, and communicate in a meaningful manner. That way, you can use a single mailbox (or port) and keep all your communications working properly. That's the neat thing about TCP. It adds some overhead, but makes sure that everything is ordered and properly delivered.

If you're not a fan of these analogies, do not despair—we'll cut to the chase by seeing how to use TCP and UDP sockets with Erlang right now.

UDP Sockets

There are only a few basic operations with UDP: setting up a socket, sending messages, receiving messages, and closing a connection. The possibilities are a bit like this:

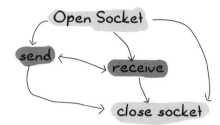

The first operation, no matter what, is to open a socket. This is done by calling gen_udp:open/1-2. The form {ok, Socket} = gen_udp:open(PortNumber) is the simplest.

The port number will be any integer between 1 and 65535.

From 0 to 1023, the ports are known as *well-known ports*. Most of the time, your operating system will make it impossible to listen to a well-known port unless you have administrative rights.

Ports from 1024 through 49151 are registered ports. They usually require no permissions and are free to use, although some of them are registered to well-known services (see *http://www.iana.org/assignments/service-names-port-numbers/service-names-port-numbers.xml*).

The rest of the ports are known as *dynamic* or *private*. They're frequently used for *ephemeral* ports, which are ports randomly assigned for a single session by the caller connecting to a given service.

For our tests, we'll take port numbers that are somewhat safe, such as 8789, which are unlikely to be taken by other applications.

But before that, what about gen_udp:open/2? The second argument can be a list of options, specifying what type of data we want to receive (list or binary) and how we want to receive it: as messages ({active, true}) or as results of a function call ({active, false}). There are more options, such as whether the socket should be set with IPv4 (inet4) or IPv6 (inet6), whether the UDP socket can be used to broadcast information ({broadcast, true | false}), the size of buffers, and so on. For now, we'll stick with the simple stuff, and then you can look into the other socket options on your own.

Now let's open a UDP socket. First start a given Erlang shell:

```
1> {ok, Socket} = gen_udp:open(8789, [binary, {active,true}]).
{ok,#Port<0.676>}
2> gen_udp:open(8789, [binary, {active,true}]).
{error,eaddrinuse}
```

In the first command, we open the socket, order it to return binary data, and tell it we want it to be active. You can see a new data structure being returned: #Port<0.676>. This is the representation of the socket we have just opened. Sockets can be used a lot like pids. You can even set up links to them so that failure is propagated to the sockets in case of a crash!

The second function call tries to open the same socket over again, which is impossible. That's why {error, eaddrinuse} is returned. Fortunately, the first socket is still open.

Next, we'll start a second Erlang shell. In this one, we'll open a second UDP socket, with a different port number:

```
1> {ok, Socket} = gen_udp:open(8790).
{ok,#Port<0.587>}
2> gen_udp:send(Socket, {127,0,0,1}, 8789, "hey there!").
ok
```

Ah, a new function! In the second call, gen_udp:send/4 is used to send messages (what a wonderfully descriptive name). The arguments are, in order: gen_udp:send(OwnSocket, RemoteAddress, RemotePort, Message). The RemoteAddress can be either a string or an atom containing a domain name ("example.org"), a 4-tuple describing an IPv4 address, or an 8-tuple describing an IPv6 address. Next we specify the receiver's port number (the mailbox in which we are going to drop our slip of paper), and then the message, which can be a string, a binary, or an IO list.

Did the message ever get sent? Go back to your first shell and try to flush the data:

```
3> flush().
Shell got {udp,#Port<0.676>,{127,0,0,1},8790,<<"hey there!">>}
ok
```

Fantastic. The process that opened the socket will receive messages of the form {udp, Socket, FromIp, FromPort, Message}. Using these fields, we'll be able to know where a message is from, what socket it went through, and what the contents are.

We've covered opening sockets, sending data, and receiving data in an active mode. What about passive mode? For this, we need to close the socket from the first shell and open a new one:

```
4> gen_udp:close(Socket).
ok
5> f(Socket).
ok
6> {ok, Socket} = gen_udp:open(8789, [binary, {active,false}]).
{ok,#Port<0.683>}
```

Here, we close the socket, unbind the Socket variable, and then bind it as we open a socket again, in passive mode this time. Before sending a message back, try the following:

```
7> gen_udp:recv(Socket, 0).
```

And your shell should be stuck. The function here is recv/2. This is the function used to poll a passive socket for messages. The 0 here is the length of the message we want. The funny thing is that the length is completely ignored with gen_udp. (gen_tcp has a similar function, but in that case, it does have an impact.) Anyway, if we never send a message to the socket, recv/2 will never return. Go back to the second shell, and send a new message:

```
3> gen_udp:send(Socket, {127,0,0,1}, 8789, "hey there!").
ok
```

The first shell should have printed {ok,{{127,0,0,1},8790,<<"hey there!">>}} as the return value. What if you don't want to wait forever? Just add a timeout value:

```
8> gen_udp:recv(Socket, 0, 2000).
{error,timeout}
```

And that's most of it for UDP. No, really!

TCP Sockets

While TCP sockets share a large part of their interface with UDP sockets, there are some vital differences in how they work. The biggest one is that clients and servers are two entirely different things. A client will behave with the following operations:

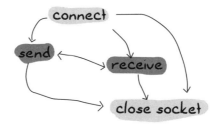

While a server will follow this scheme:

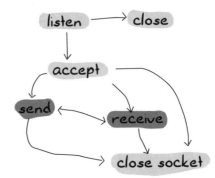

Weird looking, huh? The client acts a bit like gen_udp does. You connect to a port, send and receive, and then stop. When serving, however, we have one new mode there: listening. That's because of how TCP works to set up sessions.

First of all, we open a new shell and start something called a *listen socket* with gen_tcp:listen(Port, Options):

```
1> {ok, ListenSocket} = gen_tcp:listen(8091, [{active,true}, binary]).
{ok,#Port<0.661>}
```

The listen socket is simply in charge of waiting for connection requests. You can see that we used options similar to those we used with gen_udp. That's because most options are going to be similar for all IP sockets. The TCP ones do have a few more specific options, such as a connection backlog ({backlog, N}), keepalive sockets ({keepalive, true | false}), and packet framing ({packet, N}, where N is the length, in bytes, of each packet's header to be stripped and parsed for you), to name a few.

Once the listen socket is open, any process (and more than one) can take the listen socket and fall into an "accepting" state, locked up until some client asks to talk with it:

```
2> {ok, AcceptSocket} = gen_tcp:accept(ListenSocket, 2000).
** exception error: no match of right hand side value {error,timeout}
3> {ok, AcceptSocket} = gen_tcp:accept(ListenSocket).
** exception error: no match of right hand side value {error,closed}
```

Damn. We timed out and then crashed. The listen socket got closed when the shell process it was associated with disappeared. Let's start over again, this time without the 2 seconds (2000 milliseconds) timeout:

```
4> f().
ok
5> {ok, ListenSocket} = gen_tcp:listen(8091, [{active, true}, binary]).
{ok,#Port<0.728>}
6> {ok, AcceptSocket} = gen_tcp:accept(ListenSocket).
```

And then the process is locked. Great! Let's open a second shell:

```
1> {ok, Socket} = gen_tcp:connect({127,0,0,1}, 8091, [binary, {active,true}]).
{ok,#Port<0.596>}
```

This one takes the same options as usual, and you can add a Timeout argument in the last position if you don't want to wait forever. Your first shell should have returned with {ok, SocketNumber}. From this point on, the accept socket and the client socket can communicate on a one-on-one basis, similar to using gen_udp. Take the second shell and send messages to the first one:

```
3> gen_tcp:send(Socket, "Hey there first shell!").
ok
```

And from the first shell, enter this:

```
7> flush().
Shell got {tcp,#Port<0.729>,<<"Hey there first shell!">>}
ok
```

Both sockets can send messages in the same way, and can then be closed with gen_tcp:close(Socket). Note that closing an accept socket will close that socket alone, and closing a listen socket will close all of the related accept sockets.

That's it for most of TCP sockets in Erlang! But is it really?

Ah yes, of course, there is more that can be done. If you've experimented with sockets a bit on your own, you might have noticed that there is some kind of ownership to sockets. By this, I mean that UDP sockets, TCP client sockets, and TCP accept sockets can all have messages sent through them from any process in existence, but messages received can be read only by the process that started the socket:

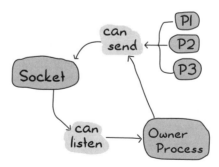

That's not very practical, is it? It means that we must always keep the owner process alive to relay messages, even if it has nothing to do with our needs. Wouldn't it be neat to be able to do something like the following?

1. Process A starts a socket
2. Process A sends a request

3. Process A spawns process B
   with a socket
4a. Gives ownership of the   4b. Process B handles the response
    socket to Process B
5a. Process A sends a request 5b. Process B Keeps handling
                                   the response
6a. Process A spawns process C 6b. ...
    with a socket
    ...

Here, Process A would be in charge of running a bunch of requests, but each new process would take charge of waiting for the response, processing it, and whatnot. Because of this, it would be clever for Process A to delegate a new process to run the task. The tricky part here is giving away the ownership of the socket.

Here's the trick: Both gen_tcp and gen_udp contain a function called controlling_process(Socket, Pid). This function must be called by the current socket owner. Then the process tells Erlang, "You know what? Just let this Pid guy take over my socket. I give up." From now on, the pid in the function is the one that can read and receive messages from the socket. That's it.

More Control with Inet

So now we have covered how to open sockets, send messages through them, change ownership, and so on. We also know how to listen to messages both in passive and active mode. Back in the UDP example, when we wanted to switch from active to passive mode, we restarted the socket, flushed variables, and went on. This is rather impractical, especially when we desire to make this switch while using TCP, because we would need to break an active session.

Fortunately, there's an Erlang module named inet that takes care of handling all operations that can be common to both gen_tcp and gen_udp sockets. For our problem at hand—changing between active and passive modes—there's a function named inet:setopts(Socket, Options). The option list can contain any terms used at the setup of a socket.

WARNING *Be careful! There is a module named inet and a module named inets. inet is the module we want here. inets is an OTP application that contains a bunch of pre-written services and servers (including FTP, TFTP, HTTP, and so on). An easy way to differentiate them is that inets is about services built on top of inet, or if you prefer, inet + s(ervices).*

Start a shell to be a TCP server:

```
1> {ok, Listen} = gen_tcp:listen(8088, [{active,false}]).
{ok,#Port<0.597>}
2> {ok, Accept} = gen_tcp:accept(Listen).
```

And in a second shell, enter the following:

```
1> {ok, Socket} = gen_tcp:connect({127,0,0,1}, 8088, []).
{ok,#Port<0.596>}
2> gen_tcp:send(Socket, "hey there").
ok
```

Then back at the first shell, the socket should have been accepted. We flush to see if we got anything:

```
3> flush().
ok
```

Of course not; we're in passive mode. Let's fix this:

```
4> inet:setopts(Accept, [{active, true}]).
ok
5> flush().
Shell got {tcp,#Port<0.598>,"hey there"}
ok
```

Yes! With full control over active and passive sockets, the power is ours. But how do we pick between active and passive modes?

In general, if you're expecting a message right away, passive mode will be much faster. Erlang won't need to toy with your process's mailbox to handle things, and you won't need to scan said mailbox, fetch messages, and so on. Using recv will be more efficient, especially if the size of the data to be received is unknown. However, recv changes your process from something event-driven to active polling. If you need to play middleman between a socket and some other Erlang code, this might make things a bit complex between blocking and handling incoming messages.

In that case, switching to active mode will be a good idea. If packets are sent as messages, you just need to wait in a receive (or a gen_server's handle_info function) and play with them, just as with any other messages. The downside of this, apart from speed, has to do with rate limiting.

The idea is that if all data coming from the outside world is blindly accepted by Erlang and then converted to messages, it is somewhat easy for someone outside the VM to flood it and kill it. Passive mode has the advantage of restricting how and when messages can be put into the Erlang VM, and delegating the task of blocking, queuing, and discarding messages to the lower-level implementations.

So what if we need active mode for the semantics, but passive mode for the safety? We could try to quickly switch between passive and active mode with inet:setopts/2, but that would be rather risky for race conditions. Instead, there's a mode called *active once*, with the option {active, once}. Let's try it to see how it works.

Keep the shell with the server from earlier and enter this:

```
6> inet:setopts(Accept, [{active, once}]).
ok
```

Now go to the client shell and run two more send/2 calls:

```
3> gen_tcp:send(Socket, "one").
ok
4> gen_tcp:send(Socket, "two").
ok
```

Then go back to the server shell and add the following:

```
7> flush().
Shell got {tcp,#Port<0.598>,"one"}
ok
8> flush().
ok
9> inet:setopts(Accept, [{active, once}]).
ok
10> flush().
Shell got {tcp,#Port<0.598>,"two"}
ok
```

See? Until we ask for {active, once} a second time, the packet containing "two" hasn't been converted to a message, which means the socket was back to passive mode. So the active once mode allows us to do that back-and-forth switch between active and passive modes in a safe way. This offers nice semantics plus safety.

There are other nice functions that are part of inet: stuff to read statistics, get current host information, inspect sockets, and so on. The documentation to the inet module contains more details about what can be done.

Well, that's most of what you need to know about sockets. Now let's put all this knowledge into practice.

NOTE   *Out in the wilderness of the Internet, there are libraries available to handle a truckload of protocols: HTTP, ZeroMQ, raw Unix sockets, and more. The standard Erlang distribution, however, comes with two main options: TCP and UDP sockets. It also comes with some HTTP servers and parsing code, but that's not the most efficient approach around.*

Sockserv, Revisited

I won't be introducing that much new code in this example. Instead, we'll look back at the `sockserv` server from Process Quest, introduced in Chapter 22, which is a perfectly viable server. We'll look at how to deal with serving TCP connections within an OTP supervision tree, in a gen_server.

A naive implementation of a TCP server might look a bit like this:

```
-module(naive_tcp).
-compile(export_all).

start_server(Port) ->
    Pid = spawn_link(fun() ->
        {ok, Listen} = gen_tcp:listen(Port, [binary, {active, false}]),
        spawn(fun() -> acceptor(Listen) end),
        timer:sleep(infinity)
    end),
    {ok, Pid}.

acceptor(ListenSocket) ->
    {ok, Socket} = gen_tcp:accept(ListenSocket),
    spawn(fun() -> acceptor(ListenSocket) end),
    handle(Socket).

%% Echoing back whatever was obtained.
handle(Socket) ->
    inet:setopts(Socket, [{active, once}]),
    receive
        {tcp, Socket, <<"quit", _/binary>>} ->
            gen_tcp:close(Socket);
        {tcp, Socket, Msg} ->
            gen_tcp:send(Socket, Msg),
            handle(Socket)
    end.
```

To understand how this works, a little graphical representation might be helpful:

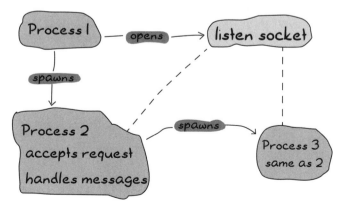

The start_server function opens a listen socket, spawns an acceptor, and then just idles forever. The idling is necessary because the listen socket is bound to the process that opened it, so that one needs to remain alive as long as we want to handle connections. Each acceptor process waits for a connection to accept. Once one connection comes in, the acceptor process starts a new, similar process and shares the listen socket with it. Then it can move on and do some processing while the new guy is working. Each handler will repeat all messages it gets until one of them starts with "quit"—then the connection is closed.

NOTE   *The pattern «"quit", _/binary» means that we first want to match on a binary string containing the characters q, u, i, and t, plus some binary data we don't care about (_).*

Start the server in an Erlang shell by calling naive_tcp:start_server(8091). Then open a telnet client (remember that telnet clients are technically not for raw TCP, but act as good clients to test servers without needing to write one) to localhost, and you can see the following taking place:

```
$ telnet localhost 8091
Trying 127.0.0.1...
Connected to localhost.
Escape character is '^]'.
hey there
hey there
that's what I asked
that's what I asked
stop repeating >:(
stop repeating >:(
quit doing that!
Connection closed by foreign host.
```

Hooray. Now it's time to start a new company called Poople Inc. and launch a few social networks with our server. However, as the name of the module mentions, this is a naive implementation. The code is simple, and it wasn't conceived with parallelism in mind. If all the requests come one by one, then the naive server works fine. But what happens if we have a queue of 15 people wanting to connect to the server at once?

Then only one query at a time can be replied to, and this involves each process first waiting for the connection, setting it up, and then spawning a new acceptor. The fifteenth request in the queue will have needed to wait for 14 other connections to have been set up to even get the chance of asking for a right to communicate with our server. If you're working with production servers, it might be closer to 500 to 1000 queries per second! That's impractical.

What we need to do is change the sequential workflow we have:

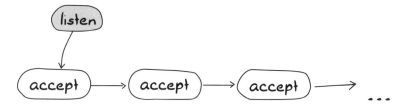

to something more parallel:

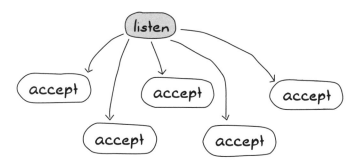

By having many acceptors already on standby, we'll be cutting down on a lot of delays to answer new queries.

Now, rather than going through another demo implementation, we'll study sockserv-1.0.1 from Chapter 22. It will be nicer to explore something based on real OTP components and real-world practice. In fact, the general pattern of sockserv is the same one used in servers like cowboy (although cowboy is no doubt more reliable than sockserv) and etorrent's torrent client and server.

To build Process Quest's sockserv, we'll go top-down. The scheme we'll need is a supervisor with many workers. If we look at the parallel drawing above, the supervisor should hold the listen socket and share it with all workers, which will be in charge of accepting things.

How do we write a supervisor that can share things across all workers? There is no way to do it with regular supervision; all children are entirely independent, no matter whether you use one_for_one, one_for_all, or rest_for_one supervision. A natural reflex might be to turn to some global state—a registered process that just holds the listen socket and hands it over to the handlers. You must fight this reflex and be clever. Use the force (and the ability to refer back to Chapter 17, which covers supervisors). You have 2 minutes to think of a solution (the 2-minute limit is based on the honor system; time it yourself).

The secret is in using a simple_one_for_one supervisor. Because simple_one_for_one supervisors share the child specification with all of their children, all we need to do is shove the listen socket in there for all the children to access it!

Here's the supervisor in all its glory:

```erlang
%%% The supervisor in charge of all the socket acceptors.
-module(sockserv_sup).
-behavior(supervisor).

-export([start_link/0, start_socket/0]).
-export([init/1]).

start_link() ->
    supervisor:start_link({local, ?MODULE}, ?MODULE, []).

init([]) ->
    {ok, Port} = application:get_env(port),
    %% Set the socket into {active_once} mode.
    %% See sockserv_serv comments for more details.
    {ok, ListenSocket} = gen_tcp:listen(Port, [{active,once}, {packet,line}]),
    spawn_link(fun empty_listeners/0),
    {ok, {{simple_one_for_one, 60, 3600},
        [{socket,
         {sockserv_serv, start_link, [ListenSocket]}, %Pass the socket!
         temporary, 1000, worker, [sockserv_serv]}
        ]}}.

start_socket() ->
    supervisor:start_child(?MODULE, []).

%% Start with 20 listeners so that many multiple connections can
%% be started at once, without serialization. In best circumstances,
%% a process would keep the count active at all times to insure nothing
%% bad happens over time when processes get killed too much.
empty_listeners() ->
    [start_socket() || _ <- lists:seq(1,20)],
    ok.
```

What is going on in there? The standard start_link/0 and init/1 functions are there. You can see sockserv getting the simple_one_for_one restart strategy, and the child specification having ListenSocket passed around. Every child started with start_socket/0 will have it as an argument by default. Magic!

Just having that won't be enough, though. We want the application to be able to serve queries as soon as possible. That's why we added that call to spawn_link(fun empty_listeners/0). The empty_listeners/0 function will start 20 handlers to be locked and waiting for incoming connections. We've put it inside a spawn_link/1 call for a simple reason: The supervisor process is in its init/1 phase and cannot answer any messages. If we were to call ourselves from within the init function, the process would deadlock and never finish running. An external process is needed just for this reason.

In the preceding snippet, notice that we pass the option {packet, line} to gen_tcp. This option will make it so all received packets will be broken into separate lines and queued up based on that (the line ends will still be part of the received strings). This will help make sure we avoid some common errors with telnet clients in our case.

So yeah, that was the whole tricky part. We can now focus on writing the workers themselves.

If you recall the Process Quest sessions from Chapter 22, interacting with the game followed these steps:

1. The user connects to the server.
2. The server asks for the character's name.
3. The user sends in a character name.
4. The server suggests stats.
5a. The user refuses; go back to point 4.
5b. The user accepts; go to point 6.
6. The game sends events to the player, until . . .
7. The user sends quit to the server or the socket is forced to close.

This means we will have two kinds of input to our server processes: input coming from the Process Quest application and input coming from the user. Data coming from the user will be doing so from a socket and so will be handled in our gen_server's handle_info/2 function. Data coming from Process Quest can be sent in a way we control, and so a cast handled by handle_cast will make sense there.

First, we must start the server module:

```
-module(sockserv_serv).
-behavior(gen_server).

-record(state, {name, % player's name
                next, % next step, used when initializing
                socket}). % the current socket

-export([start_link/1]).
-export([init/1, handle_call/3, handle_cast/2, handle_info/2,
        code_change/3, terminate/2]).
```

Here we have a pretty standard gen_server callback module. The only special thing is the state containing the character's name, the socket, and a field called next. The next part is a bit of a catchall field to store temporary information related to the state of the server. A gen_fsm could also have been used here without too much trouble.

For the actual server startup, we use the following:

```
-define(TIME, 800).
-define(EXP, 50).
```

```
start_link(Socket) ->
    gen_server:start_link(?MODULE, Socket, []).

init(Socket) ->
    %% Properly seeding the process.
    <<A:32, B:32, C:32>> = crypto:rand_bytes(12),
    random:seed({A,B,C}),
    %% Because accepting a connection is a blocking function call,
    %% we can not do it in here. Forward to the server loop!
    gen_server:cast(self(), accept),
    {ok, #state{socket=Socket}}.

%% We never need you, handle_call!
handle_call(_E, _From, State) ->
    {noreply, State}.
```

The two macros defined here (?TIME and ?EXP) are special parameters that make it possible to set the baseline delay between actions (800 milliseconds) and the amount of experience required to reach the second level (50, doubled after each level).

You'll notice that the start_link/1 function takes a socket. That's the listen socket passed in from sockserv_sup.

The bit about the random seed is for making sure a process is properly seeded to later generate character statistics. Otherwise, some default value will be used across many processes, and we don't want that. The reason we're initializing in the init/1 function rather than in whatever library that uses random numbers is that seeds are stored at a process level (damn it—mutable state!), and we wouldn't want to set a new seed on each library call.

The important bit here is that we're casting a message to ourselves. This is because gen_tcp:accept/1-2 is a blocking operation, combined with the fact that all OTP init functions are synchronous. If we wait 30 seconds to accept a connection, the supervisor starting the process will also be locked 30 seconds. So we cast a message to ourselves, and then add the listen socket to the state's socket field.

DON'T DRINK TOO MUCH KOOL-AID

If you read code from other people, you will often see programmers calling random:seed/1 with the result of now(). now() is a nice function because it returns monotonic time (always increasing; never twice the same). However, it's a bad seed value for the random algorithm used in Erlang. For this reason, it's better to use crypto:rand_bytes(12) to generate 12 crypto-safe random bytes (use crypto:strong_rand_bytes(12) if you want even more safety). By doing <<A:32, B:32, C:32>>, we're casting the 12 bytes to three integers to be passed in.

Enough fooling around. Now we need to accept that connection:

```erlang
handle_cast(accept, S = #state{socket=ListenSocket}) ->
    {ok, AcceptSocket} = gen_tcp:accept(ListenSocket),
    %% Remember that thou art dust, and to dust thou shalt return.
    %% We want to always keep a given number of children in this app.
    sockserv_sup:start_socket(), % A new acceptor is born, praise the lord.
    send(AcceptSocket, "What's your character's name?", []),
    {noreply, S#state{socket=AcceptSocket, next=name}};
```

We accept the connection, start a replacement acceptor (so that we always have about 20 acceptors ready to handle new connections), and then store the accept socket as a replacement to ListenSocket and note that the next message we receive through a socket is about a name with the next field.

But before moving on, we send a question to the client through the send function, defined as follows:

```erlang
send(Socket, Str, Args) ->
    ok = gen_tcp:send(Socket, io_lib:format(Str++"~n", Args)),
    ok = inet:setopts(Socket, [{active, once}]),
    ok.
```

Trickery! Because we expect to pretty much always need to reply after receiving a message, we do the active once routine within that function, and also add line breaks in there. This is just laziness locked in a function. It isn't necessarily optimal design, given it means that we need to always reply to any message received by the user if we don't want to ever lock them out (by being in {active, false} after dropping a message) and that the rate-limiting nature of {active, once} is now regulated by how fast we send data, rather than how fast we can digest it. As I said, it's laziness locked in a function.

We've completed steps 1 and 2, and now we need to wait for user input coming from the socket:

```erlang
handle_info({tcp, _Socket, Str}, S = #state{next=name}) ->
    Name = line(Str),
    gen_server:cast(self(), roll_stats),
    {noreply, S#state{name=Name, next=stats}};
```

We have no idea what's going to be in the Str string, but that's all right, because the next field of the state lets us know whatever we receive is a name. Because we are expecting users to use telnet for the demo application, all bits of text we're going to receive will contain line ends. The line/1 function, defined as follows, strips them away:

```erlang
%% Let's get rid of the white space and ignore whatever's after.
%% Makes it simpler to deal with telnet.
line(Str) ->
    hd(string:tokens(Str, "\r\n ")).
```

Once we've received that name, we store it and then cast a message to ourselves (roll_stats) to generate stats for the player, the next step in line.

If you look in the file, you'll see that instead of matching on entire messages, I've used a shorter ?SOCK(Var) macro. The macro is defined as -define(SOCK(Msg), {tcp, _Port, Msg}) and is just a quick way for someone as lazy as I am to match on strings with slightly less typing.

The stats rolling comes back into a handle_cast clause:

```
handle_cast(roll_stats, S = #state{socket=Socket}) ->
    Roll = pq_stats:initial_roll(),
    send(Socket,
        "Stats for your character:~n"
        "  Charisma: ~B~n"
        "  Constitution: ~B~n"
        "  Dexterity: ~B~n"
        "  Intelligence: ~B~n"
        "  Strength: ~B~n"
        "  Wisdom: ~B~n~n"
        "Do you agree to these? y/n~n",
        [Points || {_Name, Points} <- lists:sort(Roll)]),
    {noreply, S#state{next={stats, Roll}}};
```

The pq_stats module contains functions to roll stats, and the whole clause is being used only to output the stats there. The ~B format parameters mean we want an integer to be printed out. The next part of the state is a bit overloaded here. Because we ask the users whether they agree or not, we will need to wait for them to respond, and either drop the stats and generate new ones or pass them to the Process Quest character we'll no doubt start very soon.

Let's listen to the user input, this time in the handle_info function:

```
handle_info({tcp, Socket, Str}, S = #state{socket=Socket, next={stats, _}}) ->
    case line(Str) of
        "y" ->
            gen_server:cast(self(), stats_accepted);
        "n" ->
            gen_server:cast(self(), roll_stats);
        _ -> % Ask again because we didn't get what we wanted.
            send(Socket, "Answer with y (yes) or n (no)", [])
    end,
    {noreply, S};
```

It would have been tempting to start the character in this direct function clause, but I decided against it. handle_info is to handle user input, and handle_cast is for Process Quest things. Separation of concerns! If the user denies the stats, we just call roll_stats again. This is nothing new. When the user accepts, we can start the Process Quest character and begin waiting for events from there:

```erlang
%% The player has accepted the stats! Start the game!
handle_cast(stats_accepted, S = #state{name=Name, next={stats, Stats}}) ->
    processquest:start_player(Name, [{stats,Stats},{time,?TIME},
                                    {lvlexp, ?EXP}]),
    processquest:subscribe(Name, sockserv_pq_events, self()),
    {noreply, S#state{next=playing}};
```

These are regular calls defined for the game. You start a player and subscribe to the events with the sockserv_pq_events event handler. The next state is playing, which means that all messages received are more than likely to be from the game:

```erlang
%% Events coming in from process quest.
%% We know this because all these events' tuples start with the
%% name of the player as part of the internal protocol defined for us.
handle_cast(Event, S = #state{name=N, socket=Sock}) when element(1, Event) =:= N ->
    [case E of
        {wait, Time} -> timer:sleep(Time);
        IoList -> send(Sock, IoList, [])
     end || E <- sockserv_trans:to_str(Event)], % Translate to a string.
    {noreply, S}.
```

Here, sockserv_trans:to_str(Event) converts some game event to lists of IO lists or {wait, Time} tuples that represent delays to wait between parts of events (we print "executing a . . ." messages a bit before showing what the item dropped by the enemy is).

In our list of steps to follow, we've covered all except one: quitting when users tell us they want to. Put the following clause as the top one in handle_info:

```erlang
handle_info({tcp, _Socket, "quit"++_}, S) ->
    processquest:stop_player(S#state.name),
    gen_tcp:close(S#state.socket),
    {stop, normal, S};
```

Stop the character, close the socket, and terminate the process.

Other reasons to quit include the TCP socket being closed by the client:

```erlang
handle_info({tcp_closed, _Socket, _}, S) ->
    {stop, normal, S};
handle_info({tcp_error, _Socket, _}, S) ->
    {stop, normal, S};
handle_info(E, S) ->
    io:format("unexpected: ~p~n", [E]),
    {noreply, S}.
```

You could also check for similar special cases when calling gen_tcp:send/3 (it wouldn't return ok) or inet:setopts/2, although by virtue of being active most of the time, we'll get the message shown here anyway, although possibly later.

We also added an extra clause to handle unknown messages. If the user types in something we don't expect, we don't want to crash.

Only the terminate/2 and code_change/3 functions are left to write:

```
code_change(_OldVsn, State, _Extra) ->
    {ok, State}.

terminate(normal, _State) ->
    ok;
terminate(_Reason, _State) ->
    io:format("terminate reason: ~p~n", [_Reason]).
```

If you followed through this whole example, you can try compiling this file and substituting it for the corresponding BEAM file in the release we had and see if it runs correctly. It should, if you copied things right (and if I did, too).

Where to Go from Here?

Your next assignment, should you choose to accept it, is to add a few more commands of your choice to the client. Why not add things like "pause" that will queue up actions for a while and then output them all once you resume the server? Or if you're badass enough, try noting the levels and stats you have so far in the sockserv_serv module and adding commands to fetch them from the client side. I've always hated exercises left to the reader, but sometimes it's just too tempting to drop one here and there, so enjoy!

Reading the source of existing server implementations and programming some yourself are also good exercises. Rare are the languages where doing things like writing a basic web server is an exercise for amateurs, but Erlang is one of them. Practice a bit, and it will become second nature. Erlang communicating with the outside world is just one of the many steps we've taken toward writing useful software. Chapter 24 will give us some tools to make sure that useful software remains useful over time, with the intervention of unit tests.

24

EUNITED NATIONS COUNCIL

The software we've written has gotten progressively bigger and somewhat more complex. When that happens, it becomes rather tedious to start an Erlang shell, type things in, look at results, and make sure things work after code has been changed. As time passes, it becomes simpler for everyone to run tests that are prepared and ready in advance, rather than following lists of stuff to check by hand all the time. It's also possible that you're a fan of test-driven development and so will find tests useful.

When we created an RPN calculator in Chapter 8, we wrote a few tests manually. They were simply a set of pattern matches of the form `Result = Expression` that would crash if something went wrong and succeed

otherwise. That works for simple bits of code you write for yourself, but when you get to more serious tests, you will definitely want something better, like a framework.

For unit tests, we'll tend to stick with EUnit. For integration tests, EUnit and Common Test can both do the job. In fact, Common Test can do everything from unit tests up to system tests, and even testing of external software not written in Erlang. For now, we'll go with EUnit, given how simple it is and the good results it yields. We'll look into using Common Test in Chapter 28.

EUnit—What's an EUnit?

EUnit, in its simplest form, is just a way to automate running functions that end in _test() in a module by assuming they are unit tests. If you dig out that RPN calculator we wrote in Chapter 8, you'll find the following code:

```
rpn_test() ->
    5 = rpn("2 3 +"),
    87 = rpn("90 3 -"),
    -4 = rpn("10 4 3 + 2 * -"),
    -2.0 = rpn("10 4 3 + 2 * - 2 /"),
    ok = try
        rpn("90 34 12 33 55 66 + * - +")
    catch
        error:{badmatch,[_|_]} -> ok
    end,
    4037 = rpn("90 34 12 33 55 66 + * - + -"),
    8.0 = rpn("2 3 ^"),
    true = math:sqrt(2) == rpn("2 0.5 ^"),
    true = math:log(2.7) == rpn("2.7 ln"),
    true = math:log10(2.7) == rpn("2.7 log10"),
    50 = rpn("10 10 10 20 sum"),
    10.0 = rpn("10 10 10 20 sum 5 /"),
    1000.0 = rpn("10 10 20 0.5 prod"),
    ok.
```

This is the test function we wrote to make sure the calculator worked. Find the old module and try this:

```
1> c(calc).
{ok,calc}
2> eunit:test(calc).
  Test passed.
ok
```

Calling eunit:test(Module) was all we needed! Yay, we now know EUnit! Pop the champagne and let's head to a different chapter!

Obviously, a testing framework that does this little wouldn't be very useful, and in technical programmer jargon, it might be described as "not very good."

EUnit does more than automatically export and run functions ending in _test(). For one, you can move the tests to a different module so that your code and its tests are not mixed together. This means you can't test private functions anymore, but also that if you develop all your tests against the module's interface (the exported functions), you won't need to rewrite tests when you refactor your code.

Let's try separating tests and code with two simple modules:

```
-module(ops).
-export([add/2]).

add(A,B) -> A + B.
```

```
-module(ops_tests).
-include_lib("eunit/include/eunit.hrl").

add_test() ->
    4 = ops:add(2,2).
```

So we have ops and ops_tests, where the second includes tests related to the first. Here's something EUnit can do:

```
3> c(ops).
{ok,ops}
4> c(ops_tests).
{ok,ops_tests}
5> eunit:test(ops).
  Test passed.
ok
```

Calling eunit:test(Mod) automatically looks for Mod_tests and runs the tests within that module.

Let's change the test a bit (make it 3 = ops:add(2,2)) to see what failures look like:

```
6> c(ops_tests).
{ok,ops_tests}
7> eunit:test(ops).
ops_tests: add_test (module 'ops_tests')...*failed*
::error:{badmatch,4}
  in function ops_tests:add_test/0


===========================================================
  Failed: 1.  Skipped: 0.  Passed: 0.
error
```

We can see which test failed (ops_tests: add_test...) and why it failed (::error:{badmatch,4}). We also get a full report on how many tests passed or failed.

The output is pretty bad though—at least as bad as regular Erlang crashes. It doesn't have a clear explanation (4 didn't match with what, exactly?), for example. We're left helpless by a test framework that runs tests but doesn't tell you much about them.

For this reason, EUnit introduces a few macros to help us. Each of them will give us cleaner reporting (including line numbers) and clearer semantics. These macros are the difference between knowing that something goes wrong and knowing *why* something goes wrong:

?assert(Expression) and ?assertNot(Expression)

These will test for Boolean values. If any value other than true makes it into ?assert, an error will be shown. The same is true for ?assertNot, but for negative values. These macros are somewhat equivalent to true = X and false = Y.

?assertEqual(A, B)

This does a strict comparison (equivalent to =:=) between two expressions, A and B. If they are different, a failure will occur. This is roughly equivalent to true = X =:= Y. The macro ?assertNotEqual is available to do the opposite of ?assertEqual.

?assertMatch(Pattern, Expression)

This allows you to match in a form similar to *Pattern = Expression*, without variables ever binding. This means that you could do something like ?assertMatch({X,X}, some_function()) and assert that you receive a tuple with two elements being identical. Moreover, you could later run ?assertMatch(X,Y), and X would not be bound.

Actually, rather than behaving like *Pattern = Expression*, this macro's semantics are closer to (fun (Pattern) -> true; (_) -> erlang:error(nomatch) end)(Expression). Variables in the pattern's head *never* get bound across multiple assertions. The macro ?assertNotMatch was added to EUnit in R14B04.

?assertError(Pattern, Expression)

This tells EUnit that *Expression* should result in an error. As an example, ?assertError(badarith, 1/0) would be a successful test.

?assertThrow(Pattern, Expression)

This is the same as ?assertError, but with throw(Pattern) instead of erlang:error(Pattern).

?assertExit(Pattern, Expression)

This is the same as ?assertError, but with exit(Pattern) (and not exit/2) instead of erlang:error(Pattern).

?assertException(Class, Pattern, Expression)

This is a general form of the three previous macros. As an example, ?assertException(error, Pattern, Expression) is the same as ?assertError(Pattern, Expression). Starting with R14B04, there is also the macro ?assertNotException/3 available for tests.

Using these macros, we could write better tests in our module, as follows:

```
-module(ops_tests).
-include_lib("eunit/include/eunit.hrl").

add_test() ->
    4 = ops:add(2,2).

new_add_test() ->
    ?assertEqual(4, ops:add(2,2)),
    ?assertEqual(3, ops:add(1,2)),
    ?assert(is_number(ops:add(1,2))),
    ?assertEqual(3, ops:add(1,1)),
    ?assertError(badarith, 1/0).
```

Let's try running them:

```
8> c(ops_tests).
./ops_tests.erl:12: Warning: this expression will fail with a 'badarith' exception
{ok,ops_tests}
9> eunit:test(ops).
ops_tests: new_add_test...*failed*
::error:{assertEqual_failed,[{module,ops_tests},
                             {line,11},
                             {expression,"ops : add ( 1 , 1 )"},
                             {expected,3},
                             {value,2}]}
  in function ops_tests:'-new_add_test/0-fun-3-'/1
  in call from ops_tests:new_add_test/0


=========================================================
  Failed: 1.  Skipped: 0.  Passed: 1.
error
```

See how much nicer the error reporting is? We know that the ?assertEqual on line 11 of ops_tests failed. When we called ops:add(1,1), we thought we would receive 3 as a value, but we instead got 2. Of course you must read these values as Erlang terms, but at least they're there.

What's annoying with this, however, is that even though we had five assertions and only one failed, the whole test was still considered a failure. It would be nicer to know that some assertion failed without behaving as if all the others after it failed, too. Our test is equivalent to taking an exam, and as soon as you make a mistake, you fail and get thrown out of school. Then your dog dies, and you just have a horrible day.

Because of this common need for flexibility, EUnit supports something called *test generators*.

Test Generators

Test generators are pretty much shorthand for assertions wrapped in functions that can be run later, in clever manners. Instead of having functions ending with _test() with macros that are of the form ?assertSomething, we use functions that end in _test_() and macros of the form ?_assertSomething. Those are very small changes, but they make tests much more powerful.

The following two tests would be equivalent:

```
function_test() -> ?assert(A == B).
function_test_() -> ?_assert(A == B).
```

Here, function_test_() is called a *test generator function*, while ?_assert(A == B) is called a *test generator*. It's called that because, secretly, the underlying implementation of ?_assert(A == B) is fun() -> ?assert(A,B) end; that is to say, it's a function that generates a test.

The advantage of test generators, compared to regular assertions, is that they are funs. This means that they can be manipulated without being executed. We could, in fact, have *test sets* of the following form:

```
my_test_() ->
    [?_assert(A),
     [?_assert(B),
      ?_assert(C),
      [?_assert(D)]],
     [[?_assert(E)]]].
```

Test sets can be deeply nested lists of test generators. We could have functions that return tests! Let's add the following to ops_tests:

```
add_test_() ->
    [test_them_types(),
     test_them_values(),
     ?_assertError(badarith, 1/0)].

test_them_types() ->
    ?_assert(is_number(ops:add(1,2))).

test_them_values() ->
    [?_assertEqual(4, ops:add(2,2)),
     ?_assertEqual(3, ops:add(1,2)),
     ?_assertEqual(3, ops:add(1,1))].
```

Because only add_test_() ends in _test_(), the two functions test_them_types() and test_them_values() will not be seen as tests. In fact, they will be called by add_test_() to generate tests:

```
1> c(ops_tests).
./ops_tests.erl:12: Warning: this expression will fail with a 'badarith' exception
./ops_tests.erl:17: Warning: this expression will fail with a 'badarith' exception
{ok,ops_tests}
2> eunit:test(ops).
ops_tests:25: test_them_values...*failed*
[...]
ops_tests: new_add_test...*failed*
[...]


=========================================================
  Failed: 2.  Skipped: 0.  Passed: 5.
error
```

So we still get the expected failures, and now you see that we jumped from two tests to seven—the magic of test generators.

What if we want to test only some parts of the suite—maybe just add_test_/0? Well, EUnit has a few tricks up its sleeve.

```
3> eunit:test({generator, fun ops_tests:add_test_/0}).
ops_tests:25: test_them_values...*failed*
::error:{assertEqual_failed,[{module,ops_tests},
                             {line,25},
                             {expression,"ops : add ( 1 , 1 )"},
                             {expected,3},
                             {value,2}]}
  in function ops_tests:'-test_them_values/0-fun-4-'/1


=========================================================
  Failed: 1.  Skipped: 0.  Passed: 4.
error
```

Note that this works only with test generator functions. What we have here as {generator, Fun} is what EUnit parlance calls a *test representation*. EUnit provides the following test representations:

* {module, Mod} runs all tests in Mod.
* {dir, Path} runs all the tests for the modules found in Path.
* {file, Path} runs all the tests found in a single compiled module.
* {generator, Fun} runs a single generator function as a test, as seen in the preceding example.
* {application, AppName} runs all the tests for all the modules mentioned in AppName's .app file.

These different test representations can make it easy to run test suites for entire applications or even releases.

Fixtures

It would still be pretty hard to test entire applications just by using assertions and test generators. This is why *fixtures* were added. Fixtures, while not being a catchall solution to getting your tests up and running to the application level, allow you to build a certain scaffolding around tests.

The scaffolding in question is a general structure that allows you to define setup and teardown functions for each of the tests. These functions will allow you to build the state and environment required for each of the tests to be useful. Moreover, the scaffolding will let you specify how to run the tests (do you want to run them locally, in separate processes, or some other way?).

Several types of fixtures are available, with variations to them. The first type is simply called the setup fixture. A setup fixture takes one of the following forms:

```
{setup, Setup, Instantiator}
{setup, Setup, Cleanup, Instantiator}
{setup, Where, Setup, Instantiator}
{setup, Where, Setup, Cleanup, Instantiator}
```

Argh! It appears we need a bit of EUnit vocabulary in order to understand how fixtures work.

Setup

A function that does not take any arguments. Each of the tests will be passed the value returned by the setup function, which will be called once per instantiator.

Cleanup

A function that takes the result of a setup function as an argument and takes care of cleaning up whatever is needed. If an OTP terminate does the opposite of init, cleanup functions are the opposite of setup functions for EUnit. For each setup function call, the cleanup function will be called.

Instantiator

A function that takes the result of a setup function and returns a test set (remember that test sets may be deeply nested lists of ?_Macro assertions). You can also return a list of instantiators, and the setup and cleanup function will be called for each one.

Where

A function that specifies how to run the tests, as in local, spawn, {spawn, node()}.

All right, so what does this look like in practice? Well, let's imagine some test to make sure that a fictive process registry correctly handles trying to register the same process twice, with different names:

```
double_register_test_() ->
    {setup,
     fun start/0,               % setup function
     fun stop/1,                % cleanup function
     fun two_names_one_pid/1}.  % instantiator

start() ->
    {ok, Pid} = registry:start_link(),
    Pid.

stop(Pid) ->
    registry:stop(Pid).

two_names_one_pid(Pid) ->
    ok = registry:register(Pid, quite_a_unique_name, self()),
    Res = registry:register(Pid, my_other_name_is_more_creative, self()),
    [?_assertEqual({error, already_named}, Res)].
```

This fixture first starts the registry server within the start/0 function. Then the instantiator two_names_one_pid(ResultFromSetup) is called. In that test, the only thing we do is try to register the current process twice.

That's where the instantiator does its work. The result of the second registration is stored in the variable Res. The function will then return a test set containing a single test (?_assertEqual({error, already_named}, Res)). That test set will be run by EUnit. Then the cleanup function stop/1 will be called. Using the pid returned by the setup function, stop/1 will be able to shut down the registry that we started beforehand.

What's even better is that this whole fixture itself can be put inside a test set:

```
some_test_() ->
    [{setup, fun start/0, fun stop/1, fun some_instantiator1/1},
     {setup, fun start/0, fun stop/1, fun some_instantiator2/1},
     ...
     {setup, fun start/0, fun stop/1, fun some_instantiatorN/1}].
```

And this will work!

What's annoying here is the need to always repeat that setup and teardown functions, especially when they're always the same. That's where the second type of fixture, the foreach fixture, enters the stage.

The foreach fixture is quite similar to the setup fixture, with the difference that it takes lists of instantiators.

```
{foreach, Where, Setup, Cleanup, [Instantiator]}
{foreach, Setup, Cleanup, [Instantiator]}
```

```
{foreach, Where, Setup, [Instantiator]}
{foreach, Setup, [Instantiator]}
```

Here's the some_test_/0 function written with a foreach fixture:

```
some_test2_() ->
    {foreach
     fun start/0,
     fun stop/1,
     [fun some_instantiator1/1,
      fun some_instantiator2/1,
      ...
      fun some_instantiatorN/1]}.
```

That's better. The foreach fixture will then take each of the instantiators and run the setup and teardown function for them.

Now we have covered how to use a fixture for one instantiator and a fixture for many instantiators (each getting their setup and teardown function calls). What if we want to have one setup function call and one teardown function call for many instantiators?

In other words, what if we have many instantiators, but want to set some state only once? There's no easy way for this, but here's a little trick that might do it:

```
some_tricky_test_() ->
    {setup,
     fun start/0,
     fun stop/1,
     fun (SetupData) ->
        [some_instantiator1(SetupData),
         some_instantiator2(SetupData),
         ...
         some_instantiatorN(SetupData)]
     end}.
```

By using the fact that test sets can be deeply nested lists, we wrap a bunch of instantiators with an anonymous function behaving like an instantiator for them.

More Test Control

Tests can also have some finer-grained control as to how they should be running when you use fixtures. Four options are available:

{spawn, TestSet}
> This runs tests in a separate process than the main test process. The test process will wait for all of the spawned tests to finish.

{timeout, *Seconds*, TestSet}

The tests will run for *Seconds* number of seconds. If they take longer than *Seconds* to finish, they will be terminated without further ado.

{inorder, TestSet}

This tells EUnit to run the tests within the test set strictly in the order they are returned.

{inparallel, Tests}

Where possible, the tests will be run in parallel.

As an example, the `some_tricky_test_/0` test generator could be rewritten as follows:

```
some_tricky_test2_() ->
    {setup,
     fun start/0,
     fun stop/1,
     fun(SetupData) ->
         {inparallel,
          [some_instantiator1(SetupData),
           some_instantiator2(SetupData),
           ...
           some_instantiatorN(SetupData)]}
     end}.
```

Test Documentation

That's really most of it for fixtures, but there's one more nice trick to show you. You can add descriptions of tests in a neat way. Check this out:

```
double_register_test_() ->
    {"Verifies that the registry doesn't allow a single process to "
     "be registered under two names. We assume that each pid has the "
     "exclusive right to only one name",
     {setup,
      fun start/0,
      fun stop/1,
      fun two_names_one_pid/1}}.
```

Nice, huh? You can wrap a fixture by doing {Comment, Fixture} in order to get readable tests. Let's put this in practice.

Testing Regis

Because seeing fake tests isn't the most entertaining thing to do, and because pretending to test software that doesn't exist is even worse, we'll instead study the tests I have written for the *regis-1.0.0* process registry, the one used by Process Quest.

The development of regis was done in a test-driven manner. Hopefully you don't hate test-driven development (TDD), but even if you do, it shouldn't be too bad because we'll look at the test suite after the fact. By doing this, we cut through the few trial-and-error sequences and backpedaling that I might have experienced when writing it the first time, and I'll look like I'm really competent, thanks to the magic of text editing.

The regis application is made of three processes: a supervisor, a main server, and an application callback module. Knowing that the supervisor will check only the server, and that the application callback module will do nothing except behave as an interface for the two other modules, we can safely write a test suite focusing on the server itself, without any external dependencies.

Being a good TDD fan, I began by writing a list of all the features I wanted to cover:

- Implement an interface similar to the Erlang default process registry.
- The server will have a registered name so that it can be contacted without tracking its pid.
- A process can be registered through our service and can then be contacted by its name.
- A list of all registered processes can be obtained.
- A name that is not registered by any process should return the atom undefined (much like the regular Erlang registry) in order to crash calls using it.
- A process cannot have two names.
- Two processes cannot share the same name.
- A process that was registered can be registered again if it was unregistered between calls.
- Unregistering a process never causes a process crash.
- A registered process's exit will unregister its name.

That's a respectable list. Doing the elements one by one and adding cases as I went, I transformed each of the specifications into a test.

The final file obtained was *regis_server_tests*. I wrote things using a basic structure a bit like this:

```erlang
-module(regis_server_tests).
-include_lib("eunit/include/eunit.hrl").


%%%%%%%%%%%%%%%%%%%%%%%%%%%%%
%%% TESTS DESCRIPTIONS %%%
%%%%%%%%%%%%%%%%%%%%%%%%%%%%%


%%%%%%%%%%%%%%%%%%%%%%%%%%%
%%% SETUP FUNCTIONS %%%
%%%%%%%%%%%%%%%%%%%%%%%%%%%


%%%%%%%%%%%%%%%%%%%%%%%
%%% ACTUAL TESTS %%%
%%%%%%%%%%%%%%%%%%%%%%%


%%%%%%%%%%%%%%%%%%%%%%%%%%%%
%%% HELPER FUNCTIONS %%%
%%%%%%%%%%%%%%%%%%%%%%%%%%%%
```

Yes, this does look weird when the module is empty, but as you fill it up, it makes more and more sense.

After adding a first test—that it should be possible to start a server and access it by name—the file looked like this:

```erlang
-module(regis_server_tests).
-include_lib("eunit/include/eunit.hrl").


%%%%%%%%%%%%%%%%%%%%%%%%%%%%%%%%
%%% TESTS DESCRIPTIONS %%%
%%%%%%%%%%%%%%%%%%%%%%%%%%%%%%%%
start_stop_test_() ->
    {"The server can be started, stopped and has a registered name",
     {setup,
      fun start/0,
      fun stop/1,
      fun is_registered/1}}.


%%%%%%%%%%%%%%%%%%%%%%%%%%%%%
%%% SETUP FUNCTIONS %%%
%%%%%%%%%%%%%%%%%%%%%%%%%%%%%
start() ->
    {ok, Pid} = regis_server:start_link(),
    Pid.

stop(_) ->
    regis_server:stop().
```

```
%%%%%%%%%%%%%%%%%%%%%
%%% ACTUAL TESTS %%%
%%%%%%%%%%%%%%%%%%%%%
is_registered(Pid) ->
    [?_assert(erlang:is_process_alive(Pid)),
     ?_assertEqual(Pid, whereis(regis_server))].


%%%%%%%%%%%%%%%%%%%%%%%%%%
%%% HELPER FUNCTIONS %%%
%%%%%%%%%%%%%%%%%%%%%%%%%%
```

See the organization now? It's already so much better. The top part of
the file contains only fixtures and top-level descriptions of features. The
second part contains setup and cleanup functions that we might need. The
last part contains the instantiators returning test sets.

In this case, the instantiator is is_registered(Pid), which will make sure
the server can be started and stopped. We'll actually revisit it in a short while.

In the final file for the tests, if you've downloaded it with the rest of the
code in this book, the first two sections would look more like this:

```
-module(regis_server_tests).
-include_lib("eunit/include/eunit.hrl").

-define(setup(F), {setup, fun start/0, fun stop/1, F}).


%%%%%%%%%%%%%%%%%%%%%%%%%%%%
%%% TESTS DESCRIPTIONS %%%
%%%%%%%%%%%%%%%%%%%%%%%%%%%%


start_stop_test_() ->
    {"The server can be started, stopped and has a registered name",
     ?setup(fun is_registered/1)}.


register_test_() ->
    [{"A process can be registered and contacted",
      ?setup(fun register_contact/1)},
     {"A list of registered processes can be obtained",
      ?setup(fun registered_list/1)},
     {"An undefined name should return 'undefined' to crash calls",
      ?setup(fun noregister/1)},
     {"A process cannot have two names",
      ?setup(fun two_names_one_pid/1)},
     {"Two processes cannot share the same name",
      ?setup(fun two_pids_one_name/1)}].


unregister_test_() ->
    [{"A process that was registered can be registered again iff it was "
      "unregistered between both calls",
      ?setup(fun re_un_register/1)},
     {"Unregistering never crashes",
      ?setup(fun unregister_nocrash/1)},
     {"A crash unregisters a process",
      ?setup(fun crash_unregisters/1)}].
```

```
%%%%%%%%%%%%%%%%%%%%%%%%%
%%% SETUP FUNCTIONS %%%
%%%%%%%%%%%%%%%%%%%%%%%%%
start() ->
    {ok, Pid} = regis_server:start_link(),
    Pid.

stop(_) ->
    regis_server:stop().


%%%%%%%%%%%%%%%%%%%%%%%%%%
%%% HELPER FUNCTIONS %%%
%%%%%%%%%%%%%%%%%%%%%%%%%%
%% nothing here yet
```

Nice, isn't it? Note that as I was writing the suite, I ended up seeing that I never needed any other setup and teardown functions than start/0 and stop/1. For this reason, I added the ?setup(Instantiator) macro, which makes things look a bit better than if all the fixtures were fully expanded.

It's now pretty obvious that I turned each point of the feature list into a bunch of tests. You'll note that I divided all tests depending on whether they had to do with starting and stopping the server (start_stop_test_/0), registering processes (register_test_/0), and unregistering processes (unregister_test_/0).

By reading the test generators' definitions, we can know what the module is supposed to be doing. The tests become documentation (although they should not replace proper documentation).

We'll study the tests a bit and see why things were done in a certain way. Here's the first test in the list, start_stop_test_/0, with the simple requirement that the server can be registered:

```
start_stop_test_() ->
    {"The server can be started, stopped and has a registered name",
     ?setup(fun is_registered/1)}.
```

The implementation of the test itself is put in the is_registered/1 function, which hasn't changed:

```
%%%%%%%%%%%%%%%%%%%%%%%%%
%%% ACTUAL TESTS %%%
%%%%%%%%%%%%%%%%%%%%%%%%%
is_registered(Pid) ->
    [?_assert(erlang:is_process_alive(Pid)),
     ?_assertEqual(Pid, whereis(regis_server))].
```

This is the same instantiator as earlier. There's nothing really special about the test, although the function erlang:is_process_alive(Pid) might be new to you. As its name says, the function checks whether a process is currently running. I've put that test in there for the simple reason that it might be possible that the server crashes as soon as we start it, or that it's never

started in the first place. This would give
confusing test results if we assumed the
registration failed due to some code error,
when the server wasn't started in the first
place. We don't want that.

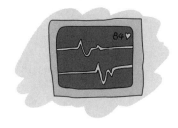

The second test is related to being able
to register a process:

```
{"A process can be registered and contacted",
 ?setup(fun register_contact/1)}
```

Here's what the test looks like:

```
register_contact(_) ->
    Pid = spawn_link(fun() -> callback(regcontact) end),
    timer:sleep(15),
    Ref = make_ref(),
    WherePid = regis_server:whereis(regcontact),
    regis_server:whereis(regcontact) ! {self(), Ref, hi},
    Rec = receive
        {Ref, hi} -> true
        after 2000 -> false
    end,
    [?_assertEqual(Pid, WherePid),
     ?_assert(Rec)].
```

Granted, this isn't the most elegant test around. The timers are the biggest
eyesore, and they could be avoided by using some sort of synchronous process
initialization (either a behavior or functions such as proc_lib:start_link and its
related synchronization functions, which are described in the proc_lib module's documentation). The test spawns a process that will do nothing but
register itself and reply to some message we send it. This is all done in the
callback/1 helper function, which is defined as follows:

```
%%%%%%%%%%%%%%%%%%%%%%%%
%%% HELPER FUNCTIONS %%%
%%%%%%%%%%%%%%%%%%%%%%%%
callback(Name) ->
    ok = regis_server:register(Name, self()),
    receive
        {From, Ref, Msg} -> From ! {Ref, Msg}
    end.
```

So the function has the module register itself, receives a message, and
sends a response back. Once the process is started, the register_contact/1
instantiator waits 15 milliseconds (just a tiny delay to make sure the other
process registers itself), and then tries to use the whereis function from
regis_server to retrieve a pid and send a message to the process. If the regis
server is functioning correctly, a message will be returned, and the pids will
match in the tests at the bottom of the function.

The next tests are introduced as follows:

```
{"A list of registered processes can be obtained",
 ?setup(fun registered_list/1)}
```

So when a bunch of processes have been registered, it should be possible to get a list of all the names. This is a functionality similar to Erlang's registered() function call:

```
registered_list(_) ->
    L1 = regis_server:get_names(),
    Pids = [spawn(fun() -> callback(N) end) || N <- lists:seq(1,15)],
    timer:sleep(200),
    L2 = regis_server:get_names(),
    [exit(Pid, kill) || Pid <- Pids],
    [?_assertEqual([], L1),
     ?_assertEqual(lists:sort(lists:seq(1,15)), lists:sort(L2))].
```

First, we make sure that the first list of registered processes is empty (?_assertEqual(L1, [])) so that we have something that works even when no process has ever tried to register itself. Then 15 processes are created, all of which will try to register themselves with a number (1 through 15). We make the test sleep a bit to make sure all processes have the time to register themselves, and then call regis_server:get_names(). The names should include all integers between 1 and 15, inclusively. Then a slight cleanup is done by eliminating all the registered processes—we don't want to be leaking them, after all.

You'll notice the tendency of the tests to store state in variables (L1 and L2) before using them in test sets. The reason for this is that the test set that is returned is executed well after the test initiator (the whole active bit of code) has been running. If you were to try to put function calls that depend on

other processes and time-sensitive events in the ?_assert* macros, you would get everything out of sync, and things would generally be awful for you and the people using your software.

The next test is simple:

```
{"An undefined name should return 'undefined' to crash calls",
 ?setup(fun noregister/1)}
...
noregister(_) ->
    [?_assertError(badarg, regis_server:whereis(make_ref()) ! hi),
     ?_assertEqual(undefined, regis_server:whereis(make_ref()))].
```

As you can see, this tests for two things: we return undefined and the specification's assumption that using undefined does indeed crash attempted calls. Here, there is no need to use temporary variables to store the state; both tests can be executed at any time during the life of the regis server, given we never change its state.

Let's keep going:

```
{"A process cannot have two names",
 ?setup(fun two_names_one_pid/1)},
...
two_names_one_pid(_) ->
    ok = regis_server:register(make_ref(), self()),
    Res = regis_server:register(make_ref(), self()),
    [?_assertEqual({error, already_named}, Res)].
```

This is pretty much the same test we used in a demo earlier in the chapter. In this one, we're just looking to see whether we get the right output and that the test process can't register itself twice with different names.

The next test is the opposite of two_names_one_pid:

```
{"Two processes cannot share the same name",
 ?setup(fun two_pids_one_name/1)}].
...
two_pids_one_name(_) ->
    Pid = spawn(fun() -> callback(myname) end),
    timer:sleep(15),
    Res = regis_server:register(myname, self()),
    exit(Pid, kill),
    [?_assertEqual({error, name_taken}, Res)].
```

Here, because we need two processes and the results of only one of them, the trick is to spawn one process (the one whose results we do not need), and then do the critical part ourselves.

You can see that timers are used to make sure that the other process tries registering a name first (within the callback/1 function), and that the test process itself waits to take its turn, expecting an error tuple ({error, name_taken}) as a result.

This covers all the features for the tests related to the registration of processes. Only those related to unregistering processes remain:

```
unregister_test_() ->
[{"A process that was registered can be registered again iff it was "
  "unregistered between both calls",
  ?setup(fun re_un_register/1)},
 {"Unregistering never crashes",
  ?setup(fun unregister_nocrash/1)},
 {"A crash unregisters a process",
  ?setup(fun crash_unregisters/1)}].
```

Let's see how they are to be implemented. The first one is kind of simple:

```
re_un_register(_) ->
    Ref = make_ref(),
    L = [regis_server:register(Ref, self()),
         regis_server:register(make_ref(), self()),
         regis_server:unregister(Ref),
         regis_server:register(make_ref(), self())],
    [?_assertEqual([ok, {error, already_named}, ok, ok], L)].
```

This way of serializing all the calls in a list is a nifty trick I like to do when I need to test the results of all the events. By putting them in a list, I can then compare the sequence of actions to the expected [ok, {error, already_named}, ok, ok] to see how things went. Note that there is nothing specifying that Erlang should evaluate the list in order, but this trick has pretty much always worked for me.

The following test—the one about never crashing—goes like this:

```
unregister_nocrash(_) ->
    ?_assertEqual(ok, regis_server:unregister(make_ref())).
```

Whoa, slow down here, buddy! That's it? Yes it is. The re_un_register function already handles testing the "unregistration" of processes. For unregister_nocrash, we really only want to know if it will work to try to remove a process that's not there.

Then comes the last test, and one of the most important ones for any test registry you'll ever have: A named process that crashes will have the name unregistered. This has serious implications, because if you don't remove names, you'll end up having an ever-growing registry server with an ever-shrinking name selection.

```
crash_unregisters(_) ->
    Ref = make_ref(),
    Pid = spawn(fun() -> callback(Ref) end),
    timer:sleep(150),
    Pid = regis_server:whereis(Ref),
    exit(Pid, kill),
    timer:sleep(95),
    regis_server:register(Ref, self()),
    S = regis_server:whereis(Ref),
    Self = self(),
    ?_assertEqual(Self, S).
```

This one reads sequentially:

1. Register a process.

2. Make sure the process is registered.

3. Kill that process.

4. Steal the process's identity (the true spy way).

5. Check whether we do hold the name ourselves.

In all honesty, the test could have been written in a simpler manner:

```
crash_unregisters(_) ->
    Ref = make_ref(),
    Pid = spawn(fun() -> callback(Ref) end),
    timer:sleep(150),
    Pid = regis_server:whereis(Ref),
    exit(Pid, kill),
    ?_assertEqual(undefined, regis_server:whereis(Ref)).
```

That whole part about stealing the identity of the dead process was nothing but a petty thief's fantasy.

That's it! If you've done things right, you should be able to compile the code and run the test suite:

```
$ erl -make
Recompile: src/regis_sup
... <snip> ...
$ erl -pa ebin/
```

```
1> eunit:test(regis_server).
  All 13 tests passed.
ok
2> eunit:test(regis_server, [verbose]).
======================= EUnit ========================
module 'regis_server'
  module 'regis_server_tests'
    The server can be started, stopped and has a registered name
      regis_server_tests:49: is_registered...ok
      regis_server_tests:50: is_registered...ok
      [done in 0.006 s]
... <snip> ...
  [done in 0.520 s]
======================================================
  All 13 tests passed.
ok
```

Oh yeah, see how adding the verbose option will add test descriptions and runtime information to the reports? That's neat.

He Who Knits EUnits

We've now covered how to use most of EUnit's features to run test suites. More important, you've seen a few techniques related to writing tests for concurrent processes, using patterns that make sense in the real world.

You should know one last trick. When you feel like testing processes such as gen_server and gen_fsm, you might want to inspect their internal state. Here's a nice way to do this, courtesy of the sys module:

```
3> regis_server:start_link().
{ok,<0.160.0>}
4> regis_server:register(shell, self()).
ok
5> sys:get_status(whereis(regis_server)).
{status,<0.160.0>,
        {module,gen_server},
        [[{'$ancestors',[<0.31.0>]},
          {'$initial_call',{regis_server,init,1}}],
         running,<0.31.0>,[],
         [{header,"Status for generic server regis_server"},
          {data,[{"Status",running},
                 {"Parent",<0.31.0>},
                 {"Logged events",[]}]},
          {data,[{"State",
                  {state,{1,{<0.31.0>,{shell,#Ref<0.0.0.333>},nil,nil}},
                          {1,{shell,{<0.31.0>,#Ref<0.0.0.333>},nil,nil}}}}]}]]}
```

Neat, huh? Everything that has to do with the server's innards is given to you, and you can now inspect everything you need, all the time!

If you feel like getting more comfortable with testing servers and whatnot, I recommend reading the tests written for Process Quest's player module at *http://learnyousomeerlang.com/static/erlang/processquest/apps/processquest-1.1.0/test/pq_player_tests.erl*. They test the gen_server using a different technique, where all individual calls to handle_call, handle_cast, and handle_info are tried independently. It was still developed in a test-driven manner, but the needs of that approach forced things to be done differently.

You'll see the true value of tests in Chapter 25, when we rewrite the process registry to use ETS, an in-memory database available for all Erlang processes.

25

BEARS, ETS, BEETS: IN-MEMORY NOSQL FOR FREE!

Something we've been doing time and time again has been implementing some kind of storage device as a process. We've made fridges to store things, built regis to register processes, seen key/value stores, and so on. If we were programmers doing object-oriented design, we would have a bunch of singletons floating around, special storage classes, and whatnot. In fact, wrapping data structures like dicts and GB trees in processes is a bit like that.

This chapter introduces ETS, an in-memory database that provides an alternative data storage approach.

Why ETS

Holding data structures in a process is actually fine for a lot of cases, such as when you need that data to do some task within the process, as internal state, and so on. This will be the majority of our use cases. There is one case where it may not be the best choice: when the process holds a data structure for the sake of sharing it with other processes and little more.

One of the applications we've written is guilty of that. Can you guess which one? Of course you can. I mentioned it at the end of the previous chapter. regis (part of the Process Quest game we developed in Chapter 22) needs to be rewritten. That is not because it doesn't work or can't do its job well, but because it acts as a gateway to share data with potentially a lot of other processes.

regis is the central application to do messaging in Process Quest (and anything else that would use it), and pretty much every message going to a named process must go through it. This means that even though we took great care to make our applications very concurrent with independent actors and made sure our supervision structure could be scaled up, all of our operations will depend on a central regis process that will need to answer messages one by one:

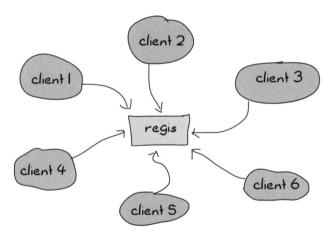

If we have a lot of message-passing going on, regis risks getting busier and busier. If the demand is high enough, our whole system will become sequential and slow. That's pretty bad.

NOTE *We have no direct proof that* regis *is a bottleneck within Process Quest. In fact, Process Quest does very little messaging compared to many other applications in the wild. If we were using* regis *for something that required a lot more messaging and lookups, then the problems would be more apparent.*

To get around this problem, we could either split regis into subprocesses to make lookups faster (*sharding* the data) or find a way to store the data in some database that will allow for parallel and concurrent access of the data. While the first way would be very interesting to explore, we'll take an easier path by doing the latter.

Erlang has Erlang Term Storage (ETS) tables, which are an efficient in-memory database included with the Erlang VM. This database sits in a part of the VM where destructive updates are allowed and where garbage collection dares not approach, in a part of memory not shared by processes. ETS tables are generally fast, and they provide a pretty easy way for Erlang programmers to optimize some of their code when parts of it get too slow.

ETS tables allow limited concurrency in reads and writes (much better than none at all for a process's mailbox) in a way that could let us optimize away a lot of the pain, but that could also add problems. This is because their use throws away most of the concepts that make Erlang safe for concurrency in the first place.

DON'T DRINK TOO MUCH KOOL-AID

While ETS tables are a nice way to optimize applications, they should be used with some care. By default, the VM is limited to 1,400 ETS tables. While it is possible to change that number (by using `erl -env ERL_MAX_ETS_TABLES Number`), this default low level is a good sign that you should try to avoid having one table per process in general.

But before we rewrite regis to use ETS, we should try to understand a bit of ETS's principles.

The Concepts of ETS

ETS tables are implemented as BIFs in the ets module. ETS was designed to provide a way to store large amounts of data in Erlang with constant access time (functional data structures tend to flirt with logarithmic access time), and to have such storage look as if it were implemented as processes in order to keep their use simple and idiomatic.

NOTE   *Having tables look like processes doesn't mean that you can spawn them or link to them. It means that they can respect semantics of nothing shared, wrapping calls behind functional interfaces, having them handle any native data type for Erlang, and making it possible to give them names (in a separate registry). Also, while you can't link to tables, they do have a similar mechanism available, as mentioned near the end of this section.*

All ETS tables natively store Erlang tuples, and only tuples. The tuples can contain whatever you want, and one of the tuple elements will act as a primary key that you use to sort things. For example, having tuples of people of the form {Name, Age, PhoneNumber, Email} will let you have a table that looks like this:

```
{Name, Age, PhoneNumber, Email},
{Name, Age, PhoneNumber, Email},
{Name, Age, PhoneNumber, Email},
{Name, Age, PhoneNumber, Email},
{Name, Age, PhoneNumber, Email},
...
```

So if we want to have the table's index be the email addresses, we can do this by telling ETS to set the key position to 4 (as described in "Creating and Deleting Tables" on page 423). Once you've decided on a key, you can choose different ways to store data in tables:

set

A set table will tell you that each key value must be unique. There can be no duplicate email in the preceding database example. Sets are great when you need to use a standard key/value store with constant time access.

ordered_set

There can still be only one key instance per table, but ordered_set adds a few other interesting properties. The first is that elements in an ordered_set table will be ordered (who would have thought?). The first element of the table is the smallest one, and the last element is the largest one. If you traverse a table iteratively (jumping to the next element over and over again), the values should be increasing, which is not necessarily true of set tables. Using ordered_set tables is great when you frequently need to operate on ranges (for example, "I want entries 12 to 50"). They do, however, have the downside of being slower in their access time ($O(\log N)$, where N is the number of objects stored).

bag

A bag table can have multiple entries with the same key, as long as the tuples themselves are different. This means that the table can contain {key, some, values} and {key, other, values} without any problems, which would be impossible with set tables (they have the same key). However, you couldn't have {key, some, values} twice in the table, as those entries would be entirely identical.

duplicate_bag

The tables of this type work like bag tables, except that they allow entirely identical tuples to be held multiple times within the same table.

The ordered_set *tables will see the values 1 and 1.0 as identical for all operations. Other tables will see them as different. Although it's nice to be able to use both integers and floating-point numbers together, it is somewhat rare that a given function can return both. You will generally avoid a lot of problems if your programs restrict their return values to one or the other.*

Another general concept related to ETS tables involves table ownership. When a process calls a function that starts a new ETS table, that process is the owner of the table.

By default, only the owner of the table can write to it, but everyone can read from it. This is known as the protected level of permissions. You can also choose to set the permissions to public, where everyone can read and write, or private, where only the owner can read or write.

The concept of table ownership goes a bit further. The ETS table is intimately linked to the process. If the process dies, the table disappears (and so does all of its content). However, the table can be given away, similar to sockets and their controlling processes, or an heir can be determined so that if the owner process dies, the table is automatically given away to the heir process.

ETS Phone Home

Now that we've covered some ETS concepts, we're ready to move on to the basics of handling tables. ETS functions allow you to create and destroy tables, as well as insert and look up data.

Creating and Deleting Tables

To start an ETS table, call the function ets:new/2. This function takes the argument Name (as an atom) and then a list of options. In return, you get a unique identifier necessary to use the table, comparable to a pid for processes.

The options can be any of the following:

Type = set | ordered_set | bag | duplicate_bag
   This sets the type of table you want to have, as described earlier. The default value is set.

Access = private | protected | public
   This sets permissions on the table, as described earlier. The default option is protected.

named_table

Funnily enough, if you call ets:new(some_name, []), you'll be starting a protected set table without a name. For the name to be used as a way to contact a table (and to be made unique), the option named_table must be passed to the function. Otherwise, the name of the table will be purely for documentation purposes and will appear in functions such as ets:i(), which prints information about all ETS tables in the system.

{keypos, Position}

As you may (and should) recall, ETS tables work by storing tuples. The Position parameter holds an integer from 1 to N, telling which of each tuple's elements should act as the primary key of the database table. The default key position is set to 1. This means you must be careful if you're using records, as each record's first element will always be the record's name (remember what they look like in their tuple form). If you want to use any field as the key, use {keypos, #RecordName.FieldName}, as it will return the position of FieldName within the record's tuple representation.

{heir, Pid, Data} | {heir, none}

ETS tables have a process that acts as their parent. If the process dies, the table disappears. If the data attached to a table is something you might want to keep alive, then defining an heir can be useful. If the process attached to a table dies, the heir receives a message saying {'ETS-TRANSFER', TableId, FromPid, Data}, where Data is the element passed when the option was first defined. The table is automatically inherited by the heir. By default, no heir is defined. It is possible to define or change an heir at a later time by calling ets:setopts(Table, {heir, Pid, Data}) or ets:setopts(Table, {heir, none}). If you simply want to give the table away, call ets:give_away(Tab, Pid, Data).

{read_concurrency, true | false}

This is an option to optimize the table for read concurrency. Setting this option to true means that reads become way cheaper to do, but switching to writes becomes a lot more expensive. Basically, this option should be enabled when you do a lot of reading and little writing, and need an extra kick of performance. If you do some reading and some writing, and they are interleaved, using this option might even hurt performance.

{write_concurrency, true | false}

Usually, writing to a table will lock the whole thing and no one else can access it, either for reading or writing, until the writing is done. Setting this option to true lets both reads and writes be done concurrently, without affecting the ACID properties of ETS. Doing this, however, will reduce the performance of sequential writes by a single process and also the capacity of concurrent reads. You can combine this option with read_concurrency when both writes and reads come in large bursts.

ACID stands for atomicity, consistency, isolation, and durability. ACID properties are those defined for a reliable database transaction system. See http://en.wikipedia.org/wiki/ACID *for more information.*

compressed

Using this option will allow the data in the table to be compressed for most fields, but not the primary key. This comes at the cost of performance when inspecting entire elements of the table.

Then, the opposite of table creation is table destruction. For that one, all that's needed is to call ets:delete(Table), where Table is either a table ID or the name of a named table. If you want to delete a single entry from the table, a very similar function call is required: ets:delete(Table, Key).

Inserting and Looking Up Data

Two other functions are required for basic table handling: ets:insert(Table, ObjectOrObjects) and ets:lookup(Table, Key). In the case of insert/2, ObjectOrObjects can be either a single tuple or a list of tuples to insert.

```
1> ets:new(ingredients, [set, named_table]).
ingredients
2> ets:insert(ingredients, {bacon, great}).
true
3> ets:lookup(ingredients, bacon).
[{bacon,great}]
4> ets:insert(ingredients, [{bacon, awesome}, {cabbage, alright}]).
true
5> ets:lookup(ingredients, bacon).
[{bacon,awesome}]
6> ets:lookup(ingredients, cabbage).
[{cabbage,alright}]
7> ets:delete(ingredients, cabbage).
true
8> ets:lookup(ingredients, cabbage).
[]
```

You'll notice that the lookup function returns a list. It will do that for all types of tables, even though set-based tables will always return one item at most. It just means that you should be able to use the lookup function in a generic way, even when you use bag or duplicate_bag tables (which may return many values for a single key).

Another thing that takes place in the preceding snippet is that inserting the same key twice overwrites it. This will always happen in set and ordered_set tables, but not in bag or duplicate_bag tables. If you want to avoid this, the function ets:insert_new/2 might be what you need, as it will insert elements only if they are not already in the table.

NOTE *The tuples do not need to all be the same size in an ETS table, though that is consid-ered the best practice. It is, however, necessary that the tuple is at least of the same size (or greater) than whatever the key position is.*

There's another lookup function available if you need to fetch only part of a tuple: ets:lookup_element(TableID, Key, PositionToReturn). It will return the element that matched (or a list of them if there is more than one in a bag or duplicate_bag table). If the element isn't there, the function errors out, with badarg as a reason.

Let's try our previous example again with a bag table:

```
9> TabId = ets:new(ingredients, [bag]).
16401
10> ets:insert(TabId, {bacon, delicious}).
true
11> ets:insert(TabId, {bacon, fat}).
true
12> ets:insert(TabId, {bacon, fat}).
true
13> ets:lookup(TabId, bacon).
[{bacon,delicious},{bacon,fat}]
```

As this is a bag table, {bacon, fat} is there only once, even though we inserted twice, but you can see that we can still have more than one bacon entry. The other thing to look at here is that without passing in the named_table option, we must use TabId to use the table.

NOTE *If at any point while copying these examples your shell crashes, the tables are going to disappear, as their parent process (the shell) has disappeared.*

The last basic operations we can make use of will be about traversing table entries one by one, ordered_set tables are the best fit for this task:

```
14> ets:new(ingredients, [ordered_set, named_table]).
ingredients
15> ets:insert(ingredients,
15>            [{ketchup, "not much"}, {mustard, "a lot"},
15>             {cheese, "yes", "goat"}, {patty, "moose"},
15>             {onions, "a lot", "caramelized"}]).
true
16> Res1 = ets:first(ingredients).
cheese
17> Res2 = ets:next(ingredients, Res1).
ketchup
18> Res3 = ets:next(ingredients, Res2).
mustard
19> ets:last(ingredients).
patty
20> ets:prev(ingredients, ets:last(ingredients)).
onions
```

As you can see, elements are now in sorting order, and they can be accessed one after the other, both forward and backward.

Oh yeah, we need to see what happens in boundary conditions:

```
21> ets:next(ingredients, ets:last(ingredients)).
'$end_of_table'
22> ets:prev(ingredients, ets:first(ingredients)).
'$end_of_table'
```

When you see atoms starting with a $, you should know that they're some special value (chosen by convention by the OTP team) telling you about something. Whenever you're trying to iterate outside the table, you'll see these $end_of_table atoms. Other than cases like this, you should avoid using atoms starting with $ in order to prevent confusion or possible clashes with OTP's own atoms.

We've now covered how to use ETS as a basic key/value store. Next, we'll look at some more advanced uses.

Meeting Your Match

What if you want to do more than just match on keys when doing lookups? When you think about it, the best way to select things would be with pattern matching, right? The ideal scenario would be to somehow store a pattern to match on within a variable (or as a data structure), pass that to some ETS function, and let said function do its thing.

This is called *higher-order pattern matching*, and sadly, it is not available in Erlang. In fact, very few languages have it. Instead, Erlang has a kind of sublanguage that Erlang programmers have agreed to use to describe pattern matching as a bunch of regular data structures.

This notation is based on tuples to fit nicely with ETS. It simply lets you specify variables (regular and "don't care" variables), that can be mixed with the tuples to do pattern matching. Variables are written as '$0', '$1', '$2', and so on (the number has no importance except in how you'll get the results) for regular variables. The "don't care" variable can be written as '_'. All these atoms ('_', '$0', '$1', and so on) can be used to represent the pattern for a table entry when placed in a tuple like so:

```
{items, '$3', '$1', '_', '$3'}
```

This is roughly equivalent to saying {items, C, A, _, C} with regular pattern matching. As such, you can guess that the first element needs to be the atom items, the second and fifth slots of the tuple need to be identical, and so on.

To make use of this notation in a more practical setting, two functions are available: match/2 and match_object/2. (match/3 and match_object/3 are available as well, but their use is outside the scope of this chapter—readers are encouraged to check the docs for details.)

The match/2 function returns the variables of the pattern, and the match_object/2 function returns the whole entry that matched the pattern:

```
1> ets:new(table, [named_table, bag]).
table
2> ets:insert(table, [{items, a, b, c, d}, {items, a, b, c, a},
2>                     {cat, brown, soft, loveable, selfish},
2>                     {friends, [jenn,jeff,etc]}, {items, 1, 2, 3, 1}]).
true
3> ets:match(table, {items, '$1', '$2', '_', '$1'}).
[[a,b],[1,2]]
4> ets:match(table, {items, '$114', '$212', '_', '$6'}).
[[d,a,b],[a,a,b],[1,1,2]]
5> ets:match_object(table, {items, '$1', '$2', '_', '$1'}).
[{items,a,b,c,a},{items,1,2,3,1}]
6> ets:delete(table).
true
```

The nice thing about match/2 as a function is that it returns only what is strictly necessary. This is useful because, as mentioned earlier, ETS tables follow the nothing-shared ideals. If you have very large records, copying only the necessary fields might be a good thing to do.

Anyway, you'll also notice that while the numbers in variables have no explicit meaning, their order is important. In the final list of values returned, the value bound to $114 will always come after the values bound to $6 by the pattern. If nothing matches, empty lists are returned.

It is also possible that you might want to delete entries based on such a pattern match. In these cases, the function ets:match_delete(Table, Pattern) is what you want.

This is all fine and lets us do pattern matching of any literal value, albeit in a funny-looking way. It would be pretty neat if it were possible to have things like comparisons and ranges, explicit ways to format the output (maybe lists aren't what we want), and so on. Oh wait, you can!

You Have Been Selected

Erlang provides an approach that gives us something more equivalent to true function heads–level pattern matching, including very simple guards. If you've ever used a SQL database, you might have seen ways to do queries where you compare elements that are greater than, equal to, or smaller than other elements. This is the kind of good stuff we want here.

The people behind Erlang thus took the syntax for matches and augmented it in crazy ways until it was powerful enough. Sadly, they also made
it unreadable. Here's what it can look like:

```
[{{'$1','$2',<<1>>,'$3','$4'},
  [{'andalso',{'>','$4',150},{'<','$4',500}},
   {'orelse',{'==','$2',meat},{'==','$2',dairy}}],
  ['$1']},
 {{'$1','$2',<<1>>,'$3','$4'},
  [{'<','$3',4.0},{is_float,'$3'}],
  ['$1']}]
```

This is pretty ugly—not the data structure you would want your children
to look like. Believe it or not, we'll learn how to write these things called
match specifications, but not in the preceding form—no, that would be a bit
too hard for no reason. But we'll still learn how to read them, though!
Here's what match specifications look like from a higher-level view:

```
[{InitialPattern1, Guards1, ReturnedValue1},
 {InitialPattern2, Guards2, ReturnedValue2}].
```

And from a yet higher view, we see this:

```
[Clause1,
 Clause2]
```

These things represent, roughly, the pattern in a function head, then
the guards, and then the body of a function. The format is still limited to
'$N' variables for the initial pattern, just as it was for match functions. The
new sections are the guard patterns, which allow us to do something quite
similar to regular guards. If we look at the guard [{'<','$3',4.0},{is_float,'$3'}],
we can see that it is quite similar to ... when Var < 4.0, is_float(Var) -> ... as
a guard.
The next guard, more complex this time, is as follows:

```
[{'andalso',{'>','$4',150},{'<','$4',500}},
 {'orelse',{'==','$2',meat},{'==','$2',dairy}}]
```

Translating it gives us a guard that looks like ... when Var4 > 150
andalso Var4 < 500, Var2 == meat orelse Var2 == dairy -> .... Got it?
Each operator or guard function works with a prefix syntax, meaning that we use the order {FunctionOrOperator, Arg1, ..., ArgN}. So is_list(X)
becomes {is_list, '$1'}, X andalso Y becomes {'andalso', X, Y}, and so on.
Reserved keywords such as andalso and orelse, and operators like ==, need
to be turned into atoms so the Erlang parser won't choke on them.
The last section of the pattern is what you want to return. Just put
the variables you need in there. If you want to return the full input of

the match specification, use the variable '$_' to do so. A full specification of match specifications can be found in the Erlang documentation at *http://www.erlang.org/doc/apps/erts/match_spec.html.*

As I said earlier, we won't learn how to write patterns that way, since there's a nicer way to do it. ETS comes with what is called a *parse transform.* A parse transform is an underdocumented (and officially not supported by the OTP team for whatever problems you encounter) way of accessing the Erlang parse tree halfway through the compiling phase. They let ballsy Erlang programmers transform the code in a module to a new alternative form. A parse transform can be pretty much anything and change existing Erlang code to almost anything else, as long as it doesn't change the language's syntax or tokens.

The parse transform coming with ETS must be enabled manually for each module that needs it. The way to do it in a module is as follows:

```
-module(SomeModule).
-include_lib("stdlib/include/ms_transform.hrl").
...
some_function() ->
    ets:fun2ms(fun(X) when X > 4 -> X end).
```

The line -include_lib("stdlib/include/ms_transform.hrl"). contains some special code that will override the meaning of ets:fun2ms(SomeLiteralFun) whenever it's being used in a module. Rather than being a higher-order function, the parse transform will analyze what is in the fun (the pattern, the guards, and the return value), remove the function call to ets:fun2ms/1, and replace it all with an actual match specification. Weird, huh? The best thing is that because this happens at compile time, there is no overhead to using this way of doing things.

We can try it in the shell, without the include file this time:

```
1> ets:fun2ms(fun(X) -> X end).
[{'$1',[],['$1']}]
2> ets:fun2ms(fun({X,Y}) -> X+Y end).
[{{'$1','$2'},[],[{'+','$1','$2'}]}]
3> ets:fun2ms(fun({X,Y}) when X < Y -> X+Y end).
[{{'$1','$2'},[{'<','$1','$2'}],[{'+','$1','$2'}]}]
4> ets:fun2ms(fun({X,Y}) when X < Y, X rem 2 == 0 -> X+Y end).
[{{'$1','$2'},
  [{'<','$1','$2'},{'==',{'rem','$1',2},0}],
  [{'+','$1','$2'}]}]
5> ets:fun2ms(fun({X,Y}) when X < Y, X rem 2 == 0; Y == 0 -> X end).
[{{'$1','$2'},
  [{'<','$1','$2'},{'==',{'rem','$1',2},0}],
  ['$1']},
 {{'$1','$2'},[{'==','$2',0}],['$1']}]
```

All of these are written so easily now! And, of course, the funs are much simpler to read.

How about that complex example from the beginning of the section? Here's what it would be like as a fun:

```
6> ets:fun2ms(fun({Food, Type, <<1>>, Price, Calories})
6>     when Calories > 150 andalso Calories < 500,
6>         Type == meat orelse Type == dairy;
6>         Price < 4.00, is_float(Price) ->
6> Food end).
[{{'$1','$2',<<1>>,'$3','$4'},
  [{'andalso',{'>','$4',150},{'<','$4',500}},
   {'orelse',{'==','$2',meat},{'==','$2',dairy}}],
  ['$1']},
 {{'$1','$2',<<1>>,'$3','$4'},
  [{'<','$3',4.0},{is_float,'$3'}],
  ['$1']}]
```

The match specification doesn't entirely make sense at first glance, but at least it's much simpler to figure out what it means when the variables actually have names rather than numbers.

One thing to be careful about is that not all funs are valid match specifications:

```
7> ets:fun2ms(fun(X) -> my_own_function(X) end).
Error: fun containing the local function call 'my_own_function/1' (called in body)
 cannot be translated into match_spec
{error,transform_error}
8> ets:fun2ms(fun(X,Y) -> ok end).
Error: ets:fun2ms requires fun with single variable or tuple parameter
{error,transform_error}
9> ets:fun2ms(fun([X,Y]) -> ok end).
Error: ets:fun2ms requires fun with single variable or tuple parameter
{error,transform_error}
10> ets:fun2ms(fun({<<X/binary>>}) -> ok end).
Error: fun head contains bit syntax matching of variable 'X', which cannot be
 translated into match_spec
{error,transform_error}
```

The function head needs to match on a single variable or a tuple, no nonguard functions can be called as part of the return value, and assigning values from within binaries is not allowed. Try some stuff in the shell to see what you can do.

To make match specifications useful, it would make sense to use them. This can be done with these functions:

- ets:select/2 to fetch results
- ets:select_reverse/2 to get results in reverse in ordered_set tables (for other types, it's the same as select/2)
- ets:select_count/2 to know how many results match the specification
- ets:select_delete(Table, MatchSpec) to delete records matching a match specification

Let's try it. We'll define a record for our tables, and then populate them with various goods:

```
11> rd(food, {name, calories, price, group}).
food
12> ets:new(food, [ordered_set, {keypos,#food.name}, named_table]).
food
13> ets:insert(food, [#food{name=salmon, calories=88, price=4.00, group=meat},
13>   #food{name=cereals, calories=178, price=2.79, group=bread},
13>   #food{name=milk, calories=150, price=3.23, group=dairy},
13>   #food{name=cake, calories=650, price=7.21, group=delicious},
13>   #food{name=bacon, calories=800, price=6.32, group=meat},
13>   #food{name=sandwich, calories=550, price=5.78, group=whatever}]).
true
```

We can then try to select food items under a given number of calories:

```
14> ets:select(food, ets:fun2ms(fun(N = #food{calories=C}) when C < 600 -> N end)).
[#food{name = cereals,calories = 178,price = 2.79,group = bread},
 #food{name = milk,calories = 150,price = 3.23,group = dairy},
 #food{name = salmon,calories = 88,price = 4.0,group = meat},
 #food{name = sandwich,calories = 550,price = 5.78,group = whatever}]
15> ets:select_reverse(food, ets:fun2ms(fun(N = #food{calories=C}) when C < 600 -> N end)).
[#food{name = sandwich,calories = 550,price = 5.78,group = whatever},
 #food{name = salmon,calories = 88,price = 4.0,group = meat},
 #food{name = milk,calories = 150,price = 3.23,group = dairy},
 #food{name = cereals,calories = 178,price = 2.79,group = bread}]
```

Or maybe what we want is just delicious food:

```
16> ets:select(food, ets:fun2ms(fun(N = #food{group=delicious}) -> N end)).
[#food{name = cake,calories = 650,price = 7.21,group = delicious}]
```

Deleting has a little special twist to it. You need to return true in the pattern instead of any kind of value:

```
17> ets:select_delete(food, ets:fun2ms(fun(#food{price=P}) when P > 5 -> true end)).
3
18> ets:select_reverse(food, ets:fun2ms(fun(N = #food{calories=C}) when C < 600 -> N end)).
[#food{name = salmon,calories = 88,price = 4.0,group = meat},
 #food{name = milk,calories = 150,price = 3.23,group = dairy},
 #food{name = cereals,calories = 178,price = 2.79,group = bread}]
```

As the last selection shows, items over $5.00 were removed from the table. ETS has a lot more functions, such as ways to convert the table to lists or files (ets:tab2list/1, ets:tab2file/1, ets:file2tab/1) and get information about all tables (ets:i/0, ets:info(Table)). Head over to the official documentation to learn more about these functions.

There's also a module called tv (Table Viewer) that can be used to visually manage the ETS tables on a given Erlang VM. Just call tv:start(), and a window will be opened, showing your tables.

DETS

DETS is a disk-based version of ETS, with a few key differences:

- There are no longer ordered_set tables.
- There is a disk-size limit of 2GB for DETS files.
- Operations such as prev/1 and next/1 are not nearly as safe or fast.
- Starting and stopping tables has changed a bit. A new database table is created by calling dets:open_file/2, and is closed by calling dets:close/1. The table can later be reopened by calling dets:open_file/1.

Otherwise, the API is nearly the same, and it is thus possible to have a simple way to handle writing and looking for data inside files.

DON'T DRINK TOO MUCH KOOL-AID

DETS risks being slow, as it is a disk-only database. You might feel like coupling ETS and DETS tables into a somewhat efficient database that stores both in RAM and on disk.

If you feel like doing so, it might be a good idea to look into Mnesia (covered in Chapter 29) as a database, which does exactly the same thing, while adding support for sharding, transactions, and distribution.

A Little Less Conversation, a Little More Action, Please

Following this rather long section title (and long previous sections), we'll turn to the practical problem that brought us here in the first place: updating regis so that it uses ETS and gets rid of a few potential bottlenecks.

Before we get started, we need to think about how we're going to handle operations, and what is safe and unsafe. Things that should be safe are those that modify nothing and are limited to one query (not three or four over time). They can be done by anyone at any time. Everything else that has to do with writing to a table, updating records, deleting them, or reading in a way that requires consistency over many requests is to be considered unsafe.

Because ETS has no transactions whatsoever, all unsafe operations should be performed by the process that owns the table. The safe ones should be allowed to be public—done outside the owner process. We'll keep this in mind as we update regis.

The first step will be to make a copy of *regis-1.0.0* as *regis-1.1.0* (you can get a copy of *regis-1.1.0* at *http://learnyousomeerlang.com/static/erlang/regis-1.1.0.zip*). I'm bumping up the second number and not the third one here because our changes shouldn't break the existing interface and are technically not bug fixes, so we're going to consider this version to be only a feature upgrade.

The Interface

In that new directory, we'll need to operate only on *regis_server.erl* at first. We'll keep the interface intact so all the rest, in terms of structure, should not need to change too much.

```
%%% The core of the app: the server in charge of tracking processes.
-module(regis_server).
-behavior(gen_server).
-include_lib("stdlib/include/ms_transform.hrl").

-export([start_link/0, stop/0, register/2, unregister/1, whereis/1,
         get_names/0]).
-export([init/1, handle_call/3, handle_cast/2, handle_info/2,
         code_change/3, terminate/2]).

%%%%%%%%%%%%%%%%%
%%% INTERFACE %%%
%%%%%%%%%%%%%%%%%%
start_link() ->
    gen_server:start_link({local, ?MODULE}, ?MODULE, [], []).
```

```
stop() ->
    gen_server:call(?MODULE, stop).

%% Give a name to a process.
register(Name, Pid) when is_pid(Pid) ->
    gen_server:call(?MODULE, {register, Name, Pid}).

%% Remove the name from a process.
unregister(Name) ->
    gen_server:call(?MODULE, {unregister, Name}).

%% Find the pid associated with a process.
whereis(Name) -> ok.

%% Find all the names currently registered.
get_names() -> ok.
```

For the public interface, only whereis/1 and get_names/0 will change and be rewritten. That's because, as mentioned earlier, they are single-read safe operations. The rest will require to be serialized in the process owning the table.

That's it for the API so far. Let's head for the inside of the module.

Implementation Details

We're going to use an ETS table to store stuff, so it makes sense to put that table into the init function. Moreover, because our whereis/1 and get_names/0 functions will give public access to the table (for speed reasons), naming the table will be necessary for it to be accessible to the outside world. By naming the table, much like what happens when we name processes, we can hardcode the name in the functions, so we won't need to pass around an ID.

```
%%%%%%%%%%%%%%%%%%%%%%%%%%%%%%
%%% GEN_SERVER CALLBACKS %%%
%%%%%%%%%%%%%%%%%%%%%%%%%%%%%%
init([]) ->
    ?MODULE = ets:new(regis, [set, named_table, protected]),
    {ok, ?MODULE}.
```

The next function will be handle_call/3, handling the message {register, Name, Pid} as defined in register/2.

```
handle_call({register, Name, Pid}, _From, Tid) ->
    %% Neither the name or the pid can already be in the table
    %% so we match for both of them in a table-long scan using this.
    MatchSpec = ets:fun2ms(fun({N,P,_Ref}) when N==Name; P==Pid -> {N,P} end),
    case ets:select(Tid, MatchSpec) of
        [] -> % free to insert
            Ref = erlang:monitor(process, Pid),
            ets:insert(Tid, {Name, Pid, Ref}),
            {reply, ok, Tid};
```

```
      [{Name,_}|_] -> % maybe more than one result, but name matches
          {reply, {error, name_taken}, Tid};
      [{_,Pid}|_] -> % maybe more than one result, but Pid matches
          {reply, {error, already_named}, Tid}
  end;
```

This is by far the most complex function in the module. There are three basic rules to respect:

- A process cannot be registered twice.
- A name cannot be taken twice.
- A process can be registered if it doesn't break the first two rules.

This is what the preceding code does. The match specification derived from fun({N,P,_Ref}) when N==Name; P==Pid -> {N,P} end will look through the whole table for entries that match either the name or the pid that we're trying to register. If there's a match, we return both the name and pid that were found. This may be weird, but it makes sense to want both when we look at the patterns for the case ... of after that.

The first pattern means nothing was found, and so insertions are good. We monitor the process we have registered (to unregister it in case of failure), and then add the entry to the table. In case the name we are trying to register was already in the table, the pattern [{Name,_}|_] will take care of it. If it was the pid that matched, then the pattern [{_,Pid}|_] will take care of it. That's why both values are returned: It's simpler to match on the whole tuple later on, not caring whether it was Pid or Name that matched in the match specifications.

Why is the pattern of the form [Tuple|_] rather than just [Tuple]? The explanation is simple enough: If we're traversing the table looking for either pids or names that are similar, it is possible the list returned will be [{NameYouWant, SomePid},{SomeName,PidYouWant}]. If that happens, then a pattern match of the form [Tuple] will crash the process in charge of the table and ruin your day.

Oh yeah, don't forget to add the -include_lib("stdlib/include/ms_transform.hrl"). in the module; otherwise, fun2ms will die with a weird error message:

```
** {badarg,{ets,fun2ms,
          [function,called,with,real,'fun',should,be,transformed,with,
           parse_transform,'or',called,with,a,'fun',generated,in,the,
           shell]}}
```

That's what happens when you forget the include file. Consider yourself warned. Look before crossing the streets, don't cross the streams, and don't forget your include files.

The next bit handles when we ask to manually unregister a process:

```
handle_call({unregister, Name}, _From, Tid) ->
    case ets:lookup(Tid, Name) of
        [{Name,_Pid,Ref}] ->
            erlang:demonitor(Ref, [flush]),
            ets:delete(Tid, Name),
            {reply, ok, Tid};
        [] ->
            {reply, ok, Tid}
    end;
```

This is similar to what's in the old version of the code. The idea is simple: Find the monitor reference (with a lookup on the name), cancel the monitor, and then delete the entry and keep going. If the entry is not there, we pretend we deleted it anyway, and everyone will be happy. Oh, how dishonest we are.

The next bit is about stopping the server:

```
handle_call(stop, _From, Tid) ->
    %% For the sake of being synchronous and because emptying ETS
    %% tables might take a bit longer than dropping data structures
    %% held in memory, dropping the table here will be safer for
    %% tricky race conditions, especially in tests where we start/stop
    %% servers a lot. In regular code, this doesn't matter.
    ets:delete(Tid),
    {stop, normal, ok, Tid};
handle_call(_Event, _From, State) ->
    {noreply, State}.
```

As the comments in the code say, we could have been fine just ignoring the table and letting it be garbage-collected. However, because the test suite we wrote in Chapter 24 starts and stops the server all the time, delays can be a bit dangerous.

This is what the timeline of the process looks like with the old one:

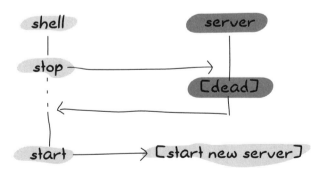

And here's what sometimes happens with the new one:

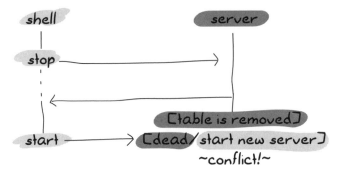

By using this scheme, we're making it a lot more unlikely for errors to happen by doing more work in the synchronous part of the code:

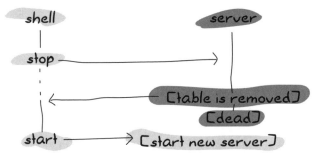

If you don't plan on running the test suite very often, you can just ignore the whole thing. I've decided to show it to avoid nasty surprises, although in a non-test system, this kind of edge case should rarely occur.

Here are the other OTP callbacks:

```
handle_cast(_Event, State) ->
    {noreply, State}.

handle_info({'DOWN', Ref, process, _Pid, _Reason}, Tid) ->
    ets:match_delete(Tid, {'_', '_', Ref}),
    {noreply, Tid};
handle_info(_Event, State) ->
    {noreply, State}.

code_change(_OldVsn, State, _Extra) ->
    {ok, State}.

terminate(_Reason, _State) ->
    ok.
```

We don't care about any of them, except receiving a DOWN message, meaning one of the processes we were monitoring died. When that happens, we delete the entry based on the reference we have in the message, and then move on.

You'll notice that code_change/3 could actually work as a transition between the old regis_server and the new regis_server. Implementing this function is left as an exercise for the reader. I hate books that give exercises for the reader without solutions, so here's at least a little pointer so I'm not just being a jerk like all the other writers out there: You need to take either of the two GB trees from the older version, and use gb_trees:map/2 or the gb_trees iterators to populate a new table before moving on. The downgrade function can be written by doing the opposite.

All that's left to do is fix the two public functions we have left unimplemented. Of course, we could write a %% TODO comment, call it a day, and go drink until we forget we're programmers, but that would be a bit irresponsible. Let's fix stuff:

```erlang
%% Find the pid associated with a process.
whereis(Name) ->
    case ets:lookup(?MODULE, Name) of
        [{Name, Pid, _Ref}] -> Pid;
        [] -> undefined
    end.
```

This one looks for a name, and returns the pid or undefined depending on whether the entry has been found or not. Note that we use regis (?MODULE) as the table name here—that's why we made it protected and named in the first place.

Here's the next one:

```erlang
%% Find all the names currently registered.
get_names() ->
    MatchSpec = ets:fun2ms(fun({Name, _, _}) -> Name end),
    ets:select(?MODULE, MatchSpec).
```

We use fun2ms again to match on the name and keep only that. Selecting from the table will return a list and do what we need.

That's it! You can run the test suite in test/ to make things go:

```
$ erl -make
... <snip> ...
Recompile: src/regis_server
$ erl -pa ebin
... <snip> ...
1> eunit:test(regis_server).
  All 13 tests passed.
ok
```

Hell, yes—I think we can consider ourselves pretty good at ETSing now.

You know what would be really nice to do next? We could actually explore the distributed aspects of Erlang. Maybe we can bend our minds in a few more twisted ways before being finished with the Erlang beast. Let's see.

26

DISTRIBUNOMICON

Oh, hi! Please have a seat. I was expecting you.

When you first heard of Erlang, there were two or three attributes that likely attracted you. Erlang is a functional language, it has great semantics for concurrency, and it supports distribution. We've covered the first two attributes, and spent time exploring a dozen more you possibly didn't expect. Now we're at the last big thing: distribution.

We've waited quite a while before getting here because it's not exactly useful to get distributed if we can't make things work locally to begin with. We're finally up to the task and have come a long way to get where we are.

Like almost every other feature of Erlang, the distributed layer of the language was first added in order to provide fault tolerance. Software running on a single machine is always at risk of having that single machine dying and taking your application offline. Software running on many machines makes it easier to handle hardware failure if, and only if, the application was built correctly. There is no benefit regarding fault tolerance if your application runs on many servers but cannot deal with one of them being taken down.

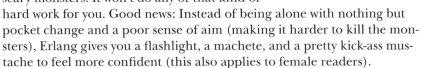

Distributed programming is like being left alone in the dark, with monsters everywhere. It's scary, and you don't know what to do or what's coming at you. Bad news: Distributed Erlang is still leaving you alone in the dark to fight the scary monsters. It won't do any of that kind of hard work for you. Good news: Instead of being alone with nothing but pocket change and a poor sense of aim (making it harder to kill the monsters), Erlang gives you a flashlight, a machete, and a pretty kick-ass mustache to feel more confident (this also applies to female readers).

That's not especially due to how Erlang is written, but more or less due to the nature of distributed software. Erlang provides the few basic building blocks of distribution: ways to have many nodes (VMs) communicating with each other, serializing and deserializing data in communications, extending the concepts of multiple processes to many nodes, ways to monitor network failures, and so on. However, it will not provide solutions to software-specific problems such as "what happens when stuff crashes."

This is the standard "tools, not solutions" approach you've seen before in OTP. You rarely get full-blown software and applications, but you do get many components you can use to build systems. You'll have tools that tell you when parts of the system go up or down and tools to do a bunch of stuff over the network, but hardly any silver bullet that takes care of fixing things for you.

Let's see what kind of flexing we can do with these tools.

This Is My Boomstick

To tackle all these monsters in the dark, we've been granted a very useful thing: pretty complete network transparency.

An instance of an Erlang VM that is up and running, ready to connect to other VMs, is called a *node*. Whereas some languages or communities will consider a server to be a node, in Erlang, each VM is a node. You can have 50 nodes running on a single computer, or 50 nodes running on 50 computers. It doesn't really matter.

When you start a node, you give it a name, and it will connect to an application called Erlang Port Mapper Daemon (EPMD), which will run on each of the computers that are part of your Erlang cluster. EPMD will act as a name server that lets nodes register themselves, contact other nodes by name rather than port numbers, and warn you about any name clashes.

From this point on, a node can decide to set up a connection to another node. When it does so, both nodes automatically start monitoring each other, and they can tell if the connection is dropped or a node disappears. More importantly, when a new node joins another node that is already part of a group of nodes connected together, the new node automatically connects to the entire group.

To illustrate how Erlang nodes set up their connections, let's take the idea of a group of survivors during a zombie outbreak. The survivors are Zoey, Bill, Rick, and Daryl. Zoey and Bill know each other and communicate on the same frequency on walkie-talkies. Rick and Daryl are each on their own, as shown here:

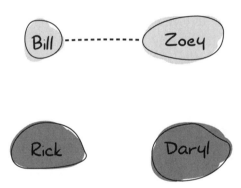

Now let's say Rick and Daryl meet on their way to a survivor camp. They share their walkie-talkie frequency and can now stay up to date with each other before splitting ways again, like this:

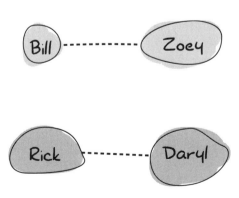

At some point, Rick meets Bill. Both are pretty happy about that, and so they decide to share frequencies. At this point, the connections spread, and the final graph looks like this:

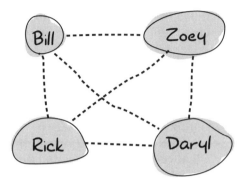

That means that any survivor can contact any other directly. This is useful because in the event of the death of any survivor, no one is left isolated. Erlang nodes are set up in this way: Everyone connects to everyone.

DON'T DRINK TOO MUCH KOOL-AID

Connecting nodes in this manner, while nice for some fault-tolerance reasons, has a pretty bad drawback with regard to how much you can scale. It will be hard to have hundreds and hundreds of nodes part of your Erlang cluster, simply because of how many connections are required and how much chatter is involved. In fact, you will require one ephemeral port per node. While some large-scale projects have managed to do this, you may find it easier to just split groups of nodes into smaller clusters.

If you were planning on using Erlang to do that kind of heavy setup, please read on in this chapter to see why things are that way and what might be done to work around the problem, if possible.

Once the nodes are connected, they remain fully independent. They keep their own process registry and ETS tables (with their own names for tables), and the modules they load are independent from each other. A connected node that crashes won't bring down the other nodes in the cluster.

Connected nodes can then start exchanging messages. The distribution model of Erlang was designed so that local processes can contact remote processes and send them regular messages. How is this possible if nothing is shared and all the process registries are unique? As we'll see when we get into the specifics of distribution in "Connecting Nodes" on page 459, there is a way to access registered processes on a particular node. From that point on, a first message can be sent.

Erlang messages are serialized and unserialized automatically for you in a transparent manner. All data structures, including pids, will work the same remotely and locally. This means that we can send pids over the network, and then the other side can communicate with them by sending messages. Even better, links and monitors can be set up across the network if you can access the pids!

So if Erlang is doing so much to make everything that transparent, why am I saying it's only giving us a machete, a flashlight, and a mustache?

Fallacies of Distributed Computing

Much like a machete is meant to kill only a given type of monster, Erlang's tools are meant to handle only some kinds of distributed computing. To understand the tools Erlang gives us, it will be useful to first have an idea of what kind of landscape exists in the distributed world, and which assumptions Erlang makes in order to provide fault tolerance.

Some very smart guys took their time in the past few decades to categorize the kind of stuff that goes wrong with distributed computing. They came up with eight major assumptions people make (some of which Erlang's designers made for various reasons) that end up biting them in the ass later.

NOTE *The fallacies of distributed computing were introduced in "Fallacies of Distributed Computing Explained," by Arnon Rotem-Gal-Oz, available online at* http://www .rgoarchitects.com/Files/fallacies.pdf.

The Network Is Reliable

The first fallacy of distributed computing is assuming that the application can be distributed over the network. That's kind of weird to say, but there will be plenty of times where the network will go down for annoying reasons: power failures, broken hardware, someone tripping over a cord, vortex to other dimensions engulfing mission-critical components, headcrabs infestation, copper theft, and so on.

One of the biggest errors you can make is to think you can always reach remote nodes and talk to them. This is somewhat possible to handle by adding more hardware and gaining redundancy, so that if hardware fails, the application can still be reached somewhere else. The other thing to do is to be ready to suffer a loss of messages and requests, and also be ready for things to become unresponsive. This is especially true when you depend on some kind of third-party service that's no longer there, while your own software stack keeps working well.

Erlang doesn't have any special measures to deal with network reliability, as usually the decisions made will be application specific. After all, who else but you can know how important a specific component will be? Still, you're not totally alone, as a distributed Erlang node will be able to detect other nodes getting disconnected (or becoming unresponsive). There are specific functions to monitor nodes, and links and monitors will also be triggered upon a disconnection.

The best thing Erlang has in this case is its asynchronous communication mode. By sending messages asynchronously and forcing developers to send a reply back when things work well, Erlang pushes for all message-passing activities to intuitively handle failure. If the process you're talking to is on a node that disappears due to some network failure, you handle it as naturally as any local crash. This is one of the many reasons why Erlang is said to scale well (scaling not only in performance but also in design).

> ### DON'T DRINK TOO MUCH KOOL-AID
>
> Linking and monitoring across nodes can be dangerous. In the case of a network failure, all remote links and monitors are triggered at once. This might then generate thousands and thousands of signals and messages to various processes, which puts a heavy and unexpected load on the system.
>
> Preparing for an unreliable network also means preparing for sudden failures and making sure your system doesn't get crippled by part of the system suddenly disappearing.

There Is No Latency

One of the double-edged aspects of seemingly good distribution systems is that they often end up hiding the fact that the function calls you are making are remote. While you expect some function calls to be really fast, that will not be the case when they are made over the network. It's the difference between ordering a pizza from within the pizzeria and getting one delivered from another city to your house. While there will always be a basic wait time, it's possible that your pizza will be delivered cold because delivery took too long.

Forgetting that network communications make things slower even for really small messages can be a costly error if you always expect really fast results. Erlang's model treats us well there. Because of the way we set up our local applications with isolated processes, asynchronous messages, and time-outs, and we're always thinking about the possibility of processes failing, there is little adaptation required to go distributed. The timeouts, links, monitors, and asynchronous patterns remain the same, and still are as reliable. Erlang doesn't implicitly assume there is no latency, and in fact, always expects it by design.

You, however, might make that assumption in your design and expect replies faster than realistically possible. Just keep an eye open.

Bandwidth Is Infinite

Although network transfers are getting faster and faster all the time, and generally speaking, each byte transferred over the network is cheaper as time goes by, it is risky to assume that sending copious amounts of data is simple and easy.

Because of how we build applications locally, we generally won't have too many problems with that in Erlang. Remember that one good trick is to send messages about what is happening, rather than moving new states around ("player X found item Y," rather than sending player X's entire inventory over and over again).

If, for some reason, you need to send large messages, be extremely careful. The way Erlang distribution and communication work over many nodes is especially sensitive to large messages. If two nodes are connected, all of their communications will tend to happen over a single TCP connection. Because we generally want to maintain message ordering between two processes (even across the network), messages will be sent sequentially over the connection. That means that if you have one very large message, you might be blocking the channel for all the other messages.

Worse than that, Erlang knows whether nodes are alive by sending *heartbeats*. Heartbeats are small messages sent at a regular interval between two nodes, basically saying, "I'm still alive. Keep on keepin' on!" They're like our zombie survivors routinely pinging each other with messages. "Bill, are you there?" And if Bill never replies, you might assume he is dead (or out of batteries), and he won't get your future communications. Heartbeats are sent over the same channel as regular messages.

The problem is that a large message can hold back heartbeats. Too many large messages keeping heartbeats at bay for too long will eventually result in either of the nodes assuming the other is unresponsive and closing its connection to it. That's bad.

The good Erlang design lesson to keep in mind to prevent such problems is to keep your messages small. Everything will be better that way.

The Network Is Secure

When you get distributed, it's often very dangerous to believe that everything is safe—that you can trust the messages you receive. It can be simple things like someone fabricating messages and sending them to you, someone intercepting packets and modifying them (or looking at sensitive data), or in the worst case, someone being able to take over your application or the system on which it runs.

In the case of distributed Erlang, this is sadly an assumption that was made. Here is what Erlang's security model looks like:

```
* This box intentionally left blank *
```

Yep. This is because Erlang distribution was initially meant for fault tolerance and redundancy of components. In the old days of the language, back when it was used for telephone switches and other telecommunication applications, Erlang would often be deployed on hardware running in the weirdest places—very remote locations with odd conditions (engineers sometimes needed to attach servers to the wall to avoid wet ground or install custom heating systems in the woods in order for the hardware to run at optimal temperatures). In these cases, you had failover hardware in the same physical location as the main hardware. This is often where distributed Erlang would run, and it explains why Erlang designers assumed a safe network to operate with.

Sadly, this means that modern Erlang applications can rarely be clustered automatically across different data centers. In fact, it isn't recommended to do so. Most of the time, you will want your system to be based on many smaller, walled-off clusters of Erlang nodes, usually located in single locations. Anything more complex will need to be left to the developers using one of the following methods:

- Switching to SSL
- Implementing their own high-level communication layer
- Tunneling over secure channels
- Reimplementing the communication protocol between nodes

Using SSL is explained in the Secure Socket Layer User's Guide (Chapter 3, "Using SSL for Erlang Distribution," at *http://www.erlang.org/doc/apps/ssl/ssl_distribution.html*). Pointers on how to implement your own carrier protocol for the Erlang distribution are provided in the ERTS User's Guide (Chapter 3, "How to implement an alternative carrier for the Erlang distribution" at *http://www.erlang.org/doc/apps/erts/alt_dist.html*), which also contains details on the distribution protocol (Chapter 9, "Distribution Protocol," at *http://www.erlang.org/doc/apps/erts/erl_dist_protocol.html*).

Even in these cases, you must be careful, because someone gaining access to one of the distributed nodes then has access to all of them, and can run any command those nodes can.

Topology Doesn't Change

When first designing a distributed application made to run on many servers, it is possible that you will have a given number of servers in mind, and perhaps a given list of hostnames. Maybe you will design things with specific IP addresses in mind. This can be a mistake. Hardware dies, operations people move servers around, new machines are added, and some are removed. The topology of your network will constantly change. If your application works with any of these topological details hardcoded, then it won't easily handle these kinds of changes in the network.

In the case of Erlang, there is no explicit assumption made in that way. However, it is very easy to let it creep inside your application. Erlang nodes all have a name and a hostname, and they can constantly be changing. With Erlang processes, you not only need to think about how the process is named, but also about where it is now located in a cluster. If you hardcode both the names and hostnames, you might be in trouble at the next failure. Don't worry too much though. As discussed in "The Calls from Beyond" on page 467, we can use a few interesting libraries that let us forget about node names and topology in general, while still being able to locate specific processes.

There Is Only One Administrator

This fallacy is something a distribution layer of a language or library can't prepare you for, no matter what. The idea of this fallacy is that you do not always have only one main operator for your software and its servers, although it might be designed as if there were only one. If you decide to run many nodes on a single computer, then you might never need to think about this fallacy. However, if you run stuff across different locations, or a third party depends on your code, then you must take care.

Things to pay attention to include giving others tools to diagnose problems on your system. Erlang is somewhat easy to debug when you can manipulate a VM manually—you can even reload code on the fly if you need to, after all. Someone who cannot access your terminal and sit in front of the node will need different facilities to operate though.

Another aspect of this fallacy is that things like restarting servers, moving instances between data centers, and upgrading parts of your software stack are not necessarily controlled by a single person or team. In very large software projects, it is likely that many teams, or even many different software companies, take charge of different parts of a greater system.

If you're writing protocols for your software stack, being able to handle many versions of that protocol might be necessary, depending on how fast or slow your users and partners are to upgrade their code. The protocol might contain information about its versioning from the beginning, or be able to change halfway through a transaction, depending on your needs. I'm sure you can think of more examples of things that can go wrong.

Transport Cost Is Zero

The transport cost is zero fallacy is a two-sided assumption. The first one relates to the cost of transporting data in terms of time, and the second one is related to the cost of transporting data in terms of money.

The first case assumes that doing things like serializing data is nearly free, very fast, and doesn't play a big role. In reality, larger data structures take longer to be serialized than small ones, and then they need to be unserialized on the other end of the wire. This will be true no matter what you carry across the network, although small messages help reduce the noticeability of this effect.

The second aspect of assuming transport cost is zero has to do with how much it costs to carry data around. In modern server stacks, memory (both in RAM and on disk) is often cheap compared to the cost of bandwidth, which you need to pay for continuously, unless you own the whole network where things run. Optimizing for fewer requests with smaller messages will be rewarding in this case and many others, too.

For Erlang, due to its initial use cases, no special care has been taken to do things like compress messages going cross-node (although the functions for it already exist). Instead, the original designers chose to let people implement their own communication layer if they required it. The responsibility is thus on the programmer to make sure small messages are sent and other measures are taken to minimize the costs of transporting data.

The Network Is Homogeneous

The last assumption is thinking that all components of a networked application will speak the same language or will use the same formats to operate together.

For our zombie survivors, this can be a question of not assuming that all survivors will always speak English (or good English) when they lay their plans, or that a word will have the same meaning to different people.

In terms of programming, this is usually about not relying on closed standards but using open ones instead, or being ready to switch from one protocol to another one at any point in time. When it comes to Erlang, the distribution protocol is entirely public, but all Erlang nodes assume that people communicating with them speak the same language. Foreigners trying to integrate themselves into an Erlang cluster either must learn to speak Erlang's protocol or Erlang applications need some kind of translation layer for XML, JSON, or whatever.

Learning to speak Erlang's protocol is relatively simple. If you respect the protocol, you can pretend to be another Erlang node, even if you're not writing Erlang. If it quacks like a duck and walks like a duck, then it must be a duck. That's the principle behind *C nodes*. C nodes (or nodes in languages other than C) are programs that implement Erlang's protocol and then pretend they are Erlang nodes in a cluster, allowing you to distribute work without too much effort. More details are available at *http://www.erlang.org/doc/tutorial/cnode.html*.

Another solution for data exchange is to use BERT or BERT-RPC (documented at *http://bert-rpc.org/*). This is an exchange format like XML or JSON, but specified as something similar to the Erlang *external term format* (documented at *http://www.erlang.org/doc/apps/erts/erl_ext_dist.html*).

Fallacies in a Nutshell

We've looked at a bunch of assumptions involved in distributed computing fallacies. In short, you always need to be careful and consider the following points:

- You shouldn't assume the network is reliable. Erlang doesn't have any special measures for that, except detecting that something went wrong for you (although that's not too bad as a feature).

- The network might be slow from time to time. Erlang provides asynchronous mechanisms and knows about it, but you need to be careful that your application is also aware of this possibility.

- Bandwidth isn't infinite. Small, descriptive messages help respect this.

- The network isn't secure, and Erlang doesn't have anything to offer by default for this.

- The topology of the network can change. No explicit assumption is made by Erlang, but you might make some assumptions about where things are and how they're named.

- You (or your organization) rarely fully control the structure of things. Parts of your system may be outdated, use different versions, or be restarted or down when you don't expect that to happen.

- Transporting data has costs. Again, small, short messages help.

- The network is heterogeneous. Not everything is the same, and data exchange should rely on well-documented formats.

Dead or Dead-Alive

The fallacies of distributed computing partially explain why we're fighting monsters in the dark. Although we have some useful tools, there are still a lot of issues and things left for us to do. We need to be careful about design decisions (small messages, reducing communication, and so on) regarding these fallacies. The most problematic issue has to do with nodes dying or the network being unreliable. This issue is especially nasty because there is no good way to know whether something is dead or alive (without being able to contact it).

Let's get back to Bill, Zoey, Rick, and Daryl, our four zombie apocalypse survivors. They all met at a safe house, spent a few days resting there, eating whatever canned food they could find. After a while, they needed to move out and split across town to find more resources. They've set a rendezvous point in a small camp on the limits of the town they're in. During the expedition, they keep contact by talking with the walkie-talkies. They announce what they found, such as other survivors.

Now suppose that at some point between the safe house and the rendezvous point, Rick tries to contact his comrades. He manages to call Bill and Zoey, but Daryl isn't reachable. Bill and Zoey can't contact him either. The problem is that there is absolutely no way to know if Daryl has been devoured by zombies, if his battery is dead, if he is asleep, or if he is just underground. The group must decide whether to keep waiting for him, keep calling for a while, or assume he is dead and move forward.

The same dilemma exists with nodes in a distributed system. When a node becomes unresponsive, is it gone because of a hardware failure? Did the application crash? Is there congestion on the network? Is the network down? In some cases, the application is not running anymore, and you can simply ignore that node and continue what you're doing. In other cases, the application is still running on the isolated node; from that node's perspective, everything else is dead.

Erlang made the default decisions of considering unreachable nodes as dead nodes and reachable nodes as alive. This is a pessimistic approach that makes sense if you want to quickly react to catastrophic failures. It assumes that the network is generally less likely to fail than the hardware or the software in the system, which makes sense considering how Erlang was used originally. An optimistic approach (which assumes nodes are still alive) could delay crash-related measures because it assumes that the network is more likely to fail than hardware or software, and thus have the cluster wait longer for the reintegration of disconnected nodes.

This raises a question: In a pessimistic system, what happens when the node we thought was dead suddenly returns, and it turns out it never died? We're caught by surprise by a living dead node, which had a life of its own, isolated from the cluster in every way—data, connections, and so on. Some very annoying things can happen.

Let's imagine for a moment that you have a system with two nodes in two different data centers. In that system, users have money in their account, with the full amount held on each node. Each transaction then synchronizes the data with all the other nodes. When all the nodes are fine, users can keep spending money until their account is empty.

The software is chugging along fine, but at some point, one of the nodes gets disconnected from the other. There is no way to know if the other side is alive or dead. For all we care, both nodes could still be receiving requests from the public, but without being able to communicate with each other.

There are two general strategies that can be taken: stop all transactions or don't. The risk of picking the first one is that your product becomes unavailable and you're losing money. The risk of the second one is that a user with $1,000 in his account now has two servers that can accept $1,000 of transactions, for a total of $2,000! Whatever we do, we risk losing money if we don't do things right.

Isn't there a way to avoid the issue entirely by keeping the application available during netsplits, without losing data in between servers?

My Other Cap Is a Theorem

A quick answer to the previous question is no. There is sadly no way to keep an application alive and correct at the same time during a netsplit.

This idea is known as the *CAP theorem*. The CAP theorem first states that there are three core attributes to all distributed systems: **c**onsistency, **a**vailability, and **p**artition tolerance.

Consistency

In the previous example, consistency would be having the ability to have the entire system, whether there are 2 or 1,000 nodes that can answer queries, see exactly the same amount of money in the account at a given time. This is something usually done by adding transactions (where all nodes must agree to making a change to a database as a single unit before doing so) or some other equivalent mechanism.

By definition, the idea of consistency is that all operations look as if they were completed as a single, indivisible block, even across many nodes. This is not in terms of time, but in terms of not having two different operations on the same piece of data modifying them in ways that give multiple values reported by system during these operations. It should be possible to modify a piece of data and not need to worry about others ruining your day by fiddling with it at the same time you are.

Availability

The idea behind availability is that if you ask the system for some piece of data, you're able to get a response. If you don't get an answer back, the system isn't available to you. Note that a response that says, "Sorry, I can't figure out results because I'm dead," isn't really a response, but only a sad excuse for one. There is no more useful information in this response than in no response at all (although academics are somewhat divided on the issue).

NOTE *An important consideration in the CAP theorem is that availability is a concern only to nodes that are not dead. A dead node cannot send responses because it can't receive queries in the first place. This isn't the same as a node that can't send a reply because a thing it depends on is no longer there. If the node can't take requests, change data, or return erroneous results, it isn't technically a threat to the balance of the system in terms of correctness. The rest of the cluster just needs to handle more of the load until the dead node comes back up and can be synchronized.*

Partition Tolerance

Partition tolerance is the tricky part of the CAP theorem. It usually means that the system can keep on working (and contain useful information) even when parts of it can no longer communicate with each other. The whole point of partition tolerance is that the system can work with messages possibly being lost between components. The definition is a bit abstract and open-ended, and we'll see why.

The CAP theorem basically specifies that in any distributed system, you can have only two of the CAP attributes: consistency + availability (CA), consistency + partition tolerance (CP), or availability + partition tolerance (AP). There is no possible way to have all of them. This is both bad and good news. The bad news is that it's impossible to have both consistency and availability while the network is partitioned. The good news is that this is a theorem. If customers ask you to provide all three of them, you will have the advantage of being able to tell them it is literally impossible to do so, and won't need to lose too much time (outside of explaining to them what the hell the CAP theorem is).

Of the three possibilities, one that we can usually dismiss is the idea of CA. The only time you would really want this is if you dare to say the network will never fail, or that if it does, it does as an atomic unit (if one thing fails, everything fails at once).

Until someone invents a network and hardware that never fail, or has some way to make all parts of a system fail at once if one of them does, failure must be an option. Only two combinations of the CAP theorem remain: AP or CP. A system torn apart by a netsplit can either remain available or consistent, but not both.

NOTE *Some systems will choose to have neither A nor C. In some cases of high performance, criteria such as throughput (how many queries you can answer) or latency (how fast you can answer queries) will bend things in a way such that the CAP theorem isn't about two attributes (CA, CP, or AP), but also about two or fewer attributes. Also note that some system can be fully consistent when there is no netsplit but relax consistency requirements when netsplits happen.*

Zombie Survivors and CAP

Time passed for our group of survivors, and they fended off groups of undead for a good while. Bullets pierced brains, baseball bats shattered skulls, and infected people were left behind. Bill, Zoey, Rick, and Daryl's batteries eventually ran out, and they were unable to communicate. As luck would have it, they all found two survivor colonies populated with computer scientists and engineers enamored with zombie survival. The colony survivors were familiar with the concepts of distributed programming, as well as communicating using light signals and mirrors with homemade protocols.

Bill and Zoey found the Chainsaw colony, and Rick and Daryl found the Crossbow camp. Given that our survivors were the newest arrivals in their respective colonies, they were often delegated to go out in the wild, hunt for food, and kill zombies coming too close to the perimeters, while the rest of the people debated the merits of Vim versus Emacs (the only war that couldn't die after a complete zombie apocalypse).

On their hundredth day there, our four survivors were sent to meet halfway across the camps to trade goods for each colony. Before the survivors left for their meeting, the Chainsaw and Crossbow colonies agreed on a rendezvous point. If the destination or meeting time were to change while they were on their journey, Rick and Daryl could send a message to the Crossbow colony, or Zoey and Bill could send a message to the Chainsaw colony. Then each colony would communicate the information to the other colony, which would forward the changes to the other survivors, as shown here:

- - - - light signal

All four survivors left early on a Sunday morning for a long trip on foot, due to meet on Friday morning before dawn. Everything went fine (except the occasional skirmishes with dead people who had been alive for quite a while at this point).

Unfortunately, on Wednesday, due to heavy rain and increased zombie activity, Bill and Zoey were separated, lost, and delayed. The new situation looked a bit like this:

- - - - light signal

To make matters worse, after the rain, the usually clear sky between the two colonies got foggy, and it became impossible for the Chainsaw computer scientists to communicate with the Crossbow people. Bill and Zoey communicated their problems to their colony and asked to set a new meeting time. This would have been all right without the fog, but now they have the equivalent of a netsplit.

If both camps work under the CP approach, they will just keep Zoey and Bill from setting a new meeting time. The CP approach is usually all about stopping modifications to the data so it remains consistent, and all survivors can still ask their respective camps for the data from time to time. They will just be denied the right to change it. This ensures that there is no way for some survivors to mess up the planned meeting time; any other survivors cut off from any contact could still meet at that time.

If both camps pick AP instead of CP, then survivors could be allowed to change meeting dates. Each side of the partition would have its own version of the meeting data. So if Bill called for a new meeting for Friday night, the general state becomes as follows:

```
Chainsaw: Friday night
Crossbow: Friday before dawn
```

As long as the split lasts, Bill and Zoey will get their information from Chainsaw only, and Rick and Daryl from Crossbow only. This lets some of the survivors reorganize themselves if needed.

The interesting problem here is how to handle the different versions of the data when the split is resolved (and the fog goes away). The CP approach to this is pretty straightforward: The data didn't change, so there is nothing to do. The AP approach has more flexibility but also more problems to resolve. Usually, different strategies are employed:

- Use the *last write wins* approach, which is a conflict resolution method that keeps the last update that was made. This one can be tricky because in distributed settings, timestamps can be off, or things can happen at exactly the same time.

- A winner can be picked randomly.

- Use more sophisticated time-based methods to help reduce conflicts, such as last write wins, but with logical clocks. Logical clocks do not work with absolute time values, but with incrementing values every time someone modifies a file. If you want to know more about this approach, read up on *Lamport clocks* or *vector clocks*.

- The onus of picking what to do with the conflict can be pushed back to the application (or in our case, to the survivors). The receiving end will just need to choose which of the conflicting entries is the right one. This is a bit like what happens when you have merge conflicts with source control tools like Subversion, Mercurial, or Git.

Which one is better? The way I've described things may have led you to believe that we have the choice to be either fully AP or fully CP, like an on/off switch. In the real world, we can have various options, such as a quorum system, which changes this yes/no question into a dial we can turn to choose how much consistency we want.

A quorum system works by a few simple rules. You have N nodes in the system and require M of them to agree to modify the data to make it possible. A system with a relatively low consistency requirement could ask for only 15 percent of the nodes to be available to make a change. This means that in cases of splits, even small fragments of the network are still able to modify the data. A higher consistency rating, set to maybe 75 percent of the nodes, would mean that a larger part of the system needs to be present in order to make changes. In this situation, if a few of the nodes are isolated, they won't have the right to change the data. However, the major part of the system that's still interconnected can work fine.

By making the M value of required nodes equal to N (the total number of nodes), you can have a fully consistent system. By giving M the value 1, you have a fully AP system, with no consistency guarantees.

Moreover, you could play with these values on a per-query basis. Queries having to do with things of little importance (someone just logged on!) can have lower consistency requirements, while things having to do with inventory and money could require more consistency. Mix this in with different conflict resolution methods for each case, and you can build surprisingly flexible systems.

Combined with all the different conflict resolution solutions available, a lot of options become available to distributed systems, but their implementation remains very complex. We won't use them in detail, but I think it's important to know what's available out there and to be aware of the different options.

Now that we've looked at the issues involved with distributed computing with Erlang, let's turn to the specifics of setting up a basic distributed system.

Setting Up an Erlang Cluster

Except for handling the fallacies of distributed computing, the hardest part of distributed Erlang is managing to set up things right. Connecting nodes across different hosts is a special kind of pain. To avoid this, we'll usually try things out using many nodes on a single computer, which tends to make things easier.

Through the Desert on a Node with No Name

As mentioned earlier, Erlang gives names to each of the nodes to be able to locate and contact them. The names are of the form *Name@Host*, where the host is based on available DNS entries, either over the network or in your computer's host files (*/etc/hosts* on Mac OS X, Linux, and other Unix-like systems, and *C:\Windows\system32\drivers\etc\hosts* for most Windows installations). All names need to be unique to avoid conflicts. If you try to start a node with the same name as another one on the same hostname, you'll get a pretty terrible crash message.

Before starting any nodes, we need to talk a bit about their names. There are two types of names:

- *Long names* are based on fully qualified domain names (*aaa.bbb.ccc*). Many DNS resolvers consider domain names to be fully qualified if they contain a period (.).

- *Short names* are based on hostnames without a period. They are resolved by going through your host file or through any possible DNS entry.

It is generally easier to set up a bunch of Erlang nodes on a single computer using short names rather than long names.

Also note that nodes with short names cannot communicate with nodes that have long names, and the opposite is also true.

To use short names, start the Erlang VM with `erl -sname` *short_name@domain*. To use long names start the VM with `erl -name` *long_name@some.domain*. You can also start nodes with only the names: `erl -sname` *short_name* or `erl -name` *long_name*. Erlang will automatically attribute a hostname based on your operating system's configuration. Another option is to start a node and specify a direct IP address, such as `erl -name` *name@127.0.0.1*.

Windows users should still use `werl` *instead of* `erl`. *However, in order to start a distributed node and give it a name, the node should be started from the command line instead of by clicking some shortcut or executable.*

Connecting Nodes

Let's start two nodes:

```
$ erl -sname ketchup
... <snip> ...
(ketchup@ferdmbp)1>
```

```
$ erl -sname fries
... <snip> ...
(fries@ferdmbp)1>
```

To connect `fries` with `ketchup` (and make a delicious cluster), go to the first shell and enter the following function:

```
(ketchup@ferdmbp)1> net_kernel:connect(fries@ferdmbp).
true
```

The `net_kernel:connect(NodeName)` function sets up a connection with another Erlang node. (Some tutorials use `net_adm:ping(Node)`, but I think `net_kernel:connect/1` sounds more serious and lends me credence!) If you see `true` as the result from the function call, congratulations, you're in distributed Erlang mode now. If you see `false`, you're in for a world of hurt trying to get your network to play nice. For a very quick fix, edit your host files to accept whatever host you want to use. Then try again.

You can see your own node name by calling the BIF `node()` and see who you're connecting to by calling the BIF `nodes()`:

```
(ketchup@ferdmbp)2> node().
ketchup@ferdmbp
(ketchup@ferdmbp)3> nodes().
[fries@ferdmbp]
```

To get the nodes to communicate with each other, we'll try a simple trick. Register each shell's process as `shell` locally:

```
(ketchup@ferdmbp)4> register(shell, self()).
true
```

```
(fries@ferdmbp)1> register(shell, self()).
true
```

Now you'll be able to call the process by name by sending a message to {Name, Node}. Let's try this on both shells:

```
(ketchup@ferdmbp)5> {shell, fries@ferdmbp} ! {hello, from, self()}.
{hello,from,<0.52.0>}
```

```
(fries@ferdmbp)2> receive {hello, from, OtherShell} -> OtherShell ! <<"hey there!">> end.
<<"hey there!">>
```

So that message was apparently received, and we can send something else to the other shell:

```
(ketchup@ferdmbp)6> flush().
Shell got <<"hey there!">>
ok
```

As you can see, we can transparently send tuples, atoms, pids, and binaries without a problem. Any other Erlang data structure is fine, too.

And that's it. You know how to work with distributed Erlang!

More Tools

Several other BIFs might be useful for working with distributed Erlang. The erlang:monitor_node(NodeName, Bool) function lets the process that calls it with true as a value for Bool receive a message of the format {nodedown, NodeName} if the node dies.

NOTE *Unless you're writing a special library that relies on checking the life of other nodes, you will rarely need to use erlang:monitor_node/2. This is because functions like link/1 and monitor/2 still work across nodes. However, it may be interesting to use erlang:monitor_node/2 when you have a lot of monitors or links across many nodes. If you used the usual link/1 and monitor/2 functions in that case, a node dying could mean that thousands of monitors would fire at once, instead of only one event for the node monitor, which can then relay information locally.*

Suppose we set up the following from the fries node:

```
(fries@ferdmbp)3> process_flag(trap_exit, true).
false
(fries@ferdmbp)4> link(OtherShell).
true
(fries@ferdmbp)5> erlang:monitor(process, OtherShell).
#Ref<0.0.0.132>
```

Then we kill the ketchup node. In this case, the fries shell process should receive an 'EXIT' and monitor message:

```
(fries@ferdmbp)6> flush().
Shell got {'DOWN',#Ref<0.0.0.132>,process,<6349.52.0>,noconnection}
Shell got {'EXIT',<6349.52.0>,noconnection}
ok
```

And that's the kind of stuff you'll see.

NOTE *Instead of killing a node to disconnect it, you may also want to try the BIF erlang:disconnect_node(Node) to get rid of the node without shutting it down.*

But hey, wait a minute! Why does the pid look like that? Are we seeing things right?

```
(fries@ferdmbp)7> OtherShell.
<6349.52.0>
```

What? Shouldn't this be <0.52.0>? Nope. See, that way of displaying a pid is just some kind of visual representation of what a process identifier is really like. The first number represents the node (where 0 means the process is coming from the current node), the second one is a counter, and the third is a second counter for when you have so many processes created that the first counter is not enough. The true underlying representation of a pid is more like this:

```
(fries@ferdmbp)8> term_to_binary(OtherShell).
<<131,103,100,0,15,107,101,116,99,104,117,112,64,102,101,
  114,100,109,98,112,0,0,0,52,0,0,0,0,3>>
```

The binary sequence <<107,101,116,99,104,117,112,64,102,101,114,100,109,98, 112>> is in fact a Latin-1 (or ASCII) representation of <<"ketchup@ferdmbp">>, the name of the node where the process is located. Then we have the two counters: <<0,0,0,52>> and <<0,0,0,0>>. The last value (3) is some token value to differentiate whether the pid comes from an old node, a dead one, and so on. That's why pids can be used transparently anywhere.

NOTE *If you're unsure which node a pid is coming from, you don't need to convert it to a binary to read the node name. Just call node(Pid), and the node where it's running will be returned as an atom.*

Other interesting BIFs to use are spawn/2, spawn/4, spawn_link/2, and spawn_link/4. They work like the other spawn BIFs, except these let you spawn functions on remote nodes. Try this from the ketchup node:

```
(ketchup@ferdmbp)6> spawn(fries@ferdmbp,
(ketchup@ferdmbp)6>         fun() -> io:format("I'm on ~p~n", [node()]) end).
I'm on fries@ferdmbp
<6448.50.0>
```

This is essentially a remote procedure call. We can choose to run arbitrary code on other nodes, without giving ourselves more trouble than that! Interestingly, the function is running on the other node, but we receive the output locally. That's right—even output can be transparently redirected across the network. This is possible thanks to the idea of group leaders. Group leaders are inherited in the same way whether they're local or remote and will forward IO operations to their parents until they hit the correct output driver, in the original shell that called them.

Those are all the tools you need in Erlang to be able to write distributed code. You have just received your machete, flashlight, and mustache. You're at a level that would take a long while to achieve with other languages without such a distribution layer. Now is the time to kill monsters. Or maybe first, we need to talk about the cookie monster.

Cookies

Earlier in the chapter, I illustrated how Erlang node connections are set up as meshes. If someone connects to a node, it gets connected to all the other nodes. However, you may want to run different Erlang node clusters on the same piece of hardware. In this case, you do not want to accidentally connect two Erlang node clusters together. To help with this, the designers of Erlang added a little token value called a *cookie*.

Many references, such as the official Erlang documentation, put cookies under the topic of security. But that has to be seen as a joke, because there's no way anyone seriously considers cookies to be safe things.

The cookie is a little unique value that must be shared between nodes to allow them to connect with each other. Cookies are closer to the idea of usernames than passwords, and I'm pretty sure no one would consider having a username (and nothing else) as a security feature. Cookies make much more sense as a mechanism used to divide clusters of nodes than as an authentication mechanism.

To give a cookie to a node, just start it by adding a -setcookie *Cookie* argument to the command line. Let's try this with two new nodes:

```
$ erl -sname salad -setcookie 'myvoiceismypassword'
... <snip> ...
(salad@ferdmbp)1>
```

```
$ erl -sname mustard -setcookie 'opensesame'
... <snip> ...
(mustard@ferdmbp)1>
```

Now both nodes have different cookies, and they shouldn't be able to communicate:

```
(salad@ferdmbp)1> net_kernel:connect(mustard@ferdmbp).
false
```

This one has been denied, but we don't see many explanations as to why. Let's take a look at the mustard node:

```
=ERROR REPORT==== 10-Dec-2013::13:39:27 ===
** Connection attempt from disallowed node salad@ferdmbp **
```

Good. Now what if we did really want salad and mustard to be together? There's a BIF called erlang:set_cookie/2 to do what we need. If you call erlang:set_cookie(OtherNode, Cookie), you will use that cookie only when connecting to that other node. If you instead use erlang:set_cookie(node(), Cookie), you'll be changing the node's current cookie for all future connections. To see the changes, use erlang:get_cookie():

```
(salad@ferdmbp)2> erlang:get_cookie().
myvoiceismypassword
(salad@ferdmbp)3> erlang:set_cookie(mustard@ferdmbp, opensesame).
true
(salad@ferdmbp)4> erlang:get_cookie().
myvoiceismypassword
(salad@ferdmbp)5> net_kernel:connect(mustard@ferdmbp).
true
(salad@ferdmbp)6> erlang:set_cookie(node(), now_it_changes).
true
(salad@ferdmbp)7> erlang:get_cookie().
now_it_changes
```

There is one last cookie mechanism to see. If you tried the earlier examples in this chapter, go look in your home directory. You should see a file named *.erlang.cookie* in there. If you read that file, you'll see a random string that looks a bit like PMIYERCHJZNZGSRJPVRK. Whenever you start a distributed node without a specific command to give it a cookie, Erlang will create one and put it in *.erlang.cookie*. Then every time you start a node again without specifying its cookie, the VM will look into your home directory and use whatever is in that file.

Remote Shells

One of the first things we've learned in Erlang was how to interrupt running code by using CTRL-G (^G). In there, we saw a menu for distributed shells:

```
(salad@ferdmbp)1>
User switch command
--> h
  c [nn]            - connect to job
  i [nn]            - interrupt job
  k [nn]            - kill job
  j                 - list all jobs
  s [shell]         - start local shell
  r [node [shell]]  - start remote shell
  q         - quit erlang
  ? | h             - this message
```

The r [node [shell]] option is the one we're looking for to work with our remote shells. We can start a job on the mustard node as follows:

```
--> r mustard@ferdmbp
--> j
  1  {shell,start,[init]}
  2* {mustard@ferdmbp,shell,start,[]}
--> c
Eshell V5.9.1  (abort with ^G)
(mustard@ferdmbp)1> node().
mustard@ferdmbp
```

And there you have it. You can now use the remote shell the same way you would use a local one. There are a few differences with older versions of Erlang, where features like autocompletion are not available. This way of doing things is still very useful whenever you need to change things on a node running with the -noshell option. If the -noshell node has a name, then you can connect to it to do DevOps-related things like reloading modules, debugging some code, and so on.

By using CTRL-G again, you can go back to your original node. Be careful when you stop your session though. If you call q() or init:stop(), you'll be terminating the remote node!

Hidden Nodes

Erlang nodes can be connected by calling net_kernel:connect/1, but you need to be aware that pretty much any interaction between nodes will get them to set up a connection. Calling spawn/2 or sending a message to a foreign pid will automatically set up connections.

This might be rather annoying if you have a decent cluster and you want to communicate with a single node to change a few things there. You wouldn't want your admin node to suddenly be integrated into the cluster, making other nodes believe that they have a new coworker to send tasks to. To connect to a remote node without automatically connecting to all the other nodes it is connected to, you could call the rarely used erlang:send(Dest, Message, [noconnect]) function, which sends a message without creating a connection, but this is rather error prone.

Instead, you want to set up a node with the -hidden flag.

Let's say you're still running the mustard and salad nodes. We'll start a third node, olives, which will connect only to mustard (make sure the cookies are the same!):

```
$ erl -sname olives -hidden
... <snip> ...
(olives@ferdmbp)1> net_kernel:connect(mustard@ferdmbp).
true
(olives@ferdmbp)2> nodes().
[]
(olives@ferdmbp)3> nodes(hidden).
[mustard@ferdmbp]
```

Aha! The node didn't connect to ketchup, and at first sight, it didn't appear to connect with mustard either. However, calling nodes(hidden) shows that we do have a connection there! Let's see what the mustard node sees:

```
(mustard@ferdmbp)1> nodes().
[salad@ferdmbp]
(mustard@ferdmbp)2> nodes(hidden).
[olives@ferdmbp]
(mustard@ferdmbp)3> nodes(connected).
[salad@ferdmbp,olives@ferdmbp]
```

This is a similar view, but now we add the nodes(connected) BIF that shows all connections, regardless of their type. The ketchup node will never see any connection to olives, unless especially told to connect there.

One other interesting use of nodes/1 is calling nodes(known), which will show all nodes that the current node ever connected to.

With remote shells, cookies, and hidden nodes, managing a distributed Erlang system becomes simpler.

The Walls Are Made of Fire, and the Goggles Do Nothing

If you need to go through a firewall with distributed Erlang (and do not want to tunnel), you will likely want to open a few ports here and there for Erlang communication. In this case, you should open port 4369, the default port for EPMD (the Erlang Port Mapper Daemon application introduced earlier in the chapter). It's a good idea to use this port, because it has been officially registered for EPMD by Ericsson. This means that any standards-compliant operating system you use will have that port free, ready for EPMD.

Then you will want to open a range of ports for connections between nodes. The problem is that Erlang just assigns random port numbers to inter-node connections. There are, however, two hidden application variables that let you specify a range within which ports can be assigned. The two values are inet_dist_listen_min and inet_dist_listen_max from the kernel application.

You could, as an example, start Erlang as erl -name left_4_distribudead -kernel inet_dist_listen_min 9100 -kernel inet_dist_listen_max 9115 in order to set a range of 15 ports to be used for Erlang nodes. Alternatively, you could specify these ports with a configuration file named *ports.config* that looks a bit like this:

```
[{kernel,[
  {inet_dist_listen_min, 9100},
  {inet_dist_listen_max, 9115}
]}].
```

And then starting the Erlang node as erl -name the_army_of_darknodes -config ports. The variables will be set in the same way. Note that these ports are listen ports, so you need to keep only one per node per machine. If you are running two VMs on a given server or computer, you'll need two listen ports.

The Calls from Beyond

On top of all the BIFs and options we've covered so far, there are a few modules that can be used to help developers work with distribution.

The net_kernel Module

net_kernel is the module we used to connect and disconnect nodes earlier.

It has some other fancy functionality, such as being able to transform a nondistributed node into a distributed one:

```
$ erl
... <snip> ...
1> net_kernel:start([romero, shortnames]).
{ok,<0.43.0>}
(romero@ferdmbp)2>
```

You can use either shortnames or longnames to define whether you want to have the equivalent of -sname or -name. Moreover, if you know a node is going to be sending large messages and thus might need a long heartbeat time between nodes, a third argument can be passed to the list: net_kernel:start([Name, Type, HeartbeatInMilliseconds]). By default, the heartbeat delay (also called *tick time*) is set to 15 seconds, or 15,000 milliseconds.

Two other functions of the module are net_kernel:set_net_ticktime(S), which lets you change the tick time of the node to avoid disconnections, and net_kernel:stop(), which switches a node from being distributed back to being a normal node:

```
(romero@ferdmbp)2> net_kernel:set_net_ticktime(5).
change_initiated
(romero@ferdmbp)3> net_kernel:stop().
ok
4>
```

The global Module

The next useful module for distribution is global. The global module is an alternative process registry. It automatically spreads its data to all connected nodes, replicates data there, handles node failures, and supports different conflict-resolution strategies when nodes get back online.

You register a name by calling global:register_name(Name, Pid), and unregister with global:unregister_name(Name). In case you want to do a name transfer without ever having it point to nothing, you can call global:re_register_name(Name, Pid). You can find a pid with global:whereis_name(Name), and send a message to a process by calling global:send(Name, Message). There is everything you need. What's especially nice is that the names you use to register the processes can be *any* terms at all.

A naming conflict will happen when two nodes suddenly connect and both have two different processes sharing the same name. In these cases, global will kill one of them randomly by default. There are ways to override that behavior. Whenever you register or reregister a name, pass a third argument to the function:

```
5> Resolve = fun(_Name,Pid1,Pid2) ->
5>      case process_info(Pid1, message_queue_len) > process_info(Pid2, message_queue_len) of
5>          true -> Pid1;
5>          false -> Pid2
5>      end
5> end.
#Fun<erl_eval.18.59269574>
6> global:register_name({zombie, 12}, self(), Resolve).
yes
```

The Resolve function will pick the process with the most messages in its mailbox as the one to keep (it's the one the function returns the pid of). You could alternatively contact both processes and ask for who has the most subscribers, or keep only the first one to reply, to name a few strategies you could implement. If the Resolve function crashes or returns something other than the pids, the process name is unregistered. For your convenience, the global module already defines three functions:

1. fun global:random_exit_name/3 kills a process randomly. This is the default option.

2. fun global:random_notify_name/3 randomly picks one of the two processes as the one to survive, and it will send {global_name_conflict, Name} to the process that lost.

3. fun global:notify_all_name/3 unregisters both pids and sends the message {global_name_conflict, Name, OtherPid} to both processes. It lets them resolve the issue themselves so they reregister again.

The global module has one downside in that it is often said to be rather slow to detect name conflicts and nodes going down. It's also better for a somewhat small number of registrations that tend not to change too much over time. Other than these limitations, global is a fine module, and it's even supported by behaviors. Just change all the gen_Something:start_link(...) calls that use local names ({local, Name}) to instead use {global, Name}, and then all calls and casts (and their equivalents) to use {global, Name} instead of just Name. When you do this, things will be distributed.

NOTE *Erlang versions from R15B01 and newer allow the usage other registries than local and global. Supply the name as {via, RegistryModule, Name} to use whatever compatible process registry you want for your processes.*

The rpc Module

The next module on the list is rpc (for remote procedure call). It contains functions that let you execute commands on remote nodes, as well as a few functions that facilitate parallel operations. To test these out, let's begin by starting two different nodes and connecting them together, as demonstrated earlier in the chapter. Name the nodes cthulu and lovecraft.

The most basic rpc operation is rpc:call/4-5. It allows you to run a given operation on a remote node and get the results locally:

```
(cthulu@ferdmbp)1> rpc:call(lovecraft@ferdmbp, lists, sort, [[a,e,f,t,h,s,a]]).
[a,a,e,f,h,s,t]
(cthulu@ferdmbp)2> rpc:call(lovecraft@ferdmbp, timer, sleep, [10000], 500).
{badrpc,timeout}
```

As seen in this Call of the Cthulu node, the function with four arguments takes the form rpc:call(Node, Module, Function, Args). Adding a fifth argument gives a timeout. The rpc call will return whatever was returned by the function it ran, or {badrpc, Reason} in case of a failure.

If you've studied some distributed or parallel computing concepts before, you might have heard of *promises* or *futures*. Promises and futures are a bit like remote procedure calls, except that they are asynchronous. The rpc module lets us have this:

```
(cthulu@ferdmbp)3> Key = rpc:async_call(lovecraft@ferdmbp, erlang, node, []).
<0.45.0>
(cthulu@ferdmbp)4> rpc:yield(Key).
lovecraft@ferdmbp
```

By combining the result of the function rpc:async_call/4 with the function rpc:yield(Res), we can have asynchronous remote procedure calls and fetch the results later. This is especially useful when you know the remote procedure call you will make will take a while to return. Under these circumstances, you send it off, get busy doing other stuff in the meantime (making other calls, fetching records from a database, drinking tea, and so on), and then wait for the results when there's absolutely nothing else left to do. Of course, you can run such calls on your own node if you need to:

```
(cthulu@ferdmbp)5> MinTime = rpc:async_call(node(), timer, sleep, [30000]).
<0.48.0>
(cthulu@ferdmbp)6> lists:sort([a,c,b]).
[a,b,c]
```

```
(cthulu@ferdmbp)7> rpc:yield(MinTime).
... <long wait> ...
ok
```

If by any chance you want to use the yield/1 function with a time-out value, call rpc:nb_yield(Key, Timeout) instead. To poll for results, use rpc:nb_yield(Key) (which is equivalent to rpc:nb_yield(Key,0)):

```
(cthulu@ferdmbp)8> Key2 = rpc:async_call(node(), timer, sleep, [30000]).
<0.52.0>
(cthulu@ferdmbp)9> rpc:nb_yield(Key2).
timeout
(cthulu@ferdmbp)10> rpc:nb_yield(Key2).
timeout
(cthulu@ferdmbp)11> rpc:nb_yield(Key2).
timeout
(cthulu@ferdmbp)12> rpc:nb_yield(Key2, 1000).
timeout
(cthulu@ferdmbp)13> rpc:nb_yield(Key2, 100000).
... <long wait> ...
{value,ok}
```

If you don't care about the result, you can use rpc:cast(Node, Mod, Fun, Args) to send a command to another node and forget about it.

But what if what we want is to call more than one node at a time? Let's add three nodes to our little cluster: minion1, minion2, and minion3. Those are cthulu's minions. When we want to ask them questions, we need to send three different calls, and when we want to give orders, we must cast three times. That's pretty bad, and it doesn't scale with very large armies.

The trick is to use two rpc functions for calls and casts, respectively rpc:multicall(Nodes, Mod, Fun, Args) (with an optional Timeout argument) and rpc:eval_everywhere(Nodes, Mod, Fun, Args):

```
(cthulu@ferdmbp)14> nodes().
[lovecraft@ferdmbp, minion1@ferdmbp, minion2@ferdmbp, minion3@ferdmbp]
(cthulu@ferdmbp)15> rpc:multicall(nodes(), erlang, is_alive, []).
{[true,true,true,true],[]}
```

This tells us that all four nodes are alive (and none were unavailable for an answer). The left side of the tuple is alive, the right side isn't. Yeah, erlang:is_alive() just returns whether the node it runs on is alive or not, which might look a bit weird. Yet again, remember that in a distributed setting, alive means "can be reached," not "is running." Then let's say cthulu isn't really appreciative of its minions and decides to kill them, or rather, talk them into killing themselves. This is an order, and so it's cast.

For this reason, we use eval_everywhere/4 with a call to init:stop() on the minion nodes:

```
(cthulu@ferdmbp)16> rpc:eval_everywhere([minion1@ferdmbp, minion2@ferdmbp,
minion3@ferdmbp], init, stop, []).
abcast
(cthulu@ferdmbp)17> rpc:multicall([lovecraft@ferdmbp, minion1@ferdmbp,
minion2@ferdmbp, minion3@ferdmbp], erlang, is_alive, []).
{[true],[minion1@ferdmbp, minion2@ferdmbp, minion3@ferdmbp]}
```

When we ask again for who is alive, only one node remains: the lovecraft node. The minions were obedient creatures.

The rpc module has a few more interesting functions, but the core uses were covered here. If you want to know more, I suggest that you comb through the documentation for the module.

Burying the Distribunomicon

That's it for most of the basics on distributed Erlang. There are a lot of things to think about and a lot of attributes to keep in mind. Whenever you need to develop a distributed application, ask yourself which of the distributed computing fallacies you could potentially run into (if any). If a customer asks you to build a system that handles netsplits while staying consistent *and* available, you know that you need to either calmly explain the CAP theorem or run away (possibly by jumping through a window, for a maximal effect).

Generally, applications where a thousand isolated nodes can do their job without communicating or depending on each other will provide the best scalability. The more inter-node dependencies created, the harder it becomes to scale the system, no matter what kind of distribution layer you have. This is just like zombies (no, really!). Zombies are terrifying because of how many there are and how difficult it can be to kill them as a group. Even though individual zombies can be very slow and far from menacing, a horde can do considerable damage, even if it loses many of its zombie members. Groups of human survivors can do great things by combining their intelligence and communicating together, but each loss they suffer is more taxing on the group and its ability to survive.

That being said, you have the tools required to get going. Chapter 27 introduces distributed OTP applications. This kind of application provides a takeover and failover mechanism for hardware failures, but not general distribution. It's a lot more like respawning your dead zombie than anything else.

27

DISTRIBUTED OTP APPLICATIONS

Although Erlang leaves us with a lot of work to do to build a distributed system, it still provides a few solutions. One of these is the concept of *distributed OTP applications*. Distributed OTP applications, or just *distributed applications* in the context of OTP, allow us to define takeover and failover mechanisms. In this chapter, we'll cover what that means and how it works, and write a little app to demonstrate these concepts.

Adding More to OTP

In Chapter 19, we briefly discussed the structure of an application as something using a central application controller dispatching to application masters, each monitoring a top-level supervisor for an application, like this:

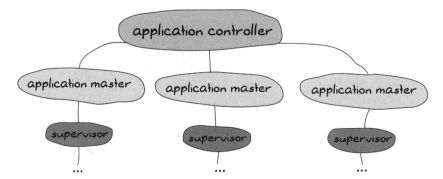

In standard OTP applications, the application can be loaded, started, stopped, or unloaded. In distributed applications, we change how things work. Now the application controller shares its work with the *distributed application controller,* another process sitting next to it (usually called dist_ac), as shown here:

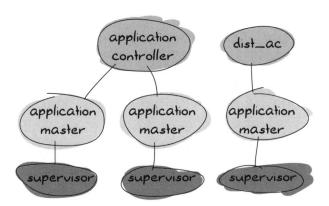

Depending on the application file, the ownership of the application will change. A dist_ac will be started on all nodes, and all dist_ac processes will communicate with each other. What they talk about is not too relevant, except for one thing. With standard applications, the four application statuses are being loaded, started, stopped, and unloaded. Distributed applications split the idea of a started application into *started* and *running.* The difference between the two is that you could define an application to be global within a cluster. An application of this kind can run on only one node at a time, while regular OTP applications don't care about what's happening on other nodes. As such, a distributed application will be started on all nodes of a cluster, but running on only one.

What does this mean for the nodes where the application is started without being run? The only thing they do is wait for the node of the running application to die. This means that when the node that runs the app dies, another node starts running it instead. This approach can avoid interruption of services by moving around different subsystems.

Taking and Failing Over

There are two important concepts handled by distributed applications: *failover* and *takeover*.

A failover is the idea of restarting an application somewhere other than where it stopped running. This is a particularly valid strategy when you have redundant hardware. You run something on a main computer or server, and if it fails, you move it to a backup one. In larger-scale deployments, you might instead have 50 servers running your software (all at maybe 60 to 70 percent load), and expect the running ones to absorb the load of the failing ones. The concept of failing over is mostly important in the former case, and somewhat less interesting in the latter one.

The second important concept of distributed OTP applications is the takeover. Taking over is the act of a dead node coming back from the dead, being known to be more important than the backup nodes (maybe it has better hardware), and deciding to run the application again. This is usually done by gracefully terminating the backup application and starting the main one instead.

NOTE   *In terms of distributed programming fallacies, distributed OTP applications assume that when there is a failure, it is likely due to a hardware failure, and not a netsplit. If you deem netsplits more likely than other hardware failures, you must be aware of the possibility that the application is running both as a backup and main one, and that funny things could happen when the network issue is resolved. Maybe distributed OTP applications aren't the right mechanism for you in these cases.*

Let's imagine that we have a system with three nodes, where only the first one is running a given application:

The nodes B and C are declared to be backup nodes in case A dies, which we pretend just happened:

For a brief moment, nothing is running. After a while, B realizes this and decides to take over the application:

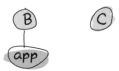

That's a failover. Then, if B dies, the application gets restarted on C:

Another failover, and all is well.

Now suppose that A comes back up. C is running the app happily, but A is the node we defined to be the main one. This is when a takeover occurs. The app is willingly shut down on C and restarted on A:

And so on for all other failures.

One obvious issue is how terminating applications all the time like this is likely to result in losing important state. Sadly, that's your problem. You'll need to think of places where to put and share all that vital state before things break down. The OTP mechanism for distributed applications makes no special case for that.

With these concepts in mind, let's move on to making things work in practice.

The Magic 8 Ball

A Magic 8 Ball is a simple toy that you shake to get divine and helpful answers. You ask questions like "Will my favorite sports team win the game tonight?" and the ball you shake replies something like "Without a doubt." You can then safely bet your house's value on the final score. Other questions like "Should I make careful investments for the future?" could return "That is unlikely" or "I'm not sure." The Magic 8 Ball has been vital in the Western world's political decision making in the past few decades, and it is only natural that we use it as an example for fault tolerance.

Our implementation won't make use of real-life switching mechanisms for automatically finding servers, such as round-robin DNS servers or load balancers. Instead, we'll stay within pure Erlang and have three nodes (denoted as A, B, and C) in a distributed OTP application. The A node will represent the main node running the Magic 8 Ball server, and the B and C nodes will be the backup nodes:

Whenever A fails, the Magic 8 Ball application should be restarted on either B or C, and both nodes will still be able to use it transparently.

Building the Application

Before setting up things for distributed OTP applications, we'll build the application itself. It's going to be mind-bogglingly naive in its design:

In total, we'll have three modules: the supervisor, the server, and the application callback module to start things.

The Supervisor Module

The supervisor will be rather trivial. We'll call it m8ball_sup (as in *Magic 8 Ball Supervisor*), and we'll put it in the *src/* directory of a standard OTP application:

```
-module(m8ball_sup).
-behaviour(supervisor).
-export([start_link/0, init/1]).

start_link() ->
    supervisor:start_link({global,?MODULE}, ?MODULE, []).

init([]) ->
    {ok, {{one_for_one, 1, 10},
          [{m8ball,
            {m8ball_server, start_link, []},
            permanent,
            5000,
```

```
            worker,
            [m8ball_server]
        }]}}.
```

This is a supervisor that will start a single server (m8ball_server), a permanent worker process. It's allowed one failure every 10 seconds.

The Server Module

The Magic 8 Ball server will be a bit more complex. We'll build it as a gen_server with the following interface:

```
-module(m8ball_server).
-behaviour(gen_server).
-export([start_link/0, stop/0, ask/1]).
-export([init/1, handle_call/3, handle_cast/2, handle_info/2,
         code_change/3, terminate/2]).

%%%%%%%%%%%%%%%%%%%
%%% INTERFACE %%%
%%%%%%%%%%%%%%%%%%%
start_link() ->
    gen_server:start_link({global, ?MODULE}, ?MODULE, [], []).

stop() ->
    gen_server:call({global, ?MODULE}, stop).

ask(_Question) -> % The question doesn't matter!
    gen_server:call({global, ?MODULE}, question).
```

Notice how the server is started using {global, ?MODULE} as a name and how it's accessed with the same tuple for each call. That's the global module we saw in Chapter 26, applied to behaviors.

Next come the callbacks, the real implementation. The Magic 8 Ball should randomly pick one of many possible replies from some configuration file. We want a configuration file because it should be easy to add or remove answers as we wish.

First, if we want to do things randomly, we'll need to set up some randomness as part of our init function:

```
%%%%%%%%%%%%%%%%%%%
%%% CALLBACKS %%%
%%%%%%%%%%%%%%%%%%%
init([]) ->
    <<A:32, B:32, C:32>> = crypto:rand_bytes(12),
    random:seed(A,B,C),
    {ok, []}.
```

We used this pattern before in Chapter 23. Here, we're using 12 random bytes to set up the initial random seed to be used with the random:uniform/1 function.

The next step is to read the answers from the configuration file and pick one. As discussed in Chapter 19, the easiest way to set up some configuration is through the app file (in the env tuple). Here's how we're going to do this:

```
handle_call(question, _From, State) ->
    {ok, Answers} = application:get_env(m8ball, answers),
    Answer = element(random:uniform(tuple_size(Answers)), Answers),
    {reply, Answer, State};
handle_call(stop, _From, State) ->
    {stop, normal, ok, State};
handle_call(_Call, _From, State) ->
    {noreply, State}.
```

The first clause shows what we want to do. We expect to have a tuple with all the possible answers within the answers value of the env tuple. Why a tuple? Simply because accessing elements of a tuple is a constant time operation, while obtaining them from a list is linear (and thus takes longer on larger lists). We then send back the answer.

NOTE *The server reads the answers with application:get_env(m8ball, answers) on each question asked. If you were to set new answers with a call like application:set_env(m8ball, answers, {"yes","no","maybe"}), the three answers would instantly be the possible choices for future calls. Reading them once at startup should be somewhat more efficient in the long run, but it will mean that the only way to update the possible answers is to restart the application or add a special call to do it.*

You should have noticed by now that we don't actually care about the question asked; it's not even passed to the server. Because we're returning random answers, it is entirely useless to copy the question from process to process. We're just saving work by ignoring it entirely. We still leave the answer there because it will make the final interface feel more natural. We could also trick our Magic 8 Ball into always returning the same answer for the same question if we felt like it, but we won't bother with that for this example.

The rest of the module is pretty much the same as usual for a generic gen_server doing nothing:

```
handle_cast(_Cast, State) ->
    {noreply, State}.

handle_info(_Info, State) ->
    {noreply, State}.

code_change(_OldVsn, State, _Extra) ->
    {ok, State}.

terminate(_Reason, _State) ->
    ok.
```

Now we can get to the more serious stuff, namely the application file and the callback module. We'll begin with the latter, *m8ball.erl*:

```erlang
-module(m8ball).
-behaviour(application).
-export([start/2, stop/1]).
-export([ask/1]).


%%%%%%%%%%%%%%%%%%
%%% CALLBACKS %%%
%%%%%%%%%%%%%%%%%%
start(normal, []) ->
    m8ball_sup:start_link().

stop(_State) ->
    ok.


%%%%%%%%%%%%%%%%%%
%%% INTERFACE %%%
%%%%%%%%%%%%%%%%%%
ask(Question) ->
    m8ball_server:ask(Question).
```

That was easy. Here's the associated app file, *m8ball.app*:

```erlang
{application, m8ball,
 [{vsn, "1.0.0"},
  {description, "Answer vital questions"},
  {modules, [m8ball, m8ball_sup, m8ball_server]},
  {applications, [stdlib, kernel, crypto]},
  {registered, [m8ball, m8ball_sup, m8ball_server]},
  {mod, {m8ball, []}},
  {env, [
    {answers, {<<"Yes">>, <<"No">>, <<"Doubtful">>,
               <<"I don't like your tone">>, <<"Of course">>,
               <<"Of course not">>, <<"*backs away slowly and runs away*">>}}
  ]}
 ]}.
```

We depend on `stdlib` and `kernel`, like all OTP applications, and also on `crypto` for our random seeds in the server. Notice how the answers are all in a tuple that matches the tuples required in the server. In this case, the answers are all binaries, but the string format doesn't really matter—a list would work as well.

Making the Application Distributed

So far, everything has been like building a perfectly normal OTP application. We have very few changes to make to our files to turn the normal application into a distributed OTP application. In fact, we have only one function clause to add, back in the *m8ball.erl* module:

```
%%%%%%%%%%%%%%%%%%%%
%%% CALLBACKS %%%
%%%%%%%%%%%%%%%%%%%%

start(normal, []) ->
    m8ball_sup:start_link();
start({takeover, _OtherNode}, []) ->
    m8ball_sup:start_link().
```

The {takeover, OtherNode} argument is passed to start/2 when a more important node takes over a backup node. In the case of the Magic 8 Ball app, it doesn't really change anything, and we can just start the supervisor all the same.

Recompile your code, and it's pretty much ready.

But hold on, how do we define which nodes are the main ones and which ones are backups? The answer is in configuration files. Because we want a system with three nodes (a@yourhost, b@yourhost, and c@yourhost), we'll need three configuration files (name them *a.config*, *b.config*, and *c.config*, and then put them all in *config/* inside the application directory):

```
[{kernel,
  [{distributed, [{m8ball,
                   5000,
                   [a@ferdmbp, {b@ferdmbp, c@ferdmbp}]}]},
   {sync_nodes_mandatory, [b@ferdmbp, c@ferdmbp]},
   {sync_nodes_timeout, 30000}
  ]}].
```

```
[{kernel,
  [{distributed, [{m8ball,
                   5000,
                   [a@ferdmbp, {b@ferdmbp, c@ferdmbp}]}]},
   {sync_nodes_mandatory, [a@ferdmbp, c@ferdmbp]},
   {sync_nodes_timeout, 30000}
  ]}].
```

```
[{kernel,
  [{distributed, [{m8ball,
                   5000,
                   [a@ferdmbp, {b@ferdmbp, c@ferdmbp}]}]},
   {sync_nodes_mandatory, [a@ferdmbp, b@ferdmbp]},
   {sync_nodes_timeout, 30000}
  ]}].
```

The general structure is always the same:

```
[{kernel,
  [{distributed, [{AppName,
                   TimeOutBeforeRestart,
                   NodeList}]},
  {sync_nodes_mandatory, NecessaryNodes},
  {sync_nodes_optional, OptionalNodes},
  {sync_nodes_timeout, MaxTime}
  ]}].
```

The NodeList value can usually take a form like [A, B, C, D] for A to be the main one, B as the first backup, C as the next one, and D as the last. Another syntax is possible, giving a list of like [A, {B, C}, D], so A is still the main node, B and C are equal secondary backups, and then comes the rest.

The sync_nodes_mandatory tuple will work in conjunction with sync_nodes_timeout. When you start a distributed VM with values set for this, the VM will stay locked up until all the mandatory nodes are also up and locked. Then they will be synchronized and things will start going. If it takes more than MaxTime to get all the nodes up, then they will all crash before starting.

There are a lot more options available, and I recommend looking into the kernel application documentation (*http://www.erlang.org/doc/man/kernel_app.html*) if you want to know more about them.

Let's try running the m8ball application. If you're not sure 30 seconds is enough to boot all three VMs, you can increase sync_nodes_timeout as you see fit. Then start three VMs:

```
$ erl -sname a -config config/a -pa ebin/
```

```
$ erl -sname b -config config/b -pa ebin/
```

```
$ erl -sname c -config config/c -pa ebin/
```

As you start the third VM, the other VMs should all unlock at once. Go into each of the three VMs, and turn by turn, start both crypto and m8ball with application:start(AppName).

Now you should be able to call the Magic 8 Ball from any of the connected nodes:

```
(a@ferdmbp)3> m8ball:ask("If I crash, will I have a second life?").
<<"I don't like your tone">>
```

```
(a@ferdmbp)4> m8ball:ask("If I crash, will I have a second life, please?").
<<"Of Course">>
```

```
(c@ferdmbp)3> m8ball:ask("Am I ever gonna be good at Erlang?").
<<"Doubtful">>
```

How motivational. To see how things are with our applications,
call application:which_applications() on all nodes. Only node a should be
running it:

```
(b@ferdmbp)3> application:which_applications().
[{crypto,"CRYPTO version 2","2.1"},
 {stdlib,"ERTS  CXC 138 10","1.18.1"},
 {kernel,"ERTS  CXC 138 10","2.15.1"}]
```

```
(a@ferdmbp)5> application:which_applications().
[{m8ball,"Answer vital questions","1.0.0"},
 {crypto,"CRYPTO version 2","2.1"},
 {stdlib,"ERTS  CXC 138 10","1.18.1"},
 {kernel,"ERTS  CXC 138 10","2.15.1"}]
```

The c node should show the same thing as the b node in this case. Now
if you kill the a node (just ungracefully close the window that holds the
Erlang shell), the application should no longer be running there. Let's see
where it is instead:

```
(c@ferdmbp)4> application:which_applications().
[{crypto,"CRYPTO version 2","2.1"},
 {stdlib,"ERTS  CXC 138 10","1.18.1"},
 {kernel,"ERTS  CXC 138 10","2.15.1"}]
(c@ferdmbp)5> m8ball:ask("where are you?!").
<<"I don't like your tone">>
```

That's expected, as b is higher in the priorities. After 5 seconds (we set
the timeout to 5000 milliseconds), b should be showing the application as
running:

```
(b@ferdmbp)4> application:which_applications().
[{m8ball,"Answer vital questions","1.0.0"},
 {crypto,"CRYPTO version 2","2.1"},
 {stdlib,"ERTS  CXC 138 10","1.18.1"},
 {kernel,"ERTS  CXC 138 10","2.15.1"}]
```

It still runs fine. Now kill b in the same barbaric manner that you used
to get rid of a, and c should be running the application after 5 seconds:

```
(c@ferdmbp)6> application:which_applications().
[{m8ball,"Answer vital questions","1.0.0"},
```

```
{crypto,"CRYPTO version 2","2.1"},
{stdlib,"ERTS   CXC 138 10","1.18.1"},
{kernel,"ERTS   CXC 138 10","2.15.1"}]
```

If you restart node a with the same command we used before, it will
hang. The configuration file specifies we need b back for a to work. If you
can't expect nodes to all be up that way, you will need to make either b or
c optional. So if we start both a and b, the application should automatically
come back, right?

```
(a@ferdmbp)4> application:which_applications().
[{crypto,"CRYPTO version 2","2.1"},
 {stdlib,"ERTS   CXC 138 10","1.18.1"},
 {kernel,"ERTS   CXC 138 10","2.15.1"}]
(a@ferdmbp)5> m8ball:ask("is the app gonna move here?").
<<"Of course not">>
```

Aw, shucks. The thing is, for the mechanism to work, the application
needs to be started *as part of the boot procedure of the node*. You could, for
instance, start node a that way for things to work:

```
$ erl -sname a -config config/a -pa ebin -eval 'application:start(crypto), application:start(m8ball)'
... <snip> ...
(a@ferdmbp)1> application:which_applications().
[{m8ball,"Answer vital questions","1.0.0"},
 {crypto,"CRYPTO version 2","2.1"},
 {stdlib,"ERTS   CXC 138 10","1.18.1"},
 {kernel,"ERTS   CXC 138 10","2.15.1"}]
```

Here's how it looks from node c's side:

```
=INFO REPORT==== 8-Jan-2013::19:24:27 ===
    application: m8ball
    exited: stopped
    type: temporary
```

That's because the -eval option is evaluated as part of the boot procedure of the VM. Obviously, a cleaner way to do it would be to use releases to
set things up right, but the example would be pretty cumbersome if it had
to combine everything we have seen before.

Just remember that, in general, distributed OTP applications work best
when working with releases that ensure that all the relevant parts of the system are in place.

As I mentioned earlier, in the case of many applications (the Magic 8
Ball included), it's sometimes simpler to just have many instances running
at once and synchronizing data, rather than forcing an application to run
in only a single place. It's also simpler to scale the system once that design
has been picked. If you need some failover/takeover mechanism, distributed OTP applications might be just what you need.

28

COMMON TEST FOR
UNCOMMON TESTS

Back in Chapter 24, we explored how to use EUnit to
do unit and module testing, and even some concurrent testing. At that point, EUnit started to show its
limits. Complex setups and longer tests that needed
to interact with each other became problematic. Plus, EUnit does not
provide any help for handling distributed Erlang and all of its power.
Fortunately, another test framework exists, and it's more appropriate
for the heavy lifting we now want to do.

What Is Common Test?

As programmers, we enjoy treating our programs as black boxes. Many of
us would define the core principle behind a good abstraction as being able
to replace whatever we've written with an anonymous black box. You put
something in the box; you get something out of it. You don't care how it
works on the inside, as long as you get what you want.

In the testing world, this has an important connection to how we like to test systems. When we were working with EUnit, we used the approach of treating a module as a black box, where we tested only the exported functions and none of the ones inside, which are not exported. I've also given examples of testing items as a white box, as in the case of the Process Quest player module's tests, where we could look at the innards  of the module to make its testing simpler. This was necessary because the interaction of all the moving parts inside the box made testing it from the outside very complex.

That was for modules and functions. What if we zoom out a bit? Let's fiddle with our scope in order to see the broader picture. What if we want to test a library? What if it's an application? Even broader, what if it's a complete system? Then we need a tool that is more adept at doing something called *system testing*.

EUnit is a pretty good tool for white box testing at a module level. It's a decent tool to test libraries and OTP applications. It's possible to use it for system testing and black box testing, but it's not optimal.

Common Test is pretty damn good at system testing. It's decent for testing libraries and OTP applications, and it's possible, but not optimal, to use it to test individual modules. So the smaller the size of what you test, the more appropriate (and flexible and fun) EUnit will be. The larger your test is, the more appropriate (and flexible and, uh, somewhat fun) Common Test will be.

You might have heard of Common Test before and tried to understand it from the documentation provided with Erlang/OTP. Then you likely gave up soon after. Don't worry. The problem is that Common Test is very powerful and has an accordingly long user guide. At the time of this writing, most of its documentation appears to be coming from internal documentation from the days when it was used only within the walls of Ericsson. In fact, its documentation is more of a reference manual for people who already understand it than a tutorial.

In order to properly learn Common Test, we'll start from the simplest parts of it and slowly grow our way to system tests. But before we get started, let's take a brief look at how Common Test is organized.

Common Test Structure

Because Common Test is appropriate for system testing, it will assume two things:

- We will need data to instantiate our stuff.
- We will need a place to store all that "side effect-y" stuff we do because we're messy people.

Because of these assumptions, Common Test will usually be organized as follows:

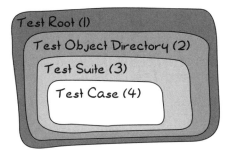

The test case is the simplest part. It's a bit of code that either fails or succeeds. If the case crashes, the test is unsuccessful (how surprising). Otherwise, the test case is considered successful.

In Common Test, test cases are single functions. All these functions live in a test suite (3), which is a module that takes care of regrouping related test cases together. Each test suite will then live in a directory—the test object directory (2). The test root (1) is a directory that contains many test object directories, but due to the nature of OTP applications often being developed individually, many Erlang programmers tend to omit that layer.

Let's go back to our two assumptions: we need to instantiate stuff, and then mess up stuff. Each test suite is a module that ends with _SUITE. If we were to test the Magic 8 Ball application from Chapter 27, we might call the suite m8ball_SUITE. Each suite is allowed to have a data directory, usually named *<Module>_SUITE_data/*. In the case of the Magic 8 Ball app, the data directory would have been *m8ball_SUITE_data/*. That directory contains anything you want that may be useful to the tests.

What about the side effects? Well, because we might run tests many times, Common Test develops its structure a bit more:

Whenever you run the tests, Common Test will find some place to log stuff (usually the current directory, but we'll cover how to configure that in "Test Specifications" on page 501). For this purpose, it will create a unique directory where you can store your data. That directory (*priv dir* in the structure diagram), along with the data directory, will be passed as part of some initial state to each of your tests. You're then free to write whatever you want in that private directory, and then inspect it later, without running the risk of overwriting something important or the results of former test runs.

Enough with this architectural material; we're ready to write our first test suite.

Creating a Simple Test Suite

We'll begin with a simple test suite with two test cases. Create a directory named *ct/* (or whatever you like—this is a free country, after all). That directory will be our test root. Inside it, make a directory named *demo/* for the simpler tests we'll use as examples. This will be our test object directory.

Inside the test object directory, we'll begin with a module named *basic_SUITE.erl*, to see the most basic stuff doable in Common Test. You can omit creating the *basic_SUITE_data/* directory—we won't need it for this run, and Common Test won't complain.

Here's what the module looks like:

```erlang
-module(basic_SUITE).
-include_lib("common_test/include/ct.hrl").
-export([all/0]).
-export([test1/1, test2/1]).

all() -> [test1, test2].

test1(_Config) ->
    1 = 1.

test2(_Config) ->
    A = 0,
    1/A.
```

Let's study it step by step. First, we need to include the file "common_test/include/ct.hrl". That file contains a few useful macros, and even though basic_SUITE doesn't use them, it's usually a good habit to include that file.

Then we have the function all/0. That function returns a list of test cases. It's basically what tells Common Test, "Hey, I want to run these test cases!" EUnit would do it based on the name (*_test() or *_test_()). Common Test does it with an explicit function call.

What about these _Config variables? They're unused for now, but for your own personal knowledge, they contain the initial state your test cases will require. That state is literally a proplist, and it initially contains two values: data_dir and priv_dir—the directory we have for our static data and the one where we can mess around.

Running the Tests

We can run the tests either from the command line or from an Erlang shell. From the command line, call ct_run -suite Name_SUITE.

NOTE   *In Erlang/OTP versions before R15 (released around December 2011), the default command was run_test instead of ct_run (although some systems had both already). The change was made to help minimize the risk of name clashes with other applications by moving to a slightly less generic name.*

By running this command, we get the following:

```
$ ct_run -suite basic_SUITE
... <snip> ...
Common Test: Running make in test directories...
Recompile: basic_SUITE
... <snip> ...
Testing ct.demo.basic_SUITE: Starting test, 2 test cases


- - - - - - - - - - - - - - - - - - - - - - - - - - - -
basic_SUITE:test2 failed on line 13
Reason: badarith
- - - - - - - - - - - - - - - - - - - - - - - - - - - -


Testing ct.demo.basic_SUITE: *** FAILED *** test case 2 of 2
Testing ct.demo.basic_SUITE: TEST COMPLETE, 1 ok, 1 failed of 2 test cases

Updating /Users/ferd/code/self/learn-you-some-erlang/ct/demo/index.html... done
Updating /Users/ferd/code/self/learn-you-some-erlang/ct/demo/all_runs.html... done
```

And we find that one of our two test cases fails. We also see that we apparently inherited a bunch of HTML files. Before looking into what this is about, let's see how to run the tests from the Erlang shell:

```
$ erl
... <snip> ...
1> ct:run_test([{suite, basic_SUITE}]).
... <snip> ...
Testing ct.demo.basic_SUITE: Starting test, 2 test cases


- - - - - - - - - - - - - - - - - - - - - - - - - - - -
basic_SUITE:test2 failed on line 13
Reason: badarith
- - - - - - - - - - - - - - - - - - - - - - - - - - - -
... <snip> ...
Updating /Users/ferd/code/self/learn-you-some-erlang/ct/demo/index.html... done
Updating /Users/ferd/code/self/learn-you-some-erlang/ct/demo/all_runs.html... done
ok
```

I've removed a bit of the output, but the shell gives exactly the same result as the command-line version.

Let's see what's going on with these HTML files:

```
$ ls
all_runs.html
basic_SUITE.beam
basic_SUITE.erl
ct_default.css
ct_run.NodeName.YYYY-MM-DD_20.01.25/
ct_run.NodeName.YYYY-MM-DD_20.05.17/
index.html
variables-NodeName
```

Oh what the hell did Common Test do to our beautiful directory? It is a shameful thing to look at. We have two directories there. Feel free to explore them if you feel adventurous, but cowards like me will prefer to instead look at either the *all_runs.html* or the *index.html* file. The former links to indexes of all iterations of the tests you ran, and the latter links to the newest runs only. Pick one, and then click around in a browser (or press around if you don't believe in a mouse as an input device) until you find the test suite with its two tests:

Num	Module	Case	Log	Time	Result	Comment
1	basic_SUITE	test1	≤ ≥	0.000s	Ok	
2	basic_SUITE	test2	≤ ≥	0.000s	FAILED	{basic_SUITE,test2,13} badarith
	TOTAL			0.139s	**FAILED**	1 Ok, 1 Failed of 2

You see that test2 failed. If you click the underlined line number, you'll see a raw copy of the module. If you click the test2 link, you'll see a detailed log of what happened:

```
=== source code for basic_SUITE:test2/1
=== Test case started with:
basic_SUITE:test2(ConfigOpts)
=== Current directory is "Somewhere on my computer"
=== Started at 2013-01-20 20:05:17
[Test Related Output]
=== Ended at 2013-01-20 20:05:17
=== location [{basic_SUITE,test2,13},
              {test_server,ts_tc,1635},
              {test_server,run_test_case_eval1,1182},
              {test_server,run_test_case_eval,1123}]
=== reason = bad argument in an arithmetic expression
  in function  basic_SUITE:test2/1 (basic_SUITE.erl, line 13)
  in call from test_server:ts_tc/3 (test_server.erl, line 1635)
  in call from test_server:run_test_case_eval1/6 (test_server.erl, line 1182)
  in call from test_server:run_test_case_eval/9 (test_server.erl, line 1123)
```

The log lets you know precisely what failed, and it is much more detailed than what we got in the Erlang shell. So, if you're a shell user, you'll find Common Test extremely painful to use. If you're a person more prone to using GUIs, then it will be more fun for you.

But enough wandering around pretty HTML files, let's see how to test with some more state.

NOTE   *If you ever feel like traveling back in time without the help of a time machine, download a version of Erlang prior to R15B and use Common Test with it. You'll be astonished to see that your browser and the logs' style brings you back to the late 1990s.*

Testing with State

As explained in Chapter 24, EUnit has these things called *fixtures*, where we give a test case some special instantiation (setup) and teardown code to be called before and after the case, respectively.

Common Test follows that concept. However, instead of having EUnit-style fixtures, it relies on two functions:

- The setup function, init_per_testcase/2
- The teardown function, end_per_testcase/2

To see how they are used, create a new test suite called state_SUITE (still under the *demo/* directory), and add the following code:

```
-module(state_SUITE).
-include_lib("common_test/include/ct.hrl").

-export([all/0, init_per_testcase/2, end_per_testcase/2]).
-export([ets_tests/1]).

all() -> [ets_tests].

init_per_testcase(ets_tests, Config) ->
    TabId = ets:new(account, [ordered_set, public]),
    ets:insert(TabId, {andy, 2131}),
    ets:insert(TabId, {david, 12}),
    ets:insert(TabId, {steve, 12943752}),
    [{table,TabId} | Config].

end_per_testcase(ets_tests, Config) ->
    ets:delete(?config(table, Config)).

ets_tests(Config) ->
    TabId = ?config(table, Config),
    [{david, 12}] = ets:lookup(TabId, david),
    steve = ets:last(TabId),
    true = ets:insert(TabId, {zachary, 99}),
    zachary = ets:last(TabId).
```

This is a little normal ETS test checking a few ordered_set concepts. What's interesting about it is the two new functions: init_per_testcase/2 and end_per_testcase/2. Both functions need to be exported in order to be called. If they are exported, the functions will be called for *all* test cases in a module. You can separate them based on the arguments. The first one is the name of the test case (as an atom), and the second one is the Config proplist that you can modify.

> **NOTE** *To read from Config, rather than using proplists:get_value/2, the Common Test include file has a ?config(Key, List) macro that returns the value matching the given key. The macro is a wrapper around proplists:get_value/2 and is documented as such, so you know you can deal with Config as a proplist without worrying about it ever breaking.*

As an example, if we had tests a, b, and c and wanted a setup and teardown function for only the first two tests, our init function might look like this:

```
init_per_testcase(a, Config) ->
    [{some_key, 124} | Config];
init_per_testcase(b, Config) ->
    [{other_key, duck} | Config];
init_per_testcase(_, Config) ->
    %% Ignore for all other cases.
    Config.
```

And we would handle the end_per_testcase/2 function similarly.

Looking back at state_SUITE, you can see the test case, but what's interesting is how we instantiate the ETS table. We don't specify an heir, and yet the tests run without a problem after the init function is finished.

As discussed in Chapter 25, ETS tables are usually owned by the process that started them. In this case, we leave the table as it is. If you run the tests, you'll see the suite succeeds.

What we can infer from this is that the init_per_testcase and end_per_testcase functions run in the same process as the test case itself. You can thus safely do things like set links or start tables within these functions without worrying about having your things breaking the way they would if they were running in different processes. What about errors in the test case? Fortunately, crashing in your test case won't stop Common Test from cleaning up and calling the end_per_testcase function, with the exception of kill exit signals.

So far, our work with Common Test is at least equal to, if not more than, what we can do with EUnit, at least in terms of flexibility. Although we don't get all the nice assertion macros, we have fancier reports, similar fixtures, and that private directory where we can write stuff from scratch. What more do we want?

If you end up feeling like outputting information to help you debug or just show progress in your tests, you'll quickly find out that io:format/1-2 prints only to the HTML logs, not to the Erlang shell. If you want to do both (with free timestamps included), use the function ct:pal/1-2. It works like io:format/1-2, but prints to both the shell and logs.

Test Groups

Right now, our test structure within a suite might look like this:

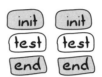

What if we have many test cases with similar needs in terms of some init functions, but some different parts in them? Well, the easy way to do it is to copy/paste and modify, but this will be a real pain to maintain. Moreover, what if we want to run many tests in parallel or in random order instead of one after the other? There's no easy way to do that based on what we've seen so far. This is pretty much the same kind of problem that could limit our use of EUnit.

To solve these issues, we have *test groups*. Common Test test groups allow us to regroup some tests hierarchically. Even more, they can regroup some groups within other groups, as shown here:

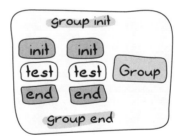

In this hierarchy, a group has its own initialization and termination functions, wrapping many tests or other groups. This allows us to define some common environment to a bunch of related tests, or even groups of other tests. For example, if half of your tests need to connect to a database with a given configuration, and the other half with another configuration, setting this configuration with different groups would be the most efficient way to do it.

Defining Test Groups

For this approach to work, we need test groups. First, we add a groups() function to declare all of the groups:

```
groups() -> ListOfGroups.
```

Here's what `ListOfGroups` should be:

```
[{GroupName, GroupProperties, GroupMembers}]
```

And in more detail, here's what this could look like:

```
[{test_case_street_gang,
  [],
  [simple_case, more_complex_case]}].
```

That's a tiny test case street gang. Here's a more complex one:

```
[{test_case_street_gang,
  [shuffle, sequence],
  [simple_case, more_complex_case,
   emotionally_complex_case,
   {group, name_of_another_test_group}]}].
```

This one specifies two properties: `shuffle` and `sequence`. We'll look at what they mean soon.

The example also shows a group including another group. This assumes that the groups() function might be a bit like this:

```
groups() ->
    [{test_case_street_gang,
      [shuffle, sequence],
      [simple_case, more_complex_case, emotionally_complex_case,
       {group, name_of_another_test_group}]},
     {name_of_another_test_group,
      [],
      [case1, case2, case3]}].
```

You can also define the group inline within another group:

```
[{test_case_street_gang,
  [shuffle, sequence],
  [simple_case, more_complex_case,
   emotionally_complex_case,
   {name_of_another_test_group,
    [],
    [case1, case2, case3]}
  ]}].
```

That's getting a bit complex, right? Read the examples carefully, and it should get simpler with time. Keep in mind that nested groups are not mandatory, and you can avoid them if you find them confusing.

But wait, how do you use such groups? By putting them in the all/0 function:

```
all() -> [some_case, {group, test_case_street_gang}, other_case].
```

This way, Common Test will be able to know whether it needs to run a single test case or a group of them.

Test Group Properties

The preceding examples used some test group properties, including shuffle, sequence, and an empty list. The following group properties are available:

empty list / no option

The test cases in the group are run one after the other. If a test fails, the others after it in the list are run.

shuffle

This runs the test in a random order. The random seed (the initialization value) used for the sequence will be printed in the HTML logs, in the form {A,B,C}. If a particular sequence of tests fails and you want to reproduce it, use that seed in the HTML logs and change the shuffle option to be {shuffle, {A,B,C}}. That way, you can reproduce random runs in their precise order if you ever need to do so.

parallel

The tests are run in different processes. Be careful, because if you forget to export the init_per_group and end_per_group functions, Common Test will silently ignore this option.

sequence

Using this option doesn't necessarily mean that the tests are run in order, but rather that if a test fails in the group's list, then all the other subsequent tests are skipped. This option can be combined with shuffle if you want any random test failing to stop the ones that follow.

{repeat, Times}

This repeats the group Times times. You could run the whole test case sequence in parallel nine times by using the group properties [parallel, {repeat, 9}]. Times can also have the value forever, although "forever" is a bit of a lie, as it can't defeat concepts such as hardware failure or heat death of the universe (ahem).

{repeat_until_any_fail, N}

This runs all the tests until one of them fails or they have been run N times. N can also be forever.

{repeat_until_all_fail, N}

This works the same as the preceding option, but the tests may run until all cases fail.

{repeat_until_any_succeed, N}

This is also the same as the preceding options, except the tests may run until at least one case succeeds.

{repeat_until_all_succeed, N}

I think you can guess what this one does, but just in case: It's the same as the preceding options, except that the test cases may run until they all succeed.

EVERY DAY I'M SHUFFLING
(test cases)

Honestly, that's quite a bit of content for test groups, and I feel an example would be appropriate here.

The Meeting Room

To use test groups, we'll create a meeting room-booking module:

```
-module(meeting).
-export([rent_projector/1, use_chairs/1, book_room/1,
         get_all_bookings/0, start/0, stop/0]).
-record(bookings, {projector, room, chairs}).

start() ->
    Pid = spawn(fun() -> loop(#bookings{}) end),
    register(?MODULE, Pid).

stop() -> ?MODULE ! stop.

rent_projector(Group) -> ?MODULE ! {projector, Group}.

book_room(Group) -> ?MODULE ! {room, Group}.

use_chairs(Group) -> ?MODULE ! {chairs, Group}.
```

These basic functions will call a central registry process. They will allow us to book the room, rent a projector, and put dibs on chairs. For the sake of the exercise, we're in a large organization with one hell of a corporate structure. Because of this, three different people are responsible for the projector, the room, and the chairs, but there is one central registry. Because of this structure, you can't book all items at once, but must do it by sending three different messages.

To know who booked what, we can send a message to the registry in order to get all the values:

```
get_all_bookings() ->
    Ref = make_ref(),
    ?MODULE ! {self(), Ref, get_bookings},
    receive
        {Ref, Reply} ->
            Reply
    end.
```

The registry itself looks like this:

```
loop(B = #bookings{}) ->
    receive
        stop -> ok;
        {From, Ref, get_bookings} ->
            From ! {Ref, [{room, B#bookings.room},
                          {chairs, B#bookings.chairs},
                          {projector, B#bookings.projector}]},
            loop(B);
        {room, Group} -> loop(B#bookings{room=Group});
        {chairs, Group} -> loop(B#bookings{chairs=Group});
        {projector, Group} -> loop(B#bookings{projector=Group})
    end.
```

And that's it.

To book everything for a successful meeting, we would need to successively call the functions:

```
1> c(meeting).
{ok,meeting}
2> meeting:start().
true
3> meeting:book_room(erlang_group).
{room,erlang_group}
4> meeting:rent_projector(erlang_group).
{projector,erlang_group}
5> meeting:use_chairs(erlang_group).
{chairs,erlang_group}
6> meeting:get_all_bookings().
[{room,erlang_group},
 {chairs,erlang_group},
 {projector,erlang_group}]
```

This doesn't seem right, though. You possibly have this lingering feeling that things could go wrong. In many cases, if we make the three calls fast enough, we should obtain everything we want without a problem. If two people do it at once and there are short pauses between the calls, it seems possible that two (or more) groups might try to rent the same equipment at the same time.

Oh no! Suddenly, the programmers might end up having the projector, while the board of directors has the room, and the human resources department managed to rent all of the chairs. All resources are tied up, but no one can do anything useful!

We won't worry about fixing that problem. Instead, we'll work on trying to demonstrate that it's present with a Common Test suite.

The suite, named *meeting_SUITE.erl*, will be based on the simple idea of trying to provoke a race condition that will mess up the registration. We'll have three test cases, each representing a group. Carla will represent women, Mark will represent men, and a dog will represent a group of animals that somehow decided it wanted to hold a meeting with human-made tools:

```erlang
-module(meeting_SUITE).
-include_lib("common_test/include/ct.hrl").
    ...
carla(_Config) ->
    meeting:book_room(women),
    timer:sleep(10),
    meeting:rent_projector(women),
    timer:sleep(10),
    meeting:use_chairs(women).

mark(_Config) ->
    meeting:rent_projector(men),
    timer:sleep(10),
    meeting:use_chairs(men),
    timer:sleep(10),
    meeting:book_room(men).

dog(_Config) ->
    meeting:rent_projector(animals),
    timer:sleep(10),
    meeting:use_chairs(animals),
    timer:sleep(10),
    meeting:book_room(animals).
```

We don't care whether these tests actually test something. They are just there to use the meeting module (which we'll put in place for the tests soon) and try to generate wrong reservations.

To find out if we have a race condition between all of these tests, we'll use the meeting:get_all_bookings() function in a fourth and final test:

```erlang
all_same_owner(_Config) ->
    [{_, Owner}, {_, Owner}, {_, Owner}] = meeting:get_all_bookings().
```

This one does pattern matching on the owners of all different objects that can be booked, trying to see whether they are actually booked by the same owner. This is a desirable thing if we are looking for efficient meetings.

How do we move from having four test cases in a file to something that works? We'll need to make clever use of test groups. First, because we want a race condition, we know we'll need to have a bunch of tests running in parallel. Second, given we have a requirement to see the problem from the race condition, we'll need to either run all_same_owner many times during the whole debacle or only after it, to look with despair at the aftermath.

I chose the latter:

```
all() -> [{group, clients}, all_same_owner].

groups() -> [{clients, [parallel, {repeat, 10}], [carla, mark, dog]}].
```

This creates a clients group of tests, with the individual tests being carla, mark, and dog. They're going to run in parallel, 10 times each.

You see that we include the group in the all/0 function, and then put all_same_owner. That's because, by default, Common Test will run the tests and groups in all/0 in the order they were declared.

But wait! We forgot to start and stop the meeting process itself. To do that, we'll need to have a way to keep a process alive for all tests, regardless of whether it's in the clients group. The solution is to nest things one level deeper, in another group:

```
all() -> [{group, session}].

groups() -> [{session, [], [{group, clients}, all_same_owner]},
            {clients, [parallel, {repeat, 10}], [carla, mark, dog]}].

init_per_group(session, Config) ->
    meeting:start(),
    Config;
init_per_group(_, Config) ->
    Config.

end_per_group(session, _Config) ->
    meeting:stop();
end_per_group(_, _Config) ->
    ok.
```

We use the init_per_group and end_per_group functions to specify that the session group (which now runs {group, clients} and all_same_owner) will work with an active meeting. Don't forget to export the two setup and teardown functions; otherwise, nothing will run in parallel.

All right, let's run the tests and see what we get:

```
1> ct_run:run_test([{suite, meeting_SUITE}]).
... <snip> ...
Common Test: Running make in test directories...
... <snip> ...
TEST INFO: 1 test(s), 1 suite(s)
Testing ct.meeting.meeting_SUITE: Starting test (with repeated test cases)
- - - - - - - - - - - - - - - - - - - - - - - - - -
meeting_SUITE:all_same_owner failed on line 50
Reason: {badmatch,[{room,men},{chairs,women},{projector,women}]}
- - - - - - - - - - - - - - - - - - - - - - - - - -
Testing ct.meeting.meeting_SUITE: *** FAILED *** test case 31
Testing ct.meeting.meeting_SUITE: TEST COMPLETE, 30 ok, 1 failed of 31 test cases
... <snip> ...
ok
```

Good! We have a badmatch with three tuples with different items owned by different people. Moreover, the output tells us it's the all_same_owner test that failed. I think that's a pretty good sign that all_same_owner crashed as planned.

If you look at the HTML log, you'll be able to see all the runs with the exact test that failed and for what reason. Click the test name, and you'll get the right test run.

NOTE *An important thing to know about test groups is that while the init functions of test cases run in the same process as the test case, the init functions of groups run in processes distinct from the tests. This means that whenever you initialize actors that get linked to the process that spawned them, you must make sure to first unlink them. In the case of ETS tables, you need to define an heir to make sure it doesn't disappear. This applies to all other items that are attached to a process, such as sockets and file descriptors.*

Test Suites Redux

Can we use our test suites in a way that is better than nesting groups and manipulating how we run things in terms of hierarchy? Not really, but even so, we'll add another level with the test suite itself:

We have two additional functions: init_per_suite(Config) and end_per_suite(Config). These, like all the other init and end functions, aim to give more control over initialization of data and processes.

The init_per_suite/1 and end_per_suite/1 functions will run only once, respectively, before and after all of the groups or test cases. They will be useful when dealing with general state and dependencies that will be required for all tests. This can include manually starting applications you depend on, for example.

Test Specifications

There's something you might have found pretty annoying if you looked at your test directory after running tests: a ton of files scattered around the directory for your logs—CSS files, HTML logs, directories, test run histories, and so on. It would be pretty neat to have a nice way to store these files in a single directory.

Another issue is that so far we've run tests from a test suite. We have not seen a good way to do it with many test suites at once, or even ways to run only one or two cases or groups from a suite (or from many suites).

Of course, if I'm bringing up these issues, it's because I have a solution for them. There are ways to handle them from both the command line and the Erlang shell, and you can find them in the documentation for ct_run (*http://www.erlang.org/doc/man/ct_run.html*). However, instead of going into ways to manually specify everything for each time you run the tests, we'll employ *test specifications.*

Test specifications are special files that let you detail everything about how you want to have the tests run, and they work with the Erlang shell and the command line. The test specification can be put in a file with any extension you want (although I personally fancy *.spec* files).

Specification File Contents

The spec files will contain Erlang tuples, much like a consult file (a file containing Erlang terms, which can be parsed by using file:consult/1). Here are some of the items a spec file can contain:

{include, IncludeDirectories}
> When Common Test automatically compiles suites, this option lets you specify where it should look for include files in order to make sure they are there. The IncludeDirectories value must be a string (list) or a list of strings (list of lists).

{logdir, LoggingDirectory}
> When logging, all logs should be moved to the LoggingDirectory, a string. Note that the directory must exist before the tests are run; otherwise, Common Test will complain.

{suites, Directory, Suites}

    This finds the given suites in Directory. Suites can be an atom (some_SUITE), a list of atoms, or the atom all to run all the suites in a directory.

{skip_suites, Directory, Suites, Comment}

    This subtracts a list of suites from those previously declared and skips them. The Comment argument is a string explaining why you decided to skip them. This comment will be put in the final HTML logs. The tables will show, in yellow, "SKIPPED: *Reason*," where *Reason* is whatever Comment contained.

{groups, Directory, Suite, Groups}

    This is an option to pick only a few groups from a given suite. The Groups variable can be a single atom (the group name) or all for all groups. The value can also be more complex, letting you override the group definitions inside groups() within the test case by picking a value like {GroupName, [parallel]}, which will override GroupName's options for parallel, without needing to recompile tests.

{groups, Directory, Suite, Groups, {cases,Cases}}

    This option is similar to the previous one, but it lets you specify some test cases to include in the tests with Cases, which can be a single case name (an atom), a list of names, or the atom all.

{skip_groups, Directory, Suite, Groups, Comment}

    This command was added in R15B and documented in R15B01. It allows you to skip test groups, much like the skip_suites for suites.

{skip_groups, Directory, Suite, Groups, {cases,Cases}, Comment}

    This is similar to the previous option, but with specific test cases to skip on top of it. It also has been available only since R15B.

{cases, Directory, Suite, Cases}

    This runs specific test cases from a given suite. Cases can be an atom, a list of atoms, or all.

{skip_cases, Directory, Suite, Cases, Comment}

    This is similar to skip_suites, except you choose specific test cases to avoid with this one.

{alias, Alias, Directory}

    Because it gets very annoying to write all these directory names (especially if they're full names), Common Test lets you replace them with aliases (atoms). This is pretty useful way to be concise.

Creating a Spec File

Let's try a simple example. First, add a *ct/logs/* directory, on the same level as *ct/demo/*. Unsurprisingly, that's where our Common Test logs will be moved.

Here's a possible test specification for all our tests so far, saved under the imaginative name *spec.spec*:

```
{alias, demo, "./demo/"}.
{alias, meeting, "./meeting/"}.
{logdir, "./logs/"}.

{suites, meeting, all}.
{suites, demo, all}.
{skip_cases, demo, basic_SUITE, test2, "This test fails on purpose"}.
```

This spec file declares two aliases: demo and meeting, which point to the two test directories we have. We put the logs inside *ct/logs/*, our newest directory. Then we ask to run all suites in the *meeting* directory, which, coincidentally, is the meeting_SUITE suite.

Next on the list are the two suites inside the *demo* directory. We ask to skip test2 from the basic_SUITE suite, given it contains a division by zero that we know will fail.

Running Tests with a Spec File

To run the tests, you can use ct_run -spec spec.spec (or run_test for versions of Erlang before R15) from the command line, or you can use the function ct:run_test([{spec, "spec.spec"}]). from the Erlang shell:

```
Common Test: Running make in test directories...
... <snip> ...
TEST INFO: 2 test(s), 3 suite(s)

Testing ct.meeting: Starting test (with repeated test cases)


- - - - - - - - - - - - - - - - - - - - - - - - - - -
meeting_SUITE:all_same_owner failed on line 51
Reason: {badmatch,[{room,men},{chairs,women},{projector,women}]}
- - - - - - - - - - - - - - - - - - - - - - - - - - -

Testing ct.meeting: *** FAILED *** test case 31
Testing ct.meeting: TEST COMPLETE, 30 ok, 1 failed of 31 test cases

Testing ct.demo: Starting test, 3 test cases
Testing ct.demo: TEST COMPLETE, 2 ok, 0 failed, 1 skipped of 3 test cases

Updating /Users/ferd/code/self/learn-you-some-erlang/ct/logs/index.html... done
Updating /Users/ferd/code/self/learn-you-some-erlang/ct/logs/all_runs.html... done
```

If you take the time to look at the logs, you'll see two directories for the different test runs. One of them will have a failure—that's the meeting that failed as expected. The other one will have one success and one skipped case, of the form *1 (1/0)*. Generally, the format is *TotalSkipped (IntentionallySkipped/SkippedDueToError)*. In this case, the skip happened from the spec file, so it goes on the left. If it happened because one of the many init functions failed, then it would be on the right.

Common Test is starting to look like a pretty decent testing framework, but it would be nice to be able to use our distributed programming knowledge and apply it.

Large-Scale Testing

Common Test supports having distributed tests. Before going hog wild and writing a bunch of code, let's see what's offered. Well, there isn't *that* much. The gist of it is that Common Test lets you start tests on many different nodes, but also has ways to dynamically start these nodes and have them watch each other.

As such, the distributed features of Common Test are really useful when you have large test suites that should be run in parallel on many nodes. This is often worth the effort to save time or because the code will run in production environments that are on different computers—automated tests that reflect this are desired.

When tests go distributed, Common Test requires the presence of a central node (the *CT master*) in charge of all the other nodes. Everything will be directed from there, from starting nodes, ordering tests to be run, gathering logs, and so on.

The first step to get things going that way is to expand our test specifications so they become distributed. We're going to add a couple new tuples: {node, NodeAlias, NodeName} and {init, NodeAlias, Options}.

{node, NodeAlias, NodeName} is much like {alias, AliasAtom, Directory} for test suites, groups, and cases, except it's used for node names. Both NodeAlias and NodeName need to be atoms. This tuple is especially useful when NodeName needs to be a long node name, since it would be quite annoying to have it duplicated in its entire form dozens of times over a given spec file.

{init, NodeAlias, Options} is a more complex tuple. This is the option that lets you start nodes. NodeAlias can be a single node alias or a list of many of them. The Options are those available to the ct_slave module.

Here are a few of the options available:

{username, UserName} and {password, Password}

Using the host part of the node given by NodeAlias, Common Test will try to connect to the given host over SSH (on port 22) using the username and password, and run from there.

{startup_functions, [{M,F,A}]}

This option defines a list of functions to be called as soon as the other node has booted.

{erl_flags, String}

This sets standard flags that you would want to pass to the erl application when you start it. For example, if you wanted to start a node with erl -env ERL_LIBS ../ -config conf_file, the option would be {erl_flags, "-env ERL_LIBS ../ -config config_file"}.

{monitor_master, true | false}

If the CT master stops running and this option is set to true, the slave node will also be taken down. I recommend using this option if you're spawning the remote nodes; otherwise, they will keep running in the background if the master dies. Moreover, if you run tests again, Common Test will be able to connect to these nodes, and there will be some state attached to them.

{boot_timeout, Seconds}, {init_timeout, Seconds}, and {startup_timeout, Seconds}

These three options let you wait for different parts of the starting of a remote node. The boot timeout is about how long it takes before the node becomes pingable, with a default value of 3 seconds. The init timeout is an internal timer where the new remote node calls back the CT master to say that it's up. By default, it lasts 1 second. Finally, the startup timeout tells Common Test how long to wait for the functions you defined earlier as part of the startup_functions tuple.

{kill_if_fail, true | false}

This option will react to one of the three preceding timeouts. If any of them are triggered, Common Test will abort the connection, skip tests, and so on, but not necessarily kill the node, unless the option is set to true. Fortunately, that's the default value.

NOTE *All these options are provided by the ct_slave module. It is possible to define your own module to start slave nodes, as long as it respects the right interface.*

So, we have a lot of options for remote nodes, which contributes to giving Common Test its distributed power. You're able to boot nodes with about as much control as what you would get doing it by hand in the shell. Still, there are more options for distributed tests, although they're not for booting nodes:

```
{include, Nodes, IncludeDirs}
{logdir, Nodes, LogDir}
{suites, Nodes, DirectoryOrAlias, Suites}
{groups, Nodes, DirectoryOrAlias, Suite, Groups}
{groups, Nodes, DirectoryOrAlias, Suite, GroupSpec, {cases,Cases}}
{cases, Nodes, DirectoryOrAlias, Suite, Cases}
```

```
{skip_suites, Nodes, DirectoryOrAlias, Suites, Comment}
{skip_cases, Nodes, DirectoryOrAlias, Suite, Cases, Comment}
```

These are similar to the options we've already seen, except that they can optionally take a node argument to add more detail. That way, you can decide to run some suites on a given node, others on different nodes, and so on. This could be useful when doing system testing with different nodes running different environments or parts of the system (such as databases or external applications).

Creating a Distributed Spec File

As a simple way to see how distributed testing works, let's turn the previous *spec.spec* file into a distributed one. Copy it as *dist.spec*, and then change it to look like this:

```
{node, a, 'a@ferdmbp.local'}.
{node, b, 'b@ferdmbp.local'}.

{init, [a,b], [{node_start, [{monitor_master, true}]}]}.

{alias, demo, "./demo/"}.
{alias, meeting, "./meeting/"}.

{logdir, [all_nodes, master], "./logs/"}.

{suites, [b], meeting, all}.
{suites, [a], demo, all}.
{skip_cases, [a], demo, basic_SUITE, test2, "This test fails on purpose"}.
```

In this version, we define two slave nodes, a and b, that need to be started for the tests. They do nothing special but make sure to die if the master dies. The aliases for directories remain the same as they were.

The logdir values are interesting. We did not declare a node alias as all_nodes or master, but yet, here they are. The all_nodes alias stands for all non-master nodes for Common Test; master stands for the master node itself. To truly include all nodes, [all_nodes, master] is required. (There's no clear explanation as to why these names were picked.)

The reason we used these logdir values is that Common Test will generate logs (and directories) for each of the slave nodes, and it will also generate a master set of logs, referring to the slave ones. We don't want any of these in directories other than *logs/*. Note that the logs for the slave nodes will be stored on each of the slave nodes

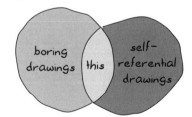

individually. In that case, unless all nodes share the same filesystem, the HTML links in the master's logs won't work, and you'll need to access each of the nodes to get their respective logs.

Last of all are the suites and skip_cases entries. They're pretty much the same as the previous ones, but adapted for each node. This way, you can skip some entries only on given nodes (which you know might be missing libraries or dependencies), or maybe more intensive ones where the hardware isn't up to the task.

Running Distributed Tests

To run distributed tests, we must start a distributed node with -name and use ct_master to run the suites (there is no way to run such tests using ct_run.):

```
$ erl -name ct
Erlang R15B (erts-5.9) [source] [64-bit] [smp:4:4] [async-threads:0] [hipe] [kernel-poll:false]

Eshell V5.9  (abort with ^G)
(ct@ferdmbp.local)1> ct_master:run("dist.spec").
=== Master Logdir ===
/Users/ferd/code/self/learn-you-some-erlang/ct/logs
=== Master Logger process started ===
<0.46.0>
Node 'a@ferdmbp.local' started successfully with callback ct_slave
Node 'b@ferdmbp.local' started successfully with callback ct_slave
=== Cookie ===
'PMIYERCHJZNZGSRJPVRK'
=== Starting Tests ===
Tests starting on: ['b@ferdmbp.local','a@ferdmbp.local']
=== Test Info ===
Starting test(s) on 'b@ferdmbp.local'...
=== Test Info ===
Starting test(s) on 'a@ferdmbp.local'...
=== Test Info ===
Test(s) on node 'a@ferdmbp.local' finished.
=== Test Info ===
Test(s) on node 'b@ferdmbp.local' finished.
=== TEST RESULTS ===
a@ferdmbp.local_____finished_ok
b@ferdmbp.local_____finished_ok

=== Info ===
Updating log files
Updating /Users/ferd/code/self/learn-you-some-erlang/ct/logs/index.html... done
Updating /Users/ferd/code/self/learn-you-some-erlang/ct/logs/all_runs.html... done
Logs in /Users/ferd/code/self/learn-you-some-erlang/ct/logs refreshed!
=== Info ===
Refreshing logs in "/Users/ferd/code/self/learn-you-some-erlang/ct/logs"... ok
[{"dist.spec",ok}]
```

Note that Common Test will show all results as ok whether or not the tests actually succeeded. That is because ct_master shows only if it could contact all the nodes. The results themselves are actually stored on each individual node.

Also note that Common Test shows that it started nodes, and with what cookies it did so. If you try running tests again without first terminating the master, the following warnings are shown instead:

```
WARNING: Node 'a@ferdmbp.local' is alive but has node_start option
WARNING: Node 'b@ferdmbp.local' is alive but has node_start option
```

That's all right. It only means that Common Test is able to connect to remote nodes, but found no use for calling our init tuple from the test specification, given the nodes are already alive. There is no need for Common Test to actually start any remote nodes it will run tests on, but I usually find it useful to do so.

That's really the gist of distributed spec files. Of course, you can get into more complex cases, where you set up more complicated clusters and write amazing distributed tests. But as the tests become more complex, you can have less confidence in their ability to successfully demonstrate the properties of your software, simply because the tests themselves might contain more errors as they become more convoluted.

Integrating EUnit Within Common Test

Because sometimes EUnit is the best tool for the job, and sometimes Common Test is, it might be desirable for you to include one into the other.

While it's difficult to include Common Test suites within EUnit ones, the opposite is quite easy. The trick is that when you call eunit:test(SomeModule), the function can return either ok when things work or error in case of any failure.

This means that to integrate EUnit tests into a Common Test suite, all you need to do is have a function a bit like this:

```
run_eunit(_Config) ->
    ok = eunit:test(TestsToRun).
```

And all your EUnit tests that can be found by the TestsToRun description will be run. If there's a failure, it will appear in your Common Test logs, and you'll be able to read the output to see what went wrong. It's that simple.

Is There More?

You bet there's more. Common Test is a very complex beast. There are ways to add configuration files for some variables; add hooks that run at many points during the test executions; use callbacks on events during the suites; and use modules to test over SSH (ct_ssh), telnet (ct_telnet), SNMP (ct_snmp), and FTP (ct_ftp).

This chapter only scratched the surface, but it is enough to get you started if you want to explore Common Test in more depth. A more complete document is the Common Test User's Guide, which comes with Erlang/OTP (*http://www.erlang.org/doc/apps/common_test/users_guide.html*). As I mentioned at the beginning of this chapter, the guide is hard to read on its own, but understanding the material covered in this chapter will help you figure out the documentation, without a doubt.

29

MNESIA AND THE ART OF REMEMBERING

You're the closest friend of a man with many friends. He has known some of those friends for a very long time, as have you. These friends come from all around the world, ranging from Sicily to New York. They pay their respects, and care about you and your friend, and you both care about them back.

In exceptional circumstances, they ask for favors because you're people of power and trust. They're your good friends, so you oblige. However, friendship has a cost. Each favor realized is duly noted, and at some point in the future, you may ask for a service in return.

You always keep your promises—you're a pillar of reliability. That's why they call your friend *boss*, and they call you *consigliere*. You're helping to lead one of the most respected Mafia families.

However, it becomes a pain to remember all your friendships, and as your areas of influence grow across the world, it is increasingly harder to keep track of what friends owe to you and what you owe to friends.

Because you're a helpful counselor, you decide to upgrade the traditional system from notes secretly kept in various places to something using Erlang.

At first, you figure using ETS and DETS tables will be perfect. However, when you're out on an overseas trip away from the boss, it becomes somewhat difficult to keep things synchronized.

You could write a complex layer on top of your ETS and DETS tables to keep everything in check. You could do that, but being human, you know that you might make mistakes and write buggy software. Such mistakes are to be avoided when friendship is so important, so you look online to find how to make sure your system works correctly.

This is when you start reading this chapter, which explains Mnesia, an Erlang distributed database built to solve such problems.

What's Mnesia?

Mnesia is a layer built on top of ETS and DETS to add a lot of functionality to those two databases, which were introduced in Chapter 25. It mostly contains features that many developers might end up creating on their own if they wanted to use ETS and DETS intensively. Mnesia allows you to write to both ETS and DETS automatically, to have both DETS's persistence and ETS's performance, and to be able to replicate the database to many different Erlang nodes automatically.

Another useful feature provided by Mnesia is *transactions*. Basically, transactions let you perform multiple operations on one or more tables as if the process doing them were the only one to have access to the tables—something ETS doesn't allow. This proves vital when you need to have concurrent operations that mix read and writes as part of a single unit. One example would be reading in the database to see if a username is taken, and then creating the user if that name is available. Without transactions, looking inside the table for the value and then registering it counts as two distinct operations that can be messing with each other. Given the right timing, more than one process might believe it has the right to create the unique user, which will lead to a lot of confusion. Transactions solve this problem by allowing many operations to act as a single unit.

Mnesia is pretty much the only full-featured database available that will natively store and return any Erlang term out of the box (at the time of this writing). The downside is that it will inherit all the limitations of DETS tables in some modes, such as not being able to store more than 2GB of data for a single table on disk (but this can be bypassed with a feature called *fragmentation*, described at *http://www.erlang.org/doc/apps/mnesia/ Mnesia_chap5.html#id75194*).

If we consider the CAP theorem (discussed in Chapter 26), Mnesia sits on the CP side, rather than the AP side. This means that it won't do eventual consistency and will react rather badly to netsplits in some cases, but it will give you strong consistency guarantees if you expect the network to be reliable (and you sometimes shouldn't).

Mnesia is not meant to replace your standard SQL database, nor is it meant to handle terabytes of data across a large number of data centers, as often claimed by the giants of the NoSQL world. Mnesia is made for smaller amounts of data, on a limited number of nodes. While it is possible to use it on a ton of nodes, most people find that their practical limits center around 10 or so. You will want to use Mnesia when you know it will run on a fixed number of nodes, have an idea of how much data it will require, and know that you will primarily need to access your data from Erlang in ways ETS and DETS would allow in usual circumstances.

Just how close to Erlang is it? Mnesia is centered on the idea of using a record to define a table's structure. Each table can store a bunch of similar records, and anything that goes in a record can be stored in an Mnesia table, including atoms, pids, references, and so on.

What Should the Store Store?

The first step in using Mnesia is to figure out the information you'll need and the table structure you'll use for storing that information.

The Data to Store

For our Mafia friend-tracking application (which I decided to name `mafiapp`), the information we might want to store includes the following:

- The friend's name, to know who we're talking to when we ask for a service or provide one.

- The friend's contact information, to know how to reach that friend. This might take various forms, such as an email address, a cell phone number, or even notes regarding where that person likes to hang out.

- Additional information, such as when the person was born, occupation, hobbies, special traits, and so on.

- A unique expertise—our friend's forte. This field stands on its own because it's something we want to know explicitly. If someone's expertise is in cooking, and we're in dire need of a caterer, we know who to call. If we are in trouble and need to disappear for a while, we may look for friends who are pilots, camouflage experts, or excellent magicians.

Then we need to think about the services being exchanged. What will we want to know about them? Here are a few items:

- Who gave the service. Maybe it's you, the *consigliere*. Maybe it's the *padrino*. Maybe it's a friend of a friend, on your behalf. Maybe it's someone who then becomes your friend. We need to know.

- Who received the service.

- When the service was given. It's generally useful to be able to refresh someone's memory, especially when asking for a favor payback.

- Details regarding the services. It's much nicer (and more intimidating) to remember every tiny detail of the services we gave, as well as the date.

Table Structure

As I mentioned in the previous section, Mnesia is based on records and tables (ETS and DETS). To be exact, you can define an Erlang record and tell Mnesia to turn its definition into a table.

For example, suppose we're working on a recipe app, and we decided to have our record take this form:

```
-record(recipe, {name, ingredients=[], instructions=[]}).
```

We can then tell Mnesia to create a recipe table, which would store any number of #recipe{} records as table rows. We could have a recipe for pizza noted as follows:

```
#recipe{name=pizza,
        ingredients=[sauce,tomatoes,meat,dough],
        instructions=["order by phone"]}
```

And a recipe for soup might look like this:

```
#recipe{name=soup,
        ingredients=["who knows"],
        instructions=["open unlabeled can, hope for the best"]}
```

We could insert both of these in the recipe table, as is. We could then fetch the same records from the table and use them in the same way as any other records.

The primary key—the unique field by which it is the fastest to look up things in a table—would be the recipe name. That's because name is the first item in the record definition for #recipe{}. You'll also notice that in the pizza recipe, we use atoms as ingredients, and in the soup recipe, we use a string. As opposed to SQL tables, Mnesia tables *have no built-in type constraints*, as long as you respect the structure of the table itself (all entries in an Mnesia table must be the same kind of record, or tuples of the same size with the same first element).

So, how should we represent our friends and services information for our mafia application? Maybe as one table doing everything?

```
-record(friends, {name,
                   contact=[],
                   info=[],
                   expertise,
                   service=[]}). % {To, From, Date, Description} for services?
```

But this isn't the best choice possible. Nesting the data for services within friend-related data means that adding or modifying service-related information will require us to change friends at the same time. This might be annoying, especially since services imply at least two people. For each service, we would need to fetch the records for two friends and update them, even if there is no friend-specific information that needs to be modified.

A more flexible model is to use one table for each kind of data we need to store:

```
-record(mafiapp_friends, {name,
                          contact=[],
                          info=[],
                          expertise}).
-record(mafiapp_services, {from,
                           to,
                           date,
                           description}).
```

Having two tables should give us all the flexibility we need to search for information and modify it, with little overhead.

DON'T DRINK TOO MUCH KOOL-AID

You'll notice that I prefixed both the `friends` and `services` records with `mafiapp_`. While records are defined locally within our module, Mnesia tables are global to all the nodes that will be part of its cluster. This implies a high potential for name clashes if you're not careful. Therefore, it is a good idea to manually namespace your tables.

From Record to Table

Now that we know what we want to store, the next logical step is to decide how we're going to store it. Remember that Mnesia is built using ETS and DETS tables. This gives us two means of storage: on disk or in memory. We need to pick a strategy!

Here are the options:

ram_copies

This option makes it so all data is stored exclusively in ETS, so in memory only. Memory should be limited to a theoretical 4GB (and practically around 3GB) for VMs compiled on 32 bits, but this limit is pushed further away on 64-bit (and half-word) VMs, assuming there is more than 4GB of memory available.

disc_only_copies

This option means that the data is stored only in DETS, on disk only, and the storage is limited to DETS's 2GB limit.

disc_copies

This option means that the data is stored both in ETS and on disk, so both in memory and on the hard disk. disc_copies tables are not restricted by DETS limits, as Mnesia uses a complex system of transaction logs and checkpoints that allow creating a disk-based backup of the table in memory.

For our current application, we will go with with disc_copies. The relationships we built with our friends need to be long-lasting, so it makes sense to be able to store things persistently. It would be quite annoying to wake up after a power failure, only to find out you've lost all the friendships you worked so hard to make. "Why just not use disc_only_copies?" you might ask. Well, having copies in memory is usually nice when we want to do more somewhat complex queries and searches, given they can be done without needing to access the disk, which is often the slowest part of any computer memory access, especially if it's a hard disk.

There's another hurdle on our path to filling the database with our precious data. Because of how ETS and DETS work, we need to define a table type. The types available bear the same definition as their ETS and DETS counterparts. The options are set, bag, and ordered_set, although ordered_set is not supported for disc_only_copies tables. (Tables of type duplicate_bag are not available for any of the storage types.) If you don't remember what these types do, look them up in Chapter 25.

The good news is that we're pretty much finished deciding how we're going to store things. The bad news is that there are still more things to understand about Mnesia before truly getting started.

Of Mnesia Schemas and Tables

Although Mnesia can work fine on isolated nodes, it does support distribution and replication to many nodes. To know how to store tables on disk, how to load them, and which other nodes they should be synchronized with, Mnesia needs to have a *schema* that holds all that information.

By default, Mnesia creates a schema directly in memory when it's started. It works fine for tables that need to live in RAM only, but when your schema needs to survive across many VM restarts, on all the nodes that are part of the Mnesia cluster, things get a bit more complex.

Mnesia depends on the schema, but Mnesia should also create the schema. This sets up a weird situation where the schema needs to be created by Mnesia without running Mnesia first! Fortunately, it's rather simple to deal with this in practice. We just need to call the function  `mnesia:create_schema(ListOfNodes)` *before* starting Mnesia. It will create a bunch of files on each node, storing all the table information required. You don't need to be connected to the other nodes when calling the function, but the nodes need to be running; the function will set up the connections and get everything working for you.

By default, the schema will be created in the current working directory, wherever the Erlang node is running. To change this, the Mnesia application has a `dir` variable that can be set to pick where the schema will be stored. You can start your node as `erl -name SomeName -mnesia dir` *where/to/store/the/db*, or set it dynamically with `application:set_env(mnesia, dir, "`*where/to/store/the/db*`")`.

NOTE   *A schema may fail to be created because one already exists, Mnesia is running on one of the nodes the schema should be on, you can't write to the directory Mnesia wants to write to, or another common file-handling problem occurred.*

Once the schema has been created, we can start Mnesia and begin creating tables. The function `mnesia:create_table/2` is what we need to use for this task. It takes two arguments: the table name and a list of options. The following are some of the options available:

{attributes, List}
This is a list of all the items in a table. By default, it takes the form [*key, value*], meaning you would need a record of the form *-record(TableName, {key,val}).* to work. Pretty much everyone cheats a little and uses a special construct (a compiler-supported macro) that extracts the element names from a record. The construct looks like a function call. To do it with our friends record, we would pass it as {attributes, record_info(fields, mafiapp_friends)}.

{disc_copies, NodeList}, {disc_only_copies, NodeList}, and {ram_copies, NodeList}
This is where you specify how to store the tables, as explained in the previous section. Note that you can have many of these options present at once. As an example, you could define a table to be stored on disk and RAM on your master node, only in RAM on all of the slaves, and only on disk on a dedicated backup node by using all three of the options.

{index, ListOfIntegers}
Mnesia tables let you have *indexes* on top of the basic ETS and DETS functionality. This is useful in cases where you are planning to build searches on record fields other than the primary key. As an example, our friends table will need an index for the expertise field. We can declare such an index as {index, [#mafiapp_friends.expertise]}. In general—and

this is true for many, many databases—you want to build indexes only on fields where the data is not too similar across all records. On a table with hundreds of thousands of entries, if your index at best splits your table in two groups to sort through, indexing will take a lot of resources (RAM and processor time) for very little benefit. An index that would split the same table in N groups of 10 or fewer elements, as an example, would be more useful for the resources it uses. Note that you do not need to put an index on the first field of the record (the second element of the tuple), as this is done for you by default.

{record_name, Atom}

This is useful if you want to have a table that has a different name than the one your record uses. However, using this option forces you to use different functions to operate on the table than those commonly used. I don't recommend using this option, unless you really know you need it.

{type, Type}

Type can be set, ordered_set, or bag, which are the same as the types used by ETS and described in Chapter 25.

{local_content, true | false}

By default, all Mnesia tables have this option set to false. You should leave it that way if you want the tables and their data replicated on all nodes that are part of the schema (and those specified in the disc_copies, disc_only_copies, and ram_copies options). Setting this option to true will create all the tables on all the nodes, but the content will be the local content only; nothing will be shared. In this case, Mnesia becomes an engine to initialize similar empty tables on many nodes.

Here's the sequence of events that can happen when setting up your Mnesia schema and tables:

- Starting Mnesia for the first time creates a schema in memory, which is good for ram_copies. Other kinds of tables won't work with it.
- If you create a schema manually before starting Mnesia (or after stopping it), you will be able to create tables that sit on disk.
- Start Mnesia, and you can then start creating tables. Tables can't be created while Mnesia is not running.

NOTE *There is another way to do things. Whenever you have an Mnesia node running and tables created that you would want to port to disk, the function mnesia:change_table_copy_type(Table, Node, NewType) can be called to move a table to disk. More particularly, if you forgot to create the schema on disk, by calling mnesia:change_table_copy_type(schema, node(), disc_copies), you'll be taking your RAM schema and turning it into a disk schema.*

Now it's time to get started with our application and see Mnesia in action.

Creating Tables

We'll handle creating the application and its tables with some weak TDD-style programming, using Common Test. Now you might dislike the idea of TDD, but stay with me, we'll do it in a relaxed manner, just as a way to guide our design more than anything else. None of that "run tests to make sure they fail" business (although you can feel free to do it that way). That we have tests in the end will just be a nice side effect, not an objective in itself. We'll mostly care about defining the interface of how mafiapp should behave and look, without doing it all from the Erlang shell. The tests won't even be distributed, but this example will still be a decent opportunity to get some practical use out of Common Test while learning Mnesia at the same time.

For this example, create a directory named *mafiapp-1.0.0* following the standard OTP structure:

```
ebin/
logs/
src/
test/
```

Installing the Database

We'll start by figuring out how we want to install the database. Because there is a need for a schema and initializing tables the first time around, we'll set up all the tests with an installation function that will ideally install things in Common Test's *priv_dir* directory. Let's begin with a basic test suite, mafiapp_SUITE, stored under the *test/* directory:

```erlang
-module(mafiapp_SUITE).
-include_lib("common_test/include/ct.hrl").
-export([init_per_suite/1, end_per_suite/1,
         all/0]).
all() -> [].

init_per_suite(Config) ->
    Priv = ?config(priv_dir, Config),
    application:set_env(mnesia, dir, Priv),
    mafiapp:install([node()]),
    application:start(mnesia),
    application:start(mafiapp),
    Config.

end_per_suite(_Config) ->
    application:stop(mnesia),
    ok.
```

This test suite doesn't have any tests yet, but it gives us our first specification of how things should be done. We first pick where to put the Mnesia schema and database files by setting the dir variable to the value of priv_dir. This will put each instance of the schema and database in a private directory generated with Common Test, guaranteeing that we will not have problems and clashes from earlier test runs.

We named the installation function install and gave it a list of nodes on which to install the records. Using this type of list is generally a better way to do things than hardcoding the information within the install function, as it is more flexible. Once this is done, Mnesia and mafiapp should be started.

We can now get into *src/mafiapp.erl* and start figuring out how the install function should work. First, we'll need to take the record definitions we had earlier and bring them back in:

```erlang
-module(mafiapp).
-export([install/1]).

-record(mafiapp_friends, {name,
                          contact=[],
                          info=[],
                          expertise}).
-record(mafiapp_services, {from,
                           to,
                           date,
                           description}).
```

This looks good enough. Here's the install/1 function:

```erlang
install(Nodes) ->
    ok = mnesia:create_schema(Nodes),
    application:start(mnesia),
    mnesia:create_table(mafiapp_friends,
                        [{attributes, record_info(fields, mafiapp_friends)},
                         {index, [#mafiapp_friends.expertise]},
                         {disc_copies, Nodes}]),
    mnesia:create_table(mafiapp_services,
                        [{attributes, record_info(fields, mafiapp_services)},
                         {index, [#mafiapp_services.to]},
                         {disc_copies, Nodes},
                         {type, bag}]),
    application:stop(mnesia).
```

First, we create the schema on the nodes specified in the Nodes list. Then we start Mnesia, which is a necessary step in order to create tables. We create the two tables, named after the records #mafiapp_friends{} and #mafiapp_services{}. There's an index on the expertise field because we do expect to search friends by expertise.

You'll also see that the services table is of type bag. This is because it's possible to have multiple services with the same senders and receivers. Using a set table, we could deal with only unique senders, but bag tables handle this fine. Then there's an index on the to field of the table. That's because we expect to look up services either by who received them or who gave them, and indexes allow us to make any field faster to search.

The last thing to note is that the code stops Mnesia after creating the tables. This is just to match the behavior I decided I wanted in the test. What was in the test is how I expect to use the code, so I better make the code fit that idea. There is nothing wrong with just leaving Mnesia running after the installation, though.

Now, if we had successful test cases in our Common Test suite, the initialization phase would succeed with this install function. However, trying it with many nodes would bring failure messages to our Erlang shells. Do you have any idea why? Here's what it would look like:

```
Node A                   Node B
------                   ------
create_schema ----------> create_schema
start Mnesia
creating table ----------> ???
creating table ----------> ???
stop Mnesia
```

For the tables to be created on all nodes, Mnesia needs to run on all nodes. For the schema to be created, Mnesia must not be running on any nodes. Ideally, we could start Mnesia and stop it remotely. The good news is we can. Remember the rpc module introduced in Chapter 26? We have the function rpc:multicall(Nodes, Module, Function, Args) to do it for us. Let's change the install/1 function definition to this one:

```
install(Nodes) ->
    ok = mnesia:create_schema(Nodes),
    rpc:multicall(Nodes, application, start, [mnesia]),
    mnesia:create_table(mafiapp_friends,
                        [{attributes, record_info(fields, mafiapp_friends)},
                         {index, [#mafiapp_friends.expertise]},
                         {disc_copies, Nodes}]),
    mnesia:create_table(mafiapp_services,
                        [{attributes, record_info(fields, mafiapp_services)},
                         {index, [#mafiapp_services.to]},
                         {disc_copies, Nodes},
                         {type, bag}]),
    rpc:multicall(Nodes, application, stop, [mnesia]).
```

Using rpc allows us to do the Mnesia action on all nodes. The scheme now looks like this:

```
Node A                   Node B
------                   ------
create_schema ----------> create_schema
start Mnesia ------------> start Mnesia
creating table ----------> replicating table
creating table ----------> replicating table
stop Mnesia -------------> stop Mnesia
```

Good, very good.

Starting the Application

The next part of the init_per_suite/1 function we need to take care of is starting mafiapp. Actually, we don't need to do this, because our entire application depends on Mnesia. Starting Mnesia starts our application. However, there can be a noticeable delay between the time Mnesia starts and the time it finishes loading all tables from disk, especially if they're large. In such circumstances, a function such as mafiapp's start/2 might be the perfect place to do that kind of waiting, even if we need no process at all for normal operations.

We'll make *mafiapp.erl* implement the application behavior (-behavior(application).) and add the two following callbacks in the file (remember to export them):

```
start(normal, []) ->
    mnesia:wait_for_tables([mafiapp_friends,
                            mafiapp_services], 5000),
    mafiapp_sup:start_link().

stop(_) -> ok.
```

The secret is the mnesia:wait_for_tables(TableList, TimeOut) function. This function will wait for at most 5 seconds (an arbitrary number; replace it with what you think fits your data) or until the tables are available.

This doesn't tell us much regarding how the supervisor should behave, because mafiapp_sup doesn't have much to do at all:

```
-module(mafiapp_sup).
-behaviour(supervisor).
-export([start_link/1]).
-export([init/1]).

start_link(Tables) ->
    supervisor:start_link(?MODULE, Tables).

%% This does absolutely nothing, only there to
%% allow waiting for tables.
init(Tables) ->
    {ok, {{one_for_one, 1, 1}, []}}.
```

The supervisor does nothing, but because the starting of OTP applications is synchronous, it's actually one of the best places to put such synchronization points.

Last, add the following *mafiapp.app* file in the *ebin/* directory to make sure the application can be started:

```
{application, mafiapp,
 [{description, "Help the boss keep track of his friends"},
  {vsn, "1.0.0"},
  {modules, [mafiapp, mafiapp_sup]},
  {applications, [stdlib, kernel, mnesia]}]}.
```

We're now ready to write actual tests and implement our application. Or are we?

Access and Context

Before getting to the implementation of our app, let's take a look at how to use Mnesia to work with tables.

All modifications, or even reads, to a database table must be done in an *activity access context*. These contexts represent different types of transactions, or ways to run queries. Here are the options:

transaction
> A Mnesia transaction allows you to run a series of database operations as a single functional block. The whole block will run on all nodes or none of them; it succeeds entirely or fails entirely. When the transaction returns, we're guaranteed that the tables were left in a consistent state, and that different transactions didn't interfere with each other, even if they tried to manipulate the same data.
>
> This type of activity context is partially asynchronous. It will be synchronous for operations on the local node, but it will wait only for the confirmation from other nodes that they *will* commit the transaction, not that they *have* done it. With Mnesia, if the transaction worked locally and everyone else agreed to do it, it should work everywhere else. If it doesn't, possibly due to failures in the network or hardware, the transaction will be reverted at a later point in time. The protocol tolerates this for some efficiency reasons, but might give you confirmation that a transaction succeeded when it will be rolled back later.

sync_transaction
> This activity context is pretty much the same as transaction, but it is synchronous. If the guarantees of transaction aren't enough for you because you don't like the idea of a transaction telling you it succeeded when it may have failed due to weird errors, especially if you want to do things that have side effects (like notifying external services, spawning processes, and so on) related to the transaction's success, sync_transaction is what you want. Synchronous transactions will wait for the final confirmation for all other nodes before returning, making sure everything went fine 100 percent of the way.
>
> An interesting use case is that if you're doing a lot of transactions—enough to overload other nodes—switching to a synchronous mode should force things to go at a slower pace with less backlog accumulation, pushing the problem of overload up a level in your application.

async_dirty
> The async_dirty activity context basically bypasses all the transaction protocols and locking activities (although it will wait for active transactions to finish before proceeding). It will, however, keep on doing

everything that includes logging, replication, and so on. An async_dirty activity context will try to perform all actions locally, and then return, leaving other nodes' replication to take place asynchronously.

sync_dirty

This activity context is to async_dirty what sync_transaction is to transaction. It will wait for the confirmation that things went fine on remote nodes, but will still stay out of all locking or transaction contexts. Dirty contexts are generally faster than transactions, but absolutely riskier by design. Handle these with care.

ets

The ets activity context is basically a way to bypass everything Mnesia does and perform a series of raw operations on the underlying ETS tables, if there are any. No replication will be done. The ets activity context isn't something you usually need to use. It's yet another case of "you'll know when you need it; if in doubt, don't use it."

These are all the contexts within which common Mnesia operations can be run. These operations themselves are wrapped in a fun and executed by calling mnesia:activity(Context, Fun). The fun can contain any Erlang function call, but be aware that it is possible for a transaction to be executed many times in case of failures or interruption by other transactions.

This means that if a transaction that reads a value from a table also sends a message before writing something back, it is entirely possible for the message to be sent dozens of times. As such, *no side effects of the kind should be included in the transaction.*

Reads, Writes, and More

I've referred to the table-modifying functions a lot, and it is now time to define them. Most of them are unsurprisingly similar to what ETS and DETS offer.

write

By calling mnesia:write(Record), where the name of the record is the name of the table, we're able to insert Record in the table. If the table is of type set or ordered_set, and the primary key (the second field of the record, not its name, under a tuple form), the element will be replaced. For bag tables, the whole record will need to be similar.

If the write operation is successful, `write/1` will return `ok`. Otherwise, it throws an exception that will abort the transaction. Throwing such an exception shouldn't be something that occurs frequently. It should mostly happen when Mnesia is not running, the table cannot be found, or the record is invalid.

delete

This function is called as `mnesia:delete(TableName, Key)`. The record(s) that share this key will be removed from the table. It either returns `ok` or throws an exception, with semantics similar to `mnesia:write/1`.

read

Called as `mnesia:read({TableName, Key})`, this function will return a list of records with their primary key matching `Key`. Much like `ets:lookup/2`, it will always return a list, even with tables of type set that can never have more than one result that matches the key. If no record matches, an empty list is returned. Similar to `delete` and `write` operations, in case of a failure, an exception is thrown.

match_object

This function is similar to ETS's `match_object` function. It uses patterns such as those described in Chapter 25 to return entire records from the database table. For example, a quick way to look for friends with a given expertise is to use `mnesia:match_object(#mafiapp_friends{_ = '_', expertise = given})`. It will return a list of all matching entries in the table. Once again, failures end up in exceptions being thrown.

select

This is similar to the ETS select function. It works using match specifications or `ets:fun2ms` as a way to do queries. (If you don't remember how this works, see "You Have Been Selected" on page 428 to brush up on your matching skills.) The function can be called as `mnesia:select(TableName, MatchSpec)`, and it will return a list of all items that fit the match specification. And again, in case of failure, an exception will be thrown.

Many other operations are available for Mnesia tables. However, those explained so far constitute a solid base for us to move forward. If you're interested in other operations, you can head to the Mnesia reference manual to find functions such as `first`, `last`, `next`, and `prev` for individual iterations, and `foldl` and `foldr` for folds over entire tables. You might also be interested in functions to manipulate tables themselves, such as `transform_table` (which is especially useful to add or remove fields in a record or a table) and `add_table_index`.

That makes for a lot of functions. To see how to use them realistically, we'll drive the tests forward a bit.

Implementing the First Requests

Now we'll add some test cases for adding data to our mafia application and for using it to look up friends and services.

A Test for Adding Services

To implement the requests, we'll first write a somewhat simple test demonstrating the behavior we want from our application. The test will be about adding services, but will contain implicit tests for more functionality.

We begin with the standard initialization stuff we need to add in most Common Test suites.

```
...
-export([init_per_suite/1, end_per_suite/1,
         init_per_testcase/2, end_per_testcase/2,
         all/0]).
-export([add_service/1]).

all() -> [add_service].
...

init_per_testcase(add_service, Config) ->
    Config.

end_per_testcase(_, _Config) ->
    ok.
```

Now for the test itself:

```
%% Services can go both ways: from a friend to the boss, or
%% from the boss to a friend! A boss friend is required!
add_service(_Config) ->
    {error, unknown_friend} = mafiapp:add_service("from name",
                                                  "to name",
                                                  {1946,5,23},
                                                  "a fake service"),
    ok = mafiapp:add_friend("Don Corleone", [], [boss], boss),
    ok = mafiapp:add_friend("Alan Parsons",
                            [{twitter,"@ArtScienceSound"}],
                            [{born, {1948,12,20}},
                             musician, 'audio engineer',
                             producer, "has projects"],
                            mixing),
    ok = mafiapp:add_service("Alan Parsons", "Don Corleone",
                             {1973,3,1}, "Helped release a Pink Floyd album").
```

Because we're adding a service, we should include both of the friends who will be part of the exchange. We'll use the function mafiapp:add_friend(Name, Contact, Info, Expertise) for that. Once the friends are added, we can actually add the service.

If you've ever read other Mnesia tutorials, you'll find that some people are very eager to use records directly in the functions (say mafiapp:add_friend(#mafiapp_friend{name=...})). This is something that I try to avoid, as records are often better kept private. Changes in implementation might break the underlying record representation. This is not a problem in itself, but whenever you'll be changing the record definition, you'll need to recompile and, if possible, atomically update all modules that use that record so that they can keep working in a running application. Simply wrapping things in functions gives a somewhat cleaner interface that won't require any module using your database or application to include records through .hrl files, which is frankly annoying.

You'll notice that the test we just defined doesn't actually look for services. This is because we'll search for them when looking up users. For now, we can try to implement the functionality required for the test using Mnesia transactions. The first function we'll add to *mafiapp.erl* will be used to add a user to the database:

```erlang
add_friend(Name, Contact, Info, Expertise) ->
    F = fun() ->
        mnesia:write(#mafiapp_friends{name=Name,
                                      contact=Contact,
                                      info=Info,
                                      expertise=Expertise})
    end,
    mnesia:activity(transaction, F).
```

We're defining a single function that writes the record #mafiapp_friends{}. This is a somewhat simple transaction. add_services/4 should be a little more complex:

```erlang
add_service(From, To, Date, Description) ->
    F = fun() ->
        case mnesia:read({mafiapp_friends, From}) =:= [] orelse
             mnesia:read({mafiapp_friends, To}) =:= [] of
            true ->
                {error, unknown_friend};
            false ->
                mnesia:write(#mafiapp_services{from=From,
                                               to=To,
                                               date=Date,
                                               description=Description})
        end
    end,
    mnesia:activity(transaction,F).
```

In the transaction, we first do one or two reads to see if the friends we're trying to add are already in the database. If either friend is not there, the tuple {error, unknown_friend} is returned, as per the test specification.

If both members of the transaction are found, we'll write the service to the database instead.

NOTE *Validating the input is left to your discretion. Doing so requires only writing custom Erlang code like anything else you would program with the language. If it is possible, doing as much validation as possible outside the transaction context is a good idea. Code in the transaction might run many times and compete for database resources.*

Based on this, we should be able to run the first test batch. To do so, we'll use the following test specification, *mafiapp.spec* (placed at the root of the project):

```
{alias, root, "./test/"}.
{logdir, "./logs/"}.
{suites, root, all}.
```

And we need the following Emakefile (also at the root):

```
{["src/*", "test/*"],
 [{i,"include"}, {outdir, "ebin"}]}.
```

Then we can run the tests:

```
$ erl -make
Recompile: src/mafiapp_sup
Recompile: src/mafiapp
$ ct_run -pa ebin/ -spec mafiapp.spec
... <snip> ...
Common Test: Running make in test directories...
Recompile: mafiapp_SUITE
... <snip> ...
Testing learn-you-some-erlang.mafiapp: Starting test, 1 test cases
... <snip> ...
Testing learn-you-some-erlang.mafiapp: TEST COMPLETE, 1 ok, 0 failed of 1 test
cases
... <snip> ...
```

All right, it passes. That's good. Let's move on to the next tests.

NOTE *When running the Common Test suite, you might get errors saying that some directories are not found. The solution is to use* ct_run -pa ebin/ *or* erl -name ct -pa `pwd`/ebin *(or full paths). While starting the Erlang shell makes the current working directory the node's current working directory, calling* ct:run_test/1 *changes the current working directory to a new one. This breaks relative paths such as ./ebin/. Using absolute paths solves the problem.*

Tests for Lookups

The add_service/1 test lets us add both friends and services. The next tests should focus on making it possible to look up information. For the sake of simplicity, we'll add the boss to all possible future test cases:

```
init_per_testcase(add_service, Config) ->
    Config;
init_per_testcase(_, Config) ->
    ok = mafiapp:add_friend("Don Corleone", [], [boss], boss),
    Config.
```

The use case we'll want to emphasize is looking up friends by their name. While we could very well search through services only, in practice, we might want to look up people by name more than actions. Very rarely will the boss ask, "Who delivered that guitar to whom, again?" No, he will more likely ask, "Who is it that delivered the guitar to our friend Pete Cityshend?" and try to look up this friend's history through his name to find details about the service. For this case, the next test is friend_by_name/1:

```
-export([add_service/1, friend_by_name/1]).

all() -> [add_service, friend_by_name].
...
friend_by_name(_Config) ->
    ok = mafiapp:add_friend("Pete Cityshend",
                            [{phone, "418-542-3000"},
                             {email, "quadrophonia@example.org"},
                             {other, "yell real loud"}],
                            [{born, {1945,5,19}},
                             musician, popular],
                            music),
    {"Pete Cityshend",
     _Contact, _Info, music,
     _Services} = mafiapp:friend_by_name("Pete Cityshend"),
    undefined = mafiapp:friend_by_name(make_ref()).
```

This test verifies that we can insert a friend and look him up, as well as what should be returned when we don't know any friend by that name. We'll have a tuple structure returning all kinds of details, including services, which we do not care about for now. We mostly want to find people, although duplicating the information would make the test stricter.

We can implement mafiapp:friend_by_name/1 by using a single Mnesia read. Our record definition for #mafiapp_friends{} put the friend name as the primary key of the table (the first one defined in the record). By using mnesia:read({Table, Key}), we can get things going easily, with minimal wrapping to make it fit the test:

```
friend_by_name(Name) ->
    F = fun() ->
```

```
    case mnesia:read({mafiapp_friends, Name}) of
        [#mafiapp_friends{contact=C, info=I, expertise=E}] ->
            {Name,C,I,E,find_services(Name)};
        [] ->
            undefined
    end
end,
mnesia:activity(transaction, F).
```

This function alone should be enough to get the tests to pass, as long as you remember to export it. We do not care about find_services(Name) for now, so we'll just stub it out:

```
%%% PRIVATE FUNCTIONS
find_services(_Name) -> undefined.
```

That being done, the new test should also pass:

```
$ erl -make
... <snip> ...
$ ct_run -pa ebin/ -spec mafiapp.spec
... <snip> ...
Testing learn-you-some-erlang.wiptests: TEST COMPLETE, 2 ok, 0 failed of 2
test cases
... <snip> ...
```

It would be nice to put a bit more details into the services area of the request. Here's the test to do that:

```
-export([add_service/1, friend_by_name/1, friend_with_services/1]).

all() -> [add_service, friend_by_name, friend_with_services].
...
friend_with_services(_Config) ->
    ok = mafiapp:add_friend("Someone", [{other, "at the fruit stand"}],
                            [weird, mysterious], shadiness),
    ok = mafiapp:add_service("Don Corleone", "Someone",
                            {1949,2,14}, "Increased business"),
    ok = mafiapp:add_service("Someone", "Don Corleone",
                            {1949,12,25}, "Gave a Christmas gift"),
    %% We don't care about the order. The test was made to fit
    %% whatever the functions returned.
    {"Someone",
     _Contact, _Info, shadiness,
     [{to, "Don Corleone", {1949,12,25}, "Gave a Christmas gift"},
      {from, "Don Corleone", {1949,2,14}, "Increased business"}]} =
    mafiapp:friend_by_name("Someone").
```

In this test, Don Corleone helped a shady person with a fruit stand to grow his business. Said shady person at the fruit stand later gave a Christmas gift to the boss, who never forgot about it.

You can see that we still use friend_by_name/1 to search entries. Although the test is overly generic and not too complete, we can probably figure out what we want to do. Fortunately, the total absence of maintainability requirements kind of makes it okay to do something this incomplete.

The find_service/1 implementation will need to be a bit more complex than the previous one. While friend_by_name/1 could work just by querying the primary key, the friend's name in services is only the primary key when searching in the from field. We still need to deal with the to field. There are many ways to handle this one, such as using match_object many times or reading the entire table and filtering data manually. I chose to use match specifications and the ets:fun2ms/1 parse transform:

```
-include_lib("stdlib/include/ms_transform.hrl").
...
find_services(Name) ->
    Match = ets:fun2ms(
            fun(#mafiapp_services{from=From, to=To, date=D, description=Desc})
                when From =:= Name ->
                    {to, To, D, Desc};
               (#mafiapp_services{from=From, to=To, date=D, description=Desc})
                when To =:= Name ->
                    {from, From, D, Desc}
            end
        ),
    mnesia:select(mafiapp_services, Match).
```

This match specification has two clauses: whenever From matches Name, we return a {to, ToName, Date, Description} tuple. Whenever Name matches To instead, the function returns a tuple of the form {from, FromName, Date, Description}, allowing us to have a single operation that includes both services given and received.

Note that find_services/1 does not run in any transaction. That's because the function is called only within friend_by_name/1, which runs in a transaction already. Mnesia can run nested transactions, but it's useless to do so in this case.

NOTE *When writing larger applications that use Mnesia, it can be interesting to separate the operations on the data stored in Mnesia from the part of the code that actually runs the operations (using mnesia:activity/2). That way, you can specify multiple operations independently, and have calling code decide whether to run them as synchronous or asynchronous transactions, or use any other context.*

Running the tests again should reveal that all three of them work.

The last use case is in regard to searching for friends through their expertise. The following test case illustrates how we might find our friend the red panda when we need a climbing expert for some task:

```
-export([add_service/1, friend_by_name/1, friend_with_services/1,
         friend_by_expertise/1]).
```

```
all() -> [add_service, friend_by_name, friend_with_services,
          friend_by_expertise].
...
friend_by_expertise(_Config) ->
    ok = mafiapp:add_friend("A Red Panda",
                            [{location, "in a zoo"}],
                            [animal,cute],
                            climbing),
    [{"A Red Panda",
      _Contact, _Info, climbing,
      _Services}] = mafiapp:friend_by_expertise(climbing),
    [] = mafiapp:friend_by_expertise(make_ref()).
```

To implement this, we'll need to read something other than the primary key. We could use match specifications, but we've already done that. Plus, we need to match on only one field. The mnesia:match_object/1 function is well adapted for this:

```
friend_by_expertise(Expertise) ->
    Pattern = #mafiapp_friends{_ = '_',
                               expertise = Expertise},
    F = fun() ->
        Res = mnesia:match_object(Pattern),
        [{Name,C,I,Expertise,find_services(Name)} ||
            #mafiapp_friends{name=Name,
                             contact=C,
                             info=I} <- Res]
    end,
    mnesia:activity(transaction, F).
```

In this case, we first declare the pattern. We need to use _ = '_' to declare all undefined values as a match-all specification ('_'). Otherwise, the match_object/1 function will look only for entries where everything but the expertise is the atom undefined.

Once the result is obtained, we format the record into a tuple, in order to respect the test. Again, compiling and running the tests will reveal that this implementation works. Hooray, we implemented the whole specification!

Accounts and New Needs

No software project is ever really finished. Users using the system bring new needs to light or break it in unexpected ways. The boss, even before using our brand-new software, decided that he wants a feature that lets him quickly go through all of our friends and see who we owe things to, and who owes us things.

Here's the test for that one:

```
...
init_per_testcase(accounts, Config) ->
    ok = mafiapp:add_friend("Consigliere", [], [you], consigliere),
    Config;
```

```
...
accounts(_Config) ->
    ok = mafiapp:add_friend("Gill Bates", [{email, "ceo@macrohard.com"}],
                            [clever,rich], computers),
    ok = mafiapp:add_service("Consigliere", "Gill Bates",
                             {1985,11,20}, "Bought 15 copies of software"),
    ok = mafiapp:add_service("Gill Bates", "Consigliere",
                             {1986,8,17}, "Made computer faster"),
    ok = mafiapp:add_friend("Pierre Gauthier", [{other, "city arena"}],
                            [{job, "sports team GM"}], sports),
    ok = mafiapp:add_service("Pierre Gauthier", "Consigliere", {2009,6,30},
                             "Took on a huge, bad contract"),
    ok = mafiapp:add_friend("Wayne Gretzky", [{other, "Canada"}],
                            [{born, {1961,1,26}}, "hockey legend"],
                            hockey),
    ok = mafiapp:add_service("Consigliere", "Wayne Gretzky", {1964,1,26},
                             "Gave first pair of ice skates"),
    %% Wayne Gretzky owes us something so the debt is negative.
    %% Gill Bates' services and debts are equal.
    %% Gauthier is owed a service.
    [{-1,"Wayne Gretzky"},
     {0,"Gill Bates"},
     {1,"Pierre Gauthier"}] = mafiapp:debts("Consigliere"),
    [{1, "Consigliere"}] = mafiapp:debts("Wayne Gretzky").
```

We're adding three test friends: Gill Bates, Pierre Gauthier, and hockey Hall of Famer Wayne Gretzky. There is an exchange of services going on with each of them and you, the consigliere. (We didn't pick the boss for this test because he is being used by other tests, and it would mess with the results!)

The mafiapp:debts(Name) function looks for a name, and counts all the services where the name is involved. When someone owes us something, the value is negative. When we're even, it's 0. When we owe something to someone, the value is 1. We can thus say that the debt/1 function returns the number of services owed to different people.

The implementation of this function is going to be a bit more complex:

```
-export([install/1, add_friend/4, add_service/4, friend_by_name/1,
         friend_by_expertise/1, debts/1]).
...
debts(Name) ->
    Match = ets:fun2ms(
        fun(#mafiapp_services{from=From, to=To}) when From =:= Name ->
            {To,-1};
           (#mafiapp_services{from=From, to=To}) when To =:= Name ->
            {From,1}
        end),
    F = fun() -> mnesia:select(mafiapp_services, Match) end,
    Dict = lists:foldl(fun({Person,N}, Dict) ->
                        dict:update(Person, fun(X) -> X + N end, N, Dict)
                    end,
```

```
                dict:new(),
                mnesia:activity(transaction, F)),
    lists:sort([{V,K} || {K,V} <- dict:to_list(Dict)]).
```

Whenever Mnesia queries become more complex, match specifications are usually going to be part of your solution. They let you run basic Erlang functions, which make them invaluable when it comes to specific result generation. In this function, the match specification is used to find that whenever the service given comes from `Name`, its value is -1 (we gave a service; they owe us one). When `Name` matches `To`, the value returned will be 1 (we received a service; we owe one). In both cases, the value is coupled to a tuple containing the name.

Including the name is necessary for the second step of the computation, where we'll try to count all the services given for each person and give a unique cumulative value. Again, there are many ways to obtain this value. I picked one that required me to stay as little time as possible within a transaction, to allow as much as possible of my code to be separated from the database, which allows more transactions to be done in general. This is useless for `mafiapp`, but in high-performance cases, it can reduce the contention for resources in major ways.

The solution I picked is to take all the values, put them in a dictionary, and use the function `dict:update(Key, Operation, Dict)` to increment or decrement the value based on whether a move is for us or from us. By putting this into a fold over the results given by Mnesia, we get a list of all the values required.

The final step is to flip the values around (from {Key, Debt} to {Debt, Key}) and sort based on this, which will give the results desired.

Meet the Boss

Our software product should at least be tried once in production. We'll do this by setting up the node the boss will use, and then the consigliere's node.

```
$ erl -name corleone -pa ebin/
```

```
$ erl -name genco -pa ebin/
```

Once both nodes are started, you can connect them and install the app:

```
(corleone@ferdmbp.local)1> net_kernel:connect('genco@ferdmbp.local').
true
(corleone@ferdmbp.local)2> mafiapp:install([node()|nodes()]).
{[ok,ok],[]}
(corleone@ferdmbp.local)3>
```

```
=INFO REPORT==== 8-Apr-2013::20:02:26 ===
    application: mnesia
    exited: stopped
    type: temporary
```

You can then start running Mnesia and mafiapp on both nodes by calling application:start(mnesia), application:start(mafiapp). Once it's running, you can see if everything is working as it should by calling mnesia:system_info(), which will display status information about your whole setup:

```
(genco@ferdmbp.local)2> mnesia:system_info().
===> System info in version "4.7", debug level = none <===
opt_disc. Directory "/Users/ferd/.../Mnesia.genco@ferdmbp.local" is used.
use fallback at restart = false
running db nodes   = ['corleone@ferdmbp.local','genco@ferdmbp.local']
stopped db nodes   = []
master node tables = []
remote             = []
ram_copies         = []
disc_copies        = [mafiapp_friends,mafiapp_services,schema]
disc_only_copies   = []
[{'corleone@...',disc_copies},{'genco@...',disc_copies}] = [schema,
mafiapp_friends,
mafiapp_services]
5 transactions committed, 0 aborted, 0 restarted, 2 logged to disc
0 held locks, 0 in queue; 0 local transactions, 0 remote
0 transactions waits for other nodes: []
yes
```

You can see that both nodes are in the running database nodes, and that both tables and the schema are written to disk and in RAM (disc_copies). We can start writing and reading data from the database. Of course, adding Don Corleone to the database is a good starting step:

```
(corleone@ferdmbp.local)4> ok = mafiapp:add_friend("Don Corleone", [], [boss], boss).
ok
(corleone@ferdmbp.local)5> mafiapp:add_friend(
(corleone@ferdmbp.local)5>     "Albert Einstein",
(corleone@ferdmbp.local)5>     [{city, "Princeton, New Jersey, USA"}],
(corleone@ferdmbp.local)5>     [physicist, savant,
(corleone@ferdmbp.local)5>         [{awards, [{1921, "Nobel Prize"}]}]],
(corleone@ferdmbp.local)5>     physicist).
ok
```

All right, we added friends from the corleone node. Let's try adding a service from the genco node:

```
(genco@ferdmbp.local)3> mafiapp:add_service("Don Corleone",
(genco@ferdmbp.local)3>                     "Albert Einstein",
(genco@ferdmbp.local)3>                     {1905, '?', '?'},
(genco@ferdmbp.local)3>                     "Added the square to E = MC").
ok
```

```
(genco@ferdmbp.local)4> mafiapp:debts("Albert Einstein").
[{1,"Don Corleone"}]
```

And all these changes can also be reflected back to the corleone node:

```
(corleone@ferdmbp.local)6> mafiapp:friend_by_expertise(physicist).
[{"Albert Einstein",
  [{city,"Princeton, New Jersey, USA"}],
  [physicist,savant,[{awards,[{1921,"Nobel Prize"}]}]],
  physicist,
  [{from,"Don Corleone",
       {1905,'?','?'},
       "Added the square to E = MC"}]}]
```

Now, if you shut down one of the nodes and start it again, things should still be fine:

```
(corleone@ferdmbp.local)7> init:stop().
ok

$ erl -name corleone -pa ebin
... <snip> ...
(corleone@ferdmbp.local)1> net_kernel:connect('genco@ferdmbp.local').
true
(corleone@ferdmbp.local)2>
application:start(mnesia), application:start(mafiapp).
ok
(corleone@ferdmbp.local)3> mafiapp:friend_by_expertise(physicist).
[{"Albert Einstein",
... <snip> ...
       "Added the square to E = MC"}]}]
```

Isn't it nice? We've now used Mnesia successfully!

 NOTE *If you end up working on a system where tables start to get messy, or if you're just curious about looking at entire tables, call the function tv:start(). It will start a graphical table viewer that lets you interact with tables visually, rather than through code.*

Deleting Stuff, Demonstrated

Wait—did we just entirely skip over deleting records from a database? Oh no! Let's add a table and use it to see how to get rid of stuff.

We'll create a little feature for you and the boss that lets you store personal enemies, for personal reasons:

```
-record(mafiapp_enemies, {name,
                          info=[]}).
```

Because this is personal information, we'll need to use slightly different table settings, with local_content set as an option when installing the table. This will let the table be private to each node, so that no one can read anyone else's personal enemies accidentally (although rpc would make it trivial to circumvent).

Here's the new install function, preceded by mafiapp's start/2 function, changed for the new table:

```
start(normal, []) ->
    mafiapp_sup:start_link([mafiapp_friends,
                            mafiapp_services,
                            mafiapp_enemies]).
...
install(Nodes) ->
    ok = mnesia:create_schema(Nodes),
    application:start(mnesia),
    mnesia:create_table(mafiapp_friends,
                        [{attributes, record_info(fields, mafiapp_friends)},
                         {index, [#mafiapp_friends.expertise]},
                         {disc_copies, Nodes}]),
    mnesia:create_table(mafiapp_services,
                        [{attributes, record_info(fields, mafiapp_services)},
                         {index, [#mafiapp_services.to]},
                         {disc_copies, Nodes},
                         {type, bag}]),
    mnesia:create_table(mafiapp_enemies,
                        [{attributes, record_info(fields, mafiapp_enemies)},
                         {disc_copies, Nodes},
                         {local_content, true}]),
    application:stop(mnesia).
```

The start/2 function now sends mafiapp_enemies through the supervisor to keep things alive there. The install/1 function will be useful for tests and fresh installations, but if you're doing things in production, you can call mnesia:create_table/2 in production to add tables. Depending on the load on your system and how many nodes you have, you might want to have a few practice runs in staging first, though.

Now, we can write a simple test to work with our database and see how it goes, still in mafiapp_SUITE:

```
...
-export([add_service/1, friend_by_name/1, friend_by_expertise/1,
         friend_with_services/1, accounts/1, enemies/1]).

all() -> [add_service, friend_by_name, friend_by_expertise,
          friend_with_services, accounts, enemies].
...
enemies(_Config) ->
    undefined = mafiapp:find_enemy("Edward"),
    ok = mafiapp:add_enemy("Edward", [{bio, "Vampire"},
                                      {comment, "He sucks (blood)"}]),
```

```
{"Edward", [{bio, "Vampire"},
           {comment, "He sucks (blood)"}]} =
    mafiapp:find_enemy("Edward"),
ok = mafiapp:enemy_killed("Edward"),
undefined = mafiapp:find_enemy("Edward").
```

This is going to be similar to previous runs for add_enemy/2 and find_enemy/1. All we'll need to do is a basic insertion for the former, and an mnesia:read/1 based on the primary key for the latter:

```
add_enemy(Name, Info) ->
    F = fun() -> mnesia:write(#mafiapp_enemies{name=Name, info=Info}) end,
    mnesia:activity(transaction, F).

find_enemy(Name) ->
    F = fun() -> mnesia:read({mafiapp_enemies, Name}) end,
    case mnesia:activity(transaction, F) of
        [] -> undefined;
        [#mafiapp_enemies{name=N, info=I}] -> {N,I}
    end.
```

The enemy_killed/1 function is the one that's a bit different:

```
enemy_killed(Name) ->
    F = fun() -> mnesia:delete({mafiapp_enemies, Name}) end,
    mnesia:activity(transaction, F).
```

And that's pretty much it for basic deletions. You can export the functions and run the test suite, and all the tests should still pass.

When trying the tests on two nodes (after deleting the previous schemas, or possibly just calling the create_table function), we should be able to see that data between tables isn't shared:

```
$ erl -name corleone -pa ebin
```

```
$ erl -name genco -pa ebin
```

With the nodes started, reinstall the database:

```
(corleone@ferdmbp.local)1> net_kernel:connect('genco@ferdmbp.local').
true
(corleone@ferdmbp.local)2> mafiapp:install([node()|nodes()]).
=INFO REPORT==== 8-Apr-2013::21:21:47 ===
... <snip> ...
{[ok,ok],[]}
```

Start the apps and get going:

```
(genco@ferdmbp.local)1> application:start(mnesia), application:start(mafiapp).
ok
```

```
(corleone@ferdmbp.local)3> application:start(mnesia), application:start(mafiapp).
ok
(corleone@ferdmbp.local)4> mafiapp:add_enemy("Some Guy", "Disrespected his family").
ok
(corleone@ferdmbp.local)5> mafiapp:find_enemy("Some Guy").
{"Some Guy","Disrespected his family"}
```

```
(genco@ferdmbp.local)2> mafiapp:find_enemy("Some Guy").
undefined
```

And you can see that no data is shared. Deleting the entry is also as simple:

```
(corleone@ferdmbp.local)6> mafiapp:enemy_killed("Some Guy").
ok
(corleone@ferdmbp.local)7> mafiapp:find_enemy("Some Guy").
undefined
```

Finally!

Query List Comprehensions

If you've followed this chapter (or worse, skipped right to this part!), thinking to yourself, "Damn, I don't like the way Mnesia looks," you might like this section. If you liked how Mnesia looked, you might also like this section. And if you like list comprehensions, you'll definitely like this section.

Query list comprehensions (QLCs) are basically a compiler trick using parse transforms that let you use list comprehensions for any data structure that can be searched and iterated through. They're implemented for Mnesia, DETS, and ETS, but can also be implemented for things like gb_trees.

Once you add -include_lib("stdlib/include/qlc.hrl"). to your module, you can start using list comprehensions with something called a *query handle* as a generator. The query handle allows any iterable data structure to work with QLCs. In the case of Mnesia, you can use mnesia:table(TableName) as a list comprehension generator, and from that point on, you can use list comprehensions to query any database table by wrapping them in a call to qlc:q(...).

This will return a modified query handle, with more details than the one returned by the table. This newest one can subsequently be modified some more by using functions like qlc:sort/1-2, and can be evaluated by using qlc:eval/1 or qlc:fold/1.

Let's experiment with this approach. We'll rewrite a few of the mafiapp functions. You can make a copy of *mafiapp-1.0.0* and call it *mafiapp-1.0.1* (don't forget to bump the version in the *.app* file).

First, we'll rework `friend_by_expertise`. This function is currently implemented using `mnesia:match_object/1`. Here's a version using a QLC:

```erlang
friend_by_expertise(Expertise) ->
    F = fun() ->
        qlc:eval(qlc:q(
            [{Name,C,I,E,find_services(Name)} ||
                #mafiapp_friends{name=Name,
                                 contact=C,
                                 info=I,
                                 expertise=E} <- mnesia:table(mafiapp_friends),
                E =:= Expertise]))
        end,
    mnesia:activity(transaction, F).
```

You can see that except for the part where we call `qlc:eval/1` and `qlc:q/1`, this is a normal list comprehension. You have the final expression in `{Name,C,I,E,find_services(Name)}`, the generator in `#mafiapp{...} <- mnesia:table(...)`, and finally, a condition with `E =:= Expertise`. Searching through database tables is now a bit more natural, Erlang-wise.

Now let's try a slightly more complex example. We'll take a look at the `debts/1` function. It was implemented using a match specification and then a fold over to a dictionary. Here's how that might look using a QLC:

```erlang
debts(Name) ->
    F = fun() ->
        QH = qlc:q(
            [if Name =:= To -> {From,1};
                Name =:= From -> {To,-1}
             end || #mafiapp_services{from=From, to=To} <-
                    mnesia:table(mafiapp_services),
                    Name =:= To orelse Name =:= From]),
        qlc:fold(fun({Person,N}, Dict) ->
                     dict:update(Person, fun(X) -> X + N end, N, Dict)
                 end,
                 dict:new(),
                 QH)
        end,
    lists:sort([{V,K} || {K,V} <- dict:to_list(mnesia:activity(transaction, F))]).
```

The match specification is no longer necessary. The list comprehension (saved to the `QH` query handle) does that part. The fold has been moved into the transaction, and it is used as a way to evaluate the query handle. The resulting dictionary is the same as the one that was formerly returned by `lists:foldl/3`. The last part, sorting, is handled outside the transaction by taking whatever dictionary `mnesia:activity/1` returned and converting it to a list.

And there you go. If you write these functions in your *mafiapp-1.0.1* application and run the test suite, all six tests should still pass.

Remember Mnesia

That's it for Mnesia. It's quite a complex database, and we've covered only a moderate portion of everything it can do. Pushing further ahead will require you to read the Erlang manuals and dive into the code. Programmers who have true production experience with Mnesia in large, scalable systems that have been running for years are rather rare. You can find a few of them on mailing lists, sometimes answering a few questions, but they're generally busy people.

Otherwise, Mnesia is always a very nice tool for smaller applications where you find picking a storage layer to be very annoying, or even larger ones where you will have a known number of nodes. Being able to store and replicate Erlang terms directly is a very neat thing—something other languages tried to write for years using object-relational mapping.

Interestingly enough, if you put your mind to it, you could likely write QLC selectors for SQL databases or any other kind of storage that allows iteration.

Mnesia and its toolchain have all the potential to be very useful in some of your future applications. For now though, we'll move on to additional tools to help you develop Erlang systems with Dialyzer.

30

TYPE SPECIFICATIONS AND DIALYZER

This chapter focuses on Dialyzer, which is a very effective tool when it comes to analyzing Erlang code. It's used to find all kinds of discrepancies, such as code that will never be executed, but its main use is to detect type errors in your Erlang code base. We'll look at why Dialyzer was created, the guiding principles behind it, and its capabilities to find type-related errors. Of course, we'll also work through a few examples of Dialyzer in use.

PLTs Are the Best Sandwiches

Our first step is to create Dialyzer's *persistent lookup table (PLT)*, which is a compilation of all the details Dialyzer can identify about the applications and modules that are part of your standard Erlang distribution, as well as code outside OTP.

It takes quite a while to compile everything, especially if you're working on a platform that does not provide native compilation through HiPE (namely Windows) or on older versions of Erlang. Fortunately, things tend to get faster with time, and the newest releases of Erlang (R15B02 onward) have parallel PLT building to make it even faster.

Enter the following command into a terminal, and let it run as long as it needs (in my case, that tends to be under 10 minutes):

```
$ dialyzer --build_plt --apps erts kernel stdlib crypto mnesia sasl common_test eunit
Compiling some key modules to native code... done in 1m19.99s
Creating PLT /Users/ferd/.dialyzer_plt ...
eunit_test.erl:302: Call to missing or unexported function eunit_test:nonexisting_function/0
Unknown functions:
compile:file/2
compile:forms/2
... <snip> ...
xref:stop/1
Unknown types:
compile:option/0
done in 6m39.15s
done (warnings were emitted)
```

This command builds the PLT by specifying which OTP applications we want to include in it. You can ignore the warnings if you want, as Dialyzer can deal with unknown functions when looking for type errors (this has to do with how its type inference algorithm works, as discussed in the next section). Some Windows users will see an error message saying "The HOME environment variable needs to be set so that Dialyzer knows where to find the default PLT." This is because Windows doesn't always come with the HOME environment variable set, and Dialyzer doesn't know where to dump the PLT. Set the variable to wherever you want Dialyzer to place its files.

If you want, you can include applications like ssl or reltool by adding them to the sequence that follows --apps, or if your PLT is already built, by calling the following:

```
$ dialyzer --add_to_plt --apps ssl reltool
```

If you want to add your own applications or modules to the PLT, you can do so by using -r Directories, which will look for all *.erl* or *.beam* files (as long as they are compiled with debug_info).

Moreover, Dialyzer lets you have many PLTs by specifying them with the --plt Name option in any of the commands you use, and pick a specific PLT. Alternatively, if you built many *disjoint* PLTs, where none of the included modules are shared between PLTs, you can "merge" them by using --plts Name1 Name2 ... NameN. This is especially useful when you want to have different PLTs in your system for different projects or Erlang versions.

While the PLT is still building, let's get acquainted with Dialyzer's mechanism for finding type errors.

Success Typing

As with most other dynamic programming languages, Erlang programs are always at risk of suffering from type errors. A programmer passes in some arguments to a function he shouldn't have, and maybe he forgot to test things properly. The program gets deployed, and everything seems to be going okay. Then at four in the morning, your company's operations guy's cell phone starts ringing because your piece of software is repeatedly crashing— enough that the supervisors can't cope with the sheer weight of your mistakes.

The next morning, you get to the office, and you find your computer has been reformatted, your car is keyed, and your commit rights have been revoked, all by the operations guy who has had enough of you accidentally controlling his work schedule.

That entire debacle could have been prevented by a compiler that has a static type analyzer to verify programs before they run.

While Erlang doesn't crave a type system as much as other dynamic languages, thanks to its reactive approach to runtime errors, it is definitely nice to benefit from the additional safety provided by early type-related error discovery.

Usually, languages with static type systems are designed that way. The semantics of the languages is heavily influenced by what their type systems allow and don't allow. For example, consider this function:

```
foo(X) when is_integer(X) -> X + 1.
foo(X) -> list_to_atom(X).
```

Most type systems are unable to properly represent the types of this function. They can see that it can take an integer or a list and return an integer or an atom, but they won't track the dependency between the input type of the function and its output type (conditional types and intersection types are able to, but they can be verbose). This means that writing such functions, which is entirely normal in Erlang, can result in some uncertainty for the type analyzer when these functions are used later in the code.

Generally speaking, analyzers will want to actually prove that there will be no type errors at runtime, as in *mathematically* prove. This means that in a few circumstances, the type checker will disallow certain practically valid operations for the sake of removing uncertainty that could lead to crashes.

Implementing such a type system would likely mean forcing Erlang to change its semantics.

The problem is that by the time Dialyzer came around, Erlang was already well in use for very large projects. For any tool like Dialyzer to be accepted, it needed to respect Erlang's philosophies. If Erlang allows pure nonsense in its types that can be solved only at runtime, so be it. The type checker doesn't have a right to complain. No programmer likes a tool that tells him his program cannot run when it has been doing so in production for a few months already!

The other option is to have a type system that will not prove the absence of errors, but will do a best effort at detecting whatever it can. You can make such detection really good, but it will never be perfect—it's a trade-off.

Dialyzer's type system designers made the decision not to prove that a program is error-free when it comes to types, but only to find as many errors as possible without ever contradicting what happens in the real world. As the "Practical Type Inference Based on Success Typings" paper (*http://www.it.uu.se/research/group/hipe/papers/succ_types.pdf*) behind Dialyzer explains, a type checker for a language like Erlang should work without type declarations being there (although it accepts hints), should be simple and readable, should adapt to the language (and not the other way around), and complain only about type errors that would guarantee a crash.

> Our main goal is to make uncover [sic] the implicit type information in Erlang code and make it explicitly available in programs. Because of the sizes of typical Erlang applications, the type inference should be completely automatic and faithfully respect the operational semantics of the language. Moreover, it should impose no code rewrites of any kind. The reason for this is simple. Rewriting, often safety critical, applications consisting of hundreds of thousand lines of code just to satisfy a type inferencer is not an option which will enjoy much success. However, large software applications have to be maintained, and often not by their original authors. By automatically revealing the type information that is already present, we provide automatic documentation that can evolve together with the program and will not rot. We also think that it is important to achieve a balance between precision and readability. Last but not least, the inferred typings should never be wrong.

Dialyzer begins each analysis optimistically, assuming that all functions are good. It will see them as always succeeding, accepting anything, and possibly returning anything. No matter how an unknown function is used, it's a good way to use it. This is why warnings about unknown functions are not a big deal when generating PLTs. It's all good anyway; Dialyzer is a natural optimist when it comes to type inference.

As the analysis goes, Dialyzer gets to know your functions better and better. As it does so, it can analyze the code and see some interesting things.

Suppose that one of your functions has a + operator between both of its arguments and that it returns the value of the addition. Dialyzer no longer assumes that the function takes anything and returns anything, but will now expect the arguments to be numbers (either integers or floating-point values), and the returned values will similarly be numbers. This function will have a basic type associated with it saying that it accepts two numbers and returns a number.

Now let's say one of your functions calls the one described previously with an atom and a number. Dialyzer will think about the code and say, "Wait a minute, you can't use an atom and a number with the + operator!" It will then freak out because where the function could return a number before, it cannot return anything given how you use it.

In more general circumstances, though, you might find that Dialyzer keeps silent about many things that you know will *sometimes* cause an error. For example, consider the following snippet of code:

```
main() ->
    X = case fetch() of
        1 -> some_atom;
        2 -> 3.14
    end,
    convert(X).

convert(X) when is_atom(X) -> {atom, X}.
```

This bit of code assumes the existence of a fetch/0 function that returns either 1 or 2. Based on this, we either return an atom or a floating-point number.

From our point of view, it appears that at some point in time, the call to convert/1 will fail. We would likely expect a type error there whenever fetch() returns 2, which sends a floating-point value to convert/1. Dialyzer doesn't think so. Remember that Dialyzer is optimistic. It has figurative faith in your code, and because there is the possibility that the function call to convert/1 succeeds at some point, Dialyzer will keep silent. No type error is reported in this case.

Type Inference and Discrepancies

For a practical example of the principles described in the previous section, let's try Dialyzer on a few modules: *discrep1.erl*, *discrep2.erl*, and *discrep3.erl*. Here's *discrep1.erl*:

```
-module(discrep1).
-export([run/0]).

run() -> some_op(5, you).

some_op(A, B) -> A + B.
```

The error in this example is kind of obvious. You can't add 5 to the you atom. We can try Dialyzer on that piece of code, assuming the PLT has been created:

```
$ dialyzer discrep1.erl
  Checking whether the PLT /home/ferd/.dialyzer_plt is up-to-date... yes
  Proceeding with analysis...
```

```
discrep1.erl:4: Function run/0 has no local return
discrep1.erl:4: The call discrep1:some_op(5,'you') will never return
since it differs in the 2nd argument from the success typing arguments:
(number(),number())
discrep1.erl:6: Function some_op/2 has no local return
discrep1.erl:6: The call erlang:'+'(A::5,B::'you') will never return
since it differs in the 2nd argument from the success typing arguments:
(number(),number())
  done in 0m0.62s
done (warnings were emitted)
```

Oh bloody fun—Dialyzer found stuff. What the hell does it mean?

The first one is an error you will see a lot when using Dialyzer. "Function Name/Arity has no local return" is the standard Dialyzer warning emitted whenever a function provably doesn't return anything (other than perhaps raising an exception) because one of the functions it calls happens to trip Dialyzer's type-error detector or raises an exception itself. When this happens, the set of possible types of values the function could return is empty; it doesn't actually return. This error propagates to the function that called it, giving us the "no local return" error.

The second error is somewhat more understandable. It says that calling some_op(5, 'you') breaks what Dialyzer detected would be the types required to make the function work, which are two numbers (number() and number()). Granted the notation is a bit foreign, but we'll explore it in more detail soon enough.

The third error is yet again a "no local return." The first one was because some_op/2 would fail; this one is because the + call will fail. This is what the fourth and last error is about. The plus operator (actually the function erlang:'+'/2) can't add the number 5 to the atom you.

What about *discrep2.erl*? Here's what it looks like:

```
-module(discrep2).
-export([run/0]).

run() ->
    Tup = money(5, you),
    some_op(count(Tup), account(Tup)).

money(Num, Name) -> {give, Num, Name}.
count({give, Num, _}) -> Num.
account({give, _, X}) -> X.

some_op(A, B) -> A + B.
```

If you run Dialyzer on that file again, you'll get similar errors to those found in *discrep1.erl*:

```
$ dialyzer discrep2.erl
  Checking whether the PLT /home/ferd/.dialyzer_plt is up-to-date... yes
  Proceeding with analysis...
discrep2.erl:4: Function run/0 has no local return
```

```
discrep2.erl:6: The call discrep2:some_op(5,'you') will never return
since it differs in the 2nd argument from the success typing arguments:
(number(),number())
discrep2.erl:12: Function some_op/2 has no local return
discrep2.erl:12: The call erlang:'+'(A::5,B::'you') will never return
since it differs in the 2nd argument from the success typing arguments:
(number(),number())
 done in 0m0.69s
done (warnings were emitted)
```

During its analysis, Dialyzer can see the types right through the count/1 and account/1 functions. It infers the types of each of the elements of the tuple, and then figures out the values they pass. It can then find the errors again, without any problems.

Let's push it a bit further, with *discrep3.erl*:

```
-module(discrep3).
-export([run/0]).

run() ->
    Tup = money(5, you),
    some_op(item(count, Tup), item(account, Tup)).

money(Num, Name) -> {give, Num, Name}.

item(count, {give, X, _}) -> X;
item(account, {give, _, X}) -> X.

some_op(A, B) -> A + B.
```

This version introduces a new level of indirection. Instead of having a function clearly defined for the count and the account values, this one works with atoms and switches to different function clauses. If we run Dialyzer on it, we get this:

```
$ dialyzer discrep3.erl
  Checking whether the PLT /home/ferd/.dialyzer_plt is up-to-date... yes
  Proceeding with analysis... done in 0m0.70s
done (passed successfully)
```

Uh-oh—somehow the new change to the file made things complex enough that Dialyzer got lost in our type definitions. The error is still there though. We'll get back to understanding why Dialyzer doesn't find the errors in this file and how to fix it in "Typing Functions" on page 556, but for now, there are a few more ways to run Dialyzer that we need to explore.

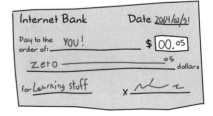

If we wanted to run Dialyzer over, say, our Process Quest release, we could do it as follows:

```
$ cd processquest/apps
$ ls
processquest-1.0.0  processquest-1.1.0  regis-1.0.0
regis-1.1.0  sockserv-1.0.0  sockserv-1.0.1
```

So, we have a bunch of libraries. Dialyzer wouldn't like it if we had many modules with the same names, so we'll need to specify directories manually:

```
$ dialyzer -r processquest-1.1.0/src regis-1.1.0/src sockserv-1.0.1/src
  Checking whether the PLT /home/ferd/.dialyzer_plt is up-to-date... yes
  Proceeding with analysis...
dialyzer: Analysis failed with error:
No .beam files to analyze (no --src specified?)
```

Oh, right—by default, Dialyzer will look for *.beam* files. We need to add the --src flag to tell Dialyzer to use *.erl* files for its analysis:

```
$ dialyzer -r processquest-1.1.0/src regis-1.1.0/src sockserv-1.0.1/src --src
  Checking whether the PLT /home/ferd/.dialyzer_plt is up-to-date... yes
  Proceeding with analysis... done in 0m2.32s
done (passed successfully)
```

Notice that we added the *src* directory to all requests. We could have done the same search without it, but then Dialyzer would have complained about a bunch of errors related to EUnit tests, based on how some of the assertion macros work with regard to the code analysis—we do not really care about these. Plus, if you sometimes test for failures and make your software crash on purpose inside of tests, Dialyzer will pick up on that, and you might not want it to.

Typing About Types of Types

As seen with *discrep3.erl*, Dialyzer will sometimes not be able to infer all the types in the way we intended. That's because Dialyzer cannot read our minds. To help Dialyzer in its task (and mostly help ourselves), we can declare types and annotate functions in order to both document them and help formalize the implicit expectations about types we put in our code.

Singleton Types

Erlang types can be as simple as, say, the number 42, noted 42 as a type (nothing different from usual), or specific atoms, such as cat or molecule. Those are called *singleton types*, as they refer to a value itself. Table 30-1 lists the singleton types.

Table 30-1: Erlang Singleton Types

Type	Description
'some atom'	Any atom can be its own singleton type
42	A given integer
[]	An empty list
{}	An empty tuple
<<>>	An empty binary

You can see that it could be annoying to program Erlang using only these types. There is no way to express things such as ages, much less "all the integers" for our programs, by using singleton types. And then, even if we had a way to specify many types at once, it would be irritating to express things such as "any integer" without writing them all by hand, which isn't possible anyway. Because of this, Erlang has union types and built-in types.

Union and Built-in Types

Union types allow you to describe more complex ideas, such as a type that has two atoms in it. *Built-in types* are predefined types, which are not necessarily possible to build by hand.

Union types and built-in types generally share a similar syntax, and they're noted with the form *TypeName*(). For example, the type for all possible integers would be noted as integer(). The reason parentheses are used is that they let us differentiate between, say the type atom() for all atoms, and atom for the specific atom atom. Moreover, to make code clearer, many Erlang programmers choose to quote all atoms in type declarations, giving us 'atom' instead of atom. This makes it explicit that 'atom' was meant to be a singleton type, rather than a built-in type where the programmer forgot the parentheses.

Table 30-2 lists the built-in types provided with the language. Note that they do not all have the same syntax as union types do. Some of them, like binaries and tuples, have a special syntax to make them friendlier to use.

Given the built-in types listed in the table, it becomes a bit easier to imagine how we would define types for our Erlang programs. Some of it is still missing though. Maybe things are too vague or not appropriate for our needs. Remember one of the discrep*N* modules' errors mentioning the type number()? That type is neither a singleton type nor a built-in type. It would be a union type, which means we could define it ourselves.

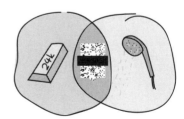

Table 30-2: Erlang Built-in Types

Type	Description
any()	Any Erlang term at all.
none()	A special type that means that no term or type is valid. Usually, when Dialyzer boils down the possible return values of a function to none(), it means the function should crash. It is synonymous with "this stuff won't work."
pid()	A process identifier.
port()	A port is the underlying representation of file descriptors (which we rarely see unless we dig deep inside the innards of Erlang libraries), sockets, or generally things that allow Erlang to communicate with the outside world, such as the erlang:open_port/2 function. In the Erlang shell, they look like #Port<0.638>.
reference()	Unique values returned by make_ref() or erlang:monitor/2.
atom()	Atoms in general.
binary()	A blob of binary data.
<<_:Integer>>	A binary of a known size, where Integer is the size.
<<_:_*Integer>>	A binary that has a given unit size, but of unspecified length.
<<_:Integer, _:_*OtherInteger>>	A mix of both previous forms to specify that a binary can have a minimum length.
integer()	Any integer.
N..M	A range of integers. For example, if you wanted to represent a number of months in a year, you could define the range 1..12. Note that Dialyzer reserves the right to expand this range into a bigger one.
non_neg_integer()	Integers that are greater or equal to 0.
pos_integer()	Integers greater than 0.
neg_integer()	Integers up to –1.
float()	Any floating-point number.
fun()	Any kind of function.
fun((...) -> Type)	An anonymous function of any arity that returns a given type. A given function that returns lists could be noted as fun((...) -> list()).
fun(() -> Type)	An anonymous function with no arguments, returning a term of a given type.
fun((Type1, Type2, ..., TypeN) -> Type)	An anonymous function taking a given number of arguments of a known type. For example, a function that handles an integer and a floating-point value could be declared as fun((integer(), float()) -> any()).

Table 30-2: Erlang Built-in Types *(continued)*

Type	Description
[Type()]	A list containing a given type. A list of integers could be defined as [integer()]. Alternatively, it can be written as list(Type()). Lists can sometimes be improper (like [1, 2 | a]). As such, Dialyzer has types declared for improper lists with improper_list(TypeList, TypeEnd). The improper list [1, 2 | a] could be typed as improper_list(integer(), atom()), for example. Then, to make matters more complex, it is possible that you will not be sure whether or not the list will be proper. In such circumstances, the type maybe_improper_list(TypeList, TypeEnd) can be used.
[Type(), ...]	A special case of [Type()] that mentions that the list cannot be empty.
tuple()	Any tuple.
{Type1, Type2, ..., TypeN}	A tuple of a known size, with known types. For example, a binary tree node could be defined as {'node', any(), any(), any(), any()}, corresponding to {'node', LeftTree, RightTree, Key, Value}.

The notation to represent the union of types is the pipe (|). Basically, this lets us say that a given type *TypeName* is represented as the union of *Type1* | *Type2* | ... | *TypeN*. As such, the number() type, which includes integers and floating-point values, could be represented as integer() | float(). A Boolean value could be defined as 'true' | 'false'. It is also possible to define types where only one other type is used. Although it looks like a union type, it is actually an *alias*.

In fact, many such aliases and type unions are predefined for you. Table 30-3 lists some of them.

Table 30-3: Predefined Union Types and Aliases

Type	Definition
term()	Equivalent to any(). It was added because other tools used term() before. Alternatively, the _ variable can be used as an alias of both term() and any().
boolean()	Defined as 'true' | 'false'.
byte()	Defined as 0..255. It's any valid byte in existence.
char()	Defined as 0..16#10ffff, but it isn't clear whether this type refers to specific standards for characters. It's extremely general in its approach to avoid conflicts.
number()	integer() | float()
maybe_improper_list()	A quick alias for maybe_improper_list(any(), any()) for improper lists in general.

(continued)

Table 30-3: Predefined Union Types and Aliases *(continued)*

Type	Definition
`maybe_improper_list(T)`	An alias for `maybe_improper_list(T, any())`, where `T` is any given type.
`string()`	Defined as `[char()]`, a list of characters. There is also `nonempty_string()`, defined as `[char(), ...]`. Sadly, there is so far no string type for binary strings only, but that's more because they're blobs of data that are to be interpreted in whatever type you choose.
`iolist()`	Defined as `maybe_improper_list(char()	binary()	iolist(), binary()	[])`. You can see that the iolist is itself defined in terms of iolists. Dialyzer does support recursive types, starting with R13B04. Before then, types like iolists could be defined only through some arduous gymnastics.
`module()`	A type that stands for module names, and is currently an alias of `atom()`.
`timeout()`	`non_neg_integer()	'infinity'`, to represent the values accepted by the `after` part of a `receive` expression.
`node()`	An Erlang's node name, which is an atom.
`no_return()`	An alias of `none()` intended to be used in the return type of functions. It is particularly meant to annotate functions that loop (hopefully) forever, and thus never return.

Defining Types

Well, that makes a few types already. Table 30-2 mentions a type for a tree written as `{'node', any(), any(), any(), any()}`. Now let's see how we could declare it in a module. The syntax for type declaration in a module is as follows:

```
-type TypeName() :: TypeDefinition.
```

As such, our tree could be defined like this:

```
-type tree() :: {'node', tree(), tree(), any(), any()}.
```

Alternatively, we could define it with a special syntax that allows us to use variable names as type comments, like this:

```
-type tree() :: {'node', Left::tree(), Right::tree(), Key::any(), Value::any()}.
```

But that definition doesn't work, because it doesn't allow for a tree to be empty. A better tree definition can be built by thinking recursively, much as we did with our *tree.erl* module back in Chapter 5. In that module, an empty tree is defined as `{node, 'nil'}`. Whenever we hit such a node in a recursive function, we stop. A regular node (that is not empty) is noted as {node, Key, Val, Left, Right}. Translating this into a type gives us a tree node of the following form:

```erlang
-type tree() :: {'node', 'nil'}
              | {'node', Key::any(), Val::any(), Left::tree(), Right::tree()}.
```

That way, we have a tree that is either an empty node or a node with contents. Note that we could have used 'nil' instead of {'node', 'nil'}, and Dialyzer would have been fine with it. I just wanted to respect the way we had written our tree module.

There's another piece of Erlang code we might want to give types to, but that we haven't covered yet.

Types for Records

What about records? They have a somewhat convenient syntax to declare types. To see it, let's imagine a #user{} record. We want to store the user's name, some specific notes (to use our tree() type), the user's age, a list of friends, and a short biography.

```erlang
-record(user, {name="" :: string(),
               notes :: tree(),
               age :: non_neg_integer(),
               friends=[] :: [#user{}],
               bio :: string() | binary()}).
```

The general record syntax for type declarations is Field :: Type, and if there's a default value to be given, it becomes Field = Default :: Type. In the #user{} record, we can see that the name needs to be a string, the notes must be a tree, and the age can be any integer from 0 to infinity (who knows how old people can get?).

An interesting field is friends. The [#user{}] type means that the user records can hold a list of zero or more other user records. It also tells us that a record can be used as a type by writing it as #RecordName{}. The last part tells us that the biography can be either a string or a binary.

Furthermore, to give a more uniform style to type declarations and definitions, people tend to add an alias such as -type Type() :: #Record{}.. We could also change the friends definition to use the user() type, ending up as follows:

```erlang
-record(user, {name = "" :: string(),
               notes :: tree(),
               age :: non_neg_integer(),
               friends=[] :: [user()],
               bio :: string() | binary()}).

-type user() :: #user{}.
```

Here, we defined types for all fields of the record, but some of them have no default value. If we were to create a user record instance as #user{age=5}, there would be no type error. All record field definitions have an implicit 'undefined' union added to them if no default value is provided for them. With earlier versions, the declaration would have caused type errors.

Typing Functions

While we could be defining types all day and night, filling files and files with them, and then printing the files, framing them, and feeling strongly accomplished, they won't be used automatically by Dialyzer's type inference engine. Dialyzer doesn't work from the types you declare to narrow down what is possible or impossible to execute.

Why the hell would we declare these types then? For documentation? Partially. There is an additional step to making Dialyzer understand the types we've declared. We need to pepper type signature declarations over all the functions we want augmented, bridging our type declarations with the functions inside modules.

So far, we have looked at things like "here is the syntax for this and that," but now it's time to get practical. A simple example of things needing to be typed could be card games. There are four suits: spades, clubs, hearts, and diamonds. Cards can then be numbered from 1 to 10 (where the ace is 1), and then be a Jack, Queen, or King.

Without Dialyzer, we would probably represent cards as {Suit, CardValue} so that we could have the ace of spades as {spades, 1}. Now, instead of just having this up in the air, we can define types to represent this:

```
-type suit() :: spades | clubs | hearts | diamonds.
-type value() :: 1..10 | j | q | k.
-type card() :: {suit(), value()}.
```

The suit() type is simply the union of the four atoms that can represent suits. The values can be any card from one to ten (1..10), or j, q, or k for the face cards. The card() type joins them together as a tuple.

These three types can now be used to represent cards in regular functions and give us some interesting guarantees. Take the following *cards.erl* module for example:

```
-module(cards).
-export([kind/1, main/0]).

-type suit() :: spades | clubs | hearts | diamonds.
-type value() :: 1..10 | j | q | k.
-type card() :: {suit(), value()}.
```

```
kind({_, A}) when A >= 1, A =< 10 -> number;
kind(_) -> face.

main() ->
    number = kind({spades, 7}),
    face   = kind({hearts, k}),
    number = kind({rubies, 4}),
    face   = kind({clubs, q}).
```

The kind/1 function should return whether a card is a face card or a number card. You will notice that the suit is never checked. In the main/0 function, you can see that the third call is made with the rubies suit, something we obviously didn't intend in our types, and likely not in the kind/1 function:

```
$ erl
... <snip> ...
1> c(cards).
{ok,cards}
2> cards:main().
face
```

Everything works fine. That shouldn't be the case. Even running Dialyzer does not show any problems. Now let's add the following type signature to the kind/1 function:

```
-spec kind(card()) -> 'face' | 'number'.
kind({_, A}) when A >= 1, A =< 10 -> number;
kind(_) -> face.
```

Then something more interesting will happen. But before we run Dialyzer, let's see how that works.

Type signatures are of the form -spec *FunctionName(ArgumentTypes)* -> *ReturnTypes*.. In the preceding specification, we say that the kind/1 function accepts cards as arguments, according to the card() type we created. It also says the function returns either the atom face or number.

Running Dialyzer on the module yields the following:

```
$ dialyzer cards.erl
  Checking whether the PLT /home/ferd/.dialyzer_plt is up-to-date... yes
  Proceeding with analysis...
cards.erl:12: Function main/0 has no local return
cards.erl:15: The call cards:kind({'rubies',4}) breaks the contract (card()) -> 'face' | 'number'
 done in 0m0.80s
done (warnings were emitted)
```

Oh bloody fun. Calling kind/1 with a "card" that has the rubies suit isn't valid according to our specifications.

In this case, Dialyzer respects the type signature we gave, and when it analyzes the main/0 function, it figures out that there is a bad use of kind/1 in there. This prompts the warning from line 15 (number = kind({rubies, 4}),). Dialyzer from there on assumes that the type signature is reliable, and that if the code is to be used according to that signature, it would logically not be valid. This breach in the contract propagates to the main/0 function, but there isn't much that can be said at that level as to why it fails—just that it does.

NOTE *Dialyzer complained about this only once a type specification was defined. Before a type signature was added, Dialyzer couldn't assume that you planned to use kind/1 only with card() arguments. With the signature in place, it can work with that as its own type definition.*

Here's a more interesting function to type, in *convert.erl*:

```
-module(convert).
-export([main/0]).

main() ->
    [_,_] = convert({a,b}),
    {_,_} = convert([a,b]),
    [_,_] = convert([a,b]),
    {_,_} = convert({a,b}).

convert(Tup) when is_tuple(Tup) -> tuple_to_list(Tup);
convert(L = [_|_]) -> list_to_tuple(L).
```

When reading the code, it is obvious that the two last calls to convert/1 will fail. The function accepts a list and returns a tuple, or it accepts a tuple and returns a list. The two last calls to the function don't respect that, expecting a tuple from a tuple, and a list from a list. If we run Dialyzer on the code, though, it will find nothing.

That's because Dialyzer infers a type signature similar to the following:

```
-spec convert(list() | tuple()) -> list() | tuple().
```

Or to put it in words, the function accepts lists and tuples, and returns lists and tuples. This is true—sadly, a bit too true. The function isn't as permissive as the type signature would imply. This is one of the places where Dialyzer sits back and tries not to say too much without being 100 percent sure of the problems.

To help Dialyzer a bit, we can send in a fancier type declaration:

```
-spec convert(tuple()) -> list();
             (list()) -> tuple().
convert(Tup) when is_tuple(Tup) -> tuple_to_list(Tup);
convert(L = [_|_]) -> list_to_tuple(L).
```

Rather than putting tuple() and list() types together into a single union, this syntax allows us to declare type signatures with alternative clauses. If we call convert/1 with a tuple, we expect a list, and the opposite in the other case.

With this more specific information, Dialyzer can now give more interesting results:

```
$ dialyzer convert.erl
  Checking whether the PLT /home/ferd/.dialyzer_plt is up-to-date... yes
  Proceeding with analysis...
convert.erl:4: Function main/0 has no local return
convert.erl:7: The pattern [_, _] can never match the type tuple()
 done in 0m0.90s
done (warnings were emitted)
```

Ah, this time it finds the error. Success! We can now use Dialyzer to tell us what we knew. Of course, putting it that way sounds useless, but when you type your functions correctly and make a tiny mistake that you forget to check, Dialyzer will have your back, which is definitely better than an error-logging system waking you up at night (or having your car keyed by your operations guy).

NOTE *Some people prefer the following syntax for a multiple-clause type signature:*

```
-spec convert(tuple()) -> list()
    ;       (list()) -> tuple().
```

This is the same as the syntax we used but puts the semicolon on another line because it might be more readable. There is no widely accepted standard at the time of this writing.

By using type definitions and specifications in this way, we're able to let Dialyzer find errors with our earlier discrep modules. Let's see how *discrep4.erl* does it:

```
-module(discrep4).
-export([run/0]).
-type cents() :: integer().
-type account() :: atom().
-type transaction() :: {'give', cents(), account()}.
```

```
run() ->
    Tup = money(5, you),
    some_op(item(count,Tup), item(account,Tup)).

-spec money(cents(), account()) -> transaction().
money(Num, Name) -> {give, Num, Name}.

-spec item('count', transaction()) -> cents();
          ('account', transaction()) -> account().
item(count, {give, X, _}) -> X;
item(account, {give, _, X}) -> X.

some_op(A,B) -> A + B.
```

The especially useful definition here is about how item/2 is typed using two alternative clauses. This will help Dialyzer to track the return values in relation to the input values and find type errors.

Typing Practice

Now we'll look at a queue module for FIFO operations. You should know what queues are, given Erlang's mailboxes are queues. The first element added will be the first one to be popped (unless we do selective receives). The module works like this:

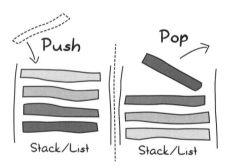

To simulate a queue, we use two lists as stacks. One list stores the new elements, and one list lets us remove them from the queue. We always add to the same list and remove from the second one. When the list we remove from is empty, we reverse the list we add items to, and it becomes the new list to remove from. This generally guarantees better average performance than using a single list to do both tasks.

Here's our FIFO module, with a few type signatures added to check it with Dialyzer:

```
-module(fifo_types).
-export([new/0, push/2, pop/1, empty/1]).
-export([test/0]).
```

```
-spec new() -> {fifo, [], []}.
new() -> {fifo, [], []}.

-spec push({fifo, In::list(), Out::list()}, term()) -> {fifo, list(), list()}.
push({fifo, In, Out}, X) -> {fifo, [X|In], Out}.

-spec pop({fifo, In::list(), Out::list()}) -> {term(), {fifo, list(), list()}}.
pop({fifo, [], []}) -> erlang:error('empty fifo');
pop({fifo, In, []}) -> pop({fifo, [], lists:reverse(In)});
pop({fifo, In, [H|T]}) -> {H, {fifo, In, T}}.

-spec empty({fifo, [], []}) -> true;
           ({fifo, list(), list()}) -> false.
empty({fifo, [], []}) -> true;
empty({fifo, _, _}) -> false.

test() ->
    N = new(),
    {2, N2} = pop(push(push(new(), 2), 5)),
    {5, N3} = pop(N2),
    N = N3,
    true = empty(N3),
    false = empty(N2),
    pop({fifo, [a|b], [e]}).
```

This defines a queue as a tuple of the form {fifo, list(), list()}. You'll notice we didn't define a fifo() type, mostly to make it easy to create different clauses for empty queues and filled queues. The empty(...) type specification reflects that.

> **MUCH ADO ABOUT NONE()**
>
> You will notice that in the function pop/1, we do not specify the none() type, even though one of the function clauses calls erlang:error/1.
>
> The type none() means a given function will not return. If the function might either fail or return a value, it is useless to type it as returning both a value and none(). The none() type is always assumed to be there, and as such, the union Type() | none() is the same as Type() alone.
>
> none() is warranted whenever you're writing a function that always fails when called, such as if you were implementing erlang:error/1 yourself.

All of our type specifications appear to make sense. Just to make sure, let's run Dialyzer and check the results:

```
$ dialyzer fifo_types.erl
  Checking whether the PLT /home/ferd/.dialyzer_plt is up-to-date... yes
  Proceeding with analysis...
```

```
fifo_types.erl:16: Overloaded contract has overlapping domains; such contracts are currently
unsupported and are simply ignored
fifo_types.erl:21: Function test/0 has no local return
fifo_types.erl:28: The call
  fifo_types:pop({'fifo',nonempty_improper_list('a','b'),['e',...]})
    breaks the contract
    ({'fifo',In::[any()],Out::[any()]}) -> {term(),{'fifo',[any()],[any()]}}
 done in 0m0.96s
done (warnings were emitted)
```

So, we have a bunch of errors, and curses, they are not so easy to read. The second one, "Function test/0 has no local return," is at least something we know how to handle. If we just skip to the next one, it should disappear.

For now, let's focus on the first error—the one about contracts with overlapping domains. If we go into fifo_types, on line 16, we see this:

```
-spec empty({fifo, [], []}) -> true;
           ({fifo, list(), list()}) -> false.
empty({fifo, [], []}) -> true;
empty({fifo, _, _}) -> false.
```

So what are said overlapping domains? We need to refer to the mathematical concepts of *domain* and *image* (also *range*). To put it simply, the domain is the set of all possible input values to a function, and the image is the set of all possible output values of a function. "Overlapping domains" refers to two sets of input that overlap.

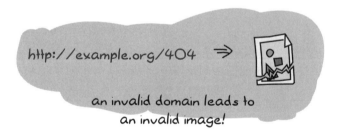

an invalid domain leads to
an invalid image!

To find the source of the problem, we need to look at list(). list() is pretty much the same as [any()], and both of these types also include empty lists. And there's your overlapping domain. When list() is specified as a type, it overlaps with []. To fix this, we need to replace the type signature as follows:

```
-spec empty({fifo, [], []}) -> true;
           ({fifo, nonempty_list(), nonempty_list()}) -> false.
```

Alternatively, we could use this form:

```
-spec empty({fifo, [], []}) -> true;
          ({fifo, [any(), ...], [any(), ...]}) -> false.
```

Then running Dialyzer again will get rid of the warning.

Let's move on to the next error (which I broke into multiple lines):

```
fifo_types.erl:28:
The call fifo_types:pop({'fifo',nonempty_improper_list('a','b'),['e',...]})
breaks the contract
({'fifo',In::[any()],Out::[any()]}) -> {term(),{'fifo',[any()],[any()]}}
```

Translated into human, this means that on line 28, there's a call to pop/1 that has inferred types breaking the one specified in the file:

```
pop({fifo, [a|b], [e]}).
```

That's the call. Now, the error message says that it identified an improper list (that happens to not be empty), which is entirely right—[a|e] is an improper list. It also mentions that it breaks a contract. We need to match the type definition that is broken between the following, coming from the error message:

```
{'fifo',nonempty_improper_list('a','b'),['e',...]}
{'fifo',In::[any()],Out::[any()]}
{term(),{'fifo',[any()],[any()]}}
```

The issue can be explained in one of three ways:

- The type signatures are right, the call is right, and the problem is the return value expected.
- The type signatures are right, the call is wrong, and the problem is the input value given.
- The call is right, but the type signatures are wrong.

We can eliminate the first one immediately. We're not actually doing anything with the return value. This leaves the second and third options. The decision boils down to whether or not we want improper lists to be used with our queues. This is a judgment call to be made by the writer of the library, and I can say without a doubt that I didn't intend improper lists to be used with this code. In fact, programmers very rarely want improper lists. The winner is number 2: The call is wrong. To solve the problem, drop the call or fix it:

```
test() ->
    N = new(),
    {2, N2} = pop(push(push(new(), 2), 5)),
    ...
    pop({fifo, [a, b], [e]}).
```

And run Dialyzer again:

```
$ dialyzer fifo_types.erl
  Checking whether the PLT /home/ferd/.dialyzer_plt is up-to-date... yes
  Proceeding with analysis... done in 0m0.90s
done (passed successfully)
```

That makes more sense.

Exporting Types

Things have gone very well. We have types, we have signatures, and we have additional safety and verifications. So what would happen if we wanted to use our queue in another module? What about any other module we frequently use, such as dict, gb_trees, or ETS tables? How can we use Dialyzer to find type errors related to them?

We can use types coming from other modules. Doing so usually requires rummaging through documentation to find them. For example, the ets module's documentation (*http://www.erlang.org/doc/man/ets.html*) has the following entries under "DATA TYPES":

continuation()
> Opaque continuation used by select/1 and select/3.

match_spec() = [{match_pattern(), [term()], [term()]}]
> A match specification, see above.

match_pattern() = atom() | tuple()
tab() = atom() | tid()
tid()
> A table identifier, as returned by new/2.

Those are the data types exported by ets. If we had a type specification that accepted ETS tables and a key, and returned a matching entry, we could define it like this:

```
-spec match(ets:tab(), Key::any()) -> Entry::any().
```

And that's about it.

Exporting our own types works pretty much the same as with functions. All we need to do is add a module attribute of the form -export_type([*TypeName/Arity*]).. For example, we could have exported the card() type from our cards module by adding the following line:

```
-module(cards).
-export([kind/1, main/0]).

-type suit() :: spades | clubs | hearts | diamonds.
-type value() :: 1..10 | j | q | k.
-type card() :: {suit(), value()}.

-export_type([card/0]).
...
```

And from then on, if the module is visible to Dialyzer (either by adding it to the PLT or analyzing it at the same time as any other module), we can reference it from any other bit of code as cards:card() in type specifications.

Some things are better left unseen

Doing this will have one downside, though: Using a type like this doesn't forbid anyone using the card module from ripping the types apart and toying with them. Anyone could be writing pieces of code that match on the cards, a bit like {Suit, _} = ... This isn't always a good idea, because it prevents us from being able to change the implementation of the cards module in the future. We would especially like to enforce this in modules that represent data structures, such as dict and fifo_types (if it exported types).

Dialyzer allows you to export types in a way that tells your users, "You know what? I'm fine with you using my types, but don't you dare look inside them!" It's a question of replacing a declaration like this:

```
-type fifo() :: {fifo, list(), list()}.
```

with this:

```
-opaque fifo() :: {fifo, list(), list()}.
```

Then you can still export it as -export_type([fifo/0]).

Declaring a type as -opaque means that only the module that defined the type has the right to look at how it's made and make modifications to it. This forbids other modules from pattern matching on the values other than the whole thing, guaranteeing (if they use Dialyzer) that they will never be bitten by a sudden change of implementation.

Sometimes the implementation of opaque data types is either not strong enough to do what it should or is actually problematic (that is, buggy).

Dialyzer does not take the specification of a function into account until it has first inferred the success typing for the function.

This means that when your type looks rather generic without any -type information taken into account, Dialyzer might get confused by some opaque types. For example, when analyzing an opaque version of the card() data type, Dialyzer might see it as {atom(), any()} after inference. Modules using card() correctly might see Dialyzer complaining because they're breaking a type contract, even if they aren't. This is because the card() type itself doesn't contain enough information for Dialyzer to connect the dots and realize what's really going on.

Usually, if you see errors when using an opaque data type, tagging your tuple helps. Moving from a type of the form -opaque card() :: {suit(), value()}. to -opaque card() :: {card, suit(), value()}. might get Dialyzer to work fine with the opaque type.

The Dialyzer implementers are currently trying to make the implementation of opaque data types better and strengthen their inference. They are also trying to make user-provided specs more important and to trust them better during Dialyzer's analysis, but this is still a work in progress.

Typed Behaviors

Back in Chapter 14, we explored how to declare behaviors using the behavior_info/1 function. The module exporting this function would give its name to the behavior, and a second module could implement callbacks by adding -behavior(ModName). as a module attribute.

The behavior definition of the gen_server module, for example, is as follows:

```
behavior_info(callbacks) ->
    [{init, 1}, {handle_call, 3}, {handle_cast, 2}, {handle_info, 2},
     {terminate, 2}, {code_change, 3}];
behavior_info(_Other) ->
    undefined.
```

The problem here is that there is no way for Dialyzer to check type definitions for that. In fact, there is no way for the behavior module to specify which kinds of types it expects the callback modules to implement, and thus there's no way for Dialyzer to do something about it.

Starting with R15B, the Erlang/OTP compiler was upgraded so that it now handles a new module attribute, named -callback. The -callback module attribute has a similar syntax to spec. When you specify function types with it, the behavior_info/1 function will be declared automatically, and the specifications are added to the module metadata in a way that lets Dialyzer do its work. For example, here's the declaration of the gen_server starting with R15B:

```
-callback init(Args :: term()) ->
    {ok, State :: term()} | {ok, State :: term(), timeout() | hibernate} |
    {stop, Reason :: term()} | ignore.
-callback handle_call(Request :: term(), From :: {pid(), Tag :: term()},
                      State :: term()) ->
    {reply, Reply :: term(), NewState :: term()} |
    {reply, Reply :: term(), NewState :: term(), timeout() | hibernate} |
    {noreply, NewState :: term()} |
    {noreply, NewState :: term(), timeout() | hibernate} |
    {stop, Reason :: term(), Reply :: term(), NewState :: term()} |
    {stop, Reason :: term(), NewState :: term()}.
-callback handle_cast(Request :: term(), State :: term()) ->
    {noreply, NewState :: term()} |
    {noreply, NewState :: term(), timeout() | hibernate} |
    {stop, Reason :: term(), NewState :: term()}.
-callback handle_info(Info :: timeout() | term(), State :: term()) ->
    {noreply, NewState :: term()} |
    {noreply, NewState :: term(), timeout() | hibernate} |
    {stop, Reason :: term(), NewState :: term()}.
-callback terminate(Reason :: (normal | shutdown | {shutdown, term()} | term()),
                    State :: term()) ->
    term().
-callback code_change(OldVsn :: (term() | {down, term()}), State :: term(),
                      Extra :: term()) ->
    {ok, NewState :: term()} | {error, Reason :: term()}.
```

And none of your code should break from the behavior changing things. Do realize, however, that a module cannot use both the -callback form and the behavior_info/1 function at once—only one or the other. This means if you want to create custom behaviors, there is a rift between what can be used in versions of Erlang prior to R15 and what can be used in later versions.

The upside is that newer modules will have Dialyzer able to do some analysis to check for errors on the types of whatever is returned.

NOTE *During version R15B exclusively, Dialyzer would check types of callbacks only when the callback module included -behaviour, not when it included -behavior. This is a bug that was later resolved.*

Polymorphic Types

Oh boy, what a section title. If you've never heard of *polymorphic types* (alternatively called *parameterized types*), this might sound a bit scary. It's fortunately not as complex as the name would lead you to believe.

The need for polymorphic types comes from the fact that when we're typing different data structures, we might find ourselves wanting to be more specific about what they can store. For example, we may want our queue from earlier in the chapter to sometimes handle anything, sometimes handle only playing cards, or sometimes handle only integers. In the latter two cases, the issue is that we might want Dialyzer to be able to complain that we're trying to put floating-point numbers in our integer queue, or tarot cards in our playing cards queue.

This is impossible to enforce by strictly using types the way we have been so far.

A polymorphic type is a type that can be "configured" with other types. Luckily for us, we already know the syntax to use it. Earlier, I said we could define a list of integers as [integer()] or list(integer())—these are polymorphic types. A polymorphic type accepts a type as an argument.

To make our queue accept only integers or cards, we could have defined its type as follows:

```
-type queue(Type) :: {fifo, list(Type), list(Type)}.
-export_type([queue/1]).
```

When another module wishes to make use of the fifo/1 type, it needs to parameterize that type. So a new deck of cards in the cards module could have had the following signature:

```
-spec new() -> fifo:queue(card()).
```

And Dialyzer would try to analyze the module to make sure that it submits and expects only cards from the queue it handles.

We Bought a Zoo

As a demonstration of the use of polymorphic type, let's say that we decided to buy a zoo to congratulate ourselves for being nearly finished with *Learn You Some Erlang*. In our zoo, we have two animals: a red panda and a squid (yes, it is a rather modest zoo, although that shouldn't keep us from setting the entry fee sky-high).

We've decided to automate the feeding of our animals, because we're programmers, and programmers like to automate stuff, often out of laziness. After doing a bit of research, we've found that red pandas can eat bamboo, some birds, eggs, and berries. We've also found that squids can fight with sperm whales, so we decided to feed them just that with our *zoo.erl* module:

```
-module(zoo).
-export([main/0]).

feeder(red_panda) ->
    fun() ->
        element(random:uniform(4), {bamboo, birds, eggs, berries})
    end;
```

```
feeder(squid) ->
    fun() -> sperm_whale end.

feed_red_panda(Generator) ->
    Food = Generator(),
    io:format("feeding ~p to the red panda~n", [Food]),
    Food.

feed_squid(Generator) ->
    Food = Generator(),
    io:format("throwing ~p in the squid's aquarium~n", [Food]),
    Food.

main() ->
    %% Random seeding
    <<A:32, B:32, C:32>> = crypto:rand_bytes(12),
    random:seed(A, B, C),
    %% The zoo buys a feeder for both the red panda and squid.
    FeederRP = feeder(red_panda),
    FeederSquid = feeder(squid),
    %% Time to feed them!
    %% This should not be right!
    feed_squid(FeederRP),
    feed_red_panda(FeederSquid).
```

This code makes use of feeder/1, which takes an animal name and
returns a feeder (a function that returns food items). Feeding the red
panda should be done with a red panda feeder, and feeding the squid
should be done with a squid feeder. With function definitions such as
feed_red_panda/1 and feed_squid/1, there is no way to be alerted by the wrong
use of a feeder. Even with runtime checks, it's impossible to do. As soon as
we serve food, it's too late:

```
1> zoo:main().
throwing bamboo in the squid's aquarium
feeding sperm_whale to the red panda
sperm_whale
```

Oh no, our animals are not meant to eat that way! Maybe types can
help. The following type specifications could be devised, using the power
of polymorphic types:

```
-type red_panda() :: bamboo | birds | eggs | berries.
-type squid() :: sperm_whale.
-type food(A) :: fun(() -> A).

-spec feeder(red_panda) -> food(red_panda());
            (squid) -> food(squid()).
-spec feed_red_panda(food(red_panda())) -> red_panda().
-spec feed_squid(food(squid())) -> squid().
```

The food(A) type is the one of interest here. A is a free type, to be decided later. We then qualify the food type in feeder/1's type specification by declaring food(red_panda()) and food(squid()). The food type is then seen as fun(() -> red_panda()) and fun(() -> squid()), instead of some abstract function returning something unknown. If we add these specs to the file, and then run Dialyzer on it, the following happens:

```
$ dialyzer zoo.erl
  Checking whether the PLT /Users/ferd/.dialyzer_plt is up-to-date... yes
  Proceeding with analysis...
zoo.erl:18: Function feed_red_panda/1 will never be called
zoo.erl:23: The contract zoo:feed_squid(food(squid())) -> squid() cannot be right because
 the inferred return for feed_squid(FeederRP::fun(() -> 'bamboo' | 'berries' | 'birds' |
'eggs'))
 on line 44 is 'bamboo' | 'berries' | 'birds' | 'eggs'
zoo.erl:29: Function main/0 has no local return
 done in 0m0.68s
done (warnings were emitted)
```

And the error is right. Hooray for polymorphic types!

Some Cautions

Although our example is pretty useful, minor changes in the code can have unexpected consequences in what Dialyzer is able to find. For example, suppose the main/0 function had the following code:

```
main() ->
    %% Random seeding
    <<A:32, B:32, C:32>> = crypto:rand_bytes(12),
    random:seed(A, B, C),
    %% The zoo buys a feeder for both the red panda and squid.
    FeederRP = feeder(red_panda),
    FeederSquid = feeder(squid),
    %% Time to feed them!
    feed_squid(FeederSquid),
    feed_red_panda(FeederRP),
    %% This should not be right!
    feed_squid(FeederRP),
    feed_red_panda(FeederSquid).
```

Things would not be the same. Before the functions are called with the wrong kind of feeder, they're first called with the right kind. As of R15B01, Dialyzer would not find an error with this code. The observed behavior is that as soon as a call to a given function succeeds within the function's body, Dialyzer will ignore later errors within the same unit of code.

Even if this is a bit sad for many static typing fans, we have been thoroughly warned. The following quote comes from the "Practical Type Inference Based on Success Typings" paper referenced earlier in the chapter:

> . . . A success typing is a type signature that over-approximates the set of types for which the function can evaluate to a value. The domain of the signature includes all possible values that the function could accept as parameters, and its range includes all possible return values for this domain. . . .
>
> . . . However weak this might seem to aficionados of static typing, success typings have the property that they capture the fact that if the function is used in a way not allowed by its success typing (e.g., by applying the function with parameters $\bar{p} \notin \bar{\alpha}$) this application will definitely fail. This is precisely the property that a defect detection tool which never "cries wolf" needs. Also, success typings can be used for automatic program documentation because they will never fail to capture some possible—no matter how unintended—use of a function.

Again, keeping in mind that Dialyzer is optimistic in its approach is vital to working efficiently with it.

Who cares about food poisoning when
supervisors have your back?

You're My Type

Dialyzer will often prove to be a true friend when programming in Erlang, although the frequent nagging might tempt you to just drop it. One thing to remember is that Dialyzer is practically never wrong, and you will likely make mistakes now and then. You might feel like some errors mean nothing, but contrary to many type systems, Dialyzer speaks out only when it knows it's right, and bugs in its code base are rare. Dialyzer might frustrate you and force you to be humble, but it is very unlikely to be the source of bad, unclean code.

That's All, Folks

So hey, that's about it for *Learn You Some Erlang for Great Good!* Thanks for reading it. There's not much more to say, but if you feel like getting a list of more topics to explore and some general words from me, you can read the book's afterword.

AFTERWORD

I see you chose to read the afterword after all. Good for you. Before I point you to a bunch of interesting topics that you might want to explore if you've decided Erlang is a development language that you want to learn more about, I would like a moment to talk about writing *Learn You Some Erlang*. It has been one hell of a ride. It took me three years of hard labor while studying and working full time, and juggling everyday life needs (if I had children, they would have died of neglect a while ago).

    This book's site, coupled with some luck and some more work, allowed me to get jobs as an Erlang trainer, a course material writer, and a developer. It allowed me to travel around the world and meet a load of interesting people. It drained a lot of energy, and cost me a decent chunk of money and time, but it paid me back tenfold in most ways imaginable.

Then this book became reality, with more work needed. Even though I thanked these people in the thanks section of the book, I want to stress my appreciation of the Erlang community in general. They helped me learn stuff, reviewed pages and pages of material for free, fixed my typos, and helped me get better at writing English and writing in general. I also want to thank the whole team at No Starch Press, who put in even more time, bringing professional editing to *Learn You Some Erlang*. Finally, thanks again to Jenn (my girlfriend), who took the time to re-trace all my drawings so they would be suitable for print.

Other Erlang Applications

There are only so many topics I could cover without going over the top. This book is already large enough as it is. It has taken years to complete, and I'm tired and glad it's over (what am I gonna do with all that free time?), but there are still plenty of other topics I would have loved to include. Here's a quick list of applications you can look up in the documentation that ships with Erlang:

Tracing BIFs and DBG
The Erlang VM is traceable inside and out. Got a bug or some stack trace you can't make sense of? Turn on a few trace flags, and the VM opens up to you. DBG, an application that comes with Erlang, takes these BIFs and builds an app on top of them. Messages, function calls, function returns, garbage collections, process spawning and dying, and so on are all traceable and observable. DBG also tends to work much better than any debugger for a concurrent language like Erlang. What's the best part about it? It's traceable within Erlang, so you can make Erlang programs that trace themselves! If you look into these functions and find them a bit hard to digest, you might be okay staying with the sys module's tracing functions. They work only on OTP behaviorized processes, but they're often good enough to get going.

Profiling
Erlang comes with a bunch of different profiling tools to analyze your programs and find all kinds of bottlenecks. The fprof and eprof tools can be used for time profiling, cprof for function calls, lcnt for locks, percept for concurrency, and cover for code coverage. Most of them are built using the tracing BIFs of the language, funnily enough.

More introspection
Unix top-like tools exist for Erlang, such as etop, part of the observer application. You can also use the Erlang debugger, but I recommend DBG instead of that one. The observer application also allows you to explore entire supervision trees for your nodes.

Documentation

EDoc is a tool that lets you turn your Erlang modules into HTML documentation. It supports annotations and ways to declare specific pages that allow you to build small websites to document your code. It's similar to Javadoc for Java users.

GUIs

The wx application is the new standard for multiplatform GUI writing with Erlang. I'm terrible at GUI stuff, so it's probably better for everyone that I didn't cover this app.

Erlang libraries

Plenty of nice libraries come by default with Erlang: cryptography tools, web servers, web clients, all kinds of protocol implementations, and so on. You can get a general list of them at *http://www.erlang.org/doc/applications.html*.

Community Libraries

There are a ton of libraries coming from the Erlang community. I didn't cover them because they tend to change, and I didn't want to favor one over the other. Here's a quick list (links don't carry over very well in a book, so you can get the actual links at *http://learnyousomeerlang.com/conclusion*):

- Rebar and Sinan if you want to build systems
- Redbug for a friendlier approach to tracing
- Gproc for a very powerful and flexible process registry
- Mochiweb, Cowboy, and Yaws if you need web servers
- riak_core for a very powerful distribution library for Erlang
- lhttpc as a web client
- PropEr, QuickCheck, and Triq for kick-ass, property-based testing tools (you need to try one of them)
- Entop for a top-like tool
- A billion JSON libraries (mochijson2, jsx, ejson, and more)
- UX for Unicode handling and common Unicode-related algorithms pending their addition to the language (planned for R16B)
- Seresye and eXAT for some artificial intelligence (AI) tools
- Database client libraries
- Lager as a robust logging system that binds itself to Erlang's error logger
- Poolboy for some generic message-based pools

Many more libraries are out there. Community libraries could easily fill their own book.

Your Ideas Are Intriguing to Me and I Wish to Subscribe to Your Newsletter

I have a blog at *http://ferd.ca* where I discuss all kinds of stuff (or at least I want to) but inevitably come back to Erlang topics, due to using it all the time.

Is That It?

No, there's still an appendix and the index!

ON ERLANG'S SYNTAX

Many newcomers to Erlang manage to understand the syntax and program around it without ever getting comfortable with it. I've read and heard many complaints regarding the syntax and the "ant turd tokens" (a subjectively funny way to refer to ,, ;, and .), how annoying it is, and so on.

Erlang draws its syntax from Prolog. While this gives a reason for the current state of things, it doesn't magically make people like the syntax. I don't expect anyone to respond to this by saying, "Oh, it's Prolog, I get it. Makes complete sense!" As such, I'll suggest three ways to read Erlang code to possibly make it easier to understand.

The Template

The template way is my personal favorite. To understand it, you must first get rid of the concept of lines of code and think in expressions. An *expression* is any bit of Erlang code that returns something. In the shell, the period (.) ends an expression. After writing 2 + 2, you must add a period (and then press ENTER) to run the expression and return a value.

In modules, the period ends forms. *Forms* are module attributes and function declarations. Forms are not expressions, as they don't return anything. This is why they're terminated in a different manner than everything else. Given forms are not expressions, it could be argued that the shell's use of . to terminate expression is what is *not* standard here. Consequently, I suggest not caring about the shell for this method of reading Erlang.

The first rule is that the comma (,) separates expressions:

```
C = A+B, D = A+C
```

This is easy enough. However, it should be noted that if ... end, case ... of ... end, begin ... end, fun() -> ... end, and try ... of ... catch ... end are all expressions. As an example, it is possible to run this:

```
Var = if X > 0  -> valid;
        X =< 0 -> invalid
     end
```

And you'll get a single value out of the if ... end. This explains why we will sometimes see such language constructs followed by a comma. It just means there is another expression to evaluate after it.

The second rule is that the semicolon (;) has two roles. The first one is separating different function clauses:

```
fac(0) -> 1;
fac(N) -> N * fac(N-1).
```

The second one is separating different branches of expressions like if ... end, case ... of ... end, and others:

```
if X < 0  -> negative;
   X > 0  -> positive;
   X == 0 -> zero
end
```

It's probably the most confusing role because the last branch of the expression doesn't need to have the semicolon following it. This is because the ; separates branches; it doesn't terminate them. Think in expressions, not lines. Some people find it easier to illustrate the role of a separator by writing the preceding expression in the following way, which is arguably more readable:

```
if X < 0  -> negative
 ; X > 0  -> positive
 ; X == 0 -> zero
end
```

This makes the role of separator more explicit. It goes in between branches and clauses, not after them.

Now, because the semicolon is used to separate expression branches and function clauses, it becomes possible to have an expression such as a case construct followed by , when followed by another expression, a ; when in the last position of a function clause, or a . when at the last position of a function.

The line-based logic for terminating lines such as in C or Java must go out the window. Instead, see your code as a generic template you fill (hence the name the *template* way):

```
head1(Args) [Guard] ->
    Expression1, Expression2, ..., ExpressionN;
head2(Args) [Guard] ->
    Expression1, Expression2, ..., ExpressionN;
headN(Args) [Guard] ->
    Expression1, Expression2, ..., ExpressionN.
```

The rules make sense, but you need to get into a different reading mode. That's where the heavy lifting needs to be done—moving from lines and blocks toward a predefined template. If you think about it, things like for (int i = 0; i >= x; i++) { ... } (or even for (...);) have a weird syntax when compared to most other constructs in languages supporting them. We're just so used to seeing these constructs that we don't mind them anymore.

The English Sentence

The English sentence approach is about comparing Erlang code to English. Although this manner is not the one I prefer, I do realize that people have different ways to make sense of logical concepts, and this is one approach I've heard being praised many times.

Imagine you're writing a list of things. Well, no. Don't imagine it, read it.

```
I will need a few items on my trip:
  if it's sunny, sunscreen, water, a hat;
  if it's rainy, an umbrella, a raincoat;
  if it's windy, a kite, a shirt.
```

An Erlang translation can remain a bit similar:

```
trip_items(sunny) ->
    sunscreen, water, hat;
trip_items(rainy) ->
    umbrella, raincoat;
trip_items(windy) ->
    kite, shirt.
```

Here, just replace the items by expressions, and you have it. Expressions such as if ... end can be seen as nested lists.

And, Or, Done.

Another variant of the English sentence approach has been suggested to me on *#erlang*, and I think it's the most elegant one. The user simply reads the ant turd tokens as follows:

- , as *and*
- ; as *or*
- . as *being done*

A function declaration can then be read as a series of nested logical statements and affirmations.

In Conclusion

Some people will just never like ant turd tokens or being unable to swap lines of code without changing the token at the end of the line. I guess there's not much to be done when it comes to style and preferences, but I still hope this appendix was useful. After all, the syntax is only intimidating; it's far from difficult.

INDEX

applications (OTP), *continued*
  currently running, 312
  dependencies, 307, 317, 337
  distributed, 473
    example, 480
  finding versions, 338–339
  included applications, 333
  library applications
    (process-free), 314
  loading, 331
  named processes, 468
  overriding, 317, 332, 341, 361,
    481–482
  restart strategy (temporary,
    transient, permanent), 313
    with reltool, 343
  statuses, 474
  start, 310, 311–312, 313
  stop, 312, 333
application controller, 309, 474
application master, 309–310
appups
  definition, 357
  file definition, 365–366
  file example, 366–367
arithmetic operations, 10
arity, 33
arrays, 129
assertion macros, 400–401.
    See also EUnit
asynchronous message passing, 139,
    445–446
atoms, 12–13
atom table, 13
availability, 453–454. *See also* CAP
    theorem

B

backward compatibility notice
  recursive types, 553–554
  simple_one_for_one child restart
    strategy, 270
  stack traces, 101
  supervisor:terminate_child
    function, 280
  typed behaviors, 566, 567

bad argument error, 91
bad arithmetic error, 92
bad arity error, 92
bad function error, 92
band operator, 26–27
band supervisor, 271, 274
bandwidth, 446–447
bang (!), 144–145. *See also* message
    passing
BEAM (virtual machine), 37
.beam files, 36. *See also*
    compiling code
behavior. *See also* applications
    (OTP); gen_event behavior;
    gen_fsm behavior; gen_server
    behavior; supervisor (OTP)
  defining behaviors, 214
  principles, 200–201
  typed behaviors, 566–567
Berard, Edward V., 176
BERT and BERT-RPC, 450
BIFs. *See* built-in functions
binaries
  bit packing, 24
  bit syntax, 23–24
  compared to atoms, 28
  pattern matching, 24–26
  strings, 27–28
  TCP segment example, 27
  type specifiers, size, endianness,
    25–26
binary comprehension, 28–29
binary generator (<=), 28
binary tree, 72–75, 103–104
binding, 46, 91
bnot operator, 26
Boolean, 14
-boot shell argument, 340–341
boot file, 339, 340–341, 369
boot script, 339–340
bor operator, 26–27
bottlenecks. *See* sequential
    bottlenecks
bsl operator, 26–27
bsr operator, 26–27

image, of a function, 562
imported functions, 35
improper lists, 21
included applications, 333
inet module
    active once, 384–386
    vs. inets application, 384
    socket options, 385
inet:setopts function, 385
installing Erlang, 5–6
integers. *See* numbers
IO lists, 375–377
is_alive() function, 470
is_process_alive(Pid) function, 411

J

jobs management, 9, 155, 464

K

kernel (OTP application
        configuration), 482
key/value storage, 127–130,
        306, 419
killing a process
    exit/2 function, 163
    kill signal, 167

L

lambda calculus, 78
last call optimization
        (elimination), 70
last write wins, 457
latency, 446
leak, processes or memory, 265,
        363, 413
Learn You A Haskell for Great Good!
        (Miran Lipovača), 1, 105
let it crash, 4
    crash-only software, 138
    mechanisms for handling errors,
        87–88
libraries
    community, 575
    path, 331
linear scaling, 4, 140–142
links
    cross-node, 446, 460–461
    definition, 162–164

to establish dependencies, 179
    unlinking, 162, 164
Lipovača, Miran, 1, 105
list comprehensions
    for database queries, 539–540
    filters, 23
    generator expressions, 22
    set theory origins, 21
    syntax, 22–23
list generator (<-), 22
lists
    basic operations, 19–20
    improper, 21
    modification costs, 367
    operations, 53, 86, 328
    order of evaluation, 415
    pattern matching, 20
    recursive definition, 20–21
    strings, 18–19
    syntax, 18, 20–21
load balancing, processes by
        the VM, 140
logical clocks (lamport, vector
        clocks), 457
logic errors, 89–90
loops, 61

M

macros
    calling, 39
    defining, 38–39
    predefined, 39
mafiapp (Mnesia example), 513–514
Magic 8 Ball example, 476–484
mailbox
    mechanisms, 151
    rationale, 139
    reading messages, 145 (*see also*
        receive expression)
make module. *See* compiling code:
        Emakefiles
make_ref() function
    request/response, 173
    unique values, 415
map (higher-order function), 79, 83
match. *See* pattern matching

net_kernel module, 467
netsplits
    definition, 452
    zombie survivors example,
        454–456
network topology, 448–449
network reliability, 445–446
node() function, 459
node(PidPortOrRef) function, 461
nodes, 458
nodes(Flag) function, 465
node synchronization (OTP
        applications), 481–482
nonlocal returns, 103–104
not operator, 14
now() function, 392
number crunching, 27
numbers
    arithmetic, operators for, 10
    bases, 11
    floating-point, 10
    integers, 10
    in RPN, 109

O

Okasaki, Chris, *Purely Functional
    Data Structures*, 133
O'Keefe, Richard, 52
one_for_all child restart strategy, 267
one_for_one child restart strategy,
        266–267
    vs. simple_one_for_one, 268
onion-layered system, 283–284
Open Telecom Platform (OTP),
        199–200, 209–210. *See
        also individual behaviors*;
        application (OTP)
operators
    arithmetic, 10
    bitwise, 26–27
    Boolean, 14
    comparison, 14–16
    message passing, 144–145
orddicts module, 127–128
ordsets module, 130–131
orelse operator, 14, 48–49

or operator, 14
output, printing with io:format/2-3,
        45, 394

P

packages, applications
        (.ez files), 345
packaging (releases), 340
packets, TCP/IP and UDP, 377
parametrized types. *See* Dialyzer:
        polymorphic types
parse transform, 430
partition tolerance, 454. *See also*
        CAP theorem
-pa shell argument, 194–195
pattern matching
    binary tree example, 73–74
    case ... end, 53
    exceptions, 96–98
    in functions, 43–44
    greeting example, 44
    lists, 20
    lists in functions, 45–46
    match operator (=), 12
    records, 124
    tuples, 17–18
    variable bindings, 46–47
persistent data structures, 73
persistent lookup table (PLT),
        543–544
pid (process identifier)
    definition, 143
    global ordering, 242
    internal representation, 461
    pid/3 shell command, 153
    self() function, 144
PLT (persistent lookup table),
        543–544
polymorphic types, 567–570
port. *See also* UDP
    controlling process, 383–384
    definitions, 379
    inet module, 384
portability, 341
postfix notation (RPN), 106
ppool application, 282–283, 325–326

run queue, 140
run_test executable, 489, 503–504
runtime errors, 90–93

S

The Electronic Frontier Foundation (EFF) is the leading organization defending civil liberties in the digital world. We defend free speech on the Internet, fight illegal surveillance, promote the rights of innovators to develop new digital technologies, and work to ensure that the rights and freedoms we enjoy are enhanced — rather than eroded — as our use of technology grows.

PRIVACY EFF has sued telecom giant AT&T for giving the NSA unfettered access to the private communications of millions of their customers. eff.org/nsa

FREE SPEECH EFF's Coders' Rights Project is defending the rights of programmers and security researchers to publish their findings without fear of legal challenges. eff.org/freespeech

INNOVATION EFF's Patent Busting Project challenges overbroad patents that threaten technological innovation. eff.org/patent

FAIR USE EFF is fighting prohibitive standards that would take away your right to receive and use over-the-air television broadcasts any way you choose. eff.org/IP/fairuse

TRANSPARENCY EFF has developed the Switzerland Network Testing Tool to give individuals the tools to test for covert traffic filtering. eff.org/transparency

INTERNATIONAL EFF is working to ensure that international treaties do not restrict our free speech, privacy or digital consumer rights. eff.org/global

EFF.ORG

ELECTRONIC FRONTIER FOUNDATION

Protecting Rights and Promoting Freedom on the Electronic Frontier

EFF is a member-supported organization. Join Now! www.eff.org/support

Learn You Some Erlang for Great Good! is set in New Baskerville, TheSansMono Condensed, Futura, and Dogma.

This book was printed and bound at Edwards Brothers Malloy in Ann Arbor, Michigan. The paper is 60# Williamsburg Smooth, which is certified by the Sustainable Forestry Initiative (SFI). The book uses a RepKover binding, which allows it to lie flat when open.